Global Wesleyan Dictionary of Theology

Global Wesleyan

DICTIONARY
of THEOLOGY

Al Truesdale, PhD, Editor

ASSOCIATE EDITORS
Henry H. Knight III, PhD
Karen Strand Winslow, PhD
Kent E. Brower, PhD

BEACON HILL PRESS
O F K A N S A S C I T Y

Copyright 2013 by Beacon Hill Press of Kansas City

ISBN 978-0-8341-2837-8

Printed in the
United States of America

Cover Design by J.R. Caines
Interior Design by Sharon Page

Library of Congress Cataloging-in-Publication Data
Global Wesleyan dictionary of theology / Al Truesdale, editor ;
associate editors, Henry H. Knight III, PhD, Karen Strand Winslow, PhD, Kent E. Brower, PhD.
pages cm
Includes bibliographical references and index.
ISBN 978-0-8341-2837-8 (hardcover)
1. Theology—Dictionaries. 2. Wesleyan Church—Doctrines—Dictionaries. 3. Holiness churches—
Doctrines—Dictionaries. I. Truesdale, Albert, 1941- II. Knight, Henry H.
III. Winslow, Karen Strand, 1952- IV. Brower, K. E. (Kent E.)
BV2.5.G56 2013
230'.703—dc23
2012043328

10 9 8 7 6 5 4 3 2 1

RELIGION / BIBLICAL REFERENCE / DICTIONARIES & ENCYCLOPEDIAS

CONTENTS

PREFACE AND PURPOSE

The Methodist family of denominations composes one part of the church catholic. The Wesleyan theological tradition marks the theological orientation of well over one hundred denominations. Together they present a picture of the global character of the Christian faith. This dictionary was conceived as a "family project" that reflects the theological and global character of the Wesleyan tradition. Users of the dictionary will observe this in the denominational and regional identity of the contributors. Although it is not the primary purpose of the dictionary to define the many features of Wesleyan theology, its users will notice a common theological orientation that characterizes the work throughout.

The purpose of the *Global Wesleyan Dictionary of Theology* is (1) to define major biblical and theological terms, themes, and movements and, where appropriate, to offer a characteristically Wesleyan assessment of each; (2) to define terms that are basic for understanding the Wesleyan tradition and theology; (3) to reflect the global character of Christian faith and doctrine by the choice of terms to be defined and by the global character of its contributors; (4) to provide a characteristically Wesleyan assessment of, and response to, the sciences, technology, the arts, religious and cultural pluralism, and major global social forces/movements that bear directly on human life; and (5) to provide a guide for understanding the richness of the Wesleyan tradition and how it can help Christians in that tradition live and articulate their faith in a global context.

HOW TO USE THE DICTIONARY

The dictionary has been designed to provide numerous ways to investigate a topic: (1) There is the essay itself in which the author discusses the topic. (2) In most of the essays some terms are in **bold**. These terms are treated elsewhere in the dictionary and constitute an internal cross-reference. (3) At the end of most essays there is a *See also* section that lists related terms defined in the dictionary. These terms constitute the dictionary's external cross-reference. (4) Resources for further study are listed at the end of most essays in a **Resources** section. Most of the resources are either books or journal articles. But some resources are located on the Internet. In these instances the website is identified. (5) Many topics not treated in essays are nevertheless identified in the dictionary body. The topics direct users to where similar topics are treated. (6) The Scripture Index provides a ready reference to the Scriptures authors have used to compose their definitions.

CONTRIBUTORS

William Abraham, PhD
Albert Cook Outler Professor of Wesley Studies
Altshuler Distinguished Teaching Professor
Perkins School of Theology
Southern Methodist University
Dallas, Texas
Entries: **Atonement; Baptism with the Holy Spirit; Christology; Evangelism; God, Doctrine of.**

Thomas R. Albin, MTh
Dean of the Upper Room Ministries and Ecumenical Relations
Nashville, Tennessee
Entry: **Holiness Denominations Worldwide.**

Patrick Allen, PhD
Provost
George Fox University
Newberg, Oregon
Entry: **University, Christian.**

Cyndi Allison, MA
Instructor in Communication Arts
Catawba College
Salisbury, North Carolina
Entry: **Media.**

Kevin L. Anderson, PhD
Associate Professor of Bible and Theology
Asbury University
Wilmore, Kentucky
Entries: **Glossolalia; Kingdom of God; Mystery Religions; New Birth (Regeneration).**

Klaus Arnold, MDiv
Rector, European Nazarene College
Principal and Senior Lecturer in Pastoral and Social Theology
Büsingen, Switzerland
Entries: **Mysticism/Mystical Theology; Pietism; Socialism.**

Clarence (Bud) Bence, PhD
Emeritus Professor of Church History
Indiana Wesleyan University
Marion, Indiana
Entries: **Pilgrim Holiness Church; Wesleyan Church; Wesleyan Methodism.**

Robert D. Branson, PhD
Emeritus Professor of Biblical Literature
Olivet Nazarene University
Bourbonnais, Illinois
Entries: **Cosmology/Cosmogony; Covenant; Holiness; Love.**

Kent E. Brower, PhD
Vice-Principal and Senior Research Fellow in Biblical Studies
Nazarene Theological College
Manchester, United Kingdom
Entries: **Bible; Biblical Metaphors for Salvation; Biblical Theology; Eschatology, Biblical; Scripture, Wesleyan Approach to.**

Warren S. Brown, PhD
Professor of Psychology
Travis Research Institute
Fuller Graduate School of Psychology
Pasadena, California
Entries: **Determinism and Free Will; Neuroscience and Religion.**

Barry E. Bryant, PhD
Associate Professor of United Methodist and Wesleyan Studies
Director, United Methodist Center for the Study of Ministry
Garrett-Evangelical Theological Seminary
Evanston, Illinois
Entry: **Holiness Movements: American, British, and Continental.**

Barry Callen, EdD
University Professor Emeritus of Christian Studies
Anderson University School of Theology
Anderson University
Anderson, Indiana
Entries: **Church of God (Anderson); Fatalism; Fundamentalist Theology; Practical Theology.**

Ted A. Campbell, PhD
Associate Professor of Church History
Perkins School of Theology
Southern Methodist University
Dallas, Texas
Entries: **Counter-Reformation (Catholic Reformation); Historical Theology; Methodist History and Historiography; World Methodism.**

Davide Cantarella, MA
District Superintendent, Russia North District
Education Coordinator, Commonwealth of Independent States Field
Moscow, Russian Federation
Entry: **Principalities and Powers.**

Jonathan P. Case, PhD
Associate Professor of Theology
Houghton College
Houghton, New York
Entries: **Luther, Martin; Roman Catholicism.**

Filimão M. Chambo, DLitt et Phil
Regional Director, Africa Region
Church of the Nazarene
Roodepoort, South Africa
Entries: **Polygamy; Ubuntu.**

Constance M. Cherry, DMin
Professor of Worship and Christian Ministries
Indiana Wesleyan University
Marion, Indiana
Entries: **Liturgical Theology; Liturgy and Worship; Music/Hymns/Hymnology.**

Young-Ho Chun, PhD
Professor of Systematic Theology
Saint Paul School of Theology
Kansas City, Missouri
Entries: **Asian Theology; Asian-American Theology; Hope, Christian; Humanism; Reformed Tradition.**

Gregory S. Clapper, PhD
Professor of Religion and Philosophy
University of Indianapolis
Indianapolis, Indiana
Entries: **Narrative Theology; Religious Pluralism; Scripture, Theology of; Virtues.**

Elisa Bernal Corley, PhD
Independent Scholar
New Berlin, Wisconsin
Entry: **Mujerista Theology.**

J. Gregory Crofford, PhD
Regional Education Coordinator, Africa Region
Church of the Nazarene
Entries: **Classes, Bands, Conference, Connectionalism, Society; Covenant Service; Jacobite Church; Predestination and Election; Prevenient Grace; Sin.**

Howard Culbertson, DMin
Garner Chair of Missions
Professor of Missions
Southern Nazarene University
Bethany, Oklahoma
Entries: **Indigenous Theologies; Miracles/Signs and Wonders; New Church Movements; New Religions; Westernization of the Gospel.**

John Culp, PhD
Professor of Philosophy
Azusa Pacific University
Azusa, California
Entries: **Apologetics; Belief; Neo-paganism; New Age Spirituality; Panentheism.**

Magali do Nascimento Cunha, PhD
Professor of Communications and Ecumenism
School of Theology
Universidade Metodista de São Paulo (Methodist University of São Paulo)
São Bernardo do Campo, Brazil
Entry: **Spiritual Warfare.**

Floyd T. Cunningham, PhD
President and Professor of Church History
Asia-Pacific Nazarene Theological Seminary
Taytay, Philippines
Entries: **Church of the Nazarene; Reformation; Revivalism.**

Dennis C. Dickerson, PhD
James M. Lawson, Jr. Professor of History
Department of History
Vanderbilt University
Nashville, Tennessee
Entries: **African-American Methodism; Black Theology; Social Gospel.**

Patti L. Dikes, JD (PhD student, Claremont Graduate University)
Adjunct Professor
Point Loma Nazarene University
San Diego, California
Entry: **Feminist Theology.**

H. Ray Dunning, PhD
Professor Emeritus Systematic Theology
Trevecca Nazarene University
Nashville, Tennessee
Entries: **Deism; Dispensationalism; Doctrine/Dogma; Free Will; Laity; Monism, Dualism, Pluralism; Ordination;** *Ordo Salutis;* **Pantheism; Religious Freedom; Witness of the Spirit.**

Andrew M. Eason, PhD
Assistant Professor of Religion
Booth University College
Winnipeg, Manitoba
Entry: **Salvation Army.**

Arseny Ermakov, PhD
Head of Discipline and Lecturer in Biblical Studies
School for Christian Studies
Booth College
Sydney, Australia
Entries: **Church of the East; Coptic Orthodoxy; Icons, Images, Iconoclasm.**

Terry Fach, MA, MPhil
Regional Education Coordinator, Canada
Church of the Nazarene
Calgary, Alberta
Entries: **Experience, Phenomenon of; Technology; Technology, Ethic of.**

Darrel Falk, PhD
President, The BioLogos Foundation
Professor of Biology
Point Loma Nazarene University
San Diego, California
Entry: **Evolution/Evolutionary Biology.**

Rubén Fernández, DMin
President, Seminario Nazareno de las Américas
Regional Education Coordinator, Mesoamerica Region
Church of the Nazarene
San José, Costa Rica
Entry: **Latin American Missiology/Liberation Struggle.**

Dean Flemming, PhD
Professor of New Testament and Missions
MidAmerica Nazarene University
Olathe, Kansas
Entries: **Contextualization; Idolatry; Mission, Theology of.**

Peter S. Forsaith, PhD
Research Fellow, Oxford Centre for Methodism and Church History
Oxford Brookes University
Oxford, United Kingdom
Entry: **Methodism, British.**

Kerry Fulcher, PhD
Provost and Chief Academic Officer
Former Chair, Biology Department
Point Loma Nazarene University
San Diego, California
Entry: **Natural Science.**

Karl Ganske, PhD
Lead Pastor, Springwater Church of the Nazarene
Entries: **Moravians; Orthodox Church; Puritanism.**

Jamie Gates, PhD
Professor of Sociology
Director, Center for Justice and Reconciliation
Point Loma Nazarene University
San Diego, California
Entries: **Globalization; Green Theology; Sexualization of a Culture; Wealth.**

R. Hollis Gause, PhD
Professor of New Testament and Theology
Pentecostal Theological Seminary
Cleveland, Tennessee
Entries: **Charismatic Theology; Pentecostalism.**

Justo L. González, PhD
Professor of Historical Theology, Retired
Decatur, Georgia
Entry: **Latino/Latina (Hispanic) Theology.**

W. Stephen Gunter, PhD
Associate Dean for Methodist Studies
Research Professor of Evangelism and Wesleyan Studies
Duke Divinity School
Duke University
Durham, North Carolina
Entries: **Arminian Theology; Arminius, Jacob.**

Amy Laura Hall, PhD
Associate Professor of Christian Ethics
Duke Divinity School
Duke University
Durham, North Carolina
Entry: **Justice.**

Geordan Hammond, PhD
Director, Manchester Wesley Research Centre
Senior Lecturer in Church History and Wesley Studies
Nazarene Theological College
Manchester, United Kingdom
Entry: **Radical Reformation.**

Brannon Hancock, PhD
Xenia Nazarene Church
Xenia, Ohio
Entries: **Arts, The; Literature and the Christian Faith; Popular Culture.**

Douglas S. Hardy, PhD
Professor of Spiritual Formation
Nazarene Theological Seminary
Kansas City, Missouri
Entries: **Contemplative Spirituality; Discernment; Empathy.**

Steven Harper, PhD
Professor of Spiritual Formation and Wesley Studies
Asbury Theological Seminary
Wilmore, Kentucky
Entries: **Renovaré; Self-Denial; Spiritual Direction/Spiritual Director; Spiritual Disciplines.**

Achim Härtner, MA
Professor of Practical Theology
E. Stanley Jones Chair of Evangelism
Reutlingen School of Theology
Reutlingen, Germany
Entries: **Prayer; Preaching.**

MaryAnn Hawkins, PhD
Associate Professor of InterCultural Studies
Dean of the Chapel
Anderson University School of Theology
Anderson University
Anderson, Indiana
Entries: **Indigenous Christian Groups; Missionary Movements; Polytheism; Word of Faith Theology.**

Antonie Holleman, Drs
Academic Dean and Lecturer in Church History
European Nazarene College
Büsingen, Switzerland
Entries: **Mary/Mariology; Monasticism; State Religion.**

Daryl Ireland, MDiv (ThD Candidate, Boston University School of Theology)
Francisca Ireland-Verwoerd, MDiv (PhD student, Boston University)
Quincy, Massachusetts
Entry: **New Religious Movements.**

Jon P. Johnston, PhD
Professor of Sociology/Anthropology
Pepperdine University
Malibu, California
Entries: **Ethnicity; Social Sciences; Sociobiology.**

Jorge L. Julca, DMin
Rector, Seminario Teológico Nazareno del Cono Sur
Regional Education Coordinator, South America Region
Church of the Nazarene
Buenos Aires, Argentina
Entry: **Discipleship.**

Israel Kamudzandu, PhD
Assistant Professor of New Testament Studies, Lindsey P. Pherigo Chair
Saint Paul School of Theology
Kansas City, Missouri
Entries: **Biblical Interpretation, Ancient and Modern Methods; Jesus of Nazareth;**
  Pharisees/Sadducees.

Craig Keen, PhD
Professor of Systematic Theology
Azusa Pacific University
Azusa, California
Entries: **Anthropology, Theological; Arianism; Creeds (Nicene, Chalcedonian,**
  Apostles', Athanasian); Incarnation.

Nathan R. Kerr, PhD
Associate Professor of Religion
Trevecca Nazarene University
Nashville, Tennessee
Entries: **Radical Orthodox Theology; Religions, Theology of; Theopolitical Theology.**

Melanie Starks Kierstead, PhD
Professor of Bible and Theology
Asbury University
Wilmore, Kentucky
Entries: **Faith; Family, Christian.**

Kenneth C. Kinghorn, PhD
Emeritus Professor of Church History
Asbury Theological Seminary
Wilmore, Kentucky
Entries: **Evangelical United Brethren Tradition; Methodism, American; Orthodoxy/**
  Orthopraxis/Orthopathy; World Methodist Council.

Kevin Kinghorn, PhD
Associate Professor of Philosophy and Religion
Asbury Theological Seminary
Wilmore, Kentucky
Entries: **Natural Theology; Philosophical Theology; Philosophy of Religion.**

Dennis F. Kinlaw, PhD
The Francis Asbury Society
Past President of Asbury University
Wilmore, Kentucky
Entry: **Christian Perfection (Entire Sanctification).**

Henry H. Knight III, PhD
Donald and Pearl Wright Professor of Wesleyan Studies
Saint Paul School of Theology
Kansas City, Missouri
Entries: **Canonical Theism; Involuntary Transgressions; Means of Grace; Orthopathy/
Orthokardia; Pentecostal Theology; Postconservative Evangelical Theology;
Sanctified Church; Tempers and Affections; Wesley, John, Theology of.**

Musa Victor Kunene, PhD
St Helens Church of the Nazarene
Sutton, St Helens
Merseyside, United Kingdom
Entries: **African Indigenous Church Theologies; Demons/Unclean Spirits.**

John Wesley Z. Kurewa, PhD
Kurewa Chair: E. Stanley Jones Professor of Evangelism
Africa University
Mutare, Zimbabwe
Africa
Entries: **Ancestors; Indigenization; Proselytism; Religious Conflict.**

Kristina LaCelle-Peterson, PhD
Associate Professor of Religion
Houghton College
Houghton, New York
Entries: **Armenian Apostolic Church; Asceticism; Free Methodism; Women's Role in
the Church.**

Philip N. LaFountain, ThD
Assistant Professor of Religion and Philosophy
Eastern Nazarene College
Quincy, Massachusetts
Entries: **Logical Positivism; Neoplatonism.**

Robert K. Lang'at, PhD
Bishop of the Africa Gospel Church
Kericho, Kenya
East Africa
Entries: **Ordinary and Extraordinary Ministries of the Church; Testimony/Witness.**

Deirdre Brower Latz, PhD
Lecturer in Pastoral and Social Theology
Nazarene Theological College
Manchester, United Kingdom
Entries: **Love Feast; Works of Mercy; Works of Piety.**

Terry LeBlanc, PhD
Chair and Director of the North American Institute for Indigenous Theological Studies
    (NAIITS)
Evansburg, Alberta
Canada
Entry: **North American Native Theologies.**

Carl M. Leth, PhD
Professor of Theology
Dean, School of Theology and Christian Ministry
Olivet Nazarene University
Bourbonnais, Illinois
Entries: **Anabaptists; Democracy; Keswick Movement; Via Media.**

James W. Lewis, PhD
Professor of Theology and Ethics
Anderson University School of Theology
Anderson, Indiana
Entries: **Bioethics; Creation, Care for the (Ecology); Ethics; Social Ethics.**

Michael Lodahl, PhD
Professor of Theology
Point Loma Nazarene University
San Diego, California
Entries: **Interfaith Dialogue; Islam.**

D. Stephen Long, PhD
Professor of Systematic Theology
Marquette University
Milwaukee, Wisconsin
Entries: **Altruism/Natural Morality; Christian Ethics/Moral Theology; Economics and
    the Use of Money; Holy Spirit (Pneumatology); Thomas Aquinas.**

Russell Lovett, PhD
Africa Nazarene University
Nairobi, Kenya
East Africa
Entries: **Creation/New Creation; Cross; Fruit of the Spirit; Gifts of the Spirit.**

Tim Macquiban, PhD
Minister, Wesley Methodist Church
Cambridge, United Kingdom
Entry: **Pseudo-Macarius.**

Beauty R. Maenzanise, PhD
Dean, Faculty of Theology
Africa University
Mutare, Zimbabwe
Africa
Entries: **African Theology; African Traditional Religions; Marriage; Traditional
    Religions.**

Mark Mann, PhD
Director, Wesleyan Center for 21st Century Studies
Associate Professor of Theology
Point Loma Nazarene University
San Diego, California
Entries: **Church and State; Human Sexuality.**

K. Steve McCormick, PhD
Professor of Historical Theology
William M. Greathouse Chair of Wesleyan-Holiness Theology
Nazarene Theological Seminary
Kansas City, Missouri
Entries: **Methodist Connectionalism; Theosis (Deification).**

David McEwan, PhD
Director of Research
Senior Lecturer in Theology, Pastoral Theology and Practice
Director, Australasian Centre for Wesleyan Research
Nazarene Theological College
Thornlands, Queensland
Australia
Entries: **Cult; Penance; Syncretism, Religious; Zionism, Christian.**

Philip R. Meadows, PhD
Lecturer in Missiology and Wesleyan Studies
Cliff College
Calver, Hope Valley
United Kingdom
Entry: **Wesley, Charles, Theology of.**

Kevin Mellish, PhD
Professor of Biblical Studies
Olivet Nazarene University
Bourbonnais, Illinois
Entries: **Devil/Satan; Lament; Legalism; Temple.**

Gift Mtukwa, MA
Assistant Lecturer
Africa Nazarene University
Nairobi, Kenya
East Africa
Entries: **Conscience; Poverty.**

Larry Murphy, PhD
Professor of Biblical Literature
Olivet Nazarene University
Bourbonnais, Illinois
Entries: **Angels; Hell.**

Thomas A. Noble, PhD
Professor of Systematic Theology
Nazarene Theological Seminary
Kansas City, Missouri
Entries: **Justification; Person; Systematic Theology (Dogmatics); Trinity.**

Thomas J. Oord, PhD
Professor of Theology and Philosophy
Northwest Nazarene University
Nampa, Idaho
Entries: **Existentialism; Metaphysics; Process Theology; Social Justice.**

Terence Paige, PhD
Professor of New Testament
Houghton College
Houghton, New York
Entries: **Repentance; Resurrection; Second Coming of Christ/Parousia.**

Blanches de Paula, PhD
Professor of Pastoral Theology
Universidade Metodista de São Paulo (Methodist University of São Paulo)
São Bernardo do Campo, Brazil
Entry: **Popular Religiosity.**

Priscilla Pope-Levison, PhD
Professor of Theology
Seattle Pacific University
Seattle, Washington
Entry: **Ecumenism.**

F. Douglas Powe Jr., PhD
E. Stanley Jones Associate Professor of Evangelism
Saint Paul School of Theology
Kansas City, Missouri
Entries: **Emergent Church Theology; Global South.**

Samuel M. Powell, PhD
Professor of Philosophy and Theology
Point Loma Nazarene University
San Diego, California
Entries: **Modernity; Pelagianism; Philosophy of Science; Postliberal Theology; Public Theology; Revelation; Salvation (Soteriology); Sanctification; Tradition, Evangelical Retrieval of.**

David Rainey, PhD
Senior Lecturer in Theology
Nazarene Theological College
Manchester, United Kingdom
Entries: **Eschatology; Evangelical Theology; Grace; Science and the Bible.**

Harold E. Raser, PhD
Professor of the History of Christianity
Director, Master of Arts (Theological Studies) Program
Nazarene Theological Seminary
Kansas City, Missouri
Entries: **Anglicanism; Palmer, Phoebe; Protestantism; Vatican Council II.**

James E. Read, PhD
Associate Professor of Philosophy and Ethics
William and Catherine Booth University College
Winnipeg, Manitoba
Canada
Entry: **Greek Philosophy.**

Terence B. Read, PhD
Professor Emeritus of Missiology
Nazarene Theological Seminary
Kansas City, Missouri
Entries: **Animism; Contextual Theology; Holistic Mission; Lausanne Movement and Covenant; Persecution and Martyrdom.**

Rodney L. Reed, PhD
Deputy Vice Chancellor, Academic Affairs
Senior Lecturer
Africa Nazarene University
Nairobi, Kenya
East Africa
Entries: **Capitalism; Obedience.**

Keith H. Reeves, PhD
Professor of New Testament and Early Christian Literature
Department of Biblical Studies
Azusa Pacific University
Azusa, California
Entries: **Kenosis; Metaphors and Names for God in the Bible; Stewardship.**

Helmut Renders, PhD
Professor for Theology and History
School of Theology
Universidade Metodista de São Paulo (Methodist University of São Paulo)
São Bernardo do Campo, Brazil
Entry: **Folk Religion.**

Claudio de Oliveira Ribeiro, PhD
Professor of Systematic Theology and History
Diretor da Faculdade de Humanidades e Direito
Universidade Metodista de São Paulo (Methodist University of São Paulo)
São Paulo, Brazil
Entry: **Latin American Theologies.**

Gregory Robertson, ThD
Associate Professor of Christian Theology
School of Theology
Anderson University
Anderson, Indiana
Entries: **Church (Ecclesiology); Liberal Theology; Secular/Secularism/Secularization.**

Theodore Runyon, Dr. Theol.
Emeritus Professor of Systematic Theology
Emory University
Atlanta, Georgia
Entries: **Augustine; Calvin, John; Church Fathers; Sacraments.**

Lester Ruth, PhD
Research Professor of Christian Worship
Duke Divinity School
Duke University
Durham, North Carolina
Entry: **Christian Year.**

John Sanders, ThD
Professor of Religion
Hendrix College
Conway, Arkansas
Entries: **Destiny of the Unevangelized; Liberation Theology; Open Theology/Theism; Postmodernity; Theodicy/Evil.**

Kenneth Schenck, PhD
Dean and Professor of New Testament
Wesley Seminary at Indiana Wesleyan University
Marion, Indiana
Entries: **Gospel; Heaven; Humility; Myth/Mythos.**

William L. Selvidge, DMiss
Associate Professor of Intercultural Studies
Nazarene Theological Seminary
Kansas City, Missouri
Entry: **Parachurch Institutions.**

Mary Lou Shea, ThD
Associate Professor of Religion
Eastern Nazarene College
Quincy, Massachusetts
Entries: **Millennium Development Goals (MDGs); New Apostolic Reformation/New Apostolic Movements; Womanist Theology.**

Susie Stanley, PhD
Professor of Historical Theology, Retired
Messiah College
Grantham, Pennsylvania
Entries: **Evangelical Feminism; Wesleyan Feminism.**

Lincoln Stevens, PhD
Professor of Philosophy
Mount Vernon Nazarene University
Mount Vernon, Ohio
Entries: **Epistemology; Reductionism; Terrorism.**

Kenton Stiles, PhD
Assistant Professor of Art History
Indiana Wesleyan University
Marion, Indiana
Entries: **Aesthetics; Dance; Film/Cinema.**

Catherine Stonehouse, PhD
Orlean Bullard Beeson Professor of Christian Discipleship
Asbury Theological Seminary
Wilmore, Kentucky
Entries: **Childhood, Wesleyan Theology of; Spiritual Formation/Growth; Vocation and Calling.**

Brent A. Strawn, PhD
Associate Professor of Old Testament
Candler School of Theology
Emory University
Atlanta, Georgia
Entries: **Hiddenness of God; Israel.**

Merle D. Strege, ThD
Professor of Historical Theology
Department of Religious Studies
Anderson University
Anderson, Indiana
Entries: **Desert Fathers and Mothers; Early African Christianity; Early Church; Ecumenical Councils; Universalism.**

Patrick Streiff, PhD
Bishop, Central and Southern Europe Episcopal Area
United Methodist Church
Zürich, Switzerland
Entry: **Fletcher, John, Theology of.**

Joseph Suray, PhD
Professor in Contemporary and Wesleyan Theology
Minister in the Methodist Church
Member of the British Methodist Council
Leicester, United Kingdom
Entries: **Deliverance/Exorcism; Divination; Mission and Social Justice; Reincarnation.**

Dwight D. Swanson, PhD
Senior Research Fellow and Senior Lecturer in Biblical Studies
Nazarene Theological College
Manchester, United Kingdom
Entries: **Dead Sea Scrolls; Messianic Judaism; Second Temple Judaism; Zionism.**

Elsa Tamez, PhD
Emeritus Professor, Universidad Bíblica Latinoamericana (Latin American Biblical University)
San José, Costa Rica
Entry: **Latin American Women's Theology.**

Richard P. Thompson, PhD
Professor of New Testament
Chair, Department of Religion
School of Theology and Christian Ministries
Northwest Nazarene University
Nampa, Idaho
Entries: **Healing, Theology of; Soul.**

Don Thorsen, PhD
Professor of Theology and Chair of Advanced Studies
Azusa Pacific Graduate School of Theology
Azusa Pacific University
Azusa, California
Entries: **Personalism/Personalist Theology; Quadrilateral, Wesleyan; Sect; Time and Eternity; Work, Theology of.**

Kevin Timpe, PhD
Associate Professor
Department of Philosophy
Northwest Nazarene University
Nampa, Idaho
Entries: **Enlightenment; Intelligent Design.**

Alex Varughese, PhD
Professor of Old Testament
Mount Vernon Nazarene University
Mount Vernon, Ohio
Entries: **Biblicism/Bibliolatry; Land; Prophecy/Prophet.**

Robert W. Wall, PhD
Paul T. Walls Professor of Scripture and Wesleyan Studies
Seattle Pacific University
Seattle, Washington
Entries: **Intertextuality; Law and Gospel; Reconciliation; Righteousness.**

Kenneth L. Waters Sr., PhD
Associate Dean of the Division of Religion and Philosophy
Professor of New Testament
Azusa Pacific University
Azusa, California
Entries: **Christology, New Testament; Ecclesiology, New Testament; Principalities and Powers.**

Sarah Whittle, PhD
Lecturer in Biblical Studies
Nazarene Theological College
Manchester, United Kingdom
Entries: **Hermeneutics; Hospitability/Hospitality; Immortality/Life After Death.**

L. Bryan Williams, PhD
Social Ethicist
Pastor, McCall Church of the Nazarene
McCall, Idaho
Entries: **Atheism/Agnosticism; Communism; Just War/War; Peacemaking; Rights, Human.**

Norman Wilson, PhD
Associate Professor of Intercultural Studies
Indiana Wesleyan University
Marion, Indiana
Entries: **Christianity and Global Cultures; Fundamentalisms; Postcolonialism; Student Volunteer Movement; Tentmakers.**

Karen Strand Winslow, PhD
Professor of Old Testament
Azusa Pacific Graduate School of Theology
Director, Free Methodist Center
Azusa Pacific University
Azusa, California
Entries: **Shalom; Sheol/Death/Gehenna; Torah; Wisdom; Women in the Bible.**

John Wright, PhD
Professor of Theology and Scripture
Point Loma Nazarene University
San Diego, California
Entries: **Apocalyptic/Apocalypticism; Creationism; Judaism.**

Lee San Young, PhD
Academic Dean
Asia-Pacific Nazarene Theological Seminary
Taytay, Philippines
Entry: **Honor/Shame Culture.**

William T. Young, PhD
Chief of Chaplains, California State Military Reserve
Adjunct Professor of Missiology
Chinese International Theological Seminary
Hacienda Heights, California
Entries: **Chinese Church, Contemporary; Mission and Theological Education; Parliament of the World's Religions; Third Wave Theology; Underground Churches in China; World Missionary Conference, Edinburgh 1910.**

DICTIONARY TOPICS
BY CATEGORIES

BIBLE, GENERAL

Bible
Biblical Interpretation, Ancient and
    Modern Methods
Biblical Metaphors for Salvation
Biblical Theology
Biblicism/Bibliolatry
Covenant
Destiny of the Unevangelized
Devil/Satan
Eschatology, Biblical
Hell
Hermeneutics
Hospitability/Hospitality
Idolatry
Immortality/Life After Death
Intertextuality
Metaphors and Names for God in the
    Bible
Righteousness
Second Temple Judaism
Temple
Women in the Bible

BIBLE, NEW TESTAMENT

Christology, New Testament
Creation/New Creation
Cross
Demons/Unclean Spirits
Ecclesiology, New Testament
Fruit of the Spirit
Gifts of the Spirit
Glossolalia
Gospel
Heaven
Jesus of Nazareth
Kingdom of God
Law and Gospel

Love
Pharisees/Sadducees
Principalities and Powers
Reconciliation
Repentance
Resurrection
Second Coming of Christ/Parousia
Soul

BIBLE, OLD TESTAMENT

Angels
Apocalyptic/Apocalypticism
Dead Sea Scrolls
Hiddenness of God
Israel
Lament
Land
Prophecy/Prophet
Shalom
Sheol/Death/Gehenna
Torah
Wisdom

CHRISTIANITY AND OTHER RELIGIONS

African Traditional Religions
Ancestors
Cult
Fundamentalisms
Interfaith Dialogue
Islam
New Religious Movements
Parliament of the World's Religions
Reincarnation
Religions, Theology of
Religious Conflict
Religious Pluralism
Syncretism, Religious

CHURCH AND CULTURE

Aesthetics
Arts, The
Dance
Film/Cinema
Literature and the Christian Faith
Media
Popular Culture

CHURCH AND SOCIETY

Capitalism
Christianity and Global Cultures
Church and State
Democracy
Public Theology
Religious Freedom
Secular/Secularism/Secularization
Sexualization of a Culture
State Religion
Technology
Technology, Ethic of
Terrorism
University, Christian

CHURCH/ECCLESIOLOGY

Church (Ecclesiology)
Laity
Ordination
Parachurch Institutions
Sacraments
Sect
Women's Role in the Church

DENOMINATIONS IN THE WESLEYAN FAMILY

African-American Methodism
Church of God (Anderson)
Church of the Nazarene
Evangelical United Brethren Tradition
Free Methodism
Holiness Denominations Worldwide
Methodism, American
Methodism, British
Pilgrim Holiness Church
Salvation Army
Sanctified Church
Wesleyan Church
Wesleyan Methodism

EARLY METHODISM

Classes, Bands, Conference, Connectionalism, Society
Covenant Service
Fletcher, John, Theology of
Love Feast
Means of Grace
Methodist Connectionalism
Ordinary and Extraordinary Ministries of the Church
Tempers and Affections
Wesley, Charles, Theology of
Wesley, John, Theology of
Works of Mercy
Works of Piety

ETHICS

Altruism/Natural Morality
Bioethics
Christian Ethics/Moral Theology
Creation, Care for the (Ecology)
Economics and the Use of Money
Ethics
Humanism
Human Sexuality
Humility
Justice
Just War/War
Marriage
Obedience
Peacemaking
Poverty
Rights, Human
Social Ethics
Social Justice
Ubuntu
Virtues
Wealth

HISTORICAL TRADITIONS AND TOPICS

Anabaptists
Anglicanism
Arianism
Armenian Apostolic Church
Arminius, Jacob
Augustine
Calvin, John
Chinese Church, Contemporary

Church Fathers
Church of the East
Coptic Orthodoxy
Counter-Reformation (Catholic
    Reformation)
Creeds (Nicene, Chalcedonian,
    Apostles', Athanasian)
Deism
Desert Fathers and Mothers
Early African Christianity
Early Church
Ecumenical Councils
Ecumenism
Historical Theology
Icons, Images, Iconoclasm
Jacobite Church
Judaism
Luther, Martin
Mary/Mariology
Monasticism
Moravians
Mystery Religions
Mysticism/Mystical Theology
New Apostolic Reformation/New
    Apostolic Movements
New Church Movements
Orthodox Church
Pelagianism
Penance
Persecution and Martyrdom
Pietism
Protestantism
Pseudo-Macarius
Puritanism
Radical Reformation
Reformation
Reformed Tradition
Revivalism
Roman Catholicism
Social Gospel
Thomas Aquinas
Underground Church in China
Vatican Council II
Zionism

LITURGY/WORSHIP

Christian Year
Liturgy and Worship
Music/Hymns/Hymnology
Preaching

MISSIONS/MISSIOLOGY

Animism
Contextualization
Contextual Theology
Deliverance/Exorcism
Divination
Evangelism
Family, Christian
Folk Religion
Globalization
Global South
Holistic Mission
Honor/Shame Culture
Indigenization
Indigenous Christian Groups
Indigenous Theologies
Latin American Missiology/Liberation
    Struggle
Lausanne Movement and Covenant
Millennium Development Goals
    (MDGs)
Miracles/Signs and Wonders
Mission, Theology of
Mission and Social Justice
Mission and Theological Education
Missionary Movements
Polygamy
Popular Religiosity
Postcolonialism
Proselytism
Student Volunteer Movement
Tentmakers
Traditional Religions
Westernization of the Gospel
World Missionary Conference,
    Edinburgh 1910

PHILOSOPHY

Atheism/Agnosticism
Belief
Communism
Determinism and Free Will
Epistemology
Existentialism
Experience, Phenomenon of
Fatalism
Greek Philosophy
Logical Positivism
Metaphysics

Modernity
Monism, Dualism, Pluralism
Myth/Mythos
Natural Theology
Neoplatonism
New Religions
Panentheism
Pantheism
Person
Philosophy of Religion
Polytheism
Postmodernity
Reductionism
Socialism

SCIENCES, NATURAL

Cosmology/Cosmogony
Creationism
Enlightenment
Ethnicity
Evolution/Evolutionary Biology
Intelligent Design
Natural Science
Neuroscience and Religion
Philosophy of Science
Science and the Bible

SCIENCES, SOCIAL

Social Sciences
Sociobiology

SPIRITUAL DISCIPLINES/ FORMATION

Asceticism
Contemplative Spirituality
Discernment
Discipleship
Empathy
Prayer
Renovaré
Self-Denial
Spiritual Direction/Spiritual Director
Spiritual Disciplines
Spiritual Formation/Growth
Stewardship
Testimony/Witness
Vocation and Calling

SYSTEMATIC THEOLOGY

Anthropology, Theological
Apologetics
Atonement
Baptism with the Holy Spirit
Childhood, Wesleyan Theology of
Christian Perfection (Entire
    Sanctification)
Christology
Conscience
Destiny of the Unevangelized
Dispensationalism
Doctrine/Dogma
Eschatology
Faith
Free Will
God, Doctrine of
Grace
Healing, Theology of
Holiness
Holy Spirit (Pneumatology)
Hope, Christian
Incarnation
Involuntary Transgressions
Justification
Kenosis
Legalism
New Birth (Regeneration)
Ordo Salutis
Orthodoxy/Orthopraxis/Orthopathy
Orthopathy/Orthokardia
Philosophical Theology
Predestination and Election
Prevenient Grace
Revelation
Salvation (Soteriology)
Sanctification
Scripture, Theology of
Scripture, Wesleyan Approach to
Sin
Spiritual Warfare
Systematic Theology (Dogmatics)
Theodicy/Evil
Theosis (Deification)
Time and Eternity
Trinity
Universalism
Via Media
Witness of the Spirit
Work, Theology of

THEOLOGICAL MOVEMENTS

African Indigenous Church Theologies
African Theology
Asian-American Theology
Asian Theology
Black Theology
Canonical Theism
Charismatic Theology
Emergent Church Theology
Evangelical Feminism
Evangelical Theology
Feminist Theology
Fundamentalist Theology
Green Theology
Latin American Theologies
Latin American Women's Theology
Latino/Latina (Hispanic) Theology
Liberal Theology
Liberation Theology
Liturgical Theology
Messianic Judaism
Mujerista Theology
Narrative Theology
Neo-paganism
New Age Spirituality
North American Native Theologies
Open Theology/Theism

Pentecostalism
Pentecostal Theology
Personalism/Personalist Theology
Postconservative Evangelical Theology
Postliberal Theology
Practical Theology
Process Theology
Radical Orthodox Theology
Theopolitical Theology
Third Wave Theology
Tradition, Evangelical Retrieval of
Wesleyan Feminism
Womanist Theology
Word of Faith Theology (Health and
    Prosperity)
Zionism, Christian

WESLEYAN TRADITION

Arminian Theology
Holiness Movements: American,
    British, and Continental
Keswick Movement
Methodist History and Historiography
Palmer, Phoebe
Quadrilateral, Wesleyan
World Methodism
World Methodist Council

ABBREVIATIONS

GENERAL

LXX	Septuagint
NT	New Testament
OT	Old Testament

BIBLE TRANSLATIONS

ESV	*English Standard Version*
KJV	King James Version
NASB	*New American Standard Bible*
NET	*New Testament—New Evangelical Translation*
NIV	*New International Version*
NJPS	*Tanakh: The Holy Scriptures: The New JPS Translation to the Traditional Hebrew Text*
NKJV	*New King James Version*
NRSV	*New Revised Standard Version*

ABBREVIATIONS FOR BOOKS OF THE BIBLE

Old Testament

Gen.	Genesis	Neh.	Nehemiah	Hos.	Hosea
Exod.	Exodus	Esther	Esther	Joel	Joel
Lev.	Leviticus	Job	Job	Amos	Amos
Num.	Numbers	Ps. (pl. Pss.)	Psalms	Obad.	Obadiah
Deut.	Deuteronomy	Prov.	Proverbs	Jon.	Jonah
Josh.	Joshua	Eccles.	Ecclesiastes	Mic.	Micah
Judg.	Judges	Song of Sol.	Song of Songs	Nah.	Nahum
Ruth	Ruth	Isa.	Isaiah	Hab.	Habakkuk
1–2 Sam.	1–2 Samuel	Jer.	Jeremiah	Zeph.	Zephaniah
1–2 Kings	1–2 Kings	Lam.	Lamentations	Hag.	Haggai
1–2 Chron.	1–2 Chronicles	Ezek.	Ezekiel	Zech.	Zechariah
Ezra	Ezra	Dan.	Daniel	Mal.	Malachi

New Testament

Matt.	Matthew	Gal.	Galatians	Philem.	Philemon
Mark	Mark	Eph.	Ephesians	Heb.	Hebrews
Luke	Luke	Phil.	Philippians	James	James
John	John	Col.	Colossians	1–2 Pet.	1–2 Peter
Acts	Acts	1–2 Thess.	1–2 Thessalonians	1–2–3 John	1–2–3 John
Rom.	Romans			Jude	Jude
1–2 Cor.	1–2 Corinthians	1–2 Tim.	1–2 Timothy	Rev.	Revelation
		Titus	Titus		

APOCRYPHA

| 1–2 Esd. | 1–2 Esdras |
| 1–2 Macc. | 1–2 Maccabees |

OT PSEUDEPIGRAPHA

2 Bar.	2 Baruch (Syriac Apocalypse)
1 En.	1 Enoch (Ethiopic Apocalypse)
Jos. Asen.	Joseph and Aseneth

DEAD SEA SCROLLS

| 1QS | Rule of the Community |
| 4Q510 | Songs of the Sage |

PHILO

| QE 1, 2 | Questions and Answers on Exodus 1, 2 |

JOSEPHUS

| Ant. | Jewish Antiquities |

RABBINIC LITERATURE

| Gen. Rab. | Genesis Rabbah |

OTHER ANCIENT SOURCES

Hippolytus

| Haer. | Refutation of All Heresies |

WORKS BY JOHN WESLEY

Outler	Outler, Albert C., ed. *John Wesley*. New York: Oxford University Press, 1964.
Wesley, *Journal*	Wesley, John. *The Journal of the Rev. John Wesley, A.M.* 8 vols. 1905-16. Bicentenary edition. London: Epworth Press, 1938.
Wesley, *Library*	———. *A Christian Library*. 30 vols. 1821. Wesley Center Online. Nampa, ID: Wesley Center for Applied Theology, c/o Northwest Nazarene University, 1993–2011. http://wesley.nnu.edu/john-wesley/a-christian-library/.
Wesley, *NT Notes*	———. *Explanatory Notes upon the New Testament*. 2 vols. London: Thomas Cordeux, 1813.
Wesley, *Works*	———. *The Works of John Wesley*. 14 vols. 3rd ed. London: Wesleyan Methodist Book Room, 1872. Reprint, Grand Rapids: Baker Books, 2002.

TRANSLITERATION OF HEBREW AND GREEK

Hebrew/ Aramaic	Letter	English
א	alef	ʾ
ב	bet	b
ג	gimel	g
ד	dalet	d
ה	he	h
ו	vav	v or w
ז	zayin	z
ח	khet	kh
ט	tet	t
י	yod	y
כ/ך	kaf	k
ל	lamed	l
מ/ם	mem	m
נ/ן	nun	n
ס	samek	s
ע	ayin	ʿ
פ/ף	pe	p
צ/ץ	tsade	ts
ק	qof	q
ר	resh	r
שׂ	sin	s
שׁ	shin	sh
ת	tav	t

Greek	Letter	English
α	alpha	a
β	bēta	b
γ	gamma	g
γ	gamma nasal	n (before γ, κ, ξ, χ)
δ	delta	d
ε	epsilon	e
ζ	zēta	z
η	ēta	ē
θ	thēta	th
ι	iōta	i
κ	kappa	k
λ	lambda	l
μ	mu	m
ν	nu	n
ξ	xi	x
ο	omicron	o
π	pi	p
ρ	rhō	r
ρ	initial rhō	rh
σ/ς	sigma	s
τ	tau	t
υ	upsilon	y
υ	upsilon	u (in diphthongs: au, eu, ēu, ou, ui)
φ	phi	ph
χ	chi	ch
ψ	psi	ps
ω	ōmega	ō
ʽ	rough breathing	h (before initial vowels or diphthongs)

INTRODUCING THE WESLEYAN THEOLOGICAL TRADITION

The many churches of the Wesleyan family, spread around the globe, trace their roots to an eighteenth-century movement of spiritual renewal within the Church of England led by John and Charles Wesley. The Wesley brothers typically rejected attempts to define their "Methodist" movement by its distinctive doctrines, emphasizing instead a distinctive concern for spiritual life (as in their 1742 tract *The Character of a Methodist*). This has sometimes been cited as evidence that they dismissed the value of doctrinal convictions or of engaging in theological instruction and debate. Nothing could be further from the truth! Indeed, when John Wesley capped his long ministry with his "Thoughts upon Methodism" in 1786, his primary exhortation was for Methodists to keep central the "doctrine, spirit, and discipline with which they first set out" (*Works*, 13:258)

This interconnection of doctrine, spiritual vitality, and disciplines/practices of Christian life is at the heart of Wesleyanism.* In downplaying *distinctive* doctrines, the Wesley brothers were emphasizing their concurrence with the *core* Christian doctrines handed down through the ages and affirmed in the Articles of Religion of the Church of England. This included a clear endorsement of the primacy of Scripture for theological reflection, combined with the Anglican appreciation for the insights of tradition, reason, and experience in interpreting Scripture. The brothers also embraced the Anglican conviction that the most important forms of doctrinal expression are those that directly impact all believers—sermons, liturgies, hymns, catechisms, and the like. They devoted their lives to gifting the Wesleyan tradition with such materials.

While insisting on the breadth of what they shared with their Anglican peers (and the historic church), the Wesley brothers admitted that they placed special emphasis on some traditional doctrines, because of their connection to spiritual vitality and Christian practice.

The doctrinal area the Wesleys highlighted most often was soteriology (the nature of salvation). Their concern was to maintain a balanced understanding of the human problem and of God's saving response. On one front this meant defending the universal reality of spiritual need, in the face of idealized accounts

---

*For more detail and documentation of the following summary, see Randy L. Maddox, "Theology of John and Charles Wesley," in Charles Yrigoyen Jr., ed., *T and T Clark Companion to Methodism* (New York: T and T Clark, 2010), 20-35.

of human nature by some Enlightenment thinkers. John's *Doctrine of Original Sin* (1757) was devoted to this concern, demonstrating the shared human experience of spiritual infirmity and bondage.

Turning the focus around, the Wesleys were equally concerned to reject depictions of depravity as the final word about humanity. Convinced that God's mercy is over all God's works (Ps. 145:9), they insisted that God reaches out in love to *all* persons in their fallen condition. Through that encounter, which they termed "prevenient grace," God awakens sufficient awareness and upholds sufficient ability to respond so that we can *either* embrace God's deeper saving work in our lives *or* culpably resist it.

This brings us to the dominant Wesleyan soteriological concern—countering the tendency of many to restrict the present benefits of salvation largely to forensic (legal) justification. Both John and Charles placed *sanctification* at the center of God's saving work, valuing justification as the doorway into this larger focus. They called their Methodist followers to "holiness of heart and life" (*Works*, 12:241), nurtured in the full range of the means of grace.

Given the coherence of the Christian worldview, these focal concerns in soteriology were reflected in characteristic emphases within the other dimensions of Christian theology. For example, both John and Charles rejected any model of predestination that assumed limited atonement and unconditional reprobation (where some are never offered a real opportunity for salvation). Likewise, they emphasized valuing Christ "in all his offices"—not just as the priest who atones for guilt but also as the prophet who teaches the ways in which we are to live and as the king who oversees the restoration of wholeness in our lives.

These and other emphases of the Wesley brothers have left an impact on their heirs. They have also made a significant contribution to the broader church. To cite just one example, the Wesleys focused more attention on the work of the Holy Spirit than had been common through much of the history of the Western church. This emphasis, continuing through their Wesleyan heirs, played a significant role in the renewal of fully Trinitarian theology in recent decades.

Its heritage places Wesleyan theology in a particularly favorable position in the twenty-first century. It has rich theological and practical resources for ministry in a postmodern world. We may note some of these.

1. Wesleyanism's emphasis on soteriology, undergirded by a rich doctrine of prevenient grace, offers constructive ways to address the growing awareness of religious diversity globalization has fostered.

2. The Wesleyan commitment to a "catholic spirit" allows multiple interpretations of nonessential doctrines. It can help Christ's church avoid unnecessary theological polarization, even while remaining faithful to the historic Christian faith. John Wesley can teach us that love must buffer our differences and that Christian communion is sacred and indispensable.

3. The Wesleyan emphasis on "warmhearted" spirituality can provide spirit *and* structure for an experientially hungry postmodern generation.

4. The Wesleyan emphasis on sanctification, grounded in optimism regarding God's grace, offers hope for the transformation of individuals and Christian community. Optimism regarding transforming grace extends to social structures as well. Through the power of the Holy Spirit, Wesleyan theology can inspire incarnational and missional ministry in society.

5. The Wesleyan call to a holy life lives and breathes in all cultural and historical contexts. It is not dependent upon any philosophical, economic, or political system. Its vision of Christian faith and practice remains pertinent as the world shifts from a modern to a postmodern cast of spirit.

6. A driving and relentless compassion for the poor and dispossessed distinguished John and Charles Wesley's ministry and understanding of the gospel. For them, the gospel and the dispossessed were inseparable. When true to their heritage, Wesleyans will proclaim and live the gospel as good news to all those whom structures of privilege would leave behind.

John Wesley's exhortation to his twenty-first-century descendants would surely be the same as it was for his Methodist people in 1786—that we keep central the "doctrine, spirit, and discipline" of the movement. He would encourage us to this task, not so much to *distinguish* ourselves from other Christian traditions, but so that we might *share* the characteristic wisdom of our tradition with our people and with the broader church. Our prayer is that this volume will prove a helpful resource that serves this end.

Randy L. Maddox, PhD
William Kellen Quick Professor of Theology and Wesleyan Studies
Divinity School
Duke University
Durham, North Carolina

Diane Leclerc, PhD
Professor of Historical Theology
Northwest Nazarene University
Nampa, Idaho

Aa

ADOPTION METAPHORS
See NEW BIRTH (REGENERATION).

AESTHETICS
The field of aesthetics is commonly defined as the philosophy of fine art, critical theory, and aesthetic experience. Its development is recent; in the eighteenth century a poetic theorist coined the term "aesthetics." That was the golden era of aesthetics, when British and German thinkers stated the defining characteristics of beauty, taste, artistic genius, and the sublime. But the foundations of aesthetic theory lie in the thinking of Plato, Aristotle, and other classical philosophers.

Early Christian and medieval theology was profoundly shaped by aesthetic interests. **Augustine**'s early writings (ca. 386–400) describe Being and all existence as consisting of a numbering (ratio) that gives measure, form, and order to all things. Augustine was responding positively to Plotinian and Pythagorean aesthetics but negatively to Manichean antimaterialism. Denys the Areopagite (late fifth to early sixth century) expanded the vision of numbered order leading to God. His cosmology describes a created hierarchy of Being/Beauty/Goodness. God, as Highest Beauty, gives each creature a subjective perfection or beauty relative to its location in the scale/chain of existence. Bonaventure (1221-74) expanded this aesthetic by applying it to humanity's cultural and intellectual disciplines. As the soul journeys *anagogically* (ascending understanding) "up" the ladder of Being, it draws closer to union with divine Beauty. **Thomas Aquinas** (ca. 1225-74) described Beauty as harmony among the three transcendentals: Unity, Truth, and Goodness. But his writings on the **metaphysics** of divine Light and earthly color are equally important as expressing then contemporary Gothic aesthetics (e.g., soaring cathedral design and luminous stained glass).

Reformation iconoclasm (destroying icons) established a rule of aesthetic austerity. Not until nineteenth-century idealism and romanticism was the rule broken. However, John Calvin recommended creation as the "book of nature" for educating and inspiring the elect. Jonathan Edwards was an important exception to rejecting aesthetic methods and themes. His writings describe God philosophically as Primary Beauty and Being itself. By his aesthetic worldview, ideal human existence consists in harmonious "consent" of individuals to themselves, others, existence itself, and God. Life is most perfect and holy when centered in and at peace with divine Beauty.

John Wesley developed a basic aesthetics, utilizing the work of Addison, Shaftesbury, Gerard, Duff, Edwards, and possibly Hume and Hutcheson. Believing the physical senses serve their five spiritual parallels, Wesley located beauty in a tripartite hierarchy: (1) appreciation of physical beauty engendered (2) moral sense and beauty, which (3) then encouraged a "taste" for God. Wesley never denied natural and artistic beauty's inherent values, although he regretted how their "pleasantness" distracted from evangelism. His sermons warn against detectable and imagined worldly pleasures (1 John 2:16). Nevertheless, this educated man of taste felt qualified to write aesthetic essays on genius, taste, and music's power.

Twentieth-century aesthetics became an isolated and specialized branch of critical philosophy. Interest in transcendental ideas and art's relationship to other disciplines (e.g., ethics and metaphysics) dissolved. Discussion now focuses on aesthetic experience, originality, hermeneutics, semiotics, multiculturalism, and voices/perspectives of the "Other." Christians must learn the new vocabulary to employ contemporary aesthetics in liturgical theory and practice. Additionally, evangelicals have yet to incorporate theological aesthetics into systematic theology.

See also Liturgy and Worship; Music/Hymns/Hymnology.

Resources

Thiessen, Gesa Elsbeth, ed. *Theological Aesthetics: A Reader*. Grand Rapids: Eerdmans, 2004.

Treier, Daniel J., Mark Husbands, and Roger Lundin. *The Beauty of God: Theology and the Arts*. Downers Grove, IL: IVP Academic, 2007.

KENTON STILES, PHD

AFFECTIONS

See TEMPERS AND AFFECTIONS.

AFRICAN-AMERICAN METHODISM

People of African descent belonged to the first generation of Methodists in American society. After they arrived in New York City in 1766, Betty, a slave, may have been the first Methodist convert. Moreover, the earliest black preachers in the Methodist movement, Harry Hoosier and Richard Allen, both former slaves, attended the Christmas Conference in 1784 in Baltimore, where the denomination was established. Because of their Wesleyan spirituality, antislavery convictions, and readiness to license blacks to preach, Methodists attracted hundreds of African-Americans in the late 1700s. Because blacks were founding ministers and members of the Methodist movement, they viewed themselves as legitimate critics of Wesleyan whites and their flawed religious witness. Richard Allen, for example, recalled that clergy at the Christmas Conference wore vestments in imitation of pretentious Anglicans. He described this practice as a sign of spiritual declension that presaged increased racism and retreats from abolitionism. Hence, the founding of autonomous black religious bodies, though expressed as responses to racism and pro-slavery practices, also owed to black perceptions that white Methodists were losing their spiritual fervor.

Between 1787 and 1821 black Methodists, mainly in the Northeast, organized scores of separate congregations and formed three autonomous denominations. Richard Allen and other Philadelphia blacks in 1787 founded the Free African Society (FAS). After whites at St. George Church, also in 1787, mistreated them, Allen led a remnant out of the FAS to form Bethel African Methodist Episcopal Church, dedicated in 1794. Despite persistent white efforts to control the congregation, Allen in 1816 united Bethel with other congregations to found the African Methodist Episcopal (AME) Church. Allen was elected and consecrated the first bishop. Similar racial troubles in New York City compelled blacks at John Street Church to withdraw and establish their own congregation in 1796.

In 1821 another group of congregations formed the African Methodist Episcopal Zion (AMEZ) Church with James Varick as their first superintendent/bishop. Peter Spencer led a third group of black Methodists out of Ezion Church in Wilmington, Delaware, in 1805, and they founded the Union Church of Africans (UCA) in 1813. Jarena Lee and Sojourner Truth, originally AME and AMEZ evangelists, mainly starting in the 1820s, encountered intense sanctification/perfectionist experiences and explicitly articulated these core Methodist doctrines. All three bodies (AME, AMEZ, and UCA) and those blacks still in the Methodist Episcopal Church operated mainly in the North and Canada. After the Civil War, all of these groups, except the Spencer churches, evangelized among ex-slave blacks in the South. They competed with the Colored Methodist Episcopal (CME) Church, a body formed in 1870 out of the Methodist Episcopal Church, South. These initiatives placed most black Methodists in the AME, AMEZ, and CME bodies, though significant numbers joined and were segregated, for a time, in the Methodist Episcopal Church.

African-American Methodists pursued a liberationist theology focused on freeing slaves, fighting for black civil rights, and identifying with Africa. Their emancipationist ethos, grounded in Wesleyan social holiness, aimed at renewing American society to reflect equity and justice. Wesleyan blacks who realized these liberationist legacies included A. Philip Randolph, founder of the March on Washington Movement in 1941, and Rosa Parks, who inspired the Montgomery (Alabama) bus boycott in 1955. Black Methodists, regardless of denomination, became carriers of a freedom tradition.

See also Black Theology; Methodism, American; Social Ethics; Social Justice; Wesley, John, Theology of.

Resources

Campbell, James T. *Songs of Zion: The African Methodist Episcopal Church in the United States and South Africa.* Chapel Hill: University of North Carolina Press, 1998.
Dickerson, Dennis C. *African Methodism and Its Wesleyan Heritage: Reflections on AME Church History.* Nashville: AMEC Sunday School Union/Legacy Publishing, 2009.

DENNIS C. DICKERSON, PHD

AFRICAN INDIGENOUS CHURCH THEOLOGIES

Defining African **indigenous** church theologies is a complex task. The complexity appears immediately upon discovering that (1) African indigenous churches (AICs) do not share the Western practice of writing theology or even articulating clear boundaries between **orthodoxy** and heresy and that (2) African involvement with Christianity has produced over eight thousand theologically diverse movements, with over nine million members. Consequently no single definition of AICs is adequate. Nevertheless, some recurrent and characteristic emphases are identifiable.

First, AICs revere one supreme God, a reverence often combined with belief in a hierarchy of lesser spirits or beings through whom believers approach God. African indigenous churches consider the one supreme God as the Creator, Source, and Support of life. The lesser spirits or beings are God's emissaries, often having mediatory responsibility.

Second, AICs emphasize the power of the **Holy Spirit** to inspire particular individuals and endow them with powers of **divination**, **healing**, and prophecy. For example, Isaiah Shembe, founder of the Nazarite Church (1911), had visions before starting his church. Engenas Barnabas Lekganyane, founder of the Zion Christian Church (ZCC) (1924), received instructions from God to start a new church while praying on Mount Thabakgone.

Third, AIC theologies are committed to maintaining social and communal order rather than encouraging personal salvation and developing doctrinal dogmas. They emphasize that **ubuntu**, the community, rather than an individual, has priority. God, the intermediary beings, humans, and even animals form a network of mutual support in which community and tribal identity are paramount.

Fourth, AICs stress the importance of **ancestors**. It is commonly believed that ancestors are closer to God and also continue to be related to their ongoing families as guardians. They remain part of their respective families until removed by the expanding gap created by succeeding generations. Therefore, just as one must respect living members of one's family for the sake of order and harmony, so one must also respect members of one's family who are now ancestors.

See also Folk Religion; Indigenization; Indigenous Christian Groups; Indigenous Theologies.

Resources

Bowker, John, ed. *The Oxford Dictionary of World Religions*. Oxford, UK: Oxford University Press, 1997.

Partridge, Christopher, ed. *New Religions: A Guide: New Religious Movements, Sects, and Alternative Spiritualities*. New York: Oxford University Press, 2004.

MUSA VICTOR KUNENE, PHD

AFRICAN THEOLOGY

African theology, like other theologies, is the study of God and God's people. The primary task of African theology is to articulate the Christian faith for Christians living in the African context. African theologians interpret the Christian faith while carefully studying contemporary currents affecting the lives of Africans. They work to make the Christian faith relevant to African life while maintaining fidelity to apostolic Christianity.

African theology brings the Christian faith into dialogue with **African traditional religions**. Commonalities between the two include a creator God, an emphasis upon community, the reality of evil, the unseen realm, and God the Covenant Maker. Hence, African theology is Christian and African. Wesleyan theologians use the Wesleyan emphasis on tradition as a bridge between the past and present for African Christianity. Church fathers such as **Augustine**, Tertullian, and Cyprian compose part of African Christian history.

Gwinyai Muzorewa has summarized current African theology by pulling together some of its major themes. African theology is theological reflection on and an expression of African Christianity (John Mbiti); a contextual African biblical theology (Francis Appiah-Kubi); a theology emerging from the life, culture, tradition, and faith of the African people in their particular African context (Rogate Mshana); a theology based on the biblical faith that speaks to the African soul (All Africa Conference of Churches [AACC]).

In its efforts to address the full range of African life—political, social, economic, cultural and religious—African theologians are open to shifts in theological methodology. African theology and theologians were heavily influenced by the end of colonialism and the birth of African nationalism after World War II. It was also heavily influenced by Pan-Africanism, the context within which a distinctive African theology arose. It emerged within the context of the church and so is now the backbone of the rapid growth of the Christian faith and the deep spirituality of indigenous churches.

The AACC maintained that the spiritual dynamics of the African revolution derives from the impact of the gospel and Christian education. It held that the church must provide spiritual direction for the revolution. This means that African independence from colonialism was largely motivated by proclaiming the Christian gospel and by interpreting the Christian faith for Africa through Christian education.

The purpose of Pan-Africanism is to give all persons of African descent a sense of identity, self-determination, and emancipation. This has provided a context for African theologians to formulate African Christian theology. African nationalism promoted freedom.

The gospel of Jesus Christ can be effectively communicated only when taken seriously by a people and their culture. African theologians believe that "enculturation" of the gospel is an essential aspect of liberation. This has become a principal focus of African theology. Enculturation promotes Christian emancipation of culture under the inspiration and impact of the gospel. Enculturation also means that African theologians work to provide a genuine African understanding of God, human life, and the world. This is in contrast to the Western missionaries, who usually viewed African culture as an incarnation of evil needing to be replaced by Western civilization.

Many Africans see in the Christian Scriptures a platform for addressing the multiple challenges Africans face. Wesleyan theologians see this conviction as consistent with John Wesley's insistence that the Scriptures are the primary witness to God's self-disclosure, a spiritual guide, and the source of human liberation. Archbishop Desmond Tutu has described the Bible as an unintended gift of liberation Europeans and North Americans gave to Africans. To paraphrase Bishop Tutu, "When the white man came to Africa, we had the land and he had the Bible. The white man said, 'Let us pray.' When we opened our eyes, he had the land and we had the Bible. But who says that was a bad bargain? When we were given the Bible, we received the one thing that most powerfully subverts oppression and injustice" (see Gish 2004, 101).

See also Contextualization; Contextual Theology; Evangelism; Global South; Indigenization; Indigenous Theologies; Postcolonialism; Scripture, Wesleyan Approach to; Syncretism, Religious; Westernization of the Gospel.

Resources

Essamuah, Casely B. *Genuinely Ghanaian: A Postcolonial History of the Methodist Church, Ghana, 1961–2000*. Trenton, NJ: Africa World Press, 2010.

Gish, Steven. *Desmond Tutu: A Biography*. Westport, CT: Greenwood Press, 2004.

Maina, Wilson Muoha. *Historical and Social Dimensions of African Christian Theology*. Eugene, OR: Wipf and Stock, 2009.

Muzorewa, Gwinyai H. *The Origins and Development of African Theology*. Eugene, OR: Wipf and Stock, 2000.

Noll, Mark A., and Carolyn Nystrom. *Clouds of Witnesses: Christian Voices from Africa and Asia*. Downers Grove, IL: InterVarsity Press, 2011.

BEAUTY R. MAENZANISE, PHD

AFRICAN TRADITIONAL RELIGIONS

The title African traditional religions (ATR) is nomenclature used for studying several traditional religions indigenous to Africa. Thinking of Africa as a single culture has been superseded by a more accurate consideration of how diverse African peoples understand and live within the spiritual dimensions of creation.

In spite of the diversity of African cultures, some features are common among the various African traditional religions.

The *first* common feature is a concept of one God, the Creator of all there is. This God alone is worshipped. Missionaries did not bring this concept to Africa but rather found it already present in many different linguistic groups. Each group had its own name for and traditional theology regarding this God.

Second, the one God communicates with human beings through several layers of lesser deities and other spirits, including ancestors. They maintain a mediatory function, and they influence daily life among the people. These beings are highly respected and/or feared but not worshipped. Spirits may take on human form as needed. This feature of ATR found affinity with forms of Christianity that presented saints and angels as intermediaries.

The *third* feature common to most ATR is the role of the ancestors as mediators between their family and the lesser deities. People do not actually die; as spirits they continue to participate in a community's life, according to the level of respect they receive after they "die." An expensive funeral is often part of that respect.

The *fourth* feature is witchcraft. According to F. O. Awolalu, witches are humans who have very strong, determined wills with a diabolical bent. Witchcraft is understood as evil, as connected to evil spirits. When found out, people who practice witchcraft are punished. Traditional healers (formerly called witch doctors) fulfill the function of discerning who in a society is performing witchcraft and of bringing them to discipline. Traditional healers are also responsible for discerning the spiritual, social, and physical causes of illnesses. They use rituals and knowledge of herbs to provide cures.

When divorced from the spiritual rituals and other fetishes associated with them, many of the herbal cures are quite effective and scientifically sound. Medical missions found a ready audience for the presentation of the gospel by bringing together the spiritual and physical aspects of healing.

Many elements of Christianity were seen as somewhat compatible with ATR. However, the presentation of Jesus as a sacrifice of atonement for sins does not fit into the theology of most ATR. Some African theologians are experimenting with presentations of Jesus that might generate greater compatibility.

See also Ancestors; Traditional Religions.

Resources

Awolalu, F. O. *Yoruba Beliefs and Sacrificial Rites.* London: Longman Group, 1979.
Mbiti, John S. *African Religions and Philosophy.* London: Heinemann, 1969.
———. *Introduction to African Religion.* 2nd ed. Johannesburg, ZA: Heinemann International Literature and Textbooks, 1991.
Muzorewa, Gwinyai H. *MWARI: The Great Being God: God is God.* Lanham, MD: University Press of America, 2001.
Thomas, Douglas E. *African Traditional Religion in the Modern World: An Introduction.* Jefferson, NC: McFarland and Company, 2005.

BEAUTY R. MAENZANISE, PHD

AGNOSTICISM
See ATHEISM/AGNOSTICISM.

ALIENS AND SOJOURNERS
See CHURCH (ECCLESIOLOGY); ISRAEL.

ALTRUISM/NATURAL MORALITY

The role of natural morality in Christian tradition generally, and the Wesleyan tradition particularly, is complex, largely due to **Augustine**'s anti-Pelagian writings. Pelagius, a British monk, supposedly taught that we already possess adequate natural resources to fulfill God's will and achieve what is good. Augustine thought this diminished the role of baptism in healing the will before properly desiring God and the Good.

John Wesley thought Augustine may have misinterpreted Pelagius. He did not defend **Pelagianism**; he questioned whether Pelagius truly taught Pelagianism. Behind Wesley's concern lay the rigid Augustinianism of certain kinds of Calvinism that almost always saw in Wesley a form of Pelagianism. Calvinism's insistence on total depravity, forensic justification, the denial of any human cooperation in salvation, and a doctrine of double predestination seemed to call into question natural morality altogether. If there is no good remaining in human nature, how could any natural morality be possible?

Augustine famously said pagan virtues were only splendid vices, which appears to make no room even for the natural morality of the ancients like Aristotle. But this is not Augustine's complete story. He also used the ancient virtue tradition to explain Christian morality, as did Wesley. Aristotle taught that every nature is given an end (purpose) and with it comes the natural means to achieve it. The end of human creatures is happiness, a natural moral end that includes friendship and fulfilling one's nature. Virtues are the cultivation of habits that give one the ability to achieve one's end. Because happiness is our end, we have the *natural* means to achieve it.

Aristotle's natural morality is called eudaemonistic, which is from the Greek term for "happiness." Although **Thomas Aquinas** found much to appreciate in Aristotle's eudaemonistic ethic, he also taught that our true end is friendship with God and that this cannot be achieved without supernatural grace. Nature is the presupposition for grace; grace comes and perfects a nature by supernatural virtues, gifts, and fruits from the Holy Spirit, and the beatitudes. But nature in itself can at best achieve only limited moral goods.

Later Catholic scholastic theology emphasized natural morality and divided it from the supernatural, arguing we have the natural means to achieve moral goods. Oddly enough, many see this as one of the origins of secularism. Toward the end of his life, Wesley worried about what this natural morality was doing, calling it nothing more than atheism ("The Unity of the Divine Being," *Works*, 7:270-71). Wesley also held to a eudaemonistic ethic and certainly had a place for a natural morality within God's gracious initiative. But for him, true morality requires happiness *and holiness*. That comes from the work of the Holy Spirit, to which the believer must freely respond.

See also Fruit of the Spirit; Hospitability/Hospitality; Justice; Poverty; Rights, Human; Social Justice; Virtues; Works of Mercy.

D. STEPHEN LONG, PHD

ANABAPTISTS

The name Anabaptist (rebaptizer) identifies a number of similar "radical" movements emerging out of the sixteenth-century Protestant Reformation. While there is no single historical source for these groups, the most prominent is the Swiss Brethren, which could be found in and around Zurich during the mid-1520s. Conrad Grebel and Felix Manz were leaders of an expanding group dissatisfied with the Zurich reforms initiated by Huldrych Zwingli. Persuaded that Zwingli was unwilling to follow the call to reform without compromising with the civil authorities, and increasingly influenced by more radical thinkers such as Thomas Müntzer and Andreas Karlstadt, they broke formally with Zwingli and the Zurich reform in January 1525. They publicly rebaptized believers on the basis of their confession of faith and created an independent congregation.

Because the Zurich reforms (as in all the magisterial **reformations**) were closely tied to civil authority, religious dissent was, by definition, civil dissent. As a result, arrests and prosecution (and persecution) of the Anabaptists soon followed. The Peasants War of 1525 also heightened fears of anarchy and the prospect of the breakdown of social order. The threat diminished civic tolerance for religious dissent. In 1534-35 a radical strain of Anabaptism tried to establish a spiritual kingdom (a New Jerusalem) in the city of Münster. The resulting social disorder, highlighted by introducing polygamy and practicing communism, validated general fears of the destructive effect of Anabaptist influence.

While the different streams of Anabaptism reflect a diversity of theological and political understanding, there are recurring themes that may serve generally to identify this tradition: (1) a common emphasis on personal faith and commitment to Christian discipleship (which forms the basis of adult baptism), (2) an affirmation of the church as a voluntary association of confessing disciples that recreate the primitive NT church, and (3) an expectation of lifestyle changes that reflect Christian commitment. Implicit in all three is an affirmation of the freedom of the will and the decisive role of human response to God.

While early Anabaptists (e.g., Hubmaier, Grebel) hoped for a civic Anabaptist reform, the negative experiences of Anabaptists quickly moved them to adopt a posture that opposed **secular** powers. Reflecting this self-understanding, and based on their experiences in the world, martyrdom and the expectation of persecution became part of the Anabaptist worldview. An ethic of peace also became a recurring theme.

The Anabaptist affirmation of the primary authority of Scripture is neither unique nor distinctive but is tied to their practice of an egalitarian and literal **hermeneutic**.

In the twentieth century a scholarly reconsideration of Anabaptist history and influence highlighted its significance since the sixteenth century in shaping Christian doctrine and practice. The Anabaptist tradition directly influenced **John Wesley** through his relationship with the **Moravians** and their witness to vital personal faith.

See also Church and State; Free Will; Moravians; Peacemaking; Persecution and Martyrdom; Radical Reformers.

Resources

Kraybill, Donald B. *Who Are the Anabaptists? Amish, Brethren, Hutterites, and Mennonites.* Scottdale, PA: Herald Press, 2003.

Weaver, J. Denny. *Becoming Anabaptist: The Origin and Significance of Sixteenth-Century Anabaptism.* 2nd ed. Scottdale, PA: Herald Press, 2005.

CARL M. LETH, PHD

ANAMNESIS

See SACRAMENTS.

ANCESTORS

Ancestors are thought to be spirits of the dead that exist in a disembodied state. In some cases, they include both genders; in others, only fathers or forefathers. They roam for a time but eventually must depart for their eternal destiny. The very wicked are never an object of veneration or worship. In some world areas, ancestors are considered partly human and partly spirit. African theologian John Mbiti describes them as the *living dead*. Feared, respected, and venerated, they are specifically remembered and are part of the extended family.

Because ancestors are not regarded as gods, many non-Western scholars object to the term "ancestor worship." In some parts of the world the term "ancestral veneration" has become more widely accepted.

The influence of ancestors upon the living is a major component of **African traditional religions**. Ancestors, spirits, and gods are believed to be ever present and to influence all human decisions. Through rituals and careful attention to offerings, feasts, and celebrations, a relationship with the departed is established. If rituals are neglected, ancestors may visit their descendants, bringing sickness, crop failure, disease, or even death. The powers in this middle world have good or evil intentions that need to be ascertained and managed. Rituals serve this purpose.

The creator God, who is not an ancestor or spirit, is often seen as distant and detached.

Ancestor worship in some form is widespread. Bishop Stephen Neill maintained that 40 percent of the world's population practices ancestor worship to some extent. However, there are significant variations in both belief and practice.

In some world areas no important family decisions are made until the ancestors have spoken, either through divination, dreams, or intervention by a medium. Clan and tribal ancestors are thought to be the guardians of their own people. In some cultures, ownership of the land is believed to be held by ancestors, just as the Israelites saw Yahweh as the owner of the Holy Land; it could not be the permanent possession of anyone.

Some Christian communities see ancestor veneration as obedience to the fifth commandment ("Honor your father and your mother" [Exod. 20:12]). In this way the strong cultural belief in family can be respected without violating the warnings against idolatry and contact with the departed (Lev. 19:31; Deut. 18:9-13). Response by missionaries to ancestor worship has ranged from acceptance to unqualified rejection.

Among all the major religions, animists are most receptive to the Christian **gospel**. This is because they constantly live in pervasive fear of ancestors, spirits, magic, and witchcraft. The gospel declares that **Jesus Christ** has overcome the threatening powers; he can liberate, cleanse, and heal.

See also African Theology; Animism; Mission, Theology of.

Resources

Moreau, A. Scott. *Evangelical Dictionary of World Missions*. Grand Rapids: Baker, 2000.

Neill, Stephen, ed. *Concise Dictionary of the Christian World Mission*. Nashville: Abingdon Press, 1971.

Van Rheenen, Gailyn. *Communicating Christ in Animistic Contexts*. Grand Rapids: Baker, 1991.

JOHN WESLEY Z. KUREWA, PHD

ANGELS

The English word "angels" refers to human and heavenly messengers who appear in the OT and NT. "Angel" translates the Hebrew word *mal'ak* and the Greek word *angelos*. In the OT, references to angels as human and heavenly beings are almost balanced. But in the NT, with few exceptions (Mark 1:2; Luke 7:24), the word "angels" refers to heavenly beings.

In the OT, *mal'ak* often refers to persons sent by an authoritative figure to perform a task or deliver a message. In Josh. 6:25, Rahab hides human messengers or angels "whom Joshua sent to spy out Jericho." In 1 Sam. 16:19, Saul sends "messengers to Jesse," commanding that Jesse send his son David to Saul. On other occasions, however, the messengers or angels are diverse heavenly beings in God's service. Though creatures, angels are powerful and act as free moral agents.

Developments in angelology occurred in Jewish writings during the intertestamental period. Fallen angels or **demons** under the leadership of **Satan** came to exercise freedom to rebel against God. The "host of heaven," however, remained faithful to God. The "host" is differentiated between diverse types of heavenly beings such as seraphim (Isa. 6:2) and cherubim (Exod. 25:20; Ezek. 10:1-5), who are distinguished from other angels in general. At times, angels are called "the holy ones" (Dan. 4:17) or "sons of God" (Job 2:1). In addition, references are made to "the angel of the LORD" (Gen. 16:11) or "the angel of God" (21:17), who is assigned particular tasks. At times, a clear distinction between God and this angel is difficult (Gen. 21:17-19; Judg. 6:11-23).

Angels serve as God's messengers to humanity (Gen. 16:10; Judg. 13:2-14). They are involved in God's acts of protection and deliverance (Exod. 23:20; Ps. 34:7; Dan. 3:28). Angels also participate in executing God's judgment on **sin** (Gen. 19:1-29; 2 Sam. 24:16-17).

ANGLICANISM • 51

In the NT, OT concepts about angels prevail, although the influence of later developments is visible. Angels are "sent to serve for the sake of those who are to inherit salvation" (Heb. 1:14). They participate in events accompanying the return of the "Son of Man" at the end of the age (Mark 13:26-27). Angels are active throughout the **apocalyptic** book of Revelation (Rev. 2:1; 7:1-3; 12:7-8; 20:1-3). In Rev. 12:7-9 and elsewhere (Jude v. 6), the idea of fallen angels headed by **Satan** is present.

See also Apocalyptic/Apocalypticism; Demons/Unclean Spirits; Devil/Satan; Principalities and Powers; Sin.

LARRY MURPHY, PHD

ANGLICANISM

The Anglican tradition in Christianity has its roots in the English **Reformation** of the sixteenth century. Anglicanism is composed of churches that have historical connections to the Church of England fashioned during that Reformation.

The term "Anglican" derives from the Medieval Latin phrase *ecclesia anglicana*, which simply means "English church." It was part of the **Roman Catholic Church** in England. In fact, England was one of the first areas of Europe to embrace Christianity, as shown by the presence of bishops from Britain at the Council of Arles in 314. However, the Roman withdrawal from England, the fall of the Roman Empire in the West, and the Germanic invasions of the fifth century and later resulted in the near disappearance of Christianity from England until missionaries began the reconversion of England in the late sixth and early seventh centuries.

Given that the British Isles were so far from Rome and separated even from the European mainland, the authority of the papacy in England was always somewhat tenuous throughout the Middle Ages. In some periods, papal authority prevailed, but in others, it was weak. A significant measure of independence from Rome was asserted by leaders of the English church. Thus the events of the sixteenth century in which the English church asserted and then established its complete independence from Rome were not entirely surprising.

With efforts to reform the Roman Catholic Church underway in Europe, England's King Henry VIII (reigned 1509-47) tried and failed to get papal support for annulling his marriage to Catherine of Aragon. She had failed to produce a male heir to the English throne. In response, Henry and the English parliament rejected papal primacy over the English church and asserted the supremacy of the English monarch over the church in England. Ironically, Pope Leo X had earlier bestowed on Henry the title Defender of the Faith because of his opposition (expressed in the treatise "Defense of the Seven Sacraments" [1521]) to Martin Luther's theology.

Even though papal authority was rejected, no major changes were made in the teachings or practices of the church at the time. However, under Henry's successor, Edward VI (reigned 1547-53), a group of church leaders who were in sympathy with the Protestant movement in Europe helped push the English church further away from Rome and closer to the Protestants. This movement was squelched, however, by Queen Mary I (reigned 1553-58), who succeeded temporarily in reestablishing papal authority over the English church. Her violent suppression of some of the most outspoken Protestants earned her the title Bloody Mary. Numerous English Protestants fled to the Continent, taking refuge among Protestants in Germany and Switzerland. Many returned to England after Mary's brief reign, intending to model the English church after Continental Protestant churches.

Under Elizabeth I (reigned 1558–1603) Anglicanism acquired much of its present shape. Elizabeth sought, and largely achieved, a compromise that would be acceptable to the largest number of English Christians. This consisted of an attempt to embrace and balance both Protestant reforms and pre-Reformation elements within the English church. The Elizabethan Settlement (1559) created a Church of England that was definitely Protestant in **doctrine** (articulated in the Thirty-Nine Articles of Religion, which reached their present form in 1571). But it retained much of the pre-Reformation structure of the English church, as evidenced in such offices as archbishop, bishop, dean, and canon. The Elizabethan Settlement also retained historic forms of **worship** now contained in the Book of Common Prayer, which first appeared in 1549 and has undergone numerous revisions.

This laid the groundwork for the claim, pressed particularly since the seventeenth and eighteenth centuries, that Anglicanism represents a *via media* ("middle way" or "middle road") between the extremes of Rome and Geneva (where **John Calvin** presided over the Reformation for twenty-five years). The Anglican tradition is *both* Catholic and **Reformed**. It thus constitutes a unique tradition within Christianity and stands alongside **Roman Catholicism**, **Eastern Orthodoxy**, and Protestantism. This emphasis on balance, compromise, and charting a middle way has given rise to lively debate among Anglicans ever since the sixteenth century. The degree of distinction between Protestant and Catholic elements within the Anglican tradition, and the implications of this for the life and practice of Anglican churches, is an enduring source of controversy.

Since the sixteenth century, Anglicanism has been exported from England to many parts of the world through British emigration, **missionary** activity, and colonialism. This has resulted in Anglican churches throughout the world. Generally these churches have organized themselves into national or regional bodies that govern themselves. Since the first Lambeth Conference (met in 1867 at Lambeth Palace in London), there has been an attempt to build and maintain ties among these churches and to sustain a worldwide Anglican Communion. This is encouraged by conferences of representatives from the churches "in communion" that meet every ten years. Currently this communion includes those churches throughout the world that are direct heirs of the Anglican Reformation and that stand in full communion (voluntary) with the Archbishop of Canterbury, the primary archbishop in the Church of England.

See also Doctrine/Dogma; Calvin, John; Liturgy and Worship; Missionary Movements; Orthodox Church; Reformed Tradition; Reformation; Roman Catholicism.

Resources

Chapman, Mark. *Anglicanism: A Very Short Introduction.* New York: Oxford University Press, 2006.
Neill, Stephen. *Anglicanism.* New York: Oxford University Press, 1978.
Ramsey, Michael. *The Anglican Spirit.* New York: Seabury Books, 2004.

HAROLD E. RASER, PHD

ANIMISM

Animism is belief in numerous personal spirit beings, including angels, demons, ghosts, souls of the dead, and other forms of the spirit world thought to inhabit humans, objects, and sacred locations. They supposedly exert strong influence on the devotee's existence. Whereas *animism* is belief in personal spirits, an*imatism* is belief in impersonal spiritual forces (e.g., the "evil eye" in folk Islam). In animism, the deities are ranked. Belief in a great God, the Creator, is found in some forms of animism, but God is considered aloof and distant. The gods, spirits, and departed ancestors of the middle world are active in everyday life, such as causing sickness in children, assuring soil fertility, and crop production. Sacrifices—including appeasement of the spirits through blood sacrifice—and special celebrations on certain days are often called for by the *medium* to influence these spirit beings and, in some cases, to manipulate their power for the worshipper's benefit.

Santeria in Cuba and Umbanda in Brazil are animistic systems. In Haitian voodoo there are both malevolent and benevolent spirits.

The term "animism" was coined by British anthropologist Edward B. Tylor (1873). He defined "animism" as "the doctrine of Spiritual Beings" (1970, 9), which in its full development "includes the belief in souls and in a future state, in controlling deities and subordinate spirits, . . . resulting in some kind of active worship" (11).

Animists are found on all continents and (in some form) in Islam, Hinduism, Buddhism, and Christianity. Bishop Stephen Neill observed that 40 percent of the world's population practices animism in some form. The more functionally animistic people are, the more receptive they are to the Christian message.

For some scholars today "preliterary religions" or "primal religions" are preferable to the term "animism."

See also African Traditional Religions; Ancestors; Principalities and Powers; Syncretism, Religious; Traditional Religions.

Resources
Hiebert, Paul. "Flaw of the Excluded Middle." *Missiology* 10, no. 1 (January 1982): 35-47.

Tylor, Edward B. *Religion in Primitive Culture.* 1873. Reprint, Gloucester, MA: Peter Smith, 1970.

Van Rheenen, Gailyn. *Communicating Christ in Animistic Contexts.* Grand Rapids: Baker, 1991.

TERENCE B. READ, PHD

ANTHROPOLOGY
See SOCIAL SCIENCES.

ANTHROPOLOGY, THEOLOGICAL

Theological anthropology denotes the consideration of human life in the light of God's work. It focuses on humans as created in God's image, enslaved to sin, called to redemption, and often as spirit, soul, and body.

Genesis 1:27 states that humans are creatures "in the image of God." What the verse signifies is unclear, however. It has been taken to indicate a special power or trait: reason, freedom of will, immortality, desire, or the inclination to morality or spirituality. It has also been regarded as a special status: the representatives or attorneys of God or those with power over other creatures or especially responsible for them. Irenaeus (d. ca. 200) distinguished "image" from "likeness." The former, retained after humans fell into sin, indicates a vague similarity with God; the latter, lost after the fall, is a "perfection" emerging from open communion with God's Spirit. Karl Barth (d. 1968) maintained that the image of God is not something *in* us but our being created to give ourselves as a whole to God, to live "toward God," as God's "counterpart." It has also been taught that since the true "image of God," as Paul says (e.g., 2 Cor. 3:5–4:6), is Jesus Christ, even Adam and Eve were created "*in* Christ," that is, having fellowship with Christ as their end (Westermann 1994, 155).

The most significant recent critique of earlier interpretations is found in Claus Westermann's massive commentary on Gen. 1–11. He argues compellingly that Gen. 1:27 is not chiefly anthropological. Rather, it points *first* to God's sovereignty, *second* to God as Creator, and then finally to humans, never as they are in themselves, but only as they are with reference to God.

Humans have been equally strongly understood as having fallen into and become captivated by sin, that is, godlessness. The mainstream of the church has variously affirmed that all human beings are in themselves, from birth, enslaved to godlessness, unable by their own power to break free from it. The work of Jesus Christ and the Holy Spirit is to bring the human heart and human work into fellowship with God. Different positions have been articulated concerning the extent of human cooperation with God in this work. It is widely affirmed, however, that the grace of God works to call forth faith, hope, love, and good works in the redeemed.

Finally, it is widely acknowledged by the teachers of the church that human beings are body, **soul**, and spirit. Since the fifth century, under Platonism's influence, the body has often been sharply distinguished from soul and spirit. However, closer to the OT and NT is the view that body, soul, and spirit are different ways of regarding the same complex whole. Thus soul may be a bodily yearning especially for God; spirit, that aspect of bodily life most directly evoked by the Holy Spirit; and body, what is enlivened by the Spirit and yearns for God.

See also Black Theology; Feminist Theology; Humanism; Justice; New Birth (Regeneration).

Resources

Barth, Karl. *Church Dogmatics.* Vol. 3, Pt. 2, *The Doctrine of Creation.* Translated by H. Knight, G. W. Bromiley, J. K. S. Reid, and R. H. Fuller. Edited by G. W. Bromiley and T. F. Torrance. Edinburgh: T and T Clark, 1960.
Westermann, Claus. *Genesis 1–11.* Translated by John J. Scullion. Minneapolis: Fortress Press, 1994.

CRAIG KEEN, PHD

APOCALYPTIC/APOCALYPTICISM

"Apocalyptic" and "apocalypticism" are terms that arose in the nineteenth and twentieth centuries in Western culture. The words describe a particular understanding of history that emerged within **Second Temple Judaism.** The English terms come from the Greek word for "revelation." Some scholars include accounts of mystical, heavenly journeys in their definition of "apocalypticism." Most scholars, however, usually understand the main feature of Jewish apocalyptic thought as directly related to a common pattern that describes the end of all things: God brings God's righteous judgment to pass on earth with an abrupt suddenness. In an apocalyptic framework, history does not move steadily and progressively into the future. Rather, a sudden rift occurs that brings God's judgment upon all people.

In apocalypticism, a righteous group stands starkly opposed to those who have accommodated themselves to the norms of the nations. As a result, the scribes look forward to a coming time of God's judgment and vindication, a cataclysmic event in which the righteous receive their eternal reward and the unrighteous receive a parallel, negative judgment.

Apocalypticism seems to have originated among Jewish wisdom teachers during the time of the Greek domination of Judah. Displaced from Judah during the exile, these teachers were influenced by Iranian dualism and the interests and wisdom traditions associated with the Mesopotamian calendar. On their return they brought the teachings back to Judah. Some Jewish scribes promoted a view of history that saw a coming abrupt change of situations through God's judgment—often accompanied by great conflict and suffering. In this conflict, the scribes saw a coming reversal of fortunes for the righteous. The **Torah**-abiding Jews, those outside the networks of power and status, would then receive an eternal reward for faithfulness practiced amid sufferings. But those who had accommodated to the Gentiles would receive God's judgment.

In apocalypticism, sudden judgment confirms God's justice. This conviction encouraged and empowered the continued faithfulness of those who had lost status and even suffered for refusing to adopt the practices of new foreign rulers. This viewpoint is found in books such as *1 Enoch*, many of the **Dead Sea Scrolls**—particularly the *War Scroll*—and the book of Daniel in the OT.

Early Christianity was deeply influenced by Jewish apocalypticism. For them **Jesus** becomes the hinge point in history. Jesus' bodily **resurrection** marks God's singular defeat of evil, death, and **Satan**. Those who believe in Jesus and submit to baptism participate in this "new age." God calls them to be holy, to live lives distinct from those dominated by this "present evil age." They will be found blameless at the coming judgment. Jesus' resurrection is a sign of what will eventually impact all creation when Jesus returns.

Such apocalypticism is in the background of most, if not all, NT writings. In continuity with its Jewish origins, Christian apocalyptic provides a framework for understanding the life of **the church**, and believers within it, during the "time between the times."

Apocalyptic speculation has occasionally occurred throughout Christian history. Though directly opposing the gospel teaching that "about that day and hour no one knows" (Matt. 24:36), recent Christian teachers have tried to read the imagery of apocalyptic biblical texts as a type of fortune-telling in the light of contemporary news. This neoapocalyptic transformation of biblical apocalyptic picked up momentum with the 1948 establishment of **Israel** as a contemporary nation-state, set within the context of cold-war tensions. This new apocalyptic differs from biblical apocalyptic because it focuses on contemporary national politics rather than on exhorting the church to faithfulness grounded in the faithfulness, crucifixion, and resurrection of Jesus.

See also Eschatology, Biblical; Kingdom of God; Second Coming of Christ/ Parousia.

JOHN WRIGHT, PHD

APOLOGETICS

"Apologetics" derives from the Greek word *apologia*, which means "to give an answer for or a defense of." Generally it refers to giving reasons for saying a belief is true. The word comes from pre-Christian Greek legal practices. Socrates' *Apology* was a defense against charges that finally led to his death. Later Greek apologies gave accounts of a philosopher's life without attempting to persuade readers to live by that person's teaching.

However, early Christian apologies did seek to persuade their hearers to accept the Christian faith. Justin Martyr (ca. 103-ca. 165), Athenagoras (ca. 177), Theophilus of Antioch (ca. 180), Tertullian (ca. 160–ca. 225), and Origen (ca. 185–ca. 254) wrote important Christian apologies. They defended Christian beliefs against attacks coming from the dominant culture. Their apologies also challenged the adequacy of Greek thought.

Contemporary Christian apologetics uses arguments based on generally accessible ideas and principles to convince people that Christian beliefs are true or defensible. While often addressed to opponents of Christianity, apologists also seek to influence committed Christians. Apologetics in postmodern cultures attempts to answer challenges to Christian belief posed by horrible evils, the natural sciences, religious pluralism, and moral relativism.

Today's Christian apologists differ among themselves over what reason, logic, or nature can "prove." Some, such as William Lane Craig, believe God's existence can be deductively proved. Others, such as Alister McGrath, limit their goal to demonstrating that Christianity makes better sense of the empirical evidence than its rivals.

Apologetics may be either negative or positive. Negative apologetics defends Christian beliefs by showing why criticisms of specific beliefs fail. Alvin Plantinga's defense of the possibility of belief in God in spite of the actuality of evil does not claim to prove God's existence but asserts that evil does not disprove it. Positive apologetics gives arguments to support a position. Plantinga's argument that if any moral claims at all are true, then naturalistic evolution is self-defeating provides positive evidence for Christian belief.

Apologetics as a type of theology differs from systematic theology and philosophy of religion. The goal of apologetics distinguishes it from systematic theology because apologetics uses claimed evidence to support Christian belief. Systematic theology, which is "confessional," creates a systematic, comprehensive presentation of Christian doctrine. Apologetics differs from philosophy of religion by presupposing the truth of specific religious convictions, while philosophy does not. Philosophy is open to and examines diverse beliefs, not privileging any religious commitments.

The use of reason to defend Christian beliefs has led many to criticize apologetics. Most famously, Karl Barth charged that the use of reason to justify Christian faith is incompatible with revelation; it subverts faith and limits God to human comprehension. The charge is that Christian apologetics is unnecessary, impossible, and harmful: unnecessary because faith does not depend upon reason, impossible because limited human reason cannot comprehend an unlimited God, and harmful because it leads to trust in one's own powers rather than trust in God's saving actions.

See also Greek Philosophy; Historical Theology; Natural Theology; Philosophical Theology; Religious Pluralism; Science and the Bible.

Resource
Edwards, Mark. "Apologetics." In *The Oxford Handbook of Early Christian Studies*, edited by Susan Ashbrook Harvey and David G. Hunter, 549-64. Oxford, UK: Oxford University, 2008.

JOHN CULP, PHD

APOSTASY
See CREEDS (NICENE, CHALCEDONIAN, APOSTLES', ATHANASIAN); DOCTRINE/DOGMA.

ARIANISM
Arianism is the most significant heresy in Christian history. It systematically dismisses the deity of Jesus Christ, while diluting much traditional language about Christ's deity. It is most closely associated with Arius (250/256–336), an Alexandrian presbyter. Arianism spread quickly, supported by the logic of God's self-enclosed (undifferentiated) identity, a selective reading of Scripture, and the writings of some earlier church leaders.

There was a strong response to Arianism by the church's mainstream. It was condemned at the Council of Nicaea (325), the first **ecumenical council**. The controversy nonetheless raged for decades. It has surfaced repeatedly since then, partly due to the work of Arian missionaries among Germanic tribes in late antiquity. Further, it remains a tempting theological option if one begins with an abstract, speculative idea of God, even if the idea claims to be relational. In response to Arianism, in the fourth century the church affirmed that the One worshipped through the **liturgies**, **prayers**, Scriptures, mission, and martyrdom of the faithful is the God inseparable from **Jesus Christ** and the **Holy Spirit**.

The most vital phrase in the Nicene Creed and the one Arians rejected is that Jesus Christ is *homoousion tō patri*, signifying that what Jesus Christ is *as God* is the same as what the Father is *as God*. The term *homoousios* translates into English as "consubstantial" or "same in substance/essence/being/reality." There is no difference between the deity of the Son and the deity of the Father. This the Arians could not affirm. To them God is so self-identical (undifferentiated) that holding that Jesus Christ is fully God either compromises God's integrity (oneness) or sets up a second God. A God who is truly one, they maintained, could never come into direct contact with a creature, let alone be a creature. According to Arius, what becomes **incarnate** is that *creature* God *made* in order to create and sustain all else. This, Arius taught, is the "word" of John 1 or the "wisdom" of Prov. 8. Although this first creature is in some sense divine, it is not *fully* divine. It is a "third thing," "lower" than God but "higher" than other creatures.

Versions of Arianism have appeared in recent times. Three examples may be noted. *First*, there are pluralists, who advocate a general notion of religion. They take Christianity to be but one instance of religion. Pluralists typically maintain that Jesus Christ is one of many mediators of the divine, none of whom is or could be fully God. *Second*, there are **process** theists, who begin with an abstract notion of God as holding all possibilities and preserving all experiences. They are restricted by theory from affirming that any creature, including Jesus Christ, could incarnate God's fullness. *Third*, some advocates of **radical orthodoxy** so stress the social and political work of God that Jesus Christ becomes but "the first of many sons" or the "foundation" of that **church** that is itself the incarnation of God.

See also Creeds (Nicene, Chalcedonian, Apostles', Athanasian); God, Doctrine of; Mission, Theology of; Religions, Theology of; Religious Pluralism; Trinity.

Resources

Kelly, J. N. D. *Early Christian Doctrines*. 5th ed. New York: Continuum International Publishing Group, 2000.
Rusch, William G. *The Trinitarian Controversy*. Minneapolis: Augsburg Fortress, 1980.
Williams, Rowan. *Arius: Heresy and Tradition*. Rev. ed. Grand Rapids: Eerdmans, 2002.

CRAIG KEEN, PHD

ARMENIAN APOSTOLIC CHURCH

The Armenian Apostolic Church is the primary church in the Republic of Armenia. Over 90 percent of its four million inhabitants are members. Worldwide the number may reach nine million adherents.

Armenia was the first Christian country; its king declared Christianity the religion of his realm around 313 (traditional date, 301). According to church tradition, the apostles Thaddeus and Bartholomew evangelized Armenia, though earliest evidence suggests a second-century arrival of both Greek and Syriac Christianity. The tide turned when the monk Gregory helped King Tiridates convert, who then purged the country of Zoroastrian and pagan practices. Gregory directed that the Etchmiadzin cathedral be built where, in a vision, he saw Christ's hand pointing. It became the seat of the catholicos, the head of the church. In 406 another monk developed the Armenian alphabet to facilitate translating the Bible, liturgy, and theological texts into Armenian.

The Armenian Church rejected the Council of Chalcedon's formulation of Christ's two natures (451), earning it the appellation *monophysite*, meaning "one nature." Some Armenians, however, prefer the term *miaphysite*, meaning "compound nature," derived from Cyril of Alexandria's articulation of the two natures united.

With other Eastern churches, the Armenian Church celebrates Christmas on January 6 and allows married men to enter the priesthood.

In the early tenth century, the catholicos and many others fled political upheaval in Armenia. They reestablished the church in Cilicia, southeast Turkey. When Cilicia was invaded, some Armenians returned to Etchmiadzin and elected a new catholicos (1441). Since then, two catholicos have presided over two autonomous bodies: the Holy See of Etchmiadzin and the Holy See of Cilicia, which moved to Lebanon after the 1915 genocide in Turkey. This division repeats in the worldwide Armenian diaspora, though leaders have discussed reunification since Armenia regained independence (1991).

Resources

Fortescue, Edward. *The Armenian Church*. New York: AMS Press, 1970.
Parry, Ken, ed. *The Blackwell Companion to Eastern Christianity*. Hoboken, NJ: Wiley-Blackwell, 2010.

KRISTINA LACELLE-PETERSON, PHD

ARMINIANISM
See ARMINIAN THEOLOGY.

ARMINIAN THEOLOGY

The term "Arminianism" is derived from the name of the Dutch theologian Jacobus (James) **Arminius** (1559–1609). He was one of the first enrollees at the University of Leiden, the Netherlands, founded in 1575. The theological faculty represented the university's premiere academic discipline, Arminius's chosen field. Graduating in 1581, Arminius studied in Geneva and Basel, Switzerland, as well as in Padua, Italy. In 1587 he returned to Amsterdam, where on August 27, 1588, he was installed as pastor, thereby fulfilling his promise to the city fathers who had financed his theological education abroad.

Typical of the day, Arminius's sermons were theological treatises that handled with exegetical precision pressing theological issues. Having studied with Theodore Beza, John Calvin's successor in Geneva, Arminius's peers and parishioners thought him the obvious person to refute "erroneous" doctrine about predestination then making the rounds in Holland. Especially offensive was the position advanced by Delft minister Dirck Coornheert. Church leaders and a university professor urged Arminius to refute Coornheert's liberalizing tendencies.

In a sermon on Rom. 7, Arminius was on record as teaching that the pilgrim described therein was not the apostle Paul. As one already converted, already "in Christ Jesus" (8:1) and already having had the "old man" crucified (see 6:6, KJV), Paul was no longer sold under sin but in a state of "no condemnation." This interpretation in his sermonic exegesis seemed to place Arminius outside the standard Protestant teaching regarding *simul justus et peccator* (simultaneously justified and still a sinner). In later writings Arminius made it clear that he did not reject the *simul justus et peccator* position of Calvin and Luther.

On the exegetical question at hand, Arminius believed that if "sold under sin" (see 7:14, KJV) referred to the converted as habitually sinning, then it would undercut the power of converting grace. But if he were to say it referred to the unconverted, he would be attributing too much good intention and ability to sinful humanity. Arminius's "unorthodox" position on Rom. 7 was also that held by Erasmus and Socinius. The suspicions this raised were exacerbated when Arminius did not produce a refutation of Coornheert's teachings on predestination.

This is the context for understanding Arminius's evangelical doctrine of **prevenient grace**, later embraced by **John Wesley**. Christ is the light that lights all people (John 1:9). Even though all are born into sin, everyone receives grace sufficient for sensitivity to God's gracious overtures. If humans were absolutely dead in trespasses and sin, totally devoid of **grace**, then there would be no capacity for responding to God.

So in Arminian theology there is a consistent emphasis on the universality of human sinfulness and on the universality of God's offer of saving grace. Sinful humanity makes no move toward salvation apart from grace. We should not refer to free will toward God as intrinsic to humanity, for apart from God's grace there is only bondage of the will. We may, however, speak of a "freed will"—made so by divine grace.

Although Arminius never explicitly refuted those who were modifying hyper-Calvinist predestinarian doctrine, we can discern his position. Those who believe in Christ will be saved, and those who do not are damned. Those who believe do so solely through Christ's grace and saving work. Those who do not believe overtly reject the overtures of saving grace.

While not teaching universalism (all will be saved), Arminius did teach that the offer of salvation is universal; he rejected the teaching that some are elected beforehand for salvation. He strenuously rejected the notion that God decides beforehand to deny salvation to some.

Arminianism must not be understood as only concerned with free will, election, and predestination. Though these emphases are better known among Wesleyans, two additional trajectories are important. *First*, in the Netherlands, Arminius's student Simon Episcopius embraced his teachings. He was the spokesperson for the Arminians (the Remonstrants) at the Synod of Dort (1618-19). But with Episcopius, the Remonstrant trajectory of Arminianism began to embrace Enlightenment sympathies, thereby placing decreasing emphasis on the soteriological center that characterized Arminius and, later, Wesleyanism.

The *second* trajectory is traceable through the high church tradition emanating from the Anglican archbishop William Laud (1573–1645), namely, Erastianism. Laud insisted the state has rightful supervision over religious and ecclesial matters, a position Arminius consistently defended against efforts by religious synods to control his teachings as a university professor.

Among the three trajectories, the most successful in number of devotees and lasting influence is that which led John Wesley to choose *The Arminian Magazine* (1778-97) as the name for the periodical that characterized the theological identity of early **Methodism**.

See also Calvin, John; Election/Predestination; Enlightenment; Free Will; Luther, Martin; Prevenient Grace; Salvation (Soteriology).

Resources
Gunter, W. Stephen. "John Wesley, A Faithful Representative of Jacobus Arminius." *Wesleyan Theological Journal* 42, no. 2 (Fall 2007): 65-82.
———. *The "Sentiments" of James Arminius: A Reformed Theologian*. Waco, TX: Baylor University Press, 2011.

W. STEPHEN GUNTER, PHD

ARMINIUS, JACOB

Jacob Arminius (1559–1609). The precise date of Arminius's death is known (October 19) but not his birth. He was born in Oudewater, South Holland, to Hermans Jacobsz (a smithy who probably made cutlery and weaponry) and Angelika (Engeltje) Jacobsdr. Arminius's father died (1558/59) before the child's birth. Arminius was baptized Hermansz (Herman's son). On September 16, 1590, in the Oude Kerk in Amsterdam, Arminius married Lijsbet Reael (1569–1648), daughter of Laurens Jacobsz Reael, head of a well-connected Amsterdam family. Arminius says nothing about Lijsbet, but her influential family connections proved providential during nineteen years of marriage. By 1590 Arminius was a university graduate, a respected Amsterdam minister married to a woman of means, and no longer dependent on charity.

Arminius's early life predicted otherwise. After the death of Arminius's father, a local priest with Protestant sympathies, Theodore Aemilius, cared for the boy. For safety's sake Aemilius removed Arminius to nearby Utrecht, Oudewater then being under Spanish (Roman Catholic) control. Gradually, Oudewater adopted Dutch Protestant loyalties, thus inviting Catholic reprisal. In 1575 Spanish forces invaded Oudewater, killing Arminius's family.

The earlier move to Utrecht proved providential. Aemilius had died shortly before the Oudewater massacre; Arminius was taken in by an Oudewater native—Rudolphus Snellius—who had fled Holland to Marburg. While visiting Utrecht, Snellius became acquainted with Arminius, a bright and needy teenager who was then probably a student at the Hieronymusschool (St. Jerome School), where Arminius most likely received the classical education that prepared him for university studies.

Snellius took Arminius to Marburg, where Arminius learned of the Oudewater massacre. In 1575 Arminius walked 250 miles to Oudewater, "to look once more upon his native town." That year William of Orange decreed the founding of the University of Leiden, where on October 23, 1576, Arminius became a student of the liberal arts and adopted his Latinized name, Jacobus Arminius, borrowed from a first-century Germanic warrior.

When in 1581 (age twenty-two) Arminius completed his Leiden studies, he was considered too young to become a pastor. The burgomasters and pastors of Amsterdam recommended him to the Merchants' Guild for financial aid for further study. So Arminius went to Geneva (1582) to study with Theodore Beza—**John Calvin**'s successor. Beza taught a derivative Calvinism in which the doctrine of predestination achieves a prominence most scholars agree cannot be found in Calvin's thinking; that is, for Beza, Calvinism becomes a decree-centered system where predestination becomes an end in itself.

In 1587, after returning to Amsterdam as a pastor (1587–1603), Arminius was called on to defend the "high Calvinism" learned from Beza. The wrinkle in this situation was that after leaving Leiden, Arminius had been theologically influenced not only by Geneva but also by extended visits to Basel, Switzerland, and Padua, Italy.

Arminius's years in Amsterdam as pastor were theologically his most productive. Almost all the theological positions he expressed in public and private disputations, and in his "Declaration of Sentiments," delivered in The Hague (1608), were developed there.

In 1603 Arminius became professor of theology at Leiden. Theological debates characterized his professorship until his death. They began in earnest during the second year. On October 31, 1604, Professor Franciscus Gomarus gave an unscheduled (and out-of-turn) public lecture on predestination. He consistently represented Beza's high Calvinism. Afterward, against his wishes, Arminius was forced into a series of controversial exchanges. They culminated in the "Declaration of Sentiments," a succinct presentation of the conflict and of his own theological position. This treatise was delivered before the High Court in The Hague, May 30, 1608. Arminius died shortly thereafter. Peter Bertius, a university classmate and lifelong friend, delivered the eulogy: "There lived in Holland a man whom they who did not know could not sufficiently esteem, whom they who did not esteem had never sufficiently known. . . . Beloved, let us love one another."

See also Arminian Theology; Predestination and Election; Reformed Tradition; Wesley, John, Theology of.

Resources

Bangs, Carl. *Arminius: A Study in the Dutch Reformation.* Eugene, OR: Wipf and Stock, 1998.
Olson, Roger E. *Arminian Theology: Myths and Realities.* Downers Grove, IL: IVP Academic, 2006.

W. STEPHEN GUNTER, PHD

ARTS, THE

While the term "art" is usually restricted to visual forms (e.g., painting, sculpture, architecture, literature), "the arts" encompass both fine and performing arts (e.g., dance, music, drama).

The boundaries of art have long been debated, but the consensus is that all forms of art involve creative and imaginative composition. Contemporary use of the term tends to exclude the more utilitarian processes of creation (i.e., the mechanical, technical, or scientific, such as carpentry and engineering). Distinguishing between artists and artisans (or craftsmen) was unheard of before the Renaissance.

From prelinguistic times, humans have employed the arts to record their experiences, express themselves, and add beauty to their lives. From a Christian perspective, this creative spark within humankind links to the biblical doctrine of the *imago Dei*; we are created in the image of God, first revealed as Creator. Humans are given the capacity to relate to God as Covenant Partner.

In the poetry of Gen. 1, God is a poet who speaks creation into existence as the spirit or breath of God hovers over the face of the deep. The prose of Gen. 2 depicts God as a sculptor, fashioning man from the dust of the ground and animating him with the divine Spirit, which breathes life into everything that lives and inspires acts of human creation.

While the OT prohibition against "graven images" (see Exod. 20:4, KJV) complicates the Judeo-Christian tradition's posture toward the arts, early Christianity did not resist images (**icons**). Food and drink symbolism, the *ichthys* (fish), and depictions of Jesus as the Good Shepherd adorn Christian meeting places and burial sites. The cross emerged as a prominent Christian symbol in the fifth century, following its perceived role in Constantine the Great's (ca. 274–337) military victories. The irony that the instrument of Jesus' execution would become the central symbol of the faith of his followers is not lost.

Church architecture, sculpture, and stained glass flourished during the Middle Ages. When the church was the dominant social institution, the arts served a pedagogical role, instructing the illiterate in the faith. In some ways, the church has always erred on the side of regarding the arts as having a purely illustrative function and as being potentially dangerous apart from their role as a handmaiden to doctrine.

The **iconoclastic** controversies of the eighth century divided the Eastern and Western churches over the use of images in worship. Eastern theologians, most notably John of Damascus (ca. 676–749), defended the veneration—but not the worship—of **icons** on the basis that the bread and wine of the Eucharist are rightly venerated. Through matter God's grace is manifested within the created order. To deny the validity of icons is to deny the incarnation of God in Jesus Christ. At the Second Council of Nicaea (787), the defenders of icons prevailed, deeming the **iconoclasts** heretical.

In the sixteenth century, however, the Western disdain for images resurfaced, this time violently, as the Reformers destroyed vast amounts of Christian art in Europe in their zeal to purify the church. Most Protestant groups have inherited strong reservations and, in some cases, antipathy toward the visual arts. Oddly, the validity of music—the most mystical and mysterious of the performing arts—is seldom questioned.

While the church's role as producer and patron of the arts has steadily declined over the past five hundred years, much art since the Renaissance has remained obsessed with the sacred. The poetry of John Milton and George Herbert reveal a vision of the world as charged with sacramentality. The intimate paintings of Caravaggio and Rembrandt are transfixed with the physical reality of Christ. By contrast, spacious landscapes of Caspar David Friedrich and the nonrepresentational canvases of the twentieth-century American abstract expressionists (e.g., Jackson Pollock and Mark Rothko) are haunted by the perceived withdrawal of the divine.

See also Aesthetics; Creation/New Creation; Creeds (Nicene, Chalcedonian, Apostles', Athanasian); Dance; Film/Cinema; Idolatry; Literature and the Christian Faith; Music/Hymns/Hymnology; Popular Culture.

Resources

Jensen, Robin M. *The Substance of Things Seen: Art, Faith, and the Christian Community.* Grand Rapids: Eerdmans, 2004.

Viladesau, Richard. *Theology and the Arts: Encountering God Through Music, Art, and Rhetoric.* New York: Paulist Press, 2000.

BRANNON HANCOCK, PHD

ASCETICISM

Asceticism refers to practices and religious movements that renounce physical comfort for the sake of spiritual development. Christian ascetic groups have asserted that bodily pleasures, including enjoying food, a good night's sleep, comfortable clothing, and expressions of sexuality, distract from seeking God. Stated positively, they have taught that denying the flesh opens space in one's life for communion with God. Ascetics have also deprived themselves of things because of remorse for sin and a desire to identify with Christ's sufferings. In extreme forms, ascetics move beyond self-denial to engage in practices harmful to their bodies, including self-flagellation and standing on a pillar for decades, as Simon (or Simeon) the Stylite did in Syria in the fifth century.

In the early church, many Christians embraced a disjointed view of the human person and a negative assessment of the body. Their culture assumed that spiritual things are good and the material world is evil. When they read that Christians should resist the "desires of the flesh" (Gal. 5:16), for instance, they heard the Bible calling for a spiritual battle against their bodies. To them renouncing the body seemed to be a principal Christian value. (This passage in Galatians and other similar ones refer not to a battle against a person's skin and bones but to one against the sinful nature that opposes the Spirit of God.) Accordingly, a higher spiritual value was placed on living as a hermit in the desert or, later, as a monk or nun in a monastic house, with the vows of poverty, humility, and chastity.

Throughout church history Christians have responded differently to the question of how best to connect life in the mundane world with the hope for life in heaven. The modern movement to incorporate classic spiritual disciplines, such as fasting, extended prayer times, and the observance of Lent, into daily life affirms the link between the physical and spiritual. The body's essential goodness is still affirmed. In other words, many Protestants engage in ascetic practices without believing that the body is evil or that the infliction of pain on oneself is required for spiritual growth.

See also Contemplative Spirituality; Desert Fathers and Mothers; Penance; Renovaré; Self-Denial; Spiritual Direction/Spiritual Director; Spiritual Disciplines.

Resources

Brown, Peter. *The Body and Society: Men, Women, and Sexual Renunciation in Early Christianity.* 2nd ed. New York: Columbia University Press, 2008.

Clark, Elizabeth. *Reading Renunciation: Asceticism and Scripture in Early Christianity.* Princeton, NJ: Princeton University Press, 1999.

KRISTINA LACELLE-PETERSON, PHD

ASEITY
See GOD.

ASIAN-AMERICAN THEOLOGY

The US Census Bureau identifies an Asian-American as a naturalized citizen born in a region related to Northeast Asia, Southeast Asia, Central Asia, the Indian Subcontinent or the South Pacific Islands, and/or his or her biological and legal descendants. Many share a common experience of being estranged from their native cultural heritage. Asian-American theology serves this heterogeneous context.

Early in Asian-American theology, some theologians tried to interpret Christian theology in the light of Buddhism, Confucianism, Taoism, and Hinduism. But most Asian-American theologians were faithful to the theologies of the missionaries who had proclaimed the gospel to them.

With changes in US immigration policy toward Asians in the mid-1960s, many immigrants arrived. In a strange land many immigrants suffered estrangement and religious dislocation. Reflecting on these experiences, recent Asian-American theologians have raised questions about identity, the meaning of life, the importance of faith, and the role of religious communities. Other themes have included the relation between ethnic and religious identity, the meaning of suffering, God's existence, and the relationship between native religious belief and the Christian faith.

Under the influence of Latin American **liberation theology**, some Asian-Christian theologians have formulated their own liberation theologies, including **minjung theology**, **dalit theology**, and coconut theology.

*The **postcolonial** context.* Under the influence of Edward Said, who critiqued orientalism and provided a basis for postcolonial studies, many Asian-American thinkers awakened to their being consigned by Western interests to a colonial status. Now they strive to speak in their own voice. They create their own space for articulating their *Asian* voice. A third space is required, different from native space and adopted space. Native space is still subject to the category of inferiority and poverty. Adopted space, representing alienation and subjugation, does not permit authenticity. In the third space (a hybrid), genuine cultural crosscurrents occur. The power of assimilation can be resisted, and space for creativity and originality can be created.

See also Asian Theology; Honor/Shame Culture.

Resources

Lee, Sang Hyun. *From a Liminal Place: An Asian American Theology.* Minneapolis: Fortress Press, 2010.

Phan, Peter C. *Christianity with an Asian Face: Asian American Theology in the Making.* Maryknoll, NY: Orbis Books, 2003.

YOUNG-HO CHUN, PHD

ASIAN THEOLOGY

Asia is the world's largest continent. It occupies the eastern part of the Eurasian landmass and its adjacent islands. It is marked by a vast variety of cultures, religions, and ethnicities.

Similarly, Asian Christian theologies are too diverse for a simple definition. Much of the diversity results from a history of various missionary agencies and confessional loyalties. For example, churches in Indonesia show the influence of the Dutch Reformed tradition. Philippine churches reveal their Spanish Roman Catholic heritage. Korean churches were deeply influenced by Presbyterian and Methodist polities and spiritualties. In India, churches display the influences of the Church of England. All of these still carry indelible marks made by Western ecclesial and theological traditions. So "Asian theology" is in fact many theologies, characterized by diverse perspectives, orientations, and practices. Its general theological character is biblical in outlook and spiritually conservative.

The term "Asian theology" here refers to the postcolonial theological awakening of Asian churches. In important ways it diverges from the Western theologies missionaries brought to Asia. Asian theologies have grown out of a recently developed consciousness of indigenous cultural roots. This disposition replaces an older one that cast Asian theologians as guardians of the theology inherited from Western missionaries. Formerly, Asian theologians were educated in the West, returned home, and faithfully transmitted what they had learned there.

After World War II the world was reshaped in many ways. Decolonization of Africa and Asia occurred. Newly won political independence was, however, countered by continued economic dependence. To break this pattern, in 1955, in Bandung, Indonesia, a group of third-world thinkers initiated the Non-Aligned Movement (NAM).

Inspired by NAM, third-world countries began freeing themselves from Western guardianship. Indigenous theologies played a significant role. Since the late 1960s and early 1970s *contextual theologies* have appeared throughout the third world. There are two schools of contextual theology, both of which are represented in Asia: (1) **liberation theology**, which addresses the socioeconomic and political dimensions of a particular context. Illustrations are *minjung* theology in South Korea, *dalit* theology and tribal theology in India, and *burakumin* theology in Japan; and (2) inculturation and dialogue theologies that attend to cultural and religious contexts. They place a local stamp on the Christian faith and may incorporate some aspects of other religions. Dialogue with other religions may contribute to making a church more indigenous.

The emergence of contextual theologies marks an empirical and **hermeneutical** turn. The local situation and experience assume a major role in theological reflection. The artificial distinction between salvation history and world history is removed. God is rediscovered as acting in all history. Hermeneutically, all theological scholarship is recognized as biased to some extent and embedded in particular cultures.

In South Korea, **minjung** theologians developed a narrative theology that connects biblical stories with the stories of suffering people. They focus on Jesus Christ, who radically identified with the "least of these" (see Matt. 25:40). The Sino-Korean word *minjung* is composed of the syllables *min* (people) and *jung* (mass). But minjung theologians say the term cannot be adequately translated. It is identical to the Greek term *ochlos* (a crowd) in the Gospels. Operationally, the minjung are politically oppressed, economically exploited, and socially alienated. They are culturally and intellectually uneducated. They are saddled with *han*. *Han* is a "lump" in one's heart that obstructs fruitful relationships with God and others. Minjung theologians insist the gospel must be preached as good news to women and men—the powerless minjung. New life in Christ and claiming one's human rights go hand-in-hand.

Minjung theologians do not construct a systematic theology. What they have developed remains fragmented. It more effectively analyzes the problem than stipulates solutions. But minjung theologians have successfully sounded theological voices that would have otherwise been muted. Minjung theology is not the church's theology but rather the public's theology. Even though minjung churches provide a significant prophetic voice, they are not flourishing in number.

In India, dalit theology critiques the older dialogue theology for neglecting the problem of caste. *Dalit* is the name for the casteless people. A growing body of literature is emerging from this theological movement. It applies not only to people of unscheduled castes but also to indigenous landless people in India. The word *burakumin* in Japanese means "outcasts." The ghettos of the burakumin were the only places where the remnants of the conscripted World War II laborers were permitted to live. Korea was a Japanese colony from 1910 to 1945. Their descendants in Japan continue to face discrimination and ostracism. Burakumin theology addresses their plight.

Dalit and burakumin theologies share a theme found in minjung theology: mirroring Jesus' identification with those who are dispossessed, marginalized, poor, oppressed, voiceless, and forgotten. The goal of all three is restoration of the *imago Dei* in all people through the gospel of Jesus Christ.

See also Contextualization; Contextual Theology; Holistic Mission; Honor/ Shame Culture; Indigenization; Indigenous Theologies; Mission and Social Justice; Monism, Dualism, Pluralism; Postcolonialism.

Resources

Lee, Jung Young, ed. *An Emerging Theology in World Perspective: Commentary on Korean Minjung Theology*. Mystic, CT: Twenty-Third Publications, 1988.

Prabhakar, M. E., ed. *Towards a Dalit Theology*. Delhi, India: ISPCK, 1989.

Sugirtharajah, R. S. *Asian Biblical Hermeneutics and Postcolonialism: Contesting the Interpretations*. Maryknoll, NY: Orbis Books, 1998.

YOUNG-HO CHUN, PHD

ATHEISM/AGNOSTICISM

Belief in God (theism) can be inverted to belief in no God or no belief in God (a-theism). Between these two options is a third possibility: there may or may not be a God or gods. Current knowledge (gnosis) and evidence are inconclusive. This option is known as agnosticism. Some atheists refer to themselves as "brights" (a worldview void of supernatural and mystical qualities). But not all brights are atheists.

The meaning of atheism has changed through the ages. In ancient history, if a person or group rejected another person's or group's understanding of the gods and the heavens—typically many gods (polytheism) and many heavens—they would be charged with impiety and antitheism (or atheism). The charge would be vindicated if the gods in question were to abandon the questioners and expose them to catastrophe. When the Egyptian pharaoh Akhenaton (ca. 1353-1336 BC), father of Tutankhamen (ca. 1341-1323 BC), wanted to worship only one god—the sun—instead of the many gods of his fathers, he was repudiated, and history records his destruction. He was judged to be atheistic because he eliminated the gods. In Greek history, the famed philosopher Socrates (ca. 469-399 BC) was condemned to death for allegedly teaching youth about gods Athens did not recognize. For that, Socrates was executed as an atheist.

In his *First Apology* (mid-second century AD), Justin Martyr (ca. 103- ca. 165) says atheism was the primary charge Romans leveled against Christians; they rejected the Roman gods. Justin countered by saying Christians in fact worship the "Most True God."

Modern atheism is heavily dependent on the writings of Karl Marx (1818-83), Friedrich Nietzsche (1844–1900), Sigmund Freud (1856–1939), and Jean-Paul Sartre (1905-80). Atheism is practically rooted in what many people see as conclusions necessitated by modern science and by the absence of scientifically convincing evidence for God's existence. Many people believe that efforts to prove God's existence based upon reason and religious experience are rationally, morally, and empirically unconvincing. In fact, many people, such as the "new atheists" (e.g., Richard Dawkins, Christopher Hitchens, and Sam Harris) believe reason, science, and morality do just the opposite; these prove there is no God. Many believers counter that the kind of evidence applicable to scientific research is grossly inapplicable to God.

Arguments in support of atheism often stem from what many believe to be irreconcilable conflicts between belief in an all-powerful and all-loving God, on the one hand, and the immense and irrational suffering and pain observed in the world, on the other.

In the tradition of philosopher Ludwig Feuerbach (1804-72), God is explained as but a human projection. The human mind "creates" or projects God; God is just "human" writ large.

In societies where religion plays a prominent role and belief in God is strong, atheists are often subject to discrimination. Because they do not believe in God, they are sometimes unjustly dismissed as immoral. In many countries, belief in God and patriotism are almost inseparable; God seems to exist to bolster the state.

Agnosticism is usually more open to the possibility of God's existence; there is simply insufficient evidence to endorse either atheism or theism. The term was coined in 1860 by Thomas Huxley, an English biologist.

Agnosticism is closely associated with skepticism where only knowledge of the natural world can be certain. Philosopher David Hume rejected the possibility of knowledge not based upon reason that relies on quantity and number or upon empirical verification. Supposed knowledge of any entity, such as God, that does not submit to these criteria is but an illusion.

See also Apologetics; Deism; Enlightenment; Evolution/Evolutionary Biology; Humanism; Intelligent Design; Logical Positivism; Modernity; Natural Science; Philosophy of Science; Postmodernity; Reductionism; Science and the Bible; Secular/Secularism/Secularization; University, Christian.

Resources

Aronson, Ronald. *Living Without God: New Directions for Atheists, Agnostics, Secularists, and the Undecided*. Berkeley, CA: Counterpoint Press, 2008.

Beattie, Tina. *The New Atheists: The Twilight of Reason and the War on Religion*. London: Darton, Longman and Todd, 2007. Reprint, Maryknoll, NY: Orbis Books, 2008.

The Brights' Net. http://www.the-brights.net/.

McGrath, Alister. *The Twilight of Atheism: The Rise and Fall of Disbelief in the Modern World*. New York: Doubleday, 2004. Reprint, New York: Galilee, 2006.

L. BRYAN WILLIAMS, PHD

ATONEMENT

"Atonement" is an Anglo-Saxon word that literally means "at-one-ment." The doctrine deals with how sinful human agents are to be made one again with a holy and just **God**. Although the early church developed a canonical account of the person of Christ, it never officially adopted one theory of atonement. It was content to permit a wide range of options, so long as its **Christology** was not compromised.

The standard views on atonement were well known to **John Wesley**, who readily deployed the full range of options. Some of **Charles Wesley**'s hymns are stunning in their capacity to use the traditional language to draw the believer into intimacy with the suffering and love of the crucified Savior. For John, the doctrine of the atonement was a point of sharp contention with William Law; the differences led him to castigate the prevailing forms of passive **mysticism**. Atonement was also the distinguishing mark of Christianity over against **deism**; in Christ, in his person and death, we are offered costly **salvation** rather than **humanistic** moralism.

Even so, Wesley never developed a systematic account of the doctrine, deploying the various images and their theories (propitiation, satisfaction, substitution) in apt ways in his preaching and teaching. He was adamantly opposed to views of limited atonement, made it clear that the benefits of atonement were entirely of **grace**, and ensured that atonement did not undercut the imperative of growth in grace through the means of grace. Some scholars have found echoes of the East in his views, but these are muted and do not inhibit his **Augustinian** convictions about inherited guilt and the need for appropriate satisfaction.

More generally, Wesley accepted a version of penal substitution, refusing to accept the ensuing logic that readily led to either limited atonement or **universalism**. Penal substitution dovetails with his robust emphasis on the subjective side of atonement, where the merits of Christ's death are applied by the **Holy Spirit** to the sinner. Even then, Wesley took up the wider narrative in which the fall was used by God to display his **love** in ways not otherwise possible. Seen as a whole, the atoning work of Christ evoked the highest joy, love, and gratitude from his children.

This richness has served the tradition well, not least in inhibiting nasty divisions. Theologians were free to appropriate the inherited tradition and to explore its full ramifications. On the one hand, this could lead to complacency, which, when coupled with the loss of a high vision of the person of Christ, could easily lead to pious sentimentalism and moralism. This readily took root when coupled with a quest for the "historical" Jesus. On the other hand, under the inspiration of Robert Traina, the search for a coherent account that integrated the actual historical death of Christ with a deep vision of atonement has led to a fresh exploration of the old images in a new key. This reflects a return to the broad vision of atonement reflected in its Anglo-Saxon etymology.

See also Biblical Metaphors for Salvation; Calvin, John; Christology, New Testament; Creation/New Creation; Justification; Predestination and Election; Reconciliation; Righteousness.

Resources

Beilby, James, and Paul R. Eddy, eds. *The Nature of the Atonement: Four Views.* Downers Grove, IL: IVP Academic, 2006.

Dunning, H. Ray. *The Whole Christ for the Whole World: A Wesleyan Perspective on the Work of Christ.* Eugene, OR: Wipf and Stock, 2008.

Shelton, R. Larry. *Cross and Covenant: Interpreting the Atonement for 21st Century Mission.* Tyrone, GA: Paternoster, 2006.

WILLIAM ABRAHAM, PHD

ATTRIBUTES OF GOD
See GOD, DOCTRINE OF.

AUGUSTINE

Augustine was born in Tagaste in present-day Algeria to a pagan father and a Christian mother, Monica, who prayed consistently for his conversion. He was educated in Carthage, where he had a concubine who bore him a son, Adeodatus. Augustine remained a devoted father. He studied and taught rhetoric in Carthage. During this time he was attracted to Manichaeism, but then became disillusioned with it. Augustine went to Rome and then to Milan to teach rhetoric. Here he encountered Ambrose, bishop of Milan. Ambrose was an eloquent rhetorician and interpreter of Christianity.

Augustine's spiritual autobiography, *Confessions* (a unique example in the ancient world), tells of his conversion. He was in a garden when over the wall came the voice of a child saying, "Take up and read." Augustine opened Paul's letter to the Romans. This marked a turning point in his life. In 387 Ambrose baptized Augustine along with his son and a close friend. He returned to his native North Africa where he was ordained (391). Augustine was made bishop of Hippo in 396.

His theological treatises followed. They subsequently shaped the theology of the Western church. His *On the Trinity* emphasized the unity of the Godhead, with the Son and the Spirit participating in the substance of the Father, and the Spirit proceeding from the Son as well as the Father. This was the basis of the later controversy over the *filioque* clause the West inserted into the Nicene Creed, a clause the East rejected.

Augustine was caught up in the Donatist controversy, which resulted from the persecution under Diocletian (303-5). Christians were ordered to surrender all copies of the Scriptures to be destroyed. Some bishops refused and were martyred; others complied. The Donatists questioned the compliant bishops' sanctity and the validity of the ordinations they performed. According to the Donatists, the church must be pure to be valid. But Augustine argued that a bishop's authority depends on his office, not on his personal holiness. The church *invisible* is holy, even though sin may mar the church *visible*.

Augustine spelled out his philosophy of history—from creation and fall to new creation—in *The City of God*. The fall of Rome in 410 caused many to claim that Christianity had undermined loyalty to the gods who protected the city. Augustine claimed instead that Roman imperial power flourished under the providence of God and had brought the peace necessary for the expansion of Christianity. Once this was accomplished, Rome's long-standing sin of pride was punished with destruction.

The major controversy during Augustine's later years was with the British monk **Pelagius**. Pelagius argued that if humans are to be held accountable, they must be free to decide for the good and not be bound by the forces of sin—original or actual. But Augustine emphasized divine **grace** as necessary to enable human decisions. Following the logic of his position, Augustine felt required to presuppose **predestination** and irresistible grace.

Considerable opposition to Augustine's position arose. Opponents were described as semi-Pelagian. The Council of Orange (529) decided in favor of a modified Augustinian position.

John Wesley's relation to Augustine was mixed. He much preferred some of the other early fathers, primarily because Augustine championed predestination. But Wesley repeatedly quoted one of Augustine's maxims: "He that made us without ourselves, will not save us without ourselves" (*Works*, 6:513). Both Wesley and Augustine emphasized grace as necessary for every stage of salvation. Wesley cannot be accurately accused of semi-Pelagianism; his doctrine of prevenient grace stresses that grace prompts even the first step along the way to salvation.

See also Church Fathers; Creeds (Nicene, Chalcedonian, Apostles', Athanasian); Early African Christianity; Faith; Free Will; Reformed Tradition; Trinity.

Resources
Brown, Peter. *Augustine of Hippo: A Biography*. Berkeley, CA: University of California Press, 2000.
Wills, Gary. *Saint Augustine: A Life*. New York: Penguin, 2005.

THEODORE RUNYON, DR. THEOL.

Bb

BAPTISM
See SACRAMENTS.

BAPTISM WITH THE HOLY SPIRIT
Few doctrines have been more controversial or more fertile in the Wesleyan tradition than that of the baptism with the **Holy Spirit**. This is not surprising, since the hallmark of the tradition as a whole is its marked emphasis on the doctrine of the Christian life. The debates are historical, exegetical, and theological. They also cut into self-involving issues of identity.

Seen as a distinct work of **grace** subsequent to **justification**, the experience of **entire sanctification** naturally invites further elaboration and defense. For **John Wesley**, **sanctification**, while seen as the work of the Holy Spirit, is rooted in **Christology**. **John Fletcher** shifted the focus from Christology to that of pneumatology, looking especially to Acts 2 as an exegetical site that would at once defend and begin to fill out what was involved in sanctification. While Wesley may well have endorsed this move, it was not one he favored linguistically. However, language matters in theology; so the scene was set for trouble down the road.

The tradition of Fletcher was picked up in the **holiness movement**; this created its own momentum, so much so that the bishops of mainstream Methodism virtually rejected the whole tradition of **perfection**, turning instead to social dimensions of perfection that eclipsed the **personalist** side of faith. Fletcher's turn to Acts 2 was taken one step further in the work of William Arthur, whose rhetorically brilliant little book *The Tongue of Fire* became a classic of Wesleyan spirituality. Once the exegetical move was made to Acts, it became natural to treat entire sanctification as the functional equivalent of baptism with the Holy Spirit. The originating tension represented in the different languages of Wesley and Fletcher was now out in the open, and the future of the tradition was on the line. **Pentecostalism** was birthed; Wesley now has some very interesting grandchildren.

One can easily read the debate as a verbal dispute. The underlying spiritual reality is seen now from this angle, now from that. Certainly the emergence of speaking in tongues as a proof of baptism with the Holy Spirit adds an explosive element, creating an unhappy disjunction between purity and power that are best seen as generous gifts of the Holy Spirit in the Christian life. Later Pentecostalism, as it morphed into the **charismatic** movement, played down the role of tongues; more recent forms give it even less billing. The search is now on for a fully comprehensive doctrine of the Christian life that will transcend the old divisions.

The most dramatic recent development is the work of Elaine Heath. She has relocated the experience of **Phoebe Palmer** in the world of classical **ascetic** theology, showing that Palmer replicated the theology of Teresa of Avila and other mystics of the Western tradition. This brings the debate of baptism with the Holy Spirit into a whole new arena, creating space for genuinely fresh and more apt accounts of the work of God in the life of the Christian.

See also Doctrine/Dogma; Gifts of the Spirit; Glossolalia; God, Doctrine of; *Ordo Salutis;* Pentecostal Theology.

Resources
Brand, Chad, ed. *Perspectives on Spirit Baptism: Five Views.* Nashville: Broadman and Holman, 2004.

Dayton, Donald W. *Theological Roots of Pentecostalism.* Grand Rapids: Francis Asbury, 1987. Reprint, Peabody, MA: Hendrickson, 1991.

Wood, Laurence W. *The Meaning of Pentecost in Early Methodism.* Lanham, MD: Scarecrow Press, 2002.

WILLIAM ABRAHAM, PHD

BEAUTY
See AESTHETICS.

BELIEF

Belief has numerous meanings. In popular usage, a belief is less certain than knowledge. The *APA Dictionary of Psychology* (VandenBos 2007, 112) defines belief as the "acceptance of the truth, reality or validity of something," especially in the absence of support for the belief's accuracy.

In psychology, belief is viewed as a state of mind or as patterns of behavior. Evolutionary psychology describes belief as a psychological structure linking abstract ideas as states of mind with stimuli that arouse emotions. Union between the abstract and emotional results in behavior that facilitates survival.

In philosophy, a belief is an attitude or intentional expression in which something is affirmed or denied—a proposition. Philosophical discussions about knowledge and religion include the concept of belief. In knowledge, belief is an active response to a claim to know. Complex theories exist about the extent to which, if at all, we consciously (willfully) control belief formation. In many cases, beliefs appear to be nonvoluntary (e.g., honey tastes sweet). Some philosophers think that beliefs are voluntary, at least to some extent, and that individuals are responsible for their beliefs. If beliefs are chosen, then a person's responsibility for what is believed becomes morally important. In contemporary discussions, a morally valid belief is warranted if a basis can be given for holding it. The validity of religious beliefs is debated in philosophy and popular culture. Nihilism, or epistemological skepticism, rejects the possibility of knowledge, which makes belief impossible and morally wrong.

John Wesley and other evangelicals distinguished between belief and **faith**. One might believe Christian doctrines to be true and still not experience evangelical, transforming faith (trust) in Jesus Christ. But Christian beliefs, such as are stated in the ecumenical **creeds**, explicate Christian faith and nourish Christian **discipleship**.

See also Determinism and Free Will; Epistemology; Ethics; Evangelical Theology; New Birth (Regeneration); Salvation (Soteriology); Spiritual Formation/Growth; Wesley, John, Theology of.

Resources

Amesbury, Richard. "The Virtues of Belief: Toward a Non-Evidentialist Ethics of Belief-Formation." *International Journal for Philosophy of Religion* 63, nos. 1-3 (2008): 25-37.
Schwitzgebel, Eric. "Belief." In *Stanford Encyclopedia of Philosophy*, edited by Edward N. Zalta. Fall 2008 ed. Stanford University. Article first published August 14, 2006. http://plato.stanford.edu/archives/fall2008/entries/belief/.
VandenBos, Gary R. *APA Dictionary of Psychology*. Washington, DC: American Psychological Association, 2007.

JOHN CULP, PHD

BIBLE

The Bible is the collected documents of the OT and NT that Christians regard as sacred. The different genres or types of literature within it include narratives, poems, biographies, epistles, wisdom texts, parables, and **apocalyptic** writings. It is holy, not in and of itself, but because it reveals the holy **triune** God who creates a holy people by the power of the **Holy Spirit**. Wesleyans believe the Bible's writers were Spirit-inspired so that the Bible is the written Word of God containing all that is necessary for salvation. The Bible is the supreme authority in matters of faith and practice, the foundation and touchstone of reason, tradition, and experience. The texts that form the Bible were written, transmitted, preserved, collected, translated, and interpreted within the community of the people of God. Christians call it the canon, meaning the recognized standard or rule.

Christians believe that God speaks through Scripture, challenging, guiding, and judging them. The Bible tells the story of God's self-revelation throughout history and supremely in Jesus, the Word made flesh. Humans learn the truth about God and themselves, their alienated condition, what God has done and is doing about this condition, and the direction of God's ultimate good purposes. This gives the Bible its inner coherence. Because Jesus is God's full and final revelation, the Bible's storyline only makes sense in the light of Jesus. Wesleyans are therefore Christocentric in their reading of Scripture. They avoid the extreme of biblical **fundamentalism** in which the Bible's words are thought to be dictated by God. Wesleyans regard this view as bibliolatry. But they also reject the view that the Bible is only one authority among others.

The process of arriving at the canon (authoritative standard) of Scripture was long and complex. Much of the OT was regarded as authoritative before the Christian era, although what it contained is uncertain. The Hebrew canon was finally fixed by the rabbis well into the second century AD. Most in the early church, including the NT writers, used a second-century BC Greek OT called the Septuagint, at least until the fourth century. It included the apocryphal books. While most of the texts in the NT canon were included early in the lists of authoritative books, only by the late second century were all twenty-seven books considered Scripture.

During the **Reformation** the precise identity of Scripture became an issue. Protestants now include sixty-six books in their Bibles as Scripture. They exclude the Apocrypha. The Eastern Church includes the apocryphal books as a second-level authority. Since the Council of Trent (1546), Roman Catholics have accepted the apocryphal books as Scripture.

The Bible in translation has been faithfully transmitted by the people of God. No original texts exist. Thousands of copies of parts of the Hebrew Bible have been found at the site of the Qumran community in Israel. The earliest NT text is a fragment of John (P^{52}) from about AD 120. But the earliest extant complete Greek manuscript (MS) is the fourth-century AD Codex (book) Sinaiticus. Scholars now have access to a wide range of early texts and have established criteria for arriving at the earliest recoverable form of a text. Believing that the earliest texts are the most reliable, most Christians insist that translations into modern languages be based on the most reliable Hebrew and Greek manuscripts available.

See also Apocalyptic/Apocalypticism; Biblical Theology; Biblicism/Bibliolatry; Dead Sea Scrolls; Hermeneutics; Intertextuality.

Resources

Beckwith, Roger T. *The Old Testament Canon of the New Testament Church and Its Background in Early Judaism.* Eugene, OR: Wipf and Stock, 2008.

Bruce, F. F. *The Canon of Scripture.* Downers Grove, IL: IVP Academic, 1988.

Codex Sinaiticus. www.codexsinaiticus.org.

Hengel, Martin. *The Septuagint as Christian Scripture.* London: T and T Clark, 2002.

BIBLICAL CRITICISM
See HERMENEUTICS.

BIBLICAL ESCHATOLOGY
See ESCHATOLOGY, BIBLICAL.

BIBLICAL INTERPRETATION
See BIBLICAL INTERPRETATION, ANCIENT AND MODERN METHODS; HERMENEUTICS.

BIBLICAL INTERPRETATION, ANCIENT AND MODERN METHODS

While hermeneutics in general studies human understanding, biblical hermeneutics focuses on understanding Scripture. Methods of interpretation have changed and developed throughout church history.

Patristic and medieval Christianity commonly distinguished between the *literal* and *spiritual* meanings of texts, with the latter subdivided into the allegorical, moral, and anagogical senses. *Literal* interpretation, often linked to historical meaning, determines what the text directly says. *Allegorical* interpretation assumes a meaning other than (though related to) the literal. *Moral* interpretation refers to ethical meaning. *Anagogical* interpretation deals with eternal or eschatological meaning. In the late medieval period, *typology*, in which one figure or event in the OT prefigures another in the NT, became common. During the Renaissance and **Reformation**, strong emphasis was placed on the literal (historical) meaning over the spiritual, although typology continued to be used by some, especially the Puritans.

For the last three hundred years hermeneutics has been done through Euro-American perspectives influenced by the Enlightenment. Many conservative scholars use a *grammatico-historical* method that seeks to identify the text's original meaning intended by the author. This method examines the text's structure and historical context. But since the nineteenth century, the *historical-critical method* has been dominant, with the goal of understanding the text within its historical, cultural, and social settings. Following Enlightenment rationalist assumptions, historical criticism does not assume the text means what it says; instead, historical criticism seeks to get behind the text to establish its meaning. Within this method, *source criticism* is concerned with when and where the text in question was written, who wrote it, to whom, and why. *Form criticism* studies the way different literary forms such as psalms or parables functioned in the life of the community prior to their being written down. *Redaction criticism* examines the changes and manner of composition of the biblical books to discover the authors' distinctive purposes and theologies. *Canonical criticism* counters the tendency of these historical methods by focusing on the background behind the text; it examines the books in their finished form and meaning for communities of believers.

In recent years, the prominence of historical criticism has been challenged by newer methods, some of which originated in the non-Western world. They deny that texts can be read objectively as historical criticism claimed, instead proposing various lenses through which readers can discern God's message for their own social settings. These new readings often move people to act on behalf of the poor and marginalized.

A range of liberationist approaches have emerged. In *liberation* readings, God is understood as the Lord of the oppressed, calling humans to create communities of peace, justice, and reconciliation. *Feminist criticism* seeks to identify features of the Bible that have a negative and repressive impact on women in order to liberate readers from patriarchal bias. *Postcolonial criticism* examines the text from the standpoint of peoples who are emerging from colonialist domination, drawing upon their previously suppressed cultural traditions as well as their colonial and postcolonial experiences. The NT is seen as reflecting the experience of a people living under Roman subjugation.

Socio-rhetorical criticism is a recent and promising method of NT interpretation pioneered by Vernon K. Robbins and others. Socio-rhetorical interpretation combines the methods of rhetorical criticism and social-scientific criticism. Social-scientific methodology is employed to study issues associated with the network of social relations (cultures and customs) in relation to the biblical text. The rhetorical method explores ancient or classical writings and strategies of persuasion to understand meaning in the NT. Socio-rhetorical criticism interprets the NT within the larger social context in which it was written and read.

Literary or narrative methods add to rhetorical criticism and have been embraced by believers in most parts of the world. Telling stories helps readers enter the world of the text and encourages imaginative thinking. Narrative readings are text centered, inviting the reader to participate in what the gospel writers are creating, thus encouraging new perspectives.

Narrative readings are linked to *reader-response criticism*, which focuses on the way readers experience the text. By attending to the characters, images, metaphors, gaps, and turns in the plot, the critic creates meaning as the story unfolds.

Behind these diverse methods of interpretation stand three different frames of reference for understanding a text's meaning: (1) authorial intention—the text *means what the author intended*; (2) the text *means what it says*—meaning is found in a text's literary structure; and (3) *readers determine the meaning of the text.*

Because no single interpretation can be considered final or definitive, scholars within the Wesleyan tradition may use any and all of these tools.

Wesleyans have also inherited several distinctive hermeneutical perspectives from John Wesley. When interpreting a passage of Scripture, Wesley insisted its meaning must be consistent with the *whole tenor of Scripture*, centered in God's love and grace meant to redeem the whole creation. The purpose of Scripture is soteriological. Wesley rejected the Zwinglian prohibition against doing anything not explicitly commanded in Scripture, and agreed with Luther that we are free to do what Scripture does not prohibit, so long as it bears good fruit. Wesley understood God's commands, such as "You shall love the Lord your God with all your heart" and "You shall love your neighbor as yourself" (Mark 12:30-31), to be God's promise to enable Christians, through **grace**, to do what God commands. Wesley also taught that biblical admonitions against accumulating wealth, along with the command that we serve the poor, are indispensable characteristics of holiness.

Wesley was always aware of being part of a community of past and current interpreters. All interpretation of the Scriptures must help readers find what Africans call a mythical home, or heaven, as identified by Euro-Americans. Thus for Wesleyans, biblical interpretation is analogous to the way of salvation (Green 2010, vii-x, 1-13).

See also Biblical Theology; Christology, New Testament; Hermeneutics; Scripture, Wesleyan Approach to; Wesley, John, Theology of.

Resource
Green, Joel B. *Reading Scripture as Wesleyans*. Nashville: Abingdon Press, 2010.
ISRAEL KAMUDZANDU, PHD

BIBLICAL METAPHORS FOR SALVATION

The Bible uses diverse metaphors to describe salvation, an all-encompassing reality. They point to the restoration of health and wholeness in our relationship with God, each other, and within God's creation.

First, there are three major metaphors, all of which describe being *in Christ*:

1. **Justification.** Christians have been brought into a right relationship with God. They have been made righteous and will be confirmed in Christ's **righteousness** when **God's kingdom** is consummated. The future verdict is already anticipated.
2. **Sanctification.** Believers are already the sanctified or holy ones. They have been sanctified in Christ by the **Spirit**. And they are being sanctified as they journey. Some day they will be holy in Christ's presence.
3. Glorification. Christians have already been drawn into the glory of the risen Christ. Now they are being transformed "from glory to glory" (2 Cor. 3:18, KJV). But they long for final glorification—**resurrection** of the body and a final end to tears, sickness, and death.

Second, a constellation of metaphors explicates the content of justification, sanctification, and glorification. They appear as *four* overlapping clusters.

1. New creation. The range of **new creation** is vast, including **new birth** into a new family that does God's will, transferal from the realm of darkness to light, and renewal of the whole of creation.
2. Participation. This includes John's language of mutual indwelling and believers abiding in the hospitable embrace of the loving triune God. It also includes Paul's prominent "in Christ" phrase (Rom. 8:1; 1 Cor. 1:30; 2 Cor. 5:17; Phil. 3:14). Believers are crucified *with* Christ, raised *with* Christ, alive *in* Christ, and sanctified *in* Christ. They walk in newness of life, in the light, and in fellowship. They are alive to God but dead to sin and the deeds of the body.
3. Freedom. Israel's defining narrative is liberation from Egyptian slavery. It spawns a wide range of metaphors. Salvation offers *freedom* from condemnation and guilt. It gives *freedom* from slavery to sin, the fear of death, and the power and tyranny of the law. Salvation offers *freedom* in Christ so that people can become who they are created to be, namely, children and heirs rather than slaves. They are created for good works, walk by the Spirit, and serve each other in love.
4. Reconciliation/restoration. *Through* Christ's faithfulness and *in* him, believers are reconciled to God. They have peace with God in a new covenantal relationship in and through the blood of Christ. Hostility and enmity toward God is ended. Alienation from God, each other, and the whole creation is healed. In the renewed and transformed **ecclesia**, the dividing walls of gender, ethnicity, and class hostility are obliterated. In Christ and through the Spirit our minds are renewed and our lives are transformed into the image of Christ. Our lives now are truly human.

See also Church (Ecclesiology); Discipleship; Eschatology, Biblical; God, Doctrine of; Heaven; Hope, Christian.

KENT E. BROWER, PHD

BIBLICAL THEOLOGY

Biblical theology involves the **Bible**'s overall theological message. It depends upon sound exegesis, namely, accepting that texts must be allowed their own voice. When the diverse voices are heard together as **God**'s story of redemptive interaction with creation, they reveal a coherence that transcends diversity.

Biblical theology as a distinct effort began with Irenaeus (late second century AD). Even before the rise of modern historical criticism, the Bible's diversity presented challenges for biblical unity. A perceived tension exists between the Bible as a collection of documents to be analyzed using literary critical tools and the Bible as the church's authoritative Scripture. The risk of imposing unifying themes on Scripture's diverse genres remains. Nevertheless, biblical theology is essential for the ecclesia.

Several assumptions undergird biblical theology. First, the whole Bible is Christian Scripture. The OT is essential for a coherent account of God's scheme of salvation. Second, Wesleyans read Scripture Christologically. Only in the light of the incarnation does its storyline become clear. Third, an overall picture of God's good purposes is requisite for understanding the details. Fourth, God calls a people to be holy. This thread runs throughout Scripture. Finally, God speaks and acts in history. Thus the storyline is the focus of interpretation rather than individual words or treating Scripture as an ahistorical series of propositions.

In the biblical story God is revealed as all-loving and redeeming. The story begins with creation. Humankind, created as male and female, is in the Creator's image and likeness. God is Being-in-Communion. Human community within creation mirrors God's care. In this harmonious relationship, creation is "very good" (Gen. 1:31). By contrast, isolation is "not good" (2:18).

But with disastrous effects humans refuse to accept their creatureliness. All relationships are distorted—the man and the woman are estranged; fratricide soon follows. Existence itself becomes distressed. Humans wrest sustenance from a recalcitrant creation. Most importantly, the relationship between God and humankind is marred. Thus sin abounds in creation, but God still cares and preserves creation. He establishes a covenant with Noah and calls Abraham—the ancestor of the people through whom God would rescue creation. When Abraham's children are enslaved in Egypt, God rescues them and makes of them "a kingdom of priests and a holy nation" (Exod. 19:6, NASB). The reign of David is Israel's golden era. But the subsequent story is riddled with failure. Holiness as separation becomes an end in itself, and election gives way to misplaced superiority and false security. Repeatedly God warns the people. They refuse to hear, and exile follows.

Amid desperate conditions, hope is reborn. The promise of return and restoration anticipates God's new thing—a new covenant written on the heart by God's Spirit. Indeed, "in the last days" the Spirit would be poured out "upon all flesh" (Acts 2:17; see Joel 2:28). Israel would rediscover its mission as "a light to the nations" (Isa. 49:6), and the nations would flock to Zion.

Into this context comes Jesus. All NT writers see his coming in continuity with God's past activity. With the coming of Jesus, God's kingdom is arriving. He is the obedient Son, even "unto death" (Phil. 2:8, KJV). He calls and creates a renewed people. This renewed people of God participate in the new covenant in the Messiah's blood. They join God's grand scheme of rescue, restoration, redemption, and re-creation. In the power of the Spirit, Jesus' followers bear witness to him, continue his mission, and engage the powers of this present age. They live as God's holy people. They hasten the day when God's good purposes will, beyond human contemplation, be accomplished in a new and renewed creation (Rom. 8:21; Col. 1:20).

See also Biblical Interpretation, Ancient and Modern Methods; Biblicism/Bibliolatry; Christology, New Testament; Ecclesiology, New Testament; Fundamentalist Theology; Hermeneutics; Scripture, Wesleyan Approach to.

Resources
Bauckham, Richard. *The Bible and Ecology.* London: DLT, 2010.
Brower, Kent E. "Eschatology." In *The New Dictionary of Biblical Theology,* edited by T. Desmond Alexander and Brian S. Rosner, 459-64. Downers Grove, IL: IVP Academic, 1999. Material from this source is used with permission.

KENT E. BROWER, PHD

BIBLICAL WORLDVIEW
See BIBLICAL THEOLOGY.

BIBLICISM/BIBLIOLATRY

Biblicism or biblical fundamentalism conveys the perspective that the literal meaning intended by the authors of biblical texts is the only legitimate meaning of **Scripture**. Biblicism in its extreme form promotes reading the Bible for its plain meaning without giving any attention to its literary or linguistic aspects. In its moderate and conservative form, it seeks to discover the literal meaning through the study of the historical, cultural, and linguistic aspects of the text.

Emphasizing the literal meaning as the only legitimate meaning of a text fails to account for Scripture's complexity as God's revealed Word. It also fails to appreciate the Bible as a theological and literary work produced by inspired writers. It ignores the need for additional methods for interpreting the Bible. For example, reading Gen. 1 as a theological and literary account that requires a theological interpretation would be objectionable to biblical literalists. A literal reading of the genealogies in the early chapters of Genesis leads biblical literalists to assume that creation took place around 4000 BC. For them, the "day" in the creation account is literally a twenty-four hour day. Numbers are interpreted literally. However, biblical literalists would not think of the sky as a solid vault that supports waters above it, even though that is the meaning the Hebrew term in Gen 1:6 conveys. Neither would they say there is water above the sky.

Biblicism limits the human involvement in writing Scripture; human writers simply wrote down what God dictated to them. Biblical literalists read Scripture without seeking to understand a text's literary and theological context. They often treat the literal meaning of Scripture as binding Christian doctrine. Some may even argue that since the Bible is clear enough to be understood, it does not require any interpretation and that Scripture is totally inerrant because it is free from *any* human error, including in matters of science, history, and geography and in other technical or nondoctrinal issues.

Biblicism often leads to bibliolatry (worshipping the Bible), assigning holiness to the form of biblical words and phrases, and treating the Bible in the same way one would worship God. Regarding a certain translation as more authoritative than others because it is an "authorized" version or because it follows a literal, word-for-word rendering of the original languages of the Bible is another form of bibliolatry.

See also Hermeneutics; Scripture, Theology of.

ALEX VARUGHESE, PHD

BIOETHICS

Bioethics is the branch of ethics that treats ethical questions and decisions associated with life-and-death issues. It studies the moral implications of biological and biomedical research, development, and application. Its range of topics is almost unlimited, stretching from the fertilization of a human egg to morally acceptable ways of dying, from private decisions about health care to public debates about medical policy. Christian ethicists are intensely involved in bioethics. But the field is dominated by nonreligious or secular moral reasoning.

Bioethics has a relatively brief history. It emerged in the last thirty-five years, with the ascendance and intersection of advances in health-related sciences, genetics, medical technology, and the extraordinarily complex moral questions they raise. But its roots are as old as medicine, going back at least to the Greek physician Hippocrates (late fifth century BC), who is often credited with the Hippocratic oath. The immediate predecessor of "bioethics" was "medical ethics," a term that became too narrow for the expanding field of investigation.

Historically, theologians have engaged medicine and science in substantial ways. But since the late 1970s the voice of Christian theologians in bioethics has become less audible. Theological reflection on bioethics influences Christians, but it has little impact in the public square.

Bioethics relies on at least four principles: (1) *Autonomy* seeks to protect the right of all persons freely to make decisions involving their own care. The requirement for informed consent comes from this principle, a principle increasingly difficult to administer, especially as it relates to children. (2) *Nonmaleficence* expresses the obligation not to cause harm. This principle protects patients and their families against the misuse of power by the bearers of technical and medical knowledge. (3) *Beneficence* expresses the general duty to help and not to harm persons. (4) *Justice* is the final principle. Medical resources are finite; demands are seemingly limitless. How are limited resources to be distributed in an equitable and just manner?

These principles offer a broad framework for bioethics. Each principle aims at achieving a beneficent result. Yet there is often debate both inside and outside the medical establishment about how to apply and balance the principles. For Christians additional questions involving the distinctive content and implications of their faith also come into play.

People in the West usually enjoy excellent medical care and access to the latest technologies. But people in many parts of the world lack this access. Since context matters, in a global context, application of the four principles becomes ever more ethically problematic for patients, health care workers and administrators, researchers, governments, and insurance companies.

A Christian valuation of human life, Christian hope as it relates to life and death, and life in the body of Christ are fundamental considerations to a Christian approach to bioethics. Along with other Christians, Wesleyans recognize that God is the Source of human life and that humans are created in God's image and hence have inviolable value bestowed on them by God that must be safeguarded. One of the greatest challenges for Christians and their teachers is to resolve questions associated with bioethics from the perspective of Christian values and the hope of the resurrection. Christians are secure *in* Christ, not *in* physical health and life's duration. Unlike those who have no hope, Christians who find themselves and their families in situations where bioethical decisions must be made should remember that their valuation of life and death is formed by the risen Christ, not by the restricted confines of human existence.

See also Anthropology, Theological; Christian Ethics/Moral Theology; Justice; Social Ethics.

Resources

Meilaender, Gilbert. *Bioethics: A Primer for Christians*. Grand Rapids: Eerdmans, 2005.
National Institutes of Health. "Bioethics Resources on the Web." http://bioethics.od.nih.gov/.
Shannon, Thomas A., and Nicholas J. Kockler. *An Introduction to Bioethics*. New York: Paulist Press, 2009.

JAMES W. LEWIS, PHD

BIRTH/LIFE/DEATH/RESURRECTION/ASCENSION OF JESUS
See JESUS OF NAZARETH.

BLACK THEOLOGY

Black theology teaches that African-Americans, though dehumanized in American slavery and segregation, were created in God's image as bearers of full human dignity. Blacks derive their value as a divine gift. Whites, when justifying their subjugation of blacks, often questioned the humanity of blacks and their divine identity as God's children. Black theology rebukes this historic heresy and affirms that God is no respecter of persons. Additionally, black theology requires its advocates to challenge and undermine sinful structures that oppress vulnerable and subject peoples. It asserts that love, while mandated in the Bible, cannot flourish if power arrangements that perpetuate poverty and injustice go undisturbed. Unless human worth, which all of humankind receives from God, is permitted to challenge the social sin of oppression, then expressions of love are empty.

Henry Turner, a bishop in the African Methodist Episcopal (AME) Church, might have provided the earliest articulation of black theology. In 1898, a period of escalating racial violence and disenfranchisement in America, Turner declared that "God is a Negro." Blacks, he said, have as much right to view God as resembling them as do Caucasians. Blacks were hopeless, he said, if they thought they did not look like their Creator. James Cone, another AME minister and theologian, deepened Turner's black theology in his book *Black Theology and Black Power* (1969). Although black self-worth was important to Cone, he also argued that insurgency against white hegemony was a crucial objective of black theology. Jesus' ministry, he declared, focused on liberation. Moreover, black churches exemplify this emancipationist theology and understanding of Jesus. Gayraud Wilmore, a black Presbyterian clergyman, contended that these emphases established a tradition of black radicalism within African-American religion.

Current scholarly activity among black theologians treats issues demanding greater elaboration and exploration. They include theodicy, Marxist praxis, reconciliation, gender, and the search for black religious sources.

Jacquelyn Grant, a **womanist theologian**, has observed that black churches possess the same sexist heritage as white churches. Unless black theology includes female religious experiences, then black theology is incomplete. Cecil Cone, James's brother, lamented that black theology initially developed in conversation with leading white theologians but then failed to continue. He believes black theology will have greater authenticity when sources within the African religious heritage and in slave testimonies receive more attention. These ongoing developments show that black theology remains an unfinished project.

See also African-American Methodism; Justice; Rights, Human; Social Justice; Womanist Theology.

Resources

Cone, James H. *Black Theology and Black Power*. New York: Seabury Press, 1969. Reprint, Maryknoll, NY: Orbis Books, 1997.

Roberts, J. Deotis. *Liberation and Reconciliation: A Black Theology.* 2nd ed. Louisville, KY: Westminster John Knox Press, 2005.

DENNIS C. DICKERSON, PHD

BODY OF CHRIST
See CHURCH (ECCLESIOLOGY).

Cc

CALVIN, JOHN

John Calvin was born in France. He studied theology and law at the universities of Paris, Bourges, and Orleans. Attracted by the interpretations of Scripture coming from the Protestant **Reformation** in Germany and Switzerland, he became critical of Catholic teaching. When King Francis I of France sided with the **Roman Catholics**, Calvin fled to Switzerland. In Basel he wrote his major work, *Institutes of the Christian Religion*, first published (in Latin) in 1536. Calvin was twenty-six. The *Institutes* provided a comprehensive Protestant theology. With **Luther**, Calvin agreed that humans are saved only through God's **grace** and Christ's merits, not by meritorious works of piety as in the Catholic tradition. He undergirded this with God's absolute sovereignty. Calvin faced the implications of sovereignty and concluded that God foreknows and preordains everything. This is the proper interpretation of Rom. 8:28-30.

Moving to Geneva, Calvin helped establish the Reformation there. He published a doctrinal statement of twenty-one articles. Geneva citizens were required to assent. He established a theocratic government that proved unpopular. Banished from Geneva, Calvin later returned to consolidate his power and authority. He wrote commentaries on the Scriptures and expanded the *Institutes* with a treatise on the Lord's Supper. Calvin disagreed with Roman Catholic and Lutheran interpretations of transubstantiation and consubstantiation and also with Zwingli's memorialism. For Calvin, by *virtue* (power) of the Spirit, when the bread is placed in our hands, because "we ought to seek Christ in heaven, our thoughts ought to be carried thither" (Wallace 1953, 164-65). **John Wesley** reversed the direction. Rather than our thoughts rising to heaven, the Spirit brings Christ to us. **Charles Wesley**'s hymn says, "To every faithful soul appear, / and show thy real presence here" (Rattenbury 1990, 52).

Calvin's influence spread to other countries in Europe, especially to the English **Puritans** and to Scotland through John Knox. Many Calvinists were in the Methodist movement, including George Whitefield, Lady Selina Huntingdon, and the growing Methodist movement in Wales. To recognize this, Wesley said he came "within a hair's breadth" of Calvinism in ascribing all good to God's free grace and excluding human merit (*Works*, 8:284-85). But on one crucial point—**predestination**—Wesley differed sharply: the belief that God foreknows and preordains everything.

Wesley agreed that God foreknows everything, for time is a dimension of the created order. All moments in time are, therefore, for God simultaneous. There is no foreknowledge or subsequent knowledge because God sees at once whatever was, is, or will be. Wesley taught that God's foreknowledge is not deterministic. God carefully guards human free will and an open future. Humans are not predestined or coerced to respond to grace, or predestined to resist it. Wesley's stand against predestination, most notably expressed in his sermon "Free Grace" (7:373-86), caused a rift among the Methodists. Eventually this was overcome when Whitefield and Wesley followed Wesley's admonition "to think and let think" (5:246).

Wesley continued his fight against the doctrine of predestination, believing it counter to the "whole scope and tenor of Scripture" (7:380). "And here I fix my foot. . . . [Christ] 'is the propitiation for our sins; and not for ours only, but for the sins of the whole world' [1 John 2:2]" (383-85). God "'is the Saviour of all men' [1 Tim. 4:10]" (381). "'The Lord is loving unto *every* man; and his mercy is over *all his* works' [Ps. 145:9]" (380, emphasis added).

Then why is not everyone saved? Although God is not willing that any should perish, God pays a price for human freedom; some "will not be healed" (381). They will persist in rejecting God's grace. Still, we are called to proclaim the good news to all.

See also Arminian Theology; Arminius, Jacob; Augustine; Determinism and Free Will; Free Will; Justification; *Ordo Salutis*.

Resources
Johnson, William. *John Calvin: Reformer for the 21st Century*. Louisville, KY: Westminster John Knox Press, 2009.
Rattenbury, J. Ernest. *Eucharistic Hymns of John and Charles Wesley*. Akron, OH: Order of St. Luke Publications, 1990.
Stewart, Kenneth. *Ten Myths About Calvinism*. Downers Grove, IL: IVP Academic, 2011.
Wallace, Ronald S. *Calvin's Doctrine of the Word and Sacrament*. Edinburgh: Oliver and Boyd, 1953.

THEODORE RUNYON, DR. THEOL.

CANONICAL THEISM

"Canonical theism" is a term coined by William J. Abraham to designate faith in the Trinitarian God in and through the rich canonical heritage of the church. Understanding "canon" to mean "an authoritative list," canonical theism argues that this heritage includes not only a canon of Scripture but also canons of creeds, councils, saints, theologians, liturgies, icons, and bishops.

Brought into existence by the **Holy Spirit**, these persons, practices, and materials are **means of grace** through which the Spirit enables persons with open and receptive hearts to know the triune God and be nurtured in that faith. Because these canons have distinctive yet overlapping functions, differences between Christian traditions in their exact contents or even in the absence of some of the canons does not prevent this work of the Spirit. While retrieving the fullness of this canonical heritage is emphasized, even more important is recognizing its soteriological purpose.

Because the canons are authoritative, over time their use in the church shifted from being means of grace to becoming epistemological criteria for adjudicating and defending truth claims. The Protestant Reformation appeal to the authority of Scripture alone against Roman Catholic appeals to church teaching is one example; some modern scholars using interpretations of Scripture to challenge traditional teachings on the incarnation and the Trinity is another. Canonical theists argue that while **epistemology** is a vital and necessary concern, turning canons into primarily epistemic criteria had the detrimental effect for the church of obscuring or losing the soteriological purpose of the canonical heritage.

One concern expressed even by sympathetic Protestant critics is this loss of the primacy of Scripture. They wonder why retrieval of a wider canonical heritage as means of grace necessarily entails no longer accepting the authority of Scripture as a criterion (or norming norm) as well. Canonical theists argue that they do not rule out such an epistemological use of Scripture but that it should function this way not outside but *within* the wider canonical heritage in which lives are being shaped by the Spirit.

Canonical theism resonates with Wesleyan emphases on sanctification, means of grace, and the work of the Holy Spirit.

See also Tradition, Evangelical Retrieval of.

Resources
Abraham, William J. *Canon and Criterion in Christian Theology.* New York: Oxford University Press, 1998.
Abraham, William J., Jason E. Vickers, and Natalie B. Van Kirk, eds. *Canonical Theism: A Proposal for Theology and the Church.* Grand Rapids: Eerdmans, 2008.
Vickers, Jason E. *Minding the Good Ground: A Theology for Church Renewal.* Waco, TX: Baylor University Press, 2011.

HENRY H. KNIGHT III, PHD

CAPITALISM

Capitalism, or economic individualism, is an economic system in which ownership of the means of production, the distribution of goods and ser vices, and the exchange of wealth rests primarily with private individuals and corporations who intend to profit from their investments. Proponents claim that self-interest and the right to own and enrich private property are morally and legally defensible.

Capitalism creates great wealth. But often the wealth is concentrated in the hands of relatively few people. Capitalism has been severely criticized by persons such as Karl Marx and **liberation theologians** for creating wide disparities between the rich and poor and for allowing the rich to oppress the poor. Marx predicted the revolutionary overthrow of capitalist societies and their replacement by scientific socialism, or communist economic systems and governments that would evenly redistribute wealth. Many Christians have argued that capitalism is unchristian because it seems to be based on self-interest and competition.

Advocates of capitalism, on the other hand, argue that in countries where free and fair competition is enforced by just systems of government, capitalism has benefitted society in general, especially by encouraging entrepreneurial creativity and individual industriousness and by creating large middle classes. Freedom to make one's own economic choices and capitalism's affinity for **democracy** place it in a morally superior position over its main rival, **socialism**. Further, they argue that capitalism's superiority over socialism was historically demonstrated in the twentieth century by the failure of socialism in its Communist forms to deliver on its economic and social promises, and the subsequent abandonment of Communism by most countries that experimented with it (e.g., the Soviet Union).

However, post-Communist claims for the triumph of capitalism are challenged by events like the global financial collapse of 2008 and the difficulty of sustaining capitalism on a planet with finite natural resources. Today, most national economies and the emerging global economy are of a "mixed" nature; they are economies in which markets are generally free but regulated with varying degrees of government oversight and intervention.

While the Bible does not address all the complexities of modern capitalism, it does address issues of economics that bear on capitalism:

1. All wealth and resources ultimately belong to God. We are merely their stewards.
2. The Scriptures recognize the right (not absolute) of individuals to own and dispose of property. They encourage hard work and self-discipline that may result in the accumulation of wealth—all necessary for capitalism.
3. God has a special concern for the poor. Christians must oppose any economic system that fails in this regard or that exploits the poor and defenseless.

4. God's people, especially the socially or economically privileged, must use their affluence for the betterment of others. The accumulation of wealth for wealth's sake (covetousness and greed), though not wealth as such, is unambiguously condemned in the Scriptures (Job 20:15; Ps. 10:3; Mark 4:19; Rom. 1:29; James 4:13-17).

See also Democracy; Economics and the Use of Money; Globalization; Latin American Missiology/Liberation Struggle; Poverty; Socialism; Wealth; Work, Theology of.

Resources
Hill, Austin, and Scott Rae. *The Virtues of Capitalism: A Moral Case for Free Markets.* Chicago: Northfield Publishing, 2010.

Wesley, John. "On the Danger of Increasing Riches." In *Works*, 7:355-62.

RODNEY L. REED, PHD

CARE FOR THE ELDERLY AND VULNERABLE
See HOLISTIC MISSION.

CHARISMATIC MOVEMENT
See CHARISMATIC THEOLOGY.

CHARISMATIC THEOLOGY

Charismatic theology identifies the worship and ministry of non-Pentecostal adherents of the Christian faith that emphasize the *charismata* (the gifts of the **Holy Spirit**) in **doctrine**, **worship**, and ministry. **Gifts of the Spirit** include speaking in tongues, discernment of spirits, word of knowledge, word of wisdom, healing, and other miraculous manifestations of the Holy Spirit in the course of **witness** and **worship**. Other descriptive terms are used, but the language of gifts (charismata) preserves the emphasis on **grace** as their origin.

Charismatic theology recognizes that the dramatic demonstrations of the gifts of the Spirit do not occur when Christian life begins. These demonstrations are experienced as a special work of the Holy Spirit—an endowment with power—that occurs in the process of one's Christian life and ministry. Charismatics believe the endowment marks a release of the power and manifestations of the Spirit in his presence and work. They believe this to be a baptism-like experience evidenced by speaking in tongues (**glossolalia**).

Ministry—both personal and corporate—is believed to be the purpose of speaking in tongues. As personal, it is held to be a private prayer language freely accessible at the will/initiation of the worshipper. As corporate, speaking in tongues occurs in public worship. For prophetic ministry to occur, charismatics teach that the Holy Spirit, through the gift of interpretation, must interpret the message. Speaking in tongues may be corporate when the congregation prays and sings in tongues simultaneously.

Charismatic experiences are present in many Christian denominations, liturgical and nonliturgical. In Pentecostal denominations the initiating charismatic experience is identified as baptism with the Holy Spirit, accompanied by the initial oral evidence of speaking in tongues. In non-Pentecostal charismatic communions the experience is most often referred to as renewal in the Holy Spirit. The initial oral evidence is most often identified as speaking in tongues.

Non-Pentecostal denominations in which these charismata occur usually define them from within their accepted patterns of worship and ministry, without making major theological changes. Consequently, there is no single charismatic theology. Instead, each community of faith retains its traditional identity and adapts charismatic nomenclature accordingly. Hence, it is legitimate to use such designations as Roman Catholic charismatics, Episcopalian/Anglican charismatics, Lutheran charismatics, and Protestant charismatics.

Charismatics teach that manifestations of the gifts of the Holy Spirit highlight experiential theology as an appropriate component in theological formulation. Although congregations in many non-Pentecostal denominations allow these gifts in worship and practice, few have developed statements of faith that show the effects of charismatic experience and worship on their theologies. For example, common to non-Pentecostal theologies is the belief that baptism with the Holy Spirit occurs at Christian initiation. According to liturgical communions this happens through sacraments of initiation such as baptism (e.g., Anglican); confirmation, also called chrismation (e.g., Roman Catholic); and chrismation (e.g., Eastern Orthodox). For some nonliturgical churches, such as Southern Baptists, baptism with the Holy Spirit is a singular/unrepeatable experience that occurs at conversion. A Christian may be filled with the Spirit many times but baptized only once.

Instead of using the language of baptism with the Holy Spirit, as in Pentecostal communions, non-Pentecostal charismatics prefer such terms as "release in the Holy Spirit" or "renewal in the Holy Spirit." Charismatics have largely retained speaking in tongues as the initial oral evidence of this renewal. The chief interest of charismatic theology is not speaking in tongues but renewed and continued ministry through all the Spirit's gifts.

See also Christology; Gifts of the Spirit; Pentecostal Theology; Repentance; Sanctification; Trinity; Wesley, John, Theology of.

Resources

Cartledge, Mark J. *Encountering the Spirit: The Charismatic Tradition.* Maryknoll, NY: Orbis Books, 2007.

Lederle, Henry I. *Theology with Spirit: The Future of the Pentecostal and Charismatic Movements in the 21st Century.* Tulsa, OK: Word and Spirit Press, 2010.

R. HOLLIS GAUSE, PHD

CHILDHOOD, WESLEYAN THEOLOGY OF

From the beginning, Wesleyan theology has taken seriously the faith and spiritual nurture of children. **John Wesley** recognized God's gracious activity in children and affirmed the validity of their faith responses. He spoke of **salvation** as the "way of salvation" (*Works*, 6:43-54); childhood is a foundational, twelve-year part of that lifelong journey.

From infancy God comes to every child with what Wesley called "preventing" or **prevenient grace** (*Works*, 6:43-54). He saw evidence of **prevenient grace** in a child's initial awareness of and desire for God, the early sense of right and wrong, and the first awareness of God's will (Outler, 273). But original **sin** is also present in all persons from birth, infecting children with a tendency toward acts of sin. God's purpose in prevenient grace is for each child to become aware of God's love and then, as he or she grows in the understanding of right and wrong, to become aware of his or her sin and God's loving offer of forgiveness through Jesus.

A Wesleyan view of the way of salvation pictures the continual gracious work of God preparing persons for times of critical response. Each response is a step into a deeper relationship with God and leads into continual growth in Christ.

In their ministry with children churches have often focused on calling them to **conversion** but have inadequately valued God's work of preparation for response or the ongoing nurture of a child's faith.

Although God initiates his relationship with the child and does the transforming, God does not act without assistance. The **church** and parents are responsible partners with God to nurture a child's faith. Significant formation takes place, not just during intentional instruction but also in the flow of life at home and in the body of Christ.

Wesley directed Methodist preachers to pay attention to children, spend time with them, and instruct them (*Works*, 8:316). Before the beginning of Sunday schools in the 1780s, Methodists were conducting classes to instruct children. They took seriously their spiritual well-being.

Children need to be with adults—worshipping, praying, and serving together with them. They need to observe adults living the Christian life. And they need places where they can learn God's story. As children spend time in the biblical narrative, God speaks to them and by grace they can come to know him. Children are blessed when at church and in the home they are led to encounter God in the biblical story.

Wesley understood the important role families play in nurturing a child's faith. He and the Methodists provided instructional resources for parents. They encouraged both parents to contribute to their children's spiritual nurture, beginning in infancy.

To parents and congregations in the eighteenth and twenty-first centuries, Wesley declares that children are "immortal spirits whom God hath, for a time, entrusted to [our] care, that [we] may train them up in holiness, and fit them for the enjoyment of God in eternity. This is a glorious and important trust" (*Works*, 7:79).

See also Conscience; Spiritual Formation/Growth.

Resources
Stonehouse, Catherine. "Children in Wesleyan Thought." In *Children's Spirituality: Christian Perspectives, Research, and Applications*, edited by Donald Ratcliff, 133-48. Eugene, OR: Wipf and Stock Publishers, 2004.
Wesley, John. "On Family Religion." In *Works*, 7:76-86.
———."On the Education of Children." In *Works*, 7:86-98.
———. "A Treatise on Baptism." In *Works*, 10:188-201.

CATHERINE STONEHOUSE, PHD

CHILDREN OF GOD
See CHURCH (ECCLESIOLOGY); ISRAEL.

CHINESE CHRISTIANITY
See CHINESE CHURCH, CONTEMPORARY.

CHINESE CHURCH, CONTEMPORARY
Christianity's growth in China since 1976 is unparalleled. When driven out in 1949-50, the missionaries left behind approximately 1 million Protestant Christians. By the 1970s many thought Chairman Mao, the Red Guard, the Cultural Revolution (1966-76), and the Gang of Four had effectively eliminated Chinese Christianity. Instead, in spite of intense persecution, Christians multiplied. By the mid-1980s their numbers stood at 40 to 54 million. Today, three and a half decades after the Cultural Revolution, mainland China is home to the world's seventh-largest Christian population. There are roughly 67 million Christians in mainland China, representing about 5 percent of the country's total population. Of these, roughly 9 million (0.7 percent of China's total population) are Catholics, including 5.7 million who are affiliated with the state-approved Patriotic Catholic Association and a conservatively estimated 3.3 million who are affiliated solely with unregistered Catholic congregations (PRC 2011). Over forty-eight thousand churches and meeting places are available for public worship. Approximately 70 percent of these are newly built.

The faithfulness and courage of Chinese Christians during the Cultural Revolution, and since, demonstrate the price to be paid and the fruit to be harvested when taking up the cross of Jesus Christ.

The Chinese government officially permits persons eighteen years old and above to attend Christian meetings approved either by the China Christian Council (CCC)/National Three-Self Movement Committee (NTSMC) or the Chinese Patriotic Catholic Association (CPCA). But millions of Christians attend unregistered house churches. "Official" and "house" churches are theologically **evangelical**. The latter is more conservative and **charismatic** than the former.

In 2010 the NTSMC, once known as the Three-Self Movement (TSM), celebrated its sixtieth anniversary. Begun in 1950 by Protestant Christians, it works to make the Chinese church truly indigenous through self-government, self-support, and self-propagation. Christian churches have historically been seen as tools of imperialism. So practicing self-reliance is important for many reasons, not the least of which is avoiding political suspicion. Maintaining mutual respect in matters of faith and worship and emphasizing unity in diversity are also important. Protestant churches in China are postdenominational; they do not identify denominationally.

The CCC was formed in 1980. It works hand in hand with the NTSMC to oversee the spiritual and theological interests of government-recognized Protestant churches. The CCC and the NTSMC have twelve commissions, ranging from Church Administration and Rural Ministries to Propagation of the Gospel and Promotion for Self-Support.

To meet the demands for more church workers, the CCC has expanded opportunities for theological education. Since 1981, eighteen seminaries and Bible schools have opened. By July 2001, more than four thousand seminarians had graduated. Over fifty provincial training centers had been established. More than five hundred thousand lay leaders had received first-time training. Since 1980 over thirty million Bibles have been printed and distributed.

Resources and facilities for theological education of house-church leaders are quite limited. Theological education and training occur mostly in local settings. House churches depend heavily on irregular instruction delivered by teachers from all over the world. Many would-be pastors enroll in radio Bible schools, including that of the Far East Broadcasting Company.

Chinese Roman Catholic underground churches recognize the authority of the pope. The government-approved CPCA does not. The existence of Catholic underground churches is a major obstacle to establishing diplomatic relations between the Holy See and the People's Republic of China.

Rapid church growth and greater openness present new challenges and opportunities. These include a rising divorce rate in many parts of China and an increase in intergenerational tensions. Others are a crisis in elder care as traditional family patterns erode in the new urbanized culture and the weakening of support systems that have been in place for generations. The Chinese church must also find ways to bear witness to its faith by engaging in Chinese society. It must show that being faithful to Christ includes good citizenship. Chinese Christians must bear witness to their faith by working with others to promote social harmony and well-being without betraying their faithfulness to Jesus Christ.

See also Asian Theology; Communism; Indigenization; Indigenous Christian Groups; Indigenous Theologies; Underground Church in China.

Resources

Aikman, David. *Jesus in Beijing: How Christianity Is Transforming China and Changing the Global Balance of Power.* Washington, DC: Regnery, 2006.

Faries, Nathan. *The "Inscrutably Chinese" Church: How Narratives and Nationalism Continue to Divide Christianity.* Lanham, MD: Lexington Books, 2010.

PRC (Pew Research Center). "Global Christianity: A Report on the Size and Distribution of the World's Christian Population." *Pew Forum on Religion and Public Life.* December 19, 2011. http://www.pewforum.org/Christian/Global-Christianity-exec.aspx.

Yu, Danny, ed. *Breaking Down the Dividing Wall.* Beijing: Beijing Culture Publishing House, 2007.

WILLIAM T. YOUNG, PHD

CHRISTIAN ETHICS/MORAL THEOLOGY

"Christian ethics" and "moral theology" are often used interchangeably. However, "moral theology" is an older term. It originated at the end of the sixth century after the **Roman Catholic** Council of Trent (1545-63). No theologian before that time would have used the term as a distinct theological discipline. After that, moral theology becomes one of two systematic disciplines in Catholic theology. The other is speculative or dogmatic theology.

This division rested on Aristotle's distinction between practical and theoretical knowledge. Dogmatic theology was concerned with theory; moral theology with practice. Moral theology dealt with, among other matters, virtues, laws, and sacraments. Protestants also pursued moral theology, but once the European Enlightenment occurred, they began to embrace the discipline of ethics more so than Catholics. A central thinker in the development of ethics was Immanuel Kant. He rephrased Jesus' Golden Rule, "Do to others as you would have them do to you" (Luke 6:31; see also, Matt. 7:12), into his categorical imperative. One version of it said, "Act only on that maxim which you can at the same time will that it be a universal law" ([1788] 1993, pt. 1, bk. 1, 1.7). A "maxim" is a law an autonomous agent embraces as a basis for action.

With this development, ethics became primarily concerned with acts. For Kant, the agent must be autonomous, or self-legislative, in acting. For an act to qualify as moral, no one will act to gain rewards, to satisfy a tradition to which he or she belongs, or to carry out what he or she has been told to do. An individual, autonomous moral act should be capable of being universalized. Any individual in any circumstance should be able at least to *will* the moral act.

Kant interpreted Christianity through his emphasis on ethics. Although the term "Christian ethics" has diverse approaches, Kant's ethics profoundly affected it. He identified a discrete realm of action that could be assessed independent of theological doctrines, traditions, or history. Subsequently, "Christian" could be added to "ethics," the latter understood as independent of, and larger than, Christianity.

Kant was roughly a contemporary of John Wesley. Most of his work occurred at the end of Wesley's life. Unlike Kant, Wesley did not produce a Christian ethics separate from theological doctrine. His sermons on the Sermon on the Mount, on law, and on the sacraments would be closest to a Christian ethics. But even they more closely resemble the older tradition of moral theology than the modern understanding of Christian ethics. However, Wesley did not maintain the rigid distinction between moral and dogmatic theology found in post-Tridentine Catholicism. He knew Aristotelian moral philosophy. He tutored students using Gerard Langbaine's commentary on Aristotle's *Nicomachean Ethics*. Nothing indicates Wesley believed this an improper course of study for Christians, even from this "man of one book"—the Bible (*Works*, 5:3). Langbaine's work, like the Catholic tradition, divided into the theoretical and the practical. But Wesley never adopted that distinction.

After Wesley, many successors adopted ethics as a distinct field of study. Sometimes this followed more the lines of Kant than Wesley, which is to say, ethics was pursued as a discipline independent of theology. Knowledge of the Good was no longer directly related to knowledge of God. Once this separation occurred, nontheological disciplines such as sociology could be given autonomy over the subject matter of ethics. Nontheological disciplines became more important for articulating a Christian ethics than dogmatic theology. For instance, the early Wesleyans patterned their ethical life after their General Rules based on two crucial principles of the natural law, "do no harm" and "do good." But they were not viewed as constituting an autonomous ethic achievable in one's own power. The first two rules were indissolubly linked to a third: "[Attend] upon all the ordinances of God" (*Works*, 8:271). This included worship, Scripture, prayer, fasting, and the Lord's Supper.

Sharp distinctions between ethics, theology, and spirituality had not yet crept into the Wesleyan tradition. The General Rules, which are similar to moral theology, are in contrast to the 1908 Methodist Episcopal Church adoption of a "social creed." Its language resembles Kant more than Wesley.

See also Conscience; Ethics; Greek Philosophy; Justice; Social Ethics; Social Justice; Theosis (Deification); Works of Mercy.

Resources

Hays, Richard B. *The Moral Vision of the New Testament: Community, Cross, New Creation: A Contemporary Introduction to New Testament Ethics.* San Francisco: HarperOne, 1996.

Kant, Immanuel. 1788. *Critique of Practical Reason.* Translated by Lewis White Beck. 3rd ed. Upper Saddle River, NJ: Prentice Hall, 1993.

Long, D. Stephen. *John Wesley's Moral Theology: The Quest for God and Goodness.* Nashville: Kingswood Books, 2005.

Marquardt, Manfred. *John Wesley's Social Ethics: Praxis and Principles.* Nashville: Abingdon Press, 1992.

D. STEPHEN LONG, PHD

CHRISTIANITY AND GLOBAL CULTURES

Even though the Christian faith transcends all cultures, it is at home and flourishing in more cultures today than ever before. Worldwide, Jesus' disciples are crossing cultural boundaries at an unprecedented pace to proclaim the good news, make disciples, and plant churches. With more adherents than any other religion, Christianity continues to expand into new regions with the goal of reaching all peoples to make them Jesus' disciples and citizens of God's kingdom.

Moving beyond cultural boundaries has characterized Christianity from its beginning. The origin of Christianity's sense of universal mission is rooted in God's promise to Abraham: in him "all the families of the earth" would be blessed (Gen. 12:3). Jesus spoke of reaching "other sheep" so there would "be one flock, one shepherd" (John 10:16). He told his disciples to go "and make disciples of all nations" (Matt. 28:19). At Pentecost peoples of multiple cultures and tongues understood and responded to the gospel message (Acts 2). Following a report from missionaries Paul and Barnabas that Gentiles had been converted, a church council convened in Jerusalem and decided to accept these believers into the young church without their having to become Jews (Acts 15). Paul summarized the importance of this decision: "There is no longer Jew or Greek . . . for all of you are one in Christ Jesus" (Gal. 3:28).

Andrew Walls has offered fresh analyses of how the Christian faith is transmitted across cultures and is contextualized. He talks about the gospel as both prisoner and liberator of culture; he describes how the gospel as *prisoner* is subject to the particular realities of each host culture, while the gospel as *liberator* brings new life and freedom to the host culture. Walls calls the ability of the gospel to move into and adapt to each host culture the *indigenizing principle*. He calls the tendency of the gospel never to be completely at home in the host culture the *pilgrim principle*. As the Christian faith became contextualized in new cultures over time—the Hellenistic-Romans, the barbarians of the north, the nation-states of Western Europe, and new peoples and lands abroad—distinctive worldviews, values, thought patterns, and practices were encountered and had to be addressed on the basis of the gospel of Jesus Christ.

Recent discoveries of the history of the church in the Middle East, Africa, and Asia have brought a new awareness of the broad cultural character of early and medieval Christianity. The discoveries have greatly challenged the Western bias regarding church history.

Recent demographic data and analyses show a resurgence of Christianity among non-Western, nonwhite believers throughout Africa, Asia, and Latin America. This contrasts with a waning vitality in the West. These developments have prompted discussions about the future character of global Christianity, so long shaped in the West by Western thought, structures, and practices.

Contemporary insights from sociology, psychology, anthropology, linguistics, communication theory, missiology, and intercultural studies are enriching our understanding of how Christianity best reaches global cultures. We are becoming aware that everyone is immersed in and shaped by a specific culture. This should make us keenly aware of how the Christian message must be interpreted and applied in each cultural context, yet without compromising its essence.

A better understanding of similarities and differences between global cultures can facilitate more meaningful and effective cross-cultural interaction, enabling Christians to serve God more effectively in proclaiming the gospel to diverse cultures.

See also Contextualization; Contextual Theology; Globalization; Indigenization; Indigenous Theologies; Postcolonialism; Westernization of the Gospel.

Resources

Jenkins, Philip. *The Next Christendom: The Coming of Global Christianity.* Oxford, UK: Oxford University Press, 2002.

Noll, Mark. *The New Shape of World Christianity: How American Experience Reflects Global Faith.* Downers Grove, IL: IVP Academic, 2009.

Walls, Andrew. *The Missionary Movement in Christian History: Studies in the Transmission of Faith.* Maryknoll, NY: Orbis Books, 1996.

NORMAN WILSON, PHD

CHRISTIANITY AND THE WORLD RELIGIONS
See RELIGIONS, THEOLOGY OF.

CHRISTIAN PERFECTION (ENTIRE SANCTIFICATION)

The doctrine of **sanctification** or Christian holiness more completely expresses God's being and purposes for creation than any other doctrine. Scriptural language about holiness is uniquely God language, expressing God's very being. Thus God is separate from all evil and is characterized by justice, truth, and mercy. God's holiness is inextricably linked with God's love, which John Wesley describes as God's "reigning attribute . . . that sheds an amiable glory on all his other perfections" (*NT Notes*, 2:341; comment on 1 John 4:8). This holy love is most fully revealed in the cross of Jesus Christ.

Humans are created in God's image and are therefore meant to be pure from sin, holy, and loving, a reflection of God's own holy love. This image became totally corrupted by sin, but God seeks through sanctification to restore us to the image in which we were created. That full restoration is Christian perfection or entire sanctification, also known as full salvation or perfect love.

Wesley defines Christian perfection as "neither more nor less than pure love; love expelling sin, and governing both the heart and life of a child of God" (*Works*, 12:432; February 21, 1771, letter to Walter Churchey). Christian perfection is when love for God becomes the ruling **temper** in our hearts, ordering and infusing love for our neighbor and all other holy tempers.

God commands his people to "be holy, for [he is] holy" (Lev. 11:44-45). Jesus identifies the two greatest commandments as loving God "with all your heart . . . soul and . . . mind" and to "love your neighbor as yourself" (Matt. 22:37-39). What God commands, God also enables persons to be and do through grace, that is, through the **Holy Spirit** working in them. Thus Christian perfection is a gift of grace, enabling us to recover the loving image of God and, through becoming holy, also to regain the happiness or the well-being that comes from being who we were meant to be.

Some understand the attainment of sanctification or holiness to be by human performance through self-discipline or asceticism. Although important as **means of grace**, such efforts in themselves are powerless to sanctify. All holiness in created objects results from God's sanctifying presence and action. Paul encourages the church at Thessalonica by promising that "the one who calls you is faithful, and he will do this" (1 Thess. 5:24). Sanctification and Christian perfection are always God's gracious gifts, never a human achievement.

Some insist that sanctification in this life can be only partial or gradual and that Christian perfection is only for the life to come. But Paul prays that the Thessalonians be sanctified "wholly," "entirely" (aorist tense, "presently and decisively") so that they will be blameless when Christ appears. His confidence rested on the sanctifying God. The fruits of Christ's **atonement** and **Pentecost** are meant for Christians now, as well as for eternity. Through **faith**, justified Christians who are growing in sanctification seek to receive Christian perfection and, through the Spirit, to permit the Savior to possess them fully. God wants persons to receive and be filled with his sanctifying presence; all that Christ's presence fills, it sanctifies. Thus Wesley insisted

Christian perfection is an instantaneous work of God, both preceded and followed by a gradual work.

Entire sanctification's importance and urgency are clear in the Scriptures. God wills that Christians be sanctified, made holy (1 Thess. 4:3; Lev. 20:26; 22:31-33). Christ suffered and died to sanctify us (Heb. 13:12). "Without [holiness] no one will see the Lord" (12:14). Nothing unholy will enter heaven (Rev. 21:27; 22:11, 15). Christian perfection is thus a gift of God that fits us for life in the kingdom of heaven as well as transforms us for life in the present age.

See also Ordo Salutis; Reformed Tradition; Salvation (Soteriology); Spiritual Formation/Growth; Theosis (Deification); Wesley, John, Theology of.

Resources

Leclerc, Diane. *Discovering Christian Holiness: The Heart of Wesleyan-Holiness Theology.* Kansas City: Beacon Hill Press of Kansas City, 2010.

Lindström, Harald. *Wesley and Sanctification.* Grand Rapids: Zondervan, 1980.

Oswalt, John. *Called to Be Holy.* Nappannee, IN: Evangel Publishing House, 1999.

DENNIS F. KINLAW, PHD

CHRISTIAN YEAR

The Christian year is a remembrance of major events in the history of salvation, especially as accomplished through Christ. This remembrance uses Scripture to provide the distinctive commemoration for each occasion and season. Commemoration is not only accomplished through Scripture but also in other acts of worship such as prayers, music, and creeds. Churches also use changes in sanctuary decorations to narrate God's activity. Some churches use a yearly rotation of commemorated saints to supplement event-related remembrances.

The major development in the Christian year occurred in the fourth century when regions began to emphasize specific feasts in the year and shared these feasts with one another. Within a few centuries, the year had developed into a shape recognizable to modern Christians.

The year begins with Advent, a season anticipating the coming of Jesus Christ, in his birth and **second coming**. In its current shape, this season lasts four Sundays and ends at Christmas, a feast on December 25 celebrating Jesus' birth and **incarnation**. Christmas begins a twelve-day season that ends with Epiphany on January 6. Whereas Western churches adopted an Epiphany that emphasizes the coming of the magi, some Eastern churches emphasize Christ's baptism. Both emphases remember the revealing of God.

The time after Epiphany consists of two periods called Ordinary Time. "Ordinary" doesn't mean commonplace but that the Sundays are designated by ordinal numbers (e.g., the Second Sunday after Epiphany).

Another anticipatory season is Lent, whose first day (in the West) is Ash Wednesday. Lent's origins (as well as Advent's) appear connected to Christians preparing for baptism on a feast day. Thus Lent commemorates the opportunity for salvation through God's activity, especially in the **cross**. Lent concludes in Holy Week, a commemoration of the last week of Jesus' life. Easter follows and begins the celebratory season of remembering Christ's resurrection. Lasting fifty days, it commemorates his ascension on the fortieth day and the outpouring of the Holy Spirit at Pentecost, the fiftieth day.

Other feasts punctuate the year, including the Baptism of Christ, the Transfiguration, and Trinity Sunday.

Approaches to the year can employ either simple or dynamic remembrance. In *simple remembrance*, the church is conscious of the separation between past and present. In *dynamic remembrance*, however, worshipping churches will speak of past events as presently occurring (e.g., Christ *is* born in Bethlehem) or of the ongoing power of the event to shape experience (e.g., Christians *are* raised with Christ to new life). A dynamic sense of remembrance was what undergirded the placement of baptisms on major feast days in the early church. The Christian concept of *anamnesis* (a-nam-nē-sis)—a *remembrance* in which, through the Holy Spirit, God in Christ is present and active in baptism and the Eucharist—undergirds dynamic remembrance.

Churches birthed from the Wesleyan movement have observed diverse levels of keeping the year. Christmas and Easter probably have been the most consistently celebrated. These classic commemorations have often been supplemented with annual events whether in Wesleyanism's early history (e.g., watch-night and covenant services on New Year's Eve) or more recently (e.g., Missions Sunday or Mother's Day).

See also Covenant Service; Cross; Incarnation; Second Coming of Christ/ Parousia.

Resources

Connell, Martin. *Eternity Today: On the Liturgical Year.* New York: Continuum, 2006.

Stookey, Laurence Hull. *Calendar: Christ's Time for the Church.* Nashville: Abingdon Press, 1996.

Talley, Thomas J. *The Origins of the Liturgical Year.* Collegeville, MN: Liturgical Press, 1991.

Webber, Robert E., ed. *The Services of the Christian Year.* Vol. 5, *The Complete Library of Christian Worship.* Peabody, MA: Hendrickson, 1993.

LESTER RUTH, PHD

CHRISTOCENTRISM

See CHRISTOLOGY; CHRISTOLOGY, NEW TESTAMENT.

CHRISTOLOGY

Christology covers the person and work of **Jesus Christ** as Lord and Savior. Because of the inevitable complexity, the latter topic is picked up in the doctrine of **atonement**. Aside from dealing with Christ's person as human and divine, the former includes discussions of the offices and states of Christ.

While the Wesleys inherited the classical tradition of Chalcedon as **Anglicans**, some scholars have worried that John Wesley had monophysite and docetic tendencies, leading him to see Christ's human nature absorbed in the divine nature or seriously downplayed. These claims do not fit well with the brilliant orthodoxy of **Charles Wesley**'s hymns, which were approved by John. This development is best understood as a corrective reaction to tendencies in the theology of his day to downplay this dimension of the canonical faith of the church. Indeed, **John Fletcher** and Joseph Benson vigorously defended a high Christology. They appealed to the practices of piety and, in patristic fashion, to the soteriological necessity of the **incarnation**. Adam Clarke's Christology was so high that it led him to challenge the standard doctrine of the **Trinity** in denying the eternal procession of the Son from the Father. This initiated a flurry of work in the nineteenth century, represented best by Richard Watson and Miner Raymond, which defended a balanced high Christology within a wider defense of the early **ecumenical creeds** and **councils**. The latter became a hallmark of Wesleyan theology as a whole as seen in the work of T. O. Summers and W. B. Pope. This was a profoundly healthy development, signaling both a corrective to the early tradition and a reiteration of the critical background faith without which the tradition can readily lose its bearings.

The shift to political and philosophical concerns in the late nineteenth century spawned a more critical attitude toward the great tradition of the church. Moral and intellectual relevance took center stage, as seen most dramatically in Boston **personalism**. In this approach, Christology was eclipsed by the doctrine of God. More significantly, the revisions created tension with the received Christological convictions. The canons of credibility in play and the metaphysics adopted undercut the high Christology of the tradition. Various efforts, not unlike those that arose later in England in the 1970s in the work of Maurice Wiles, were made to make a certain vision of divine action the core solution. God was uniquely present and active in Christ as a human agent, but he is also present and active in the saints; hence, in time the full divinity of Christ is in jeopardy. Jesus is the best window for understanding God; but somehow we can maintain this without the intellectual mysteries and conundrums of the earlier Christology.

In the successor process tradition there is a much greater openness to the tradition of Nicaea and Chalcedon. However, it is an open question how far the ontology of that tradition is honored. Where personalists worried about credibility, the **process theologians** worry about **metaphysics**. In the end, there is a renewed effort to think of Christ as the intensity of divine presence and action. Processists worry that the humanity of Christ is sacrificed in the tradition; critics worry that they have no real place for the full divinity of Christ in their metaphysics. In the end, Christ differs from other human agents only in degree.

Liberation theologians in the Wesleyan tradition approach the issues in terms of the dangers of oppression. A high Christology is thought to downplay the historicity of Jesus as Liberator. For James Cone the crucial issue is one of race; for Jose Miguez-Bonino the challenge is that of class; for feminists and womanists such as Jacquelyn Grant, it is gender. The most recent reiteration of liberation theology takes empire as the central theme, looking for surplus meaning in Christology that will aid resistance to oppression even as complicity with oppression in the originating formulation is acknowledged. The besetting danger is that Christology will reflect more than anything else the political ideology of the theologian.

The foregoing explorations have not eclipsed the ongoing appropriation of the robust Christology of early Methodism and its ancestral versions in the ecumenical faith of the church. The rich theological heritage of Nicaea and Chalcedon are heartily embraced as fitting expositions of what God did in Christ for the salvation of the world. They provide a splendid home for the distinctive soteriological themes of the Wesleyan tradition. Received as means of grace and not just as explanatory theory, they are given a whole new lease of life.

See also Atonement; Christology, New Testament; God, Doctrine of; Incarnation; Jesus of Nazareth; Kenosis; Liberal Theology.

Resources

Deschner, John. *Wesley's Christology: An Interpretation.* Dallas: Southern Methodist University Press, 1960.

Kärkkäinen, Veli-Matti. *Christology: A Global Introduction.* Grand Rapids: Baker, 2003.

O'Collins, Gerald. *Christology: A Biblical, Historical, and Systematic Study of Jesus.* 2nd ed. Oxford, UK: Oxford University Press, 2009.

Oden, Thomas C. *The Word of Life.* Vol. 2, *Systematic Theology.* San Francisco: Harper and Row, 1989.

Schweitzer, Don. *Contemporary Christologies: A Fortress Introduction.* Minneapolis: Fortress Press, 2010.

WILLIAM ABRAHAM, PHD

CHRISTOLOGY, NEW TESTAMENT

In the NT Jesus is the prophesied Messiah who came to reveal the **kingdom of God** in word and deed. His death saved us from sin and its consequences. His **resurrection** vindicated Jesus' life, validated his word, and guaranteed the **salvation** of all who believe in him. Having ascended to the right hand of God, Jesus shall return to consummate the kingdom of God.

Scholars like N. T. Wright argue that **Christology** as a discipline should not be restricted to a survey of biblical titles for Jesus but should also take into account the pattern of his works and teachings even where no title is given.

In Matthew, Jesus is the messianic King who gathers up in his being the purposes of Israel. He is also the presence of God with his people. Matthew has a doctrine of the two advents to explain that while Jesus did not fulfill all the messianic prophecies at his first coming, he will do so at his second.

In Mark, Jesus is the secret Son of God and Son of Man. While the first title highlights the divine origin and commission of Jesus and from a political point of view subverts the divinity of the Roman emperor, the second title defines Jesus' messiahship by evoking Jewish **apocalyptic** expectations. Jesus is a Son-of-Man-must-suffer kind of Messiah. Mark's secrecy motif combines with the hardness-of-heart theme to explain why Jesus is rarely recognized as the Son of God.

Luke presents Jesus as the Savior of Israel and all flesh, in that order. His concern is to show that the salvation promised to Israel has been extended to the Gentiles. Jesus' words and deeds, empowered by the Spirit, embody the boundary-breaking character of the kingdom of God.

John's **gospel** proclaims Jesus as the Incarnate Word and Son of God, a witness both to the divine origin and humanity of Jesus. While Jesus is Son of God in a way in which no one else is a child of God, he invites all to become children of God. John highlights Jesus' uniqueness, and at the same time combats late first-century docetic tendencies that denied that Jesus was a real flesh and blood person.

Paul's dominant term for Jesus is "[the] Messiah," but this is closely linked to the rarer "Son" as signifying Jesus' unique relationship with God. The notion of Jesus as Lord is also prominent in Paul. "Lord" is used in the Greek OT in place of "Yahweh." Paul's application to Jesus of Scripture originally referring to Yahweh is facilitated by this use of "Lord," an extraordinary move for Paul. The term also has the implication that Jesus is Lord, not the divine Caesar.

There are two affirmations held in common by the NT writers: first, Christ is Jesus of Nazareth, and second, Jesus Christ is Lord. Although both affirmations emerge at the earliest stage of Christian proclamation, the latter seems to have more currency in missionary preaching. Jesus both fulfills messianic expectations and deserves worshipful devotion.

Recent scholarship has shown that belief in the lordship and imminent return of Jesus occurs in the earliest stages of Christian history. In Philippians, the hymn of Christ (2:6-11) also demonstrates very early belief in the lordship and deity of Jesus. So understanding Jesus as Lord, Christ, and Son of God are not retrojections imposed by later disciples but were in fact present in Jesus' own consciousness, as argued forcefully by N. T. Wright.

John Wesley affirmed traditional belief in the atoning death, resurrection, and lordship of Jesus Christ. However, he tended also to espouse a distinctive moral Christology. Jesus was the "model of Christianity" (*Works*, 1:73).

See also Atonement; Christology; Jesus of Nazareth; Resurrection; Second Coming of Christ/Parousia.

Resources
Dunn, James D. G. *Jesus Remembered*. Vol. 1, *Christianity in the Making*. Grand Rapids: Eerdmans, 2003.

Hurtado, Larry. *Lord Jesus Christ: Devotion to Jesus in Earliest Christianity*. Grand Rapids: Eerdmans, 2003.

Marshall, I. Howard. *New Testament Theology*. Downers Grove, IL: InterVarsity Press, 2004.

———. *The Origins of New Testament Christology*. Downers Grove, IL: InterVarsity Press, 1976.

Moule, C. F. D. *The Origin of Christology*. New York: Cambridge University Press, 1977.

Wright, N. T. *Jesus and the Victory of God*. Vol. 2, *Christian Origins and the Question of God*. Minneapolis: Fortress Press, 1996.

KENNETH L. WATERS SR., PHD

CHURCH (ECCLESIOLOGY)

"Ecclesiology" is a term that denotes the doctrine of the church. It is derived from the NT Greek word used for the early Christian community, *ekklēsia*. Although this was the term the **early church** used for self-identification, in Greco-Roman culture the term denoted a group of persons called out from the remainder of a community. In Greek and Roman societies, those who held the status of citizen were privileged with the power of self-determination in discussion with other citizens. In the Septuagint (Greek version of the OT), *ekklēsia* translates the Hebrew *qahal*. *Qahal* refers to an assembly or the act of assembling. So it seems to refer more to the call to assembly or the act of assembling. *Qahal* is used of Israel as it is actually assembled at one time, though in later writings of the OT (e.g., Nehemiah; Chronicles) it is used for the nation also. Sometimes, *qahal* carries a religious connotation, such as in Deut. 9:10 when it denotes the assembly of Israel on the day God gave Moses the law, or when Israel is called the assembly of God/Lord (*qahal-Yahweh/ekklēsia kyriou*, Deut. 23:2-8, 1 Chron. 28:8; Mic. 2:5). This suggests that salvation in both the OT and NT is never simply an individual matter but is invariably communal in character. God acts not just to save persons but also to create a redeemed community.

As such, the church is the new community of believers created by God's action in **Jesus** through the **Holy Spirit**. The NT therefore speaks of it as the people of God, those constituted by God to worship and witness to God in concrete human situations (1 Pet. 2:9-11). But the church is this new reality only in relation to **Jesus Christ**. The relationship is so intense that the NT speaks of the church as the "body of Christ" (e.g., 1 Cor. 12:27; Rom. 12:4-5; Eph. 4:12). God in Christ has acted to create one new community and humanity, not a multiplicity of unrelated groups and individuals. Unity with all other Christians is God's gift to his people. There is thus one church, concretely present in many communities that worship the Lord Jesus Christ (see Eph. 4).

This suggests that the church is universal and is intended to encompass all humanity, for it is the new reality that God is bringing to pass in the world. Nonetheless, its universality is concretely expressed in each congregation. In Christ, believers are brought into fellowship and unity with Christians extending from the **early church** to Christ's return. Additionally, the church is holy. It is holy because of God's actions and because the church is sanctified "in" Christ (1 Cor. 1:2), not because it can claim perfection. God has called the church to share in the divine life and glory (Eph. 1:15-23), thereby setting humankind apart and giving to Christians a mission to represent God's **kingdom** in the world.

The church, therefore, is comprehended, not by looking first at itself, but by looking to the apostolic witness of Jesus' resurrection. The church is accordingly apostolic; it is established upon the witness of the early apostles who saw the risen Lord. Through its fidelity to the Scriptures and the ecumenical creeds, the church shows its faithfulness to the "faith that was once for all entrusted to the saints" (Jude v. 3) by the apostles.

On this basis Christians can proclaim God's forgiveness and coming kingdom. Since the church is bound to **Jesus'** resurrection, its task is to bear witness to the gospel's reality (see Matt. 28:18-20). From this obedience and thanksgiving for God's new creation, the church also focuses on worshipping its Lord. It also seeks to build up those who come to faith. Edification is a central principle by which one may determine what should and what should not be included in the church's life (see Eph. 4:29; Col. 3:12-16). As the church dwells in God, it must resist the temptation to become narcissistic; in mission, the church must be turned to the world.

Because God established the church in Jesus Christ rather than upon human merit, membership in the church occurs through regeneration. This highlights the church's nature as founded in divine **grace**. Christians are called to recognize and affirm their commitment to one another as sisters and brothers, as members of Christ's body, in a concrete place and time as mandated by the gospel of Jesus. Here the gospel is **preached** and celebrated in the **sacraments** that unite Christians to their Lord, each other, and to the world that is its mission.

See also Bible; Church and State; Covenant; Kingdom of God; Liturgy and Worship; Mission, Theology of.

Resources

Kärkkäinen, Veli-Matti. *An Introduction to Ecclesiology: Ecumenical, Historical, and Global Perspectives.* Downers Grove, IL: InterVarsity Press, 2002.

Küng, Hans. *The Church.* Translated by Ray and Rosaleen Ockenden. London: Burns and Oates, 1967.

GREGORY ROBERTSON, THD

CHURCH AND STATE

There are multiple definitions for church and state and multiple ideals for relationships between them. Here, "church" means the worldwide community of Christians. "State" refers to the institutionalized governance of a nation or society.

In Western antiquity there was little distinction between state and religion, as illustrated by the ancient Israelite theocracy and Roman imperial cult. Faith was not a private matter as it is today. Religion involved a nation's or people's commonly held practices and beliefs about deity and almost all aspects of life. Religious diversity is not new. It emerged with the rise of empires, even though the ideal of a common faith often persisted. In the Roman Empire, for example, other religions were permitted if they presented no challenge to the imperial cult.

Christianity arose in that context, a minority religion in an officially "pagan" culture. Under Emperor Constantine I (ca. 274–337), Christianity received protection and extensive imperial sponsorship (recognized as the official religion in 380). This partnership between church and state is called Constantinianism. The term describes subsequent state-sponsored Christianity.

Christianity in some form remained officially sanctioned in Europe, Russia, and many European colonies until the rise of the modern secular nation-state in the seventeenth and eighteenth centuries. Normally, secular states do not officially support a particular religion but instead endorse religious toleration. However, some scholars argue that **secularism** has achieved the status of a semiofficial quasi-religion in some nations.

Many nations still identify with particular religions, including many Arab countries where Christianity is either prohibited or persecuted. There are still countries where Christianity retains official or semiofficial status, especially in Europe and Latin America. Among these, state and church relate to each other in diverse ways with varying degrees of toleration for minority religions.

New Testament teachings about church-state relations are best understood in the light of the early church's minority status in the Roman Empire. In the Synoptic Gospels, Jesus teaches his followers to "give . . . to the emperor the things that are the emperor's, and to God the things that are God's"

(Matt. 22:21; Mark 12:17; Luke 20:25). In John's gospel Jesus declares that his **kingdom** is "not of this world" (18:36, KJV). These sayings can be understood in many ways. Taken alone, they provide limited value for identifying any ideal Christian position on the relationship between church and state.

Paul's teachings on this subject are also inconclusive. In Rom. 13:1-7 Paul advocates submitting to rulers, whose authority God has established. But how to integrate Paul's counsel with Jesus' teachings is not immediately clear. Are Christians to submit to rulers whose aims are clearly at odds with God's? Can we even be certain that Christian leaders will never succumb to the temptations to misuse power or oppose God's will?

The most influential Christian response to these questions is **Augustine** of Hippo's famous book *The City of God*. It was written (AD 413-26) after Christianity became the Roman Empire's official religion. In it Augustine replies to pagans claiming that Rome was declining because of Christianity's official imperial status. Rome was being punished for neglecting its pagan gods. Augustine's response builds upon Jesus' teachings by distinguishing between God's kingdom and human kingdoms. God's kingdom includes all believers in Christ destined for eternal salvation. They are pilgrims in this world. Human kingdoms contain persons and institutions of this world that will, with God's final victory, pass away. For this reason, Christians should be wary about forging allegiances with the finally futile kingdoms of this world. Of course, Christians should participate in society and contribute to the common social good. But their hope rests in Christ alone. Christians' chief allegiance must be to Christ and the church instead of political factions, governmental systems, or nation-states. Nation-states are temporary and sinful institutions. But Christ's church, though imperfect, transcends nationality; it will never pass away.

See also Anabaptists; Church (Ecclesiology); Democracy; Kingdom of God; Modernity; Principalities and Powers; Religious Pluralism; Sect; Secular/Secularism/Secularization; State Religion; Theopolitical Theology; Zionism, Christian.

Resources
Niebuhr, H. Richard. *Christ and Culture.* New York: Harper and Row, 1951.
Yoder, John Howard. *The Politics of Jesus.* 2nd ed. Grand Rapids: Eerdmans, 1994.

MARK MANN, PHD

CHURCH FATHERS
The term "church fathers" refers to the early Christian writers dating from the first to the sixth centuries. Among the early fathers was Clement (d. 101), traditionally the third bishop of Rome, who wrote to the Corinthian church asking it to recognize the primacy of Rome. Ignatius (d. ca. 98-117) wrote epistles to the churches on his way to martyrdom in Rome. Polycarp

(ca. 69–ca. 155) was also a martyr, as was Justin Martyr (ca. 103–ca. 165), whose *Apologies* spelled out the relationship of Christianity to Judaism and to classical culture. Athenagorus (second half of the second century) wrote his *Apology* in the mid-second century. Directed to the emperor, it asked him to defend Christians against accusations they were atheists and practiced cannibalism (eating the body and blood of Christ).

Clement of Alexandria (ca. 150–ca. 215), writing at the end of the second century, wrote theological reflections titled *Stromateis*. Tertullian (ca. 150–ca. 225), writing in the same period, developed an early version of the doctrine of the Trinity, one substance in three persons.

One of the most prolific writers in the third century was Origen (ca. 185–ca. 254), whose Platonic themes and allegorical biblical interpretations were widely influential, especially in the East.

Many of the early writings, such as *Adversus haereses* by Irenaeus (d. ca. 200), were directed against the heresies of Gnosticism and Docetism. Irenaeus helped establish the direction toward orthodoxy as affirmed in the Council of Nicaea (325). Athanasius (ca. 296–373), another church father, prevailed over the Arians, who taught that the Word (the Son) is secondary to God—God's first and highest creation. Largely because of Athanasius, the Christological formula, "true God from true God," was included in the creed.

In the Eastern Church the Cappadocian Fathers (Basil the Great [d. 379], Gregory of Nyssa [d. ca. 394], and Gregory of Nazianzus [ca. 330-ca. 390]) were especially influential. Writing after Nicaea, they developed the doctrine of the Holy Spirit and made a distinction between the one substance (*ousia*) of God and the three persons (*hypostases*). The distinction enabled them to claim the full participation of the Spirit in God, while drawing a distinction in the personhood. Their work led to the Council of Constance (381) adding to the Nicene Creed "the Holy Spirit, the Lord and Giver of life, who proceeds from the Father [the Western church later added "and the son" (*filioque*)], who with the Father and the Son is worshipped and glorified." The Council of Constantinople ratified belief in the Spirit's deity.

Augustine (354–430) was the main figure in the Latin (Western) branch of the church fathers. Also important was Jerome (ca. 347–420), the translator of the Bible into Latin—the Vulgate.

John Wesley thought that knowledge of the fathers was essential because they were closest to the original sources of Christianity. They were more trustworthy than later generations when corruption crept into the church. In their battles with the early heresies, such as Gnostics and Docetists, Marcionites and Monophysites, and Sabellians and Apollinarians, the Holy Spirit taught the fathers to discern and guard against dangers to the faith. In the seventeenth century the Eastern fathers had been largely rediscovered and published. The Church of England found them helpful in making its case against the Catholics; it was reestablishing "primitive Christianity" and eradicating the errors of the medieval Roman Church.

Especially important for Wesley were two early Eastern fathers, Macarius (**Pseudo-Macarius**, ca. 300-390) and Ephraem Syrus (ca. 320-73). Wesley published his version of Macarius's *Homilies* in the first volume of his fifty-volume *Christian Library*. Both fathers emphasized gifts of the Spirit and experiential dimensions of Christian faith.

See also Augustine; Creeds (Nicene, Chalcedonian, Apostles', Athanasian); Gifts of the Spirit; Orthodox Church; Pseudo-Macarius; Trinity; Wesley, John, Theology of.

Resources

Campbell, Ted A. *John Wesley and Christian Antiquity: Religious Vision and Cultural Change*. Nashville: Kingswood Books, 1991.
Early Church Fathers. Christian Classics Ethereal Library. http://www.ccel.org/fathers.html.

THEODORE RUNYON, DR. THEOL.

CHURCH OF GOD (ANDERSON)

The Church of God movement (Anderson) is a recent example of the radical tradition in Christianity (the term "radical" meaning a return to the faith's apostolic roots). Following the Civil War of the 1860s, American society underwent extensive industrialization and urbanization. The religious scene often featured a neglect and even denial of much of what most Christians previously held as basic. One reaction was the **holiness movement**. The Church of God "reformation" movement emerged in this context, seeking to "come out" of the competitive and compromising chaos of divisive denominationalism. It reacted against human organization of church life and championed the unifying work of the Holy Spirit.

Daniel S. Warner (1842-95), a primary pioneer, proclaimed the "morning light" of the **early church** shining again in the "evening time" of the church's troubled history. His divine commission was to return to the apostolic faith as defined by the NT and to emphasize an open fellowship of sanctified and unified believers. John W. V. Smith's narrative history of this movement is titled *The Quest for Holiness and Unity*. Most early adherents were from **Wesleyan** and **Anabaptist** traditions, forming a distinctive holiness **ecumenism**.

For this movement, the Bible was the only creed. Gifting and guidance by the Holy Spirit were emphasized as central in all church life. Its original periodical, *The Gospel Trumpet*, launched in 1881, carried on its masthead: "DEFINITE, RADICAL, and ANTI-SECTARIAN . . . For the Publication of full Salvation . . . [and] Unity of all true Christians in 'the faith once delivered to the saints.'" These radical, holiness, and unity-minded church reformers were initially "come-outers" determined to separate from all that was not godly. They meant to be heralds of God's ultimate will for the church. Revivalistic in ways similar to the larger Wesleyan-holiness camp meeting tradition, movement leaders have been "orthodox" in general belief, preaching-oriented, and focused more on spiritual experience than on formal theology.

Today this fellowship numbers about 850,000 people who worship in some seven thousand congregations distributed throughout eighty-five countries. In North America, the movement sponsors three universities, one college, and a graduate-level seminary. It functions primarily through twenty-two hundred congregations that maintain a nondenominational attitude and that practice congregational polity. Nearly 20 percent of the North American adherents are African-Americans. The majority of all adherents live outside North America. A distinctive has been **women's role in the church.** Women have always been affirmed as appropriate leaders at all levels of church life as God chooses and calls.

North American congregations cooperate with each other in state, regional, and national organizations. The general assembly is their most representative voice in the United States. It meets annually in Anderson, Indiana, and establishes policies for the cooperative work of the church that are administered through Church of God Ministries. It adopts the unified World Ministries Budget of the Church of God, which totaled about $12.5 million in 2010.

See also Anabaptists; Church (Ecclesiology); Early Church; Ecclesiology, New Testament; Ecumenism; Gifts of the Spirit; Radical Reformation; Women's Role in the Church.

Resources

Callen, Barry L., ed. *Following Our Lord: Understanding the Beliefs and Practices of the Church of God Movement (Anderson)*. Anderson, IN: Warner Press, 2008.

Smith, John W. *The Quest for Holiness and Unity*. 1980. 2nd ed. Revised and expanded by Merle D. Strege. Anderson, IN: Warner Press, 2009.

BARRY CALLEN, EDD

CHURCH OF THE EAST

Church of the East (the so-called Nestorian Church) is the name given to the church that developed to the east of the boundaries of the Roman Empire. Christian groups started to appear in the first century AD among the Aramaic-speaking populations of Syria and Mesopotamia, controlled at that time by Parthians and later the Persians. In the fourth century AD the bishop of Seleucia-Ctesiphon united the churches of the Persian Sassanid Empire under his authority and accepted the title patriarch of the East.

The Church of the East was influenced by the Syrian-Antiochian Christological tradition as formulated by Bishop Theodore of Mopsuestia (ca. 350–428) and later developed by Nestorius and others. Theodore was highly regarded in the East. Not until after his death, not until the Pelagians and Nestorians appealed to his writings, and not until the condemnation of Nestorius did Theodore's Christology begin to become controversial (eventually resulting in him being unfairly anathematized at the Fifth General Synod [553]). The Syrian theologians insisted on the perfect deity and the unimpaired humanity of Christ. The charge was that they too sharply separated the two natures. Nestorius (d. 451) taught that within the incarnate Christ there existed two persons, one human and one divine. His teaching was condemned at the Council of Ephesus in 431. He was banished to Upper Egypt, where he died in 451. His followers fled the Roman Empire and were welcomed in the East on the basis of similar Christological views. For that reason the Church of the East is often misleadingly called the Nestorian Church. Due to Christological disagreements and geopolitical situations, by the sixth century the church lost connection with the Latin-Western and Greek Byzantine churches.

In spite of being cut off from Western Christianity and oppressed by the Zoroastrians of Persia, and later by Muslim conquerors, the Church of the East developed rapidly. It was known for its scholarly work at the School of Nisibis and for its missionary zeal. By the sixth century, Christianity was brought to South India, the Arabian Peninsula, and Afghanistan by the Church of the East. In the seventh century Syrian monks preached the gospel in the imperial courts of China and established the church known in Chinese as the Religion of Light. In the eleventh century the church reached the tribes of Central Asia, Turks and Mongols. At its peak the Church of the East had 230 dioceses and 27 metropolitans. But it was almost wiped out by Tamerlane's conquests in the fourteenth century.

The Church of the East uses Syriac as its liturgical language and treats baptism and Eucharist as the most important sacraments. They believe in the goodness of human nature and reject the idea of original sin. In their liturgy, through symbolism, the whole of salvation history is celebrated and accompanied by three distinct Eucharistic prayers attributed to Addai and Mari (the apostles of the church), Theodore of Mopsuestia, and Nestorius himself.

Due to schisms in the past, the ancient tradition of the church today is represented by the Chaldean Catholic Church (650,000 members), the Assyrian Church of the East (400,000 members), and the Ancient Church of the East (70,000 members). They consist mostly of Assyrians, many of whom immigrated to the West (United States and Canada) during wars and persecutions in the Middle East in the twentieth and twenty-first centuries.

See also Christology; Church Fathers; Creeds (Nicene, Chalcedonian, Apostles', Athanasian); Ecumenical Councils; Mary/Mariology.

Resources

Baum, Wilhelm, and Dietmar W. Winkler. *The Church of the East: A Concise History.* Translated by Miranda G. Henry. New York: RoutledgeCurzon, 2003.

Baumer, Christoph. *The Church of the East: An Illustrated History of Assyrian Christianity.* New York: I. B. Tauris, 2006.

ARSENY ERMAKOV, PHD

CHURCH OF THE NAZARENE

The Church of the Nazarene emerged from the nineteenth-century holiness movement. The church united several holiness groups from different parts of North America and Great Britain. The Association of Pentecostal Churches of America, centered in Brooklyn and Boston, was made up of strong independent congregations and pastors. The Church of the Nazarene (from which the denomination received its name) began in Los Angeles in 1895, under former Methodist minister Phineas Bresee, and aimed to reach the poor. Understanding that alcohol abuse destroyed homes, and optimistic that the grace of God might eradicate social evil, Bresee was an outspoken proponent of Prohibition. The Holiness Church of Christ included small rural congregations scattered chiefly in Texas and Tennessee. These three groups came together in Pilot Point, Texas, in October 1908—an event considered the birth date of the church. The Pentecostal Mission, centered in Nashville, joined in 1915, as did the Pentecostal Church of Scotland, started in Glasgow by George Sharpe. All of these groups understood that holiness impelled concern for those neglected by not only society but also the churches. From these mostly urban areas of origin, by the second generation the church's strength shifted to rural areas.

The Church of the Nazarene reaped members from holiness camp meetings, including not only Methodists but also Quakers, Baptists, and other Protestants, all adhering to Wesleyan doctrine. The reason for the church's coming to be was the doctrine and experience of entire sanctification. This teaching had been neglected, holiness people thought, in Methodist churches.

Though retaining their right to call pastors, under strong general and district superintendents, local churches sacrificed congregational autonomy for the sake of denominational organization.

Districts elect delegates to a quadrennial general assembly, the church's highest legislative body. The general assembly elects general superintendents (six in recent years) and determines changes to the church's *Manual.* Articles of faith, indebted to the Methodist articles, ground the church in the historic teachings of the church. Broad in its understanding of essentials, the church takes no hard line on eschatological timetables and limits the inerrancy of the Bible to "all things necessary to our salvation." The church retains a place for infant as well as believer's baptism, but membership is open only to those who testify to personal conversion. The *Manual* contains guidelines for Christian living. New members pledge to "seek earnestly to perfect holiness of heart and life" (*Church of the Nazarene Manual 2009-2013*, para. 801).

An element central to the church's core is internationalism. All three of the original groups had missions in India, the first being the Association of Pentecostal Churches, which had missionaries near Bombay in 1898. Other early missionaries, sent out by these groups, were in Cape Verde, Mexico, and Japan. Policy architects such as Hiram F. Reynolds determined not to establish national churches but to allow districts around the world participation in the church's governmental processes proportional to membership rather than country.

The six international regions have administrative rather than legislative functions. In 2010 Nazarene membership stood at more than two million, of which two-thirds were outside North America. More than 20 percent resided in Africa, and more than 20 percent spoke Spanish as their first language.

See also Arminian Theology; Arminius, Jacob; Christian Perfection (Entire Sanctification); Church (Ecclesiology); Holiness Movements: American, British, and Continental; Missionary Movements; Palmer, Phoebe; Wesley, John, Theology of.

Resources

Church of the Nazarene Manual 2009-2013. Kansas City: Nazarene Publishing House, 2009.

Cunningham, Floyd T., Stan Ingersol, Harold E. Raser, and David P. Whitelaw. *Our Watchword and Song: The Centennial History of the Church of the Nazarene.* Edited by Floyd T. Cunningham. Kansas City: Beacon Hill Press of Kansas City, 2009.

Smith, Timothy L. *Called unto Holiness: The Story of the Nazarenes: The Formative Years.* Kansas City: Nazarene Publishing House, 1962.

FLOYD T. CUNNINGHAM, PHD

CITIZENSHIP AND THE KINGDOM OF GOD
See KINGDOM OF GOD.

CLASSES, BANDS, CONFERENCE, CONNECTIONALISM, SOCIETY

The nature of Christian faith is communal. **John Wesley** (1703-91) advised that "'holy solitaries' is a phrase no more consistent with the gospel than holy adulterers" (*Works*, 14:321). Methodism devised an interlocking system of accountability for individuals and groups that fostered "holiness of heart and life" (12:241). This was in harmony with the practice of the early Christians in Jerusalem (Acts 2:43-47).

Society was the name for the groupings of Methodists that sprang up under the preaching of John and **Charles Wesley** and their associates. This was no innovation, since religious societies had a history in England, including the first **Anglican** society founded by Anthony Horneck in 1678. Horneck borrowed the idea from Jakob Spener, the German Pietist, whose *ecclesiolae in ecclesia* (little churches within the church) met in homes. An expression of the **Protestant** principle of the priesthood of all believers, it was intended to bring renewal to the church at large. Similarly, Methodist societies were conceived as a renewal movement within the Church of England. Societies met for singing, prayer, and preaching. Methodists received the sacraments in their local parishes.

Classes grew out of the need for pastoral care. As more Methodist societies formed and as attendance climbed, society members were assigned to a weekly class of a dozen or so members, a forum for prayer and mutual encouragement. When John Wesley insisted that there was "no holiness but social holiness" (*Works*, 14:321), it was not a rally cry for **social justice**, though Wesley cared passionately for the sick and the poor and later was outspoken against slavery. Rather, the phrase acknowledged that holiness is best pursued in community, where accountability discourages backsliding. During class meetings, tickets for quarterly society meetings were issued, thereby assuring that all society members would be active in a class. Wesley fearlessly "put out" members from the society when they habitually neglected class meetings.

Bands were a refinement of the classes. Whereas classes were compulsory, consisting of men and women, bands were voluntary and divided by gender, age, and marital status. The bands were more exclusive, averaging five to ten members. The weekly meetings included five questions:

1. What known sins have you committed since our last meeting?
2. What temptations have you met with?
3. How were you delivered?
4. What have you thought, said, or done of which you doubt whether it be sin or not?
5. Have you done nothing you desire to keep secret? (Outler, 181)

An annual *conference* began in 1744. John Wesley set the three-point agenda as "What to teach; . . . How to teach; and . . . What to do" (*Works*, 8:275). It was an opportunity to instruct his lay preachers, many of whom had little theological education. The conference also strategized for the creation of new societies and afforded mutual encouragement.

Connectionalism refers to "connection," the network of Methodist societies that sprang up, which John Wesley and others supervised. As Methodism grew and reached new areas—including what was to become the United States—the principle of mutual encouragement and accountability continued. In America, Francis Asbury—like Wesley before him—fostered connection through a circuit system, horseback riding on a schedule between

Methodist outposts. An annual conference or assembly convened by denominations is a form of **Methodist connectionalism.**

See also Covenant Service; Love Feast; Methodism, British; Methodist Connectionalism; Spiritual Direction/Spiritual Director; Works of Piety.

Resources

Campbell, Ted A. *Wesleyan Beliefs: Formal and Popular Expressions of the Core Beliefs of Wesleyan Communities.* Nashville: Kingswood Books, 2010.

Henderson, D. Michael. *A Model for Making Disciples: John Wesley's Class Meeting.* Nappanee, IN: Evangel Publishing House, 1997.

Heitzenrater, Richard P. *Wesley and the People Called Methodists.* Nashville: Abingdon Press, 1995.

Watson, David Lowes. *The Early Methodist Class Meeting: Its Origins and Significance.* Nashville: Discipleship Resources, 1985.

J. GREGORY CROFFORD, PHD

COMMUNISM

The term "communism" can refer to any one of three streams of social philosophy and organization. First, it can refer to a social pattern in which all property and other assets are held in common for a community, such as a church or state. Second, "communism" can refer to a type of social organization in which all economic and social activity is managed by the state and dominated by a single political party. Third, it can refer to the political, social, and economic theory and actions of a political party identified as Communist.

Communism is sometimes associated with "communalism," which means "the communal ownership of assets and the association with one's ethnic group."

When used broadly, communism characterized many ancient societies where property and assets were generally held in common. The Mosaic law required communal awareness and sharing of one's goods with the poor. God, not individuals, not even a king, owned the land and all in it. Early Christianity is noted for its social mandate about communal assets. Peter's early instructions for Christians included a rejection of private ownership and the holding of everything "in common" (Acts 2:44; 4:32). Later, the apostle Paul seems to have moved away from Peter's "communism."

The Eucharist or Lord's Supper is a communal sharing in the body and blood of Christ. Many monastic and utopian societies developed around the concept of communally shared assets. The early Methodist communities, shaped under John Wesley's (1703-91) leadership, were expected to bring all they could spare into the "common stock" (*Works*, 8:261). Methodist communities were energized by Wesley's compassion for the victims of British industrialization. The eighteenth-century Wesleyan revival has been cited as delaying the more violent nineteenth-century European political upheaval properly called the Communist revolution.

When the term "communism" is used to refer to a dominating political power such as exists in China, North Korea, and Cuba, social control by elites often results in hardship for persons not in power.

The early twentieth-century Communist revolution in Europe was inspired by Karl Marx (1818-83) and Friedrich Engels (1820-95). They reacted against the excesses of capitalism, religion, and industrialization. Concentrating political and economic power in the working class (proletariat) was supposed to have placed political control in the hands of the working people. In a Communist society, private property would not be needed, and workers—alienated from the product of their labor, from themselves, and from others—would be reunited with all three. Social structures that place elites in control would be abolished. Work would result in freedom, and creativity would serve the well-being of all persons. The rewards of labor would be equitably distributed to all on the basis of need, not ability.

Others used these ideas to transform countries. Vladimir Lenin (1870–1924) changed Russia. Mao Zedong (1893–1976) shaped China.

The collapse of Communism in the late twentieth century was caused by numerous factors: pressure from the Christian church; the weaknesses of the Communist economic and industrial infrastructure; and cynicism toward a leadership that was supposed to herald the new Communist order but in fact became new elites who, as in the case of Joseph Stalin in Russia, ruled oppressively.

See also Atheism/Agnosticism; Capitalism; Natural Science; Philosophy of Science; Postcolonialism; Religious Freedom; Sacraments; Secular/Secularism/Secularization; Social Justice; State Religion; Terrorism; Wealth.

Resources
DeKoster, Lester. *Communism and Christian Faith*. Grand Rapids: Eerdmans, 1962.
Holmes, Leslie. *Communism: A Very Short Introduction*. Very Short Introductions. New York: Oxford University Press, 2009.
Miranda, José Porfirio. *Communism in the Bible*. Maryknoll, NY: Orbis Books, 1982.

L. BRYAN WILLIAMS, PHD

COMMUNITY
See CHURCH (ECCLESIOLOGY); HOSPITABILITY/HOSPITALITY; ISRAEL.

COMMUNITY DEVELOPMENT
See HOLISTIC MISSION.

COMPASSION

See HOLISTIC MISSION; SPIRITUAL FORMATION/GROWTH; STEWARDSHIP.

CONSCIENCE

Conscience is the human moral dimension that assesses action(s), either contemplated or taken, as being right or wrong, good or bad, commendable or blameworthy. Its normal signature is an immediate sense of duty or oughtness. Conscience authoritatively holds people accountable to perceived moral norms. It entails a measure of freedom. The Greek word often translated "conscience" is *syneidēsis*, meaning "to know together."

Conscience can be an instrument of God's will but is not God's direct voice. It can be in error and can fall far short of God's will. Its specific content can come from sources contrary to God's will. Conscience can be good or bad, well developed or feeble and badly flawed. In Christian life, the conscience waits to be cleansed and shaped by the **Holy Spirit.**

Although the word "conscience" does not appear in the OT, the idea is prominent. It is usually treated as the immediate voice of God. Cain hears the voice of God asking him to reconsider his intention to kill his brother (Gen. 4:6-7), but Cain disregards God's voice. David's language about a clean heart anticipates the notion of a good conscience: "Create in me a clean heart, O God, and put a new and right spirit within me" (Ps. 51:10).

The NT says conscience can become distorted or so abused that it effectively dies (amoral or psychopathic—completely lacking in conscience and feelings for others). Paul says of the Cretans, "Their very minds and consciences are corrupted" (Titus 1:15). The writer of Hebrews offers a solution for the distorted conscience: the blood of Jesus cleanses the conscience "from dead works to worship the living God" (9:14).

According to **John Wesley,** conscience is theologically grounded in **prevenient grace.** What appears to be merely a natural inheritance is in fact God's gracious gift.

> No man . . . is in a state of mere nature; there is no man . . . that is wholly void of the grace of God. No man living is entirely destitute of what is vulgarly called *natural conscience.* But this is not natural: It is more properly termed, *preventing grace.* (*Works,* 6:512)

Conscience's intent is to draw persons into right relationship with God and help them live peacefully with others.

See also Christian Ethics/Moral Theology; Ethics; Free Will; Tempers and Affections; Virtues; Works of Mercy.

Resources

Kittel, Gerhard, and Gerhard Friedrich, eds. *Theological Dictionary of the New Testament: Abridged in One Volume*. Translated and abridged by Geoffrey W. Bromiley. Grand Rapids: Eerdmans, 1985.

Williams, Thomas D. *Knowing Right from Wrong: A Christian Guide to Conscience*. New York: Faith Words, 2008.

GIFT MTUKWA, MA

CONTEMPLATIVE SPIRITUAL FORMATION

See CONTEMPLATIVE SPIRITUALITY.

CONTEMPLATIVE SPIRITUALITY

Contemplative spirituality is a path of spirituality that emphasizes practices of quiet listening and a posture of open receptivity. Although contemplative spirituality and **mysticism** share some interests, the two are not to be confused or equated.

The goal of contemplative spirituality is communion with God. Meditation entails focused thinking and reflection. Contemplation means being alert to God's presence in all places and resting in the presence of God, who holds all things together (Col. 1:17). Such experiences are gifts of **grace**.

Contemplative Christians draw inspiration from the biblical witness to God's loving devotion to **creation** (Gen. 1:31) and to Jesus' choice of silence over words as an expression of trust (1 Pet. 2:23). The experiences of Moses, Elijah (Deut. 34:10; 1 Kings 19:12-13), Peter, James, John (Matt. 17:2-5), and Paul (2 Cor. 12:2) indicate that contemplative encounters with God occur for many of God's people. Many Christians through the centuries have heeded God's invitation to "be still, and know that I am God" (Ps. 46:10).

Familiar with its use in **Greek philosophy**, Christian thinkers and practitioners developed and deepened a theology of contemplation: Origen (ca. 185–ca. 254) and the threefold path of purgation, through illumination, to union; Gregory of Nyssa (ca. 335-ca. 394) and the "negative way" of moving with God into the darkness of unknowing; the **desert fathers and mothers**; John Cassian (ca. 360–436) and Bernard of Clairvaux (1090–1153) on purity of heart in **monasticism**; the personal testimony of **Augustine**'s (354–430) *Confessions*; Pseudo-Dionysius on **mystical theology** (ca. 500); medieval mystics John of the Cross (1542-91) and Teresa of Avila (1515-82) on being the bride of Christ; and scholastic theologian Thomas **Aquinas** (ca. 1225-74) on **love**. **Reformation** leaders tended to avoid both the particular language of **mysticism** and references to contemplation more broadly, but more recently **Protestantism** has sought to retrieve a contemplative spirituality.

John Wesley addressed two potential problems associated with contemplative spirituality: *First*, some persons define contemplation as only individual, interior **prayer**, as opposed to an active life of good works that proceed, by grace, from love for God and one's neighbor. Wesley—as did Ignatius of Loyola (ca. 1491-1556), who self-identified as a "contemplative-in-action," and the Quakers—rejected the dichotomy of inner holiness and outer holiness. He affirmed that all holiness is social. Thus, contemplative practice may include solitude, silence, and praying with **icons** or the **Bible** in *lectio divina* **(works of piety)** *and* **care for the creation, love** of neighbor, and working to promote **social justice (works of mercy)** for all persons. *Second,* there is the danger of thinking that contemplative spirituality is meant only for those who are spiritually advanced or spiritually elite. Such an error would be at odds with Jesus' practice of regularly associating with sinners and tax collectors and identifying them as his friends and disciples. Wesley—as did Thomas Merton (1915-68), who helped introduce contemplation to the **laity** following **Vatican Council II**—affirmed the constant, intimate connection *all believers* can have with God, a connection as close as our breathing, as emphasized in the centering **prayer** movement.

See also Desert Fathers and Mothers; Icons, Images, Iconoclasm; Love; Monasticism; Mysticism/Mystical Theology; Prayer.

Resources

"Attentiveness." Special issue, *Weavings: A Journal of the Christian Spiritual Life* 17, no. 4 (July/August 2002).

"Contemplative Life." Special issue, *Weavings: A Journal of the Christian Spiritual Life* 7, no. 4 (July/August 1992).

Egan, Keith J. "Contemplation." In *The New Westminster Dictionary of Christian Spirituality,* edited by Philip Sheldrake, 211-13. Louisville, KY: Westminster John Knox Press, 2005.

DOUGLAS S. HARDY, PHD

CONTEXTUALIZATION

Contextualization concerns how **the gospel** revealed in Scripture authentically comes to life in each human situation or context. The term "contextualization" is relatively new, first appearing in the early 1970s. But the activity of telling and living the gospel in context-sensitive ways is as old as the Christian mission. The task of contextualization not only seeks to express the gospel in culturally and contextually appropriate forms but also continually challenges and transforms aspects of the context.

Contextualization is a multifaceted activity. Most commonly it is connected to theology and **evangelism**. This involves articulating the Christian faith in language and thought forms that fit a local audience. However, contextualization touches the church's life and mission even more broadly. **Hermeneutics, preaching, worship,** architecture, **discipleship, ethics,** church structures and leadership, and theological education all must be contextualized. Furthermore, contextualization encompasses the gospel's interaction, not simply with different cultures (enculturation) but also with a range of contexts, including socioeconomic, political, and ecclesial settings.

Recent interest in contextualization was prompted in part by the recognition that no expression of the gospel is context free. Contextualization challenges past assumptions that Western churches could export a "pure" understanding of theology and Christian living to churches in the majority world. The gospel is only good news when it speaks to particular groups of people in specific times and places. This includes the increasingly postmodern Western world. Current realities such as **globalization** and multicultural ministry settings present additional challenges.

Contextualizing the gospel is never easy to do well. Some of the most important resources are found in Scripture. The NT teems with examples of doing theology in authentic, context-sensitive ways. For instance, Paul's missionary speeches in Acts (13:13-52; 14:15-17; 17:22-31) offer compelling examples of tailoring proclamation of the good news to different audiences.

The NT writers also model the theological process. Each gospel contextualizes the story of Jesus for a different target audience. Paul writes letters that become words on target for diverse mission communities. The Revelation of John offers Asian churches a countercultural perspective on a world dominated by Roman power and idolatry. Above all, contextualization is patterned after the **incarnation** of Jesus. Becoming flesh, Jesus embraced the human situation in all of its scandalous particularity (Gal. 4:4).

Contextualization carries inherent risks. It is possible to pursue local relevance to the point of compromising biblical faith. Interpreting Scripture well is essential for appropriate contextualization. Several historic Wesleyan emphases can help guide the process of doing theology in context: (1) the primacy of **Scripture** in the theological process; (2) the guiding role of the **Holy Spirit**; (3) an openness to the contribution made by the human experience of God in its various expressions; (4) a willingness to test our context-specific reflections in the light of the wider Christian community (this includes the historic tradition of the church and today's global community of Christians in other cultures and life circumstances; churches throughout the world must function as *both* teachers and learners); and (5) the goal of furthering God's mission and forming individuals and communities of disciples in Christ's image.

Contextualization is not simply a task for experts. It is best done when the whole people of God wrestle with how the gospel can best intersect with and challenge their local circumstances. Incarnating the gospel is more than an academic exercise or a task limited to majority-world Christians. It is a missional and theological requirement for the whole church.

See also African Theology; Asian-American Theology; Asian Theology; Black Theology; Contextual Theology; Globalization; Hispanic Theology; Indigenous Theologies; Latin American Theologies; Syncretism, Religious.

Resources

Flemming, Dean. *Contextualization in the New Testament: Patterns for Theology and Mission.* Downers Grove, IL: InterVarsity Press, 2005.

Kraft, Charles H., ed. *Appropriate Christianity.* Pasadena, CA: William Carey Library, 2005.

DEAN FLEMMING, PHD

CONTEXTUAL THEOLOGY

The term **contextualization** first appeared at a World Council of Churches consultation in 1971. It was defined by Dr. Byang Kato at the 1974 **Lausanne Congress** on World Evangelization: "making concepts or ideals relevant to a given situation" (1975, 1217). However, the roots of contextualization go back to the apostolic church. It has been practiced by the church throughout the history of missions. *Contextualization* refers to adopting and presenting the gospel message in ways that make it acceptable and meaningful to those who hear. Proclamation of the gospel may be true, but it must also be presented in understandable terms that can be embraced by a culture.

Subsequently, a variety of *contextual theologies* began to emerge based on context and experience: **liberation theology, black theology, feminist theology**, and others. Scholars from the **Global South** began to examine Western theology and the Western world. They discovered that imported theology tends to be "theology from above," that is, based on historical and theoretical categories not representative of their cultures. Non-Western scholars saw Western theological perspectives as dominated by the rich, powerful, and elite. Such a theology could not be received as important for persons caught in contexts characterized by poverty and oppression. Contextual theology tended to be "theology from below." It was based on experience and the theologizing of scholars who are themselves living in contexts marked by suffering and oppression.

The primary methodology of contextual theology is storytelling—**narrative theology**. Thus one should not expect contextual theologies to be traditional Western systematic theologies. Rather, they recite events, experiences, drama, and narratives.

Latin American liberation theology (LALT) proponents wrote books and visited other world areas to promote their work. However, they spoke of their Latin American experience as if it were universal and of their theology as if it, too, were universal. This provoked a reaction in other world areas where liberationists' "universal" message struck many as a new form of imperialism. Scholars from the Global South agreed their people needed to be liberated but not by and to LALT. Liberation must be based on a culture's own perspective and experience.

Evangelicals believed LALT demonstrated an overreliance on context and Marxist categories and inadequately relied on the Bible. They disagreed with the notion that Christian belief derives primarily from human experience. In addition to fearing that the Bible had become captive to context, evangelicals were also alarmed that the theological reflection of millennia (tradition) had become marginalized in favor of the immediate context.

The **Wesleyan quadrilateral** of Scripture, tradition, reason, and experience is often spoken of as Wesley's theological sources, with Scripture having unrivaled primacy. These elements serve as a model for contextualization for Wesleyans.

See also Contextualization; Indigenous Theologies; Liberation Theology; Narrative Theology; Scripture, Wesleyan Approach to; Westernization of the Gospel.

Resources

Bosch, David J. *Transforming Mission: Paradigm Shifts in Theology of Mission*. Maryknoll, NY: Orbis Books, 1991.

Flemming, Dean. *Contextualization in the New Testament: Patterns for Theology and Mission*. Downers Grove, IL: InterVarsity Press, 2005.

Kato, Byang H. "The Gospel, Cultural Context, and Religious Syncretism." In *Let the Earth Hear His Voice*, edited by J. D. Douglas, 1216-23. Minneapolis: World Wide Publications, 1975.

Moon, Cyris H. "Models of Contextual Theology: The Struggle for Cultural Relevance." *The Ecumenical Review* (July 1995).

Pears, Angie. *Doing Contextual Theology*. London: Routledge, 2009.

Thorsen, Donald. *The Wesleyan Quadrilateral: Scripture, Tradition, Reason, and Experience as a Model of Evangelical Theology*. Lexington, KY: Emeth Press, 2005.

TERENCE B. READ, PHD

CONTRACEPTION

See CHRISTIAN ETHICS/MORAL THEOLOGY; HUMAN SEXUALITY.

COPTIC ORTHODOXY

Coptic Orthodoxy or the Coptic Orthodox Church is the major Christian church in Egypt. The word "copt" is a Westernized form of the Arabic *kibt*, which itself is derived from the Greek word *aigyptoi*, which means "Egyptians." After the Arab Muslim conquest in the seventh century, the word "copt" was used to distinguish Egyptians who were Christian from those who were Muslim.

Christian groups in Egypt appeared as early as the first century AD among the Jewish diaspora of Alexandria. Thus the book of Acts suggests that Apollos came from such a community (18:24-25). According to tradition, the Egyptian church was founded by Mark the Evangelist, one of the seventy apostles. At that time the Christian community was predominantly Greek, with few Jewish and Egyptian members. By the end of the second century Christianity was well established in Alexandria and was becoming famous and influential throughout Christendom. The Egyptian church gave to the world such theologians as Clement of Alexandria, Origen, and later Athanasius, Cyril, and the founder of the monastic movement—Anthony the Great. The catechetical school of Alexandria was a prominent theological center. At one point it was the only place of Christian learning in the Roman Empire.

Christianity started to flourish among the native-speaking population only in the middle of the third century, as Patriarch Dionysius the Great (AD 247-64) supported the conversion of Egyptians and the use of their language. The Egyptian church is also responsible for bringing Christianity to Ethiopian tribes in the fourth century.

In 451 the Ecumenical Council of Chalcedon excommunicated the Alexandrian Patriarch Dioscorus and declared Christ to be of "TWO NATURES . . . preserved and coming together to form one person and subsistence" (Bettenson 1971, 51-52). The majority of Egyptian bishops rejected the decisions of the council because it seemed that the doctrine of two natures leads back to Nestorianism and undermines belief in the one divine-human nature of Christ, as formulated by Cyril of Alexandria. This led to a schism from the rest of orthodox Christianity that continues up to this day.

Traditionally, the Coptic Church is led by the pope of Alexandria, who resides in Cairo. Coptic worship is organized around the **liturgies** of Basil and Gregory Nazianzus. Coptic and Arabic languages are used. Veneration of the Virgin **Mary** has a special place in Coptic spirituality; thus, about twenty church holy days are dedicated to her. Coptic churches, especially ancient ones, almost always lack **icons** and paintings.

Today about 9 percent of the Egyptian population belong to the Coptic Church, the largest Christian community in the Near East. Coptic diasporas can be found in Europe, Australia, and North America.

See also Christian Year; Christology; Church of the East; Creeds (Nicene, Chalcedonian, Apostles', Athanasian); Early African Christianity; Ecumenical Councils; Orthodox Church.

Resources

Bettenson, Henry. *Documents of the Christian Church*. New York: Oxford University Press, 1971.
Griggs, C. Wilfred. *Early Egyptian Christianity: From Its Origins to 451 C.E.* Leiden, NL: E. J. Brill, 1990.
Watterson, Barbara. *Coptic Egypt*. Edinburgh: Scottish Academic Press, 1988.

ARSENY ERMAKOV, PHD

COSMOLOGY/COSMOGONY

The Greek word *kosmos* refers to the ordered universe. Cosmology is the study of the ordered universe. What is the physical universe like? What is the relationship between humans and the physical universe? What is the relationship between the physical universe and God? Cosmogony, from *kosmos* (world) + *gonia* (to be born), asks how the ordered universe began. Often the two terms are used interchangeably. Every tribe, people group, or culture develops a cosmology to help them know how to thrive in the physical world and to answer questions about human meaning.

The **Israelite** cosmology was very similar to that of much of the ancient Near East (ANE). The universe was constructed in three layers: "heaven above . . . the earth beneath . . . [and] the water under the earth" (Exod. 20:4; Ps. 139:7-8). The earth, understood to be a rather flat disc, was situated between two bodies of water. The sky above was composed of an atmosphere and a solid dome (Gen. 1:6-7; Ezek. 1:22, 26), which held back the waters above. Upon this dome was suspended the sun, moon, and stars (Gen. 1:14). Windows or openings in the dome allowed rain, hail, and snow to nourish the earth. The earth was overwhelmed by a flood when God opened the fountains of the deep under the earth, and the windows of heaven above (7:11).

The Israelites differed from their neighbors in their belief that one God created and ordered the universe, not many gods who controlled its various parts. Also, instead of humanity being created as slaves to the gods, humans were formed in the image of **God** and given charge to continue God's work in bringing order to creation (1:26-28).

The NT reflects a view of the cosmos held by the Greeks and more fully developed by Claudius Ptolemy (ca. AD 100-170). The Ptolemaic model placed the earth at the center of the universe, with the moon, sun, planets, and stars rotating around it. Each was held in place by a "firmament" or crystal sphere. Beyond these was the heaven of God. The medieval church accepted this model and invested it with theological authority. The **church** taught that the earth does not move (Ps. 96:10) and that humanity is the special object of God's redemptive purposes.

In the sixteenth century this view of the universe was replaced by the Copernican model, which recognizes that the sun occupies the center of the galaxy. The earth is only one of eight planets revolving around it.

As scientific knowledge of the earth (geology), humanity (anthropology, psychology, sociology), and the universe (astronomy and astrophysics) expanded, modern cosmology developed. The universe is now known to be much older and larger than previously thought. It began some fifteen billion years ago and has become over fifteen billion light-years in size. Our solar system is one of over a billion in the Milky Way galaxy; there are hundreds of billions of galaxies. Humans have gained technological advances that enable them to meet much of their basic requirements of existence (e.g., food, shelter, clothing, and peaceful societies) and to travel, trade, and communicate around the globe.

This knowledge and technology have spawned new cosmologies, one of which is an atheistic cosmology that views matter as eternal and the universe devoid of the supernatural. There is no God. There is only the universe, operating according to fixed patterns or laws. Humans are products of purposeless evolution. Humans must themselves compose their own meaning.

Christians view matter as the creation of one God, who created all things out of nothing. Their concept of the majesty and power of God has expanded exponentially as our knowledge of the universe has increased. He spans unimaginable distances and rules over countless galaxies. Yet he is deeply concerned with humans, offering redemption, reconciliation, transformation, and his presence to those created in his image.

See also Creation/New Creation; Evolution/Evolutionary Biology; Modernity; Natural Science.

Resources
Liddle, Andrew R., and Jon Loveday. *The Oxford Companion to Cosmology*. Oxford, UK: Oxford University Press, 2009.
Swimme, Brian, and Thomas Berry. *The Universe Story: From the Primordial Flaring Forth to the Ecozoic Era*. San Francisco: HarperSanFrancisco, 1992.
Torrance, Thomas F. *Theological and Natural Science*. Eugene, OR: Wipf and Stock Publishers, 2001.
Walton, John H. *The Lost World of Genesis*. Downers Grove, IL: IVP Academic, 2009.
Wright, J. Edward. "Cosmogony, Cosmology." In vol. 1, *The New Interpreter's Dictionary of the Bible*, edited by Katharine Doob Sakenfeld, 755-63. Nashville: Abingdon Press, 2006.

ROBERT D. BRANSON, PHD

COUNTER-REFORMATION (CATHOLIC REFORMATION)

The term "Counter-Reformation" denotes a series of reforms of Catholic practices, theology, and spirituality in the sixteenth century. Protestants understood these measures as responses to the Protestant **Reformation**. This was only partially true. The term is inadequate because it fails to acknowledge extensive reforms the Catholic Church instituted. Consequently, many historians prefer the term "Catholic Reformation," although "Counter-Reformation" persists even among some Catholic historians.

The Catholic Church instituted reforms in numerous areas, including the development of new religious orders such as *(a)* the Theatines (1524), who worked to reform corrupt practices in the church; *(b)* the Capuchins (1529), who worked to restore the primitive simplicity of the Franciscans; and *(c)* the Barnabites (1530), who focused on education, missionary work, and the study of Paul's epistles. By far, though, the most important new order was *(d)* the Society of Jesus (Jesuits), founded by Ignatius Loyola and his companions in 1537 and authorized by the pope in 1540. The Jesuits not only took traditional monastic vows of poverty, chastity, and obedience but also vowed to go wherever the bishop of Rome might send them, all for the salvation of souls.

The Jesuits' obedient relationship with the papacy gave them considerable freedom in relation to local bishops. They developed an apostolate of educational and missionary work and a theology that stressed the availability of salvation for all people. The conflict in the 1590s between the Jesuits and the Dominicans over this doctrine parallels the later conflict between **Arminians** and orthodox **Calvinists** over a limited **atonement**.

A second focus of reform during the Counter-Reformation lay in cultivating Christian spiritualities. The Carmelite order, inspired by Teresa of Jesus (Teresa of Ávila) and her pupil John of the Cross, elaborated the medieval tradition of ascetic mysticism in Spanish monasteries. They attracted many new devotees to this spiritual tradition. Simultaneously, under the leadership of Ignatius of Loyola, the Society of Jesus developed quite a different form of spirituality designed for Catholic laypersons in secular occupations. They would be led on "retreats" enabling their "advance" into the world by using military metaphors favored by Ignatius.

A third focus of Catholic reform during the Counter-Reformation came by way of the Council of Trent (1545-63). It mandated reforms in many areas, including revised Catholic liturgies, clarification on the Bible's authority, and subsequent ecclesial teachings about the doctrine of justification and related issues raised by Protestant Reformers. The council also mandated for the first time that priests be educated in theological seminaries so they could teach the Christian faith and preach homilies at masses. In these latter aspects, French historian Jean Delumeau argued (1977) that the Counter-Reformation shared many themes with the Protestant Reformers, especially their emphasis on explaining the Christian faith to believers and forming them in it.

See also Calvin, John; Protestantism; Reformed Tradition; Roman Catholicism.

Resources

Delumeau, Jean. *Catholicism Between Luther and Voltaire: A New View of the Counter-Reformation*. London: Burns and Oates, 1977.
Lindberg, Carter. *The European Reformations*. Oxford, UK: Blackwell Publishing, 1996.

TED A. CAMPBELL, PHD

COVENANT

A covenant is an agreement of loyalty made between two parties, confirmed by oath and often sealed by ritual enactment. It is grounded in loyalty and trust. Unlike a contract, which minimizes risk, an element of risk is inherent in a covenant. Depending on the type of covenant, specific stipulations are sometimes stated to ensure its proper observance.

The two *primary* types of covenant in the OT derive from the political sphere.

1. The Abrahamic (Gen. 17:1-14) and Davidic (2 Sam. 7:11-17) covenants reflect the *covenant of grant.* A king would graciously bind his dynasty to a subject, granting land and dynasty in perpetuity. If the subject or his descendant showed disloyalty, punishment would follow, but the land would not be confiscated or the dynasty terminated. The covenant given to Noah whereby God bound himself to all living creatures is a variation of this form (Gen. 9:1-17).

2. The Sinaitic covenant (Exod. 20:1-17; the book of Deuteronomy) reflects the *international treaty* model in which a more powerful king establishes an alliance with a vassal king. Stipulations are placed on the vassal and oaths are taken in the names of the gods of both kingdoms. The purpose of this type of covenant was to establish a relationship of mutuality rather than dominance. Disloyalty by the vassal could nullify the covenant. **God** entered into covenant with Israel and bound himself to that people. The stipulations reflected the nature of God, who keeps covenant and demonstrates steadfast **love** and faithfulness but who punishes violators of the covenant (Exod. 34:6-7). Loyalty was demanded of Israel; they were to faithfully observe the laws, particularly not to worship other gods.

Secondary types of covenants were more personal, for example, (1) marriage (Prov. 2:17; Ezek. 16:8; Mal. 2:14) and (2) friendship (1 Sam. 20:42; Ps. 50:5).

The new covenant in **Jesus Christ** (Jer. 31:31-32; Heb. 8:8-12) is not patterned after the earlier covenants; however, it develops more fully their theological and ethical contents. **God** has graciously bound himself through the **sacrifice** of his Son to a new people, one called from all the nations of the earth (Matt. 28:19-20; Rev. 7:9). Similarly the **kingdom of God** is not identified with a specific land; it incorporates people from around the world into God's eternal reign.

People are incorporated into the kingdom as they respond in **repentance** and **faith** to the **prevenient grace** given by the **Holy Spirit**. Those who reject the covenant or disregard its commandments nullify God's saving grace (Heb. 2:2; 6:4-6) and may be lost. The new covenant stipulations are internalized through the work of the **Holy Spirit**. God's people are to live out the covenant's ethical requirements in the fellowship of the **church**. Although the sacrificial regulations have been fulfilled in the crucifixion of Jesus, the demand for loyalty and faithfulness to God's commandments is vital to the relationship that is based on **love** for and trust in God and love for God's people (John 14:15; 15:12).

See also Christian Ethics/Moral Theology; Christology, New Testament; Gospel; Law and Gospel; Repentance; Spiritual Disciplines; Torah.

ROBERT D. BRANSON, PHD

COVENANT SERVICE

The genius of early **Methodism** included celebrations that favored personal and corporate renewal of Christian faith. Among these was the annual covenant service.

John Wesley conducted the first Methodist covenant service in August 1755, with more than eighteen hundred in attendance (*Works*, 2:338-39). Adapted from Richard Alleine's *Vindiciae Pietatis; or, a Vindication of Godliness* (1663), the ceremony appeared in Wesley's *Christian Library*. The covenant service is a call to discipleship. Congregational responses include the lines, "Put me to doing; put me to suffering" and "Let me be full; let me be empty." Minister and congregation pray for the "death and utter destruction of all my corruptions." John Wesley concluded regarding the first covenant service, "Such a night I scarce ever saw before. Surely the fruit of it shall remain for ever."

By 1778, Methodists frequently added **Charles Wesley**'s hymn "Come, Let Us Use the Grace Divine" during the solemn rite. Because of unauthorized alterations to the service, John Wesley in 1780 published *Directions for Renewing Our Covenant with God*. Since then, its use has been traditional during New Year's watch-night services. Different twentieth-century versions of the service appeared in British and American Methodist worship publications. In 1992, the *United Methodist Book of Worship* reprinted Wesley's original *Directions*, recommending its annual celebration. Since Wesley, many have found it an inspiring **means of grace**.

See also Covenant; Liturgy and Worship; Means of Grace; Wesley, John, Theology of.

Resource
Westerfield Tucker, Karen B. *American Methodist Worship*. New York: Oxford University Press, 2001.

J. GREGORY CROFFORD, PHD

CREATION, CARE FOR THE (ECOLOGY)

Christian care for the creation is grounded in the belief that out of love the triune God created the world and is now redeeming not only persons but the natural order as well. This conviction is rooted in both Testaments. "In the beginning . . . God created the heavens and the earth . . . [and] saw . . . it was very good" (Gen. 1:1-31). "The creation itself will be set free from its bondage to decay and will obtain the freedom of the glory of the children of God" (Rom. 8:21). It is also rooted in the conviction that humans are appointed stewards of God's creation (Gen. 1:26).

Although Christians don't always agree about how they should care for God's creation, they do usually agree that "care" is God's mandate. Major threats to the earth's well-being now confront humans, including climate change, major oil spills, and industrial and agricultural pollution of the environment. Destruction of rainforests and the careless extinction of plant and animal species must be added. And the threat from nuclear weapons is particularly fearsome.

The 1960s marked the beginning of an intense public examination of, and response to, modern threats to earth's environment. Secular and religious leaders recognized the need for urgent and comprehensive action. A major catalyst was a book by American biologist/ecologist Rachel Carson, published in 1962. The book was *Silent Spring*. Among other things, Carson chronicled the harmful impact of pesticides such as DDT on the environment and its inhabitants.

Then in 1967 historian Lynn White Jr. published an essay that captured the attention of many Christians. The essay was titled "The Historical Roots of Our Ecological Crisis." White laid the blame for the environmental crisis on Western Christianity. He charged that historically, Christians have understood that "dominion over" creation (Gen. 1:26) has meant freedom to exploit and abuse the natural order.

Succeeding discussions among Christians about care for the creation have been diverse and often heated. Many Christians see care of the environment as a major Christian responsibility; others do not. Some Christians seem to believe the creation exists for human well-being alone; others sharply disagree, believing the nonhuman parts of creation carry a God-given value that must be respected. The former argue that only humans were created in the image of God. Other creatures exist to serve human well-being. The latter group disagrees, saying that humans are only part of nature and must assess environmental problems from a holistic point of view.

Other Christians, differing somewhat from the latter opinion, emphasize **stewardship** over the creation. They stress that humans have been assigned the responsibility of caring for creation in a way that reflects God's love. In Gen. 1, when God described all creation as "good" or "very good," he was saying that all parts of creation were fulfilling their divine purpose. There was once harmony amid creation's diversity. Humankind's use of and care for creation must strive to reclaim a measure of that harmony.

The eight **Millennium Development Goals (MDGs)** represent a global secular response to the contemporary environmental crisis. But while they require serious attention and cooperation from Christians, the church's doctrine of the kingdom of God should be its major motivation for caring for the creation. The **kingdom of God** is God's rule and reign in the world. The NT declares the kingdom—as a new social reality—has been inaugurated in the person of Jesus Christ. What the fall has defaced, the Son is now redeeming, recapitulating to the Father (Eph. 1:3-14). From the beginning, against persons such as second-century Marcion of Sinope, who wanted to separate creation from redemption, the church has insisted that Jesus' deed of redemption includes the redemption of the creation. So Christian care for the creation heralds the kingdom's consummation.

See also Contextual Theology; Creation/New Creation; Social Ethics.

Resources

Au Sable Institute of Environmental Studies. http://www.ausable.org/.
DeWitt, Calvin B. *Earth-Wise: A Biblical Response to Environmental Issues.* 2nd ed. Grand Rapids: Faith Alive Christian Resources, 2007.
Robinson, Tri. *Saving God's Green Earth: Rediscovering the Church's Responsibility to Environmental Stewardship.* With Jason Chatraw. Boise, ID: Ampelon Publishing, 2006.
White, Lynn, Jr. "The Historical Roots of Our Ecological Crisis." *Science* 155 (March 10, 1967): 1203-7.

JAMES W. LEWIS, PHD

CREATION/CHAOS

See COSMOLOGY/COSMOGONY; CREATION/NEW CREATION.

CREATIONISM

In its broadest sense, the term "creationism" represents all Christians who affirm historic Christian doctrine. Christians have historically confessed that **God** created all things from nothing (creation *ex nihilo*). God is not a force that somehow manages to bring order out of preexisting (primordial) stuff, as was true in some ancient accounts of creation. Creation is completely a volitional act on the part of the eternally triune creator God. It is thoroughly God's gift (grace) (John 1:1-5, 10-13; Col. 1:15-20; Heb. 11:3).

More narrowly, "creationism" refers to an understanding of God as Creator that is held in some conservative Protestant circles. From its rather obscure origins, this kind of creationism has spread globally among conservative Christians by way of publications and cultural networks. The heart of this type of creationism is its rejection of prevailing Western scientific claims about cosmology, geological histories, and evolutionary biological theories. This position argues that when properly construed, scientific data prove the world and all are organic species directly resulted from God's efficient causation (often thought to have happened in six twenty-four-hour days). For creationism, God—the direct creative Source of all things—left empirical and clearly observable footprints in the world. The Bible, especially Gen. 1–3, provides a scientific account of the origin of the world and that of human beings. Scientific data proves that the Bible's description of creation is scientifically accurate and hence that God alone is the Creator.

When seen in this way, creationism is a rationalistic defense of one particular strand of Protestant Christianity, with its attending doctrine of Scripture. The Bible is believed to be empirically and scientifically accurate in all topics it addresses. This understanding of biblical authority shifts Christianity's historic understanding of Scripture: Scripture gains its authority from faithfully pointing to Jesus Christ as Savior and to the church as Christ's body. The Scriptures inerrantly reveal everything necessary for our salvation, namely, the life, death, and resurrection of Jesus Christ and life in the body of Christ. Creationism in the more narrow sense argues that the Bible's authority resides in the very text itself. Its authority depends on its accuracy in all things, including or especially in matters relating to science and history. Therefore, one must accept only those empirical results of scientific study that correlate with what creationists draw from Scripture.

In the 1960s creationism moved from its prior emphasis on geography to biology. It did this in order to argue against Neo-Darwinism. Henry M. Morris (1918–2006), a founder of the Creation Research Society and the Institute for Creation Research, developed a theory of "young earth creationism." He and others argued that science shows the universe was created in six twenty-four-hour days. Other creationists developed a theory of "old earth creationism." They claimed that the "days" of Gen. 1 refer to an undetermined length of time but that God created in a way that rules out Neo-Darwinism. More recently, "intelligent design" has emerged as a less biblicist form of creationism. It holds that scientific evidence itself requires an immaterial intelligence—God—to account for life's origin and design in the universe.

See also Evolution/Evolutionary Biology; Fundamentalist Theology; Intelligent Design; Modernity; Natural Science; Scripture, Wesleyan Approach to.

Resources
Eve, Raymond A., and Francis B. Harrold. *The Creationist Movement in Modern America.* Social Movements Past and Present. Boston: Twayne Publishers, 1990.
Giberson, Karl W., and Francis S. Collins. *The Language of Science and Faith: Straight Answers to Genuine Questions.* Downers Grove, IL: InterVarsity Press, 2011.
Numbers, Ronald L. *The Creationists: From Scientific Creationism to Intelligent Design.* Rev. and enl., Cambridge, MA: Harvard University Press, 2006.

JOHN WRIGHT, PHD

CREATION/NEW CREATION

The OT declares and the NT confirms that God is the Creator of all things. They also affirm that unlike humans, God is not dependent upon the creation; he can intervene in it at will. The elements of the created order include time, space, matter/energy, and the "invisible" domain. Although the Western worldview denigrates the latter, the experience of many non-Westerners affirms its validity. Modern scientific efforts to understand the created order fall well within the divine charge found in Gen. 1:28: "Be fruitful and multiply, and fill the earth and subdue it." So do all human efforts to preserve the creation God placed in our care.

Several biblical texts refer to creation, most often in the Psalms and the **Wisdom** literature. Many of them enhance our worship of God as we declare his power and greatness, and recall how God accomplishes his will through his governance of the creation.

Written and oral texts describe the act of creation, two of which open the book of Genesis. They fit into genre shared by many ancient and even some contemporary societies. This genre is used to show how a deity maintains religious, philosophical, and social order. Characteristically, ancient Near Eastern texts explain who, how, and when to worship; the relationship between the world and the object of worship; knowledge of right and wrong; and the approved interpersonal relationships within society. These texts say, "Life is like this, because the gods created it thus." Word pictures familiar to the societies the texts addressed were employed to answer the questions.

Similarly, in the **Bible**, God revealed himself to be Creator by using ideas found in the worldview that characterized ancient Hebrew culture. Supposed conflicts between what the Bible says about how creation happened and reputable modern scientific accounts arise because we fail to understand the differences between an ancient worldview and modern science and because of the resulting misinterpretations of the Bible.

One fundamental difference between other ancient Near Eastern texts and the biblical accounts of creation is that the Bible declares creation "very good" (Gen. 1:31). This good creation reflects the holy, loving, perfectly good God. He stands in sharp contrast to the self-centered, capricious gods worshiped in other societies and to the chaos they created. The chaos (*tohu wa bohu* of Genesis and the "sea" of Revelation) the Bible recognizes is always under God's complete control; it functions within his purposes.

From the biblical perspective, the goodness of creation is disturbed, not by anything wrong with God's creative and sustaining abilities, but because of sin, appearing chronologically first as humans sinning against God. Only much later does sin appear as rebellion against God in the transhuman spirit or spirit domain.

The combination of a good creation disturbed by sin and rebellion with a sovereign Redeemer's direction of history inspired the exilic and postexilic prophets to proclaim and anticipate a new creation. The new creation would be one in which the people of God would be newly created. They would be possessed, not of rebellion, but of a pure desire to do God's will.

The **Prophets**, the literature of **Second Temple Judaism**, and the NT understand the new creation from three perspectives: (1) conversion (*Gen. Rab.* 39.4; *Jos. Asen.* 15.4; 2 Cor. 5:17); (2) a new community of faith (Isa. 65–66; Gal. 6:15-16; Eph. 2:14-16); and (3) the cosmic restoration of creation's goodness (Isa. 56–66; *1 En.* 51:4-5; *2 Bar.* 73–74; Rom. 8:18-25; 2 Cor. 5:16-28), including the final destruction of Satan. Much of this literature is **apocalyptic** and is best understood as not literal. But the literal must not be overlooked. The NT sees the fulfillment of this hope as having occurred in Christ. Numerous texts teach that the new creation and the new humanity happen only when once divided peoples become reconciled in Christ (Gal. 6:15-16; Eph. 2:11-22; Col. 3:10-11).

Today, the church's witness to God's creative work must include all three aspects of the new creation. As God blesses our efforts at global **evangelism**, and as new Christian communities mature, may he also bless our efforts at ecological restoration. To cite former US vice president Al Gore, "On a threatened planet faith seeks for an understanding of our ecological task to preserve the earth and to conserve its resources" (Anderson 2005, 233).

See also Cosmology/Cosmogony; Creationism; Evolution/Evolutionary Biology; Hermeneutics; Intelligent Design; Kingdom of God; Natural Science; Prophecy/Prophet; Reconciliation; Science and the Bible.

Resources

Anderson, Bernhard W. *From Creation to New Creation.* Eugene, OR: Wipf and Stock Publishers, 2005.
Knight, Henry H., III, ed. *From Aldersgate to Azusa Street: Wesleyan, Holiness, and Pentecostal Visions of the New Creation.* Eugene, OR: Pickwick Publications, 2010.
Wright, Christopher J. H. *The Mission of God.* Downers Grove, IL: InterVarsity Press, 2006.

RUSSELL LOVETT, PHD

CREEDS (NICENE, CHALCEDONIAN, APOSTLES', ATHANASIAN)

Because the church's mission requires it to engage the *whole of life*, from the beginning it has thought and spoken very carefully. From time to time the church has in creeds carefully stated its beliefs. The word "creed" is from the Latin *credo*, "I believe." Very early, creeds were incorporated into the disciplines by which converts entered the church's life. After studying a statement of belief, sometimes for years, a convert would recite it, often in answer to questions, during the liturgy of baptism. Baptismal creeds became the seeds from which grew (1) later ecumenical creeds, such as those of Nicaea and Chalcedon; (2) less official, traditional creeds, such as the Apostles', and (3) more formal and scholastic creeds, such as the Athanasian.

The Nicene Creed (325) is the first statement of belief ratified by delegates of virtually all regions of the church. It is the most widely accepted and recited creed in the whole church. It was written to clarify the relation of **Jesus Christ** to God the Father. The creed's central affirmation is that Jesus Christ is *homoousion tō Patri*. This phrase signifies that what Jesus Christ is *as God* is the same as what the Father is *as God*. The term *homoousios* is translated into English as "consubstantial," or "same in substance/essence/being/reality." That is, it affirms that there is no significant difference between the deity of the Son and the deity of the Father. When it was enlarged at the Council of Constantinople (381), the creed added that the **Holy Spirit,** "the Lord and Giver of Life," "who proceeds from the Father," is also fully divine, that is, "with the Father and the Son is worshiped and glorified." Thus the Nicene Creed is often said to be the church's first official affirmation of the doctrine of the **Trinity,** that God is Father, Son, and Holy Spirit.

The Creed of Chalcedon (451) was written to clarify the relation of the humanity and deity of Jesus Christ. It, too, affirms that he is *homoousion tō Patri*, adding that he is also *homoousion hēmin*, that is, the same in humanity as we are. He is thus in a sense *two*—divine and human. However, his natures *concur* as *one person*. Thus in Jesus Christ all that is God and all that is human *happen* as *one* lifetime, one person. Divinity and humanity are not dissolved into or separated from one another. Together they are truly the one Jesus Christ. Thus Mary gave birth to that human who is truly God. She may thus be called God-bearer (*Theotokos*). Further, since the *one* person Jesus Christ was crucified, implicitly both his humanity and deity suffer.

The Apostles' Creed emerged in the West and less officially. It seems to have grown from a second-century Roman baptismal creed and to have achieved its current form ca. 700. It acknowledges the Father and the Spirit, the church, the resurrection of the flesh, forgiveness, and unending life. But most of its attention focuses on Jesus Christ, although briefly. No details of Jesus' life between his birth and his suffering at the hands of Pilate are given. The creed stresses his crucifixion, descent into hell, resurrection, ascent to the Father, and future return to judge the world.

The Athanasian Creed was likely written by one person in the fifth or sixth century. Its theology derives from **Augustine** (d. 430). It clearly articulates Western theological commitments and is without authority in the Eastern Church. To make clear the creed was not written by Athanasius (d. 373), it is sometimes called by its first Latin words, *Quicunque vult* (whoever will [be saved]). It is a highly formal creed, written with precision and rigid balance. Most of its words are devoted to an explicit statement of Western Trinitarian orthodoxy. However, it also states the official position of the West on the person of Christ and, more briefly, his work.

See also Arianism; Doctrine/Dogma; God, Doctrine of; Incarnation; Quadrilateral, Wesleyan; Revelation; Sacraments.

Resources

Kelly, J. N. D. *Early Christian Creeds.* 3rd ed. London: Continuum, 2006.
Leith, John H., ed. *Creeds of the Churches: A Reader in Christian Doctrine from the Bible to the Present.* 3rd ed. Atlanta: John Knox Press, 1982.

CRAIG KEEN, PHD

CROSS

As a material object, the cross is an ancient tool of capital punishment. For the Romans of Jesus' day it seems to have been reserved for persons accused of political rebellion. Jews, whom the Romans crucified because of their rebellion against Rome, were not considered martyrs, however, because Jews understood crucifixion in the light of Deut. 21:22-23; such criminals were cursed of God. Thus, for the majority of Jews in the first century, Jesus' crucifixion negated any claims his followers made about his being the Messiah—he had been cursed by God. This is what Paul is referring to in Gal. 3:13, where he says, "Christ redeemed us . . . by becoming a curse for us."

The Roman accusation against Jesus was "King of the Jews" (see John 19:19), a charge of rebellion against Caesar. The Gospels suggest the Sanhedrin presented Jesus to Pilate charged with this accusation to assure his crucifixion. What had he done to warrant the cross? Jesus' triumphal entry into Jerusalem and his "cleansing" the **temple** could easily be seen as actions claiming royal authority. However, since the Romans didn't pursue Jesus' followers, it appears they didn't see the Jesus movement as a political threat. Yet Jewish leaders insisted that Jesus be crucified. Matthew 22 might help us understand. Jesus' answers to a series of "test" questions created amazement and increased his **honor,** while **shaming** the Jewish authorities. Crucifixion offered these authorities a way to restore their **honor;** they could show that Jesus was cursed by God.

For Christians, the cross is not a way to demean Jesus. Instead, the cross demonstrates God's **love** and fulfills his purposes. As Jesus dies on the cross, the Roman soldiers recognize him as the Son of God. In the book of Hebrews the cross is the place and the means of **atonement,** God's ultimate victory for all humanity (10:10-14). In Galatians Jesus takes *our* curse on himself so that "the blessing of Abraham might come to the Gentiles" (3:14). In Romans Jesus' death is a unique death. Rather than what all humans must suffer as a demonstration of the reign of sin, "the death [Jesus] died, he died *to* sin, once for all" (6:10, emphasis added). The cross, then, defeats the reign of sin in all its manifestations: **idolatry,** the power of **demons,** oppression and fear found in **traditional religions,** the power that **ancestors** have over those who view them as the living dead, and slavery to harmful substances and practices.

Finally, the cross is the symbol of **discipleship.** Our "living sacrifice" is the believers' part in the sanctifying work of God (12:1-2). Jesus' disciples are to "take up their cross and follow [him]" (Matt. 16:24; Mark 10:21; Luke 9:23; 14:27). For Jesus the cross was a literal form of execution. Throughout Christian history and especially today, many of Jesus' disciples have and are following him to their own executions as witnesses to him. The cross has forever transformed the word "witness" (Greek, *martyrion*) into the word "martyr." Stephen Motyer says "martyrdom is the essence of discipleship, not because every follower of Christ will be martyred, but because 'testimony' . . . may not stop short of it, if necessary" (1997, 262).

See also African Traditional Religions; Atonement; Demons/Unclean Spirits; Gospel; Honor/Shame Culture; Jesus of Nazareth; Principalities and Powers; Sin.

Resources
Morris, Leon. *Apostolic Preaching of the Cross*. 3rd ed. London: Tyndale Press, 1965.
Motyer, Stephen. "Cross, Theology of the." In *Dictionary of the Later New Testament and Its Developments*, edited by Ralph P. Martin and Peter H. Davids, 262. Downers Grove, IL: InterVarsity Press, 1997.
New Testament: Mark 15:39; Rom. 6:5-11; Gal. 3:10-13; Heb. 8–10.

RUSSELL LOVETT, PHD

CULT

The meaning of "cult" is imprecise, but within Christianity it is normally used to refer to groups that have departed from historic orthodoxy. The related term, **sect**, refers more narrowly to groups within Christianity that seek to preserve their understanding of doctrinal purity or Christian behavior. Many Christian cults do not, at least initially, see themselves as departing from historic Christian doctrine. Often within **Roman Catholicism**, groups later considered cults initially saw their practices as enriching the parent body by focusing on a particular person (such as **Mary** or one of the saints) or a devotional practice (such as **prayer** and the rosary). They define and emphasize a relationship with God contrary to what orthodoxy permits. Some forms of **mysticism** illustrate this. In Protestantism a broad range of cults are identified on historical or doctrinal grounds. The most common are the Church of Latter Day Saints (Mormons) and the Jehovah's Witnesses.

The term is popularly applied to groups characterized by devotion to a person or practice that is significantly different from the norms of the original religion from which it came. For example, the Unification Church combines Christian belief with Korean folk belief and faith in technology; the Hare Krishna movement in the West is derived from Hinduism; The Church of Scientology combines Christianity with pseudoscience and Eastern religion. Such cults offer their members a sense of belonging to something profound, giving them an identity and a sense of meaning they had not previously known. Communicants often find a high level of social support and acceptance. In many cults there is a tendency to synthesize a wide range of otherwise unconnected mythologies, beliefs, and **traditional religions**, such as mystic healing, astrology, and **reincarnation**.

Membership in a cult can become unthinking dependency. This can make it very difficult for a devotee to exit a cult. A glaring example of this occurred in Jonestown, Guyana, in November 1978; at the instruction of Jim Jones, the cult's leader, mass suicide of members of the People's Temple cult followed. Partly because of such memories, "cult" is commonly used as a derogatory term. It connotes authoritarian control, a rigid belief structure, exploitation, and possibly living in a close-knit community under tight control. Recent books dealing with cults have pointed to the fraudulent claims of cults, their aims, their leadership, and how their followers are deceived.

See also Folk Religion; Neo-paganism; New Age Spirituality; New Religious Movements; Popular Religiosity.

Resource
Martin, Walter, and Ravi Zacharias. *The Kingdom of the Cults*. Rev. ed. Minneapolis: Bethany House, 2003.

DAVID MCEWAN, PHD

CULTURE OF ACCUMULATION
See ECONOMICS AND THE USE OF MONEY.

Dd

DALIT THEOLOGY
See ASIAN THEOLOGY.

DAMNATION
See DESTINY OF THE UNEVANGELIZED; HELL.

DANCE

Dance is the intentional artistic design and rhythmic performance of bodily movement. It is often proposed as culture's oldest aesthetic form. A universal or near-universal practice in human history, dance is common to most religious systems. Whether as worship or communal rite, dance has figured prominently in Jewish, Hindu, Muslim, classical, and indigenous tribal religious practices. Christian dance was fairly common during the early and medieval centuries. It declined during the **Reformation** and **Puritan** eras.

Dance's forms are nearly as broad and diverse as its history. As *gestural,* it imitates life's forms; while as *symbolic,* it re-presents ideas and signs. When *lyrical,* dance either incarnates or illuminates music—dance's aesthetic counterpart. As *plastic,* it sculpturally shapes aesthetic forms and geometries. In *social* forms, dance enacts personal and communal identity rituals, while its *spiritual* forms serve liturgical, ecstatic, meditative, or shamanistic functions. Dance, whether public or private, may be performed by individuals, pairs, small companies, or large congregations.

This art form moves between two impulses, the *formalistic-imitative* and the *idealistic-expressive,* with improvisation mediating between them. Churches that embrace dance can benefit from each of these rhythmic varieties and functions.

As an art form, dance has suffered many abuses, chief among them being its subjugation to music and drama. While dance often complements or illuminates these arts, it is independent of them; it is its own art. Regrettably, dance has often been categorized according to hierarchical and colonial structures: from ballet one proceeds "down" to theatrical, jazz, folk, and popular dance and then to its (supposedly) most "primitive" form, ethnic or non-Western dance. Consequently, a "high versus low" dualism and pro-Western art ideologies have artificially aligned dance's "superior" forms with politically, educationally, and economically powerful social structures. In the last half century, Western professional dancers have embraced world dance, overcoming cultural bias. Dance is showing how it can be prophetic, egalitarian, and transformational.

A final abuse of dance has been its moral suffocation by pietistic **Protestantism**. Rather than praise dance's inherent beauty or explore its potential for inspired creativity, expression, and praise, many Christians accuse dance of promoting moral decay. These well-meaning but ill-informed persons ignore the importance of a practice that emphasizes physicality's goodness (e.g., creation, incarnation, and salvation), engages faith's ritual-sacramental dimensions, and commends beauty as a means of grace. Dance can accent the imaginative dimension of divine and human creativity, promote worship that engages the whole body and senses, and show how all human actions can be transformed by and for God.

If all of heaven dances when individuals are saved, then surely this establishes precedence for exploring the positive dimensions of dance.

See also Aesthetics; Arts, The; Liturgy and Worship.

KENTON STILES, PHD

DEAD SEA SCROLLS

The Dead Sea Scrolls are manuscripts found in caves along the western shore of the Dead Sea. They date between the third century BC and the second century AD. The locations of discovery range from Jericho to Ein Gedi, but the eleven caves above Khirbet Qumran contained the largest number. In 1947 a bedouin shepherd boy accidentally discovered ancient manuscripts written in Hebrew. This led to the recovery of nearly nine hundred fragmentary texts, written on leather and papyrus. They opened a window on Judaism that overlapped the lifetime of Jesus Christ.

The discovery became public when a scroll brought to the American School for Oriental Research (Jerusalem) was identified as the book of Isaiah. Based on the Hebrew script, scholars determined the date to be no later than the second half of the second century BC—making it over one thousand years older than the previously known manuscript. Other scrolls in the same cave proved equally exciting. There were titles such as *The Rule of the Community, The War of the Sons of Light with the Sons of Darkness, Thanksgiving Hymns,* and a new form of commentary, *pesher,* on prophetic books such as

Habakkuk. The documents were immediately recognized as belonging to the Essenes, a group previously known only through the works of Josephus and Philo.

This identification, as is true of most aspects of Qumran interpretation, is contested. But the Essenes remain the most persuasive, identified in the documents as the "Community," or the "Unity" (*Yahad*). They judged the then current temple practice and sacrifice corrupt. Their community was established as a spiritual temple, a holy place. The Essenes followed strict laws of purity.

The identity of the scrolls as belonging to this monastic, sectarian group led many NT scholars to diminish their significance for understanding Christianity. However, the nearly eight hundred manuscripts in Cave 4 have led to the conclusion that the manuscripts constituted a library, many actually composed away from Qumran. Whereas the number of scrolls thought to have originated within the sectarian group is significant, it is small compared with the one-third of manuscripts of biblical works (from Christian and Jewish canons) and works based on or related to the biblical books (commentary, citation, or rewrites of the text).

Some books in the library were previously known, such as the books of *Jubilees*, Judith, and *Enoch*. Some, such as the *Temple Scroll*, may have been considered Scripture, giving insight into developmental stages of authoritative canonical texts completed well into the Christian era.

The biblical manuscripts show that the older the manuscripts, the more diverse the texts. Modern translations rely on the Masoretic Text, not settled as the primary Hebrew version before the late first century AD.

One of the Dead Sea Scrolls' most valuable contributions has been to our knowledge of **Second Temple Judaism.** For Christians, this shines a brighter light on the context into which Jesus was born and the NT written. Now we have firsthand documents from that period, whereas before, scholars depended on translated accounts and medieval manuscripts.

Of similar importance is a better understanding of biblical interpretation in Jesus' day. We can see that when interpreting the OT as pointing to Jesus as Christ and Son of God, NT writers were actually using interpretive techniques common in Judaism. They followed the "rules" when persuading others their interpretation of Jesus' death and resurrection was correct. This applies even when the intended audience was Greek speaking.

Resources

Davies, Philip R., George J. Brooke, Phillip R. Callaway. *The Complete World of the Dead Sea Scrolls*. London: Thames and Hudson, 2002.

Vermes, Geza. *The Complete Dead Sea Scrolls in English*. Rev. ed. London: Penguin, 2004.

DWIGHT D. SWANSON, PHD

DEEPER LIFE MOVEMENT

See KESWICK MOVEMENT.

DEIFICATION

See THEOSIS (DEIFICATION).

DEISM

Deism is a view of the divine that emphasizes **God**'s transcendence at the expense of divine immanence (current presence and activity). Deism is sometimes referred to as the "watchmaker" view of God; after God perfectly created the world, he withdrew and no longer intervenes in its operation. God created a set of laws that cause the world to function in an orderly manner, like a watch. Deism is also sometimes referred to as the "absentee God" theory. Deism flourished in the seventeenth and eighteenth centuries. It is the opposite of **pantheism**, which emphasizes God's complete immanence.

Although deistic thinking existed among Greek philosophers since ancient times (Heraclitus, Epicurus, **Plato**, and **Aristotle**), with the arrival of the explanatory power of the **natural sciences**, things once attributed to God's presence came to be explained by natural law. Based on the popularity of Isaac Newton's view of the universe as a vast self-regulating machine, many deists used the teleological argument (the argument from design) to prove God's existence.

Lord Herbert of Cherbury (d. 1648) is generally considered the father of English deism. His book *De Veritate* was its first major statement. Lord Herbert attempted to provide a basis for tolerance in a time of severe religious contention.

The deists of the eighteenth century Enlightenment proposed a "rational religion." They denied the reality of any supernatural events such as miracles, predictive prophecy, and the inspiration of Scripture. They rejected as irrational the Christian concept of the **Trinity**. John Toland in his *Christianity Not Mysterious* declared, "The first thing I shall insist upon is, that if any doctrine of the New Testament be contrary to Reason, we have no manner or idea of it."

The deists were not atheists; they just rejected the aspects of theism not amenable to reason. Influential deists of this period included John Locke, Matthew Tindal, and William Paley, whose essay *The Watch and the Human Eye* was a classic expression of the teleological argument. Several American founding fathers were deists, including Benjamin Franklin and, somewhat ambiguously, Thomas Jefferson and George Washington.

See also Greek Philosophy; Incarnation; Intelligent Design; Panentheism.

H. RAY DUNNING, PHD

DELIVERANCE/EXORCISM

Deliverance and exorcism refer to persons, places, or things being liberated from demons. **Demons** are considered supernatural beings not under human control. The term "exorcism" is derived from *exorcismus* (Latin), "a calling up or driving out of evil spirits," and *exorkizein* (Greek), "to exorcize or bind by oath." Exorcism is a religious ritual designed to cast out demons. Traditionally the person performing exorcism is called an exorcist. Such a person is believed to have a special gift from God to cast demons from people and objects. The term "deliverance" is often reserved for persons oppressed by evil spirits. More inclusive, exorcism refers to all activities meant to drive out evil spirits.

A person possessed by a demon is thought to be under the total control of an evil force. The victim behaves abnormally and suffers mentally and physically. Demons often cry with a loud voice before leaving a person (Mark 1:23, 26; 9:26; Acts 8:7).

Exorcism is practiced in primitive and modern societies. It is common in shamanistic religions and in various developed religions (Hinduism, Islam, Buddhism, and Christianity). In the Hindu Vedic tradition, for example, demons are cast out through chants and sacrifices.

Demons and exorcism play an important role in Jesus' ministry. He casts or drives out (*ekballō*, Mark 1:34) and rebukes (*epitimaō*, Luke 9:42) demons (*daimonia*, devils [KJV]) and sets their victims free (Matt. 4:24; 8:16, 28-32; Mark 1:25-26; 3:22; Luke 4:33-41). Exorcism is authoritative evidence that Jesus is inaugurating the long anticipated **kingdom of God**. The kingdom, present in Jesus, is superior to demons and Satan's power that would oppose God's kingdom (Matt. 12:22-28; Mark 3:27; Luke 11:17-18; Rom. 8:15-17). Jesus delegated authority to his disciples to cast out demons and heal in his name (Matt. 10:1, 7-8; Mark 3:15; 6:7; Luke 10:17-20; Acts 8:6-7). Demons were cast out by the disciples (Mark 9:38; Luke 10:17), Peter (Acts 5:16), Paul (Acts 16:16-18; 19:12), and Philip (Acts 8:7).

In a Christian exorcism, **Jesus Christ** is presented as the High Priest standing between the *exorcee* and the demons. Deliverance is God's work. A Christian exorcist always remains under the authority of Jesus Christ. He or she says, "The Lord Jesus Christ rebukes you" and "Come out in the name of Jesus Christ." The declaration places demons under Jesus' authority (Jude v. 9; Acts 3:6; 16:18; Eph. 6:10-12). Only in the name of Jesus can people be truly delivered from the power of evil. Only he is the Redeemer, and only he has control over demonic powers.

John Wesley recognized the reality of demons and believed that only through the power of God can they be cast out and that God uses his servants for this work. In his sermon, "A Caution Against Bigotry," Wesley states the biblical and theological conditions for "casting out devils." He writes, "In order to have the clearest view of this, we should remember, that (according to the scriptural account) as God dwells and works in the children of light, so the devil dwells and works in the children of darkness. As the Holy Spirit possesses the souls of good men, so the evil spirit possesses the souls of the wicked" (*Works*, 5:480). How are demons to be cast out? "All this is indeed the work of God. It is God alone who can cast out Satan. But he is generally pleased to do this by man, as an instrument in his hand; who is then said to cast out devils in his name, by his power and authority" (*Works*, 5:483).

See also Demons/Unclean Spirits; Divination; Principalities and Powers.

Resource
Johns, Loren L., and James R. Krabill. *Even the Demons Submit: Continuing Jesus' Ministry of Deliverance*. Occasional Papers. Elkhart, IN: Institute of Mennonite Studies, 2006.

JOSEPH SURAY, PHD

DEMOCRACY

Democracy is a political philosophy that establishes government on the "rule of the people." It places high value on the rights of persons (at least citizens) to direct the activities and policies of their government. Practically, it requires a populace possessing the knowledge, judgment, and sense of common interest necessary for effective and equitable government. In principle, it assesses a citizen's political status in terms of natural human rights.

The principle of democracy may be expressed in various forms. *Direct democracy* involves immediate participation in voting and decision making by all citizens. *Representative democracy* vests the responsibility to govern in representatives elected by voters. The government of the United States is an example of representative democracy, though the increasing practice of general referendums on specific legislation is more representative of direct democracy. *Parliamentary democracy* is a type of representative government where the ruling party in the legislature, not the populace, chooses the prime minister.

The historical roots of democracy lie in the ancient Greek city of Athens. It practiced a form of direct democracy; all citizens could vote on decisions of state. This approach to government was sharply criticized by Plato in his *Republic*, warning that democracies will succumb to those persons expert at winning elections but not at governing. The Greek experiment was superseded by forms of government that regarded rule by the people as something to be avoided (as mob rule). While democratic philosophy would not be constructively reconsidered until the eighteenth century, Stoicism, which was prominent in the Roman era, through its notions of natural law, provided a philosophical basis for developing the ideas of natural human rights that inspire modern democracies.

In the eighteenth century the reconsideration of democracy by thinkers such as Jean-Jacques Rousseau and John Locke embedded democratic ideas into the development of modern thought and political practice. Governance should, in this view, be exercised on behalf of citizens, dependent for its authority upon the consent of the governed. These ideas were especially formative in the political understanding that marked the developing colonies that later formed the United States and in shaping the French Revolution (1789-99). Entering the twenty-first century, the ideal of democracy holds a dominant position among competing political visions.

Democracy is not without its critics. The ability of democracy to represent all of the people effectively is questioned. Democracy has been frequently criticized for becoming a "tyranny of the majority" or of powerful "special interests." The critical question is, "Can democracy truly be the rule of the people if the interests of political minorities are consistently overruled by the majority?" There is also a question about participation in the democratic process. What are the limits of participation? In modern democracies, only franchised citizens can exercise the right to vote.

See also Communism; Justice; Rights, Human; Socialism; Social Justice.

CARL M. LETH, PHD

DEMONOLOGY
See DEMONS/UNCLEAN SPIRITS.

DEMONS/UNCLEAN SPIRITS

Demons (Greek, *daimonia*) or unclean (*akathartos*) spirits are evil spiritual beings whose function is to harm people and oppose God's purposes in the world, especially his work in Jesus Christ.

Although popular belief is that demons are fallen angels, the Bible never explicitly says this. In Luke, after the mission of the seventy disciples, Jesus says, "I watched Satan fall from heaven like a flash of lightning" (10:18). The statement probably refers to the victory of the seventy disciples over the demons (see also John 12:31). Second Peter speaks of angels who sinned and were cast into hell. They were committed to "chains of deepest darkness to be kept until the judgment" (2:4). Jude says the fallen angels are "kept in eternal chains" but, like Peter, does not identify them as demons (v. 6). The legend of the fallen angels and the evils they unleashed upon the earth are vividly described in the book of *1 Enoch* (chaps. 6–8), where Gen. 6:4 is freely expanded upon.

The OT contains no developed concept of demons. The KJV speaks four times of "devils" whom apostate Israel worshipped (Lev. 17:7; Deut. 32:17; 2 Chron. 11:15; Ps. 106:37, KJV). The reference is most likely to the gods of Canaan. Second Chronicles says Jeroboam I appointed priests for the "goat-demons" (11:15). The psalmist laments Israel's apostasies during the days of the judges, charging that they even "sacrificed their sons and their daughters to the demons" (106:37). Although the texts may be suggestive, there is no explicit basis in the OT for identifying "devils" or "demons" with "demons" as they appear in the NT.

Second Temple Jewish literature indicates that after the exile, with the rise of dualism, the concept of demons or unclean spirits underwent fundamental changes. The Qumran community viewed demons as wicked spirits who serve as Satan's emissaries and messengers of destruction (1QS IV, 12; 4Q510 1 5).

"Devils" or "demons" play a prominent role in the Synoptic Gospels as unsuccessful opponents of Christ and the kingdom of God. Exorcisms were a common form of healing in Jesus' ministry (Mark 3:22-27; Matt. 12:22-30; Luke 11:14-24). They authenticate Jesus' authority as the One in whom the kingdom of God has come. Even demons, representing God's archenemy, are powerless before him. Exorcisms are part of the good news that the kingdom has come to those who beforehand lived in fear of demons.

The NT identifies Beelzebub (bē-el-zi-bəb), the devil or Satan, as "prince" of the demons (Matt. 9:34; 12:24; Mark 3:22, KJV). So the relationship between the two is clear; demons do Satan's bidding. John identifies the devil as "the prince of this world" (John 12:31; 16:11, KJV). After Jesus' transfiguration he declares, "Now is the judgment of this world: now shall the prince ["ruler," NRSV] of this world be cast out" (12:31, KJV). Colossians says that on the cross, Jesus "disarmed the rulers and authorities and made a public example of them, triumphing over them in it" (2:15). Paul may or may not be speaking of demons.

Today, among many Christians there is an almost pagan preoccupation with the power and identity of demons, a preoccupation that comes close to denying that demons, whatever they are, have fallen before the Lord of lords. Victory, not fear, is the clear message of the NT.

See also Angels; Devil/Satan; Divination; Idolatry; Second Temple Judaism.

Resources

Mounce, William D., ed. *Mounce's Complete Expository Dictionary of Old and New Testament Words.* Grand Rapids: Zondervan, 2006.

Toorn, Karel van der, Bob Becking, and Pieter W. van der Horst, eds. *Dictionary of Deities and Demons in the Bible.* 2nd ed. Leiden, NL: E. J. Brill, 1999.

MUSA VICTOR KUNENE, PHD

DESERT FATHERS AND MOTHERS

Beginning in the later third century, Christians in Egypt, Syria, and Palestine began abandoning conventional forms of life in favor of a life of **ascetic** withdrawal. According to Athanasius, their model was a young Egyptian farmer named Anthony, who about the year 270 followed the teaching of Jesus and sold his possessions, giving the proceeds to the poor. He died in 356, and thanks to Athanasius' biography of him, Anthony is commonly regarded as the father of the Christian monastic life.

Monasticism is older than Christianity, but Anthony and his successors gave the institution distinctive forms. Anthony pursued the solitary life of a hermit, the earliest form of monasticism (like "monk," from *monachos*, meaning "solitary"). Later another Egyptian ascetic, Pachomius (ca. 290–346), developed the cenobitic or communal form of monasticism. Between hermit and monastery was the *lavra* or *skete*, a small group of hermits who lived in isolated cells but who were gathered under the direction of an *abba* (father). Women also adopted this way of life, living about their *amma* (mother). This third form flourished in the Egyptian desert at Nitria, a region south and west of Alexandria, and Scetis, roughly forty miles south of Nitria. Egypt was an important center of monastic withdrawal, but desert fathers and mothers were also found in unsettled regions of Palestine.

Individual ascetics devoted much of their time to meditation and **prayer**, sustaining themselves through cottage industries such as basket weaving. **Self-denial** was characteristic of their way of life, but extreme examples, such as the so-called pillar saints, were rare. Desert fathers and mothers were spiritual directors and teachers. Over time the men and women gathered about them collected and set to writing sayings of the abbas and ammas, as well as stories about them. Eventually these collections circulated among laypeople as well as monks, spreading from the eastern Mediterranean throughout Europe and Russia. Common themes among these sayings are humility before **God**, concern for the neighbor, confrontation with temptation, and chastity of body and spirit.

Leading figures at Scetis included the abbas Moses, Pambo, Poemen, and Sisoes, the amma Sarah, and the amma Syncletica of Alexandria. In 444 Berber raiders devastated the community at Scetis, but by then the lavra was also well established in Palestine. Many of the sayings of the abbas and ammas come from that region.

See also Asceticism; God, Doctrine of; Monasticism; Prayer; Self-Denial; Spiritual Direction/Spiritual Director.

Resources

Bondi, Roberta C. *To Love As God Loves*. Philadelphia: Fortress Press, 1987.

Dunn, Marilyn. *Emergence of Monasticism: From the Desert Fathers to the Early Middle Ages*. London: Blackwell Publishing, 2003.

Harmless, William. *Desert Christians: An Introduction to the Literature of Early Monasticism*. New York: Oxford University Press, 2004.

MERLE D. STREGE, THD

DESTINY OF THE UNEVANGELIZED

The final standing before **God** of those who die having never heard the **gospel of Jesus Christ** (the unevangelized) constitutes a question that traces back to the early church. Will they benefit from the eternal life made possible by Jesus? The question arises because of two widely affirmed Christian beliefs. First, God loves all humanity and desires that all persons experience redemption (1 Tim. 2:4). Second, Jesus Christ is the unique and only Redeemer (Acts 4:12). Are those who die never having heard the gospel forever excluded from redemption? The question has received numerous possible answers.

1. One answer, known as *exclusivism,* affirms that each person must know about and explicitly exercise faith in Jesus to benefit from his atonement. Exclusivism divides into four subgroups: *(a)* restrictivism (sometimes called particularism) holds that to be redeemed a person must have knowledge of and must explicitly confess faith in Jesus Christ. This must occur prior to death. Proponents appeal to texts such as Acts 4:12 and John 14:6. They argue that a person's destiny is sealed at death. Restrictivism has been popular in Augustinian-Calvinist theological circles; *(b)* a minor view among exclusivists is that if one sincerely responds to God's promptings, God will send the message of the gospel, even if by way of angels or dreams; *(c)* postmortem evangelization holds that persons who die unevangelized or insufficiently evangelized will receive an opportunity after death to hear the gospel and exercise trust in Jesus. Proponents often argue that God is not limited by human life spans for reaching persons with the gospel (1 Pet. 3:18–4:6). **Eastern Orthodox** and Lutherans have popularized this position; and *(d)* universalism affirms postmortem evangelization but goes further by saying that ultimately all persons will come to faith in Jesus. In the end God will "have no permanent problem children" (Rom. 5:18; 1 Cor. 15:22-28). Many Eastern Orthodox and a number of Protestant theologians (e.g., Karl Barth) embrace this position. They are "hopeful" universalists.

2. Perhaps the most widespread answer is *inclusivism.* It affirms that God will save the unevangelized if they respond in faith to God based on the limited revelation they receive in this life. Proponents of inclusivism include **Thomas Aquinas** and **John Wesley.** Inclusivism became the dominant view in Roman Catholicism after Vatican II.

3. Finally, a small number of theologians argue that God possesses *middle knowledge.* God knows the decision each unevangelized person would have made had he or she heard the gospel under ideal circumstances. God saves such persons because they would have trusted in Jesus had opportunity been given.

See also Prevenient Grace; Religions, Theology of; Religious Pluralism; Repentance.

Resource

Sanders, John. *No Other Name: An Investigation into the Destiny of the Unevangelized.* Grand Rapids: Eerdmans, 1992.

JOHN SANDERS, THD

DETERMINISM AND FREE WILL

Determinism is the idea that all events (including human thoughts and behaviors) are causally determined by prior events or by an outside agent (such as God). If determinism were true, it would eliminate the possibility of human moral agency and **free will.**

With respect to human thought and behavior, there are three forms of determinism: (1) **predestination** (God predetermines the fate of human beings); (2) physical/biological determinism (all causes of thought and behavior can be reduced to the laws of atomic and subatomic physics); and (3) environmental determinism (human thought and behavior cannot transcend habits learned from prior physical and social experiences).

Physical/biological determinism has gained momentum from advances in modern **neuroscience.** Neuroscience research reveals that all realms of human behavior and experience have correlates in brain activity. They can be disturbed or eliminated by brain damage. This calls into question mind-body or body-soul dualism, in favor of a more **monist** or physicalist view of human nature. However, if we were merely physical beings, how could it not be that all causes of our behavior would be reducible to, and determined by, the laws of physics (i.e., causal **reductionism**)? If the causes of every behavior and experience were nothing but the operation of the lawful activity of atoms and molecules, then all human agency and free will would disappear, along with claims about meaning, reason, and human relatedness. They would become nothing more than the outcome of physics.

Environmental determinism is the other extreme of the nature-nurture argument about the origins of human character. This view suggests that humans are physically open systems (i.e., not entirely genetically predetermined) formed by interactions with their environment. Nevertheless, everything humans are cognitively, behaviorally, and morally capable of is the direct product of earlier learning. Humans cannot transcend their developmental history.

Some philosophers and theologians maintain a body-soul **dualism** to argue for the existence of a nonmaterial soul that makes free will possible. However, one question arising from this explanation has never been resolved. How might a nonmaterial soul interact with the material body and brain to allow for free will that in turn influences behavior?

Some believe the dilemma of determinism and free will created by neuroscience can be solved by the property of *emergence*. Although humans are entirely biological organisms, they have high-level mental, social, and spiritual *causal capacities*. These capacities emerge from dynamic patterns of interaction occurring within the hypercomplex human body/brain as it interacts with a complex interpersonal and cultural environment. *Emergent capacities*, while dependent on the physics and physiology of cells, are causal in their own right. According to this explanation we are moral agents and genuinely rational and relational creatures due to what *emerges* from our biological complexity.

See also Anthropology, Theological; Christian Ethics/Moral Theology; Ethics; Experience, Phenomenon of; Fatalism; Free Will; Monism, Dualism, Pluralism; Natural Science; Person; Predestination and Election; Social Sciences; Soul.

Resources

Fischer, John Martin, Robert Kane, Derk Pereboom, and Manuel Vargas, eds. *Four Views on Free Will*. Great Debates in Philosophy. Malden, MA: Blackwell Publishing, 2007.

Murphy, Nancey, and Warren S. Brown. *Did My Neurons Make Me Do It? Philosophical and Neurobiological Perspectives on Moral Responsibility and Free Will*. Oxford, UK: Oxford University Press, 2007.

Murphy, Nancey, Warren S. Brown, and H. Newton Malony, eds. *Whatever Happened to the Soul? Scientific and Theological Portraits of Human Nature*. Philadelphia: Fortress Press, 1998.

WARREN S. BROWN, PHD

DEVIL/SATAN

In the OT the word "satan" (Hebrew, *hasatan*; Greek, *satan*) is a noun meaning "adversary," "accuser," or "obstructer," and it is applied to humans or celestial beings. The Philistines, for example, complain that David will become their "adversary" if allowed to accompany them in battle (1 Sam. 29:4; see 2 Sam. 19:22). The psalmist, who had been verbally and physically abused, requested that the person responsible for his suffering be brought before an "accuser" at a trial (109:6).

The term "satan" can also refer to divine beings. An angel is called an "adversary" as he stands in the road and blocks Balaam's path (Num. 22:22, 31-32). In Job, "the satan" (i.e., heavenly being) is allowed to take away Job's health and possessions (1–2), and in Zechariah, he appears ready to accuse Joshua the high priest (3:2). In 1 Chronicles "Satan" (a proper name) incites David "to count the people of Israel" (21:1).

During the OT period, though, the term never refers to a demonic being who functions as the antagonist or rival of God. Certain theological developments (such as those related to the problem of evil and the introduction of dualistic thinking during the Persian period), along with the influence of Greek philosophical thought, caused changes in the term's meaning. By the time of the NT, Satan emerges as the personification of the spirit of evil who actively tries to thwart God's plans.

The NT makes frequent references to Satan (Greek, *satan*) or the devil (Greek, *diabolos* [dee-ab'-ol-os]). In the Gospels, Jesus is "tempted by Satan" (Mark 1:12-13) to prove he is the Son of God (Matt. 4:1-11) or to test Jesus' faith (Luke 4:1-13). In the parable of the sower, Satan "takes away the word" as soon as it is sown in individuals (Mark 4:15). Satan can also "enter into" individuals such as Judas Iscariot (Luke 22:3; John 13:27). Satan is the author of evil (Luke 10:19) and is associated with demons that cause physical and psychological disabilities (Matt. 12:22; Luke 13:16).

References to Satan occur in Paul's letters and Revelation. Paul accuses Satan of blocking his return to Thessalonica (1 Thess. 2:18). Sexual immorality and misconduct are the characteristics of those who give into the "temptations of Satan" (1 Cor. 5:5; 7:5; 1 Tim. 1:20; 5:15). A messenger of Satan "torment[s]" Paul by giving him a thorn in his flesh (2 Cor. 12:7). Paul at times equates Satan with a fallen angel (11:14) and calls him the "lawless one" (2 Thess. 2:9). In Revelation, Satan refers to those who slander members of the churches (2:9; 3:9) and teach heresy (2:24). The devil is identified with the dragon (12:9) who will be bound (20:2, 7) and thrown into the abyss "for a thousand years."

Resource
Conrad, Edgar W. "Satan." In vol. 5, *The New Interpreter's Dictionary of the Bible*, edited by Katharine Doob Sakenfeld, 112-16. Nashville: Abingdon Press, 2009.

KEVIN MELLISH, PHD

DISCERNMENT

Christian discernment is (1) a process of **prayer** and critical reflection for identifying God's will (Rom. 12:2); (2) special graces or gifts of the Spirit that help the church know God's will (1 Cor. 12:10); and (3) an evidence of Christian maturity and wisdom exercised in the church (Heb. 5:14). Discernment assumes that God communicates his will. Even then, because all humans are constantly subjected to the ambiguities of human frailty, God's will is not always perfectly discernible. Christians must be cautious when claiming to have discerned God's will.

The OT emphasizes making distinctions between true and false prophets when listening for God's will and when making moral decisions (Deut. 13:1-5; 30:15-20). Jesus, echoing the **wisdom** tradition, encouraged a discerning spirit when evaluating the outcomes of a person's life (Matt. 7:15-20). The NT letters instruct churches to show discernment by "test[ing] everything" against the standard of the gospel (1 Thess. 5:19-22; 1 John 4:1). And Christians must exercise discernment about their own spiritual condition, God's presence, and making significant decisions.

The church has had many instructors on discernment, among them the **desert fathers and mothers**; Thomas à Kempis (ca. 1380–1471), in his *Imitation of Christ*; Francis de Sales (1567–1622), in his *Finding God's Will for You*; Quaker clearness committees; and John Bunyan (1628-88), in his *Pilgrim's Progress*. None have been more influential than Ignatius of Loyola (ca. 1491–1556) and his *Spiritual Exercises*, used by **spiritual directors** to help people know God's will. Ignatius, like John Wesley, gave instruction for hearing the Bible's guidance, sorting through movements of one's heart to distinguish between human impulses and God's Spirit, seeking freedom from disordered **affections**, and adopting the "mind of Christ" (see Phil. 2:5). True discernment is cultivated while following Jesus; it is evidenced in the **fruit of the Spirit** (Gal. 5:22-23).

See also Christian Ethics/Moral Theology; Empathy; Spiritual Direction/Spiritual Director; Spiritual Disciplines; Tempers and Affections.

Resources

Howard, Evan B. "Christian Discernment." In *The Brazos Introduction to Christian Spirituality*, 371-401. Grand Rapids: Brazos Press, 2008.
McIntosh, Mark A. *Discernment and Truth: The Spirituality and Theology of Knowledge*. New York: Crossroad, 2004.

DOUGLAS S. HARDY, PHD

DISCIPLESHIP

Discipleship is the state of having placed oneself under the instruction of a person or doctrine. The Latin origins of the word denote a pupil or student who carefully examines, grasps, and submits to what is being taught. The Greek equivalent in the NT (*mathētēs*) means a "pupil" or "learner." The verb form means to increase in knowledge or to learn by use and practice.

Christian discipleship denotes carefully studying Jesus' teaching, placing oneself under his instruction, and being transformed by him. Christian discipleship means being a pupil (Latin, *discipulus*) of Jesus Christ. In the NT, discipleship refers to the teacher-student relationship in which the learner embodies and lives the teacher's instruction. The noun "disciple[s]" is used repeatedly in the Gospels to refer to Jesus' followers. In Matt. 13:52 **Jesus** refers to those who are "instructed" in (KJV) or "trained" for (NRSV) the **kingdom of God**. In 28:19 Jesus' disciples are instructed to "teach" (KJV) or "make disciples" (NRSV). Acts 14:21 reports that Paul and Barnabas proclaimed the gospel in Derbe and "taught many" (KJV) or "made many disciples" (NRSV).

In Matthew, Jesus' most prominent activity is teaching. He is God's Son and Lord of the church. He uniquely knows his Father's will and can reveal it to others (11:25-30). As the risen Lord, "all authority" has been given to him by his Father (28:18). Jesus' teachings mediate God's presence. Jesus' final words to his disciples, known as the Great Commission, contain clear instruction on the church's mission and Christian discipleship (Matt. 28:18-20). (1) The church is to make disciples of all nations; (2) fulfilling Jesus' commission ends not with proclaiming the gospel and making converts but with the formation of disciples as members of Christ's **church**, where he is Lord; (3) discipleship entails transformation in all the dimensions of life affected by Jesus' teachings ("teaching them to obey everything" [v. 20]); and (4) Jesus is the Authority and Model for discipleship ("that I have commanded you" [v. 20]).

The promise in Matthew is that Christ who is "God with us" or "Emmanuel" (1:23) will be with the church in its mission, "to the end of the age" (28:20).

Advancing in discipleship in conformity with Jesus' instruction evidences discipleship (Mark 8:34) and shows the extent of one's dependence on Jesus (John 15:1-11).

The Gospels and Epistles repeatedly emphasize that (1) Christian discipleship is made possible by the **Holy Spirit** (John 16:12-15; Rom. 8:1-17); (2) discipleship entails transformation and discipline of the whole person by Christ (Rom. 12:1-2; 1 Thess. 4:1-8); (3) the process of being discipled and transformed by Jesus is a continual process that never ends (Luke 14:25-33; Phil. 3:12-16); and (4) discipleship has no meaning apart from the church (Matt. 16:18-20; 18:15-20; Eph. 1:15-23).

See also Ecclesiology, New Testament; Evangelism; Sanctification; Spiritual Disciplines; Spiritual Formation/Growth; Theosis (Deification); Vocation and Calling.

JORGE L. JULCA, DMIN

DISPENSATIONALISM

Dispensationalism is a system of theology that originated in Ireland during the nineteenth century among the Plymouth Brethren. Apparently it was developed by John Nelson Darby (1800-1882). A disillusioned Anglican clergyman, Darby began with the dictum "[the church] is in ruin" (1847). Dispensationalism was popularized in North America through the notes of the *Scofield Reference Bible* (1909), edited by Cyrus Ingerson Scofield (1843–1921).

The term "dispensationalism" derives from the belief that the Bible depicts seven dispensations, or periods of time in salvation history. A different basis for the divine-human relation characterizes each dispensation. Each ends in failure and is followed by a subsequent dispensation. The present dispensation is the *church age*, which will end in judgment, a reflection of Darby's negative opinion of Christendom.

Historically, this theology has been so closely related to **fundamentalism** that the two have almost become synonymous.

Like most movements, dispensationalism differs among those who subscribe to it. It has been transformed as some adherents have become more conversant with sound biblical interpretation. Dispensationalists say their commitment to the Bible remains substantially intact despite the changes.

Three phases of the movement have been identified:

1. Classic dispensationalism (ca. 1850–1940s). Distinctive features as identified by Charles C. Ryrie are *(a)* an eternal distinction between Israel and the church; *(b)* a consistently literal principle of interpretation—particularly OT prophecy; and *(c)* a belief that God's ultimate goal is his own glory, not salvation. The latter clearly contrasts with the Wesleyan understanding of divine purpose in history.

These principles resulted in believing the kingdom of God is an earthly, political kingdom that will arrive when national Israel is literally restored to the Promised Land. The church will be secretly "raptured" prior to a "great tribulation" of seven years.

2. Revised dispensationalism (ca. 1950-85). This phase essentially softens the hard distinction between Israel and the church. But it did not completely abandon the *two purposes/two peoples* theory. Some rejected the distinction between the "kingdom of heaven" and the "kingdom of God" earlier dispensationalists had asserted.

3. Progressive dispensationalism (1986–present). Although holding many of the original premises, younger dispensationalists "reject the *two purposes/two peoples* theory . . . and see the changes in redemption history as progressive toward the accomplishment of a unified holistic plan of redemption" (Blaising 1993, 161).

See also Church (Ecclesiology); Eschatology; Eschatology, Biblical; Kingdom of God; Scripture, Wesleyan Approach to.

Resources

Blaising, Craig A., and Darrell L. Bock. *Progressive Dispensationalism.* Wheaton, IL: BridgePoint, 1993.

Darby, John Nelson. "The Public Ruin of the Church: A Reading with J. N. Darby: Notes of a Meeting in London, September, 1847." In *The Collected Writings of J. N. Darby,* 32:392-407. Online Biblical Resource Library. http://www.plymouthbrethren.org/article/11357.

Ryrie, Charles C. *Dispensationalism Today.* Chicago: Moody Press, 1965.

Sandeen, Ernest R. *The Roots of Fundamentalism: British and American Millenarianism, 1800-1930.* Chicago: University of Chicago Press, 1970.

H. RAY DUNNING, PHD

DIVINATION

The term "divination" comes from the Latin word *divinare*, which means "to foresee," "to be inspired by a god." It is a way to contact supernatural spirits in order to gain answers to questions about the future. Divinization is an ancient practice and is prevalent in many cultures and religious groups. It takes many forms. Among them are tea leaf reading, cracked eggs (in ancient China), stolisomancy (how a person dresses), geomancy or earth divination (markings on the ground or the patterns formed by tossed handfuls of soil, rocks, or sand), and tarot card reading.

Those who use divination say that it is practiced to bring healing for body and mind and that sometimes it is used to find solutions to social problems.

The practice of divination was well known in the ancient Middle East, particularly among the Babylonians, who used hepatoscopy (divination by examining a liver). Other ancient methods included augury (determining the will of the gods by the flight of birds), hydromancy (the use of water [see Gen. 44:5]), casting lots (Jon. 1:7-8), astrology (2 Kings 21:5), necromancy (calling up the dead, 1 Sam. 28:7-25), and observing the Urim and Thummim in Hebrew practice (Exod. 28:30; Lev. 8:8; Deut. 33:8). The Urim and Thummim were probably gemstones and used by the high priest to discern God's will.

Although the Bible authorized use of the Urim and Thummim, God commanded the Israelites not to engage in divination (Lev. 19:26, 31; 20:6, 27).

Historically, the Christian church treated divination as pagan and often attempted to eliminate it. The Qur'an also condemns divination as something born of Satan. "O you who believe! intoxicants and games of chance and (sacrificing to) stones set up and (divining by) arrows are only an uncleanness, the Shaitan's [Satan's] work; shun it therefore that you may be successful" (5:90).

See also Deliverance/Exorcism; Demons/Unclean Spirits; Principalities and Powers.

Resources

Loewe, Michael, and Carmen Blacker, eds. *Oracles and Divination*. New York: Shambhala/Random House, 1981.

O'Brien, Paul. *Divination: Sacred Tools for Reading the Mind of God*. Portland, OR: Visionary Networks Press, 2007.

The Qur'an. Translated by M. H. Shakir. Elmhurst, NY: Tahrike Tarsile Qur'an, 1983.

JOSEPH SURAY, PHD

DIVINE COMMAND THEORY

See ETHICS.

DOCTRINE/DOGMA

Doctrine in modern use refers to a formalized statement of either a specific belief or a body of teachings. It may refer to various fields of learning, such as science or economics. In religion, it refers to a logically developed teaching about God or the divine-human relation. The English term is derived from the Latin *doctrina*, meaning "teaching" or "instruction."

The term, infrequently used in English translations of the OT, is a translation of the Hebrew term *leqakh*, which means, "what is received" (see Deut. 32:2; Isa. 29:24). In Hebrew thought, the **Torah** assumed the status of doctrine, the definitive statement of the Mosaic faith. All teachings and practices were evaluated in the light of Torah.

Doctrinal statements in the OT take the form of historical statements of God's mighty acts in delivering his people, rather than as abstract statements of intellectual belief. Deuteronomy 6:21-34 is a prime example of such a "doctrinal" recitation.

The term "doctrine" is used about fifty times in the NT. It is a translation of one of three Greek terms (*logos*, *didaskalia*, and *didachē*), the most frequent being *didachē*, which means "teaching." C. H. Dodd suggested that the NT is composed of two forms of material, *kerygma* and *didachē*, the latter being derived by implication from the *kerygma*, which is the proclamation of the gospel. Jesus' teachings were referred to as "doctrine" (see Matt. 7:28; John 7:16-17, KJV), as was the teaching of the **Pharisees**, a translation of *didaskalia*.

Didaskalia is used more frequently in the later NT writings, suggesting development of formal teachings over time to preserve the purity of the faith. Its unique use in the Pastoral Epistles (1 and 2 Timothy and Titus) has a distinctly ethical implication being qualified as "sound" doctrine. "Sound" (*hugiainō*) is a medical term implying healthful or health giving by contrast to any doctrine that results in less than holy living. This suggests that doctrine has practical implications, not merely intellectual.

Dogma usually refers to a body of teaching firmly established and embodying orthodox teaching as defined by a group. The Apostolic **Fathers** began to use the term in this way to denote the generally agreed-on Christian teachings. Origen and Ignatius did also. Historically, the term is more often used in Roman Catholic theology than in Protestant theology, where doctrinal development is more fluid, this being in the light of **Protestantism**'s deference to **Scripture** as the final authority of truth. However, most orthodox Christian bodies recognize the Apostles' Creed and the formulations of the **ecumenical councils** of Nicaea and Chalcedon as dogma.

See also Church (Ecclesiology); Church Fathers; Historical Theology; Philosophical Theology; Roman Catholicism; Scripture, Theology of; Systematic Theology (Dogmatics).

H. RAY DUNNING, PHD

DOGMA
See DOCTRINE/DOGMA.

DUALISM
See MONISM, DUALISM, PLURALISM.

Ee

EARLY AFRICAN CHRISTIANITY

By the early second century, Christianity had reached Africa and spread rapidly from Egypt to the Strait of Gibraltar. There were concentrations of churches in the Nile Valley and the Medjerda Valley in modern Algeria and Tunisia. Early African Christianity was largely Hellenistic, using Greek and Latin. However, another stream of ancient Christianity, the **Coptic Church**, originated in Egypt. Ancient African Christians contributed significantly to the theological, spiritual, and political development of Christianity throughout the Mediterranean world.

By the mid-second century, Christians at Alexandria, Egypt, had developed a school for advanced theological study. This school gave rise to Origen (ca. 185–ca. 254), one of the most influential exegetes of the ancient **church**. Origen was especially adept at the spiritual or allegorical interpretation of the Bible, a **hermeneutical** method that remained in wide use through much of the Middle Ages. A second African contributor to ancient Christian theology was the Carthaginian apologist Tertullian (ca. 160–ca. 225), who contributed the term *trinitas* and its definition to the theological vocabulary. The early fourth-century bishop Athanasius (ca. 296–373) presided over the Alexandrian church and championed what came to be Nicene orthodoxy. Another highly influential African, Augustine (354–430), presided as bishop of Hippo Regius and produced a stream of seminal theological works that helped shape Western theology for centuries.

In addition to theological contributions, early African Christianity was pivotal in developing Christian **monasticism**. About 270, an Egyptian named Anthony (ca. 251–356) sold his possessions and retreated to the desert to pursue an **ascetic** life of holiness. His disciplined life attracted others. These early monks lived individually in isolated cells. About 320, Pachomius (ca. 290–346) founded a monastery at Tabennisi in the Nile Valley and compiled a rule for the community. The communal or coenobitic form of monasticism is attributed to Pachomius. His rule influenced later monastic contributors such as Basil the Great, John Cassian, and Benedict of Nursia. Pachomius's form of monasticism spread to Greece, Italy, France, and the British Isles.

Ancient Christians used deliberative meetings called **councils** to resolve important theological issues. Here, too, may be detected the influence of early African Christianity. Aside from the Jerusalem Council (Acts 15), two of the earliest known councils were held under the guidance of Cyprian, bishop of Carthage (d. 258). Convened to consider the efficacy of baptism by heretics and the rebaptism of the lapsed, these councils of bishops largely supported Cyprian against Stephen, bishop of Rome. Although Stephen prevailed, the gathering of bishops in council established a precedent for addressing important theological controversies.

See also Asceticism; Church (Ecclesiology); Coptic Orthodoxy; Desert Fathers and Mothers; Ecumenical Councils; Hermeneutics; Monasticism.

Resource
Isichei, Elizabeth Allo. *A History of Christianity in Africa: From Antiquity to the Present.* Grand Rapids: Eerdmans, 1995.

MERLE D. STREGE, THD

EARLY CHURCH

In AD 596, Pope Gregory the Great sent Augustine of Canterbury on mission to Britain. By that year the church had grown from a handful of disciples into a far-flung, increasingly hierarchical institution. This growth can be described in terms of structure, canon and doctrine, sociopolitical setting, and geographical reach.

Structure. The NT refers to "deacons," "presbyters," and "bishops," and the Pastoral Epistles specify leadership qualifications. By the sixth century the clergy had grown into a hierarchy of deacons, priests, bishops, and metropolitans, at the very top of which stood the patriarchs of the five most important sees (jurisdictions): Rome, Alexandria, Antioch, Constantinople, and Jerusalem. Alongside the hierarchy, toward the end of the third century the **monastic** movement emerged in Egypt as another form of Christian calling. Neither truly laypersons nor priests, the **desert fathers and mothers** developed an alternative way of being Christian.

Canon and doctrine. The canon of **Scripture**, especially the NT, was formalized parallel to hierarchical development. The canon shaped the church, and the church shaped the canon. In its earliest stage the church used the Jewish Scriptures (the Septuagint). By the end of the first century Paul's letters were regarded as authoritative. Reception of the four canonical gospels and other books followed until a canon of the NT was joined to the OT as Christian Scripture no later than the mid-fourth century. Alongside the

Bible, Christian apologists employed elements of Greco-Roman thought to defend the faith against its critics. These concepts, Scripture, and the vocabulary employed in worship combined to construct a language appropriate for Christians. In the **ecumenical councils** church bishops debated, and the creeds that emerged (**Nicene** and **Chalcedonian**) eventually defined the theological implications of that language. Thus the early church formulated what became the orthodox statements of Christian faith on such doctrines as the **Trinity**, the person of **Christ**, and the **incarnation**.

Sociopolitical setting. The place of the church in society was dramatically reversed during antiquity. By AD 600 the faith of a tiny, persecuted minority had been transformed into the official religion of the Byzantine Empire. Emperor Nero's persecution of Christians in AD 64 set a precedent for persecution. By the turn of the century Christians were persecuted sporadically and regionally. Persecution formally ended with the Edict of Galerius in 311 and the more famous Edict of Milan, issued by Constantine and Licinius (313). Constantine's Christian conversion inaugurated further dramatic changes. He became the church's patron, diverting imperial funds from pagan temples to churches for projects such as producing Bibles and constructing churches. Christianity enjoyed the status of an imperially recognized religion until the reign of Theodosius (379-95), a ruthless persecutor of pagans. By the end of his reign Christianity had become the official religion of a "Christian empire," and the church its formal institution.

Geographical reach. By AD 600 the church had spread beyond the Christian empire. Until the end of the second century churches were concentrated mainly in the eastern Mediterranean. By the end of the fourth century the church had spread as far west as Roman Britain and east to Persia (tradition claims that the apostle Thomas carried the faith to India). Churches could be found north of the Rhine-Danube border among the Germanic tribes. In the fifth century Patrick carried the gospel to the Celtic peoples. Later that century Gregory the Great commissioned Augustine of Canterbury, an act which spread the authority of the Roman, papal church to England.

See also Bible; Christology; Church (Ecclesiology); Ecumenical Councils; Incarnation; Trinity.

Resources
Chadwick, Henry. *The Early Church.* The Penguin History of the Church 1. Rev. ed. London: Penguin, 1993.
González, Justo L. *The Early Church to the Dawn of the Reformation.* Vol. 1, *The Story of Christianity.* Rev. ed. San Francisco: HarperOne, 2010.

MERLE D. STREGE, THD

ECCLESIOLOGY
See CHURCH (ECCLESIOLOGY).

ECCLESIOLOGY, NEW TESTAMENT

The NT presents the **church** as the people of the new **covenant**. It does not replace **Israel** but fulfills Israel's commission to be a light of knowledge and truth to the nations. As such, God extends Israel's gifts of election, covenantal promise, messianic visitation, **Scripture**, and **salvation** to the church. The church is not equivalent to the **kingdom of God** but represents the emergence of God's kingdom on the earth.

In the **Gospels**, the church is a fellowship that bears the good news of Jesus' **resurrection** and the promise of salvation (Matt. 16:24-26; Mark 16:15; Luke 24:44-49; John 20:26-31). However, in Matthew the church is more specifically presented as Israel's expanding **mission** to the nations, that mission being embodied in the ministry of Jesus' original disciples. The Greek term *ekklēsia* that Jesus uses in Matthew, may, like the Hebrew *qahal*, be better understood as "assembly" instead of "church." On the other hand, Jesus envisioned more than a reform movement within **Judaism**. He anticipated the creation of a new community as a result of the disciples' mission to the nations.

Mark sees the followers of Jesus as the first flowering of the kingdom of God. John the Baptist and Jesus urge people to repent because the kingdom is at hand. The parable of the sower in Mark (4:3-9) eventually portrays the acceptance of Jesus' kingdom preaching, which is both the preparation for and appearance of the kingdom.

In Luke-Acts the church is the end-time community of the **Holy Spirit**. Although Luke does not see the **parousia** as imminent, clearly the church serves in the final period before the end.

In the gospel of John and the Johannine epistles the church is the elect community gathered around a core leadership of eyewitnesses to Jesus' resurrection (John 17:6-26; 1 John 1:1-4; 2 John vv. 7-11). Admittedly, the concept of the church in John and the Johannine epistles is rather sectarian. Jesus invites those who believe, but have not seen, into an insular fellowship in possession of an exclusive truth—an emphasis that seems to arise out of the gospel writer's war against false teaching.

Although Paul views the church as an expectant fellowship of saints awaiting the Lord's return, he offers a wide range of metaphors to describe the church. It is the body of Christ, the colony of heaven, the bride of Christ, the new creation, and a house of mixed utensils (1 Cor. 12:27; Phil. 3:20; Eph. 5:25-33; 2 Cor. 5:17; 2 Tim. 2:20-21). Paul addresses the relationship between the church and Israel in Romans. Clearly, God has not rejected Israel. Whether Israel will be saved as a result of the gospel mission or a special act of God, Paul still advocates a gospel mission to the Jews because those who become believers in Christ sanctify the remainder. Paul declares that after the full number of Gentiles are saved, "all Israel will be saved" (Rom.

11:26). Whether or not "all Israel" includes the church, Paul sees the church as a multicultural, gender-inclusive, socially liberating fellowship.

There are additional images of the church in the NT: the once and for all redeemed people of Christ (Heb. 7:23-28); a chosen race, a royal priesthood, a holy people (1 Pet. 2:9); and the true and faithful witnesses (Rev. 7:14; 17:6, 14).

John Wesley thought of the church as "a congregation, or body of people, united together in the service of God" (*Works*, 6:392). He emphasized the "called-out" character of the church and condemned superficial or merely formalistic identification with the church.

See also Christology; Creation/New Creation; Early Church.

Resources
Brower, Kent E., and Andy Johnson, eds. *Holiness and Ecclesiology in the New Testament.* Grand Rapids: Eerdmans, 2007.
Kimbrough, S. T., Jr., ed. *Orthodox and Wesleyan Ecclesiology.* Crestwood, NY: St Vladimir's Seminary Press, 2007.

KENNETH L. WATERS SR., PHD

ECOLOGY
See CREATION, CARE FOR THE (ECOLOGY).

ECONOMICS AND THE USE OF MONEY

"Economics" is an ancient term that originally implied much more than exchange of money. It comes from two Greek words: *oikos* (household) and *nomos* (law or rule). Its basic definition had to do with how one ruled or structured a household. This could refer to how a householder organized a house, a ruler ran an empire, or God ordered creation. Consequently, the term was closely associated with politics. It also related to understanding nature. For instance, the OT, ancient philosophers, and the NT assume God so ordered nature that certain things could not be done without provoking harmful consequences. One such harm was using money to make money—usury. Money could not legitimately have this use because doing so produced nothing. But money could be used legitimately to do other things, such as buying sheep or a farm and hoping this purchase would yield a profit. It would be unintelligible and contrary to nature to say, as is said today, "My money is working for me."

Moreover, not everything could be given a value and exchanged; some things were not for sale. The adage "everything and everyone has a price" would have been nonsensical. Likewise, not all time was to be used for exchanging goods. The expression "24/7" would have violated the Sabbath.

The early Wesleyan General Rules reflect this basic ethic of money. They prohibited practices such as buying and selling on the Sabbath, buying or selling slaves, and "giving or taking things on usury." This economic ethic changed in the modern era, especially with the rationalization of economics that occurred beginning with the publication of Adam Smith's 1776 *The Wealth of Nations*. Smith's title draws upon Isaiah's biblical prophecy concerning Israel's restoration. When God restores Israel, it will enjoy the "wealth of the nations" (Isa. 61:6). Smith extended the promise to his readers; they will inherit "the wealth of nations."

However, wealth will come not as God's gift but through free-market principles Smith laid down. *First*, each individual should act on his or her self-interest. *Second*, no one should have an unfair advantage. *Third*, if these principles are adhered to, an "invisible hand" will insure an optimum outcome. Although Smith himself was a moral philosopher, after *The Wealth of Nations* a tradition of economic theory emerged that eventually separated it from politics and morality. Economics became a supposedly neutral mathematical discipline, independent of moral and political norms.

Christian theologians debate the merits of a supposedly morally neutral free market. Some see it as "heretical" and responsible for the secularization of Western society, even the "death of God." Some economists agree. Alfred Marshall, responsible for "supply and demand curves," said modern economics "put man in the saddle," in control of our own destiny and no longer relying on nonempirical sources such as God (Skidelsky 1992, 170). Other theologians say the free market is a neutral mechanism. Its rationality can be discovered by employing social sciences and without theological intervention. Economics provides the "facts," while theology, at best, offers "values." Still others see the free market as a positive fruit of Christianity. This debate among Christian theologians has at times been strident.

See also Capitalism; Creation, Care for the (Ecology); Justice; Kingdom of God; Secular/Secularism/Secularization; Self-Denial; Social Ethics; Social Justice; Technology, Ethic of; Wealth; Works of Mercy.

Resource
Skidelsky, Robert. *John Maynard Keynes: The Economist as Savior, 1920-1937.* London: Penguin Books, 1992.

D. STEPHEN LONG, PHD

ECUMENICAL COUNCILS

Ancient church councils can be defined as meetings that gathered representatives from many individual churches to consider matters of widespread importance to the **church**. Numerous councils and synods met, but "ecumenical," from the Greek word *oikoumenē*, meaning "the whole inhabited earth," designated seven councils between 325 and 787. These councils were said to have gathered representatives of the whole church throughout the world (i.e., the Roman Empire).

The Council of Nicaea in 325 was the first to be named ecumenical. Called by Emperor Constantine, who understood himself to be head of the church as well as the empire, the council was intended to settle a dispute between the Alexandrian presbyter Arius and Alexander, bishop of that city. Arius asserted that the Word (*Logos*), which was incarnate as **Jesus**, was not divine in the same sense as **God**. Two test words, *homoiousion* (of similar substance) and *homoousion* (of one substance) formed the poles of the debate. The latter triumphed and became the anchor of the Nicene Creed.

In 381, the Council of Constantinople convened to resolve issues remaining after Nicaea. Bishops at this council substituted their own version of a general creed for the Nicene. This new version, formally known as the Niceno-Constantinopolitan Creed, is the one affirmed as the Nicene in Christian churches. It includes a larger section than the original on the **Holy Spirit** and the **Trinity**, thanks largely to the work of the Cappadocian theologians—Basil the Great, Gregory of Nyssa, and Gregory of Nazianzus.

Convened in 431 to deal with teaching associated with Nestorius, patriarch of Constantinople, the Council of Ephesus condemned this view as heresy. Nestorius was said to have taught that two separate persons, one divine and one human, resided in the incarnate Christ. Against this view the council affirmed that **Christ** was a single person simultaneously God and human. Under the domination of Cyril of Alexandria, this council also formally identified **Mary** as *Theotokos*, the "God-bearer" or "Mother of God."

In 451, bishops met at Chalcedon for the fourth ecumenical council, noteworthy on two counts. Preeminently, this council issued the Definition of Faith of the Council of Chalcedon, which defined Christ as "very God of very God" and "very man of very man," phrases that have been orthodox Christian doctrine ever since. Second, although absent, Pope Leo the Great played a key role in council deliberations by sending his famous *Tome*, a lengthy definition of the person of Christ delineating the orthodox position. That his letter served this function bolstered subsequent Roman claims for supreme papal ecclesiastical authority.

In the sixth century a lengthy controversy developed around the teachings of three Eastern theologians—Theodore of Mopsuestia, Theodoret of Cyrrhus, and Ibas of Edessa. The Emperor Justinian issued decrees against the Three Chapters, as they were called, because in his eyes they had too much in common with Nestorianism. Not all agreed with the emperor, and the matter dragged on until he convened the fifth ecumenical council, the second to be held at Constantinople, in 553. Although disputed for a time by Pope Vigilius, the council upheld the condemnation of the Three Chapters.

During 680-81, again at Constantinople, the sixth ecumenical council met to resolve another **Christological** question. At issue was whether Christ had two wills—one divine and one human—or one will for his divine-human person. The latter view is called Monothelitism (one will), and bishops at the sixth council condemned it as a heresy.

In 726 the Emperor Leo the Isaurian condemned the use of **icons**, calling them **idols**, and ordered them destroyed. His edict was met with resistance, especially in the monasteries. This Iconoclastic Controversy continued unabated in the Greek-speaking church, also reaching into the West. The seventh ecumenical council met in Nicaea in 787 and restored icons in the church even as the bishops defined appropriate veneration of images.

See also Christ; Christology; Church (Ecclesiology); Creeds (Nicene, Chalcedonian, Apostles', Athanasian); God, Doctrine of; Holy Spirit (Pneumatology); Icons, Images, Iconoclasm; Idolatry; Jesus of Nazareth; Mary/Mariology; Monasticism; Trinity.

Resources
Need, Stephen W. *Truly Divine and Truly Human: The Story of Christ and the Seven Ecumenical Councils.* Peabody, MA: Hendrickson Publishers, 2008.
Tanner, Norman P. *The Councils of the Church: A Short History.* New York: Crossroad, 2001.

MERLE D. STREGE, PHD

ECUMENISM

The term "ecumenism" (*oikoumenē*) refers in the NT to the "whole inhabited earth" (see Matt. 24:14, author's translation). A related meaning pertains to the "whole of the church" and connotes that which is accepted and authoritative throughout the whole church. "Ecumenism" also refers to engagement within history on behalf of the unity of the church. The adjective, "ecumenical," particularly in the phrase "the ecumenical movement," connects with this last meaning and underscores a deep commitment to Christian unity.

In harmony with John Wesley's "Letter to a Roman Catholic" (1749), which emphasizes mutual concern and respect between different branches of the Christian church, Methodists have been at the vanguard of ecumenism since the mid-nineteenth century. Methodists participated in the Evangelical Alliance (1846) and in ecumenical student movements such as the YMCA (1844) and YWCA (1854). In the twentieth century, Methodist leadership was pivotal for the World Missionary Conference (WMC) in Edinburgh (1910). Methodist layman John R. Mott (1865–1955) was a central twentieth-century ecumenical leader. He chaired the WMC and wrote a book on its theme (*Evangelization of the World in This Generation*). He also chaired the Continuation Committee after the WMC and the International Missionary Council, which merged four decades later with the World Council of Churches (WCC). Mott served as honorary president of the WCC.

Methodists continue to provide valuable ecumenical service under the umbrella of the WCC at every level, including three general secretaries:

Emilio Castro (1985-92), Philip Potter (1972-84), and Samuel Kobia (2004-9). Some Methodist bodies, such as the Evangelical Methodist Church, Free Methodist Church, and Primitive Methodist Church, express their ecumenism through membership in the National Association of Evangelicals instead of the WCC.

A significant portion of Methodist ecumenism relates to intra-Methodist unity, both internationally and nationally. An early international gathering of Methodist groups for cooperation and fellowship was the Ecumenical Methodist Conference. Its first meeting, in 1881, hosted delegates representing 28 Methodist bodies from 20 countries. It convened every ten years until 1931. Two decades later, another international organization for Methodists formed, the World Methodist Council. It meets every five years. During the most recent World Methodist Council meeting, 76 member churches from 132 countries were represented.

Within national borders, ecumenical work results in the reunification of Methodist bodies. Following the first meeting of the Ecumenical Methodist Conference, discussions among Methodist bodies in Canada ensued. Three years later (1884) a formal union of Canadian Methodists occurred.

American Methodism's gravest division occurred over slavery. This led to establishing separate Methodist Episcopal Church denominations in the North and in the South. In 1939, these two Methodist bodies, along with the Methodist Protestant Church, reunited to form one denomination, the Methodist Church. Then in 1968, the United Methodist Church emerged from the union of the Methodist Church and the Evangelical United Brethren Church. In the mid-1970s, the Commission on Pan-Methodist Cooperation and Union (now the Pan-Methodist Commission) organized to discuss interracial and ecumenical goals shared by the African Methodist Episcopal Church, the African Methodist Episcopal Zion Church, the Christian Methodist Episcopal Church, and the United Methodist Church. This now includes six denominations.

Within British Methodism, mergers occurred in the twentieth century. In 1907, the Methodist New Connexion, the Bible Christian Church, and the United Methodist Free Churches united to form the United Methodist Church. Then in 1932, the Methodist Union brought about a merger between the United Methodist Church, Wesleyan Methodism, and the Primitive Methodists to form the Methodist Church in Great Britain.

Methodists have joined ecumenical partnerships with other denominations to form new united churches such as the Church of South India (1947), the United Church of Christ in the Philippines (1948), the Evangelical United Church of Ecuador (1965), and the Uniting Church in Australia (1977).

See also Holiness Movements: American, British, and Continental; Pentecostalism; World Methodism; World Methodist Council.

PRISCILLA POPE-LEVISON, PHD

EDUCATION AND DISCIPLESHIP
See SPIRITUAL FORMATION/GROWTH.

EMERGENT CHURCH THEOLOGY

There are multiple definitions of emergent and what it means to be part of the emergent conversation. Most interpreters agree that it means something new coming forth out of the old (usually **modernity**). It is a movement that rethinks ecclesial practices and theology. What makes the emergent conversation unique is that it promotes a "generous orthodoxy" and refuses to be bound by one particular denominational or theological perspective (see McLaren 2004, 15-25).

The emergent conversation is characterized by four themes: (1) the importance of dialogue, (2) worship, (3) community, and (4) missional focus. Theologically, these themes have things in common with the Wesleyan tradition, especially John Wesley and the early Methodists.

First, theology involves a dialogue between the past and present **church.** "Emergents" avoid ready-made theological answers because they are in dialogue about the nuances of biblical texts as they bear on Christian practice. In addition to dialogue with contemporaries, dialogue includes theological giants of the past. John Wesley corresponded with his contemporaries about challenging theological issues and held conferences among Methodists to discuss theology and practice. But he also drew heavily on Christians of the past. For both emergents and Wesley, theology is neither simply an academic enterprise nor a matter of practice. Instead, it involves an ongoing dialogue that requires living at the intersection of thinking and doing, past and present.

Second, **worship** is more than a weekly gathering of individuals. It is participatory; it engages the whole person and enables him or her to think and act more deeply as a Christian who has encountered the risen Christ. The goal of worship is not simply to add creative elements that attract "young people." Instead, worship continues a theological dialogue that invites Christians to know Christ holistically. Wesleyan **classes and bands** often operated in a similar way. Individuals came not to observe but to participate in the Holy Spirit's ongoing work of transformation.

Third, community is more than just a voluntary association of individuals. Through an emphasis on persons as constituted by relations, emergents envision a more communal understanding of Christian faith. Early Wesleyan classes were likewise structured to promote community and accountability. Wesley believed all Christian holiness to be "social holiness." Neither the emergents nor Wesley deny the importance of the individual, but they both invite a rethinking of how we understand ourselves in relation to others.

Fourth, many in the emergent conversation urge a missional approach to theology that focuses on the importance of **discipleship**. Wesley and the early Methodists also focused on discipleship. In both instances a discipleship that transforms personal daily practices and how the body of Christ should live out those practices is promoted.

See also Mission, Theology of; Wesley, John, Theology of.

Resources

Anderson, Ray. *An Emergent Theology for Emerging Churches.* Downers Grove, IL: Inter-Varsity Press, 2006.

Jones, Tony. *The New Christians: Dispatches from the Emergent Frontier.* San Francisco: Jossey-Bass, 2008.

McLaren, Brian. *A Generous Orthodoxy.* Grand Rapids: Zondervan, 2004.

F. DOUGLAS POWE JR., PHD

EMPATHY

Empathy is (1) a capacity to identify with and participate in another's feelings, ideas, or experience; (2) the process of entering what another is experiencing; and (3) a relational skill for understanding another person's distress.

The term "empathy" is absent in the Bible and ancient Christian theology. But "sympathy" and "compassion" convey much the same meaning. "Empathy" was introduced into English vocabulary by modern relational philosophy (e.g., Martin Buber's *I and Thou* [1923]) and the **social sciences**—especially psychotherapy and counseling (Carl Rogers' *Client-Centered Therapy* [1951])—to provide a nuanced alternative to negative and limiting connotations of "sympathy" and "compassion." "Sympathy" can carry overtones of pity and condescension (see Job's "comforters").

The Scriptures disclose a relational and compassionate God who so closely identifies with the creation that he moves out to it in **love** (Ps. 103:13-14). Jesus embodies sympathy and compassion for others (Matt. 15:32; 20:32-34; Luke 7:11-13; Heb. 4:15) as an expression of his deity. The Holy Spirit communicates and facilitates God's empathy (Rom. 8:22-27) to believers. Consequently, Christians are to be empathic as God is (Phil. 2:1-4; 1 Pet. 3:8). They are to act toward others as God does—with mercy (Luke 10:33-37) and forgiveness (Eph. 4:32).

Research in **evolutionary biology**, the social psychology of altruism, the social and moral development of children, and counseling outcomes demonstrates that empathy is required for human flourishing. It is foundational for wholesome interpersonal relationships and for creating community. This is because empathy facilitates trust and **ubuntu**. The capacity for empathy originates when early experiences of being parented are marked by sensitivity and responsiveness to basic needs. Conversely, a failure to develop empathy results in an inability to relate to others (Matt. 18:23-33). In extreme instances, psychopathologies such as attachment or antisocial personality disorders occur.

To extend empathy to another, one must become self-emptying (**kenosis**) as Jesus was in order to see things from another's perspective and join in that person's suffering (Phil. 2:5-7). John Wesley noted that true empathy for the poor and afflicted requires being with them in acts or **works of mercy**.

See also Discernment; Hospitability/Hospitality; Self-Denial; Social Sciences; Works of Mercy.

Resources
Nouwen, Henri J. M. *The Wounded Healer: Ministry in Contemporary Society.* Garden City, NY: Doubleday Books, 1972.
Weavings: A Journal of the Christian Spiritual Life 5, no. 6 (November/December 1990).
DOUGLAS S. HARDY, PHD

EMPIRICISM
See EPISTEMOLOGY.

ENLIGHTENMENT

The Enlightenment (or the Age of Enlightenment), refers to the flowering of a diverse intellectual spirit and outlook that dominated much of Western Europe during the eighteenth century. Gertrude Himmelfarb identifies three branches of the Enlightenment, each with its own primary emphasis: France (reason), Britain (social virtues), and America (political liberty) (2004, 19). Many of the Enlightenment's themes were developing in the second half of the seventeenth century. Its roots are traceable to the rising humanism of the fourteenth and fifteenth centuries.

The Enlightenment is characterized more by a general outlook or attitude than by assent to particular beliefs or doctrines; its diversity can be seen among many of its leading figures: Voltaire, David Hume, Denis Diderot, Jean-Jacques Rousseau, John Locke, and Immanuel Kant. Despite its diversity, a central theme in the Enlightenment is optimism about human reason. Though medieval philosophers and theologians believed in the ability of human reason to come to truth, Enlightenment figures saw reason as independent of the need for divine revelation or ecclesial authority, traditions, and institutions. The central thrust of the Enlightenment is captured in the paradigmatic first paragraph of Immanuel Kant's *Was ist Aufklärung?* (*What Is Enlightenment?*), first published in 1784:

> Enlightenment is man's emergence from his self-incurred immaturity. Immaturity is the inability to use one's own understanding without the guidance of another. This immaturity is *self-incurred* if its cause is not lack of

understanding, but lack of resolution and courage to use it without the guidance of another. The motto of enlightenment is therefore: *Sapere Aude!* [Dare to be wise!] Have courage to use your *own* understanding!" (1991, 1)

Enlightenment figures criticized the **metaphysical** and religious starting point of medieval Christendom and began instead with **epistemology.** Their dominant epistemology was empiricism, and their focus on the "science of man" prompted a flourishing of the physical and social sciences (e.g., psychology, sociology, and economics).

The Enlightenment was not confined to intellectual concerns but also sought to bring about social change. This is best seen in France as evidenced in the clash between its entrenched aristocracy and its large and powerful middle class, namely, the bourgeoisie. The clash finally resulted in the French Revolution (1789-99). In contrast to the institution of an absolute monarch and the privilege of hereditary nobility, Enlightenment political ideals can be seen in the French Revolutionary motto "Liberty, equality, and fraternity."

Not only did the Enlightenment criticize the old social and political order, but it also hoped to establish a new order founded upon individual rights, personal autonomy, and equality before the law. Enlightenment figures also helped establish influential social groups such as the Academy of Sciences in France and the Royal Society of London, both of which helped train new scientists and increase their public social status and influence. This effort spread Enlightenment ideas even further.

See also Cosmology/Cosmogony; Deism; Epistemology; Intelligent Design; Metaphysics; Modernity; Natural Science; Religious Freedom; Social Sciences.

Resources

Brown, Stewart J., and Timothy Tackett, eds. *Enlightenment, Reawakening, and Revolution 1660–1815.* Vol. 7, *Cambridge History of Christianity.* New York: Cambridge University Press, 2007.

Frazer, Michael L. *The Enlightenment of Sympathy: Justice and the Moral Sentiments in the Eighteenth Century and Today.* Oxford, UK: Oxford University Press, 2010.

Himmelfarb, Gertrude. *The Roads to Modernity: The British, French, and American Enlightenments.* New York: Random House, 2004.

Kant, Immanuel. *An Answer to the Question: What Is Enlightenment?* Translated by H. B. Nisbet. New York: Penguin Books, 1991.

KEVIN TIMPE, PHD

ENTIRE SANCTIFICATION

See CHRISTIAN PERFECTION (ENTIRE SANCTIFICATION); SANCTIFICATION.

ENVIRONMENTALISM

See CREATION, CARE FOR THE (ECOLOGY).

EPICLESIS

See SACRAMENTS.

EPISTEMOLOGY

The term "epistemology," meaning "theory of knowledge," derives from two Greek words: *epistēmē* (knowledge) and *logos* (word, account). It is the part of philosophy that investigates knowledge—its nature, scope, sources, and structure. Much of the continuing concern over the nature of knowledge has centered on identifying the conditions that rationally justify belief. The effort began with Plato (429–347 BC) and continues in contemporary epistemological discussions.

One longstanding concern about the scope of knowledge is the challenge of epistemic skepticism. This is the view that knowledge cannot be obtained. Historically, skepticism ranges from the nearly "global" epistemic skepticisms advocated by Carneades (ca. 214-ca. 129 BC), David Hume (1711-76), and Friedrich Nietzsche (1844–1900) to the more "local" epistemic skepticisms of René Descartes (1596–1650) and Willard Van Orman Quine (1908–2000). *Global* skepticism holds there are no rationally justified, true beliefs that achieve knowledge in any sphere of investigation. This is because of the fallibility and circularity necessarily involved in human believing. Most epistemologists reject global skepticism because of its self-refuting inconsistency. If there is no knowledge in any sphere of investigation, then global skepticism cannot be known either. *Local* skepticism holds there are some rationally justified, true beliefs that obtain knowledge.

A critical examination of the sources of knowledge is primarily interested in the extent to which specific cognitive practices provide legitimate knowledge. Typically, epistemology examines such potential sources as sense perception, memory, introspection, and reason. But recently, rich investigations of religious perceptions and revelation as possible sources of knowledge have produced significant results.

Perhaps the most important epistemological problem is the debate over rationalism and empiricism. Rationalism argues that at least part of the content of knowledge is *a priori* (prior to) sense experience. Empiricism, on the other hand, holds that knowledge arises exclusively *a posteriori* (after) sense experience. The modern debate over rationalism and empiricism was initiated by the Continental rationalists, including René Descartes, Gottfried Leibniz (1646–1716), and Baruch Spinoza (1632-77), and the British empiricists, including John Locke (1632–1704), George Berkeley (1685–1753), and David Hume. The Continental rationalists favored a priori (clear, distinct, adequate, or intuitive) ideas or necessary truths (similar to those found in mathematics and deductive logic) as the basis for knowledge. The British empiricists defended knowledge based primarily on ideas resulting from sense experience. Their views increasingly narrowed knowledge to what can be derived from sense experience. This ultimately formed the basis for Hume's skepticism (*A Treatise of Human Nature* [1739]) about the external world, induction, causation, God, human immortality, and free will.

Kant's epistemology in the *Critique of Pure Reason* (1781) attempted to answer Hume's skepticism by showing that a posteriori empirical experience, combined with a priori rational thought, constructs (rather than discovers) scientific and perceptual knowledge. It does this by means of synthetic a priori judgments that are necessary and universal to rational minds. In doing this, however, Kant's proposal displaced metaphysical knowledge of God, human immortality, and human free will in favor of a more limited role for the practical world of morality.

Recent epistemology has focused on foundationalism, the view that knowledge consists in *nonbasic* beliefs ultimately based on, and justified by, *properly basic* beliefs as their foundation. The key issue is whether the criteria of properly basic beliefs are limited to incorrigibility and self-evidence or to evidence derived from the senses. Alvin Plantinga's reformed epistemology has criticized this by pointing out that what constitutes proper basicality does not itself satisfy incorrigibility, self-evidence, or being evident to the senses, thus making foundationalism self-refuting. He then develops a soft foundationalism that identifies other kinds of defeatable, grounded, and properly basic beliefs, such as believing in God on the basis of the religious perception.

John Wesley's epistemology reflects much of the distinctive outlook of modern empiricism, but with important differences. It affirms the natural empirical sources of generalized human experience, systematic science, and the inner experience of the spiritual senses. However, Wesley rejected the enthusiasm of privatized experience. He often regulated experience by using Scripture and well-developed Aristotelian logic. Scripture is the primary, legitimate source of religious knowledge (revelation), but it must be carefully interpreted by the use of reason (logic) and tradition. All of these—Scripture, tradition, reason, and experience—together form Wesley's quadrilateral epistemology for true Christian faith and life.

See also Logical Positivism; Metaphysics; Natural Theology; Quadrilateral, Wesleyan.

Resources
Alston, William P. *Perceiving God: The Epistemology of Religious Experience*. Ithaca, NY: Cornell University Press, 1991.

Audi, Robert. *Belief, Justification, and Knowledge.* Belmont, CA: Wadsworth Publishing, 1988.

Swinburne, Richard. *Revelation: From Metaphor to Analogy.* New York: Oxford University Press, 1992.

LINCOLN STEVENS, PHD

ESCHATOLOGY

The term "eschatology" comes from the Greek word *eschatos.* One meaning is "final" or "latest." In theology, eschatology refers to the "final things" associated with God completing his plan of redemption. Traditionally, eschatology was treated as the last in a series of Christian doctrines. It was almost exclusively oriented toward the future.

That is no longer true. Biblical and systematic theologians now realize that for the NT, Christ himself is God's *eschaton,* God's "final word or act." The gospel itself is eschatological because it is good news about the inauguration of the long-anticipated **kingdom of God.** John the Baptist prophesied the kingdom's arrival (Mark 1:1-11). Jesus came preaching the good news that in him the kingdom was arriving (vv. 14-15). Luke says the "Spirit of the Lord" was upon Jesus as he proclaimed the kingdom's arrival (4:14-19). Ephesians declares that in Christ, God "made known to us the mystery of his will . . . as a plan for the fullness of time" (1:9-10).

Scholars recognize in the NT a distinction between kingdom inauguration and kingdom consummation, between the "already" and the "not yet." The *eschaton* is still advancing. Only when all things have been brought under Christ's subjection (1 Cor. 15:28), and he "hands over" the completed kingdom to his Father (15:24), will the *eschaton* be "accomplished" (Eph. 1:9-11). The church lives in the "between times"; it lives *from* the "already" and *toward* the "not yet."

The creative tension between the "already" and the "not yet" doesn't ignore the past. Eschatology includes God's faithfulness in the past as a basis for understanding present and future fulfillment.

Early in the twentieth century Albert Schweitzer and Johannes Weiss developed a biblical understanding of eschatology. But not until the mid-twentieth century did eschatology acquire its current meaning, prompted largely by British theologian C. H. Dodd, who introduced the concept of "realized eschatology" as Christ's inauguration of the kingdom. He also popularized the distinction between the "already" and the "not yet." More recently, the German theologians Jürgen Moltmann (*Theology of Hope* [1967]) and Wolfhart Pannenberg (*Basic Questions in Theology* [1970]) have enriched the current understanding.

Moltmann and Pannenberg made eschatology a theological topic of the first order, rather than placing it at the end as had traditionally been done.

Eschatology as the inaugurated and future hope, yet to be fulfilled in history, provided their basis for understanding all Christian theology.

Paul approached eschatology on the basis of two events: Jesus' death and resurrection. He speaks of "Christ in you, the hope of glory" (Col. 1:27). Christ's death summed up human history. His cross and resurrection reconciled humanity to God, to creation, and to others. Through Christ, at **Pentecost** the eschatological Spirit was poured out on all Jesus' disciples (Joel 2:28-29; Acts 2:14-21), making the risen Christ present in the **church**. Through the Spirit, Christ is now effecting new creation (Rom. 8:2; 2 Pet. 3:13; Rev. 21:1-5).

Eschatology recognizes sin's destructive power. But in Christ the victory over sin has already been won (Col. 2:13-15). The church now lives to announce this reality to persons and to the creation (Rom. 8:18-25; Eph. 3:10).

Integral to eschatology is the church's mission to proclaim the good news. This places enormous responsibility on Christian theology; it must faithfully serve the mission assigned to the church by its Lord (Matt. 28:18-20).

See also Creation/New Creation; Dispensationalism; Eschatology, Biblical; Heaven; Resurrection; Second Coming of Christ/Parousia; Systematic Theology (Dogmatics); Trinity.

Resources

Bauckham, Richard, and Trevor Hart. *Hope Against Hope: Christian Eschatology in Contemporary Context.* London: Darton, Longman, and Todd, 1999.

Brower, Kent E. "'Let the Reader Understand': Temple and Eschatology in Mark." In *Eschatology in Bible and Theology: Evangelical Essays at the Dawn of a New Millennium,* edited by Kent E. Brower and Mark W. Elliott. Downers Grove, IL: InterVarsity Press, 1997.

DAVID RAINEY, PHD

ESCHATOLOGY, BIBLICAL

Eschatology is usually defined as the doctrine of last things. But biblical eschatology is better defined as the direction and goal of God's covenant faithfulness in and for his created order. This definition is Trinitarian in shape, Christocentric in focus, creation affirming, and future orientated. God's good purposes are already being realized.

Biblical eschatology begins and ends with the triune God. From creation to consummation, Scripture shows how God's purposes intersect with creation. Jesus' incarnation marks the climax of OT hopes. Thus, the kingdom is a present reality, established in Jesus' death and resurrection and publicly confirmed by the outpouring of the Spirit. Through the Spirit in the church, the power of the age to come influences the present. God's renewed people, a kingdom of priests and a holy nation, are the vanguard of God's purposes. They are on God's mission. Through the Spirit they model God's triune life communally and individually.

But God's people still live in mortal flesh and are subject to weakness, decay and death, and temptation. They live in an environment under evil's hostile dominion as manifested in diverse personal and societal forms. Christians suffer for their witness to the truth. Even the Spirit's presence is but a foretaste of God's ultimate good purposes.

This dynamic tension between the "already" and the "not yet" is at the heart of biblical eschatology: the kingdom is present *and* coming. The resurrection of the body, death's defeat, the end of all opposition, and the redemption of the created order, all await consummation in Christ.

Three elements shape biblical eschatology. *First,* Christ remains at the center, the embodiment and goal of God's purposes. *Second,* what occurs in life now matters. Judgment signals that God cares about creation and that evil will not prevail. The fate of those who put themselves outside God's ultimate purposes is described in diverse ways. Their self-chosen destiny is not God's intention for them. *Third,* the story ends in the triumph of God in Christ. The new heaven and new earth in which the holy God dwells among a holy people is the glorious hope of those who are in Christ, and for God's whole creation. With this hope in view, God's people face the present with confidence in the God who raised Jesus from the dead.

Attempts to provide a road map to the future from Scripture are misguided. No matter how popular elaborate timetables or dispensational schemes might be, they miss the genius of biblical eschatology and its breathtaking scope. They reduce it to a cryptic puzzle solvable by those who supposedly have the key.

But if details are unclear, the direction is not: God's good purposes for his created order come to rest in Christ. Herein lies the Christian hope.

See also Eschatology; Hope, Christian; Kingdom of God; Resurrection; Second Coming of Christ/Parousia.

Resources

Brower, Kent E. "Eschatology." In *The New Dictionary of Biblical Theology*, edited by T. Desmond Alexander and Brian S. Rosner, 459-64. Downers Grove, IL: IVP Academic, 1999. Material from this source is used with permission.

Brower, Kent E., and Mark Elliott, eds. *Eschatology in the Bible and Theology: Evangelical Essays at the Dawn of a New Millennium*. Downers Grove, IL: InterVarsity Press, 1997.

Wright, N. T. *Surprised by Hope: Rethinking Heaven, the Resurrection, and the Mission of the Church*. New York: HarperOne, 2008.

KENT E. BROWER, PHD

ESSENES
See DEAD SEA SCROLLS.

ETHICS

Formally, ethics is the systematic reflection on morality; morality is the practice of ethics. Ethics systematically formulates and evaluates morality. Informally, ethics and morality are used interchangeably. The Greek term for "ethics," *ēthikē* (from *ēthos*), means "character," "custom," "principles," or "standards of human conduct." Historically, the term focused on the particular ways of life and conduct specific communities embraced.

Because ethics is essential to what it means to be human, all people groups engage in ethical reflection. Standards of conduct and their justification must be established.

Since the time of the ancient Greek philosophers, the essential questions of ethics have been, "What is the good life?" and "What life is truly worth living?" These questions continue to be imperative today.

Broadly understood, ethics is a philosophical enterprise. It is a universal human concern not limited to religion. Philosophical ethics is identified by numerous types of general ethical theories. Two of the most important are (1) an ethic of doing and (2) an ethic of being.

1. An *ethic of doing*. The two following types emphasize action or decision making:

   a. *Teleological* (Greek, *telos* [design, goal, end]) *ethics* focuses on the goal or result of an action. Right and wrong depend on the goal of one's action. *Utilitarianism* is one form of teleological ethics. "The greatest good for the greatest number" is its most recognizable form. Right or wrong depend on whether one's action produces more good than evil for the greatest number of persons. For example, most American states require everyone to wear a seat belt when riding in a motorized vehicle. Doing so results in fewer deaths. Not liking seat belts is insignificant; the greatest good determines the ethical action.

   Teleological ethics is sometimes called *consequentialism* because it focuses on an action's consequences. The emphasis is not on motive or a law that must be obeyed but on an action's results or consequences. If the desired goal is achieved, the action is "good."

   b. *Deontological* (Greek, *deon* [duty]) *ethics* is rule based. Formalized by German philosopher Immanuel Kant (1724–1804), it judges an action moral or immoral based on whether it conforms to one's duty to obey the law.

   Deontology acknowledges that good results may come from bad motives. However, the moral agent should not be called morally responsible if intentions and actions are not conformable to the moral law. The point of morality has shifted from consequences (teleological) to a moral agent's intentional compliance with a moral law. That results might be beneficial does not make an action moral or immoral.

More specifically, deontology assumes that all persons, regardless of social identity, can discern which rule applies and can make morally commendable decisions. "Act," Kant advised, "only on that maxim which you can at the same time will that it be a universal law" ([1788] 1993, pt. 1, bk. 1, 1.7).

Hence, deontological ethics insists that all persons can discern which ethical principle applies in a given situation. One must choose out of unconditional respect for the intrinsic excellence of the moral law, not because of some perceived benefit (e.g., heaven). This is the *categorical imperative*, as opposed to the *hypothetical imperative*.

(1) One type of deontological ethics is *divine command*. "The good is good because God commands it; God does not command something because it is good." God alone is the Source of moral prescription. Ethics is a process of reflecting on what God has willed or prohibited. Humans have a singular duty to hear and obey God's will. Those who embrace divine command theory identify the Ten Commandments and portions of the Sermon on the Mount as divine commands.

(2) Another form of deontological ethics is *natural law*. It assumes an ordered, rational, and connected universe. God has equipped humans to discern how things *ought to be*. The workings of God's creation unfold according to rules comprehensible by everyone. A natural law ethic seems to make sense among diverse peoples who do not share certain goals and traditions.

The Wesleyan emphasis on **prevenient grace** engages natural law in illuminating ways. It recognizes that what is identified as natural law is actually the effective working of prevenient grace. The conscience, or the ability to ascertain natural law, is the product of prevenient grace.

2. An *ethic of being*. The focus of an ethic of being is on the actor or the decision maker. This is *virtue* or *character* ethics. **Virtues** are excellences of character, the possession of which enables one to become the human God intends. The decisive critical question is, "What kind of person ought I to be?" This is a question of identity. The moral focus is not on the decision but on the quality or character of the person making the decision. A second question is, "What course of action (practicing virtues) will achieve that quality?" According to Aristotle, the appropriate excellence of a person is to act rationally,

and to act rationally is to act in accordance with the best and most complete virtues.

The **fruit of the Spirit** in Gal. 5:22-23 names a cluster of Christian virtues that will shape Christians according to Jesus' character. Acquiring and growing in the fruit of the Spirit is at the heart of Wesley's understanding of **sanctification**.

See also Christian Ethics/Moral Theology; Greek Philosophy; Social Ethics; Spiritual Formation/Growth; Tempers and Affections; Theosis (Deification).

Resources

Blackburn, Simon. *Ethics: A Very Short Introduction.* New York: Oxford University Press, 2001.

Deigh, John. *An Introduction to Ethics.* Cambridge Introductions to Philosophy. Cambridge, UK: Cambridge University Press, 2010.

Kant, Immanuel. 1788. *Critique of Practical Reason.* Translated by Lewis White Beck. 3rd ed. Upper Saddle River, NJ: Prentice Hall, 1993.

JAMES W. LEWIS, PHD

ETHNICITY

Ethnicity refers to the unique cultural heritage that characterizes a social group. The distinguishing features give the group a measure of coherence. Features may include nonbiological, learned cultural traits such as shared ancestry and folklore.

Ethnicity can be resilient even when its identifying features diminish. Many of the fifteen million Italian Americans rarely speak the native language. But they proudly self-identify as Italian because of other common bonds such as history and kinship.

The meaning of ethnicity has changed over time. Once it was narrowly equated with being "Christian," "non-Anglo," "possessing heathenish superstitions" (1772), and so on. During World War II, as the idea of race became associated with racism, ethnicity assumed a more neutral tone, becoming a means of distinguishing persons according to gender, age, and religion. Most social scientists retain this understanding.

For many, ethnicity is not neutral. It takes center stage and is charged with emotion. For them, ethnicity is the primary badge for self-identification and pride.

Persons are born into ethnic groups. Later they make choices about continuing to belong. Some ethnicities as a whole either forsake or minimize their ethnic roots, preferring to blend into the dominant culture.

Conflict between ethnic groups is a serious social and national problem. Several "solutions" have been devised: (1) *assimilation/amalgamation*, which involves ethnic groups gradually surrendering their ethnicity and being absorbed into the dominant culture; (2) *accommodation*, which involves retaining only a measure of ethnic identity; (3) *extermination/ethnic cleansing*, which uses brutal measures to eliminate an undesirable ethnic group; (4) *expulsion*; (5) *imposing a caste system*; and (6) *segregation/apartheid*.

Ethnicity differs from race in that race involves inherited and some permanent biological traits such as skin color, hair texture, and head shape. But there are no universal racial categories. Brazilians subscribe to three primary races: *blanco* (white), *preto* (black), and *pardo* (mulatto). But they use dozens of additional terms to categorize people with minute physical differences. On the other hand, African-Americans visiting Ghana are shocked when they are called *obruni*—"white foreigners."

Like ethnicity, race can be linked to perception, even while physical features (e.g., skin color) remain constant. Racial identity can become ambiguous or unsettled. Upward socioeconomic mobility can change racial identification. In Brazil, "A rich Negro is a white man, and a poor white man is a Negro."

In fact, shared physical features do not give a racial group its identity, for no set of features applies to all members. Instead, the *shared experience* of being racially identified, in spite of diverse physical features, is the most important factor.

The complex task of identifying race is a complicated biological reality: Humans have always engaged in migration and crossbreeding. The result is a universal racial mixture. Some surveys indicate that at least 75 percent of blacks in the United States have some white ancestry.

See also Anthropology, Theological; Person; Social Sciences.

JON P. JOHNSTON, PHD

EUCHARIST
See SACRAMENTS.

EVANGELICAL FEMINISM

Evangelical feminism is one of several expressions of feminism founded on Christianity. Evangelical feminist theologians claim that gender equality is compatible with Christianity. They contend the Bible teaches that God gifts women and men equally for leadership in all areas of life. Two organizations best represent evangelical feminist theology.

The Evangelical Women's Caucus (EWC) sponsored its first conference in 1975 to discuss feminism from an evangelical perspective. Speakers challenged sexism in church and society. From its inception, the EWC endorsed and promoted the Equal Rights Amendment (a 1970s proposed amendment to the United States Constitution that did not succeed).

The EWC became the Evangelical and Ecumenical Women's Caucus in 1990 to reflect its broader mainline Christian constituency. Currently taking its name from its newsletter, the organization calls itself EEWC-Christian Feminism Today (EEWC-CFT). It promotes women's gifts in the **church** and provides education and encouragement.

The second feminist organization with evangelical roots is Christians for Biblical Equality (CBE), founded in 1988. It is related to a similar and prior group in Great Britain called Men, Women, and God. The CBE group claims the Bible promotes equal authority and responsibility for women and men to advance Christ's kingdom in the church, home, and world. It began disseminating its egalitarian theology by distributing a statement: *Men, Women and Biblical Equality.* The feminist message of CBE has reached a larger constituency within the evangelical community than has that of the EEWC-CFT.

Besides the diverse audiences, the two groups also approach the Bible and marriage differently. While CBE maintains that no biblical passage contradicts their understanding of feminism, members of the EEWC-CFT acknowledge that a patriarchal mind-set influenced some texts that must be interpreted in their particular contexts. Both reject male dominance (headship) within marriage, but CBE defines **marriage** as being between a woman and a man.

Both groups sponsor conferences. The EEWC-CFT publishes a newsletter, while CBE supports an online bookstore and publishes two journals and a weekly e-newsletter.

See also Christian Ethics/Moral Theology; Feminist Theology; Human Sexuality; Social Justice; Women's Role in the Church.

Resources

Pierce, Ronald W., Rebecca Merrill Groothuis, and Gordon D. Fee, eds. *Discovering Biblical Equality: Complementarity Without Hierarchy.* 2nd ed. Downers Grove, IL: InterVarsity Press, 2005.
Scanzoni, Letha Dawson, and Nancy A. Hardesty. *All We're Meant to Be: Biblical Feminism for Today.* 3rd ed. Grand Rapids: Eerdmans, 1992.

SUSIE STANLEY, PHD

EVANGELICAL THEOLOGY

The Greek word *euangelion* carries the meaning of "good news" or "**gospel**." In Christian theology the gospel refers to Jesus' life, teachings, death and resurrection, ascension, and final return. Accordingly, evangelical theology is based on *euangelion* and explicates who Jesus is and what he accomplished (1 Cor. 15:1-4).

All Christian traditions have emphasized the good news of Jesus Christ in their theology. But in the eighteenth century a movement developed that adopted the term "evangelical" and assigned it a specific meaning as the movement spread across denominational lines. Eventually some Protestant denominations used the term "evangelical" as a specific designation, distinct from some other Protestant traditions.

Although the evangelical movement identifies different predecessors in church history, the American pre-Revolutionary War pastor/theologian Jonathan Edwards (1703-58) was a major catalyst in the evangelical revival known as the Great Awakening. It spread throughout New England and parts of the other colonies.

Subsequently, two priests in the Church of England, the evangelical **Calvinist** George Whitefield (1714-70) and the evangelical **Arminian John Wesley** (1703-91), promoted a similar evangelical revival in the British Isles. Whitefield repeatedly visited and preached extensively in the North American colonies and Bermuda. Through John Wesley's efforts (and those of his brother Charles), the **Methodist** movement sought to preserve evangelical theology in the Church of England. Wesley worked to integrate orthodoxy (right faith) and orthopraxy (right practice) in Christian life. Although not all evangelicals supported Wesley's understanding of Christian holiness, holy living became a consistent feature of the evangelical revival.

Historian David Bebbington identified four characteristics of evangelical theology: (1) authority of the Scriptures, (2) a cruciform life, (3) evangelical conversion, and (4) discipleship actively expressed in works of mercy and love. Evangelical theology was also creedal in formation (stated or unstated), meaning that its doctrine is based on the Nicene Creed (AD 325). Although its creedal statements are generally brief, they affirm the doctrine of the Trinity, the full deity and humanity of Christ, the deity of the Holy Spirit, the requirement of salvation through Christ alone, the final return of Christ, and creation *ex nihilo*.

Evangelical theology and the evangelical movement developed from within existing church traditions, so there was no need to develop a new ecclesiology. However, in time numerous new denominations and **parachurch** groups emerged. Among them, attention to **ecclesiology** tended to decline, often accompanied by a declining interest in the sacraments. This departure was far removed from the movement's eighteenth-century origins—particularly John Wesley.

As the evangelical movement developed, doctrinal controversies occurred. By the middle of the twentieth century, evangelical theology attempted to distinguish itself from American fundamentalism, even though at times the distinction was difficult to maintain.

Divisions arose, not over Trinitarian theology, **Christology**, the atonement, or ecclesiology, but over the **Reformation** principle of *sola Scriptura*. Although evangelicalism and **fundamentalism** embraced biblical authority, they disagreed over its meaning. The controversy has not been resolved.

An important feature of evangelical theology, in addition to its four identifying marks and Nicene faith, is its commitment to worldwide missions. This emphasis has been supported by wide-ranging educational programs, including theological education and the liberal arts. Consequently, evangelical theology has become global. Its global reach tests doctrinal and missional unity.

Various attempts at theological and missional unity within evangelicalism have occurred. Of particular importance was the 1974 International Congress on World Evangelization in Lausanne, Switzerland, and the writing of the Lausanne Covenant. In that covenant evangelicals committed to addressing a variety of global and contextual needs. Social redemption, shared theological emphases, and an emphasis on personal salvation now characterize evangelicalism. Stewardship of the creation, in addition to personal salvation and social redemption, contributes to a holistic theology.

Today the leading edge of evangelical Christianity is more and more located in the Global South, especially among **Pentecostals. Global South** evangelicals increasingly take charge of their own theological, ecclesiastical, educational, and missional vocation.

See also Anglicanism; Charismatic Theology; Church (Ecclesiology); Creation, Care for the (Ecology); Creeds (Nicene, Chalcedonian, Apostles', Athanasian); Evangelical Feminism; Evangelism; Fundamentalist Theology; Indigenous Theologies; Lausanne Movement and Covenant; Missionary Movements; Postconservative Evangelical Theology; Puritanism; Sanctification; Social Justice; Third Wave Theology; Tradition, Evangelical Retrieval of; Trinity.

Resources
Bebbington, David. *Evangelicalism in Modern Britain: A History from the 1730s to the 1980s.* London: Routledge, 1989.
Bloesch, Donald. *Essentials of Evangelical Theology.* Peabody, MA: Hendrickson Publishers, 2005.
Dorrien, Gary J. *The Remaking of Evangelical Theology.* Louisville, KY: Westminster John Knox Press, 1998.
McGonigle, Herbert. *Sufficient Saving Grace: John Wesley's Evangelical Arminianism.* Carlisle, UK: Paternoster, 2001.

DAVID RAINEY, PHD

EVANGELICAL UNITED BRETHREN TRADITION
The Evangelical United Brethren Church tradition has roots in two denominations: the United Brethren in Christ Church (UB) and the Evangelical Church (EC), both of which were rooted in German Evangelical **Pietism**. Each denomination resembled the early American Methodists in theology, organization, and government. Only their use of the German language and some disagreements over polity prevented their merging with the Methodists.

The UB movement began in the 1760s under the evangelistic preaching of Philip William Otterbein (German Reformed) and Martin Boehm (Mennonite), both of whom ministered among German settlers in Pennsylvania, Maryland, and Virginia. Their followers formed a denomination in 1800, with the motto, "We are brothers." The EC arose in the 1790s under the leadership of Jacob Albright, who also ministered among German-speaking people, primarily in Pennsylvania. Albright's People formally organized in 1807 as the Newly Formed Methodist Conference. The UB and EC asked all new members and ordinands to confess their belief that "the Bible is the Word of God."

United Brethren in Christ Church and EC leaders were friends with Francis Asbury and the Methodists. Doctrinally, both denominations were **Arminian** and **Wesleyan**. The UB and EC considered **evangelism** their main mission. Following the pattern of the Methodists, they engaged in itinerant evangelism and organized their converts into classes (class meetings). Theologically, they stressed "**justification** by faith confirmed by a sensible assurance thereof" (UMC 2008), Christian nurture, the priesthood of all believers, and **entire sanctification**.

Both denominations had bishops and annual conferences, after the pattern of the Methodists. As the two denominations expanded west of the Alleghenies, they printed books of discipline, produced hymnals, formed colleges, established camp meetings, and supported missionaries. In 1946 at Johnstown, Pennsylvania, the UB and EC merged to form the Evangelical United Brethren Church (EUB). Its doctrines found new expression in its confession of faith (1962), which was a continuation of the creedal statements of the UB and EC. The common theological heritage of the EUB and the Methodist Episcopal Church led in 1968 to a merger, the new denomination becoming the United Methodist Church.

See also Holiness Movements: American, British, and Continental; Methodism, American.

Resource

UMC (United Methodist Communications). "Doctrinal Traditions in the Evangelical Church and the United Brethren Church." From *The Book of Discipline of the United Methodist Church*. Nashville: United Methodist Publishing House, 2008. http://www.umc.org/site/apps/nlnet/content.aspx?c=lwL4KnN1LtH&b=5068501&ct=6466459&notoc=1.

KENNETH C. KINGHORN, PHD

EVANGELISM

The term "evangelism," like that of "evangelist," was not common in **John Wesley**'s day. "Evangelist" generally meant a writer of one of the Gospels. "Evangelism" and "evangelization" arose in the wake of the evangelical awakenings of the eighteenth century; "evangelization" dropped out until recovered by **Roman Catholicism** as a contrast to the evangelistic theology and practices of twentieth-century **evangelicals,** who were seen as **fundamentalists.** The nineteenth-century precursors of evangelists were commonly known as revivalists. This reflected a shift from awakenings, seen as outpourings of the Spirit, to revivalism, seen as the effects of human effort; it also reflected the world of Christendom, where the challenge was to move church members from a nominal to a real commitment. The central practices of evangelism in this trajectory were prayer, preaching, altar calls, and minimal follow-up.

There is continuity in this revivalistic development with Wesley's practices, which focused on field preaching and intensive spiritual direction in the societies, **class meetings,** and **bands.** There is also extensive continuity with a Wesleyan theology, which emphasized the hearing of the Word of God in coming to **faith** and the indispensability of human response as enabled by **prevenient grace.** Many saw in Wesley and later revivalists the remnants of a **Pelagian** view of **salvation;** however, the real issue was the crucial place of genuine human response to the good news of the **gospel.** The use of Wesley's canonical forty-four sermons is pivotal in understanding his work. They constitute both a handbook of **spiritual direction** and a theology of the Christian life. They move seamlessly from how to become a Christian, to what it is to be a Christian, to how to remain a Christian.

The loss of these materials, especially in the United States, has left the tradition diminished in the content of its doctrinal catechesis. The latter is especially visible in the work of Harry Ward, who in the early twentieth century used the techniques honed in revival to recruit members for local trade unions. In time, he drifted toward a Marxist vision of ecclesial existence that used the **church** as a means to political ends. Others responded to problems of poverty and upward social mobility by radicalizing the emphasis on the work of the **Holy Spirit** in evangelism and inventing **Pentecostalism,** where the practices of revivalism found a new home and renewed energy.

The loss of a robust Wesleyan theology, including the wider, background music of the classical faith of the tradition, undercut over time the capacity to engage in evangelism in much of the later Wesleyan tradition. The ensuing shortfall in numbers has been the catalyst for major efforts to recover evangelistic nerve and practice. Wesleyans have borrowed from neighboring proposals in evangelicalism, such as church growth and the new monasticism. They have also been at the forefront of recent writing on evangelism, providing a rich menu of reflection and innovative practice. One can readily detect echoes of the earlier tradition in the significant place given to **preaching,** catechesis, **spiritual formation,** small groups and retreats, creative styles and settings of **worship,** and statistical records.

Finding an appropriate place for social action as it relates to evangelism has been a recurring challenge to Wesleyans. The challenge has not been just to find persons in need but to find those most in need. One way forward is to connect evangelism conceptually to the making of disciples and then actually to make the kind of robust disciples who can be salt and light in the world (see Matt. 5:13-14).

See also Evangelical Theology; Lausanne Movement and Covenant; Mission, Theology of; New Birth (Regeneration); *Ordo Salutis;* Pentecostalism; Pentecostal Theology; Proselytism; Salvation (Soteriology).

Resources

Abraham, William J. *The Logic of Evangelism.* Grand Rapids: Eerdmans, 1989.
Gunter, W. Stephen, and Elaine Robinson, eds. *Considering the Great Commission.* Nashville: Abingdon Press, 2005.
Jones, Scott J. *The Evangelistic Love of God and Neighbor.* Nashville: Abingdon Press, 2003.

WILLIAM ABRAHAM, PHD

EVOLUTION

See SOCIOBIOLOGY.

EVOLUTION/EVOLUTIONARY BIOLOGY

To biologists, "evolution" is the term that describes the process by which life's diversity arose. Although Charles Darwin is generally credited with discovering the process, the idea of evolution was not new at the time. What began with Darwin, though, was the proposal of a scientifically plausible explanation of *how* evolution occurred. He proposed that the chief driving force behind the process of evolution was *natural selection.*

Natural selection is based on the principle that organisms within a species exhibit heritable variations in traits. For example, bird beaks within a species are not all exactly the same length or exactly the same shape. What Darwin proposed was that within a species, those organisms that carried the variation best adapted to their specific environment would on average leave more offspring. If the variation was heritable, then as time went by that variant would become increasingly abundant relative to others. Through time, the entire species, in Darwin's view, would change. Hence, in our example, if there is consistent advantage in a particular environment for birds to have longer beaks, and if there are heritable variants of beak length, then as time goes by the mean beak length of the species will be longer. The trait in the species as a whole would have changed. Darwin proposed that given a very long period of time, this principle would serve as a force that could change not just single traits but all traits. Given sufficient time, the complete diversity of living organisms on earth, past and present, could be explained through selection of this sort. Although biologists have been working out the details ever since, Darwin's ideas remain at the core of evolutionary theory. Evolution is widely regarded as the unifying theme that undergirds the science of biology.

Evolutionary theory implies that all organisms, including humans, are related to each other through descent from single-celled organisms through a process that occurred over the past approximate 3.5 billion years, beginning when single-celled organisms first appeared in the fossil record.

Although **fundamentalists**, including scientific **atheists** and biblical literalists, understand evolution to be incompatible with Christian theology, this is not the case for a **Wesleyan** understanding of **God**, Scripture, and the natural world. The laws that govern nature are not something distinct from the activity of God. The natural laws of the universe reflect the ongoing presence of God's activity. If that activity were to cease, the universe would vanish.

So "natural" does not imply God's absence. Quite the opposite is true. God working through natural processes to bring about life's diversity does not imply the absence of *super*natural activity in life's history. Science is only able to study effectively that aspect of God's activity that is regular and predictable. All that has happened in life's history has happened in response to God's creative command. All life—eminently human life—is God's creation regardless of whether it took place over millions of years or in an instant.

> For in him all things in heaven and on earth were created, things visible and invisible, whether thrones or dominions or rulers or powers—all things have been created through him and for him. He himself is before all things, and in him all things hold together. (Col. 1:16-17)

See also Creationism; Intelligent Design; Natural Science; Philosophy of Science; Science and the Bible; Wesley, John, Theology of.

Resources
Ayala, Francisco J. *Darwin and Intelligent Design.* Facets Series. Minneapolis: Fortress Press, 2006.

Falk, Darrel R. *Coming to Peace with Science: Bridging the Worlds Between Faith and Biology.* Downers Grove, IL: InterVarsity Press, 2004.

Giberson, Karl. *Saving Darwin: How to Be a Christian and Believe in Evolution.* New York: HarperOne, 2008.

DARREL FALK, PHD

EXISTENTIALISM

Existentialism is a philosophy that enjoyed considerable influence during the twentieth century. Difficult to define precisely, existentialism affirms the concise but technical phrase "existence precedes essence." This means that language, ideas, or rational systems cannot fully explain life and are not even the proper place to begin. Living comes prior to and transcends our attempts to understand reality. Existentialists typically believe that humans must attend to the concerns of life and allow these concerns to guide understanding rather than let rational preconceptions guide our explanations of life.

Existentialism comes in both Christian and non-Christian forms. Among the most famous non-Christian existentialists are Albert Camus, Martin Heidegger, Karl Jaspers, Friedrich Nietzsche, and Jean-Paul Sartre. The most famous Christian existentialist is Søren Kierkegaard.

Existentialism teaches that much Western philosophy has been preoccupied with trying to explain the general and universal features of reality. It has been overly rationalist. Existentialism insists we pay closer attention and give priority to individual experience or personal subjectivity.

Existentialists typically emphasize the particularities of what it means to be human, chief among them being human decisions and perplexities, genuine freedom, and personal authenticity. Existentialists insist on the value and ultimacy of the individual, often contrasting the individual with the "herd," namely, mass culture, machines, hierarchies, or external authorities. Writers of existentialist literature often have as their literary theme the idea that humans have a tendency to deny their own responsibility. Humans wrongly try to flee from the truth of their inescapable freedom.

Existentialism calls on people to renounce their own alienation and endorse the quest for authentic selfhood. This quest entails dealing honestly with anxiety, the possibility of death, the concerns of life, and the reality of self-consciousness.

Existentialists recognize they cannot obtain absolute certainty. They call upon humans to live bravely despite uncertainty. They attempt to come to terms with being affected by others and "thrown" into the world by no decision of their own.

Many important twentieth-century Christian theologians were influenced directly or indirectly by existentialism, including Karl Barth, Emil Brunner, Rudolf Bultmann, Gabriel Marcel, Reinhold Niebuhr, and Paul Tillich. They emphasized the finality of a decision for faith and embraced paradoxical formulations of some Christian doctrine.

The influence of existentialism extends into the twenty-first century, although few scholars embrace the label "existentialist" as their primary identification. Many ideas of existentialism are present in deconstructive philosophy, phenomenology, **process** philosophy, and **postmodernism**.

See also Experience, Phenomenon of; Faith; Free Will; Hermeneutics; Humanism; Metaphysics.

Resources
Kaufmann, Walter. *Existentialism from Dostoevsky to Sartre*. New York: Plume, 1975.
Solomon, Robert C., ed. *Existentialism*. 2nd ed. New York: Oxford University Press, 2004.

THOMAS J. OORD, PHD

EXODUS AND EXILE
See ISRAEL; SECOND TEMPLE JUDAISM.

EXPERIENCE, PHENOMENON OF

Generally, experience is a mental state of awareness of a felt (or phenomenal) character that may or may not represent something about the world (as in ordinary sense perception).

Modern philosophers and psychologists have been preoccupied with experiences associated with sense perception—the awareness of objects in the world gained through the five main sense modalities (vision, touch, smell, taste, and hearing). However, there are also nonsensory kinds of awareness such as imagination, memory, emotion, and abstract thought. Empiricism is the view that knowledge can only be derived through sense experience.

In Christian theology, human experience identifies one way God reveals himself. Experience contrasts with mere rational processes or what is accepted as true or false on the basis of authority or **tradition**. **Philosophy of religion** considers the *evidential value* of religious experience.

The phenomenology of experience is the study of how we experience anything at all. Our own internal states of nonsensory consciousness ("I am excited about the game") are immediately *given* to us and not mediated *through* anything. Sensory perception of an object ("the football") is presented or given through a state of consciousness ("the way it appears to me") distinguishable from the external object. This basic account still leaves unsettled whether there is direct awareness of the object itself (direct realism), an indirect awareness through some kind of internal object (medium) of experience that allows one to infer from that experience the external object's existence (representative realism), or an external object that is reducible to (is nothing more than) our experiences (phenomenalism).

The **epistemological** question about experience is, "How reliable or accurate is experience in producing accurate beliefs?" Late modern philosophers argue that the human subject is always active in constructing the experiences one has. All experience is human experience. Thus even sensory experiences are already influenced by presuppositions, expectations, and culture.

A more optimistic view is that some experiential beliefs are directly justified. On this view we are prima facie justified in our perceptual beliefs insofar as we have no good reason for supposing they are unreliable. Philosopher William Alston (1921–2009) argued that because beliefs are similar in structure to sensory perceptual beliefs, beliefs about God, formed on the basis of religious experience, are similarly justified unless there is sufficient reason to believe otherwise.

See also Belief; Epistemology; Natural Theology; Quadrilateral, Wesleyan.

Resources

Alston, William P. *Perceiving God: The Epistemology of Religious Experience.* Ithaca, NY: Cornell University Press, 1991.
Romans 1:18-20.

TERRY FACH, MA, MPHIL

Ff

FAITH

The common NT term for "faith" is the Greek word *pistos*. The closely related verbal form, *pisteuein*, means "to believe." Another word for "faith" is
"trust." Although humans express faith, even the capacity to do so results
from the enabling agency of the **Holy Spirit** (Rom. 10:17; 12:6). Not only
does God initiate his self-disclosure, but he alone initiates our acceptance as
well. Even expressions of godly sorrow for one's sins prior to **regeneration** are
in response to the Spirit's convicting activity. Otherwise, faith would be an
achievement about which humans could boast. Even the *idea* of faith comes
directly from God's faithfulness. The warrant for faith is God's faithfulness,
definitively expressed by the Father, in his Son, through the Spirit's witness.
The OT repeatedly speaks of God's *khesed*, his "steadfast love" or "loving-
kindness" (Exod. 34:7; Ps. 26:3; Isa. 16:5).

Faith as understood in the NT is grounded in the OT. Luke opens his
gospel with Mary rehearsing God's faithfulness (Luke 1:46-55). Paul uses
Habakkuk (2:4), the "righteous live by their faith," to establish his doctrine
of salvation by faith alone (Gal. 3:11; Phil. 3:9). And the heroes of faith
championed by the writer of Hebrews were all OT figures (chap. 11).

In Scripture, God's people demonstrate or express their faith by obeying
his will, his commands, because they can trust everything to his unbroken
faithfulness.

The Gospels make much of Jesus' faith in his heavenly Father and of him
perfectly completing his Father's will. Unlike the first Adam, Jesus never set
his will against the Father. The author of Hebrews tells us that Ps. 40:6-8 is
speaking of Christ: "See, God, I have come to do your will, O God" (Heb.
10:5-7). Christian faith is faith in this faithful Christ (Gal. 2:16).

The NT church left no doubt about salvation coming by faith. Paul told
a Roman jailer, "Believe [*pisteuson*] on the Lord Jesus, and you will be saved"

(Acts 16:30-31). Saving faith entails that one is helplessly lost in sin but that God has graciously provided salvation through his Son, Jesus. Having faith, that is, believing, is the sole requirement for salvation stipulated by the NT. Paul's epistles declare that salvation is through faith in Christ alone; it no longer involves obedience to the whole Mosaic law.

Faith in the risen Christ will yield obedience (John 15:14). What are normally referred to as works, whether **works of piety** or **mercy**, proceed from and express radical trust in God and his gift of **reconciliation**; they neither generate trust (faith) nor achieve reconciliation. "Without faith," the author of Hebrews tells us, "it is impossible to please God, for whoever would approach him must believe that he exists and that he rewards those who seek him" (11:6).

Only by misunderstanding either faith or works can there be a conflict between the two. Works as conformity to God's will make faith concrete. "Works do not a good [person] make [a person reconciled to God]," said Martin Luther, "but a good [person] does good works" (1520).

Wesleyan-Arminian theologians are in agreement. But whereas Luther saw a conflict between the apostle Paul and the epistle of James—judging it "an epistle of straw" (1522)—Wesleyans see no conflict. What James means when he says, "You see that a person is justified by works and not by faith alone" (James 2:24), is that works must necessarily evidence one's gracious embrace of the gospel of Jesus Christ. John Wesley explained, "St. James's justification by *works*, is the fruit of St. Paul's justification by *faith*" (*NT Notes*, 2:297; comment on James 2:21). As much as repentance is a prerequisite to faith, the outcome of faith is obedient good works—a faith that works through love (Gal. 5:6).

See also Christian Ethics/Moral Theology; Free Will; Grace; Justification; New Birth (Regeneration); Revelation; Salvation (Soteriology).

Resources

Luther, Martin. *The Freedom of the Christian*. 1520. Theology Network. http://www.the-ologynetwork.org/unquenchable-flame/luther/the-freedom-of-the-christian.htm.

———. "Preface to the New Testament." 1522. In *Works of Martin Luther—Prefaces to the Books of the Bible*. God Rules.net. http://www.godrules.net/library/luther/NEW1luther_f8.htm.

Wesley, John. "The Marks of the New Birth." In *Works*, 5:212-23.

MELANIE STARKS KIERSTEAD, PHD

FALL, THE
See SIN.

FAMILY, CHRISTIAN

The natural phenomenon of family shows humanity's social nature. Scripture demonstrates that God ordained the family as the most natural and fundamental human unit: mother, father, and children bonded together to meet basic needs. In the OT setting, family included much more than the traditional nuclear family. It included the patriarchal clan (*mishpakhah*), that is, persons related by blood and marriage. Family or household even included slaves and livestock (Exod. 20:10). The oldest male relative was the "father" of the household and its ultimate authority. All who belonged to him were considered part of his family. The descendants of Abraham were members of his family.

In the ancient world, beyond the economic value of having children, the Hebrew people recognized the God-given worth of persons and saw children as gifts from God. In the ancient world there was little consideration of persons *as individuals* such as is common in the Western world today. One's identity was closely tied to his or her extended family and clan. Concern for the honor of the family/clan was foremost. And although males, females, and procreation exist in all species, Scripture teaches that God stands in relationship to the family in a way unique to humans.

The OT primarily uses the image of family to tell its story. Nearly the whole OT is a narrative of the Hebrew family, displaying functional, dysfunctional, bifurcated, and whole family structures. The OT doesn't set out to retell the story of human relationships *as such* but to show how God works among his people. Covenant is the basis. The OT illustrates the human need for God's presence and his faithfulness to humans as their beloved Creator. It shows that God desires to take part in the human family.

God's relational nature is articulated in family language. In the Bible, God, himself, is described as having familial characteristics. God is referred to as Father and, minimally, as Mother—a hen, to be precise (Ps. 91:4; Matt. 23:37; Luke 13:34)! The picture of God's involvement with the human family is so intense that in the NT God's Son physically becomes part of the human family. Although Jesus is presented as God's Son, he is born as a son in the family of Mary and Joseph. He grew up (Luke 2:52) in a human family, and he cared for his human family (John 19:26). Hebrews refers to the brotherhood of Jesus, saying Jesus is not embarrassed to call believers his "brothers and sisters" (2:11). Jesus explained that his family extends beyond bloodlines, making clear that his true family members are those "who hear the word of God and do it" (Luke 8:21). This family transcends, but also fulfills, the human family. Christ's love for the church is to be the model for love in the Christian family (Eph. 5:25–6:4). For Christians, the quality of Christ's love for the church defines the human family.

In the NT, the imagery of the family is used to denote Christian relationships—the family of God. Paul indicates that Christians are part of God's family: "I bow my knees before the Father, from whom every family [of saints] in heaven and on earth takes its name" (3:14-15). Regardless of ethnic or socio-economic situation, believers are brothers and sisters (Philem. v. 16).

Because of the rich and pervasive family imagery the NT uses to describe the relationship between God and believers, and among believers, one might argue that the family is nearly sacramental. The NT norm for family places God's blessing on a man and woman who are exclusively and mutually committed in marriage to following God's commandments of love and faithful respect (Mark 10:2-9; Eph. 5:22-31). However, today in many cultures the norm is often fractured by divorce and other tragedies, thus making the traditional nuclear family inaccessible. Nevertheless, God's supportive and instructive presence abides with single parents, grandparents, and guardians as they nurture the children in their care. In such challenging circumstances, the church can serve those in need, living out the Lord's incarnational presence.

Just as a physical relationship between a male and female is fundamental for the creation of offspring, so the ongoing collaboration between parents is needed for nurturing and raising children to adulthood. Married parents, working together, provide balanced nurture for children during the developmental years. Balancing sacrifice, responsibility, gifting, and temperament offers a model for children and demonstrates the results of cooperative efforts and accomplishments. The NT makes clear that the Christian family is to be a microcosm for understanding Christ's love for the church, for replicating Christ's love in all family relationships, and for demonstrating God-blessed community, cooperation, and accomplishment (Eph. 5:21–6:4; Col. 3:12-22).

See also Childhood, Wesleyan Theology of; Marriage.

Resources
Balswick, Jack O., and Judith K. Balswick. *The Family: A Christian Perspective on the Contemporary Home.* 3rd ed. Grand Rapids: Baker Academic, 2007.

Marsolini, Maxine. *Blended Families: Creating Harmony As You Build a New Home Life.* Chicago: Moody Publishers, 2000.

Sandford, John Loren, and Paula Sandford. *Restoring the Christian Family: A Biblical Guide to Love, Marriage, and Parenting in a Changing World.* Lake Mary, FL: Charisma House, 2009.

MELANIE STARKS KIERSTEAD, PHD

FATALISM

Fatalism is a perception of reality that views all events, including human decisions and actions, as occurring by necessity. Humans are powerless to do anything other than what they do, resulting in passive acceptance of all that happens. Responsibility for negative circumstances is attributed to forces beyond human control. Fatalism can justify indifference and inaction.

For the ancient Greeks, fatalism signified the unseen power—personified in goddesses of fate—that rules over human destiny. Even the gods could not defy this all-encompassing reality. Life is ruled by a determinism that has no purpose or meaning. Some contemporary representatives of Hinduism, Buddhism, and Islam evidence fatalistic tendencies in their thought and practice.

Naturalistic **determinism**, as seen in the work of celebrated psychologist B. F. Skinner, views human behavior as controlled by genetic or environmental factors. Philosophers entertaining similar ideas include John Stuart Mill and Arthur Schopenhauer.

Theistic determinism views all events as planned and caused by God (or gods). Therefore, some branches of Christianity have substituted **predestination and election** for the Hellenistic concept of fate.

Fatalistic tendencies in Christianity assume that God has foreknowledge of and complete control over all things, even foreordaining them. This is in contrast to the paradoxical assumption of some Christian traditions that (1) God infallibly knows and controls the entire future but that (2) humans nevertheless have a free will—God's freely given gift—that allows them to make genuine decisions not predetermined by God. Christian theologians have struggled to reconcile divine predestination with human free will.

John Wesley agreed with **John Calvin** on many things but differed over Calvin's emphasis on predestination. A prominent school of thought today is **open theology**, which affirms that a truly sovereign God has granted free will, takes it seriously, and is affected by human decisions.

See also Calvin, John; Determinism and Free Will; Open Theology/Theism; Predestination and Election; Reincarnation; Wesley, John, Theology of.

BARRY CALLEN, EDD

FEMINIST THEOLOGY

Feminist theology studies, conceptualizes, and analyzes the Divinity's nature, attributes, and relation with creation in ways that critique and reform/transform the predominantly androcentric character (approaching religion, culture, and history in a way that is centered on the masculine point of view) of traditional theology. It makes theology fully inclusive of women. It exposes, resists, and critiques the hegemony of patriarchal theology for marginalizing, effacing, and subordinating women. Androcentrism masquerading as asexual, normative, and unbiased theology is targeted.

While there is a distinct Christian feminist theology, feminist theology is not limited to Christianity; it finds expression in all major religions by offering alternative ways of thinking about Divinity and humanity. Feminist theology recovers and reclaims the place of women's lives, bodies, and voices in theology. It champions efforts to liberate and empower women.

Although the academic discipline of Christian feminist theology began in the 1960s and 1970s, its origins are much older. They include biblical references to a feminine face of God who nurses the children of her womb (Isa. 49:15), gathers the Israelites as a hen gathers her chicks under her wings (Pss. 17:8; 36:7; 91:4; Luke 13:34-35), and protects them as an angry mother bear robbed of her cubs (Hos. 13:8). The roots of feminist theology also lie in the visions of medieval mystics such as Julian of Norwich, who envisioned Christ as Mother, and in the doctrine of sin articulated in the seventeenth century by Margaret Fell, cofounder of the Quakers. She elucidated an original creation marked by gender equality and wholeness that the fall destroyed. In the Wesleyan-holiness tradition feminist theology has admirable precedent in such women as Phoebe Palmer. She transcended and transformed rigid gender roles through bold statements about God and contributed significantly to the nineteenth-century women's movement.

Based on a celebration of fluidity and multiplicity, and at times even dissonance, in recent decades feminist theological discourse has evolved and expanded rapidly in material, method, and style. The field employs numerous techniques to create space for examining the previously unexamined and for developing the dynamic theoretical fluidity and discord characteristic of feminist practice itself.

Topics of Christian feminist theology include how an inordinate use of masculine references for God, almost to the exclusion of feminine and non-anthropomorphic metaphors and images, have shaped Christianity and the larger society. Additional topics include how the female body and sexuality are negatively represented in sacred and literary texts, the destructive results of prevailing ideas and customs regarding the correct relationship between women and men, and what it means to be feminine and masculine.

Finding that women's theological contributions, insights, and genius have traditionally been neglected/misrepresented by male academics, scholars are making the theological voices of women visible. They are embracing the embodiment of women as a source of knowledge of God and are employing theological constructs that promote gender inclusivity. Although some feminist theologians regard Christian theology as irreparably tainted, others believe there is no decisive rupture between the theological past and the present, claiming it would be erroneous to reject the intellectual traditions on which Christian theology is founded. Still others map a transformative path of grace toward a reimagined theology free from sexism and gender prejudice.

Feminist theology shares the Wesleyan tradition's valuation of experience in its understanding of God, as well as its emphasis on the mutuality and interdependence of all persons. From its beginning, the Wesleyan-holiness tradition—not always consistently—has insisted on the full participation of women in Christ's church and on their rightful place in its theological enterprise.

See also Evangelical Feminism; Justice; Mujerista Theology; Wesleyan Feminism; Womanist Theology; Women in the Bible; Women's Role in the Church.

Resources

Clifford, Annie M. *Introducing Feminist Theology.* Maryknoll, NY: Orbis Books, 2001.

Fiorenza, Elisabeth Schüssler. *Wisdom Ways: Introducing Feminist Biblical Interpretation.* Maryknoll, NY: Orbis Books, 2001.

PATTI L. DIKES, JD

FESTIVALS

See ISRAEL; JUDAISM; TEMPLE.

FILM/CINEMA

Cinema or video is a popular fine art medium used by churches. In the West, as an art form its frequency of use in worship is second only to music. It has significant potential as a means for doctrinal engagement in two broad areas.

First, its different forms can be used for multiple worship applications, instruction, and other ministries. This involves a religion-*in*-film approach that positively assesses cinema's religious content. Documentary or genre films, for example, can support catechetical-historical instruction. Popular films can focus a congregation's attention on doctrinal or moral topics or illustrate sermonic content. Inspirational and art films can foster spiritual formation. Additionally, one can use the content of "weightier" films—including character studies—to help small groups reflect on social, moral, and philosophical topics. Many times films contain didactic, allegorical, or symbolic meanings.

A *second* broad approach to cinema considers it a parallel depiction of Christian faith and action. Specifically, this approach evaluates cinematic drama as analogous to the moments and movements of Christian discipleship. Such an interpretation permits speaking of salvation history as epic, Scripture as narrative plot, God as director, Christ as protagonist, the demonic/evil as antagonist, and the church as ensemble/cast. Cinema can serve as a foil for the failure of faith, conversion as the climax, growth in Christian holiness as the subsequent "falling action" that *builds* toward final resolution, and glorification as the finale. One benefit of viewing faith as a classic moral narrative, that is, as a conflict between good and evil played out on life's stage, is that it helps us reimagine on a grand scale what the Father accomplished in his Son through the power of the Holy Spirit.

Some Christian critics of cinema, and especially of "Hollywood values," resist such comparisons. They charge that cinema glorifies immorality, violence, and greed; it promotes negative political propaganda and social stereotypes. Avant-garde films are particularly problematic, for they often challenge values based on religious convictions, subvert public morality, and present anti-Christian worldviews. Many times these criticisms are accurate. But perhaps rather than lament current cinema, Christians should use it to picture human life when transformed by God.

Christians should be cautious users of film; it can often "feel" real and have a documentary appearance when in fact it is an audiovisual "text" that demands interpretation. It offers a carefully constructed world in which camera angles, framing, lighting, dialogue, movements, and even time it-self—through "flashes" forward, backward, and sideways—are manipulated. As with other art forms, the creator's vision is omnipresent and presupposed. To understand the cinematic message, its codes must be processed. We should always examine a film's implicit or connotative meanings and sym-bols, as well as its explicit expressions of ideas, values, and purposes. Even as Christians appreciate cinema's **aesthetic** strengths and cultural importance, they must try to discern its theological questions and challenge its overarch-ing goals and claims from a Christian perspective.

See also Arts, The; Humanism; Liturgy and Worship; Popular Culture; Secular/Secularism/Secularization.

Resources
Lyden, John, ed. *The Routledge Companion to Religion and Film.* London: Routledge, 2009.
Stone, Bryan P. *Faith and Film: Theological Themes at the Cinema.* St. Louis: Chalice Press, 2000.

KENTON STILES, PHD

FLETCHER, JOHN, THEOLOGY OF

John William Fletcher (Jean Guillaume de la Fléchère) was born in 1729 in Nyon, Switzerland. He went to Geneva for classical studies (Collège et Faculté des Lettres) but did no theological studies. He arrived in England in 1750, becoming a tutor in 1751. Later he met the Methodists and expe-rienced conversion early in 1754. He was ordained a priest in the Church of England in 1757.

John Wesley asked Fletcher to assume leadership of the Methodists in 1761 and again in 1773. Instead, from 1760 till his death in 1785 he remained vicar of Madeley, in early industrial Shropshire.

Fletcher's friendship with **Charles Wesley** was closer than that with John. He was also friends for many years with leading Calvinist Methodists, particularly Lady Huntingdon.

The controversy within Methodism over antinomianism and predestina-tion made Fletcher the "theologian of Wesleyan-**Arminianism**," and through his modeling of a sanctified life the "saint of Methodism." Well into the nine-teenth century, his *Checks to Antinomianism* and other writings were stan-dard reading for preachers in the Wesleyan tradition.

Fletcher equally opposed radical Arminianism and radical Calvinism. In *Scripture Scales* he published hundreds of pages of parallel Scripture quotations showing the similarity between "Bible Arminians" and "Bible Calvinists." Both parties must honor "free will" and "free grace." Fletcher agreed with the Calvinists that there is no such thing as natural **free will.** God's initial **grace** frees persons to respond (be response-able) to grace. Grace works in all, but it remains God's sovereign will for how intensely he reveals his grace (hence the differences between the revelation given to "Heathen," "Jews," and "Christians").

God is sovereign in bestowing his grace, but in his justice he acts equitably toward all. Predestination as Calvinists teach disregards equal justice. Therefore, Fletcher reiterates two axioms that he observes in John Wesley's writings and of which he never loses sight:

(1) ALL OUR SALVATION IS OF GOD IN CHRIST, and therefore OF GRACE. All opportunities, invitations, inclination, and power to believe are bestowed upon us of mere grace—most absolutely free. (2) According to the gospel dispensation, ALL OUR DAMNATION IS OF OURSELVES. By obstinate unbelief and avoidable unfaithfulness we may *neglect so great **salvation**,* desire to *be excused* from coming to the feast of the Lamb, *make light of* God's gracious offers, refuse to occupy, bury our talent, and act the part of slothful servants. In other words, BY OUR MORAL AGENCY we may *resist, grieve, do despite to,* and *quench the Spirit of grace.* (Streiff 2001, 196-97)

In Fletcher's mature theology he developed a Trinitarian dispensation of God's grace in history. Several of **John Wesley**'s later sermons reflect Fletcher's mature writings. If John Wesley was the champion of shortcut theological answers—unwilling "to split the hair," and if Charles championed theology in poetic praise, Fletcher was the champion of digging with love into theological debate.

Late in life, Fletcher married the woman to whom he had almost proposed marriage over twenty years earlier: Mary Bosanquet (1739–1815). An early female leader in Methodism, she began preaching in the 1760s. She engaged in widespread correspondence with many Methodists. Together with other women she led a community of Christians and established an orphanage—an effort that could not remain economically viable. A person of means, she invested her fortune in doing as much good as possible for persons in need.

At the time of their marriage in 1781, Fletcher had recovered from consumption, thanks to a trip to his native Switzerland. He was experiencing a fullness of God's Spirit of love unequalled so far in his spiritual journey. The marriage prolonged John's life for a few years. Mary often had dreams of deceased persons. After John's death, she regularly dreamed of him as a comforting presence, directing her thoughts in praise to God. She continued regular preaching services among the Methodist society in Madeley. At age seventy-five she was still preaching five times weekly.

See also Arminian Theology; Christian Perfection (Entire Sanctification); Free Will; Methodism, British; Predestination and Election; Prevenient Grace; Sanctification; Trinity; Wesley, Charles, Theology of; Wesleyan Feminism.

Resources

Forsaith, Peter S., ed. *Unexampled Labours: Letters of the Revd. John Fletcher to Leaders in the Evangelical Revival.* Peterborough, UK: Epworth Press, 2008.

Streiff, Patrick. *Reluctant Saint? A Theological Biography of Fletcher of Madeley.* Peterborough, UK: Epworth Press, 2001.

Wood, Laurence W. *The Meaning of Pentecost in Early Methodism: Rediscovering John Fletcher as John Wesley's Vindicator and Designated Successor.* Lanham, MD: Scarecrow Press, 2002.

PATRICK STREIFF, PHD

FOLK RELIGION

Folk religion refers to the everyday religious beliefs and practices of a people that give them spiritual support, help them combat and restrict evil, and procure for them divine favor. Folk religion is two-tiered—it claims to represent a religion but in many ways contrasts sharply with it. Folk religion modifies the official form of a religion as articulated by its scholars and priests. No religion, continent, or culture is free of folk religion.

Popular religion is reliant on the formal religion but is free to reinvent itself by blending old and new ideas and by even incorporating elements that contradict formal religion—usually unawares. It often introduces magic in its many forms.

Many elements of folk religion might be derived from sources that existed before a formal religion was introduced, such as the influence of African religions on formal Christianity. So folk religion mixes *folk* and *formal*, for neither exclusivism nor syncretism is able to control a religion at the popular level. It stands outside "official" control. Participants may or may not be aware of this.

The distinctions between folk and formal religion can include a primitive as opposed to a developed cosmology, animism as opposed to monotheism, manipulation of the divine as opposed to compliant worship, legalism as opposed to grace, and anthropocentrism as opposed to theocentrism. In addition, there are differences in leadership (lay or priestly) and where proper worship should occur. There are also sharp differences between folk and official religion over what should be considered pure and impure, profane and holy, true and false.

Judaism and Christianity are not immune to folk religion. Devotees of both religions are usually in contact with many other religious influences. Their everyday religious convictions are formed in complex processes of integration, rejection, and resignification of beliefs and symbols not controlled by either formal Judaism or Christianity. The OT bears repeated testimony to this phenomenon by showing how incessantly attractive Baal worship was to the people. The NT reveals that folk religion among Christians was already developing before the end of the NT era.

John Wesley was unwilling to settle for a cleavage between folk and formal Christianity. Instead, he confidently believed that the fullness of God's **grace** and the rich substance of the Christian faith are intended for all God's people, including the people whom he referred to as the "bulk of mankind" (*Works*, 5:1, "Preface"). He believed that the poor to whom he ministered had been largely ignored by the state church. They were without access to the gospel and its liberating power.

The Wesleys and the Methodists set out to correct that deficit by preaching the gospel in its fullness, by providing access to education, health care, and monetary guidance. Wesley selected a well-developed Christian library for Methodists that would educate them in the Christian faith. The **classes** and **bands** were also instruments. Confidence in the transforming grace of God propelled John and Charles Wesley and their followers.

See also New Religious Movements; Syncretism, Religious; Wesley, John, Theology of.

Resources
Hiebert, Paul G., R. Daniel Shaw, and Tite Tiénou. *Understanding Folk Religion: A Christian Response to Popular Beliefs and Practices*. Grand Rapids: Baker, 1999.
Van Rheenen, Gailyn, ed. *Contextualization and Syncretism: Navigating Cultural Currents*. Evangelical Missiological Society Series Number 13. Pasadena, CA: William Carey Library, 2006.

HELMUT RENDERS, PHD

FOUNDATIONALISM
See EPISTEMOLOGY.

FREE METHODISM

The Free Methodist Church (FMC) was formed from the evangelistic, reform-minded holiness branch of Methodism in the mid-nineteenth century. Benjamin Titus Roberts and other former ministers in the Methodist Episcopal Church in western New York formally organized the FMC in August 1860, in Pekin, New York. At a time when many in his conference were moving away from Methodism's revivalist and holiness roots, Roberts preached the need for conversion and a **holiness** experience (**entire sanctification**), followed by a life of total commitment to God and a concern for the outcast. He promoted abolishing slavery, treating women justly, and, borrowing from the central tenet of liberation theology, God's "preferential option for the poor" (Gutiérrez 1988, xxvi-xxvii). Roberts advocated building simple churches, plain dress, and free pews that would welcome the poor to worship. He also opposed Christian membership in secret societies. To reduce conflict, the Genesee Conference leaders removed Roberts and others from Methodist ministry; fifty years later their ordination papers were returned with apologies.

Begun in 1860, *The Earnest Christian* magazine became the vehicle for expressing Roberts's concerns, including Christian holiness. This must be possible, he argued, because God requires it. Roberts believed, therefore, that an initial purifying experience could be appropriated by faith. On the other hand, entire sanctification is not a fixed condition; it is like manna—gathered every day. Christian holiness requires daily vigilance to keep oneself constantly open to the Spirit's influences. So Roberts taught instantaneous and gradual dimensions of Christian holiness: the initial purifying experience entails placing oneself on the altar of Christ's cross, and continued growth in holiness means daily taking up Christ's cross.

The early FMC shared Roberts's commitment to justice for the enslaved and the poor but not for women. Roberts publicly supported women's suffrage, preached partnership in marriage (rather than male headship), and promoted the ordination of women, starting in 1861. His book *Ordaining Women* (1891) argued that women and men were made equally in God's image and are equally redeemed and gifted for God's service. At Roberts's death in 1893 the church still rejected his position, despite FMC women who had worked as pastors and evangelists throughout FMC history. Finally in 1911 the FMC ordained women as deacons, affirming them as pastors but barring them from leadership in their conferences or in the denomination. In 1974 the church voted to grant women ordination as elders and to open all positions in the church to qualified persons, regardless of gender. By 2008 women made up 11 percent of Free Methodist Church—USA clergy.

The FMC has valued education. In 1866 they founded an academy in North Chili, New York, now Roberts Wesleyan College, and started Spring Arbor University, Seattle Pacific University, and Greenville College (Illinois) by the turn of the twentieth century. Azusa Pacific University in California and Central Christian College in Kansas are affiliated schools. In addition, in the 1950s Osaka Christian College (Japan) and the Faculdade de Teológia Metodista Livre (Brazil) were founded. More recently, Northeastern Seminary (at Roberts Wesleyan) and Hope Africa University (Burundi) were begun.

By 2010, the FMC worldwide was composed of thirteen general conferences, freestanding national or regional churches with a membership of
about 750,000 (77,000 in North America). It was working in seventy-two
countries.

See also Holiness Denominations Worldwide; Methodism, American;
Wesley, John, Theology of.

Resources

Gutiérrez, Gustavo. *A Theology of Liberation: History, Politics, and Salvation.* Translated
    and edited by Caridad Inda and John Eagleson. 15th anniv. ed. Mayknoll, NY: Orbis
    Books, 1988.
Marston, Leslie Ray. *From Age to Age: A Living Witness: Free Methodism's First Century.*
    Winona Lake, IN: Light and Life Press, 1960.
Snyder, Howard A. *Populist Saints: B. T. and Ellen Roberts and the First Free Methodists.*
    Grand Rapids: Eerdmans, 2006.

KRISTINA LACELLE-PETERSON, PHD

FREE WILL

"Free will" is primarily a philosophical term referring to the capacity of rational agents to choose a course of action among various alternatives. It is
one of the most debated and debatable of philosophical issues among ancient
and modern philosophers. Many philosophers, as well as theologians (including John Wesley), argue for free will on moral grounds. Eighteenth-century
philosopher Immanuel Kant, for example, insisted that "if I ought, I can"
(see Kant [1788] 1993, bk. 1, 1.8). Otherwise, there is no logical basis of
accountability.

When used in a theological context, free will generally refers to humanity's relation to God. The topic is usually addressed in the context of the relation between divine sovereignty and human freedom. One's understanding
of God and human nature are significant aspects of the discussion.

The historically paradigmatic debate on the subject occurred between
Augustine and the British monk Pelagius. The debate hinged on the implications of original **sin**. Based on Pelagius's concern about the ethical implications of the teaching that humans, consequent on the fall, must inevitably sin,
he denied that persons are born with a fallen nature inherited from Adam.
Rather, each person became his or her own Adam. Thus each person was free
to sin or not to sin. Augustine, to the contrary, insisted that humanity's present state is *non posse non peccare* (not possible not to sin). Thus he attempted
to preserve the absolute necessity of grace as divine healing and enablement.

Thomas Aquinas held to a position known as semi-Pelagianism, which
became the basis for the medieval Catholic teaching about works-righteousness, against which the Protestant Reformers **Martin Luther** and **John Calvin**
reacted. They followed closely the position of Augustine for much the same
reason, namely, to reject the possibility of self-salvation by good works and to

exalt the absolute necessity of grace. This concern doubtless contributed to their embracing the teaching of unconditional election and predestination, which rejects any human contribution to one's salvation.

John Wesley accepted the Augustinian doctrine of original sin but modified it by his doctrine of **prevenient grace**. Although the capacity to turn to God on one's own initiative was lost in the fall, prevenient grace restores human "response-ability" and empowers persons to respond in faith to God's love. Wesley was able to sustain Pelagius's concern for moral accountability while retaining the priority of grace. Wesley's interpretation of the essence of the Christian life as responsive love was supported on the assumption that coerced love is a contradiction in terms. If humanity cannot respond in freedom to God's love, response is meaningless.

See also Anthropology, Theological; Conscience; Determinism and Free Will; Fatalism; Pelagianism; Predestination and Election; Repentance; Wesley, John, Theology of.

Resources

Kant, Immanuel. *Critique of Practical Reason*. 1788. Translated by Lewis White Beck. 3rd ed. Upper Saddle River, NJ: Prentice Hall, 1993.

Luther, Martin. *The Bondage of the Will*. Translated by Henry Cole. Lawrence, KS: Digireads.com, 2009.

Wesley, John. "Free Grace." In *Works*, 7:373-86.

H. RAY DUNNING, PHD

FRUIT OF THE SPIRIT

The metaphoric expression "fruit of the Spirit" is found only in Gal. 5:22 (twice if the KJV translation of Eph. 5:9 is accepted, though the best Greek manuscripts, where the word is "light" [*phōtos*], not "spirit" [*pneumatos*], do not support that translation). But its meaning appears often in the NT (e.g., Rom. 8:1-17; 1 Pet. 2:1-3; 3:8-10). The fruit of the Spirit is the fruit of Christ cultivated in Christians and the church by the Holy Spirit.

The word picture of fruit characterizing one's life is common in the Bible. In Ps. 1:3 the godly person, like a well-watered tree, bears fruit in its season. In John 15, the pruned branch that remains in Jesus will bear much fruit. Isaiah compares Israel to a fruit-bearing vine (5:1-7; 27:2-6), and Joel announces that when the **Spirit** is poured out on restored **Israel**, the trees and vine will bear fruit (2:18-32). So in Gal. 5:22 the metaphor "fruit of the Spirit" is not new and may be drawn from OT texts. But efforts to identify the text's precise origin are not convincing. The verse contrasts the lifestyle produced by living in (by) the Spirit with one produced by pursuing fleshly desires. The metaphor must be seen in that context.

The choice of "fruit" is significant because what is produced comes not from human effort, as do the "works of the flesh" (v. 19), but from the divine source of life that flows in fully committed Christians. The Spirit's fruit is the result of a person's life being centered "in Christ." The list in Galatians is not exhaustive (vv. 22-23). Christians will neither express the qualities on it equally nor develop them at the same pace. Unlike the **gifts of the Spirit**, the fruit of the Spirit cannot be falsified; it comes only through the indwelling Holy Spirit. Christians are directed or commanded to conduct their lives in harmony with and in the power of the Spirit (Rom. 8:9-11). Doing so evidences the fruit of the Spirit in sharp contrast to "works of the flesh" (Gal. 5:19-21).

The fruit of the Spirit is not just a set of individual and private virtues. Instead, the gracious qualities listed in verses 22-23 are meant to characterize the church, the community created through the Holy Spirit. They should mark the interpersonal relationships between Christians who are different in many ways but who together form Christ's body. The fact that love comes first in the list signifies its prominence above all the others; it is the impetus for the others. Love eventuates in action, manifesting the Spirit's work in the form of **peace**, gentleness, self-control, and whatever else maintains unity in the body of Christ.

See also Church (Ecclesiology); Gifts of the Spirit; Holy Spirit (Pneumatology); Love.

Resources

Dockery, David S. "Fruit of the Spirit." In *Dictionary of Paul and His Letters*, edited by Gerald Hawthorne, Ralph Martin, and Daniel Reid, 316-19. Downers Grove, IL: InterVarsity Press, 1993.

Hays, Richard B. "The Letter to the Galatians: Introduction, Commentary, and Reflections." In vol. 11, *The New Interpreter's Bible*, edited by Leander Keck, 181-348. Nashville: Abingdon Press, 2000.

RUSSELL LOVETT, PHD

FUNDAMENTALISMS

The term "fundamentalisms" normally refers to religious movements that seek unambiguously to oppose the presumed heresies unleashed by **modernism, secularism**, and other deceptive sources. They adhere to a set of premodern doctrines, behaviors, and worldviews and seek to reestablish them in society. In addition to **Protestant** fundamentalists who espouse **fundamentalist theology**, fundamentalists are found in other religions as well. Some forms of fundamentalism approve the use of violence; many do not. Fundamentalist groups are present among Hindus, Muslims, Jews, Mormons, and Buddhists. Adherents would choose the description "orthodox" over "fundamentalist."

Muslim fundamentalists, who prefer the term "Islamic fundamentalists," exist in diverse forms. These include Salafism and Wahhabism. They adhere to literal interpretations of the Qur'an and Hadith and work to replace state secular laws with Shari'a (law based on the Qur'an). Among Hindus, Hindutva fundamentalism refers to an intolerant political ideology arising out of Hinduism. It is expressed in Shiv Sena and the Bharatiya Janata Party. Jewish fundamentalists include militant **Zionists** and various forms of ultraorthodox Judaism. Mormon fundamentalists work to restore beliefs and practices, such as plural marriages, now rejected by the Church of Jesus Christ of Latter-day Saints. Buddhist fundamentalists hold radical separatist views and practices in relation to mainstream Buddhism.

Similarities in the various fundamentalisms typically include (1) sacred scriptures that stand above criticism; (2) a clear, eternal and unquestionable revelation from their god or gods; (3) adherence to a narrow understanding of their faith, consisting of clearly defined beliefs and practices considered above critique, and an intolerance of those who disagree; (4) social distinctions established with and passed down through cultural traditions; and (5) a willingness from adherents to sacrifice their lives for the faith.

Fundamentalists from various religions often share common social views and moral norms. These include the role of women in religion, home, and society; opposition to abortion, homosexuality, consumerism, and materialism; and support for law and order.

Because of their radical worldviews, some nonreligious movements can be classified as fundamentalist. These include vocally militant atheists who see religion as humankind's enemy and work to eliminate it. Their radical empiricism and secularism and intolerance of beliefs about transcendent reality qualify them as fundamentalists. The same applies to radical secularists who oppose any expression of religion in the public square.

See also Fundamentalist Theology; Islam; New Religious Movements; Polygamy; Postmodernity; Religious Pluralism.

Resources

Marty, Martin E., and R. Scott Appleby, eds. *Accounting for Fundamentalisms: The Dynamic Character of Movements.* The Fundamentalism Project 4. Chicago: University of Chicago Press, 2004.

———, eds. *Fundamentalisms Comprehended.* The Fundamentalism Project 5. Chicago: University of Chicago Press, 2004.

———, eds. *Fundamentalisms Observed.* The Fundamentalism Project 1. Chicago: University of Chicago Press, 1994.

NORMAN WILSON, PHD

FUNDAMENTALIST THEOLOGY

Fundamentalist theology is the product of fundamentalist Christianity, a reactionary movement that arose mainly within British and American Protestantism in the late nineteenth and early twentieth centuries. The irenic holiness revivalism of Dwight L. Moody (1837-99) yielded to a more disaffected, creedal, culture-fighting evangelicalism. In reaction to **liberal theology**, fundamentalists defended the "fundamentals" of Christian orthodoxy that they believed modern thought was eroding and established churches were betraying.

Targets of the fundamentalist movement were academic liberty in Christian colleges and universities, Darwinism, higher criticism of the Bible, the **social gospel**, and comparative religions. "Findings" of modern **science** that appeared to contradict the plain teaching of the Bible were rejected as misguided and arrogant. Fundamentalists tended toward intransigence and inflexibility, insisting on "orthodox" truth without always exhibiting an orthodox love for those who disagreed with them. The label "fundamentalism" became a pejorative term to some and a banner of pride to others.

An early formulation of American fundamentalist beliefs came from the Niagara Bible Conference, followed by a widely distributed series of tracts titled *The Fundamentals: A Testimony to the Truth* (1910-15). They articulated the doctrines judged fundamental to Christian faith, including the inerrancy of the Bible, the virgin birth, substitutionary atonement, and the bodily resurrection of Jesus.

The **dispensationalism** of J. N. Darby (1800-1882), popularized through the *Scofield Reference Bible*, became almost standard as the lens for viewing the future.

J. Gresham Machen (1881–1937) and Benjamin Breckinridge Warfield (1851–1921), both professors at Princeton Theological Seminary, although not dispensationalists or premillennialists, were important precursors to fundamentalism.

Some conservatives in the 1950s abandoned the fundamentalist label and style. They retained the fundamentals while being more intellectually refined, socially concerned, and cooperative in spirit. Pastor and educator Harold J. Ockenga proposed "new evangelical" as an alternative designation. American evangelist Billy Graham came from a fundamentalist background but cooperated freely with a wide range of conservative Christians. Carl F. H. Henry was a prominent "evangelical" scholar who helped institutionalize the newer evangelicalism by assisting in the establishment of Fuller Theological Seminary and founding the magazine *Christianity Today*.

Carl McIntire formed the American Council of Christian Churches in 1941, an umbrella for fundamentalist bodies. The rival National Association of Evangelicals (NAE) was formed the following year for conservative, but more moderate, Christian leaders and denominations. The NAE holds core classical theological convictions but is not reactionary or separatist in attitude and action.

Fundamentalism remains influential, a principal contemporary example being **creationism**. Its effective use of radio and television continues to reach millions.

See also Biblicism/Bibliolatry; Creationism; Ecumenism; Evolution/
Evolutionary Biology; Fundamentalisms; Hermeneutics; Modernity;
Natural Science; Religious Pluralism; Science and the Bible; Scripture,
Wesleyan Approach to; Secular/Secularism/Secularization; Social Gospel.

Resources

Barr, James. *Fundamentalism.* Philadelphia: Westminster Press, 1978.

Marsden, George M. *Fundamentalism and American Culture: The Shaping of Twentieth-Century Evangelism 1870–1925.* New York: Oxford University Press, 1980.

Rogers, Jack B., and Donald K. McKim. *The Authority and Interpretation of the Bible: An Historical Approach.* Eugene, OR: Wipf and Stock Publishers, 1999.

Sandeen, Ernest R. *The Roots of Fundamentalism: British and American Millenarianism, 1800–1930.* Chicago: University of Chicago Press, 1970.

BARRY CALLEN, EDD

Gg

GENERAL REVELATION
See REVELATION.

GIFTS OF THE SPIRIT

In definition and practice "gifts of the Spirit" is unnecessarily one of the more divisive topics in the **church**. Three passages address the topic specifically: Rom. 12:6-8; 1 Cor. 12–14; and Eph. 4:11-16. Exegesis of these texts can add to the confusion because the Greek words for "gifts" change, and at times the role of the Spirit is not clear.

Too seldom is the topic addressed in relationship to Jesus' teaching on the purpose and role of the **Holy Spirit**. When speaking of returning to his Father and of sending the Holy Spirit to the disciples, **Jesus** said, "The one who believes in me . . . will do greater works than these, because I am going to the Father" (John 14:12). The cumulative effect of these texts is that the gifts of the Spirit are specific, God-given abilities provided as needed to believers so that the purposes of Christ can be fulfilled through the church's ministry under the Spirit's leadership. The gifts of the Spirit are Christ's gifts to the church, administered by the Holy Spirit.

Accordingly, the gifts must be distinguished from natural talents inherent in a person's temperament or personality. The two may work together, but the Holy Spirit alone administers Christ's gifts and empowers the gifts he bestows.

Because of the immensely diverse and unpredictable nature of ministry for which gifts are needed, there is no exhaustive list of spiritual gifts. They do, however, seem to fall into three categories: (1) Spirit manifestations within the worshipping community, (2) deeds of service, and (3) specific ministries. Some gifts listed under Spirit manifestations represent religious phenomena at times exhibited in past and present pagan religions. These include **glossolalia** (ecstatic languages), **miracles**, and healing. Because, as was the case in Corinth, other spirits may manifest these phenomena, their expression in the church may be, but need not be, falsified and used to create confusion instead of health in the church. At other times, their apparent authenticity may be nothing more than a learned response instead of being true manifestations of the Spirit's presence and work.

The **Holy Spirit** alone, not human initiative, determines which gifts are needed and when. The Spirit decides to whom the gifts will be given. To some he gives one or more lifelong gifts, because the church always has need of them. In other instances, the Spirit gives to specific persons a unique ability only as the need exists. In all instances the Spirit gives his gifts to the church for building it up. He does not give them to individuals for personal aggrandizement or to satisfy their carnal desires. Pride associated with possessing certain gifts thought to be more important than others was a major source of division in the Corinthian church. That error remains an ever-present threat to the church.

Because the Spirit's gifts are for ministry, believers **discern** their own gifting by exercising ministry. Under supervision, new believers—especially—should be encouraged to participate in different ministry activities to discern ministries for which the Holy Spirit has gifted them.

See also Charismatic Theology; Demons/Unclean Spirits; Fruit of the Spirit; Means of Grace; Miracles/Signs and Wonders; Spiritual Formation/ Growth.

RUSSELL LOVETT, PHD

GLOBALIZATION

"Globalization" is a popular twenty-first-century term, as well as a hotly debated concept in academic literature. The word originated in twentieth-century economic and political analysis and refers generally to the increasing global social, economic, and political integration of all human culture (including technology, language, art, music, literature, traditions, customs, diet, child rearing, health care, work, and consumption).

While the term is fairly new, the roots of globalization trace back to the global trade networks established by the fifteenth-century Portuguese and Spanish conquistadores. Even further back, globalization's roots lie in the Christian Crusades of the eleventh to thirteenth centuries. And beyond that, globalization can be traced to Alexander the Great's program of Hellenization.

Modern globalization emerged from the colonization and exploitation of the world's peoples and resources by European nations. Accelerating technological sophistication, as well as the military and economic power of dominant nations, helps drive it. Modern colonization came first with the Portuguese and the Spanish (fifteenth to seventeenth centuries), then the British and the French (eighteenth to nineteenth centuries), and then the United States (twenty-first century to the present).

The meaning and merits of globalization are contested. There is wide disagreement over whether globalization is a range of processes or a series of interconnected projects, a new era or nothing new, politically the end or the revival of the modern nation-state, a creator of more of the same or a multiplier of diversity and difference.

Some argue that globalization is a natural or unalterable range of processes driven by the global integration of markets, nation-states, and technologies that enable individuals, corporations, and nation-states to reach around the world farther, faster, deeper, and cheaper than ever before. Others argue that globalization is a set of deliberate, ideologically driven projects pushing economic liberalization, spreading free-market capitalism to the benefit of the major actors that control capital and at the expense of the world's poor majority.

One line of argument maintains that globalization constrains nation-states. Supposedly, free trade limits the ability of states to set policy and protect domestic companies, capital mobility makes generous welfare states less competitive, global problems exceed the grasp of any individual state, and global norms and institutions become more powerful. Others argue that globalization is nothing new; it is but an extension of the exploitative practices of colonialism on a global scale, with a growing global class structure not confined to particular nations. Nation-states still control armies that defend and protect geographic borders and diverse corporate interests.

Also debated is the degree to which these processes/projects are bringing about less diversity and increased sameness around the world and the extent to which they are resulting in new forms of diversity and local identities. For example, young Tanzanians have embraced hip-hop culture from the United States and, to a degree, mimic the music and lifestyles inherited from global media outlets. But they also transform and use these styles locally. Even so, while no one must accept what global corporations sell, a disproportionate advantage belongs to global corporations in distributing and consuming symbols, buying habits, and popular culture.

See also Capitalism; Christianity and Global Cultures; Indigenous Theologies; Popular Culture; Secular/Secularism/Secularization; Technology, Ethic of; Social Justice.

Resources
Barrett, David B., George T. Kurian, and Todd M. Johnson, eds. World Christian Encyclopedia: A Comparative Survey of Churches and Religions in the Modern World. 2 vols. New York: Oxford University Press, 2001.

Eitzen, D. Stanley, and Maxine Baca Zinn. *Globalization: The Transformation of Social Worlds*. Wadsworth Sociology Reader Series. 3rd ed. Belmont, CA: Wadsworth, 2011.

Johnstone, Patrick. *The Future of the Global Church: History, Trends, and Possibilities.* Downers Grove, IL: InterVarsity Press, 2012.

Noll, Mark A. *The New Shape of World Christianity: How American Experience Reflects Global Faith.* Downers Grove, IL: InterVarsity Press, 2009.

JAMIE GATES, PHD

GLOBAL SOUTH

First coined by the United Nations, the term "Global South" refers to Africa, Asia, and the Southern Hemisphere of the Americas. It includes multiple continents. Demographically, Christianity is moving steadily southward and is taking on a distinctive character marked by the shift. There are continuities and pronounced differences between traditional Western churches and churches in the Global South. This is no less true of Global South churches in the Wesleyan tradition.

Some common characteristics mark the Wesleyan movement in the Global South. *First*, as whole, Wesleyan churches are growing numerically in ways other Western churches are not. *Second*, Global South churches are attuned to **Scripture** in ways that differ from many Western churches. All of life is viewed and lived through Scripture without dividing the world into sacred and secular. *Third*, Global South Wesleyan churches have a more **Pentecostal** flavor. This is often expressed in worship, styles of prayer, and belief in **miracles** and healings. *Fourth*, Global South churches, because of various aspects of colonialism, understand the social aspects of the gospel in some ways that differ from Western churches. For them the **gospel** has everything to do with social and political structures.

Given these characteristics, what marks Global South churches as Wesleyan? *First*, many of the churches in the Global South know that while salvation is consummated in **heaven**, it significantly changes the here and now. They reclaim a Wesleyan focus on **sanctification** as living out **salvation** in this world, while realizing that heaven is yet to come. A complementary emphasis on personal salvation *and* social transformation characterizes many of these churches.

The Wesleyan ideal of justification is central because a personal relationship with Jesus is foundational for being Christian. This makes social transformation possible. When regimes attempt to rule by force, because of a relationship with Jesus, communities are able to withstand oppression.

The emphasis on salvation in this world also includes a special commitment to the poor. Like Wesley, many Global South churches minister to the economic conditions of "the least among us" (see Matt. 25:31-46). For them, embodying the gospel entails caring for neighbors. Acts of piety and mercy are integrated into daily life as a part of being in community.

Many churches in the Global South expand on the Wesleyan understanding of the **means of grace** in their attitude toward healing and miracles. Showing mercy toward one's neighbor includes regularly praying for miracles and healings. Experiencing miracles and healings from God are not extraordinary events but normal parts of daily life. Fully loving one's neighbor entails concern for his or her spiritual, social, and physical well-being. Scripture and prayer shape individuals and communities.

Although Wesleyan churches in the Global South are similar to Western churches in their embrace of Wesleyan theology, because of their contexts they exhibit their own distinctive characteristics.

See also Christianity and Global Cultures; Church and State; Glossolalia; Miracles/Signs and Wonders; Mission and Social Justice; Wesley, John, Theology of; Works of Mercy; Works of Piety.

Resources

Jenkins, Philip. *The New Faces of Christianity: Believing the Bible in the Global South.* New York: Oxford University Press, 2006.

———. *The Next Christendom: The Coming of Global Christianity.* 3rd ed. New York: Oxford University Press, 2011.

Kim, Elijah J. F. *The Rise of the Global South: The Decline of Western Christendom and the Rise of Majority World Christianity.* Eugene, OR: Wipf and Stock Publishers, 2012.

F. DOUGLAS POWE JR., PHD

GLORY

See GOD, DOCTRINE OF.

GLOSSOLALIA

"Glossolalia" is a technical term coined in the late 1800s. It derives from the NT expression "to speak in tongues" (Greek, *lalein glōssais*). Glossolalia is a gift of the Spirit that enables individuals to speak in languages they have not learned. It is a sign of the Messiah's end-time outpouring of the Spirit and a supernatural way to magnify God and God's saving acts. Glossolalia is mentioned in only three NT books: Acts, 1 Corinthians, and Mark (the longer ending).

The book of Acts reports tongue speaking at Pentecost (2:4, 11), the house of Cornelius (10:46), and the conversion of followers of John the Baptist in Ephesus (19:6). These strategic events signal Christ's eschatological gift of the Holy Spirit to restore and expand Israel. In Acts, glossolalia involves speaking in actual human languages, unknown to the speakers but recognizable to visitors in Jerusalem from around the world (2:4, 6, 8-11). Its content and practice declare "God's deeds of power" (v. 11) and "[extol] God" (10:46). Though associated with prophetic speech (2:18; 19:6), tongue speaking is not a vehicle for preaching the gospel. The multilingual praise at Pentecost drew bewilderment and accusations of drunkenness (2:6, 12-13), necessitating a proper exposition of God's saving activity during Peter's sermon (vv. 14-36).

The common view that glossolalia in 1 Cor. 12–14 differs fundamentally from that in Acts can no longer be maintained. Suggested pagan origins (e.g., the oracle at Delphi or **mystery religions**) for "ecstatic utterances" at Corinth have not survived scrutiny (Forbes, *Prophecy and Inspired Speech*, 103-87). For Paul, glossolalia is the spiritual gift of speaking in unlearned human (perhaps also angelic) languages (13:1). He uses the same terminology for glossolalia as Acts does; its companion gift is the interpretation of tongues (12:10, 30; 14:5, 13, 26-28); and his illustrations relate to actual languages (14:10-11, 21).

Glossolalia was overvalued in the Corinthian church and was exercised in self-serving, divisive, and chaotic ways. Paul prefers prophecy in the assembly because it is immediately intelligible and edifies listeners (vv. 1, 3-6, 24, 31, 39). He limits the number of instances of glossolalia during corporate worship and lays down the requirement of interpreting tongues (vv. 26-28). In private, glossolalia benefits the individual as Spirit-aided praying, singing, blessing, and thanksgiving to God (vv. 2, 14-16).

The later addition to Mark (16:9-20), with its unique reference to speaking in "new tongues" (v. 17), attests to glossolalia among early Christians, perhaps into the second century AD.

Widespread practice of tongue speaking continued into the third century (Tertullian, Novatian) and perhaps into the fourth (Pachomius, Ambrose). In both East and West, Chrysostom and Augustine reported a cessation of charismatic gifts. Yet pockets of glossolalia emerged later (e.g., among the Camisards, noted by **John Wesley** in his day, and the Irvingites in the 1830s). Tongue speaking especially marks modern **Pentecostalism**, which sprang from the American holiness movement in the early 1900s. Pentecostalism deviated from the holiness movement by supplementing the second work of grace, **entire sanctification**, with the experience of the **baptism with the Holy Spirit** and its initial physical evidence of speaking in tongues.

See also Charismatic Theology; Gifts of the Spirit; Holiness Movements: American, British, and Continental; Pentecostal Theology.

Resources
Forbes, Christopher. *Prophecy and Inspired Speech in Early Christianity and Its Hellenistic Environment.* Tübingen, DE: Mohr, 1995. Reprint, Peabody, MA: Hendrickson, 1997.

Turner, Max. *The Holy Spirit and Spiritual Gifts.* Carlisle, UK: Paternoster, 1996. Reprint, Peabody, MA: Hendrickson, 1998.

KEVIN L. ANDERSON, PHD

GOD, DOCTRINE OF

John Wesley and the early Methodists inherited a broadly traditional and classical vision of God. They held a **Trinitarian** conception of God and kept intact the standard attributes of omniscience, omnipotence, omnipresence, omnibenevolence (all goodness), timelessness, and so on. Moreover, Wesleyans saw no need to alter the doctrine of the double procession (the *filioque* clause, namely, that the Holy Spirit proceeds from both the Father and the Son). This inheritance was Anglican and medieval in substance; in addition, it was believed to be biblical in its foundations. The distinctive Wesleyan move was to emphasize the **love** and **holiness** of God as the core of any doctrine of God that fully harmonized with the **gospel**. Overall, the early Wesleyans seemed content to leave the received tradition intact, focusing on the doctrine of the Christian life.

In the period after Wesley, in the great but neglected era of Methodist dogmatic theology, Wesleyan theologians worked hard to articulate the complex tradition of the Western church in a Wesleyan voice. After Methodist theologians in the nineteenth century split into "liberal" and "conservative" wings, this material was dismissed by many as aridly scholastic and out of touch with new developments in history and science. The conservative wing of Methodism helpfully preserved and mediated this inheritance, developing full-scale **systematic theologies.** They thus made available the crucial doctrinal background within which the doctrines of **justification, new birth,** assurance, and **sanctification** were lodged and without which they become transmuted into psychological and political categories. Without a robust doctrine of God the Wesleyan tradition readily becomes anthropocentric and suffocating.

The most powerful innovations began showing up in the mainstream traditions in the late nineteenth century. Influenced by idealist philosophy imported from Germany, Methodist theologians reworked their vision of God in a **liberal** Protestant direction, looking to religious experience as the relevant foundation for their proposals. This change reflected a radical turn to philosophy as a positive handmaid to theology, so much so that there was an easy transition from Boston **personalism** to the much more popular **process** tradition. The attraction for the doctrine of God was that these traditions appeared to provide a better home for personal piety than the classical tradition of the **church**. God was relational to the very core, responding temporally to events in personal experience and the world.

When the Barthian reversal of liberalism took hold, many Wesleyans turned to neoorthodoxy as a radical alternative that better reflected the God of the Bible, eschewed the God of the philosophers, and escaped the skepticism of the Anglo-American analytic tradition. The more conservative incarnations of the tradition have recently been drawn to both the process and

Barthian traditions. There is a common desire across the Wesleyan tradition to interact with wider developments in theology at large.

Some are drawn to **open theism** in order to safeguard the commitment to genuine human freedom. In this tradition, God does not know the free future decisions of human agents because these decisions as a matter of logic cannot be known in advance. This move is seen as more biblical, it fits with wider developments within **evangelicalism**, and it champions a cleansing of the classical tradition from Greek influences as reflected in the doctrine of divine impassibility. All these arguments are deeply contested. If divine foreknowledge is compatible with knowing our free future actions, as depicted in the idea of simple foreknowledge, then some of the motivation for open theism vanishes.

The most thorough effort to recover a traditional and classical vision of God is represented by Thomas Oden, whose consensual method locates Wesley and the best of the Wesleyan tradition in the wider doctrinal agreements that stretch across space and time. This option is deliberately cast as an antidote to the process tradition, seen as having sacrificed the transcendence of God, and to the **liberation** tradition, seen as having wrongly construed the God of the classical tradition as a projection of bourgeois, middle-class culture.

One unknown factor for the future is the possible impact of analytic philosophy and analytic theology on the tradition. The former tends to stick to the God of mere theism; the latter involves tentative steps to include the fullness of the Christian conception of God. Given the instability of philosophical results, we can well expect fresh if rigorously precise innovations.

See also Biblical Theology; Christology; Creeds (Nicene, Chalcedonian, Apostles', Athanasian); Hiddenness of God; Incarnation; Metaphors and Names for God in the Bible; Trinity.

Resources
Abraham, William J., Jason E. Vickers, and Natalie B. Van Kirk, eds. *Canonical Theism: A Proposal for Theology and the Church*. Grand Rapids: Eerdmans, 2008.

Knowles, Michael P. *The Unfolding Mystery of the Divine Names*. Downers Grove, IL: IVP Academic, 2012.

Leupp, Roderick T. *Knowing the Name of God*. Downers Grove, IL: InterVarsity Press, 1996.

Oden, Thomas C. *The Living God*. Vol. 1, *Systematic Theology*. San Francisco: Harper and Row, 1987.

Stone, Bryan P., and Thomas J. Oord. *Thy Nature and Thy Name Is Love: Wesleyan and Process Theologies in Dialogue*. Nashville: Kingswood Books, 2001.

WILLIAM ABRAHAM, PHD

GOD'S EXISTENCE, ARGUMENTS FOR
See NATURAL THEOLOGY.

GOSPEL

The word "gospel" has meant different things in different contexts. Most often it means "good news." Matthew, Mark, and Luke make the "gospel of the kingdom" the essence of Jesus' earthly teaching (e.g., Matt. 4:23; Mark 1:15). This suggests that Isa. 52:7 provided key background for how Jesus viewed his ministry. In particular, Jesus likely saw his ministry as part of the restoration of God's reign within Israel and the world, including the defeat of evil powers that currently rule the earth.

The original context of Isa. 52:7 was the return of Israel from captivity in Babylon around the year 538 BC. The statement in that verse, "Your God reigns," seems to connect directly to Jesus' proclaiming the kingdom of God, the rule of God returning to earth as it is in heaven. Early Christians, like Paul primarily, read this verse in its Greek translation, where they found the verb "to proclaim the good news" (*euangelizōmai*). It is thus quite possible that the early Christian use of the word "gospel" started among Greek-speaking Christians who connected Jesus' preaching of the rule of God with the Greek sense of "gospel" as being the announcement of good news of momentous importance. For example, a famous inscription from 9 BC refers to the Roman emperor Augustus as a savior whose enthronement was good news (*euangelion*) for humanity.

A major focus of the gospel in Matthew, Mark, and Luke is Jesus' ministry to the poor. Luke 4:18 pictures Jesus quoting Isa. 61:1 as part of the inaugural address of his ministry: "The Spirit of the Lord is upon me, because he has anointed me *to bring good news* to the poor" (emphasis added). Matthew 4:23 also connects Jesus' ministry of healing to his proclamation of the good news. Matthew, Mark, and Luke thus understood the gospel as referring not only to the coming reign of God over the earth but also to Jesus' liberating ministry to the oppressed and disempowered.

In Jesus' ministry, the good news was about God's reign. In Paul's writings, the gospel is about Jesus Christ himself as King. Jesus descended from King David in his humanity and was enthroned "Son of God" as part of his resurrection (Rom. 1:3-4). The title "Son of God" refers to Jesus as King, Messiah, Christ. The background for this phrase is firmly planted in OT passages such as 2 Sam. 7:14 and Ps. 2, which were originally about kings of Judah. Other NT books also picture Jesus' exaltation to God's right hand as a kind of enthronement as Son of God (e.g., Acts 13:33; Heb. 1:5).

Paul's sense of the gospel of Jesus is thus much like the inscription about Augustus. The good news is that Jesus has been enthroned as King. As King he will bring justice and salvation to the earth. The gospel thus extends beyond the fact that Jesus is King to the consequent benefits and blessings.

Mark 1:1 probably has a similar sense of the word "gospel." Mark's opening narrates the beginning of the good news that Jesus Christ is King: "The beginning of the gospel . . ." (KJV). Later readers took the phrase to mean that Mark itself was a gospel. It is thus likely a coincidence of history that the word "gospel" came to refer not just to the good news of Jesus as King but also to the genre of books such as Mark that present the good news about Jesus. We now refer to the books Matthew, Mark, Luke, and John as gospels, whereas originally their audiences would have thought of them either as biographies (Matthew, Mark, John) or as histories (Luke-Acts).

See also Atonement; Christology; Kingdom of God; Law and Gospel; Salvation (Soteriology).

Resources

Burridge, Richard. *What Are the Gospels? A Comparison with Graeco-Roman Biography.* 2nd ed. Grand Rapids: Eerdmans, 2004.

Ladd, George Eldon. *The Gospel of the Kingdom: Scriptural Studies in the Kingdom of God.* 1959. Reprint, Carlisle, UK: Paternoster, 2000.

Wright, N. T. *What Saint Paul Really Said: Was Paul of Tarsus the Real Founder of Christianity?* Grand Rapids: Eerdmans, 1997.

KENNETH SCHENCK, PHD

GRACE

"The grace of the Lord **Jesus Christ**, the **love** of God, and the communion of the **Holy Spirit** be with all of you" (2 Cor. 13:13). Paul's benediction identifies grace with Christ. Since Paul is adamant that "Christ crucified" (1 Cor. 1:23) is the **gospel** to be preached, grace's meaning must be tied to Christ's work on the **cross.**

Cognate ideas are associated with grace. The Corinthian benediction joins grace to "love" and "communion" and places it in **Trinitarian** form. Other terms associated with grace are "faith," "reconciliation," "truth," "hope," and "adoption," all of which enrich the tapestry of grace. Grace and the related terms reveal the extent of God's **salvation** offered to humanity and the creation. Clearly, grace is God's gift, void of all prior human initiative. Grace arises from God's love, not from what humanity deserves. Paul declares, "By grace you have been saved through faith, and this is not your own doing; it is the gift of God" (Eph. 2:8).

The gospel of John concurs: "The Word became flesh and lived among us, and we have seen his glory, the glory as of a father's only son, full of grace and truth" (John 1:14). That God's grace and salvation are offered to all humanity and creation is a radical declaration.

Grace is the heart of all Christian **theology**, whether biblical, doctrinal, historical, or pastoral. Since grace is revealed in Jesus Christ and proclaimed as the Father's gift, the Christian message is clear: the Father is the source of grace, given out of his love. Grace is communicated at the Holy Spirit's initiative. So grace is thoroughly Trinitarian.

The direct implication of grace is that the human condition is deeply flawed, a condition from which all persons need deliverance that they cannot generate. In response, God's unmerited grace extends to all persons as an invitation to transformation. Not only does God by grace initiate salvation, but he also graciously continues to work throughout a person's life.

God's grace has enormous social and cosmic consequences. It is active in persons and in the created order, even before its recipients are aware. God's grace isn't limited to humans; Scripture speaks of "new heavens and a new earth" (2 Pet. 3:13). All creation awaits gracious liberation and restoration (see Rom. 8:19-22).

Nevertheless, the specific sinful human condition is directly addressed. A solution is needed. **John Wesley** identified stages of God's workings. He didn't intend to suggest that a different grace is assigned in each phase but simply that God works in differing ways for differing purposes. Wesley taught **prevenient grace** (preventing grace), justifying grace, and **sanctifying** grace. Prevenient grace precedes and enables a person's response to God's call. It does not produce conversion or regeneration but initiates awareness of God and one's need for salvation. Grace can also be regenerative and reconciling if a person responds obediently to God's call. He or she repents, experiences God's forgiveness, and is restored to a right relationship (born anew from above) with God and others.

Transformation is radical; it involves transition from a self-centered life to one centered on Jesus Christ. This is life marked by fellowship with God and responsible freedom. It is energized by the Holy Spirit. God's grace subsequently works to sanctify, continually transforming a person in Christ's image.

Important to Wesley's explanation of grace is that it universally extends to all persons, with the intent of their salvation. This entails that Christ lived and died for all.

It is imperative to view the **church** in light of God's grace. It is made possible through the **reconciliation** accomplished by Christ (2 Cor. 5:17-21). Grace is manifest in the communion the Holy Spirit establishes. Not only is the church a graced fellowship (*koinōnia*), but grace is also its message—the gospel of God.

See also Biblical Theology; Creation/New Creation; Holiness; Justification; New Birth (Regeneration); *Ordo Salutis;* Spiritual Formation/Growth.

Resources

Collins, Kenneth J. *The Theology of John Wesley: Holy Love and the Shape of Grace.* Nashville: Abingdon Press, 2007.

Torrance, T. F. *The Doctrine of Grace in the Apostolic Fathers.* Edinburgh: Oliver and Boyd, 1948.

DAVID RAINEY, PHD

GREEK PHILOSOPHY

Greek philosophy flowered in the fifth and fourth centuries BC, most notably in Plato (ca. 427–ca. 348/7 BC); Socrates, his teacher (ca. 469–399 BC); and Plato's student Aristotle (384/3-322 BC). They have shaped **metaphysics**, **epistemology**, logic, **ethics**, and philosophic method in the West ever since. They relied on reason to investigate reality. Only fragments remain of the work of pre-Socratic philosophers such as Thales, Pythagoras, and Parmenides, but in them we see the beginnings of a marked shift to nontheological theories.

Plato used dialogue for doing philosophy. He often featured Socrates as the protagonist. Socrates' thought, which he himself never recorded, heavily influenced Plato's earlier dialogues. In the later dialogues Socrates serves as a mouthpiece for Plato's own ideas. Typically, the dialogues portray Socrates as engaging interlocutors to examine, in systematic fashion, a wide range of topics. The method is dialectic. The process regularly challenges inherited philosophical, moral, religious, and political dogma. It unmasks ignorance and punctures pride. Arrival at truth is the goal of dialectic.

This method led Plato to his most distinctive contribution to philosophy, the theory of forms. The empirical world, according to Plato, consists only of flawed instances of what is most real. Reality is comprised of transcendent, universal, eternal, and immutable forms. For example, a person is made just by participating in the form **Justice**. Forms are not known through sense experience, but through reason. With philosophical training, the mind can know the real. This is a capacity of the **soul**.

Plato paired the doctrine of forms with the doctrine of recollection. Before entering the body, the **soul**—by nature immortal—knows the forms. But this knowledge is lost at birth. It can be remembered (recalled) when properly guided by philosophy. The mind must be led away from believing that what the senses perceive, the empirical, is most real and led to the transcendent realm of eternal forms.

Conversely, for Aristotle, sensory **experience** was critical for acquiring knowledge of reality. He rejected Plato's theory of transcendent forms and the way of knowledge associated with them. His account of reality, set forth in the *Metaphysics*, was founded on what he observed of the natural world. Paramount for Aristotle was teleology, or the concept that all things move toward fulfilling or "perfecting" (*telos*) their essential nature. This is one of four ways of explaining why things exist, the other three being explanations in terms of efficient, material, and formal "causes." According to Aristotle, forms are fully *in* things and account for those things being the sort of things they are.

Aristotle's teleological explanation of reality is perhaps best explicated in his *Nicomachean Ethics*. He answers the question, "What is the human being for?" Aristotle thought of humans being in movement from what they are to what they are meant to be by way of appetite, will, and rational activity. He observed that individuals strive for the highest end proper to human nature: *eudaemonia* (flourishing or happiness). By Aristotle's account, *eudaemonia* is rightly perceived and cultivated through a virtuous life. Although **virtues** are particular to human nature, they are not natural characteristics like the senses. Rather, virtues must be cultivated until they are "habituated," thus becoming one's characteristic disposition. Friendship is critical for actualizing virtue; virtuous friends help friends mature and realize the good through shared projects.

The emphasis Socrates, Plato, and Aristotle placed on the rigorous exercise of reason does not limit philosophy to individualism. Philosophy expands to include community. Community, along with honoring reason as a source of wisdom and embracing the discipline necessary for becoming good or virtuous in community, is central to their pursuits.

Plato and Aristotle have profoundly influenced Christian theology, Plato through Augustine and many others, and Aristotle through Thomas Aquinas and many others.

See also Epistemology; Ethics; Metaphysics; Neoplatonism; Virtues.

Resources
Abraham, William J. *Aldersgate and Athens: John Wesley and the Foundations of Christian Belief.* Waco, TX: Baylor University Press, 2010.
Copleston, Frederick. *Greece and Rome: From the Pre-Socratics to Plotinus.* Vol. 1, *A History of Philosophy.* New York: Image Books, 1993.

JAMES E. READ, PHD

GREEN THEOLOGY
Christians marvel over the grandeur of God's creation. We are mandated to exercise stewardship over it and to recognize that it, too, is the object of Christ's redemption (Rom. 8:18-25). "Green," a late twentieth-century word, arose out of concern for environmental well-being. Green often refers to practices or policies that do not negatively affect the environment, such as preferring solar energy over nonrenewable resources. "Green" is also a term for humanity's care for God's creation; it is consistent with the Christian conviction found in Romans (similar terms are "creation care," "environmental stewardship," and "sustainability").

Green theology considers how God relates to the creation, and the role Christians should play. Green theology examines the wholeness of the biophysical environment from the perspective of God as Creator and Redeemer.

Christian valuation of our biophysical environment is grounded in creation, incarnation, the fall, and redemption. God created the world and called it good. But the creation has been marred by sin, including the relationship between humans and their physical environment. Through the incarnation, God has provisionally restored that relationship and is now, through the Holy Spirit, bringing the victory to completion (Rom. 8:19-23; Eph. 1:7-11).

Just as humanity's sin affected the creation, the gospel of Christ includes a human role in restoring the creation. In Gen. 1 God told humans to "fill the earth and to *subdue* it" (v. 28, emphasis added). We are to rule over the fish, wild animals, and "every creeping thing" (v. 26). We are to be accountable for our stewardship over God's gift. Dominion, *not domination*, was God's charge to humans. But in our sinfulness, we have acted not as stewards, not as receiving the creation as God's gift. Instead, we have distorted our relationship with the creation and have treated it as a possession for selfish exploitation.

Some Christians discount stewardship over the creation, believing instead that the world is incorrigibly evil and that God will soon destroy it and replace it with a "heavenly kingdom." For them, there is little interest in green theology. But Wesleyans cannot embrace this low estimate of the world. John Wesley's confidence was that the kingdom of God will be established "on earth as it is in heaven" (Matt. 6:10) and that God is even now working for the restoration of all things. Wesley showed negligible interest in writings that speculated on the end-time. He had no patience for **apocalyptic** speculation and was content to know that God will in his own time consummate the kingdom inaugurated in Jesus Christ.

See also Creation, Care for the (Ecology); Creation/New Creation; Technology, Ethic of.

Resources

Clatworthy, Jonathan. *Good God: Green Theology and the Value of Creation.* Charlbury, UK: Jon Carpenter, 1997.

Yordy, Laura Ruth. *Green Witness: Ecology, Ethics and the Kingdom of God.* Cambridge, UK: Lutterworth Press, 2010.

JAMIE GATES, PHD

GROWTH IN GRACE

See SANCTIFICATION; SPIRITUAL DISCIPLINES; SPIRITUAL FORMATION/GROWTH; TEMPERS AND AFFECTIONS.

Hh

HEALING, THEOLOGY OF

Throughout the Bible, healing refers generally to the restoration of health, sometimes of a people but mostly of the individual. The need for healing assumes sickness or physical impairment that hampers typical human activity. In biblical times, sickness was perceived more holistically, with its source extending beyond the human body to society and even the cosmos. Although healing was often achieved through physical care and ancient medical practices, the Bible presents God as the ultimate Source of healing. Thus, due to their association with other deities, ancient magical practices were categorically rejected as means for healing.

The OT depicts God as Healer, notably with regard to Israel as God's **covenant** people. In the Pentateuch, God promises to protect obedient Israel from the diseases sent on the Egyptians because "I am Yahweh, your healer" (Exod. 15:26, author's translation). The Psalms accredit God with healing the repentant or faithful (e.g., Pss. 30:2; 41:3; 107:19-20). The Prophets represent God as offering healing for **repentance** (e.g., Isa. 6:10; 19:22; 30:26; Jer. 3:22). Jeremiah ascribes Judah's Babylonian exile to its sickness as a nation resulting from continued **sin** in the form of unfaithfulness (e.g., Jer. 8:15, 22; 30:12-13; 46:11).

Thus healing reached beyond the physical to all human existence, including the covenant and all human interaction (e.g., social and economic). Healing was thereby understood as a sign of God's favor, and sickness as a sign of God's punishment for ritual impurity and covenantal violations. These OT perspectives provide the general background for NT understandings of healing.

Most NT references to healing are linked to Jesus' ministry, found in the Gospels and Acts. Along with Jesus' teaching and preaching, healing was central to his ministry. In John's gospel healing functions as a "sign" (*sēmeion*; e.g., John 4:46-54) of Jesus' identity—the divine Word/Logos (1:1-18). In the Synoptic Gospels and Acts healing was often associated with **faith** (e.g., Matt. 9:22; Mark 10:52) and was a sign of the coming kingdom of God that Jesus proclaimed (Matt 4:23; 9:35). Jesus' **miracles** validated him not as an ancient miracle worker per se but as God's anointed servant and agent of healing (Luke 4:18-19; Acts 2:22). Although specific terminology often refers to physical healing (*therapeuō, iaomai*) or **deliverance/exorcism**, Jesus' message also denotes healing as **salvation** (*sōzō*; e.g., Mark 5:34). Healing extended to the ministry of Jesus' representatives. They pronounced healing in Jesus' name (e.g., Acts 3:6; 4:10). Thus through Jesus God extends healing and thereby wholeness to human existence as indicative of God's kingdom coming on the earth.

See also Covenant; Deliverance/Exorcism; Faith; Kingdom of God; Miracles/Signs and Wonders; Salvation (Soteriology); Sin.

RICHARD P. THOMPSON, PHD

HEALTH AND PROSPERITY THEOLOGY
See WORD OF FAITH THEOLOGY (HEALTH AND PROSPERITY).

HEAVEN

Heaven in the Hebrew OT (*shamayim*) and the Greek NT (*ouranos*) is simply the word for "sky." The Hebrew word is always plural, and the Greek term is often plural. So persons in the Bible may have conceptualized the heavens as layers of sky. For example, the Jewish writing called the *Testament of Levi* pictures three layers of sky above (cf. 2 Cor. 12:2), with God in the highest heaven or layer. The *Ascension of Isaiah* pictures seven layers of heaven, with God again occupying the highest one.

Heaven is the place where God dwells (e.g., Rev. 13:6). It is the location of God's throne (e.g., Isa. 66:1; Acts 7:48-50) from which he rules the cosmos. Often heaven was also understood as God's true sanctuary, the model for the earthly temple, especially its innermost sanctum (see Isa. 6; Heb. 9:24). Jewish writers like Philo (e.g., QE 2.94) and Josephus (e.g., *Ant.* 3.180-81) attest to this sense that the earthly sanctuary in Jerusalem was modeled after God's heavenly temple.

According to the NT, Jesus Christ is currently in heaven in his resurrected body, where he is seated at the right hand of God the Father Almighty (e.g., Acts 2:34; Heb. 1:13; cf. Ps. 110:1). Christ ascended to heaven after his resurrection; from there he will return to judge the living and the dead (Acts 1:11; Heb. 9:28). In the meantime, Christ intercedes at God's right hand for the atonement of believers (Rom. 8:34; Heb. 4:14-15; 7:25).

Different parts of the NT seem to give differing impressions of whether or not heaven is the final destination for believers in eternity. On the one hand, significant portions of the NT picture eternity unfolding on a transformed and redeemed earth (e.g., Rom. 8:18-25; Rev. 21:1-4). Paul looks for the redemption of the earth in Rom. 8:21, and Rev. 21:2 sees a new Jerusalem coming down to a new earth. On the other hand, John speaks of Jesus going to prepare a place in heaven for his followers, a place to which he will take them after he returns (John 14:2-3). Heaven also seems the most likely location for any intermediate state (e.g., Luke 23:42; 2 Cor. 5:8; Phil. 1:23).

Some parts of the NT speak of heaven as a current reality for believers. Ephesians 2:6 speaks of our already being "seated . . . with him in the heavenly places." Hebrews 12:22-24 says Christians have already reached the "heavenly Jerusalem," the "city of the living God," where angels are in "festal gathering" and the spirits of the perfected righteous are assembled.

See also Creation/New Creation; Eschatology; Hope, Christian; Immortality/Life After Death; Resurrection; Second Temple Judaism; Soul.

Resources
Wright, N. T. *Surprised by Hope: Rethinking Heaven, the Resurrection, and the Mission of the Church*. New York: HarperOne, 2008.
———. *The Resurrection of the Son of God*. Minneapolis: Augsburg Fortress, 2003.

KENNETH SCHENCK, PHD

HELL

The Valley of (the son of) Hinnom lies just southwest of Jerusalem. The NT identifies this valley as **Gehenna**. It is metaphorically associated with a place of judgment and punishment for the wicked beyond the grave. The Greek *geenna* or *gehenna* is translated by the English word "hell."

In Israel's history, the Valley of Hinnom was associated with idolatry and murder. During the reign of such kings as Ahaz and Manasseh, child sacrifice by fire formed part of worshipping Baal and Molech (2 Chron. 28:3; 33:6; Jer. 32:35). The Valley of Hinnom was also associated with the burial of criminals or those slain in battle. Their burial there was a result of God's judgment. At times, the dead remained unburied and were devoured by carrion-eating birds and animals (Jer. 7:31-33).

During the centuries immediately before Jesus, the Valley of Hinnom became more than a place with a notorious past. In the Jewish writing *1 Enoch*, this "accursed valley" is presented as the fate of the "accursed" themselves (27:1-2). The valley is described as "a place of condemnation," "an abyss, full of fire and flaming" (90:24). This depiction represents a new emphasis within Judaism involving **life after death**, a concept not stressed in the OT.

Generally, in the OT the Hebrew word *sheol* was used to depict one's fate beyond the grave. **Sheol** was the universal destiny of the dead. In the Greek translation of the Hebrew Bible (LXX), and later Jewish literature, the Greek word *hadēs* translates *sheol*. But at times the meaning of *hadēs* changed to refer to the destiny for the wicked or a place of punishment where the wicked await the final judgment and resurrection of the dead. This idea can be seen in Rev. 20:14.

In time, the Valley of Hinnom became a garbage dump for Jerusalem. It was a place of perpetual burning. In view of its long history and continuing use, the Valley of Hinnom or Gehenna came to represent metaphorically a place of eternal punishment for the wicked.

The term *gehenna* occurs twelve times in the NT. With the exception of James 3:6 (concerning the tongue), it is found only in the sayings of Jesus. It is the place of punishment for unrighteousness or **sin** (Matt. 5:22; 23:15, 33) and is described by using the language of "eternal fire" (18:8), an "unquenchable fire" (Mark 9:43), and a place where the "worm never dies, and the fire is never quenched" (v. 48). Hell is a place to be avoided at all costs (Matt. 5:29-30; Mark 9:43-48).

In the NT, *hadēs* is also used with reference to life beyond the grave (Luke 10:15; 16:23). The extent to which *gehenna* and *hadēs* should be differentiated is debatable. However, a case can be made that *hadēs* may refer to a temporary rather than eternal abode for the wicked. In Rev. 20:13-15, a "lake of fire" describes the destination for "Death and Hades," as well as all whose names are "not found written in the book of life."

See also Immortality/Life After Death; Sheol/Death/Gehenna; Sin.

LARRY MURPHY, PHD

HERESY

See CREEDS (NICENE, CHALCEDONIAN, APOSTLES', ATHANASIAN); DOCTRINE/DOGMA; ORTHODOXY/ORTHOPRAXIS/ORTHOPATHY.

HERMENEUTICS

Hermeneutics refers to how persons understand and interpret linguistic and nonlinguistic, written and verbal, expressions. Biblical hermeneutics refers to how we read, understand, and apply biblical texts. It includes **Bible** and theology, philosophical questions about how we understand, and literary questions about the nature of texts and the process of reading. Add to that the study of linguistics and how communication occurs, along with how readers are influenced by their social location and prior beliefs. All readers and hearers of Scripture engage in hermeneutics.

The NT authors' use of **Scripture** reveals a hermeneutic in which the OT is read through the lens of Christ. The OT provides the frame of reference for understanding **Jesus**, the people of God, the progression of salvation history, and, more inclusively, the whole creation's advance toward its goal. Early Christians inherited from **Judaism** the notion of inspired exegesis and exegetical methods such as *midrash* (homiletical material), *pesher* (eschatological interpretation), allegory, and typology that functioned alongside a text's historical setting and interpretation.

The third-century Alexandrian and Antiochian schools reveal a division between an allegorical and a more literal reading of Scripture. The Alexandrians used an allegorical threefold interpretation: literal, moral, and spiritual. The Antiochians did not reject allegory but were concerned mainly with the aim or intention of the writer. The Alexandrian influence continued into medieval exegesis, where a fourfold meaning developed. During the **Reformation**, **John Calvin** favored the historical meaning over the allegorical and emphasized the plain sense of a text. The **Enlightenment** fostered a desire for objective, so-called scientific meaning, free of theology and church dogma. German philosopher G. E. Lessing (1729-81) highlighted the division between rational truth and historical truth, dismissing Christian claims about its divine origin, and similar claims by all other religions, as historically unreliable.

The historical critical method, the dominant modern Western paradigm for literary criticism, emerged in the nineteenth century. It is concerned primarily with scientific method and questions of date, authorship, and composition. The era is marked by confidence in objectivity, including skepticism about theological claims. Friedrich Schleiermacher (1768–1834), the "father of modern theology," required that hermeneutics not be understood as applying mechanistic rules for interpretation but as "the art of understanding" (1977). He is credited with identifying the hermeneutical circle, which is the theory that one cannot understand the parts without also understanding the whole and that preunderstanding is a requirement for further reflection.

The nineteenth century witnessed shattered confidence in the search for the historical Jesus. This led to the historical skepticism of William Wrede (1859–1906). This flowered in Rudolf Bultmann's (1884–1976) attempt to make the Gospels believable in a scientific age by demythologization. Form criticism, which concentrated on literary *genre*, adopted an atomistic approach to the text, often confusing form with historical reliability. Redaction criticism focused on identifying the text's sources for detecting an author's intention. Karl Barth (1886–1968) discarded form criticism's supposed value-neutral approach. Reading from a Christological and **Trinitarian** center, Barth insisted Scripture is the Word of God for the **church**. It must be heard in **faith** and **obedience**.

Literary criticism was largely responsible for a shift in emphasis to the final form of the text. Biblical interpreters made fruitful use of narrative devices that enable a reader to enter the world of the story, encouraging participation and imagination. Many literary theorists followed structuralist assumptions that texts are autonomous and generate their own meaning without reference to the author's intentions. This led to the notion of the "death of the author." Closely related to this, poststructuralism posed the question, "How is it possible to construct meaning at all?" Both approaches emphasize the polyvalence of texts (having many meanings) and the potential for pluriformity (variability) of meaning in texts. More recently, socio-rhetorical criticism focuses on values, convictions, and beliefs both in the texts we read and in the larger social world in which we live. Canonical criticism takes seriously the shape of the collection of texts as canon, either as received by the early church or in today's final form.

The reader-centered approach to interpretation is based on reader-response criticism. It emphasizes the individual as a reader-responder. Reading a text includes collaboration between the writer, text, and reader. The social location of the reader, or community of readers, consciously contributes to the hermeneutical framework. This necessarily results in contextual or ideological readings. Feminist interpreters highlight feminine language, enable the voices of women in the biblical narratives to be heard, and critique patriarchal culture.

Increasingly, contributions from the majority world mount a welcomed challenge to dominant Western experience and interpretation. **Liberation** approaches and **postcolonial** criticism highlight power relations. They analyze imperialism and colonial Christianity to read the biblical text from the perspectives of subjugated and oppressed persons. Such approaches recover submerged identities, traditions, and cultural heritage. They enable the church to hear significant voices that have been marginalized but are essential for fully hearing the Scriptures and for global theological conversation.

Many of the critical tools can be profitable for Wesleyan biblical interpretation. Returning to precritical interpretation is counterproductive and contrary to a Wesleyan understanding of biblical authority. An eclectic appropriation of the tools is most fruitful. The historical critical method remains the basis for conducting interpretation.

Wesleyans should acknowledge the impossibility of achieving a completely disinterested interpretation; they should knowingly engage Scripture theologically. A Wesleyan hermeneutic will, under guidance by the Holy Spirit, be informed by tradition. It will also employ reason and experience. A Wesleyan hermeneutic is Christocentric and ecclesiological; it takes into account the whole of Scripture and projects trajectories of meaning. A Wesleyan hermeneutic affirms women in the full range of ministry. It exposes and critiques injustice and seeks to read the Bible from the perspective of the marginalized.

A proper hermeneutic requires that we participate in Scripture from which we find our place in God's unfolding salvation. We confess that God is definitively revealed in the Word made flesh and that the Scriptures bear faithful witness. A characteristically Wesleyan interpretation of Scripture will be marked by trust in the authority of God as declared in Scripture. It is conducted in relationship with God who speaks by the Spirit through Scripture. It occurs in humility, in faithful interpretive communities, in dialogue with our theological heritage and the entire great tradition.

See also Biblical Interpretation, Ancient and Modern Methods; Biblical Theology; Biblicism/Bibliolatry; Christology; Contextualization; Epistemology; Indigenization; Intertextuality; Scripture, Wesleyan Approach to; Westernization of the Gospel; Women's Role in the Church.

Resources

Schleiermacher, Friedrich. *Hermeneutics: The Handwritten Manuscripts.* Edited by Heinz Kimmerle and translated by James Duke and Jack Forstman. Atlanta: Scholars Press, 1977.

Thiselton, A. C. *Hermeneutics: An Introduction.* Grand Rapids: Eerdmans, 2009.

Wright, N. T. *Scripture and the Authority of God: How to Read the Bible Today.* New York: HarperOne, 2011.

SARAH WHITTLE, PHD

HIDDENNESS OF GOD

Divine hiddenness is frequently encountered in the Bible. The motif is variously described, but a common phrasing conjoins the verb "to hide" (Hebrew, *satar*) with God's "face" (Hebrew, *panim*). The notion of God's face being hidden often expresses judgment: Israel sins and God hides—that is, God withdraws divine presence and help (Deut 31:17-18; 32:20). This understanding is pronounced in the Prophets (Jer. 33:5; Ezek. 39:23-24; Mic. 3:4). But the motif of divine hiddenness also appears in the Psalms. There the psalmist is not addressing the issue of sin that has caused God's hiding but rather lamenting over God's hiding that has produced the predicament the psalmist now faces, often innocently (Pss. 10:1; 13:1; 27:9).

If these two uses are directly related, it seems that the Psalms' use of the motif preceded that of the Prophets. The latter adopted the motif, expounding it further as proof of disobedience. Even if that is correct, the psalmic use remains legitimate, and so God's hiddenness must not be viewed solely as a sign of judgment. Instead, it is a real part of humanity's experience of God (Ps. 22:1; Matt. 27:46). Blaise Pascal (1623-62) famously said any religion that doesn't say God is hidden is not true ([1958] 2006, no. 584). He echoed Isa. 45:15: "Truly, you are a God who hides himself, O God of Israel, the Savior."

Some scholars have noted that God slowly withdraws through the course of the OT. While this could be a kind of divine hiding, it should be observed that explicit mention of God's hiding actually decreases in later biblical texts. Moreover, any impression of God's withdrawal in the OT is countered by a reading that includes the NT's promise of God's presence (Matt. 1:23; 3:16-17; Rev. 21:3).

Finally, even if God does slowly withdraw through the course of the OT, this could be seen in analogy with human development: God, the divine parent, allows humans to individuate and mature. Even so, the notion of judgment in the Prophets remains a significant theological perspective. Whatever the case, divine hiddenness—and the notion of God's presence and/in absence—comprises an important part of **revelation** and **the doctrine of God** in **biblical theology.**

See also Biblical Theology; God, Doctrine of; Revelation.

Resource

Pascal, Blaise. *Pascal's Pensées.* New York: E. P. Dutton and Co., 1958. Reprint, Project Gutenberg, 2006. http://www.gutenberg.org/files/18269/18269-h/18269-h.htm.

BRENT A. STRAWN, PHD

HISTORICAL THEOLOGY

Historical theology denotes critical, contemporary reflection on the historic teachings of Christian communities and Christian leaders. It is closely related to **systematic theology** in its methods of contemporary reflection, and it also draws significantly on the study of **church** history in its work toward understanding historically and contextually the objects of its reflection. Historical theology, then, attempts to integrate accurate and contextual historical reflection on Christian teachings with the application of contemporary criteria for discerning the extent to which various historic teachings are both true and truly Christian.

The traditional subjects of historical theology have included (1) patristic theology, that is, the teachings of the early Christian church as represented in its **creeds, councils,** and other doctrinal statements and in such significant church fathers as Irenaeus, Origen, the Cappadocian writers, and Augustine; (2) leading medieval theologians such as Anselm of Canterbury and Thomas Aquinas; (3) leading Protestant Reformers such as **Martin Luther, John Calvin,** and Richard Hooker, as well as the Reformation confessions of faith and the doctrines of the **Counter-Reformation;** and (4) Christian dialogue with modern **philosophies** and modern scientific developments.

Recent decades have seen a number of new developments in historical theology. *First,* historical theologians have begun to focus on such women theologians as Macrina the sister of Cappadocian writers Basil and Gregory of Nyssa, medieval abbess Hildegard of Bingen, Catholic Reformer Teresa of Jesus (Teresa of Ávila), and Methodist holiness advocate **Phoebe Palmer.** *Second,* the **ecumenical** movement has inspired examination of previously unexpected conjunctions across traditional denominational lines. Included is the interest of **Lutheran** theologians of the "Finnish school" in conjunctions between Lutheran thought and **Eastern Orthodox** teachings on sanctification, and the attempts of Albert C. Outler and others to see connections between John Wesley's thought and that of **Catholic** as well as Eastern Christian theological traditions. *Third*, cultural and geographical contexts have become new subjects of historical-theological reflection; thus for example, **Augustine** of Hippo has been reconsidered as an African theologian as well as a cardinal figure in Western (Latin) Christian thought. *Fourth*, historical theology has also been considered in relationship to popular cultures and popular spiritualities. An example would be studies of the relationship between popular Catholic devotional practices in the Southwestern United States and Mexico in relation to **theologies of liberation**.

Wesleyan communities have developed their own distinctive theological and doctrinal traditions as a subject of reflection by historical theology. The theologies of John and Charles Wesley have been subjects of reflection by Wesleyans since the eighteenth century. In the nineteenth century, Wesleyan theologians Richard Watson, Thomas N. Ralston, Thomas O. Summers, William Burt Pope, Miner Raymond, and John Miley developed multivolume systematic theologies that involved sustained reflection on Wesleyan teachings. Many of these were approved for study by preachers and thus were given a degree of doctrinal approbation by Wesleyan and Methodist denominations.

American Methodist theologians were particularly interested in responding to Calvinistic evangelicals. Building on the work of such ecumenical Methodist theologians as Colin W. Williams and Albert C. Outler, there has been since the 1970s a large-scale renewal of historical-theological reflection on John and Charles Wesley, as well as other Wesleyan theological subjects, including the historic doctrines of Wesleyan and Methodist church bodies.

See also Orthodox Church; Protestantism; Roman Catholicism; Wesley, Charles, Theology of; Wesley, John, Theology of.

Resources
Langford, Thomas A., ed. *Practical Divinity.* 2 vols. 2nd ed. Nashville: Abingdon Press, 1998.
Oden, Amy. *In Her Words: Women's Writings in the History of Christian Thought.* Nashville: Abingdon Press, 1994.
Pelikan, Jaroslav. *The Christian Tradition: A History of the Development of Doctrine.* Chicago: University of Chicago Press, 1971-89.

TED A. CAMPBELL, PHD

HOLINESS

The OT Hebrew root *qdsh* (holy) appears over 800 times as a verb (*qadash*), noun (*qodesh*), and adjective (*qadosh*). The NT Greek root *hagos* (holy) appears as an adjective (*hagios*), verb (*hagiazō*), and nouns (*hagiasmos, hagiotēs, hagiōsynē*) over 250 times. The words derive from cultic settings that signify "separate," "apart," or "sacred." Objects (Num. 4:4), places (Exod. 3:5; 1 Kings 6:16), times (Lev. 23:3-4), and persons (Exod. 19:6; Lev. 21:6) set apart or **sanctified** as belonging to God were declared holy. The antithesis is "common" or "profane."

What was removed from the sphere of *common* activity and placed in God's service gained its holiness by its association with God. Holiness was not inherent in the object itself. Yet because of being dedicated to a holy God, improperly handling holy objects could bring death (1 Sam. 6:19; 2 Sam. 6:7). Holiness was not a static quality but a personal, active force. While the Priestly tradition emphasized ritual purity, the Prophets emphasized moral living.

To speak of **God** as "the Lord God [Yahweh], the Holy One of Israel" (Isa. 30:15) or to declare "you [God] alone are holy" (Rev. 15:4) is to assert God's distinctive *otherness* from all creation. Holiness names God's innermost essence, his quintessential being, his deity in contrast to all things creaturely. God is wholly "the Other." In this sense holiness communicates God's transcendence. Yet God as holy is neither remote nor unknowable. When God reveals himself, humans can be overwhelmed by terror, fright, and awe (Exod. 3:6; Deut. 10:17-21; Isa. 6:5; Ezek. 1:28). Conversely they also are drawn to God in fascination (Exod. 33:18-29).

The ancient Near Eastern gods who also were considered holy served various functions. They brought fertility, maintained justice, and preserved the created order. They shared their holiness with their devotees, who assumed the gods' characteristics. For example, those who served fertility gods as prostitutes were considered holy (Gen. 38:21; 1 Kings 14:24).

The holiness of the God of Israel is manifest in all his attributes, particularly the moral ones. He opposed oppressors (Exod. 3:7-10; 22:21-22); required morality of those in **covenant** with him (Exod. 20:12-17); mandated that justice, especially for the poor and disenfranchised, be upheld (Exod. 22:21-27; Isa. 1:17; Amos 5:10-15); and demonstrated his love for Israel by choosing them as his people (Deut. 4:37; 7:8). In turn, his people were to reflect God's holiness by practicing justice and honesty in their dealings, showing compassion toward others, and demonstrating love for one another. One does not become holy by being moral. Rather, a person or community in covenantal relationship with God is expected to reflect God's holy character by being moral (Lev. 19:2).

The NT builds on the OT concept of holiness and makes several advances. God, who alone is holy, imparts his holiness to those who worship him and obey his commandments in the Spirit's power. The moral dimension of holiness shows little consideration for ritual purity (Eph. 4:17–5:5; 1 Thess. 4:1-8). The exceptions are baptism and observing the Eucharist. Experiencing God's holiness becomes democratized; people from every nation, tribe, and language are invited to become God's worshippers (Rev. 7:9). They are addressed as *hagioi*, which means "holy ones," "holy people," or "saints" (Rom. 1:7; 1 Cor. 1:2; 2 Cor. 1:1; Eph. 1:1; Phil. 1:1; Col. 1:2). Jesus taught that the primary expression of God's holiness in his disciples is love (*agapē*) (Matt. 10:35-40). Love for one another should distinguish them (John 13:34-35; 1 Cor. 13).

The holy life is not static or fixed. It is an ever-expanding adventure. Christ dwells in his disciples through the **Holy Spirit**, who fills them with God's presence and enables them to live in Christ's love (Eph. 3:14-19).

See also Christian Ethics/Moral Theology; Christian Perfection (Entire Sanctification); Discipleship; God, Doctrine of; Sacraments; Salvation (Soteriology); Sanctification; Spiritual Formation/Growth.

ROBERT D. BRANSON, PHD

HOLINESS DENOMINATIONS WORLDWIDE

The theological and spiritual vitality of the holiness movement is reflected in the current diversity of almost one hundred denominations, with more than thirteen million members worldwide. There are roughly four million adherents in North America and another one million in Central and South America. In Asia and Australia there are another four million adherents, with significant numbers of churches in Korea and India. In Africa, there are an estimated three million members of holiness denominations, and the numbers are growing rapidly.

The majority of the denominations named below trace their theological roots to the Wesleyan movement in Great Britain. Other traditions such as the Baptists, Quakers, United Brethren, Mennonites, and independents, though not Wesleyan, have been drawn by the same desire for a deeper experience of God, a higher life, growth in grace, full salvation, Christian perfection, and the baptism with the Holy Spirit and fire.

After World War II, the holiness traditions experienced international growth and began to establish theological seminaries in India, Africa, Korea, and the Philippines. Despite the loss of some adherents to the Pentecostal movement, which placed a greater emphasis on the baptism with the Holy Spirit as evidenced by the ability to "speak in an unknown tongue," the holiness movement has continued to grow numerically. Today the two largest associations of holiness denominations are the Interchurch Holiness Convention (IHC) and the Christian Holiness Partnership (CHP). However, the independent and missional nature of the holiness movement means that many groups choose not to participate in either organization.

A "definitive list" of denominations in the holiness movement would soon become inaccurate. However, identifying the current active communions demonstrates the holiness movement's vitality. The names below followed by an asterisk indicate predominantly black denominations. (Many Pentecostal denominations identify themselves as rooted in the nineteenth-century American holiness movement and as Wesleyan regarding the doctrine of entire sanctification; while Pentecostals could be considered another sizable wing of the holiness movement, they are not listed here.)

Advent Christian Church; Africa Gospel Church; Associated Churches of Christ (Holiness)*; Baptist: Alliance of the Reformed Baptist Church of Canada; Baptist: Free Baptist Church (South Africa); Baptist: Free Christian Baptist Church of New Brunswick; Baptist: Holiness Baptist Church; Baptist: Holiness Baptist Churches of Southwestern Arkansas; Bible Holiness Church; Brethren in Christ Church; Calvary Holiness Church; Christian and Missionary Alliance; Christian Nation Church; Christian Union; Christ's Sanctified Holy Church (nonsacramental); Christ's Sanctified Holy Church*; Churches of Christ in Christian Union; Churches of God (Independent Holiness People); Churches of God, Holiness*; Church of Christ (Holiness) USA*; Church of Daniel's Band; Church of God (Anderson, Indiana); Church of God (Gospel Spreading)*; Church of God (Guthrie, Oklahoma); Church of God (Holiness); Church of God (Sanctified Church)*; Church of the Nazarene; Emmanuel Holiness Church (Britain); Evangel Church; Evangelical Christian Church (Wesleyan); Evangelical Church in Canada; Evangelical Church of Christ (Holiness)*; Evangelical Church of North America; Evangelical Congregational Church; Evangelical Methodist Church; Evangelical Missionary Church of Canada; Evangelical United Brethren Church; Evangelistic Mission; Fellowship of Charismatic Nazarenes; Free Christian Zion Church of Christ*; Free Holiness People; Free Methodist Church; Friends: Central Yearly Meeting of Friends; Friends: Evangelical Friends International; Full Salvation Union; Gospel Mission Corps; Gospel Spreading Church of God; Gospel Tabernacle Church; Holiness Church, Donalsonville, Georgia; Holiness Church of California; Holiness Church of Texas; Holiness Movement Church; Igreja Evangelica Holiness do Brasil; Immanuel Church; Immanuel Missionary Church; Independent Holiness Church; Kidokkyo Tae-Han Songgyol Kyohoe (Korean Evangelical Holiness Church); Kodesh Church of Immanuel (USA and Liberia)*; League of Prayer (Britain); Mennonite Brethren in Christ; Methodist: Congregational Methodist Church; Methodist: Evangelical Methodist Church; Methodist: Free Methodist Church; Methodist: Holiness Methodist Church; Methodist: Holiness Methodist Church of the Lumbee River Annual Conference (North Carolina); Methodist: Methodist Church (England); Methodist: Missionary Methodist Church of America; Methodist: Primitive Methodist Church of USA; Methodist: United Methodist Church (USA); Methodist: Wesleyan Church; Methodist: Wesleyan Methodist Church of Australia; Metropolitan Church Association; Missionary Church of Canada; New Testament Church of God; Nippon Seikyokai (Japan Holiness Church); Oriental Missionary Society Holiness Church of North America (originally Japanese); Original

Church of God or Sanctified Church*; Pilgrim Holiness Church, Inc. (of the Midwest); Pilgrim Holiness Church of NY, Inc.; Pilgrim Wesleyan Holiness Church*; Pillar of Fire Church; Salvation Army; Sanctified Church of Christ*; Standard Church of America; Triumph the Church and Kingdom of God in Christ (International)*; United Brethren in Christ (Old Constitution); United Christian Church; Universal Church of God; Universal Church of God*; Volunteers of America; Wesleyan Bible Holiness Church; Wesleyan Holiness Alliance; Wesleyan Holiness Charismatic Fellowship; and Yesukyo Tae-Han Songgyol-Kyoheo (Jesus Korea Holiness Church, begun in 1962).

See also Christian Perfection (Entire Sanctification); Holiness; Holiness Movements: American, British, and Continental; Keswick Movement; Pentecostal Theology; Sanctification; Theosis (Deification); Wesley, John, Theology of; World Methodism.

Resources

Jones, Charles Edwin. *Black Holiness: A Guide to the Study of Black Participation in Wesleyan Perfectionist and Glossolalic Pentecostal Movements.* ATLA Bibliography Series, 18. Metuchen, NJ: Scarecrow Press, 1987.

———. *The Holiness-Pentecostal Movement: A Comprehensive Guide.* ATLA Bibliography Series, 54. Lanham, MD: Scarecrow Press, 2008.

———. *The Wesleyan Holiness Movement: A Comprehensive Guide.* ATLA Bibliography Series, 50. Lanham, MD: Scarecrow Press, 2005.

THOMAS R. ALBIN, MTH

HOLINESS MOVEMENTS: AMERICAN, BRITISH, AND CONTINENTAL

In 1763 **John Wesley** and his preachers boldly affirmed that God had raised up the "preachers called **Methodists** . . . to reform the nation" and the church and "to spread scriptural holiness" (*Works*, 8:299). Holiness movements are identified theologically as similar attempts to renew the church through an experience described by Wesley's teaching of **entire sanctification** as a second work of grace subsequent to justification that is wrought by the **Holy Spirit**, cleansing believers of sin and filling them with love for God and neighbor.

By the 1830s the doctrine met neglect among Methodists, causing Timothy Merritt to publish *The Christian's Manual: A Treatise on Christian Perfection* (1834). But increased resistance inside Methodism eventually gave rise to the American holiness movement outside Methodism. The following are some developments in that movement.

Palmer and "Altar Theology" (1836-37). **Phoebe Palmer**'s Tuesday Meetings for the Promotion of Holiness introduced "altar theology," by which Christ was seen as an altar that sanctified the believer. It emphasized the instantaneous nature of the experience. This offered a new paradigm for holiness preaching and revivals, making her one of the movement's most influential figures. But her altar theology resulted in what some see as an "altered theology" where Wesley was concerned, marking a theological shift. The alteration emphasized entire sanctification as more of a crisis experience and less of a process, creating a rift between Palmer and Methodist supporter and friend Nathan Bangs. Palmer would also foreshadow the importance of women in the holiness movement: Lucy Drake Osborn, Abbie Mills, Mattie Perry, Catherine Booth, Lela McConnell, and Mary Lee Cagle, among others. The Holy Spirit who cleansed believers from sin also validated women as preachers.

Oberlin and "New Theology" (1836-39). Charles Finney and Asa Mahan, of Oberlin College, also experienced entire sanctification. They concluded it was consistent with their Calvinism. Whereas the doctrine of predestination separated Calvinists from Wesleyans in the eighteenth century, the experience of entire sanctification brought some of them together in nineteenth. Furthermore, Palmer's altar theology and Oberlin's "new theology" linked holiness preaching with **revivalism**, adding a catalyst to the movement.

Higher Life Movement. William Boardman's *The Higher Christian Life* (1858) exchanged the Wesleyan concept of "perfection" for "higher living," making the doctrine more popular with non-Methodists and less objectionable to those from the Reformed tradition. His work influenced Hannah Whitall Smith, author of *The Christian's Secret of a Happy Life.* These books were important to the "higher life" movement that eventually spread to England.

Social Reform. With the help of Finney, Boardman, and others, revivalism prior to the Civil War also produced a concern for social reform. Many women (e.g., Phoebe Palmer, Almira Losee, Frances Willard, Emma Whittemore, and Jennie Smith) contributed leadership to the causes of abolition, poverty, temperance, and women's concerns (homes for unwed mothers and rescue homes for prostitutes).

Holiness Camp Meetings. Holiness revivals continued to gain momentum until the Civil War. In 1867, three Methodists, J. A. Wood, John Inskip (a Palmer devotee), and Alfred Cookman, conceived of a "new method" for promoting holiness. They convened the first camp meeting in Vineland, New Jersey, resulting in the National Camp Meeting Association for the Promotion of Holiness.

Black Holiness Leaders. Having empowered women, the holiness movement would eventually cross racial barriers, even in the South. White preachers W. B. Godbey, James Epps Jr., and Richard Baxter Hayes regularly preached to black gatherings, while Jarena Lee and Amanda Berry Smith (both members of the African Methodist Episcopal Church) often reached out to whites. Smith, a regular attendee of Palmer's Tuesday Meetings, was sanctified under Inskip's preaching (1868) and became a significant leader in the movement. Other noted leaders were Mary Magdalina Tate (founder of an early black holiness movement) and Gertrude Lightfoot (pastor of a large

New York City congregation). The black holiness conventions convened by C. P. Jones and C. H. Mason resulted in Mason forming the Church of God in Christ and Jones forming a holiness group, the Church of Christ (Holiness) USA.

Internationalization. In the mid-nineteenth century, Phoebe and Walter Palmer, Finney, Boardman, and Hannah Whitall and Robert Pearsall Smith spread the holiness and "higher life" messages to **Keswick** and Oxford, England. Pietist influences made Germany receptive to holiness teaching. Through collaboration between German, American, and English Methodists, along with Keswick evangelists, holiness teaching quickly took root as the Fellowship Movement. Through the efforts of the Oriental Missionary Society, a work begun in Tokyo eventually succeeded in Korea by 1907, resulting in the Korea Evangelical Holiness Church, the world's largest holiness denomination.

Revivalism and camp meetings helped holiness movements spread by escaping denominational bounds. From there they transcended geography, sex, race, ethnicity, socioeconomic limitations, and even national bounds. They became more nuanced by their particular historical and social locations, giving them a peculiar diversity around a common spiritual experience.

See also Holiness; Pentecostal Theology; Predestination and Election; Sanctification; Social Gospel; Social Justice; Wesley, John, Theology of; Women's Role in the Church; World Methodism.

Resources
Dieter, Melvin E. *The Holiness Revival of the Nineteenth Century.* Metuchen, NJ: Scarecrow Press, 1980.

Dupree, Sherry Sherrod. *African-American Holiness Pentecostal Movement: An Annotated Bibliography.* New York: Garland, 1996.

Smith, Timothy L. *Revivalism and Social Reform: American Protestantism on the Eve of the Civil War.* Gloucester, MA: Peter Smith, 1976.

Stanley, Susie C. *Holy Boldness: Women Preachers' Autobiographies and the Sanctified Self.* Knoxville, TN: University of Tennessee Press, 2002.

BARRY E. BRYANT, PHD

HOLISTIC MISSION

The term "holistic mission" attempts to define the relationship between evangelism and social responsibility/transformation. Its concern is the whole person in his or her broad social context, not just his or her spiritual and eternal interests. Seldom has there been agreement in the **church** on what the term should include.

Many Christians perceive the church's mission to be that of glorying God by continuing to do the works **Jesus** began to do through the **Holy Spirit** (Luke 4:18-19). They say that immediately after the church was established, it ministered in holistic ways through **evangelism**, teaching, communal worship, celebration of the Eucharist, prayer, deliverance, and compassionate ministries (Acts 2:41-47). Persons who become part of God's people become part of a community that reflects Christ's example; it addresses the gospel to the whole person.

Liberal Christianity in the nineteenth and twentieth centuries tended to define the church's mission more as working to transform political, economic, and social institutions in accordance with the **kingdom of God.** Seeking **justice** through transformation of institutions was a principal goal. Churches representing this strand of **Protestant** Christianity are sometimes referred to as the ecumenical church because they have been at the forefront of the **ecumenical** movement. Among these churches the term *missio Dei*, Latin for "God's mission," is often used to express the comprehensive mission of God in the world. The term was defined at the 1952 Willingen Conference of the International Missionary Council as mission that derives from God's nature. Delegates reexamined the theological foundations of mission and reformulated mission policy. "Social engagement" became the new watchword for churches committed to ecumenism. Evangelism ceased being part of holistic mission. According to the conference's vision, the church is sent into the world to love, serve, teach, heal, and liberate persons. Calls were even heard in the conference to bring home all missionaries.

During the post-World War II period "mission" came to include ministry to the poor, a pursuit of justice for all—especially the dispossessed of the earth—and defending the oppressed and enslaved.

Meanwhile, during the same period evangelical churches established the spiritual mandate of Matt. 28:18-20 over the cultural mandate (Gen. 9:1-3). The Lausanne Covenant, which states a clear priority for the spiritual mandate, was signed by nearly all the delegates to the **Lausanne Congress.** It is still the statement of purpose for many evangelical churches. However, there is a notable difference between the 1974 Lausanne Covenant and the 1989 Manila Manifesto (second Lausanne Conference). Both documents focus on evangelism. But the Manifesto includes social transformation as a vital part of the church's assignment. The distinction reveals an effort by the conservative wing of the church to establish a balance between evangelism and social transformation.

Internationalization of the Christian church and the impact of **liberation theology** have promoted accepting a new definition of holistic mission by much of the Christian church. The church's participation in the political process to achieve structural social change is currently seen by many evangelicals as essential to the **gospel.** Other evangelicals argue that trying to use the gospel to achieve structural change in society is contrary to the example of Jesus and the early church.

In the Wesleyan tradition, holistic ministry is seen as essential for Jesus' disciples. Wesley brought together careful attention to discipleship, a simple lifestyle, concern for the poor and enslaved, and Christian holiness, which is loving God "with all [the] heart, . . . soul, . . . mind, and . . . strength" and loving "your neighbor as yourself" (Mark 12:30-31). This combination made a profound impact on England and the early American republic. Wesley's message of "personal and social holiness" soon expanded to all of the British Isles, America, and the Caribbean. Wesleyans view John Wesley as a model of faithfulness to the apostolic tradition and continue to emphasize evangelism, holiness of heart and life, education, compassion, and deliverance from all forms of bondage. The cultural and spiritual mandates work together in a holistic way to meet the physical and spiritual needs of people. A whole gospel encompasses a full healing and full redemption in all spheres of human existence.

See also Creation, Care for the (Ecology); Early Church; Justice; Love; Mission and Social Justice; Reconciliation; Sacraments; Social Ethics; Social Gospel; Wesley, John, Theology of.

Resources

Bosch, David J. *Transforming Mission: Paradigm Shifts in the Theology of Mission.* Maryknoll, NY: Orbis Books, 1991.

Moreau, A. Scott, ed. *Evangelical Dictionary of World Missions.* Grand Rapids: Baker, 2000.

Woolnough, Brian, ed. *Holistic Mission: God's Plan for God's People.* Eugene, OR: Wipf and Stock Publishers, 2011.

TERENCE B. READ, PHD

HOLY ONE OF GOD
See JESUS OF NAZARETH.

HOLY ORDERS
See ORDINATION.

HOLY PEOPLE OF GOD
See CHURCH (ECCLESIOLOGY).

HOLY SPIRIT (PNEUMATOLOGY)

In the Farewell Discourses in John's gospel, Jesus explains to his disciples that he must leave them. He must go to Jerusalem where he will suffer and die. Jesus tells them it is to their "advantage" that he leaves. If he does not, "the [Counselor] will not come to you; but if I go, I will send him to you" (16:7). The Counselor is the Holy Spirit. Jesus explains that the Counselor will "convince," "guide," "speak," "declare," and "glorify" (vv. 13-14). The Spirit acts in judgment, righteousness, truth, and language.

Scripture speaks of the Spirit as an agent who does what God does. The Spirit makes Jesus' mission possible, and Jesus sends the Spirit. In John 20:22 Jesus "breathe[s]" on the disciples and they "receive the Holy Spirit." In Acts 1:8 Jesus tells his disciples they will receive the Holy Spirit. This happens on the day of Pentecost (Acts 2). The Spirit comes upon them, uniting them in a common language that reverses the judgment on the Tower of Babel (Gen. 11).

The church articulated the Spirit's agency in the deliberations at the **councils** of Nicaea (325) and Constantinople (381). Some Christians had argued that God the Father was the real God and that the Son and Spirit were like the Father, but not the same. After much deliberation, political squabbling, and the exile of various theologians, the church affirmed in the councils that the Father, Son, and Spirit are "of the same essence." They are distinct "persons" who act, but the actions (offices) of each person express God's single essence. In other words, the person of the Father is the essence of God, as are the Son and Spirit. The Father, Son, and Spirit together are also the essence of God. But there are not four essences, only one. This is the doctrine of the Trinity, a mystery revealed.

God is one essence in three persons. The persons are distinguished by verbs used to explain them. The Father "eternally begets" the Son but "processes" the Spirit. The original Nicene Creed stated the Spirit proceeds from the Father. Later, Western Christianity added the Spirit proceeds from the Father "and the Son." Eastern Christians objected. After much disagreement, in the eleventh century the church split between East and West. The cleavage continues. The irony should not be missed. The Spirit is known as the "principle of communion." He makes us one and draws us into the life of God. This is why at the major sacramental occasions such as baptism and the Eucharist we pray for an outpouring of the Holy Spirit. Only the Spirit can make us what we are called to be. A church divided over the Spirit remains a scandal.

The role of the Holy Spirit in Wesley's work was crucial. To be born of God assumed an *exit* and *return*. Through creation one "subsists" in God; all creation is born of God by the Spirit. But this subsistence in God is defined primarily by a sensible life (our senses), which Wesley refers to consistently as "sight." Sin misleads us into thinking sensible objects before us constitute our true being. We see only what is before us, missing its depth, which causes us to "exit" or be separated from God. Hence, we walk by sight rather than by faith. To be born of God (new creation) is to "return" and be restored to God's image—Jesus Christ. This occurs through faith, the bestowed virtue by which the newborn soul receives the Spirit's animating life. The Spirit's presence returns human life to God through love, prayer, praise, and thanksgiving. This dynamic constitutes Wesley's theme of *action-reaction*. The Spirit infuses life into the soul, and the person then cooperates by returning that life to God through specific acts of love.

See also Christology; Christology, New Testament; Ecumenical Councils; Fruit of the Spirit; Gifts of the Spirit; Theosis (Deification); Trinity.

Resources

Pinnock, Clark. *Flame of Love: A Theology of the Holy Spirit.* Downers Grove, IL: InterVarsity Press, 1996.

Tuttle, Robert G. "John Wesley and the Gifts of the Holy Spirit." *The Unofficial Confessing Movement Page.* http://www.ucmpage.org/articles/rtuttle1.html.

Wesley, John. "On the Holy Spirit," *Works,* 7:508-20.

D. STEPHEN LONG, PHD

HOMILETICS

See PREACHING.

HOMOSEXUALITY

See HUMAN SEXUALITY.

HONOR/SHAME CULTURE

Many Middle Eastern, Asian, and African cultures are primarily honor/shame based as distinguished from guilt-based cultures that largely characterize the West. In a shame-based culture shame is the primary form of social control. In a guilt-based culture a sense of guilt for having done wrong (e.g., trespassed against a moral norm) performs that role. The distinction between a "guilt culture" and a "shame culture" was first introduced by anthropologist Ruth Benedict in *The Chrysanthemum and the Sword: Patterns of Japanese Culture* (1948) to explain the differences between Japanese and American societies. The distinction has been much debated.

The Bible was written primarily to shame-based audiences, a fact that can affect how people read the Bible and even understand Jesus Christ as Savior.

In a shame-based culture all interactions between people are governed by well-defined customs and rules. Honor/shame is collective; it primarily attaches to members of a certain clan, tribe, or extended family as *a whole,* not primarily to individuals. Shame/honor results from violating/upholding mandated social codes that compose a "living web" of human relationships and functions. Compliance generates honor; violation generates shame.

In shame-based cultures a person's identity and honor are indexed to membership in, and obligation and duty to, family, clan, and tribe/nation. An individual's foremost duty toward his or her group is to bring honor and avoid shame at all costs. Failure to observe duty shames the whole community; it results in a loss of identity and exclusion from community unless amends are made.

Shame involves losing respect and honor, not in feeling individually guilty. It has little to do with a person's own conscience, with feeling guilty for wrongful acts. Instead, in shame/honor cultures a person is "shamed" only when a violation is discovered. Until then, shame does not apply. A person might go to great lengths to prove his or her innocence, even in the face of obvious evidence to the contrary.

An honor/shame culture tends to discourage individuality, whereas a guilt-based culture tends to encourage it. According to the Confucian principle of *Li*, for instance, a man "is what he is" only in relationship to his parents and elders.

Appreciating these characteristics helps us understand the Bible in many places. For example, first-century, shame-based people would have known that when Jesus' accusers slapped his mouth and struck his head, they were attempting to shame him (Matt. 26:67; Luke 22:63-64). When the high priest Ananias ordered those nearby to strike Paul on the mouth, it was an attempt to shame him (Acts 23:1-5).

See also Contextualization; Contextual Theology; Westernization of the Gospel.

Resources

Jewett, Robert, ed. *The Shame Factor: How Shame Shapes Society.* Eugene, OR: Cascade Books, 2011.

Neyrey, Jerome. *Honor and Shame in the Gospel of Matthew.* Louisville, KY: Westminster John Knox Press, 1998.

LEE SAN YOUNG, PHD

HOPE, CHRISTIAN

The Christian faith is grounded in God's definitive self-**revelation** in the life, death, and resurrection of **Jesus**, confirmed in many ways to be the Christ (Messiah). Christ as God's gift creates Christian **faith**; Christ as an example models the power of God's **love**. Christian hope is a sure confidence that what God began to do in Christ, he will complete (Eph. 1:7-14). It arises from the promises of God already fulfilled in Jesus—in whom the Father fulfilled previous covenants and messianic expectations. Christian hope springs up from the church's living memory that in Christ, God fulfilled all his promises (2 Cor. 1:15-22). Now he can be trusted to fulfill promises still in play (Rom. 8:18-39). The Father will consummate the **kingdom** Jesus inaugurated and proclaimed. Through faith in the risen and ascended Christ, Christians have the steadfast hope of eternal life with God in his fulfilled kingdom (John 14:19; Col. 1:5, 27; Titus 1:2; 2:13; 3:7; 1 Pet. 1:3, 13).

This shows that Christian hope has nothing to do with a human desire to gain material and social benefits not now possessed and nothing to do with projecting such an expectation into a fictitious heavenly afterlife. Nor does Christian hope have anything to do with a cringing fear of physical death.

Christian hope is fundamentally rooted in the promises of God that come to us in Jesus Christ. These include the **resurrection** from the dead, Christ's return, the new creation and consummation of God's kingdom, the final overcoming of all evil, and the vindication of God's people before all flesh. Christians live in, celebrate, and assess the world and are moved by a hope (confidence) founded completely on the resurrection of Jesus. Christians have experienced the **new creation** and now, in the power of the Holy Spirit, actively await its completion—a new heaven and a new earth (Rev. 21:5). The new creation will require a mighty re-creative and redemptive act of the God who never disappoints (vv. 3-5).

The "future" Christ promised is the **parousia** (Greek, *parousia*; Latin, *adventus*), not *futurus* (Greek, *phusis*), meaning nature that just repeats itself by its own resources, thus making the truly new impossible. In the crucified, risen, and ascended Christ, the new future has already been given to us. Christ is the future of all that truly matters—the very future of God. Christian hope arrives, not by human striving, but as pure gift. It emerges not from some uncertain hope that a desired outcome be achieved but rather from what has already been given, is already certain, namely, the presence of the risen and soon-coming Lord—God's gift.

So, unlike a hope constantly plagued by uncertainty, Christians are to live with unshakable confidence in God's faithfulness already confirmed in Jesus Christ. To faith is added hope and love (1 Cor. 13:13). Faith is accompanied by hope and is led by love for God and our neighbor. Hope is that excellent and certain habituation in which, because of the past, it is known in advance that God is faithful to his promises and will equip his people with a trust anchored in God's faithfulness.

See also Eschatology; Immortality/Life After Death; Second Coming of Christ/Parousia; Theosis (Deification); Trinity.

Resources

Knight, Henry H., III, ed. *From Aldersgate to Azusa Street: Wesleyan, Holiness, and Pentecostal Visions of the New Creation.* Eugene, OR: Pickwick Publications, 2010.

Moltmann, Jürgen. *Theology of Hope.* SCM Classics. London: SCM, 2010.

YOUNG-HO CHUN, PHD

HOSPITABILITY/HOSPITALITY

Welcoming or receiving others, particularly the foreigner or stranger, is prominent throughout Scripture. **God** is seen as guest and host. Abraham and Sarah entertain three strangers, welcoming them and setting a feast before them in what becomes a paradigm for hospitality (Gen. 18). Though unaware, they have entertained God. The obligation to feed and protect others is centered on the stranger and alien (Lev. 19:34). Just as God provided for Israel when they were sojourners, feeding them with manna (Exod. 16–17), they should remember those who are vulnerable, displaced, and homeless.

In the NT, Jesus' welcome to sinners often takes place over shared food. Hospitality becomes transformational, the means to **holiness**. Whereas reciprocity was common in the ancient world, the parable of the great banquet (Luke 14) contains the instruction to invite those who are unable to repay, not those who can reciprocate. Such meals enact the kingdom of God and prefigure the heavenly banquet. Jesus' Last Supper with his disciples is reenacted in the **sacrament** of the Lord's Supper. There Christians receive God's self-giving hospitality. Because the Eucharist is Christ's table, the invitation is to all who seek God's **grace.**

Participation in Christ's body entails offering the same gracious welcome to others, with an emphasis on a unity that transcends ethnic, social, and economic boundaries. All are invited into the fellowship and hospitality taking place between the Father, Son, and Spirit, as God's love makes room for all. It includes Christians in a redefined family. This loving community is also outward looking and missional, inviting the world to participate.

Recognizing God's grace and generous welcome to all, a Wesleyan understanding of holiness has hospitality at its core. Hospitality as holiness transcends cultural norms; it offers instead a vision of a relational God who seeks relationship and in whom a holy life has its source. Committed to advancing God's goals for the world, Christian hospitality entails giving and receiving, shared meals and shared lives, protection and provision, care for the needy, and a welcome into homes, families, and churches. Bearing witness to God's hospitality, we become guest and host. To receive hospitality is to know ourselves as vulnerable strangers and guests of God; to offer hospitality is to proclaim and enact the gospel, the divine welcome.

See also Mission and Social Justice; Reconciliation.

Resources

Pohl, Christine D. *Making Room: Recovering Hospitality as a Christian Tradition.* Grand Rapids: Eerdmans, 1999.

Sutherland, Arthur. *I Was a Stranger: A Christian Theology of Hospitality.* Nashville: Abingdon Press, 2006.

SARAH WHITTLE, PHD

HUMANISM

The term "humanism" was first used by nineteenth-century scholars to identify the Renaissance system of education based on the classics. They drew on the fifteenth-century term *umanista*, which refers to persons studying classical literature and philosophy, not to understand God, but to understand what it means to be human. So understood, humanism refers to a system of education that emphasizes human individuality, dignity, and the privileged place of humans in the universe.

More than a philosophy, Renaissance humanism was a comprehensive cultural movement that included poetry, art, literature, history, and moral philosophy. Many scholars say it drew its inspiration from Petrarch (1304-74) and other older Italian humanists who were not anti-Christian.

More positively, Christian humanism has a long and rich history that continues to today. It reaches as far back as Jesus, who refused to let religious laws subvert the value of any person, whether woman, child, or slave. Christian humanists teach that human freedom and dignity, creativity, the inviolability of conscience in all persons, the freedom to use the mind for critical reflection and exploration, and the appreciation of beauty and truth wherever they appear are not just compatible with Christianity but are actively promoted by the Christian gospel. The ranks of Christian humanists are long. They run from the Italian Giovanni Pico della Mirandola, who wrote *Oration on the Dignity of Man* (ca. 1486), and Erasmus of Rotterdam (1466–1536) to G. K. Chesterton (1874–1936) and Aleksandr Solzhenitsyn (1918–2008).

In spite of the rich history of Christian humanism, since the time of Jacob Burckhardt (1818-97) and Friedrich Nietzsche (1844–1900), humanism has popularly identified as anti-Christian. Nietzsche thought of humanism as a turn from the "slave morality" imposed by Judaism and Christianity to the "master morality" provided by the Greeks and Romans. The anti-Christian and antireligion form of humanism became more broadly accepted in the twentieth century and became identified as "secular humanism." In this form, humanism was attacked by Roman Catholics and Protestants as a harbinger of modern atheism.

John Wesley critically appropriated insights from John Locke's empiricist **epistemology** and also embraced **Jacob Arminius**'s notion of "responsive" freedom. He took seriously the fall and original sin. But he also emphasized humankind's freedom, made possible by grace alone, to respond actively to the gospel. Although Wesley would have soundly rejected secular humanism, he held to a high and optimistic view of what God's grace can achieve in persons completely yielded to renewal in Christ's image.

See also Greek Philosophy; Justice; Person; Rights, Human; Social Justice.

Resources

Kurtz, Paul. *What Is Secular Humanism?* New York: Prometheus Books, 2007.
Lamont, Corliss. *The Philosophy of Humanism*. 8th ed. Amherst, NY: Humanist Press, 1997.

YOUNG-HO CHUN, PHD

HUMAN SEXUALITY

Christian reflection on human sexuality addresses two distinct yet insepa-rable topics: gender and sexual behavior.

Gender is defined early in Scripture (Gen. 1:27). Humans are created in God's image as *male* and *female*. Throughout Scripture this binary view of gender is assumed and has prevailed in Christian thought into the modern era. The Bible consistently and positively affirms that God made man and woman for each other and that their sexual desires properly find fulfillment within heterosexual marriage (Mark 10:2-9; 1 Cor. 7:1-9; 1 Thess. 4:3-8; Heb. 13:4).

In recent decades, challenges to the two-gender classification have come from the natural and **social sciences**. Recent discoveries show that numerous genetic, physiological, and social factors contribute to gender formation. Ad-ditionally, some persons exhibit "intersexual" characteristics and are neither fully male nor female. Some scientists therefore conclude that traditional definitions of gender are social constructions that misconstrue the complex-ity of human physiology and gender identity formation.

Biblical teachings on gender have frequently been misused to subjugate women. Failure to read the Bible holistically in light of the gospel of Jesus Christ makes this possible. Scripture affirms that (1) men *and* women are equally created in God's image (Gen. 1:26-27); (2) patriarchal social struc-tures are not part of God's original plan (3:16); and (3) gender-role distinc-tions obstructing women from full and equal participation with men in the life of the church and society run counter to the gospel (Gal. 3:28).

Biblical and traditional teachings about sexual activity are not always so clear. The attitude toward sexuality in the OT is overwhelmingly positive. Sexual activity is endorsed in the first commandments God gives to humans (Gen. 1:28) and is an activity to be enjoyed by lovers (Song of Solomon). A slightly different picture emerges in the NT. Several NT texts speak of mar-riage in lofty terms, even as a metaphor for Christ's relationship with the church (Eph. 5:22-33; Rev. 21:9-10). However, both Jesus and Paul com-mended celibacy under certain conditions (Matt. 19:10-12; 1 Cor. 7:1-9).

The NT affirms that any form of sexual activity outside marriage con-stitutes sin. As in the OT, the NT especially condemns adultery, fornication, prostitution, and rape—including pederasty, or sex with children (1 Cor. 5:9-11; 6:9, 1 Tim. 1:10, Heb. 13:4; 1 Pet. 4:3). However, although marriage be-tween two persons is clearly the norm promoted in the creation stories (Gen. 1–3), polygamy and keeping concubines were common in ancient Israel.

There is also diversity regarding sexual ethics within Christian history. With the rise of monasticism, and the influence of **Greek philosophy** (es-pecially **Neoplatonism**) on early Christian theology, many Christians began to view any sexual activity as impeding Christian life. This helped forge attitudes toward sex in **Roman Catholicism.** Celibacy is the ideal (hence the celibate priesthood), and sexual activity is morally appropriate only within marriage and when intended for procreation (hence Catholic restrictions on birth control). **Protestants** have taught that marriage is fully commensurate with Christian life, and that sexual activity within marriage is not detrimental to Christian discipleship. They have tended to endorse marital sexual activity for pleasure and for nurturing marriage. Both traditions have agreed that sexual activity outside marriage is sinful.

Currently, controversy rages in some parts of Christianity over whether homosexual practice is compatible with Christian discipleship. Christians have traditionally viewed Scripture as prohibiting sexual activity outside *heterosexual* marriage. The Bible seldom discusses homosexual behavior. But the few texts addressing the topic of homosexual activity (Lev. 18:22; 20:13; Acts 15:28-29; Rom. 1:18-32; 1 Cor. 6:9-11; 1 Tim. 1:10) consistently condemn it as sinful.

However, other Christians, especially in the West and North, reject the traditional view of sexual ethics, particularly homosexuality. They assert that the NT condemns only pederasty, promiscuity, or homosexual acts committed by heterosexual persons. Others say the Bible's condemnation of homosexual behavior should be viewed as "outdated" Hebrew holiness codes, such as prohibitions against intercourse with a menstruating woman (Lev. 18:19-22).

Nevertheless, Scripture and Christian tradition *as a whole* are clear about the following: (1) human sexuality is a beautiful part of God's holy plan and is properly fulfilled only in accordance with God's will; (2) heterosexual marriage is the biblical norm for morally appropriate sexual intercourse; (3) homosexual orientation should not be equated with homosexual behavior; and (4) God loves all persons and expects us to do the same.

See also Anthropology, Theological; Ethics; Evolution/Evolutionary Biology; Family, Christian; Feminist Theology; Greek Philosophy; Marriage; Natural Science; Person; Polygamy; Self-Denial; Social Sciences; Sociobiology; Wesleyan Feminism; Women in the Bible; Women's Role in the Church.

Resources

Countryman, L. William. *Dirt, Greed, and Sex: Sexual Ethics in the New Testament and Their Implications for Today.* Minneapolis: Fortress Press, 2007.

Schmidt, Thomas E. *Straight and Narrow? Compassion and Clarity in the Homosexuality Debate.* Downers Grove, IL: InterVarsity Press, 1995.

Spaulding, Henry W., II. *Untangling the Sexual Revolution: Rethinking Our Sexual Ethic.* Kansas City: Beacon Hill Press of Kansas City, 1989.

MARK MANN, PHD

HUMILITY

The apostle Paul gave a good definition of humility when he told the Philippians to "regard others as better than yourselves. Let each of you look not to your own interests, but to the interests of others" (Phil. 2:3-4). He then quoted an early Christian poem about how Jesus "emptied himself" of the rights and privileges of divinity and, instead, assumed the status of a servant (vv. 6-7). Already in human form, Jesus humbled himself even further to experience one of the most shameful kinds of death—crucifixion (v. 8).

Paul's example of Jesus and of Paul's own life shows that humility is more a way of living and behaving than a matter of self-esteem. Humility for Paul meant putting the needs of others above one's own. Humility involves not thinking of oneself "more highly" than one ought but thinking with "sober judgment . . . according to the measure of faith that God has assigned" (Rom. 12:3). Christian humility is not self-effacement, for we are created in God's image, both female and male (Gen. 1:27). God made humans "a little lower than God" (Ps. 8:5); to denigrate others and/or oneself insults God who made us (e.g., James 3:9).

However, humility is also a matter of attitude, its opposite being arrogance. An arrogant person fails to see that everything he or she has is a gift from the Lord, that we entered this world naked and will exit it the same (Job 1:21). "[We] are dust, and to dust [we] shall return" (Gen. 3:19; see also Eccles. 3:20). Humble persons recognize who they are before God (see Isa. 6) and rejoice in the greatness of his love.

See also Fruit of the Spirit; Self-Denial; Virtues.

Resources
Murray, Andrew. Humility. 1895. Reprint, Bloomington, MN: Bethany House, 2001.
Thomas à Kempis. The Imitation of Christ. Edited by Harold C. Gardiner. New York: Doubleday, 2009.

KENNETH SCHENCK, PHD

HYPOSTATIC UNION
See TRINITY.

Ii

ICONS, IMAGES, ICONOCLASM

The word "icon" comes from the Greek term *eikōn/eikona*, meaning "image" or "picture." The earliest Christian pictures (third and fourth centuries AD) come from the catacombs of Rome. On their walls there could be found scenes of worship, illustrations to biblical stories, images of apostles, and symbols of Christ and the church. At this point the notion of the veneration of sacred images was unknown to the church. But by the seventh century AD icons were widely used, despite such a practice having always been seen as controversial by some theologians and church leaders.

Icons have a special place in Orthodox spirituality. They serve to communicate theological truths as well as divine grace. John of Damascus notes, "What the written word is to those who know letters, the icon is to the unlettered" (1898, 10-17). Icons explain and illustrate church theology and the interpretation of Scripture through symbolic and artistic representation. This was a crucial aspect of proclamation in the mostly illiterate societies of Late Antiquity and the Middle Ages. Icons are not mere works of art or aesthetic artifacts; they are "windows to heaven." They have a mystical dimension; holy persons represented in images become present and accessible to a believer. Leontius of Neapolis observes, "We Christians, by bodily kissing an icon of Christ . . . are in spirit kissing Christ Himself" (Schmemann [1963] 1997). According to the Orthodox tradition, God fills sacred images with his presence and power. Thus icons help Christians to communicate with God and saints and to receive grace. For this reason icons are widely used in worship and everyday life.

Iconoclasm (Greek, *eikona* [image] and *klaō* [break]; lit. "image breaking") refers to the eighth- and ninth-century movement in the Byzantine Empire against the veneration of icons. Iconoclasts regarded icons as idols and their veneration as an act of idolatry, basing their position on the Decalogue (Exod. 20:4-5). They radically rejected the mystical and liturgical aspects of icons.

The origin of the iconoclastic movement is a matter of scholarly debate. Several reasons are suggested: the rising influence of Islam; the superstitious worship of icons among laypeople; the political struggle against church influence; the attempt of secular culture to liberate art from church dominance; and an outbreak of suppressed Hellenistic spiritualism, with a negative attitude toward the material in religion.

The struggle over icons started in 726 when the Emperor Leo III ordered the removal of the image of Christ from the gates of Constantinople. Supported by emperors, state bureaucracy, and the army, iconoclasts violently persecuted the icon devotees and destroyed sacred images in churches and public places. But they were opposed by high-standing clergy and monks. The fight over icons continued throughout the eighth century with varying success.

Finally, in 843 the Council of Constantinople, with the support of Empress Theodora, condemned iconoclasm and restored the veneration of icons. The reinstatement of icons was triumphantly celebrated in the cathedral of Hagia Sophia in Constantinople and is still commemorated annually by the **Orthodox Church** as the festival of the Triumph of Orthodoxy.

See also Spiritual Disciplines; Theosis (Deification).

Resources

John of Damascus, Saint. *St. John Damascene on Holy Images.* Translated by Mary H. Allies. London: Thomas Baker, 1898. Internet Medieval Source Book. http://www.fordham.edu/halsall/source/johndam-icons.asp.

Ouspensky, Léonid. *Theology of the Icon.* 2 vols. Translated by Anthony Gythiel with selections translated by Elizabeth Meyendorff. Crestwood, NY: St Vladimir's Seminary Press, 1992.

Schmemann, Alexander. "Byzantium." Chap. 4 in *The Historical Road of Eastern Orthodoxy.* Translated by Lydia W. Kesich. New York: Holt, Rinehart, and Winston, 1963. Reprint, Crestwood, NY: St Vladimir's Seminary Press, 1997. ELPENOR. http://www.ellopos.net/elpenor/schmemann-orthodoxy-4-byzantium.asp?pg=4.

ARSENY ERMAKOV, PHD

IDOLATRY

Idolatry is of fundamental concern for the OT and NT. From the perspective of Scripture, idolatry involves the **worship** of anything other than the living God.

In the OT, Israel's life is anchored in a covenant relationship of exclusive loyalty to the one creator God. The first two commandments prohibit worshipping other gods and revering idols or **images**, including images of the Lord (Exod. 20:3-4; Deut. 5:7-8). The second commandment is closely related to the first, since pagan deities were commonly believed to be present in their images.

The OT frequently ridicules idols as lifeless and powerless human creations (e.g., Ps. 115:4-8; Isa. 44:9-20; Jer. 10:1-10). But occasionally Scripture acknowledges the presence of demonic forces behind the idols (Deut. 32:16-17; Ps. 106:35-38; cf. 1 Cor. 10:18-21; Rev. 9:20). There is no graver offense to God than idolatry. It arouses God's jealousy (zeal for what is rightfully his; Exod. 20:5; 34:14; Deut. 32:16, 21), which is tied to God's love for those he has redeemed. As a fundamental rejection of the "Godness" of God, idolatry spawns other sins, especially sexual immorality (Num. 25:1-3; 1 Kings 14:22-24; cf. 1 Cor. 10:7-8). Indeed, the dominant OT metaphor for idolatry is spiritual adultery and harlotry (e.g., Isa. 1:21; Jer. 2:20; 3:8-9, 21; Ezek. 16:28, 35; Hos. 2:12-14).

The NT also treats idolatry with utmost seriousness (e.g., Acts 17:29-31; Rom. 1:18-23; 1 Cor. 5:10-11; 10:14-22; 1 John 5:21; Rev. 2:20-23; 14:9-11; 21:8). For Gentile Christians, conversion involved "turn[ing] to God from idols, to serve a living and true God" (1 Thess. 1:9). But the NT recognizes that idolatry is more than simply worshipping images; it is a matter of the heart. An idol can be anything that claims for itself the love and devotion that belong to God alone. Greed, therefore, is a form of idolatry (Eph. 5:5; Col. 3:5; cf. Matt. 6:24).

Scripture's attitude toward idolatry assumes that God is unique and cannot be represented by any created thing. Idolatry shatters the distinction between God and **creation**. It exalts something in the created order and deposes the Creator. From a biblical perspective, idolatry not only denies God his proper honor but also dehumanizes people. We become like what we worship (Ps. 115:8; Hos. 9:10).

Today, humans practice idolatry in many ways. Pseudo-gods and their images are still worshipped throughout the world in various religious contexts. But if idols are essentially what we trust in and serve instead of the living God, then idolatry is prevalent in all societies. In the modern world, idolatry can take such forms as consumerism, nationalism, civil religion, or the veneration of **science**, celebrity, sex, or sports. Idolatry also occurs when people try to reduce God to an object they can manipulate for their own ends. God's loving mission in the world seeks to deliver humans from worshipping gods that fail. God works to restore all of creation to its rightful purpose of bringing glory to the Creator.

See also Icons, Images, Iconoclasm; Liturgy and Worship; Polytheism; Religious Pluralism; Syncretism, Religious.

Resources

Beale, Gregory K. *We Become What We Worship: A Biblical Theology of Idolatry.* Downers Grove, IL: IVP Academic, 2008.

Wright, Christopher J. H. "The Living God Confronts Idolatry." Chap. 5 in *The Mission of God: Unlocking the Bible's Grand Narrative.* Downers Grove, IL: InterVarsity Press, 2006.

DEAN FLEMMING, PHD

IDOL WORSHIP
See IDOLATRY.

IMAGE OF GOD
See ANTHROPOLOGY, THEOLOGICAL; CREATION/NEW CREATION; THEOSIS (DEIFICATION).

IMMORTALITY/LIFE AFTER DEATH

The doctrine of eternal life is rooted in the historic death and resurrection of Jesus and the future hope of the bodily resurrection of believers as part of a cosmic renewal. God's power over death is demonstrated in the resurrection of Jesus, who is the firstfruits of the general resurrection and therefore of the new creation. In contrast to the Platonic notion of the immortality of a disembodied soul, salvation history is linear: eternal life is a gift from God, who will raise the dead by the **Spirit**. Christians anticipate a transformed bodily life in a remade world. Jewish eschatology was reshaped to take account of the eschatological significance of Christ's death and resurrection.

Jesus' death and resurrection mean the power of death has been overcome and God's future brought into the present. As such, eternal life is not merely something to be hoped for but that in which we currently participate because of our being in Christ—buried with him and raised to new life, with the consequent demands of Christian life now dead to sin. Those participating in Jesus' resurrection life are vindicated in advance as recipients of God's eschatological salvation. That eternal life has begun demonstrates the reality of the new creation in the present and assures its future. Christians are now citizens of heaven, living life according to a new and different order.

Because of life in between the present and the future, Christians experience both the decay of the outward and the regeneration of the inward person. Physical transformation to a body like that of Christ remains future: human resurrection will be fully realized when the dead in Christ are raised and our mortal bodies are changed to become immortal. However, a moral transformation is currently taking place. Thus eternal life in the present is characterized by conformity to Christlikeness—that is, comprehension of, and participation in, the purposes of God for the whole of creation. The life-giving Spirit brings about both moral renewal and the final bodily transformation.

Hope has already come to life, but we continue to pray for the fullness of God's kingdom to come—anticipating the time when heaven and earth will be united. In the future we will see God face-to-face, knowing unhindered presence, experiencing the divine glory, and being fully transformed into God's likeness. In the New Jerusalem, images from the garden form a picture of eternal life in the city of God. The sure and certain hope is that death does not have the last word. This new life requires us to anticipate the final resurrection and new heaven and earth by transforming the present in the light of the future.

See also Christology, New Testament; Creation/New Creation; Eschatology; Kingdom of God.

Resources

Smalley, Stephen. *Hope for Ever: The Christian View of Life and Death*. Carlisle, UK: Paternoster, 2006.

Wright, N. T. *The Resurrection of the Son of God*. Minneapolis: Fortress Press, 2003.

———. *Surprised by Hope: Rethinking Heaven, the Resurrection, and the Mission of the Church*. New York: HarperOne, 2008.

SARAH WHITTLE, PHD

INCARNATION

The technical term "incarnation" signifies that Jesus' life is the event in which the second person of the Trinity, God's Son or Word, "became flesh" (Latin, *in-* [into, in] *carn-* [flesh]; see John 1:14). The Hebrew word for "flesh" (*basar*), when used in the OT, normally signifies human vulnerability and mortality. God is never spoken of in the OT as "flesh." Flesh and God are as different as weakness and power. That God has become flesh in Jesus signifies that the Almighty has entered into human frailty. This does not mean that the Almighty has undergone a reduction of power but that the Almighty has embraced everything frailty entails, by living it—to the point of crucifixion, and that the Almighty has been glorified in that frailty.

The doctrine is not a theological abstraction. It is an account of the concrete *lifetime* of the first-century Jewish peasant in which God "was pleased to dwell" (Col. 1:19). Jesus, the "friend of tax collectors and sinners" (Matt. 11:19), "counted among the lawless" (Luke 22:37), crucified and forsaken (Mark 15:25-34), is Lord and God (John 20:28).

The incarnation is not a doctrine about a lone individual. Instead, it tells how God in **Jesus Christ** enters into solidarity with vulnerable people. His history is inseparable from theirs. He comes in direct contact with sinners, the sick, the blind, the lame, the poor, lepers, prostitutes, the demon-possessed, political criminals, Roman collaborators, and even corpses. They and he mingle as he lives, is crucified, and is buried with them. Just as the Son loves his Father, he also loves these neighbors. They in turn become identified with his "self" (cf. Mark 12:29-31). All this happens "for us and our salvation," as the earliest creeds, such as the Nicene Creed (AD 325), affirm.

The view of salvation lying behind these creeds goes far beyond the notion of acquittal for wrongdoing. The early church understood **salvation** to be our entry into intimate fellowship with God, being made holy, our sanctification and participation in the very nature of God (2 Pet. 1:4). Since in our finitude and sin we could not ascend to God and make salvation happen, God descended to us. Athanasius (ca. 296–373) affirmed that unless God becomes what we are (while remaining truly God), we cannot become what God is (while remaining truly human). This view of salvation led to the orthodox doctrine that Jesus Christ is fully God (thus *God* becomes human), fully human (thus God becomes *human*), and one person (thus God *becomes* human). It also led to the doctrine of the Trinity: Jesus Christ works God's yes to us; the Spirit works our yes to God.

Among the errors that deny the incarnation and have been declared heresies are **Arianism** (which denies that Jesus Christ is fully divine), Apollinarianism (which denies that Jesus Christ is fully human), Nestorianism (which denies that Jesus Christ is one person), and Monophysitism (which dissolves the humanity of Jesus Christ into his deity).

See also Atonement; Christology; Christology, New Testament; Doctrine/Dogma; God, Doctrine of; Kenosis; Reconciliation; Revelation.

Resources
Norris, Richard A., Jr., ed. and trans. *The Christological Controversy.* Philadelphia: Fortress Press, 1980.
Schnackenburg, Rudolph. *Jesus in the Gospels: A Biblical Christology.* Translated by O. C. Dean Jr. Louisville, KY: Westminster John Knox Press, 1995.

CRAIG KEEN, PHD

INDIGENIZATION

The term "indigenization" refers to the modification of an idea, institution, practice, or service to suit a local culture. This requires increased local participation and control determined by the characteristic values of an indigenous group. The term is widely used in Christian missions to refer (1) to making the gospel understood in the language and thought forms of local people and (2) to efforts to make the church autonomous in its organization.

The Madras Conference, sponsored by the International Missionary Council in 1938, defined "indigenization" as

a group of believers who live out their life, including their socialized Christian activity, in a pattern of the local society and for whom any transformation of the society comes out of their felt needs under the guidance of the **Holy Spirit** and Scripture.

The concept is not new. At the Jerusalem Council (Acts 15) **early church** leaders debated the extent to which Gentile Christians should adhere to Jewish tradition. Later the church debated whether Christians should adapt to Hellenistic practices. During the Reformation era, Wycliffe, Tyndale, and Luther translated the Bible into local languages so that Christians could better understand and obey the Scriptures.

In **Roman Catholic** missions the term "accommodation" was used. Protestants preferred "indigenization." Indigenous church theory as it relates to Protestant missions was developed by three church leaders in the nineteenth century: Henry Venn, Rufus Anderson, and Roland Allen. They stated three main themes of indigenization: *self-government, self-support,* and *self-propagation.* They were intended to address a phenomenon that had developed as trained missionaries were sent to the poor and needy of many non-Western areas. A culture of dependence developed among the "younger churches." Churches in a number of countries became entirely dependent on mission agencies and became estranged from their cultural contexts. Anderson and Venn in particular urged mission agencies to turn over control of the new churches to local leadership as soon as possible to achieve self-supporting, self-governing, and self-propagating churches. The missionaries were to move on to other fields. Venn promoted the "euthanasia of a mission," meaning the end of missionary control over the younger church.

Later it was discovered that an indigenous church that was truly a biblical church would be more than the "three *selfs*" model permitted. The model was more of a Western business model than a biblical model. For example, it said nothing about the missionary responsibility of a truly apostolic **church.** As a correction to this deficiency, the percentage of missionaries from the Global South among the total number of career missionaries continues to increase.

In the early 1970s an even larger need for interpreting the Scriptures in ways that are contextually meaningful and that can result in holistic transformation was recognized. The emphasis became known as **contextualization.** It encouraged the younger churches to move beyond indigenization. Behind contextualization stands the recognition that no culture possesses a privileged understanding of the gospel. Rather it judges all cultures. All the churches in all cultures must be instructed by the whole gospel message. This establishes a relationship of interdependence and partnership in the body of Christ.

See also Contextualization; Indigenous Christian Groups; Indigenous Theologies; Postcolonialism.

Resources

Hiebert, Paul G. "Indigenization." *Global Anabaptist Mennonite Encyclopedia Online.* 1989. http://www.gameo.org/encyclopedia/contents/I54ME.html (accessed January 24, 2011).

Kim, Uichol, Kuo-Shu Yang, and Kwang-Kuo Hwang, eds. *Indigenous and Cultural Psychology: Understanding People in Context.* International and Cultural Psychology. New York: Springer Science+Business Media, 2006.

JOHN WESLEY Z. KUREWA, PHD

INDIGENOUS CHRISTIAN GROUPS

Anything that originates in, belongs to, or is native to a particular place or group is "indigenous." Its opposite is "foreign." Indigenous Christian groups are persons of a specific cultural context who have experienced salvation in Christ while living and worshipping in modes that reflect their cultures and customs.

The era of colonization allowed missionaries of European and American origin to enter many countries. They normally established churches that worshipped in ways consistent with their home cultures, whether American or European, Catholic or Protestant. Sanctuaries, cathedrals, liturgy, music, and dress were patterned after the missionaries' home cultures. For example, rather than encourage the development of church music characteristic of indigenous cultures, missionaries often banned local instruments and translated Western hymns into local languages. The general assumption was that Western Christianity was true Christianity and that introducing "pagan" (indigenous) artifacts or practices into church life would constitute **syncretism.**

Starting in the 1950s, colonized nations began overthrowing colonial powers and emerging as free nations. Since then, indigenous populations have tried to answer questions about what they believe and how they practice Christianity. Some have reaffirmed Western forms of Christianity while others have emerged as indigenous Christian groups.

Much like Protestant denominations in Western Christianity, indigenous Christian groups have assumed multiple forms, even within a single nation. They range from orthodox **contextualization** to extreme **syncretism**, which many call heresy. This raises questions about how decisions involving inclusion and exclusion in Christian worship and practice should be made and who should make them. Paul G. Hiebert has described the critical process undertaken by indigenous Christian groups. Congregations carefully assess past customs in light of how they understand the Bible and decide how the Scriptures should be obeyed. They retain customs that do not distort the gospel; they reject others that are contrary to the gospel. The Bible is interpreted in ways that can effectively convey the gospel to their cultures (Hiebert 1999, 381-82).

Two NT passages are central for a biblical understanding of this process. The first is the early church debate recorded in Acts 15, which asks the question, "Must Gentiles become Jews to be Christians?" The second is in Acts 21, which poses the opposite question, "Must Jews become Gentiles to be Christians?" Contemporary Christian anthropologists join the apostle Paul in answering no to both questions. The **incarnation** of Christ expressed God's love and desire for the salvation of all persons. It also demonstrated God's willingness to become part of human culture in order to express his love. Indigenous Christian groups are an ongoing expression of God's desire to redeem individuals and their cultures.

See also Christianity and Global Cultures; Contextualization; Contextual Theology; Indigenous Theologies; Missionary Movements; New Religious Movements; Syncretism, Religious.

Resources
Hiebert, Paul G. Understanding Folk Religion: *A Christian Response to Popular Beliefs and Practices.* Grand Rapids: Baker Books, 1999.
Pocock, Michael, Gailyn Van Rheenen, and Douglas McConnell. *The Changing Face of World Missions: Engaging Contemporary Issues and Trends.* Grand Rapids: Baker Academic, 2005.
Winter, Ralph D., and Steven C. Hawthorne, eds. *Perspectives on the World Christian Movement: A Reader.* 4th ed. Pasadena, CA: William Carey Library, 2009.

MARYANN HAWKINS, PHD

INDIGENOUS THEOLOGIES

An indigenous theology is formed when Christian **beliefs**, experiences, and practices are articulated in thought forms that reflect a particular tribal or **indigenous** people group's cultural context. What results is not the sometimes suffocating imposition of imported theology but an indigenous theology that emerges from dialogue between the **gospel**, orthodox Christian faith, and the social, economic, cultural, political, and ecological characteristics of a people group.

Some see the flowering of indigenous theologies as detrimental to Christian unity. That is a mistake. An indigenous people grappling with the meaning of the Christian faith within their context simply shows that for the gospel to flourish it must become deeply rooted in the social and intellectual soil of each people group. Indigenous theology marks a movement away from uncritically embracing theology formulated in a foreign culture or placing Western theologians on a pedestal.

Speaking about Western theology, **Asian theology**, **Latin American theology**, and **African theology** doesn't mean Christian theology and the church have splintered. Rather, it recognizes that when Christians comprehensively engage the meaning of the gospel, their theology will show evidence of the engagement. Their consideration of Scripture will help address the gospel to **human rights** violations, ethnic conflicts and atrocities, **poverty**, and **ecological** degradation. Community value systems, identification with the **land**, and a desire for authentic **shalom** may be only minimally important for Western theology, but they are profoundly important for indigenous cultures. They directly affect how theology is done.

Contrary to what some have charged, an indigenous theology need not lead to **syncretism**. Indigenous theology simply recognizes that Christian theology is not an abstraction unrelated to history and particular cultures.

Some have opposed indigenous theologies because they think of Christian theology as fixed and timeless. They seem to forget that the ecumenical **creeds** and Western theology bear the stamp of Western history and culture.

Some have used the word "hybrid" to describe indigenous theologies. However, that term carries colonialist overtones because it projects the notion that an indigenous theology does nothing more than modify Western theology.

Promoting indigenous theologies doesn't involve encouraging people to make up new **doctrines.** It simply involves recognizing that articulating the Christian faith can be both genuinely multicultural and catholic (universal). Theology can speak to diverse cultures without becoming competitive. Some motifs and themes in **Scripture** will strike more responsive chords in some cultures than in others. For instance, the marginalized will be attracted to God's love for strangers and aliens. Upwardly mobile professionals in world-class cities may be moved by the sense that God wants persons to be productive. The poor will see God's commitment to persons who have been excluded from sharing a culture's material **wealth.**

Do errors in theology and practice occur? Yes, but perhaps no more often than in the West.

See also Globalization; Holistic Mission; Indigenization; Indigenous Christian Groups; Millennium Development Goals (MDGs); Westernization of the Gospel.

HOWARD CULBERTSON, DMIN

INSPIRATION
See SCRIPTURE, THEOLOGY OF.

INSTITUTED MEANS OF GRACE
See MEANS OF GRACE; PRAYER; SACRAMENTS; WORKS OF PIETY.

INTELLIGENT DESIGN

Intelligent design (ID) refers to a subset of contemporary design arguments for God's existence. Design arguments in general, also called teleological arguments, claim that certain characteristics of the world exhibit features of purposeful design that prove God's existence.

The term "intelligent design" became common after the publication of *Of Pandas and People* (1989), a controversial American secondary school science textbook. "Intelligent design" replaces "creationism" found in earlier drafts. However, the term can be found in numerous writings dating back to the mid-nineteenth century. According to the Discovery Institute, a non-profit think tank based in Seattle and closely aligned with the American intelligent design movement, "The theory of intelligent design holds that certain features of the universe and of living things are best explained by an intelligent cause, not an undirected process such as natural selection" (2012).

A central element of ID is "irreducible complexity" in organisms, a term coined by Michael Behe in *Darwin's Black Box* (1996). Behe argues that certain biochemical systems (e.g., blood clotting, the eye, or bacterial flagella) are necessarily and irreducibly complex from the beginning. He claims that if such systems "cannot be produced gradually [they] would have to arise as an integrated unit, in one fell swoop, for natural selection to have anything to act on" (39). The existence of "irreducible complexity" argues for an intelligent designer—God.

Other strands of ID focus on the improbability of life arising simply because of naturalistic forces or on the apparent fine-tuning of the constants of physics required for making life in the universe possible.

Critics of ID say that even if arguments for intelligent design were sound, they would not prove the God of traditional Christian theology. Other critics say that instead of ID being principally a well-grounded research program, it is actually an argument for God's existence. Some scientists who are also Christians say that alleged gaps of knowledge in the evolutionary history of living organisms on which ID rests no longer exist.

Intelligent design has been the subject of debate in science, religion, and philosophy. It has also been the occasion for controversy in public school policy and curricula. In an influential 2005 United States federal court case, *Kitzmiller et al. v. Dover Area School District et al.*, Judge John E. Jones III declared it unconstitutional to teach intelligent design in publicly funded high schools. The religious nature of ID, he argued, is readily apparent to an objective observer. Teaching ID in the public schools amounts to teaching religion rather than science and is consequently unconstitutional.

See also Church and State; Creationism; Creation/New Creation; Evolution/Evolutionary Biology; Natural Science; Natural Theology; Philosophy of Religion.

Resources

Behe, Michael. *Darwin's Black Box*. New York: Free Press, 1996.

Discovery Institute (Center for Science and Culture). "Top Questions." Accessed November 16, 2012. http://www.discovery.org/csc/topQuestions.php.

Kitcher, Philip. *Living with Darwin: Evolution, Design, and the Future of Faith*. Oxford, UK: Oxford University Press, 2009.

McGrath, Alister. *A Fine-Tuned Universe: The Quest for God in Science and Theology*. Louisville, KY: Westminster John Knox Press, 2009.

Monton, Bradley. *Seeking God in Science: An Atheist Defends Intelligent Design*. Peterborough, ON: Broadview Press, 2009.

KEVIN TIMPE, PHD

INTERFAITH DIALOGUE

Interfaith dialogue refers to the demanding practice of entering mutually respectful yet frank conversation with a person or persons of a different religious tradition than one's own.

The word "dialogue" is critical. Persons who engage in interfaith dialogue must be willing to become careful listeners. Dialogue is not one person preaching to another. This does not exclude attempts to convert another; indeed, for interfaith dialogue to be authentic and honest there is no inherent reason to avoid all evangelization. Conversely, one should permit similar efforts by one's dialogue partner.

For this reason some religious traditions—perhaps most notably Orthodox Judaism—do not encourage participation in interfaith dialogue. Traditionally, Orthodox Jews do not actively seek converts. Thus there is a strong tendency among many of them to fear that people of other traditions, such as Islam or Christianity, might have an advantage over Orthodox Jews in interfaith dialogue and might use it as a pretext for proselytization.

Interfaith dialogue has a long history in Christianity. To some extent, Paul's famous sermon to the Stoic and Epicurean philosophers of Athens (Acts 17:22-31) is understandable as an example of such dialogue, particularly since Paul assessed their religious practice as somewhat positive (v. 22) and even quoted pagan religious poetry favorably (v. 28). Even Jesus' conversation with the Samaritan woman at the well can be seen as a mild form of interfaith dialogue, since their conversation revolved around Jewish-Samaritan theological differences (John 4:5-26).

Beyond the NT era, the most dramatic early proponent of interfaith dialogue was the second-century philosopher-theologian Justin Martyr, who speculated about the efficacy of divine Wisdom (Greek, *Logos*), which enlightens and instructs humans everywhere and always (cf. John 1:4, 9)—especially great Greek philosophers such as Socrates, Plato, and Heraclitus. Additionally, Justin engaged in extensive debate and dialogue with a rabbi, which he shared with his readers in *Dialogue with Trypho*.

Interfaith dialogue is an increasingly important component of Christian theological reflection, though certainly not all Christians approve. For some, to enter into dialogue already concedes too much legitimacy to non-Christian convictions and practices. However, Christians in the Wesleyan tradition have important reasons for dialogue. First, there is Wesleyanism's deep appreciation for the doctrine of prevenient grace, which states (similar to Justin Martyr) that the Spirit of God is always present everywhere, laboring patiently and quietly to draw persons of all religions to the light of God's redeeming love in Jesus Christ. Second, there is Wesleyanism's strong emphasis on love of one's neighbor as a central component of the entirely sanctified life; it is certainly arguable that loving one's neighbors includes and even requires getting to know them, including striving to know well and respectfully our neighbors' religious convictions and practices.

See also Judaism; Prevenient Grace; Religions, Theology of; Religious Pluralism.

Resources
Cobb, John B., Jr. *Beyond Dialogue: Toward a Mutual Transformation of Christianity and Buddhism.* Philadelphia: Fortress Press, 1982.
Lodahl, Michael. *Claiming Abraham: Reading the Bible and the Qur'an Side by Side.* Grand Rapids: Brazos Press, 2010.
Truesdale, Al. *With Cords of Love: A Wesleyan Response to Religious Pluralism.* With Keri Mitchell. Kansas City: Beacon Hill Press of Kansas City, 2006.

MICHAEL LODAHL, PHD

INTERTEXTUALITY

A technical definition of the term "intertextuality" is difficult. It was recently coined by literary critics to describe literary texts whose existence and meaning are predicated on their relationship with other texts. Intertextuality refers to literature's constant recourse to other literature; no text is composed in isolation. Texts are studied reciprocally. One text "reads" another and amplifies its original meaning.

Scholars use the term "intertextuality" in broad reference to how biblical writers quote or allude to Scripture for amplifying the meaning of, or providing the theological setting for, their own writing. New Testament writers found in Israel's Scripture various ways to shape Christian communities. They interpreted the new dispensation inaugurated by the risen Son's messianic mission.

But the theological subject matter of the OT doesn't change in the NT. Scripture in its different parts bears witness to the one and only God, Lord Christ, and Holy Spirit and to a single biblical plan of redemption.

Interpreters use intertextuality to note the simultaneity of Scripture as a whole. They bring texts together by their common words or incidents, even when unintended by their authors. For example, the birth stories of Jesus in Matthew and Luke are written independently but are brought together by the Bible's interpreters as complementary witnesses to the Messiah's birth. The inherent subjectivity of the interpreted Scripture, in which an interpreter seeks a meaning of Scripture pertinent to a particular situation, is constrained not by a consistent application of multiple hermeneutical rules but by core beliefs about God's gospel proclaimed and embodied by Jesus.

Scripture, in its diverse parts, when read together as a unified witness to the triune God, establishes an authoritative context in which the word of the living God becomes known to and for a particular people in the company of God's Spirit. The "canon consciousness" of biblical writers obligated them to pick up their biblical texts and stories and repeat them by citation or allusion because they were of a piece with their own compositions. John, Paul, and Peter brought their inherited Scripture into conversation with their own compositions, not only to demonstrate Scripture's continuing authority as God's Word but also to give God's word in Scripture a new and expanded meaning for ever-changing congregations and contexts.

This interpretive act of relating co-texts and texts adds depth and texture to Scripture's meaning. It also confirms the unity of Scripture, a central feature of Wesley's understanding of Scripture's nature and power.

Resources
Allen, Graham. *Intertextuality (The New Critical Idiom)*. 2nd ed. New York: Routledge, 2011.
Kristeva, Julia. *Desire in Language: A Semiotic Approach to Literature and Art*. New York: Columbia University Press, 1980.
Sweeney, Marvin A. *Form and Intertextuality in Prophetic and Apocalyptic Literature*. Eugene, OR: Wipf and Stock Publishers, 2010.

ROBERT W. WALL, PHD

INVOLUNTARY TRANSGRESSIONS

John Wesley distinguished between voluntary and involuntary transgressions of God's law, arguing that only the former are properly called **sin**. Involuntary transgressions result from the ignorance and mistakes that accompany human finitude. They thus result in mistakes in practice. While intentional or voluntary sin is absent from **Christian perfection**, persons whose hearts are filled with love for God and neighbor nonetheless commit involuntary transgressions. Because such transgressions violate God's perfect will, they require the atonement of Christ and prayer for God's forgiveness.

The growth of believers subsequent to Christian perfection focuses on overcoming ignorance and learning to avoid mistakes. Growth enables a person increasingly to love in accordance with God's will. Today involuntary transgressions can be expanded to encompass our awareness of participating in societal structures and a cultural ethos that bear the marks of sin.

See also Christian Perfection (Entire Sanctification); Discernment; Fruit of the Spirit; Holiness; Righteousness; Sanctification; Sin; Tempers and Affections.

HENRY H. KNIGHT III, PHD

ISLAM

Islam is a worldwide religious tradition and community (Arabic, *ummah wāhidah* [one community]) that comprises virtually one-fourth of the world's population. It is second in size only to Christianity and is among the world's fastest-growing religions.

The term *islam* is derived from the same Semitic root as the Hebrew word *shalom*, or "peace." But it also implies "submission." A *muslim*, accordingly, is "one who submits" to God. Muslims typically combine these meanings to stipulate that Islam is the way of *shalom* (Arabic, *salam*) that may be achieved only through collective human submission to God's will (Arabic, *Al-lah*, "the God").

According to Islamic tradition, this way of peace through submission is the original religious faith. It extends back through history to Adam and Eve and includes other Bible luminaries such as Noah, Abraham, Moses, David, the Hebrew prophets, and Jesus. Indeed, according to the Qur'an all the preceding (including Adam) are *nabi'im*—prophets. Including Adam as a prophet exemplifies the Muslim conviction that humans exist *as human* only as, and to the extent that, they receive divine revelation through prophetic address.

Thus while in one sense the story of Islam begins with the preaching of Muhammad (AD 570–632), Muslims insist the faith Muhammad proclaimed does not differ from the preceding prophets. Thus Islam is the one true and original religious faith for all humanity.

Even before Muhammad's time, most Arabs assumed they were physically descended from Ishmael, Abraham's son with Hagar (Gen. 16:15; 21:1-21). But only a few, who were called *hanifs* (people rightly inclined), practiced an Abrahamic monotheism in which God alone was worshipped. In an Islamic understanding of history, the period prior to Muhammad's prophetic ministry is called *jahiliya*, the "time of ignorance" or "barbarism" in which most Arabic peoples worshipped local deities of tribe or natural phenomena.

According to Muslim tradition, Muhammad was a spiritually sensitive seeker. During one of his frequent meditations in a cave overlooking his hometown Mecca, at age forty, he heard a commanding voice: "Recite!" Eventually this voice was identified as that of the angel Gabriel. For Muslims, the entire Qur'an (Arabic for "recitation") was dictated by God to Gabriel and then by Gabriel to Muhammad. The Qur'an is understood and experienced by Muslims as an *oral* and *aural* experience, an active "hearing" of divine speech. Indeed, in Islam the Qur'an (divided into 114 suras or chapters) is the perfect and utterly infallible divine speech, the "Manifest Book." God created it as "an Arabic Qur'an" "that perchance you may understand" (Qur'an 43:2, 3).

Not surprisingly, the "five pillars" of Islamic practice are all readily derived from the Qur'an. They are (1) *shahada*, public confession that there is only one God and that Muhammad is God's special and final prophet; (2) *salat*, the five daily prescribed sessions of prayer; (3) *zakāt*, the charitable giving of alms to care for the poor and the wayfarer; (4) *sawm*, fasting during the daytime throughout the month of Ramadan, in remembrance of Muhammad's reception of revelation; and (5) *hajj*, pilgrimage to the holy city of Mecca, if health and financial means are available for the journey.

Islamic identity is also formed by a set of core theological convictions derived from the Qur'an: (1) the reality of the one God, who is Creator of all, who (2) speaks to humanity through the prophets and the "books" or texts that result from revelation; (3) spiritual beings, most notably angels (who are not gifted with free will) but also *jinn* (from which "genie" is derived)—intelligent spirits who must choose whether or not to be Muslim—the most infamous of whom is Iblis or Satan the tempter; (4) the eschaton, including the resurrection of the dead and the day of judgment; and (5) God's sovereign power over all things.

See also Interfaith Dialogue; Religions, Theology of; Religious Pluralism.

Resources

Ayoub, Mahmoud M. *Islam: Faith and History.* Oxford, UK: Oneworld, 2004.
Lodahl, Michael. *Claiming Abraham: Reading the Bible and the Qur'an Side by Side.* Grand Rapids: Brazos Press, 2010.
Mattson, Ingrid. *The Story of the Qur'an: Its History and Place in Muslim Life.* Oxford, UK: Blackwell Publishing, 2008.

MICHAEL LODAHL, PHD

ISLAMIC FUNDAMENTALISM
See FUNDAMENTALISMS.

ISRAEL

The name "Israel" first occurs in Gen. 32:28. There, in his struggle at the river Jabbok with "a man" (v. 24), Jacob is renamed Israel. This new name is interpreted as one who has "striven with God and with humans, and have prevailed" (v. 28). The first Hebrew verb used here (*sarah*, "to strive") suggests the name "Israel" means "he who strives" (*yisra-*) "with God" (*-'el*). Hosea 12 reinforces this suggestion, adding that Jacob "strove with God" and "with the angel" (vv. 3-4). However, the verb used in verse 4 may not be *sarah* at all but another homographic verb (same spelling, different meaning)—perhaps *sarar* or *sarah*, both of which apparently mean "to rule," "to be ruler." They derive from the noun *sar*, "prince," "leader," "ruler." Given how Semitic theophoric (god-bearing) names work, it is extremely unlikely that the proper name "Israel" would mean "he who rules God" and refer to Jacob, a human. Instead, proper names with divine elements typically have the mentioned deity as the subject of the verb. An example is the proper name "Nathaniel," which means "God" (*-'el*) "gave" (*natan-*).

Consequently the accounts in Gen. 32 and Hos. 12 apparently provide a folk origin for the name "Israel" that was influenced by the broad context of Jacob's story but especially by his wrestling at Peniel. Originally, however, "Israel" probably meant something such as "God fights" or even "God rules." Even so, no account secures this explanation of the origin. More broadly, "he who strives with God" is an appropriate description of Israel, God's people, who struggle with God in various ways throughout Scripture but who never seem to release God until they have received God's blessing (Gen. 32:26, 29).

"Israel" occurs over two thousand times in the Bible. It typically has two primary referents: (1) Jacob, who goes by that name even after Gen. 32; and (2) Jacob's descendants, the "children of Israel" (Exod. 1:1; Lev. 1:2, KJV). The latter use is by far the more frequent. Indeed, the "children of Israel" commonly refers to the Israelites as a whole. The same holds for other compounds such as "house of Israel" and "people of Israel" (Exod. 40:38; Josh. 8:33). But "Israel" by itself can also refer to the larger people group or nation (Deut. 34:10). "Israel" (and its compounds) can also be used more narrowly to refer to *(a)* the northern kingdom, which split from the southern kingdom in 922 BC (1 Kings 12:16; Hos. 1:1); or *(b)* the southern kingdom, more properly called Judah (2 Chron. 11:3; Isa. 5:7).

References to "Israel" in some prophetic contexts, particularly those predating the fall of the northern kingdom (722 BC), may reflect an idealized use in which the divided nation is addressed as if it were (still) one. Later, post-722 BC texts that employ "Israel" may tend toward an eschatological use, speaking as if the once unified but now divided and partially destroyed nation will someday be whole again (Ezek. 37:15-28). So even though "Israel" became a technical term for the northern kingdom after 922 BC, it never lost its broader reference to God's people as a whole (Ezra 9:1; Gal. 6:16).

The **land** of Israel is also mentioned numerous times (1 Sam. 13:19). So "Israel" can refer to a specific geographical location. Emblematic of the land is its capital city, Jerusalem, known in poetic contexts as Zion, after the hill on which sat David's city and the **temple**. The importance of land and place to biblical faith cannot be overstated.

The NT often mentions the term "Israel" as referring to people and land (Matt. 2:20; 8:10). Many instances cite the OT or reference its stories (Mark 12:29; 2 Cor. 3:7). In Rom. 9–11 Paul discusses Israel extensively, focusing on its place in God's salvation after Christ's coming and affirming two crucial points: (1) the Gentiles are grafted into the tree that is Israel (11:17-24), and (2) all Israel will be saved (11:26).

See also Church (Ecclesiology); Eschatology; God, Doctrine of; Temple; Zionism.

Resource
Esler, Philip F., ed. *Ancient Israel: The Old Testament in Its Social Context*. Minneapolis: Augsburg Fortress, 2006.

BRENT A. STRAWN, PHD

Jj

JACOBITE CHURCH

Most likely named after the monk Jacob Baradeus (d. AD 578), the Jacobite Church is an informal designation for a grouping of historic Christian churches found primarily in Syria, Iraq, and Turkey but also represented in India, Lebanon, Jordan, Egypt, and, more recently, the United States. Consolidated in Antioch under Severus from 513 to 518, the largest contingent is the Syrian Orthodox Church, but all look to the patriarch of Antioch as their spiritual head.

The history of the Jacobite Church is complex. Its beginning stems from the fifth-century controversy over **Christology**. The Council of Chalcedon (451) ruled that Christ is of one substance with the Father in his divinity but also of one substance with us in his humanity. Dissenting from this "two natures" view were the Monophysites (Greek, "single nature"), who emphasized the divinity of Christ to the detriment of his humanity. Jacob Baradeus and his followers espoused Monophysitism, setting themselves off from their Greek Orthodox rivals, who in derision dubbed them "Jacobites," a label they accepted.

Development of a Eucharist-centered liturgy in Syriac—a close cousin of the Aramaic spoken by Christ—helped solidify the Jacobite identity. When the region later came under Muslim dominance, rulers granted the Jacobites minority status as "people of the book." Most notable among Jacobite thinkers was Gregory Bar Hebraeus (d. 1286), who composed the *Chronicle* (a world history beginning with Adam), as well as Syriac and Arabic commentaries on Aristotle.

The number of Jacobites decreased dramatically in the seventh century when many aligned themselves with Rome, taking the label "Syrian Catholics." Estimates put their numbers at two hundred thousand in Turkey, with an equal number in Syria and Iraq. In 1974, the Syrian Orthodox Church joined the Council of Churches of the Middle East.

See also Christology; Ecumenical Councils.

Resources

Bailey, Betty Jane, and J. Martin Bailey. *Who Are the Christians in the Middle East?* Grand Rapids: Eerdmans, 2003.

Pacini, Andrea, ed. *Christian Communities in the Arab Middle East: The Challenge of the Future.* Oxford, UK: Clarendon Press, 1998.

J. GREGORY CROFFORD, PHD

JESUS OF NAZARETH

The origin and development of Christianity revolves around the figure of Jesus of Nazareth. Biblical scholars often distinguish between the *historical Jesus* and the *Jesus of Christian faith,* without intending to diminish Jesus as the center of the church's faith. The distinction simply means that the Jesus we meet in the NT is already confessed to be the Christ and is not presented as a neutral figure whose importance has yet to be decided. The early church would have no interest in treating Jesus simply as a subject of historical research. Clearly, the early church had no doubt about the historical basis for its faith.

The term "historical Jesus" refers to what historians can learn about Jesus from a strictly historical perspective (prior to or apart from the church's faith in Jesus as the Christ and the formation of the NT). How scholars identify the historical Jesus depends on the sources they use, whether the Gospels or other writings and artifacts. For many scholars, what they learn about the historical Jesus only fortifies their faith.

The term "Jesus of faith" refers to what early Christians affirmed in response to their encounter with the risen Christ. Early Christians were convinced, even in the midst of persecutions, that Jesus had risen from the dead, ascended to the Father, and will live forever (Rom. 6:23; 2 Cor. 11:23-29; Gal. 6:8; 1 Thess. 2:14–3:10; 1 Tim. 1:16; Heb. 10:32-39; 1 John 5:11).

New Testament historians, whose goal it is to understand Jesus in his own Jewish context, offer various accounts of the historical Jesus. Some scholars seek to get behind the gospel portrayals of Jesus to discover the actual historical figure prior to the church's depiction of him. Other historians see a correspondence between the two and use historical research to enhance our understanding of the Jesus the church confesses as Lord. Still others say we should recognize the limits of historical research and give priority to the theological testimony of the gospel writers themselves.

The Synoptic Gospels (Matthew, Mark, Luke) portray both a historical Jesus and a Jesus of faith. Matthew (1:1-17) and Luke (3:21-38) use genealogies to locate Jesus within history. However, all three Synoptic Gospels move the historical to a second level by affirming Jesus as "Son of David" and "Son of God."

The Gospels thus describe a Jesus who lived, thought, and worked as a Jew, yet died and was resurrected as the Son of God. Each gospel writer presents Jesus as the One who sustains all life and is fully present in the community of faith. The gospel writers and early Christians experienced and witnessed the life-giving power of Jesus in his life in Palestine and as the risen Lord.

In Mark, Jesus is the "Holy One of God" (1:24), who establishes the kingdom of God. He is God's embodiment (1:15; 3:27; 4:11).

In Matthew, Jesus' historical nature is established by the genealogy (1:1-17), but he is also the "Son of God" (chaps. 3–4), "the teacher" (*didaskalos*, 8:19; 12:38; 22:16) and "Lord" (*kyrios*, 8:2, 6, 8, 21, 25; 9:28, 38) of the church. Seen from Jewish and, more specifically, Pharisaic estimates, Jesus is the personification of the Torah—the source of all wisdom and the yardstick of righteousness. Distinctive to Matthew is an overarching depiction of Jesus as Immanuel (1:23, "God with us") and as risen. Jesus confirms his name and promise by being present until the end of the age (28:20*b*).

Luke-Acts focuses on Jesus as a figure whose birth, work, death, and resurrection are overshadowed by the Holy Spirit. Readers of Luke are invited to believe in Jesus, who is filled with the power of the Spirit (Luke 4:1, 18; Acts 2:22-24). Like the other Synoptic Gospels, the mystery of Jesus is the "kingdom of God" in the life of Jesus' disciples (Luke 17:21). In Luke, the church is undergirded by the presence of Jesus in a new and mysterious way—one that invites belief from all peoples.

Jesus' ascension (24:50-51) illustrates the powerful transition from Jesus as a figure in history to an abiding presence among those who believe in him. The disciples and Christian believers are invited to believe and live within the spiritual presence of Jesus through healing and life-changing experiences (Acts 3:6; 4:29-31; 16:18). The ascension is thus not perceived as Jesus' absence from his beloved community but signals his presence in a new way through the Spirit.

According to all the Gospels, Jesus must be proclaimed to all nations, starting in Jerusalem and extending to the global world (Matt. 28:18-20). The Gospels remind the church of Jesus' continued presence in the Lord's Supper, worship, prayer, scriptural meditations, and healings. Making disciples (v. 19), life in the Spirit (Rom. 8:5-17), and recognizing Jesus in the "least of these" (Matt. 25:40) are additional signs of Jesus' presence.

Our twenty-first-century readings and interpretations of the story of Jesus continue to be informed by historical study and the presence of the risen Christ, through the Holy Spirit, in miracles, salvation, God's peace, baptism, and Eucharist. Add to that the further testimony of the Gospels and Epistles.

At its core the Christian faith begins with Jesus' followers experiencing him as the risen One in a new way after his death. The Jesus of faith is not about mythical enlightenment but about a personal encounter with the "holy Other" (see 1 Cor. 15:3-8). In life and worship, believers encounter the historical Jesus and Jesus of faith as one Lord.

See also Atonement; Biblical Theology; Christology; Christology, New Testament; Creeds (Nicene, Chalcedonian, Apostles', Athanasian).

Resources
Green, Joel B., and Max Turner, eds. *Jesus of Nazareth Lord and Christ: Essays on the Historical Jesus and New Testament Christology*. Grand Rapids: Eerdmans, 1994.

Johnson, Luke Timothy. *The Real Jesus: The Misguided Quest for the Historical Jesus and the Truth of the Traditional Gospels*. San Francisco: HarperSanFrancisco, 1996.

Wright, N. T. *The Challenge of Jesus: Rediscovering Who Jesus Was and Is*. Downers Grove, IL: InterVarsity Press, 1999.

ISRAEL KAMUDZANDU, PHD

JUDAISM

"Judaism" is the name given to the systematic way or ways of life observed by people who seek to live in continuity with Israel and the worship of God, Creator of heaven and earth, as presented in the five books or scrolls of Moses—the **Torah** (Genesis–Deuteronomy). Judaism is best understood through the forms of life Jews practiced after the first destruction of the temple (587/6 BC). As a technical term, "Judaism" is not synonymous with the history of the Jews dating back to Abraham.

Judaism is marked by four ages (see Neusner below):

1. Diversity (ca. 500 BC to AD 70)
2. Definition (AD 70 to 640)
3. Cogency (AD 640 to 1800)
4. Second Age of Diversity (AD 1800 to present)

1. The first age begins after the first destruction of Jerusalem. Basic elements of a Judaic way of life emerged among those who retained ties to Jerusalem: reconstruction of the temple, emergence and circulation of **Torah** and other ancestral scrolls, and the practice of circumcision, festivals, and Sabbath observation. Later in this period the synagogue as a place for Jewish gathering emerged.

Far from being monolithic, diverse Jewish groups configured the basic components of the **temple**, Torah, synagogue, and even worship of the Lord in different ways, a diversity that eventually included **Jesus of Nazareth** and the earliest Christian **church**.

2. The age of definition began with the Roman destruction of the Jerusalem temple (AD 70). A systematic way of life emerged that centered on Torah interpretation. This required a "dual Torah," an *oral Torah* that corresponded to the *written Torah*. The oral Torah applied to all Israel the requirements associated with the holiness of the temple priesthood—the sanctification of everyday life. Teachers, called the rabbis, wrote and com-

piled various classical documents of the oral Torah. They in turn generated their own legal documents, or halakah: the Mishnah, the Tosefta, the Jerusalem Talmud, and the Babylonian Talmud. The rabbis also developed various narrative commentaries or midrash on the biblical books, such as *Genesis Rabbah* (Great) and *Leviticus Rabbah*. These documents have retained their importance for Jews.

3. The age of cogency (AD 640–1800) developed the resources of the previous age into a coherent, consistent way of life. The accomplishments provided a way of life for Jews who lived as minorities amid Islamic and Christian majorities. Moses ben Maimon, known as Maimonides (1135–1204), may best represent this stage. Maimonides converted Jewish law into a complete logical system and reflected philosophically on how to speak of God in the light of God's revelation in the Torah. This period witnessed the flourishing of Jewish mysticism—active participation in the living God.

4. The fourth age (second age of diversity) began in the eighteenth and nineteenth centuries. Jews developed different strategies for responding to the **Enlightenment** and the challenges posed by assimilation into the Western world. *(a) Reform Judaism* sought to adapt the Jewish tradition to secular norms in order to permit Jews to live within Western societies while retaining a historic tie to Jewish tradition. *(b) Orthodox Judaism* emphasized the full observance of the law to protect Jews against modernist influences—often in very modern ways. *(c) Conservative Judaism* or Masorti Judaism emerged in the mid-nineteenth century. The movement attempts a middle way by retaining Torah observance while incorporating moderate accommodations to the contemporary world. *(d) Zionism* is a form of political Judaism that assimilates Jewish tradition to the norms of the European nation-state. After the Shoah (Holocaust), or execution of six million Jews during World War II, Zionism promoted the formation of the State of Israel (1948). Progressive Jews founded Israel over the opposition of most orthodox. The State of Israel has developed as a secular and national form of Judaism. *(e) Reconstructionist Judaism* was founded on the thought of Rabbi Mordecai Kaplan (1881–1983). A progressive, contemporary form of Judaism, it combines deep respect for traditional Judaism with insights and ideas coming from contemporary social, intellectual, and spiritual life. In addition to Jewish religion, Reconstructionist Judaism defines Judaism as the entire cultural legacy of the Jewish people. It entertains diverse ideas about God.

Judaism is an embodied discussion across time on the good of God's revelation of Torah for those who look to it in faith. Judaism remains vibrant today, even though it confronts challenges from assimilation, secularization, and intermarriage.

See also Second Temple Judaism; Secular/Secularism/Secularization; Zionism.

Resources

Gelernter, David Hillel. *Judaism: A Way of Being.* New Haven, CT: Yale University Press, 2009.

Heschel, Abraham Joshua. *God in Search of Man: A Philosophy of Judaism.* New York: Farrar, Straus and Giroux, 1976.

Neusner, Jacob, and Alan J. Avery-Peck, eds. *The Blackwell Companion to Judaism.* Malden, MA: Blackwell Publishers, 2000.

JOHN WRIGHT, PHD

JUDGMENT, THE

See ESCHATOLOGY.

JUSTICE

The OT and NT witness to the importance of justice for God and God's people. Forms of the Hebrew words *tsedeq* and *tsedaqah* (justice, rightness, righteousness) and *mishpat* (justice) and the Greek words *dikaiosynē* and *euthytēs* (righteousness) convey variances of justice, righteousness, and right dealing. When Cain questions God about keeping his brother, Scripture introduces the topic of justice (Gen. 4). When Hagar is expelled from God's protection, the narrator evokes indignation and a longing for God to correct the injustice (chap. 21). When Jesus calls Zacchaeus down from his perch to host Jesus as a neighbor, the story ends with Zacchaeus returning what he had taken unjustly (Luke 19). As Scripture closes with the book of Revelation, God's people are urged to cling to God's promise of righteousness (chap. 22).

Within one conflicted prophetic book, and even within a single contentious psalm of judgment, the **Bible**'s testimony to justice differs. But God's righteousness endures; it never fails (Pss. 7:17; 50:6; Isa. 45:22-23). Doing justice and acting righteously involves our being faithful to God's unfailing character. The Bible tells God's children that in various circumstances they must discern the precise meaning of justice and how best to execute it. So Christians will do well to be on guard when justice is maligned as unbiblical.

The most obvious extrabiblical source for discerning the meaning of justice is Aristotle's *Nicomachean Ethics*, a pre-Christian text **Thomas Aquinas** in his *Summa theologiae* draws on for his canonical discussion of justice. A contrast between the two texts is seen in Aristotle's assumption that there are *grades of humanity* according to which graded goods are distributed. Similarly, a divinely ordained or even natural hierarchy is a presupposition in thirteenth-century Christianity. But the scriptural witness repeatedly refutes a hierarchical or meritorious account of justice. God chose Israel in the form of a "wandering Aramean" (Deut. 26:5) and Christ died "while we still were sinners" (Rom. 5:8). The notion that God awards on the basis of merit is refuted by the infinite reckoning of grace.

JUSTIFICATION ♦ 277

For Thomas Aquinas, daily **worship** is an act of justice, because when Christians worship, they give to God what is rightly due: their hearts, minds, and souls. When worship is viewed this way, Christians should recognize that seeking justice in the world is a form of worship. This is a distinctive way of seeing the world and living in it. Thomas calls this way of being in the world, this "living into the world," a virtue. This requires that daily and weekly, to do what is most *worshipful*, we readjust our vision of justice.

For example, Wesleyan Christians sing inspiring hymns by which faithful justice can become a disposition and, by grace, a virtue. During a time when the English hierarchy was discriminating between persons all the way from commoners to royalty, Wesleyans sang of a different and higher justice, as illustrated in the hymn "And Can It Be?"

> No condemnation now I dread;
> Jesus, and all in Him, is mine!
> Alive in Him, my living Head,
> And clothed in righteousness divine,
> Bold I approach th' eternal throne
> And claim the crown, thro' Christ, my own.

(Wesley [1738] 1993)

Such justice as this is the fruit of unmerited grace, not of meritorious privilege or achievement. It elicits worship and sends graced worshippers back into the world to worship God by acting justly and loving mercy (Mic. 6:8).

See also Shalom; Social Ethics; Social Justice; Wesley, John, Theology of; Works of Mercy.

Resources

Enns, Elaine, and Chad Myers. *Diverse Christian Practices of Restorative Justice and Peacemaking.* Vol. 2, *Ambassadors of Reconciliation.* Maryknoll, NY: Orbis Books, 2009.

Wesley, Charles. "And Can It Be." 1738. In *Sing to the Lord*, 225. Kansas City: Lillenas Publishing, 1993.

Wolterstorff, Nicholas. *Justice in Love.* Grand Rapids: Eerdmans, 2011.

AMY LAURA HALL, PHD

JUSTIFICATION

Justification is vindication, the declaration that someone is just or righteous. Since all are unrighteous, justification is therefore unmerited pardon or forgiveness.

Justification is a major theme in Galatians and Romans, but the word itself rarely appears elsewhere in Scripture. Augustine taught against the **Pelagians** that justification was by **grace**. But he largely equated justification with sanctification as being *made* holy or righteous by grace received through the sacraments.

From his study of Paul, **Martin Luther** initiated a revolution in the doctrine of justification. He agreed with Augustine that salvation was by grace, but grace was God's unmerited favor rather than an internal influence. Justification was not to *make* but to *declare* a person righteous. God justified, not the righteous, but sinners by grace alone (*sola gratia*) through faith alone (*sola fide*). The Christian was thus "simultaneously both righteous and a sinner" (*simul iustus et peccator*). This was through **Christ** alone (*a solo Christo*), since on the cross Christ took upon himself the sinner's unrighteousness (1 Pet. 2:24) and in exchange gives his righteousness to the sinner. This was thus an "alien righteousness," only ours as we are united to Christ by faith. Justification by faith therefore *was* the gospel, the article of faith "by which the church stands or falls" (McGrath 1998, 450). Calvin and the other Reformers agreed.

John Wesley came to understand justification through the **Moravians.** Through hearing a reading from Luther's "Preface to the Romans" at Aldersgate Street in London (1738), Wesley received assurance that his sins were forgiven. He held that his doctrine of justification did "not differ from" Calvin's a "hair's breadth" (*Works*, 3:212). For Wesley, Christian salvation has "two grand branches, justification and **sanctification**" (6:509). He later charged that some Calvinists used the doctrine of justification as a cloak for antinomianism.

According to the "new perspective" on Paul presented recently by N. T. Wright and others, Protestants have too often seen justification as simply the individual's way to heaven. But Judaism in Paul's day was not legalistic or Pelagian (as Luther assumed), and Paul has a more corporate understanding. God's covenant with Israel was for the salvation of the world.

Increasing agreement between Roman Catholics and Protestants on justification began with Hans Küng's endorsement of Karl Barth's doctrine. It is agreed that salvation is by grace through faith but that justification and sanctification must not be separated in a way that turns justification into a legal fiction. The faith that saves (as Wesley emphasized) is the faith that works though love (Gal. 5:6).

See also Atonement; Augustine; Calvin, John; Covenant; Cross; Faith; Gospel; Law and Gospel; Legalism; Luther, Martin; Reformation; Righteousness; Salvation (Soteriology); Sanctification; Wesley, John, Theology of.

Resources

McGrath, Alister E. *Iustitia Dei: A History of the Doctrine of Justification*. 2nd ed. Cambridge, UK: Cambridge University Press, 1998.

Wright, N. T. *Justification: God's Plan and Paul's Vision*. Downers Grove, IL: InterVarsity Press, 2009.

THOMAS A. NOBLE, PHD

JUST WAR/WAR

As human beings live in proximity with one another, conflicts of interest often occur. Conflicts can become violent, even armed and destructive. War is one form of armed conflict; it is waged by a nation-state or another organized group against an identified enemy. War can also refer to a state of hostility peacefully resolved short of armed conflict. Moreover, it can indicate a more generalized state of conflict or competition, in the absence of armed conflict, when individuals, organizations, or nation-states compete for power in settings such as games, business, or diplomacy.

Some wars are called just. A just war is armed conflict allegedly justified by moral reasons at least one party to the conflict believes to be defensible. Such justification will often include reasons for the conflict, how the war is to be prosecuted, and how it is to be concluded. Moral justification may include stating moral limits with reference to strategies, weapons, treatment of prisoners and civilians, and escalation.

War is a tragic part of human history, as amply documented by social records. In ancient societies, religion and warfare were often partners. Conflicts were waged at the behest of and for the glory of the gods, and sometimes between the gods.

In the biblical story of Cain's murder of his brother Abel (Gen. 4:1-16), we have an account of conflict not initiated by the gods. God names Cain's action as sin and warns of the consequences of warfare. God identifies the social consequences of the intentional annihilation of another person.

Much of the OT reveals how warfare was woven into Israel's successes and failures. In Joshua and Judges, God is often reported to have commanded the elimination of Israel's enemies as the means for possessing the Promised Land. In other instances, God declares war on idolatry and its practitioners.

In Jesus' teachings about the **kingdom of God**, he completely rejects armed conflict as a way to realize the kingdom (Matt. 5:9). Jesus minimized the value of the sword for solving problems and achieving peace (Luke 22:35-38). Early Christians understood Jesus' teaching as requiring pacifism of his disciples. However, when Christianity became aligned with Roman power and its weaponry, it often justified and participated in armed conflict. The Crusades illustrate warfare blessed and encouraged by the church.

Many Christians insist that when war occurs, it must be conducted justly. A "just war" theory has developed. The theory is rooted in the thought of the Roman statesman and orator Cicero (106–43 BC). It was developed by **Augustine** (AD 354–430) and fully argued by **Thomas Aquinas** (AD ca. 1225-74). According to them, a war can be defined as just if (1) it seeks to limit damage imposed by war; (2) all other means for resolving the conflict have been exhausted; (3) success is likely; and (4) the use of tactics and weaponry does not create more evil than the evil of the aggressor. Those responsible for the common good must weigh all conditions before war can be considered just. A resolution to end conflict quickly and repair the damage of war is also contained in the theory.

Today, just actions during a war are codified by international agreements such as the Geneva Conventions. The nuclear war threat and terrorist tactics leveled against populations have made deciding the ethics by which war can be considered just much more difficult.

See also Christian Ethics/Moral Theology; Early Church; Ethics; Justice; Peacemaking; Religious Conflict; Social Ethics; Social Justice; Spiritual Warfare; Terrorism; Theodicy/Evil.

Resources

Johnson, James Turner. *Just War Tradition and the Restraint of War: A Moral and Historical Inquiry.* Princeton, NJ: Princeton University Press, 1981.

Yoder, John Howard. *Christian Attitudes to War, Peace, and Revolution.* Edited by Theodore Koontz and Andy Alexis-Baker. Grand Rapids: Brazos Press, 2009.

L. BRYAN WILLIAMS, PHD

Kk

KENOSIS

The term "kenosis" means "emptying." Since the third or fourth century the term has acquired major significance in Christian theology, owing largely to Paul's letter to the Philippians. He cites an early Christian hymn in which Jesus, "who, though he was in the form of God, did not regard equality with God as something to be exploited, but *emptied* himself, taking the form of a slave" (2:6-7, emphasis added).

What does this emptying entail? Christian theologians generally understood that kenosis refers to Jesus' voluntarily laying aside his divine prerogatives such as omnipotence and omniscience. Paul discusses kenosis in conjunction with Jesus humbling himself and becoming "obedient to the point of death" (v. 8). Paul elsewhere says of Jesus, "Though he was rich, yet for your sakes he became poor" (2 Cor. 8:9).

The idea of Jesus' kenosis clearly concerns the quality of Jesus' earthly existence. Some NT writers highlight Jesus' development. Luke, for example, indicates that Jesus grew in his understanding. Luke observes that as a boy Jesus "increased in wisdom and in years, and in divine and human favor" (2:52). He also seems to indicate that Jesus did not know everything (8:45). Similarly, Jesus would lack the divine prerogative of omniscience. The author of Hebrews indicates that Jesus "learned obedience through what he suffered" (5:8). The exact meaning of this is not clear, but apparently Jesus learned obedience through human experience. All this affirms the full humanity of Jesus.

John's gospel, on the other hand, seems to put greater emphasis on Jesus' full knowledge and power. Jesus is constantly in communion with the Father (John 5:19-24; 11:42) and is equal with him (10:30).

Kenosis introduces us to the mystery of the incarnation, the divine self-disclosure that remains no less a mystery (1 Cor. 2:7; Eph. 3:9).

See also Christology; God, Doctrine of; Incarnation; Revelation.

KEITH H. REEVES, PHD

KERYGMA
See GOSPEL; KINGDOM OF GOD.

KESWICK MOVEMENT

The **Keswick** (ke-zik) movement is a British product of the nineteenth-century American holiness movement. It is largely associated with the work and influence of three American holiness leaders. William Boardman, author of *The Higher Christian Life* (1858), cooperated with Robert Pearsall Smith and his wife, Hannah Whitall Smith, author of the widely influential *The Christian's Secret of a Happy Life* (1875). From 1873 to 1875 the Smiths were active in Great Britain and Continental Europe, advocating the message of Christian holiness. Their efforts began with small-group conversations and resulted in a series of conferences that culminated in one in Brighton, England, that lasted from May to June 1875. It was attended by as many as eight thousand persons from across Europe. Although the Smiths returned to the United States in 1875, the movement would find a permanent home in Keswick. After T. D. Harford-Battersby, vicar of St. John's in Keswick, participated in a meeting in Oxford where he encountered the "higher life," he proposed hosting a convention in 1875 in his own parish community. The Keswick conferences continue to meet annually under the auspices of Keswick Ministries. Its goal is "the promotion of practical holiness." It promotes other Keswick events around the world.

The theological character of the Keswick movement is that it connects the more characteristically Wesleyan holiness movement with Reformed evangelicals in Great Britain and Europe. The result is a modified vision of Christian holiness that emphasizes empowerment for *victory over* the flesh (by "counteraction" of sinful tendencies). This emphasis differs from the more radical eradication of original sin, as taught by Wesleyans, that results in a *changed heart* (and changed desires), not merely victory over remaining sin.

The Keswick movement has been marked by a special passion for missions and an emphasis on empowerment for service. It has been a catalyst for numerous mission initiatives. J. Hudson Taylor, founder of the China Inland Mission (now Overseas Mission Fellowship [OMF]), was an active and prominent leader in the Keswick movement. It has produced prominent and influential church leaders, such as F. B. Meyer, Andrew Murray, and A. B. Simpson. It has stimulated the writing of significant devotional literature, including Lettie Cowman's *Streams in the Desert* and Murray's *The Prayer Life*. The most enduring institutional legacy has been its influence on the Christian and Missionary Alliance church. It has also had formative influence on Columbia International University (Columbia, South Carolina).

See also Christian Perfection (Entire Sanctification); Holiness Movements: American, British, and Continental; Missionary Movements; Revivalism; Sanctification.

Resources

Jones, Charles Edwin. *The Keswick Movement: A Comprehensive Guide.* Lanham, MD: Scarecrow Press, 2007.
Pollock, John Charles. *The Keswick Story: The Authorized History of the Keswick Convention.* London: Hodder and Stoughton, 1964.

CARL M. LETH, PHD

KINGDOM OF GOD

The kingdom of God refers to God's activity as king to deliver humans from sin, overcome evil, and establish God's rule of **righteousness** and peace over the world.

The word for "kingdom" in Hebrew and Aramaic (*malkut*), as well as Greek (*basileia*), derives from the word for "king" (Hebrew and Aramaic, *melek*; Greek, *basileus*). "Kingdom" refers primarily to the exercise of royal power or authority and only secondarily to the territory or domain of such rule. Thus many scholars believe the NT expression *basileia tou theou* (kingdom of God) is more faithfully rendered "reign of God," "rule of God," or "dominion of God," emphasizing the activity rather than the realm of divine sovereignty.

The phrase "kingdom of God" does not occur in the OT. Explicit references to God's kingdom are infrequent. But the theme of God's kingdom and references to God as King are essential to OT theology, not least in the Psalms. The Lord is King over Israel and sits enthroned above the cherubim in the Jerusalem **temple**. Ultimately God does not reign from Mount Zion but from **heaven**, and his kingdom extends beyond Israel to all nations. The OT vision of God's kingdom foresaw the Lord finally bringing justice and peace to the world. God will judge and destroy those who are oppressive and evil; he will exalt the righteous who humbly serve him.

During the period between the OT and NT, sectors of early Judaism sharpened the hope for God's coming kingdom. Jewish **apocalyptic** expected God to center his universal rule in Jerusalem, rebuild the temple, and defeat Israel's enemies. These events were associated with a messianic age, when the Messiah or Son of David (Matt. 20:30-31; 21:9) would serve as God's vice-regent, followed by the **resurrection**, the final judgment, and the eternal kingdom.

The Gospels refer to the kingdom of God over one hundred times and use three expressions: "kingdom of God," "kingdom of heaven," and simply "kingdom." The phrase "kingdom of heaven" (exclusively in Matthew) bears no nuance of meaning to distinguish it from "kingdom of God." The word "heaven" is used as a reverent substitute to avoid uttering God's name.

The kingdom of God was central to Jesus' ministry and teaching. Since the late 1800s, Jesus' view of the kingdom of God has been interpreted in three ways. *First*, consistent or thoroughgoing **eschatology** asserts that Jesus saw the kingdom as an entirely future, apocalyptic event. *Second*, realized eschatology sees the kingdom as fully present in the deeds and person of Jesus himself. *Third*, most scholars today take a mediating view, seeing the kingdom of God as both present (inaugurated or fulfilled in Jesus' ministry) and future (to be consummated at the end of the age).

The urgency of Jesus' proclamation came from his bold declaration, "The kingdom of God [heaven] has come near" (Matt. 4:17; Mark 1:15). The presence of God's kingdom was already breaking into the world in Jesus' person and saving actions. In particular, his **exorcism** of **demons** was a sign that the kingdom was beginning its advance, triumphing over the powers of evil (Matt. 12:28; Luke 11:20). Jesus' parables can describe the kingdom as secretly and quietly at work in the present (e.g., Mark 4:26-32). But Jesus also spoke of the kingdom's future arrival, involving the coming of the Son of Man, the resurrection, the final judgment, and the anticipated paradise for the righteous (often depicted as a banquet or marriage feast). Participation in the kingdom requires **discipleship:** turning from one's sinful ways and devoting oneself to following Jesus the Messiah in simple and humble **faith**—even if it means personal sacrifice or persecution.

See also Christology, New Testament; Eschatology; Repentance; Second Coming of Christ/Parousia.

Resources

Marshall, I. H. "Kingdom of God (of Heaven)." In vol. 3, *The Zondervan Encyclopedia of the Bible*, edited by Merrill C. Tenney and Moisés Silva, 911-22. Grand Rapids: Zondervan, 2009.

Willis, Wendell, ed. *The Kingdom of God in 20th-Century Interpretation*. Peabody, MA: Hendrickson, 1987.

KEVIN L. ANDERSON, PHD

Ll

LAITY

The term "laity" comes from the Greek word *laos*, which means "people." In general use it refers to persons who are not members of a specialized profession. Its religious use refers to persons who are not clergy. The role and status of laypersons differs in various religious traditions.

In the pre-**Reformation Catholic Church**, the laity were considered second-class citizens. Since ordination (holy orders) was a **sacrament**, and thus a means of grace, laypersons were denied a measure of grace available only to clergy. Laypersons were generally denied access to the Bible and were thus dependent on interpretations offered by the hierarchy. Laypersons did not have full access to the Mass because they could receive only the bread; the priest alone could drink the wine. And since the Mass was said in Latin, laypersons who were not conversant in Latin were effectively excluded from participating in its meaning.

The **Protestant** Reformers emphasized the priesthood of all believers and removed the traditional limitations. All Christians are equally in Christ and all are commissioned as priests to exercise forms of ministry in the **church** and world. The distinction between clergy and laity became functional, not spiritual and hierarchical. Qualifications for clergy became a matter of professional training rather than receiving special grace.

Vatican Council II (1962-65) elevated the status of the laity by declaring that in their own way the laity are "made sharers in the priestly, prophetical, and kingly functions of Christ; and they carry out for their own part the mission of the whole Christian people in the Church and in the world." Called to ministry in the world,

> by exercising their proper function and led by the spirit of the Gospel they [laity] may work for the sanctification of the world from within as a leaven. In this way they may make Christ known to others, especially by the testimony of a life resplendent in faith, hope and charity. (Vatican 1964, 4.31, under "The Laity")

The laity act with freedom and personal responsibility, not as mere agents of the hierarchy. According to repeated statements by popes and lay Catholic leaders, the laity should say, "We are the church," just as the saints declared "Christ lives in me." The council also granted greater lay participation in the liturgy.

The twentieth-century **ecumenical** movement gave attention to the nature and mission of the church, which entails a scrutiny of the status and role of the laity. It was recognized that "secular" laity are the church's most fruitful contact with the world for evangelism and social reform. Since the mid-twentieth century, Catholic and Protestant theologians have explored a theological basis for the ministry of the laity (Yves Conger, *Lay People in the Church* [1953]; Hendrik Kraemer, *A Theology of the Laity* [1958]). Such studies highlighted the often overlooked fact that some of the most influential thinkers and leaders of significant reform movements in Christian history were laypersons. In fact, it was not until about the second century that a distinction was made between lay and clergy. The apostles themselves probably would be considered laypersons. The modern missionary movement was largely initiated by laypersons.

John Wesley made extensive use of lay leaders in his **Methodist** societies, although he maintained close supervision of their work. Most Protestant churches involve laypersons in church government and various ministries.

See also Ecumenism; Wesley, John, Theology of.

Resource
Vatican: The Holy See. Dogmatic Constitution on the Church, *Lumen Gentium*. November 24, 1964. http://www.vatican.va/archive/hist_councils/ii_vatican_council/documents/vat-ii_const_19641121_lumen-gentium_en.html.

H. RAY DUNNING, PHD

LAMENT

The lament represents one of the oldest and most attested literary genres in the ancient world. Laments constituted an integral part of daily life, since they expressed great sorrow in the face of death, calamity, devastation caused by war, consciousness of sin, intense sickness, persecution, and accusation. Laments were directed to God and thus constituted a prayer in the strict sense. A lament could also be accompanied by music (Jer. 48:36) and take the form of a dialogue, such as a refrain taken up by a choir (2 Sam. 1:19, 25, 27). Various types of laments have been identified in OT literature.

Individual laments are prominent, especially in the book of Psalms. Many individual laments originated in a liturgical context, although some could be prayed far away from the sanctuary (Pss. 42–43), such as on a sickbed (Isa. 38:10-20). Individual laments contained a basic format:

    1. Address to God, including a brief cry followed by praises

2. Presentation of the complaint
3. Confession of trust in God and plea for help
4. Exclamation of certainty that God heard the supplicant's prayer
5. Vow of praise/thanksgiving

The structure of the individual lament indicates that the lament does not stand by itself but moves from a petition based on distress to joyful praise.

Communal laments are a type of liturgical song in which the people bewailed the destruction of the city and the temple in 587/6 BC (Pss. 40; 60; 74; 79; 80; 137). Communal laments also emerged from other kinds of community crises, including military threats and natural catastrophes (Pss. 42–43; 58; 83; 106; 125). Communal laments were sung during times of mourning when the people were originally summoned to a fast.

City laments mourned the destruction of a city, as if the city were a deceased person. City laments not only described the destruction of the city and its important shrines (i.e., temple) but also attempted to ascribe a cause for the devastation. The book of Lamentations represents the quintessential example of a city lament, but this type of lament can be found elsewhere (Ps. 137; Isa. 15:1–16:14; 47:1-15; Jer. 48:1-47; Amos 5:1-3, 16-20; Mic. 1:2-16).

The *funeral dirge* was sung by surviving family members or close friends in memory of the deceased. Dirges often included short ejaculatory phrases ("O my son!"), a glorious depiction of the past, as well as denunciations of those responsible for the death (2 Sam. 3:33-34; Jer. 38:22).

See also Biblical Theology; Hiddenness of God.

Resources
Gunkel, Hermann. *An Introduction to the Psalms.* Translated by James D. Nogalski. Macon, GA: Mercer University Press, 1998.
Seybold, Klaus. *Introducing the Psalms.* Translated by R. Graeme Dunphy. 1990. Reprint, London: T and T Clark, 1997.

KEVIN MELLISH, PHD

LAND

Land is an important biblical concept (Hebrew, *'erets, 'adamah;* Greek, *gē*). In the OT, *'erets* means "earth" when referring to the place of human habitation and "land" when referring to a political territory. The term *'adamah* primarily means "tillable land" or "ground," though it sometimes refers to a political territory or the whole earth. In the creation account, humans (*'adam*) are intimately connected to the land; they are formed from the "dust of the ground [*'adamah*]" (Gen. 2:7).

The concept of land is often associated with the idea of God's promise of a land to Israel's ancestors. The idea that the "earth" (*'erets*) belongs to the Lord (Ps. 24:1) underlies this conviction. God created it to be the habitat for all plant and animal life, including humans (Gen. 1:28-30). The creational mandate to "subdue" (*kabash*) the "earth" (*'erets*) conveys the human task of preserving and cultivating the land (1:28; 2:5). The mandate is explicit in the human vocation to "till" and "keep" the garden (2:15). Biblical theology also traces the lack of productivity of the "ground" (*'adamah*) to **sin** (3:17-18).

Israel's sabbatical law (Lev. 25:1-7) is designed to promote the land's well-being. The law calls Israel to treat the land, God's gift to his people, with love and care and not to exploit it or destroy it. This covenant law thus gives specific application to the creational mandate in Gen. 1–2. Israel's tradition also traces loss of the land and the exile to Israel's covenant breaking. Biblical theology thus implicitly warns that human failure to keep the creational mandate may lead to eventual loss and destruction of the earth/land on which humans live as God's tenants.

In the NT, the concept of land relates to the Land of Promise (Acts 7:3) as well as the lands (the whole earth) where Jesus' disciples were to preach the gospel and make disciples (Matt. 28:19-20; Acts 1:8; 2 Cor. 10:16).

See also Covenant; Creation, Care for the (Ecology); Creation/New Creation.

ALEX VARUGHESE, PHD

LATIN AMERICAN MISSIOLOGY/LIBERATION STRUGGLE

In 1972, Ecuadorian-born NT scholar Rene Padilla said the evangelical church in Latin America was without a theology. The charge was largely correct. Congregations were becoming self-propagating, self-sustaining, and self-governing. But they could not say the same for theology. **Evangelical** churches had largely imported their liturgy, music, and evangelistic methods from North America. The same was true for theological education.

In a continent where more than 50 percent of the population lives in poverty, evangelical churches practiced a nonincarnate Christianity. In a context of hunger and misery, evangelicals had largely "spiritualized" Christian faith. Social action, when it occurred, was mostly superficial, not socially transforming.

As has happened before, when one part of the Christian faith appears in its extreme form, the reaction can also be extreme. This often happened in **liberation theology**'s reaction against spiritualized Christianity's lack of social critique, engagement, and transformation. Liberation theology was born in the Catholic Church in the 1960s from a deep concern for social engagement. It rapidly spread to **Protestant** churches. The Peruvian priest Gustavo Gutiérrez first used the term in 1967. He gained broad recognition with his publication of *A Theology of Liberation* (1971). Other contributors such as Juan Luis Segundo and Leonardo Boff soon joined the effort.

For liberation theology, liberation is more than mere theology (orthodoxy). Liberation theologians teach that authentic Christian salvation must include the transformation of life's social, political, and economic dimensions as well. The hermeneutical starting point for liberation theology is the social, political, and economic context, not the Bible itself. The liberationist hermeneutic intentionally employs Marxist social-historical analysis to understand context.

A criticism of liberation theology has been that it tried to speak for the poor but failed to speak with them; its realm of discourse remained the world of the intellectual. Liberation theology did not reach the people. Further, liberation theology concentrated too much on social transformation and gave inadequate attention to spiritual needs. To the surprise of liberation theologians poor people chose instead of liberation theology different forms of neo-Pentecostalism, which in many cases alienated practitioners from the larger social, political, and economic context to which liberation theology was committed.

While liberation theology's appeal was increasing, in the evangelical wing of Latin American Christianity a movement known as integral mission, or integral (holistic) mission theology, was emerging. Some of its leaders were Rene Padilla, Samuel Escobar, Orlando Costas, and Emilio Nuñez. Integral mission emerged from the Latin American Theological Fraternity (FTL). It was strengthened by the different Latin American evangelical congresses (CLADE). Their goal was to reconcile the proclamation of the gospel with social action. Integral mission resulted from becoming aware of the importance of returning to the Bible for resources to help Christians fulfill their redemptive role in history—in their concrete situations—in the light of their commitment to Jesus Christ.

In retrospect, it is fair to say that integral mission has provided an equilibrium that makes it possible for Latin American Christians to retain their emphasis on evangelical faith while also seeing Christ in the faces of the poor.

A Wesleyan contribution to integral mission has been made by Federico A. Melendez in *Ethics and Economy: The Legacy of John Wesley to the Church in Latin America* (2006). Melendez's work prompted Padilla to observe that John Wesley and Wesleyan theology provide historical precedent for integral mission.

See also Contextualization; Contextual Theology; Holistic Mission; Indigenization; Justice; Social Ethics; Social Justice.

RUBÉN FERNÁNDEZ, DMIN

LATIN AMERICAN THEOLOGIES

Latin American theology refers to distinctive work in Christian theology that emerged in Latin America in the 1960s—among Protestants and Roman Catholics. It responds to the concerns and challenges to the Christian faith posed by poverty and human suffering in Latin America. Latin American theology emerged from the practice of Christian faith amid political and ecclesial turmoil. Its distinguishing characteristics are (1) a call for a just society and (2) an appeal to theologians, ecclesiastical bodies, educational institutions, and society as a whole to give preferred attention to the needs of the poor. Some notable Latin American Roman Catholic theologians are Gustavo Gutiérrez, Juan Luis Segundo, and Hugo Assmann. Prominent among Protestants are José Miguez Bonino, Rubem Alves, and Julio de Santa Ana.

These two characteristics are not new in the church, having been present in various measures and forms throughout church history, although marginally. In the eighteenth-century Methodist movement, for example, sensitivity to human suffering—especially poverty and slavery—drove the Wesley brothers and the Methodists. The importance John Wesley assigned to the poor is evident in his life and writings.

The commitment of the early Methodists made its mark on Latin American Methodism. In the early to mid-twentieth century Hugh C. Tucker, Sante Uberto Barbieri, Guaracy Silveira, Almir dos Santos, and others contributed to an embryonic Latin American theology. From the late 1970s major opportunities for theological and pastoral renewal emerged in Latin America. Methodists played a significant role, and the Methodist environment was a privileged stage of this process. The yearning for a more characteristically "Wesleyan" Methodism that addressed the social, economic, and political needs of people distinguished Latin American Methodism from American Methodism. There was also an interest in stronger lay ecclesiastical participation, in theological renewal, and in a more public face for the church. Hence, it would intentionally be less sectarian. In addition to the theologians already mentioned are also the names of Mortimer Arias, Emilio Castro, Federico Pagura, Elsa Tamez, and Rui Josgrilberg.

In the field of theology, there are already traits in Methodism that flow agreeably in the direction described. For example, the ecumenical emphasis of Methodism requires a doctrine of the Holy Spirit that is

> *prophetic* (critical and transformative of reality); *charismatic* (based on the diversity of ministries and services provided freely by The Spirit to all); *community oriented* (God's people overcoming the bureaucratic machine and promoting individual local leadership); and *missional in disposition* (facing away from concentration on institutional Methodism, and facing toward the world). (Mattos 1987)

Current discussions have sought to respond to the theological demands expressed using the theme of new creation—one of the central points of Latin American theology today, as evidenced by the writings of Leonardo Boff. In such thinking the emphasis is on the relationship between ecology, ecclesial renewal, and social justice and the salvific understanding that affirms the necessity of renewing the image of God in creation. Because it is corrupted, the image of God in human beings must go through a renewal process. This is eminently a salvific issue that cannot be blurred by new forms of religious individualism. The social responsibility of the church, including missionary and ecological issues, requires a thorough reconstruction of the theological understanding of salvation, rejecting the logic of individualism, to perceive its personal, collective, and cosmic dimensions, as recommended by the Scriptures.

One key point is the place of the poor in theological reflection and pastoral practice. The Wesleyan emphasis in general is associated with the care, assistance, and education of the poor, along with maintaining solidarity with them. This is extremely significant, since the poor have always been outside the church and nowadays are given increasingly less attention. However, a Wesleyan theology in Latin America must move beyond this perspective. It must deepen the notion found in Wesley that gives preference to the poor in acts of care and practical assistance and extend it to embrace the biblical notion that the kingdom of God is the possession of the poor (Luke 6:20).

See also Latin American Women's Theology; Liberation Theology; Mujerista Theology.

Resources
Aguilar, Mario. *The History and Politics of Latin American Theology*. Vol. 2. London: SCM, 2008.
Mattos, Paulo Ayres. *Pastoral Metodista: Ontem, hoje, amanhã*. São Bernardo do Campo, São Paulo, BR: Faculdade de Teologia/Instituto Metodista de Ensino Superior, 1987.
Petrella, Ivan. *Latin American Liberation Theology: The Next Generation*. Maryknoll, NY: Orbis Books, 2005.

CLAUDIO DE OLIVEIRA RIBEIRO, PHD

LATIN AMERICAN WOMEN'S THEOLOGY
Women in Latin America began developing their own theology at the end of the 1970s as one expression of Latin American **liberation theology**. Their point of departure was the concrete situation of Latin American women who suffer a double and even triple oppression because of their gender, social class, and, in Brazil, race. At first, Latin American women's theology was called theology of women. It subsequently became known as Latin American feminist theology.

At the turn of this century, additional approaches developed, leading to diverse foci in Latin American feminist theology. Today there are three emphases:

1. The feminist theology of liberation is a continuation of what developed in the 1970s. It concentrates on the need to liberate women from oppression that affects their everyday lives. For them, liberation entails changing oppressive social structures in ways that eliminate discrimination against women, including economic disparities. Feminist theology of liberation

works to "de-*patriarchalize*" the Christian God by discovering new "faces of God" in solidarity with women's sufferings and struggles. It *deconstructs* biblical texts whose interpretation discriminates against women. It rereads Scripture from a liberating perspective.

2. Latin American ecofeminist theology began in Brazil and Chile at the turn of this century in dialogue with ecofeminists in the United States. It sees a similarity between the domination and violence against women and that aimed against nature. It addresses the similarity from two perspectives. The *first* is that both are treated violently. The *second* is that women and nature have a vocation to sustain and transmit life. Latin American ecofeminist theology proposes an ecofeminist Christian theo-cosmology based on identifying systems in which all living beings are interrelated.

3. Latin American black feminist theology is concentrated in Brazil, the Latin American country with the largest black population. It began and was developed as part of Latin American **black theology.** It emphasizes the struggles of black women who live amid racist and poor Latin American societies. This theology is distinct, in part, because in addition to Christianity, it dialogues with other forms of religion such as Candomblé and Santeria. Consequently, **religious pluralism** is fundamental for this theology.

See also Contextual Theology; Feminist Theology; Justice; Latin American Theologies; Liberation Theology; Mujerista Theology; New Religious Movements; Social Justice; Wesleyan Feminism; Womanist Theology.

Resources

Aquino, María Pilar. *Our Cry for Life: Feminist Theology from Latin America.* Maryknoll, NY: Orbis Books, 1993.
Fabella, Virginia, and Mercy Amba Oduyoye, eds. *With Passion and Compassion: Third World Women Doing Theology.* Maryknoll, NY: Orbis Books, 1988.

ELSA TAMEZ, PHD

LATINO/LATINA (HISPANIC) THEOLOGY

This is the name jointly given to a variety of **contextual theologies** produced by the Latino (or Hispanic) community in the United States. This community is composed of people of various Latin American descents: Mexican, Puerto Rican, Cuban, Dominican, Central American, and others. By far the largest group is the Mexican-Americans. While many are immigrants or children of immigrants, others can trace their roots in the United States to a time when the land belonged to Mexico or to Spain.

The most common theme linking Hispanic theologies is the sense of "in-betweenness." Some express this as "living on the hyphen," meaning the hyphen located in terms such as "Mexican-American" and "Cuban-American." Others refer to the experience of *nepantla*, a Nahuatl word (NAH waht 1, a language spoken by the Aztecs and belonging to a large group of Indian languages) referring to "the land in between" and therefore particularly appropriate for the borderlands; *nepantla* is used to express the common experience of many Latinos and Latinas. Others speak of exile—a condition of living where they do not fully belong, while yet not really belonging anywhere else. But by far the most common image is *mestizaje*, or the condition of being "mestizo"—literally, "of mixed blood" or "half-bred."

Leading the way to the use of *mestizaje* as a hermeneutical principle for the Latino experience was Father Virgilio Elizondo, who drew on earlier Mexican discussions of Mexico as a mestizo, which he applied to theological reflection. A mestizo belongs at once to two different places and to neither of them. As a Mexican-American, Elizondo discovered that in his native Texas he was a "Mexican" but that on crossing the border he was told he was not really Mexican. In his doctoral dissertation at the Institute Théologique de Paris (a simplified version was published as *The Galilean Journey*), Elizondo related this experience to that of Galileans whom the Gentiles considered Jews, while the Judean Jews considered them little better than Gentiles. Just as Jesus came from Galilee, renewed creation and creativity often come from the margins where cultures and races mix. Therefore, as the title of one of Elizondo's later books proclaimed, *The Future Is Mestizo*.

While the theme of in-betweenness is common to all Latino and Latina theology, it contains a wider variety. Some Latinas refer to their work as **mujerista theology**, thus trying to indicate that theirs is a theology from a Hispanic female perspective. Others prefer to speak of themselves as *feministas* in order to strengthen their links with Latin American feminist theology. Some stress the significance of popular religion as a source for theological reflection. Others fear the consequences of its wholesale acceptance.

Even so, Latino/Latina theology is highly ecumenical. The Academy of Catholic Theologians in the United States (ACHTUS) includes mainline Protestants and Pentecostals among its members. And the main institutional and programmatic channels for developing and discussing Latino/Latina theology are also ecumenical: the journal *Apuntes*, the Hispanic Summer Program (HSP), the Hispanic Theological Initiative (HTI), and the Asociación para la Educación Teológica Hispana (AETH).

See also Folk Religion; Indigenous Theologies; Latin American Missiology/ Liberation Struggle; Liberation Theology; Popular Religiosity.

Resources

Aponte, Edwin David, and Miguel A. De La Torre, eds. *Handbook of Latina/o Theologies*. St. Louis: Chalice Press, 2006.
Aquino, María, Daisy L. Machado, and Jeanette Rodríguez, eds. *A Reader in Latina Feminist Theology: Religion and Justice*. Austin, TX: University of Texas Press, 2002.
González, Justo. *Mañana: Christian Theology from a Hispanic Perspective*. Nashville: Abingdon Press, 1990.

JUSTO L. GONZÁLEZ, PHD

LAUSANNE COVENANT

See ECUMENISM; HOLISTIC MISSION; LAUSANNE MOVEMENT AND COVENANT.

LAUSANNE MOVEMENT AND COVENANT

The Lausanne Movement (LM) traces its origin to the First International Congress on World Evangelization in July 1974 in Lausanne, Switzerland, sponsored by the Billy Graham Association and *Christianity Today*. The theme for the congress was "the whole church taking the whole gospel to the whole world." The Lausanne Committee for World Evangelization (LCWE), formed following the 1974 congress, facilitates conferences, study groups, and produces printed materials. The LCWE is the continuation committee of Lausanne I, mobilizing evangelical leaders to collaborate for world evangelism.

Lausanne 1974 was evangelical in composition. However, **Roman Catholic** and World Council of Churches representatives were among the 2,300 invited participants. There were 570 observers from 150 countries. Participants were asked to sign a three-thousand-word document, the Lausanne Covenant. It was a manifesto promoting worldwide missions and urging that missionaries be sent from all six continents to all six continents.

The LCWE was appointed to study diverse topics that arose during the conference. They included the relationship of evangelism and social concern; the uniqueness of Christ; the validity of missions; and the relationship of the gospel to culture. The LCWE planned the Second International Congress on World Evangelization, Lausanne II, in Manila in 1989. This congress produced the Manila Manifesto, a document containing twenty-one affirmations in the tradition and spirit of the Lausanne Covenant, but which broadened the agenda of missions to include topics such as the "whole gospel" and "the gospel and social responsibility." The primacy of evangelism was retained, with the recognition that the whole gospel had inescapable social implications.

Lausanne III, also known as Cape Town 2010, was the latest conference sponsored by the LCWE. Delegates to the three Lausanne congresses increasingly included leaders from world areas where daily concerns were not necessarily those of the Western world.

Topics under study at Lausanne III reflected this new character: non-Christian religions, poverty, HIV/AIDS, persecution, and religious pluralism. Lausanne I and Lausanne II had emphasized the priority of evangelism over social issues, but increasingly a new spirit was taking hold in mainstream evangelism; gaining ground was a new willingness to consider the church's responsibility for justice in society and for working to balance spiritual and cultural mandates.

Wesleyans see the spiritual and cultural mandates as complementary and holistic. They believe human persons, the community, and the natural environment must be addressed as a whole. For them the "whole gospel" aims at the full healing and redemption of all spheres of human life.

See also Holistic Mission; Interfaith Dialogue; Missionary Movements; World Missionary Conference, Edinburgh 1910.

Resources

Bosch, David J. *Transforming Mission: Paradigm Shifts in Theology of Missions.* Maryknoll, NY: Orbis Books, 1991.

Moreau, A. Scott, ed. *Evangelical Dictionary of World Missions.* Grand Rapids: Baker, 2000.

TERENCE B. READ, PHD

LAW AND GOSPEL

The well-known pairing "law and gospel" involves two essential and complementary dimensions of the **covenant** community's life with God and with each other. The covenant community—ancient **Israel** and the **church**—is defined by both. The two involve a vigorous faithfulness to what God commands (law) made possible by a vital **faith** in the **God** who graciously saves or liberates from **sin** (gospel), thus making obedience to God's will possible. In the pure gift of himself as Redeemer (gospel) God makes it possible to fulfill the commandment that we love him with all our heart, mind, soul, and strength, and our neighbor as ourselves (Matt. 22:35-40; Mark 12:28-31).

Law and gospel are inseparable. Efforts to divide them result in distorted Christian life and proclamation. Trying to retain gospel without law results in moral impoverishment, while law apart from gospel results in **legalism** and an unforgiving spirit.

To avoid these errors John Wesley insisted, "There is . . . the closest connexion that can be conceived, between the law and the gospel" (*Works*, 5:313), even though at times he found it necessary to emphasize one more than the other, depending on the spiritual maturity of his audience (11:486-87). Wesley was in agreement with the sixteenth-century Protestant Reformers **Martin Luther**, Huldrych Zwingli, and **John Calvin**. He preached two sermons on Rom. 3:31 titled "The Law Established Through Faith." In the second sermon Wesley said,

> We then establish the law, when we declare every part of it, every commandment contained therein, not only in its full, literal sense, but likewise in its spiritual meaning; not only with regard to the outward actions, which it either forbids or enjoins, but also with respect to the inward principle, to the thoughts, desires, and intents of the heart. (*Works*, 5:459)

The biblical concept of law combines two important elements: (1) On the one hand, the Hebrew word *torah* means far more than a "moral code" or "legal requirement." Its root meaning is "instruction" or "curriculum." As made clear by Scripture's **Torah** story (i.e., Pentateuch), instruction includes all of life. It is formative of the chosen people who have first been graciously liberated (gospel) from slavery to live as God's "treasured possession" among the nations (Exod. 19:5). Their calling to become "a priestly kingdom and a holy nation" bears public witness to God's gracious victory over death (v. 6). (2) On the other hand, Torah includes specific rules and regulations that order a community's relationship with God and one another. The relationship is covenantal in nature—mutually committed partnerships maintained by mutual fidelity. The community's faithfulness toward God is expressed in steadfast obedience to the rules that give body to the covenant, whether for ordering worship or commerce. The covenant-keeping response to God's command (formation of the community's public identity as God's "treasured possession") is motivated by love for God (Deut. 6:5) and neighbor (Lev. 19:18) in response to his gift of calling and liberation.

The gospel of Jesus Christ is the definitive expression and fulfillment of law and gospel. On his Father's authority and through the **Holy Spirit**, Jesus freely offered God's forgiveness and reconciliation to sinners and then charged them to live out that reconciliation as transformed people (Luke 19:2-10; John 8:3-11). The gospel is, John Wesley said, the "powerful means, whereby God makes every believer a partaker of present and eternal salvation" (*Works*, 5:447). Paul defines the proclamation of the Christian gospel as "the power of God for salvation to everyone who has faith" (Rom. 1:16). Almost certainly he has in mind the strategic use of "gospel" in Isaiah (40:9; 52:7) that refers to a messenger announcing God's victory. Paul interprets this prophetic word to mean God's victory over sin and death, the result of which is eternal life with God.

Understood as commentary on the Gospels, God's promised victory was embodied in and proclaimed by **Jesus of Nazareth**, God's Messiah. His life, death, and resurrection supplied the hard evidence that the salvation God had promised Israel is now fulfilled for everyone who has faith; God has cashed in this promissory note through Jesus (2 Cor. 1:18-20; Eph. 1:3-14). When Paul speaks of the gospel's powerful result, he has in mind a manner of transformed existence that results from this act of faith. "For we are what he has made us, created in Christ Jesus for good works, which God prepared beforehand to be our way of life" (Eph. 2:10).

Law defines the moral and religious character of this transformed existence. The dialectic of law and gospel, then, is worked out in the community saved by grace alone. Christians are empowered by God's Spirit to love God and neighbor in obedience to God's command.

See also Gospel; Grace; New Birth (Regeneration); Reconciliation; Righteousness.

Resources

Luther, Martin. "The Bondage of the Will." In *Martin Luther: Selections from His Writings,* edited by John Dillenberger, 166-203. Garden City, NY: Doubleday, 1961.
———. "The Freedom of a Christian." In *Martin Luther: Selections from His Writings,* 42-85.
Wesley, John. "The Righteousness by Faith." In *Works,* 5:75-76.

ROBERT W. WALL, PHD

LEGALISM

In Christian theology, "legalism" is a pejorative term that emphasizes strict adherence to the law as the central means of attaining salvation and maintaining covenant relationship with God. Since by this measure one's standing with God is governed by obedience to prescribed rules, legalism tends to emphasize the letter of the law over the spirit. The danger in legalism is twofold: (1) more emphasis is placed on outward performance than inward motivations such as love and gratitude, and (2) there is the temptation to see oneself fulfilling the requirements of the law independent of God's grace or assistance. Legalism can lead to a works-righteousness mentality and a dangerous self-righteousness that is condescending and critical of other people who do not measure up. Legalism is the opposite of antinomianism, the belief that faith in Jesus Christ releases Christians from obeying moral laws.

Although the term "legalism" never appears in the Scriptures, the problem and the errors associated with it are repeatedly addressed in the NT. Jesus, for example, condemned many of the religious leaders of his day for their hypocrisy and the heavy demands they placed on the people (Matt. 23). Prior to his conversion, the apostle Paul epitomized the life of a legalist: "as to righteousness under the law, blameless" (Phil. 3:6). The early church also struggled with legalism, since most of the first converts came out of a strict Jewish background. Although the council at Jerusalem concluded that adherence to the law was not a prerequisite for salvation (Acts 15), legalism continued to crop up in various congregations. In his letter to the Galatians, Paul had to confront a group of teachers who were claiming converts had to observe circumcision and other Jewish customs. Paul warned the believers that submitting to the yoke of works represented a rejection of Christ (2:21) and resulted in a return to bondage and slavery (4:9; 5:1).

See also Gospel; Grace; Law and Gospel; Pharisees/Sadducees; Righteousness.

KEVIN MELLISH, PHD

LIBERAL THEOLOGY

In theology the terms "liberal" and "liberalism" must be distinguished from their popular use in political discourse. In theology, a liberal is one whose approach to Christian theology assigns priority to reason and experience over Scripture and Christian tradition. What can be accepted as Christian must first satisfy these criteria. Primacy for what can be accepted as Christian may be extended to the theory of evolution regarding the world and human existence, notions that tend toward psychological or social determinism, and the historical and cultural relativity of all scriptures and religions. Liberalism is an approach to theology that embodies this particular religious **epistemology.** It originated in Germany during the eighteenth century and was determinative of German theology through the early part of the twentieth century. It dominated Western theology through the mid-twentieth century.

Friedrich Schleiermacher (1768–1834) is generally acknowledged as the father of modern Protestant theology, a founder of liberal theology. He earned this title because of the theological methodology he used to defend Christianity against **Enlightenment** criticism. Immanuel Kant had sought to ground theology in moral experience. Schleiermacher grounded theology in another kind of experience, "feeling," what he believed to be the universal sense of absolute dependence. He did theology on the basis of human experience, not on the basis of Scripture. The "true" and acceptable in theology would have to be what human consciousness and human experience permit. Experience broadly conceived would be theology's governing norm and orientation. This approach to theology was established in Schleiermacher's early monograph *Religion: Speeches to Its Cultural Despisers* (1799). It was then systematically developed in *The Christian Faith* (1821-22).

Schleiermacher's approach was comparable to that of the second-century apologists who used Hellenistic philosophy to defend the Christian faith against its Hellenistic critics. Schleiermacher's principal critics were the romantics of the latter half of the eighteenth and early nineteenth centuries. Among other things, romanticism reacted against the intellectualism of the **Enlightenment.** Romantics gave a place to emotion that the Enlightenment denied. So instead of elevating reason as the basis for theology, Schleiermacher used the romantics' emphasis on feeling as interpreted through reason. Their deep sense of feeling, Schleiermacher said, actually pointed to the God whom they denied.

Schleiermacher's method of assigning primary theological and religious authority to human experience became determinative for liberal theology. It is found wherever a theologian privileges human existence, as experienced in modern secularity, over Scripture, the **ecumenical councils**, and tradition.

By the late mid-twentieth century liberal theologians generally shunned the name "liberal." More recently a retrieval of the title has occurred. While in the past liberal theologians assigned primary authority to Western ways of perceiving reality, newer liberals give that place to culturally specific knowledge. This might include a particular cultural perspective on morality, an embrace of **religious pluralism**, or the perspectives of a specific gender or sexual orientation. Liberal theologians say that religious beliefs, including Christianity, are inevitably parochial and must be recognized as such. Claiming that the Christian faith should be universally embraced ignores its relativity and is motivated by a desire for power over others.

See also Postliberal Theology; Public Theology; Quadrilateral, Wesleyan.

Resources

Hodgson, Peter. *Liberal Theology: A Radical Vision*. Minneapolis: Fortress Press, 2007.

Rasor, Paul. *Faith Without Certainty: Liberal Theology in the 21st Century*. Boston: Skinner House Books, 2005.

GREGORY ROBERTSON, THD

LIBERATION THEOLOGY

In the 1960s, Latin American Roman Catholic theologians developed a distinctive theology that addressed the specific socioeconomic conditions of the poor and the oppressed in that region. They self-consciously turned away from the dominant theological discussions of Europe; the urgent issue in Latin America was how to speak of God in a context characterized by crushing poverty, not how to talk about God in a secularizing world. They built on the premise that God wants to liberate people from economic destitution and install righteous economic and social relationships between persons. Consequently, they expounded a theology of liberation and became known as liberation theologians.

The orienting principle of liberation theologians is the "preferential option for the poor" (Gutiérrez 1988, xxvi-xxvii). God is for the poor and oppressed, not because they are morally superior, but because they are poor and voiceless among the powerful.

To achieve their goal, liberation theologians used Marxist social analysis to understand the inequalities between people. However, their efforts sparked conflict with ecclesiastical leadership in the Vatican. The oppressive and antichurch nature of Marxism in Europe prompted Vatican opposition.

However, that was not true of the Latin American context. Liberation theologians observed that most Latin American lands and businesses were controlled by a few wealthy people and multinational corporations. Many liberation theologians concluded that capitalism was inherently evil.

Conflict with the Vatican increased in 1968 at the Medellín conference of Latin American bishops (CELAM II). Catholic clergy condemned their church's historical alliance with Latin America's ruling authorities. Liberation theologians charged the Roman Catholic Church with overemphasizing *orthodoxy* (right belief) and depreciating *orthopraxy* (right practice). It is insufficient, they said, to have correct doctrine without correct practice. The church has highlighted God's transcendence of the world and neglected biblical teaching where God identifies with the poor.

Liberation theologians thus accentuate the Exodus motif; God liberated the Israelites from an oppressive regime. That precedent highlights Jesus' inauguration of the kingdom of God in which he identified with the marginalized. The crucified God is immersed in the miseries of life, identifying with the disenfranchised.

Consequently, liberation theologians seek to restate the church's teaching on sin and salvation, noting that sin has primarily been treated as personal moral failures instead of unjust social institutions, a lack of political rights, and the oppression of the poor. Salvation has concentrated on quantity (eternal existence in heaven) instead of qualitatively transforming society now. This led to ecclesiastical criticism that liberation theologians are uninterested in personal salvation. A number of them have affirmed personal salvation but have also insisted that salvation not be limited to personal interests. God is working in history to establish his kingdom. This includes redeeming individuals and their social structures and addressing material as well as spiritual needs.

Liberation theology has significantly influenced African-American and feminist theologies.

See also Capitalism; Contextualization; Contextual Theology; Early Church; Economics and the Use of Money; Justice; Latin American Missiology/ Liberation Struggle; Mujerista Theology; Poverty; Social Ethics; Social Justice.

Resources

Berryman, Phillip. *Liberation Theology: Essential Facts About the Revolutionary Movement in Latin America and Beyond*. New York: Pantheon, 1987.

Gutiérrez, Gustavo. *A Theology of Liberation: History, Politics, and Salvation*. Translated and edited by Caridad Inda and John Eagleson. 15th anniv. ed. Mayknoll, NY: Orbis Books, 1988.

Runyon, Theodore, ed. *Sanctification and Liberation: Liberation Theologies in the Light of the Wesleyan Tradition*. Nashville: Abingdon Press, 1981.

JOHN SANDERS, THD

LITERATURE AND THE CHRISTIAN FAITH

Christianity is responsible for many of history's greatest literary works. It has also been shaped by the literary tradition—written and oral—of its own sacred text, the **Bible**. The Bible is a remarkable repository of literary genres, comprising narrative, biography, poetry, proverb, **history**, epistle, and **apocalyptic**.

Literature is commonly understood as the art of the written word, but more accurately it includes the epics, histories, and folklore of oral traditions. Before the earliest biblical narratives were inscribed, they were passed along orally, as when families gathered around the Passover meal and children asked their elders to recount the story of Israel's deliverance from Egypt. Eventually such narratives were written, preserving them for future generations.

Literature is usually classified as either fiction or nonfiction. The former, characterized by imagination and invention, includes poetry, novels, drama, short stories, and folklore (fairy tales, fables, etc.). In the digital age, this definition is extended to film, comic books, and narrative forms of video gaming. Nonfiction, which seeks accurately to portray facts, includes essays, legal documents, journals/memoirs, histories, biographies, most journalism, letters and academic writing, as well as varieties of technical and/or instructional writing. Postmodern literature often blurs the boundaries between fiction and nonfiction.

The historical development of literature may be described as a gradual movement from **myths** and epic narratives, by which cultures sought to make sense of common experience, toward increasingly particular types of writing. The Babylonian *Epic of Gilgamesh* (ca. 1900 BC) and the stories of the OT are grand in scope when compared with the apostle Paul's epistles and the Gospels. **Augustine's** *Confessions* (ca. AD 397-98) gives birth to autobiography. In the expressions of every historical epoch—from the theater of Shakespeare and the poetry of William Blake and W. B. Yeats to modern memoirs and postmodern blogs—literature has been a vehicle for religious ideas.

Christianity is no exception; it is narrative—the story of God with his people through Jesus Christ. The relationship between Christianity and literature is interdependent and mutually nurturing. The same is true of Judaism from which Christianity issued.

Reading and writing literature can play an edifying role in fostering Christian life. George Herbert (1593–1633), an **Anglican** priest, penned some of the finest poetry in the English language. **John Wesley** famously described himself as a *homo unius libri*, "man of one book" (*Works*, 5:3), yet he begins his *Plain Account of Christian Perfection* by cataloging the extrabiblical spiritual and theological literature that had shaped his spirituality. The fiction of Fyodor Dostoyevsky (1821-81), J. R. R. Tolkien (1892–1973), and Flannery O'Connor (1925-64) is inconceivable apart from an imagination profoundly influenced by the Christian faith. Likewise, their stories and allegories serve to explain and support the Christian faith.

The **gospel** comes to us as story—God's Word made flesh. Literary theorists agree that every good story follows a plot that involves a hero, the pursuit of a goal, conflict, and resolution, whether positive (e.g., comedy) or negative (e.g., tragedy). Humankind is easily mistaken as the protagonist in the biblical narrative, when, in fact, God is both its Author and Hero. His aim is covenant communion with his creation. Sin creates conflict, and God initiates action that leads to resolution in the story of Jesus Christ and the church—a grand drama now moving toward its consummation.

See also Arts, The; Bible; Hermeneutics; Intertextuality; Myth/Mythos; Narrative Theology.

Resources

Cunningham, David S. *Reading Is Believing: The Christian Faith Through Literature and Film.* Grand Rapids: Brazos Press, 2002.

Willimon, William H. *Reading with Deeper Eyes: The Love of Literature and the Life of Faith.* Nashville: Upper Room Books, 1998.

BRANNON HANCOCK, PHD

LITURGICAL THEOLOGY

Liturgical theology is theological reflection on the meaning of Christian worship. It is the art of carefully applying theological reflection to liturgical practice. Its goal is for theologically informed liturgy (Greek, *leitourgia* [the work of the people in worshipping God]) to yield true worship and orthodox theology. In principle, liturgy is considered *theologia prima* (primary theology) while **systematic theology**, as its own discipline, is considered *theologia secunda* (secondary theology). The act of worship comes first; theological reflection on worship comes second. However, liturgical theologians try to guard against separating liturgy (the practice of worship) from theological reflection (liturgical theology) and against treating one as superior to the other. Liturgics and theological reflection, though distinguishable, are organically inseparable. The challenge is to avoid letting theology dictate worship (as though the **church** simply prays what the church believes) or letting liturgy dictate theology (as though the rule of prayer, or practice of worship, determines belief or doctrine). To avoid this error liturgy and theological reflection must be partners in a complementary conversation, a united theological process of its own. Theology informs the prayer, and the prayer itself is the vehicle for theology.

The rise of liturgical theology as an identifiable discipline is fairly recent. Its appearance is typically dated from the early part of the twentieth century and coincides with the liturgical renewal movement of the same period. Prior to this time, traditional classification of theological systems failed to distinguish liturgical theology as a category all its own. Liturgics was paired with **practical theology** and was studied largely as rituals and rubrics. As such it was of interest primarily to clerics, not to "pure theologians." During the second half of the twentieth century key liturgical theologians advanced the case for liturgical theology. Notable among them were Aidan Kavanagh and Alexander Schmemann. They and others held that liturgical theology is done by the liturgical assembly (the church) as a whole and should not be left solely to clerics and academics. For them, liturgy is an *act* of theology, one whereby the believing community addresses God, dialogues with God, makes statements of belief about God, and symbolizes its belief in various forms.

Liturgical theology echoes the ancient Latin formula *Lex orandi lex credendi est* (The rule of **prayer** is the rule of belief), a maxim attributed to Prosper of Aquitaine (ca. 390–ca. 465) but already visible in the writings of earlier **church fathers**. The church of God learns to pray (engages in the liturgy, the act of worship) and from this learns what to believe. We can say that *lex orandi* is related to *lex credendi* as speech is related to grammar. First, people speak, and then come the grammarians who analyze speech.

David Fagerberg has helped show how liturgical theology is differentiated from other approaches to worship. A theology *of* worship presumes worship is the subject to which theological constructs and principles are applied. A theology *from* worship suggests a liturgical way of doing theology where all that happens in the life of the church is decided by its liturgy. Liturgical theologians do not first generalize or dictate the starting point for other theological approaches to worship. Rather, they begin by participating in and reflecting on real liturgies in motion as the basis for both explaining Christian faith and forming it in return.

See also Laity; Liturgy and Worship; Orthodoxy/Orthopraxis/Orthopathy; Preaching; Sacraments.

Resources

Davies, Horton. *Worship and Theology in England: From Watts and Wesley to Martineau, 1690–1900.* Grand Rapids: Eerdmans, 1996.

Fagerberg, David W. *Theologia Prima: What Is Liturgical Theology?* 2nd ed. Chicago: Liturgy Training Publications, 2003.

Kavanagh, Aidan. *On Liturgical Theology.* New York: Pueblo Publishing, 1984.

Schmemann, Alexander. *Introduction to Liturgical Theology.* Translated by Asheleigh Moorehouse. Crestwood, NY: St Vladimir's Seminary Press, 1966.

CONSTANCE M. CHERRY, DMIN

LITURGICS

See LITURGICAL THEOLOGY; LITURGY AND WORSHIP.

LITURGY AND WORSHIP

Liturgy and worship are two distinct, yet inseparable, dimensions of Christian faith. In Christian practice, worship is the main event, the appointed meeting between God and God's people. The liturgy, or form of worship, provides the means through which worship occurs. Worship occurs between the individual and **God** through personal devotions, the daily office, **work** as **prayer**, service to others, and so on. Popularly expressed, worship is 24-7. Yet while living all of life as an act of worship is consistent with Scripture, *corpo-*

rate worship predominates in the OT and NT. This is evident in the worship required of God's covenant people **Israel** and in the worship offered to God by Christian communities established after the day of Pentecost.

Worship is more easily described than defined. In worship the gathered community prays, sings, reads aloud from Holy Scripture, and receives the word proclaimed. The church offers gifts, testifies to God's faithfulness, and affirms creedal statements of faith. It will also receive the **sacraments**, exhort, surrender to God's will, and collect gifts for the poor. All such expressions of worship are supported by the Scriptures.

The English word "worship" derives from the Anglo-Saxon word *weorthscipe*, which means "ascribing worthiness to one to whom great honor is due." While the word "worship" is found almost 311 times in the OT and NT, depending on the English translation, it is the result of numerous Hebrew and Greek words, each with a different emphasis. Therefore the word "worship" appearing in English Bibles can have several meanings.

The English word "liturgy" is derived from the Greek word *leitourgia*, translated as the "work of the people" (from *ergon* [work] and *laos* [people]). Liturgy is the vehicle through which Christians engage in worship. It includes things that are *spoken* (words that form the prepared and spontaneous text of worship) and things *done* (actions and gestures either accompanying the text or standing alone that facilitate worship). Words and actions provide a means of communication in worship: from God to people, people to God, and people to people. Any liturgy, therefore, consists of the sum total of worship words and actions that help the community express its devotion to God.

Some Christian bodies are closely identified with their liturgies. Thus one may refer to the Byzantine liturgy or the **Anglican** liturgy or the Celtic liturgy. However, all worshipping communities have liturgies of some sort. Those communities identified with the oral tradition (worshipping communities that, having no official liturgies, worship according to their own oral/verbal worship patterns) and those within the free-church traditions who value nonprescribed worship nevertheless have liturgies. Written or oral, prescribed or not, each community employs words and actions to worship God.

John Wesley, as a devoted Anglican priest, valued the liturgy of the 1662 Book of Common Prayer (BCP). He wanted the BCP to influence **Methodists** in Europe and America. He provided for the liturgical practices of American Methodists on the frontier by developing *The Sunday Service* (1784). It consisted of an official order and text for Methodists as they gathered on Sunday for worship. While not all of the BCP was adapted, Wesley nevertheless provided an approved service so the integrity of worship could be maintained in the new world.

Theologically, worship tells the story of God—the story of **creation** and **new creation**, the story of the life, death, resurrection, ascension, and anticipated return of Jesus Christ. Worship is the occasion when in its liturgy the church proclaims the story of the triune God: Father, Son, and Holy Spirit.

See also Charismatic Theology; Contextualization; Indigenization; Liturgical Theology; Orthodoxy/Orthopraxis/Orthopathy.

Resources

Cherry, Constance M. *The Worship Architect: A Blueprint for Designing Culturally Relevant and Biblically Faithful Services.* Grand Rapids: Baker Academic, 2010.

Davies, Horton. *Worship and Theology in England: From Watts and Wesley to Martineau, 1690-1900.* Grand Rapids: Eerdmans, 1996.

Webber, Robert. *Ancient-Future Worship: Proclaiming and Enacting God's Narrative.* Grand Rapids: Baker, 2008.

White, James. *Introduction to Christian Worship.* 3rd ed. Nashville: Abingdon Press, 2000.

CONSTANCE M. CHERRY, DMIN

LOGICAL POSITIVISM

Logical positivism, also known as logical or scientific empiricism, was an early twentieth-century movement in philosophy. It attempted to appropriate the methodology and rigor of mathematics and the natural sciences for the field of philosophy, especially the philosophy of science.

The movement originated in Austria and Germany in the 1920s and 1930s among thinkers associated with the Vienna Circle, which formed around Moritz Schlick, who held the chair of philosophy at the University of Vienna (1920s). Among its members were the philosophers Friedrich Waismann, Otto Neurath, Rudolf Carnap, Herbert Feigl, and Victor Kraft. Members who were mathematicians were Hans Hahn, Carl Menger, and Kurt Gödel.

Early logical positivists were influenced by the positivism of Ernst Mach (that all knowledge is derived from observable phenomena), the logical concepts of Gottlob Frege (his concern with language), and philosopher Bertrand Russell (his emphasis on empiricism). Much of their inspiration came from Ludwig Wittgenstein, who lived near Vienna for a short time, and G. E. Moore. Wittgenstein's *Tracatus Logico-Philosophicus* shaped the basic perspective of the movement, namely, that the purpose of philosophy is the logical clarification of thought.

Philosophers influenced by the Vienna Circle are A. J. Ayer and Gilbert Ryle.

The primary emphases of the movement were the determination of meaning and the analysis of language. A statement, according to logical positivists, has meaning only if it is either an analytic a priori (tautological) or a synthetic a posteriori statement. At the heart of logical positivism lay the verifiability principle as a criterion of meaning. A. J. Ayer stated the principle: "We say that a sentence is factually significant to any given person, if, and only if, he knows how to verify the proposition which it purports to express" ([1936] 1952, 35). Statements that were true by definition or could be verified by empirical investigation were considered "meaningful"; all other statements were "meaningless."

The result was an attack on **metaphysics** (and religion and ethics). For logical positivists, metaphysical statements were "nonsensical" because they were neither necessary truths of logic nor empirically verifiable.

The immediate application of logical positivism was to scientific language by demonstrating that scientific theories could be shown to be truths of logic and mathematics, supported by propositions correlating to sense experience.

Recently postpositivism has attempted to revise and extend the insights of logical positivism by challenging the notion that logical positivism is a form of radical empiricism and by emphasizing the role of a priori knowledge in scientific investigation.

See also Epistemology; Natural Science.

Resources
Ayer, Alfred Jules. *Language, Truth and Logic*. 1936. Reprint, Mineola, NY: Dover, 1952.
———, ed. *Logical Positivism*. New York: Free Press, 1959.
Friedman, Michael. *Reconsidering Logical Positivism*. New York: Cambridge University Press, 1999.

PHILIP N. LAFOUNTAIN, THD

LOGOS
See CHRISTOLOGY; JESUS OF NAZARETH.

LORD AND MASTER
See CHRISTOLOGY, NEW TESTAMENT; JESUS OF NAZARETH.

LORD'S SUPPER
See SACRAMENTS.

LOVE
The primary OT terms for love are 'aheb (ah-HAYV) and khesed (KHE-sed). The verb 'aheb with its noun forms carries a wide range of meanings: "sexual passion," "affection," "friendship," "commitment," and "loyalty." One may love *things*: food, drink, sleep, righteousness, and faithfulness. One may also love *persons*: a spouse, children, friends, the poor, neighbors, masters, rulers, and God.

Deuteronomy 6:4-5 commands the Israelites to love God with their entire being. The literary form of Deuteronomy is that of a **covenant**, or international treaty. Just as a vassal was committed to observe conditions the overlord stipulated, even so Israelites should faithfully observe God's

LOVE • 307

commandments. Loyalty was a motivation, but so was affection based on gratitude for God's gracious acts of deliverance and giving the **law**. Observing the covenant's ethical obligations would maintain the community's life. Leviticus 19:18*b* enjoined Israelites to love their neighbors. As God's **holy** people, they must deal justly and righteously with each other. The range of love, compassion, and **justice** extended to the socially marginalized—the poor, powerless, and non-Israelites, or "strangers," who lived among them.

The OT speaks mainly of God's love for **Israel**. Because he loved their **ancestors**, God delivered Israel from Egypt and made covenant with them. He chose them to be his special people (Exod. 19:4-6; Hos. 11:1). Even when Israel repeatedly violated the covenant, God responded lovingly rather than destructively (Hos. 11:8-9).

The noun *khesed* can be translated "everlasting love," "steadfast love," "mercy," "compassion," and "pity." It can describe mutual loyalty between parties such as existed between Jonathan and David (1 Sam. 20:14-17). More often it applies to situations where one is in need and another can assist, is not obliged to do so, but nevertheless chooses to address the need. God's *khesed* is the basis of his forgiveness (Exod. 34:6-7). He creatively goes beyond the covenant's legal obligations and reconciles transgressors. Israel relied on God's *khesed* to maintain its covenant relationship. Hosea reversed the direction by requiring Israel to show *khesed* to God. God desires "[*khesed*] and not sacrifice, the knowledge of God rather than burnt offerings" (6:6). The Greek translation of the OT (LXX) often translates *khesed* as *eleos* ("mercy," "compassion," and "pity"). When the NT uses the word *eleos*, it sometimes carries the meaning of *khesed*, as when Jesus quotes Hos. 6:6 (Matt. 9:13; 12:7; see also Luke 1:50, 54, 58, 72; Rom. 11:30-31; Eph. 2:4; Titus 3:5).

These multiple expressions of God's engaging love raise the question of divine impassibility (the concept that God is incapable of emotion and suffering). Many early theologians, including Augustine and Thomas Aquinas, taught that God is impassible. They were influenced by Greek philosophers who believed that emotions exhibit *change* and therefore manifest imperfection. Emotions must not be ascribed to God, who is perfect. Suffering is an emotion. If God were to suffer, he would be less than perfect. For their own reasons, Martin Luther and John Calvin also taught the impassibility of God. But many contemporary theologians argue that love and suffering are inseparable. Through suffering love, God most truly reveals himself. The living God is immutable—unchanging—in his steadfast love and holiness, not as an impassible metaphysical perfection. This position is more in line with God's faithfulness as manifested in the OT and NT.

The primary NT terms for love are the noun *agapē* and the verb *agapaō*. They correspond to the Hebrew word *'aheb* and carry connotations of affection, loyalty, faithfulness, and commitment but not sexual passion or lust. The verb *phileō* (fi-LE-o) when translated "to love" is sometimes synonymous with *agapaō*, as in the postresurrection exchange between Jesus and Peter recorded in John 21:15-18.

In the Synoptic Gospels (Matthew, Mark, Luke), Jesus rarely speaks about love, but when he does, it is at critical points in the narrative. He accepts the OT concepts when referring to Deut. 6:4-5 and Lev. 19:18b— the first and second great commandments (Matt. 22:34-40; Mark 12:28-32; Luke 10:25-28). In Mark the core of the debate between Jesus and his opponents is these love commandments. Mark adds, "After that no one dared to ask him any question" (12:34). In Matt. 5:44 (cf. Luke 6:27-28) Jesus commands his followers to love their enemies and then continues with the command to "be perfect . . . as your heavenly Father is perfect" (Matt. 5:48). God's mercy extends to the righteous and unrighteous alike (v. 45). Jesus' disciples should act accordingly toward their enemies. They should act with compassion and should exercise **justice** and **righteousness**.

In the gospel of John, love characterizes life in the church. Love is more than an emotion; it is an action—friendship, solidarity, loyalty, and commonality—that characterizes life in community. Jesus' disciples must "love one another" (15:12) and demonstrate their love for Jesus by keeping his commandments (14:15). Jesus claims an intimate relationship with the Father (3:35); he identifies so closely with the Father that he speaks of the two as being one (10:30). God's love for humanity motivated the Son's **incarnation** and sacrifice (3:16). Claiming that "God is love" (1 John 4:8) is not a philosophical concept; it names God's active and redemptive self-sacrifice. That kind of love should characterize the community of Jesus' disciples. It comes from God, the Source of all love. All who love are born of God; those who do not are not (vv. 7-8). Indeed this love made complete in the believer's heart is the ground for assurance (vv. 17-18), a passage of great importance to **John Wesley**. But it always issues in concrete love of the other (vv. 19-20).

The apostle Paul also viewed God's love as the motivation for Christ's atonement and as the model for Christian life (Gal. 2:20; 1 Cor. 13). From eternity, God chose his people to be "holy and blameless" in love. Out of love for sinful humanity, God offered salvation (Eph. 1:4; 2:4-6).

See also Ancestors; Christian Ethics/Moral Theology; Discipleship; God, Doctrine of; Greek Philosophy; Hospitability/Hospitality; Incarnation; Justice; Justification; Neoplatonism; Reconciliation.

ROBERT D. BRANSON, PHD

LOVE FEAST

The early Methodist love feast was a meal of plain cakes and water set within a service of fellowship, conversation, and testimony. It served as a symbol of unity and provided an opportunity for closer union between believers. Participation was meant to encourage Christians to move toward **holiness**. Stories of personal conversion, fervent celebration, prayer, and joyful hymn singing marked the occasion. Hymns for the love feast were primarily written by **Charles Wesley**.

John Wesley inaugurated love feasts among Methodists, insisting they revived rites of the early church, though he had first encountered love feasts among the **Moravians**. Within Methodism the earliest use was prior to 1740. They were held frequently and were confined to the **bands**. At first, participants were separated by gender. Later (1759) the general love feast expanded to include both genders and whole **societies** (Rack 1992, 411). Entrance was confined to ticketed members. By then the larger **societies** typically held love feasts quarterly.

Love feasts were significant because Methodists often lacked opportunity to participate in the **sacrament** of the Eucharist. The Methodist leaders made clear that love feasts were not the Eucharist, but the inclusive nature, egalitarianism, and emphasis on participation led to their being understood sacramentally by some. Leadership for the love feasts was not confined to ordained priests. Stewards, who oversaw the love feasts, also collected offerings for the poor.

Love feasts were controversial. Critics perceived them as unhealthy and suspected they were meant to replace the Eucharist. Wesley defended them as sources of communal encouragement. He insisted they were a complement to, not a replacement for, the Eucharist. Love feasts did not occur at the same time as parish Eucharist services. Wesley urged Methodists to participate in the Eucharist as often as possible.

After Methodism separated from the **Anglican** Church, love feasts gradually died out, partly because the Lord's Supper was now available in Methodist chapels.

See also Christian Perfection (Entire Sanctification); Sacraments; Spiritual Formation/Growth.

Resources
Baker, Frank. *Methodism and the Love-Feast*. London: Epworth Press, 1957.
Rack, Henry. *Reasonable Enthusiast*. London: Epworth Press, 1992.

DEIRDRE BROWER LATZ, PHD

LUTHER, MARTIN

Born in Eisleben (1483), Luther enrolled at the University of Erfurt (1501), intending eventually to study law. After a terrifying experience in a thunderstorm, however, he vowed to become a monk and joined the Augustinian order. In 1508 Luther was sent to Wittenberg as lecturer in moral philosophy. While in Rome in 1510 on business for his order, he became disturbed by the corruption he saw. In 1511 Luther received his doctorate in theology and was appointed professor of Scripture at Wittenberg.

The Dominican Johannes Tetzel arrived in Saxony in 1517, selling a special plenary indulgence. It promised the complete remission of sin and punishment (part of the proceeds were used to build St. Peter's in Rome). Objecting strenuously, Luther penned his Ninety-Five Theses and, according to legend, posted them on the door of the Wittenberg castle church. Copies spread rapidly; consequently, Luther was forced to defend himself before Cardinal Cajetan (Augsburg, 1518) and Johannes Eck (Leipzig, 1519). Under protection from Elector Frederick, in 1520 Luther wrote *Address to the Christian Nobility*, *The Babylonian Captivity of the Church*, and *The Freedom of a Christian Man*. In June 1520, Leo X issued a papal bull, *Exsurge Domine* (Arise, O Lord), demanding that Luther recant. Following his refusal, Leo excommunicated Luther (January 1521).

At the Diet of Worms (April 1521) Luther refused to recant and was placed under imperial ban. Hidden by his friends in the Wartburg castle, Luther worked on translating the NT into German and eventually returned to Wittenberg. In 1525 he married a former nun, Catherine von Bora, with whom he would have six children. In 1534 Luther's German Bible was published. His Small Catechism and Large Catechism (1529) and Smalcald Articles (1537) would later be included in the Book of Concord (1580), Lutheranism's doctrinal standard. Luther died in Eisleben in 1546.

Luther disputed any ecclesiastical claims to authority or teachings lacking scriptural basis. The church can be recognized by its possession of the Word of God, the sacraments (baptism and the Lord's Supper), the office of the keys, the consecration of ministers, public worship, and the "sacred cross" or trials (*On the Councils and the Church* [1539]). Luther retained a high view of the ministry. His teaching on the "priesthood of all believers" did not mean that each Christian holds priestly authority as a private possession. Rather, because it is united with Christ, the church shares corporately in Christ's priesthood. Therefore, the community must select those able publicly to exercise its "priestly offices," but such persons are not different essentially from laypersons. Luther fully expected the devil's rage against Christ's church and that the world's end was imminent.

Luther's chief contribution lies in his "theology of the cross" (*Heidelberg Disputation* [1518]). In contrast to a "theology of glory," in which human standards of success and power are projected onto God, a theology of the cross discerns the work of God hidden under the opposite of human expectations. The passion and death of Jesus is the prime example; the proclamation of Christ crucified contradicts our attempt to manipulate God. The idea of God working opposite human expectations informs Luther's recovery of the doctrine of justification by faith, in which God declares sinners righteous apart from any human merit, an idea that set Luther at odds with conventional Roman Catholic theology. Those justified by faith in Christ remain "simultaneously justified and sinners" as God works beneath, and contrary to, present experience.

Luther's theology of the cross has been appropriated in recent years by Jürgen Moltmann and Douglas John Hall. Recent research by Finnish Lutheran scholars suggests that Luther's view of salvation is close to the **Orthodox Church**'s understanding of "union with Christ."

See also Church (Ecclesiology); Justification; Orthodox Church; Protestantism; Radical Reformation; Reformation; Roman Catholicism.

Resources

Lull, Timothy, and William R. Russell, eds. *Martin Luther's Basic Theological Writings.* Minneapolis: Fortress Press, 2005.

Marty, Martin E. *Martin Luther: A Life.* New York: Penguin, 2006.

Meistad, Tore. *Martin Luther and John Wesley on the Sermon on the Mount.* Lanham, MD: Scarecrow Press, 1999.

JONATHAN P. CASE, PHD

Mm

MAGISTERIUM
See ROMAN CATHOLICISM.

MARRIAGE
Marriage is the socially sanctioned physical, emotional, spiritual, and economic union between a man and a woman as defined in the biblical expression of the two becoming "one flesh." The Genesis account of God presenting Eve to Adam as his equal in this relationship represents the ideal of the monogamous marriage and the establishment of the family unit (2:21-24). The songs in the Song of Songs (Song of Solomon) appear to have the purpose of maintaining the romantic bond and faithfulness between a man and his wife throughout their life together. Jesus' teaching on marriage and divorce (Matt. 5:31-32; 19:3-12; Luke 16:18) assumes a one-man, one-woman marital faithfulness, with the possibility of divorce as a rare case under specific conditions. Paul's teaching on marriage in Ephesians underscores the mutual **self-denial** of both partners following the example of Christ's self-giving on the cross (5:21-33). In none of these texts is there any place for either spousal abuse or the incorporation of another person in the marital bond. Paul's teaching on celibacy for the sake of the gospel is given in the context of the immanent return of Christ and does not in any way present the lifestyle of celibacy as superior to that of marriage.

Many human cultures permit nonbiblical alternative models of marriage. The reasons may be economic, personal, or for childbearing. Options include **polygamy**, polyandry (one wife and multiple husbands), homosexuality, and repeated divorce and remarriage (also known as serial polygamy). Polygamy, although appearing often in the OT, is introduced in Gen. 4:19-24 with the story of Lamech, who belonged to the seventh generation from Cain. Here the fulfillment or completeness (symbolized by the seventh generation) of Cain's refusal to obey God includes Lamech's polygamous marriage. This is just one example of Cain's flagrant distortion of God's word and will.

Because childbearing is assumed to be a blessing of marriage, homosexual unions are not endorsed by the Bible. Add to that the unremittingly negative language the Bible uses when describing same-sex relationships (Lev. 18:22; 20:13; 1 Cor. 6:9-11; 1 Tim. 1:10). Jesus' teaching that divorce was permitted only because of the stubbornness of God's people underscores the religious importance of monogamous marriage. It would not be inappropriate to expand Jesus' teaching on divorce to alternative models of marriage as evidencing a spiritual disorder.

Many cultures recognize marriage as a social and/or economic union of the families of the bride and groom. An exchange of gifts, bride price, dowry, and so on, figure into this aspect of marriage because of the gain and/or loss of a family laborer. The model of the levirate marriage—a model in the early centuries of Jewish history by which a brother of the deceased was duty-bound to marry the widow if the deceased had left no male heir—underscores the membership of a widow in her husband's family. Thus "the firstborn whom [the former widow] bears [would] succeed to the name of the deceased brother, so that his name [would] not be blotted out of Israel" (Deut. 25:6). The institution also assured that the woman's **sexuality** would be expressed only inside the first husband's family. Levirate marriage usually resulted in polygamy.

In the Bible, parental involvement in selecting a person's marriage partner was a way to retain a stable social order. It ensured the maturity required for maintaining a stable marriage. Old Testament narratives demonstrate some of these features of marriage without prescribing them. Also present in the OT is an evolution of the criteria for selecting a suitable marriage partner.

For **traditional religions** that incorporate **ancestors** as continuing participants in society, the marriage bond may be considered permanent even after a spouse dies. The Bible, however, permits freedom to remarry after the death of a spouse (Rom. 7:2-3; 1 Tim. 5:14-16).

The definition of marriage given here assumes that a legitimate marriage takes place during a legally recognized public ceremony that incorporates vows of faithfulness between the partners.

See also African Traditional Religions; Childhood, Wesleyan Theology of; Family, Christian; Human Sexuality; Social Ethics.

Resources

Granberg, L. I., and J. R. Root. "Marriage, Theology of." In *Evangelical Dictionary of Theology*, edited by Walter Elwell, 743-44. 2nd ed. Grand Rapids: Baker Academic, 2001.
Mbiti, John S. *Love and Marriage in Africa.* London: Longman, 1973.

BEAUTY R. MAENZANISE, PHD

MARY, MARIOLOGY

Mary is identified in the **Gospels** as the mother of Jesus. A virgin and engaged to Joseph, she became pregnant through the miraculous activity of the Spirit (Matt. 1:18, 20; Luke 1:35) and gave birth under extraordinary circumstances. Beyond the nativity stories, and apart from a few references, Mary is mentioned in only two other scenes, both narrated by John: the first is the wedding at Cana (John 2:1-11), and the second is the crucifixion of Jesus (19:25-27). Acts 1:14 lists Mary as a member of the first group of Jesus' followers. No extant first-century documents contain additional information.

In the centuries following the NT period, Mary received special attention in theological reflection. Ignatius, writing in AD 107, referred to Mary's humanity to affirm the humanity of Christ in his dispute with the Docetists. Irenaeus (d. ca. 200) developed a parallel between Eve and Mary as part of his explanation of the "economy of **salvation**." In the fourth century various **church fathers** used the title *Theotokos*, meaning "God-bearer" or "Mother of God," for Mary to support the truly human and truly divine nature of Christ. The Council of Ephesus (431) accepted the title *Theotokos* as dogma. The importance of Mary in theological reflection is her role in the **incarnation** and salvation as mediator between the divine and the human world, between the OT and the NT. She received and gave birth to the divine Word, participating directly in the offer of salvation. Because of her role, she also became a model of faith for believers.

It is not clear whether the theological reflection gave rise to a culture of devotion to Mary or whether a culture of devotion developed in response to popular piety within the church. Whatever the answer, as early as the fourth century the church celebrated special feasts in honor of Mary. The second-century *Protevangelium of James* provided extrabiblical information about Mary and stimulated devotion to Mary.

In the Eastern tradition Mary was frequently depicted in **icons**, honoring her role in the mystery of the incarnation and as an example of the **theosis**, the indwelling of the Spirit that enables believers to be partakers of the divine nature.

Ambrose (d. 397) and Jerome (d. 420) were instrumental in promoting Mary in the Western Christian tradition. As advocates of the monastic-ascetic tradition, they stressed Mary's virginity as a model of special Christian devotion. During the Middle Ages, theological reflection focused on Mary's immaculate conception and her bodily assumption into heaven, which were ultimately accepted as dogma by the **Roman Catholic Church** in 1854 and 1950, respectively. This period witnessed various claims of Marian appearances (Lourdes, 1858, and Fatima, 1917). Devotion to Mary has inspired magnificent works of art from the Middle Ages to the present.

The **Protestant Reformation** reduced the status of Mary to what is explicitly mentioned in Scripture and the first **ecumenical councils**. Though **Calvin** denied the title *Theotokos*, **Luther** and Zwingli did not. All three emphasized Mary as a model of faith.

Overemphasized in popular devotion, yet underemphasized in Protestantism, an **ecumenical dialogue** on Mary emerged in the second part the twentieth century. Central in these discussions is Mary as a model of faith who was fully obedient to God and who participated in salvation (Luke 1:38).

Resource

Pelikan, Jaroslav, David Flusser, and Justin Lang, eds. *Mary: Images of the Mother of Jesus in Jewish and Christian Perspective.* Minneapolis: Fortress Press, 2005.

ANTONIE HOLLEMAN, DRS

MATERIALISM

See ECONOMICS AND THE USE OF MONEY.

MEANS OF GRACE

John Wesley defines "means of **grace**" as "outward signs, words, or actions, ordained of God, and appointed . . . to be the *ordinary* channels whereby he might convey . . . preventing [**prevenient**], justifying, or sanctifying grace" (*Works*, 5:187, emphasis added). As persons participate in the means of grace, the **Holy Spirit** works in their lives to enable their growth in **salvation**. While God also works in extraordinary ways, the means of grace are the normal ways God has promised to meet persons and graciously transform lives.

Wesley has three different categories of means of grace:

1. *Instituted* means are the five prescribed by Christ: **prayer**, searching the Scriptures, the Lord's Supper, fasting, and Christian conference. *Prudential* means are rules and practices that reason and experience have shown to be used by God for Christian growth.

2. *General* means denote spiritual practices that undergird the Christian life: universal obedience, keeping God's commandments, watching out for sin, **self-denial**, taking up one's cross daily, and exercising God's presence. *Particular* means include the instituted and prudential means of grace listed above.

3. *Works of piety* are means of grace that keep us in loving relationship with God. *Works of mercy* are means of grace that keep us in loving relationship with our neighbor.

Means of grace encompass a wide array of practices. In addition to those listed above are **covenant services**, **love feasts**, watch-night services, and accountability groups such as **classes** and **bands**. Wesley's insistence that works of mercy—by which persons meet the spiritual and physical needs of the neighbor—are means of grace that enable those who practice them to grow spiritually is an important and distinctive contribution.

Means of grace mediate the presence of God through the power of the Holy Spirit. Wesley opposed a formalist reduction of means of grace to a set of duties or to automatic dispensers of grace that in effect make God distant. He also opposed an enthusiast relativizing or setting aside the means of grace in favor of immediate and intense religious experience. Wesley insisted God is immediately present through the means of grace. To use any means of grace with any degree of **faith** results in encountering God's transforming presence.

Means of grace are central practices that enable persons to have a relationship with God. Works of piety and mercy are means through which persons *express* love for God and neighbor through worship, community, personal devotions, and service to others. As Christians participate in the means of grace, they *receive* grace through which the Spirit transforms their lives, enabling them to grow in salvation.

Through means of grace we grow in the knowledge and love of God and of our neighbor. Accountability to **spiritual disciplines** in small groups counteracts the tendency toward dissipation, in which the temptations, activities, and responsibilities of life can draw persons away from God as the center of their lives. By keeping their focus on God and the neighbor, spiritual disciplines nurture faith, enabling persons to then experience means of grace such as prayer, the Lord's Supper, and Scripture, not as mere formalities, but as means to encounter God.

Because the God whom Christians encounter is revealed through Scripture, prayer, and the Lord's Supper as the God who was incarnate in the life, death, and resurrection of Jesus Christ, by participating in the means of grace they increasingly come to know and love God as the one who first loved them, even to death on the cross. As they encounter Christ in the neighbor through works of mercy, they also grow in love for God and their neighbor.

See also Discipleship; Spiritual Formation/Growth; Wesley, John, Theology of.

Resources

Knight, Henry H., III. *The Presence of God in the Christian Life: John Wesley and the Means of Grace*. Metuchen, NJ: Scarecrow Press, 1992.

Trickett, David. "Spiritual Vision and Discipline in the Wesleyan Movement." In *Christian Spirituality: Post-Reformation and Modern*, edited by Louis Dupré and Don E. Saliers in collaboration with John Meyendorff. New York: Crossroad, 1989.

Wesley, John. "The Means of Grace." In *Works*, 5:185-201.

HENRY H. KNIGHT III, PHD

MEDIA

"Media" is the plural form of the word "medium" drawn from the Latin word *medias* (middle). The implication is that information is filtered prior to distribution. Current use of the term dates back to the 1800s and was principally applied to the newspaper industry. The definition expanded during the 1920s with the advent of radio, followed by television, and now new media, including the many uses of the Internet. Today new media are being used creatively and extensively in the Global South for worship, evangelism, and Christian teaching.

The function of media has traditionally been understood as the distribution of news, with news being broadly defined and relatively difficult to classify. The first multipage newspaper printed in the United States, *Publick Occurrences Both Forreign and Domestick*, was penned by Benjamin Harris in Boston (1690). Harris's writings incorporated religious references and themes.

Theological topics remained thematically central to nineteenth-century American newspapers. But historians have largely ignored or demonized religious themes found in the reporting of the news by early media. For example, James Melvin Lee in *History of American Journalism* (1917) characterized this period as "the darkest period in the history of American journalism."

Although religious and political views certainly influenced journalism during the early twentieth century, the penny presses forever changed the relationship between media and religion, creating a divide between theological and secular reporting. With the mainstream secular press emphasizing sensationalism to enhance sales, many Christians rejected mainstream journalism. On the other hand, media practitioners distanced themselves from religion, charging it failed the test of objectivity.

Theological resistance against mass-mediated messages often extended to new media such as radio and television. Nevertheless, to the chagrin of some religious traditionalists, some members of the religious establishment and associated communities eagerly and systematically embraced new methods for proclaiming the gospel.

When the US Federal Communication Commission (FCC) regulations requiring public service programming for television appeared, many stations satisfied the requirement by filling early Sunday morning programming with diverse religious programs. While some airtime was provided *gratis* to meet FCC requirements, a few religious leaders and communities openly embraced the new medium and created made-for-television religious programming.

Regional religious broadcasts (both radio and television) continue to enjoy various levels of popularity; however, it is more common now to see media applied locally as congregations experiment with technological tools and incorporate new methods of proclamation and teaching.

The Internet has expanded communication options worldwide. It combines the various channels of media into a single platform, along with new modes of message transmission. The Internet is being used by church leaders and the general religious populaces to create, interpret, and disseminate religious messages.

Recognizing the importance of media for evangelism, denominations and **parachurch** organizations, such as Great Commission Media Ministries (GCM), use a "symphony of media" for evangelism and teaching and for disaster relief and developmental assistance in the great population centers of Asia, the Middle East, South America, and Africa. Communication that would have in earlier times taken years to accomplish can now happen in weeks through the use of new media, and it can be professionally developed and disseminated anywhere in the world.

It is currently unclear how decentralized and unmonitored access to and use of media will impact the church specifically and society generally. Certainly, new kinds of media change the social, temporal, and spatial landscape. They contradict the notion that transmission of messages should be regulated and filtered by designated gatekeepers.

See also Christianity and Global Cultures; Film/Cinema; Popular Culture; Technology.

CYNDI ALLISON, MA

MESSIAH
See CHRISTOLOGY, NEW TESTAMENT.

MESSIANIC JUDAISM

Jews who believe Yeshua (Jesus) is the Messiah of Israel are called Messianic Jews. Although there have been Jewish believers in Jesus through the centuries, modern Messianic Jews arose from the Jesus movement (1960s and 1970s). Messianic Judaism includes Jews for Jesus but also consists of hundreds of congregations wherever there are large Jewish populations. Many more Messianic Jews identify with Christian churches—usually **evangelical** and often **charismatic**.

Messianic Jews remain strongly Jewish in their identity and lifestyle and so believe themselves to be part of **Judaism**. They believe that Yeshua fulfills Judaism, that their practice is part of the fulfillment of Jewish faith, and that through the atoning work of Yeshua they may have a personal relationship with God. Messianic Jews maintain Jewish cultural identity, continue **Torah** observance, celebrate Jewish festivals as fulfilled in Yeshua, and keep the dietary laws. They accept the Hebrew Tanak (OT) and the NT (new covenant Scriptures) as Scriptures. Beyond that, there is wide variety in practice and theology between various Messianic Jewish congregations and those whose

Christian life occurs within the traditional **church.** There is no central orga-nization, and clergy are often called rabbis, but no teacher is given privileged authority. Congregations reflect the people and gifts that compose them.

Orthodox Jews consider members of Messianic Judaism to be of another religion (Christianity). They are no longer Jews. This has repercussions for the Jewish believers themselves and for their children's identity, particularly for those in Israel. Are they Jews?

The Christian response to Messianic Judaism is more complicated. A significant part of Christian teaching through the centuries has been super-sessionist; that is, it has held that the church supersedes (replaces) Judaism as the new Israel. Christ and the church fulfill all the promises made to Abra-ham (2 Cor. 1:19-22; Eph. 1:2-14). Through the centuries this has often and improperly led to anti-Semitism and finally to the Holocaust. Much post-Holocaust Christian practice has sought to find a place for observant Jews in God's purposes. For some, this had led to reject **proselytizing** Jews to faith in Christ. Another response is Christian **Zionism,** which assigns Jews a special status as the continuing subject of unfulfilled prophecies. Supposedly, in the last days a great turn to Christ by all Jews will happen.

The distinction between the names "Christian" and "Messianic Jew" in-dicates a central disagreement. Messianic Jews say they do not cease being Jews when becoming followers of Yeshua. Faith in Yeshua as Messiah means returning to the NT (new covenant) context of Jewish and Gentile followers of Jesus as described in the book of Acts and Paul's letters before synagogue and church parted ways (second century). Becoming a Messianic Jew does not mean becoming part of the Christian church and doesn't require accept-ing the historic features of the church, such as the **ecumenical councils.**

The challenge for the "Gentile church" and Messianic congregations is to affirm as one, "There is one body and one Spirit, just as you were called to the one hope of your calling" (Eph. 4:4).

See also Christology, New Testament; Jesus of Nazareth; Judaism.

DWIGHT D. SWANSON, PHD

METAPHORS AND NAMES FOR GOD IN THE BIBLE

The Hebrew Bible in particular is rich with metaphors for **God.** From the early chapters of Genesis we see that God is characterized in anthropomor-phic terms. God creates—both by speaking (1:3) and by forming from mud (2:7); he breathes (v. 7); he plants a garden (v. 8); he performs surgery (v. 21); and he walks in his garden (3:8). These anthropomorphic ideas perme-ate the Hebrew Bible but are far more pronounced in the earlier texts.

A common metaphor for God in the Psalms is that of king (5:2; 24:7; etc.). Like a king, God is sometimes pictured as sitting on a throne (Isa. 6:1). God is a warrior; he delivers his people from bondage (Exod. 15:3).

Metaphors of protection abound. God is a fortress (2 Sam. 22:2; Ps. 31:2), a rock (Ps. 31:3), a helper (30:10), a shepherd (23:1), a shelter (91:1), and a brooding hen (v. 4).

'*Elohim* is the Hebrew term commonly used to refer to God. Technically '*elohim* is a plural form and normally refers to the God of Israel, though on occasion it refers to the gods of the nations. Occasionally the shorter form, '*el*, is used to refer to the God of **Israel**, but again this term can also refer to a Canaanite deity. The term *Yahweh* is God's personal name. Source critics suggest that the terms '*elohim* and *Yahweh* derive from two different traditions. The literature on this is extensive, and there are various schools of thought, with no consensus.

The term "Jehovah" is not an actual name for God but came about by accident. Hebrew was originally written without vowels. Vowel points were later written below the Hebrew consonants as an aid to pronunciation. Pious Jews would not pronounce God's personal name for fear of violating the commandment by using God's name in vain. They developed the practice of writing the consonants of God's personal name with the vowels of the Hebrew '*adonay*, which simply means "Lord." When they saw God's name written, they would simply say, "Lord." Later translators were not aware of this practice, so they conflated the two and created "Jehovah." Most modern English versions of the **Bible** use "Lord" when the Hebrew term is '*adonay* and the cap-and-small-cap form "Lᴏʀᴅ" (or all-cap form "LORD") when the Hebrew term is *Yahweh*.

In the NT, the dominant metaphor for God is a father. While the term "father" is hinted at in the Hebrew Bible, it is not nearly as significant there as it is in the NT, particularly on the lips of Jesus. Not only does **Jesus** make constant reference to God as "Father," but the term is also used in Jesus' prayers (Matt. 6:9-13; John 17:1-26). The early church adopted this use as one of its primary metaphors.

The Greek term *kyrios*, which is traditionally translated "lord," presents challenges for the interpreter of the NT. Sometimes it clearly refers to Yahweh of the Hebrew Bible. At other times it simply refers to the master in a master-slave relationship. Still at other times it is used as a term of polite address to one's social superior. One must be especially sensitive to the context to determine the precise meaning of this term.

See also Biblical Metaphors for Salvation.

KEITH H. REEVES, PHD

METAPHYSICS

"Metaphysics" is defined in everyday language as a comprehensive proposal for how things work. In the way we act, if not also in our language, we all presuppose that things work in particular ways and for particular reasons.

When our general ideas and experiences are critically analyzed and elaborated, explicit metaphysical thinking occurs.

The words "metaphysics" and "metaphysic" are both considered proper nouns, and the two words are identical in meaning. Using the word with or without the concluding "s" is a matter of personal preference.

The name "metaphysics" has a strange origin. Aristotle's discussion of the general features of reality came after his writing on physics. Hence, the term "metaphysics" was given for that realm of philosophy that asks about the underlying nature of everything.

The sustained endeavor to construct a metaphysics involves a rigorous attempt to offer an all-embracing hypothesis to explain the diversity of life's experiences. Because we assume some explanation exists for how things work, a rigorously constructed grand hypothesis—a metaphysics—can be profoundly helpful for assessing and addressing life's many questions.

Metaphysics investigates what it means to be, to become, and to be real. Metaphysicians have traditionally wondered which aspects of existence or features of reality are necessary and permanent. Metaphysics typically explores issues of freedom and **determinism**, the nature of time, the **philosophy of science**, and the mind-body relationship and whether things are necessary or contingent. In its broadest scope, metaphysics accounts for what we find in science and religion, including questions about God's existence.

Several criticisms have been leveled against the metaphysical enterprise. One is that metaphysics attempts the impossible: to account for everything that exists. Others criticize metaphysics for not accounting for persons at the margins, particularly those whose experience is not widely known. Still others have suggested that in its attempt to account for all reality, metaphysics inevitably acts destructively by forcing everything into a single vision.

Responses to these criticisms have been offered. Many contemporary philosophers believe the best comprehensive proposal for how things work should be empirically oriented, provisional, intentionally inclusive, speculative, and always aspiring toward greatest plausibility. Others argue that adequate metaphysics should seek factual adequacy, logical consistency, and explanatory power. While an all-encompassing explanation is likely impossible, some proposal for how things work seems better than no proposal at all.

Christian theology has traditionally been closely tied to the project of metaphysics. Early Christian theologians, such as Augustine, consciously and unconsciously drew from Neoplatonic metaphysics when formulating their understanding of Christian theology. Thomas Aquinas drew from the metaphysics of Aristotle when constructing his widely influential Christian theology. These metaphysical traditions continue to influence contemporary Roman Catholic and Protestant theologies.

In the twentieth century, the **existential** metaphysics of Martin Heidegger and the **process** metaphysics of Alfred North Whitehead greatly influenced Christian theology. Two of the most important twentieth-century Christian theologians, Paul Tillich and John B. Cobb Jr., explored metaphysical questions as they appropriated existentialism and process philosophy. These metaphysical visions continue to influence Christian theology.

An ongoing debate concerns whether metaphysics includes consideration of **God** or is altogether different from God. Some Christians believe the questions of God's person and activity have nothing to do with metaphysics, holding instead that God is *wholly other* from the categories of metaphysics.

Other Christians believe metaphysics provides general categories for talking meaningfully about the existence of anything—including God. They believe some metaphysical categories are necessary to speak meaningfully about God as acting, relating, or loving.

A particularly important and complex part of metaphysics is ontology, the study of "being itself" (Greek, *ōn, ontos* [being] and *logia, logos* [study, theory]). It is in fact the foundation of metaphysics. Ontology considers the *nature of being*, its *essence*, or the most general features of what exists or might possibly exist (possible being or existence is a type of being). It asks, "What does 'being' mean? Or what does 'to be' or 'to become' really mean, if anything at all? What, if anything, is fundamentally real, either as existing or as possibly existing?" Philosophers answer these questions in many different ways. Only after an answer has been gained can a metaphysic follow, or the effort abandoned as pointless. Only then, for example, could a metaphysic of "virtue" or "human freedom" or "human community" be developed. A related question is, "If anything were indeed fundamentally real, how might a person 'know the real'?" That question introduces the field of epistemology.

In popular culture, metaphysics refers to ghosts, sorcery, telepathy, and/or the paranormal. The popular understanding is largely different from the philosophical and theological meaning.

See also Cosmology/Cosmogony; Determinism and Free Will; Epistemology; God, Doctrine of; Greek Philosophy; Holiness; Natural Science; Natural Theology; Neoplatonism; Panentheism; Philosophical Theology; Philosophy of Religion; Postmodernity; Theodicy/Evil; Time and Eternity.

THOMAS J. OORD, PHD

METHODISM, AMERICAN

American Methodism began about 1763 when Robert Strawbridge brought Wesleyan Methodism from Ireland to Frederick County, Maryland. He started a class meeting. Methodism spread into Virginia and as far north as New Jersey and Pennsylvania. In 1766 Barbara Heck urged her cousin Philip

Embury, also an immigrant Methodist Irish lay preacher, to begin preaching again, and together they formed a society in New York City. Responding to requests for assistance, John Wesley sent two missionaries to bolster the growing Methodist movement in New York. In all, Wesley dispatched to North America eight lay preachers, including Francis Asbury. As the War of Independence approached, Wesley's missionaries, excepting Asbury, returned to England. By 1784, American Methodism had 84 itinerant preachers, many class leaders, and 14,998 members. More than three times that number attended Methodist services.

Because the American Methodists had no clergy to administer the sacraments, Wesley unsuccessfully entreated the bishop of London to ordain a Methodist ministry for America. So Wesley himself ordained Richard Whatcoat and Thomas Vasey for ministry in America and consecrated Thomas Coke, an Anglican priest, to superintend the Methodist work among the "dear Americans." Wesley directed Coke to ordain Francis Asbury and to consecrate him joint overseer. In November 1784, Coke, Whatcoat, and Vasey landed at New York City, and on December 24 they and some sixty American Methodist preachers met in Baltimore, in what became known as the Christmas Conference, to form the Methodist Episcopal Church (MEC). Coke ordained Asbury and others. Asbury, with the approval of the other preachers, was consecrated a superintendent (bishop).

From the start, the American Methodists had friendly relationships with German-speaking Christians, who in 1800, led by Philip William Otterbein and Martin Boehm, formed the Church of the United Brethren in Christ (UB). In the 1790s, in Pennsylvania, another German-speaking movement began. It was led by Jacob Albright, a recent convert who had joined a Methodist class meeting. He became a Methodist exhorter and itinerated among German-speaking Americans. In 1800 Albright organized three class meetings. In 1807 Albright's People became the Newly Formed Methodist Conference. In 1816 this movement assumed the name *Evangelische Gemeinshaft* (Evangelical Community). In 1946 at Johnstown, Pennsylvania, it united with the UB Church to form the Evangelical United Brethren Church (EUB).

Another of the early Wesleyan denominations in America was the Methodist Protestant Church. During the 1820s, a group of "reformers" led by Nicholas Snethen, William Stockton, and others campaigned for voting rights for lay preachers, an elected presiding eldership, and limited episcopal authority. Uppermost, the reformers called for a voting lay representation at Methodist conferences. To publicize their views the reformers started a publication, first called *The Wesleyan Repository* (1820) and later *The Mutual Rights and Methodist Protestant* (1824). Efforts to change the polity of the MEC were unsuccessful, and in 1830 in Baltimore these reformers founded the Methodist Protestant Church (MP).

The 1844 General Conference of the MEC experienced a division over slavery. A Southern bishop, James Osgood Andrew, inherited a slave when his wife died. Andrew's second wife had inherited slaves from her deceased husband. Because Georgia law forbade freeing slaves, Bishop Andrew renounced ownership of the slaves and legally secured them to his wife. Nonetheless the Northern delegates voted to remove him from the episcopacy. In 1845, the Methodists from the Southern states met in Louisville, Kentucky, to form the Methodist Episcopal Church, South (MECS). In 1939, in Kansas City, the MEC, the MECS, and the MP Church reunited to form the Methodist Church. Subsequently, in 1968 delegates of the Methodist Church and the EUB Church met in Dallas to unite and form the United Methodist Church.

The doctrinal standards of United Methodism consist of the early ecumenical creeds, twenty-five articles of religion, and a confession of faith. The articles of religion are John Wesley's adaption of the Thirty-Nine Articles of the Church of England. The confession of faith came from the former EUB Church. As well, the UMC looks to John Wesley's *Standard Sermons* and his *Notes Upon the New Testament* as models of doctrinal exposition. Other important guides are the *United Methodist Hymnal* and the church's General Rules, which detail three areas of behavior—doing no harm, doing good, and using the **means of grace**. The church also publishes quadrennially *The Book of Resolutions*, which contains United Methodism's social principles.

Methodism embraces **Protestant** doctrine but does not agree to deterministic predestination or a limited atonement. Rather, Methodists believe that all persons can be saved, contingent on faith in Jesus Christ as Savior. Those who receive Christ as Lord do so because God's **prevenient grace** enables them. Methodist theology also emphasizes the witness of the **Holy Spirit** and both imputed righteousness in **justification** and imparted righteousness in **sanctification**. For **John Wesley**, the essential truth of Christianity is that God's design is to restore our relationship with himself and to impart to us his moral image, which leads to the **holiness** of heart and life that Scripture requires, promises, and enables.

See also Arminian Theology; Christian Perfection (Entire Sanctification); Classes, Bands, Conference, Connectionalism, Society; Holiness Movements: American, British, and Continental; Predestination and Election; Reformed Tradition; Wesley, John, Theology of; World Methodist Council.

Resources

Kinghorn, Kenneth C. *The Heritage of American Methodism.* Lexington, KY: Emeth Press, 2009.
Norwood, Frederick. *The Story of American Methodism.* Nashville: Abingdon Press, 1974.
Richey, Russell E., Kenneth E. Rowe, and Jean Miller Schmidt, eds. *The Methodist Experience in America.* 2 vols. Nashville: Abingdon Press, 2000.

KENNETH C. KINGHORN, PHD

METHODISM, BRITISH

Methodism customarily traces its origins to a small, short-lived group at Oxford in the 1730s. In fact, its roots strike deeper in the ecclesiastical and intellectual tensions of eighteenth-century Britain: the Wesley brothers were high churchmen with **Puritan** influences. Early Methodist **societies** developed from religious societies and were initially broadly based, mostly **Calvinistic,** and within the national Church of England.

John Wesley's determined organization (opposed by his brother) of his "connexion" of societies ensured that by his death (1791) its survival and separation from the Church of England were inevitable. Multiple schisms followed as different strands sought to interpret Methodism as they understood it; the residual body (always the largest grouping) became known as "Wesleyan." Irish Methodism was (and is) independent of mainland Britain, though linked to it. It has its own history and overrides political boundaries.

The divergent strands of Methodism all shared a hybrid associational church structure embodying interdependence between national ("connexional" and conference) and local structures ("societies" within "circuits"). Most conferences elected a president annually, some of whom came to wield considerable influence. After Wesley's death the first Methodist Episcopal Church (ME) bishop, Thomas Coke (1747–1814), was a powerful figure who pioneered overseas missions. So was Adam Clarke (ca. 1760–1832), a remarkable polymath and scholar. Both might have been Wesley's obvious successors; both were forces in the polity and emerging theology of the denomination. Unlike many religious movements, Methodism was not dogmatically distinctive. Rather, it held sets of shared experiences. Thus a cult of personality evident in John Wesley remained a feature of the denominational story.

Wesley's **Arminian** and Trinitarian position became classically enunciated by Wesleyans Adam Clarke and Richard Watson (1781–1833). Denominational fault lines occurred over polity issues. The New Connexion separated in the 1790s under Alexander Kilham over lay power. The Primitive Methodists (from 1807, and the second largest grouping) headed by Hugh Bourne and William Clowes urged outdoor evangelism (as Wesley had practiced). The Bible Christians, founded by William O'Bryan and James Thorne, with an evangelical emphasis, were mostly in southwest England, although migration patterns led to a global spread. Early in the nineteenth century, power among the Wesleyans became centered in the hands of Jabez Bunting (1779–1858) and associates, leading to several smaller breakaways. The United Methodist Free Churches in 1857 under James Everett brought most of these together (although they were not strictly "connexional").

All strands developed extensive overseas missionary activities and also addressed national social problems. A distinctive Methodist identity with a conservative outlook emerged, accompanied by a social conscience and cultural prohibitions (e.g., against drink and gambling).

The twentieth century brought numerical and societal decline, although also perhaps Methodism's most influential biblical scholar, A. S. Peake (1865–1929), a Primitive Methodist. Smaller denominations united in 1907, which in turn joined Wesleyans and Primitives in the Methodist Union in 1932, though some small independent Methodist groups survive.

See also Anglicanism; Arminian Theology; Classes, Bands, Conference, Connectionalism, Society; Methodism, American; Methodist Connectionalism; Predestination and Election; Wesley, Charles, Theology of; Wesley, John, Theology of; World Methodism; World Methodist Council.

PETER S. FORSAITH, PHD

METHODIST CONNECTIONALISM

The practice of Methodist connectionalism (British, "Connexionalism") was essentially a disciplined structure of "connected fellowship" born from a conviction shared with primitive Christianity: *Unus Christianus nullus Christianus*, "One Christian, no Christian" (Robbins and Carter 1998). Aimed at remaining "connected" to the church catholic, Methodist connectionalism originated within the *koinonia* of the Methodist societies as a disciplined missionary plan to maintain uniform standards of doctrine, polity, and mission. **John Wesley** saw that by voluntarily connecting to him, the Methodists could reform the church and spread scriptural holiness throughout the land, while remaining connected to the "one holy catholic and apostolic Church" (BCP 1979, 359; Heitzenrater 1997; Robbins 1999; Robbins and Carter 1998).

The particular structures of connection were built around the episcopacy, the itinerancy, and mutual care and support. The structured practices of "connected fellowship" included conference, itinerancy (circuit preachers— lay and clergy—circulating throughout the connection of churches), class meetings, a hymnal with songs of fellowship, and bands of mutual care and support. Such structured practices were designed to practice unity in love.

The theology of Methodist connectionalism is easily mapped in the connections between Wesley's doctrine of God, church, salvation, and new creation. When the whole **Trinity** descends and pours triune love into our hearts, Christians are "connected" in God's fellowship and mission. The **church** is the new way the triune God gathers and sends the people of God into the world in the "connected fellowship" of God's mission. This was the "means" by which Methodists lived in the "hope of glory."

The promise of Methodist connectionalism is discoverable in the living contagion of *koinonia* that is the church. Many have claimed Methodist connectionalism is one of the best gifts Wesley and the Methodists gave the church catholic (Beck 1991; Rigg 1852; Robbins and Carter 1998). Methodism's structured practices of connected fellowship marked the real "Character of a Methodist" (cf. Wesley, *Works*, 8:340-47) and continue to offer a way forward in unity. The Methodists knew that only as connected to the church catholic could they be united in love as the "one holy catholic and apostolic Church" (BCP 1979, 359).

See also Church (Ecclesiology); Early Church; Ecumenism; Methodism, British; Ordinary and Extraordinary Ministries of the Church; Wesley, John, Theology of.

Resources

BCP (Book of Common Prayer). New York: Church Hymnal Corporation, 1979. http://justus.anglican.org/resources/bcp/formatted_1979.htm.

Beck, Brian E. "Some Reflections on Connexionalism." *Epworth Review* 18, no. 2 (May 1991): 48-59 and no. 3 (September 1991): 43-50.

Campbell, Dennis M., Russell E. Richey, and William B. Lawrence. *Connectionalism: Ecclesiology, Mission, and Identity*. Nashville: Abingdon Press, 1997.

Heitzenrater, Richard P. "Connectionalism and Itinerancy: Wesleyan Principles and Practice." In vol. 1, *Connectionalism: Ecclesiology Mission and Identity*, edited by Dennis M. Campbell, William B. Lawrence, and Russell E. Richey, 23-38. Nashville: Abingdon Press, 1997.

Rigg, J. H. *The Connexional Economy of Wesleyan Methodism*. London, 1852.

Robbins, Bruce. "Connection and Koinonia: Wesleyan and Ecumenical Perspectives on the Church." In vol. 3, *Doctrines and Discipline*, edited by Dennis M. Campbell, William B. Lawrence, and Russell E. Richey, 199-212. Nashville: Abingdon Press, 1999.

Robbins, Bruce, and David Carter. "Connexionalism and Koinonia: A Wesleyan Contribution to Ecclesiology." *One in Christ* 34, no. 4 (1998): 320-36.

K. STEVE MCCORMICK, PHD

METHODIST HISTORY AND HISTORIOGRAPHY

Christian scriptures and early Christian communities continued the Jewish use of historical narrative to describe "God's deeds of power" (Acts 2:11*b*). Similarly, **John Wesley** kept detailed personal diaries and used them to write *The Journal of the Reverend John Wesley, A.M.*, a serial publication beginning in the late 1730s and continuing throughout his life. The *Journal* set a precedent for using narrative in Wesleyan communities and for explaining the Methodist mission, its providential origins, and its distinctive teachings and practices. Wesley also wrote brief narratives incorporated into the minutes of early Methodist conferences and some longer historical narratives of the Methodist movement.

Immediately after Wesley's death (1791), responding to a biography by a disaffected Methodist preacher (John Hampson), Thomas Coke and Henry Moore published a biography of Wesley (1792), as did John Whitehead (1792-1793). They disagreed widely in interpreting Wesley's life and work.

Early American Methodist books of discipline began with historical statements that stressed the providential conjunction between Methodist institutions and the needs of the American continent. Similarly, early American Methodist narratives, including Jesse Lee's *Short History of Methodism* (1810) and Nathan Bangs's *History of the Methodist Episcopal Church* (1839), focused on Methodism's providential rise in North America and its distinctive institutions and practices. American Methodists who opposed the episcopal polity of the Methodist Episcopal Church also appealed to the historical narrative of Wesleyan origins. Alexander McCaine's *The History and Mystery of Methodist Episcopacy* (1827) is an illustration. By the mid-nineteenth century, the Wesleyan narrative was again contested because of controversies between **holiness** leaders and others in Methodist churches.

By the late nineteenth century scientific approaches to historical study began to influence interpretation of the Wesleyan and Methodist narrative. James Buckley's *History of Methodists in the United States* (1896) did not ascribe Methodist developments directly to divine providence but typically used quoted words of Methodist leaders to suggest such connections. William Warren Sweet's study of *Methodism in American History* (1933) argued that the Methodist use of itinerant preaching was particularly appropriate to the westward movement of the American frontier.

Evolving social-scientific theories in the early twentieth century produced new interpretations of the Wesleyan narrative, often by interpreters outside traditional Methodist or Christian cultures. French social historian Élie Halévy's article "The Birth of Methodism in England" (1906) argued that Methodism supported political stability by repressing revolutionary tendencies. G. Elsie Harrison's *Son to Susanna* (1937) employed a Freudian analysis. She saw in Wesley an oedipal attachment to his mother that inhibited subsequent relationships with women. Halévy's trajectory was followed by E. P. Thompson's *The Making of the English Working Class* (1963). It used a Marxist historical perspective to assess the Methodist movement in the eighteenth and early nineteenth centuries; supposedly Methodism was socially and politically repressive.

The historiography of the Wesleyan movement since the middle of the twentieth century has followed numerous trajectories: (1) responding to the social and political issues raised by Halévy, Thompson, and others, it defended the positive accomplishments of Methodism on behalf of the working class (Bernard Semmel) or claimed the movement had theological underpinnings that supported liberative movements (Theodore Runyon, Theodore Jennings, M. Douglas Meeks, José Miguez Bonino); (2) another trajectory follows from ecumenical insights and interprets the Wesleyan movement in light of the broader Christian community (Frank Baker, Colin W. Williams, Albert C. Outler); (3) a third trajectory, prominent since the 1980s, interprets Methodist culture as a precedent for subsequent evangelical movements, including the **holiness movement** and **Pentecostalism** (D. W. Bebbington, John H. Wigger, David Hempton).

See also Historical Theology; Wesley, John, Theology of; World Methodism; World Methodist Council.

TED A. CAMPBELL, PHD

MILLENNIUM DEVELOPMENT GOALS (MDGS)

Eight Millennium Development Goals (MDGs) were identified at the September 2000 United Nations meeting of heads of government from around the world. The goals, which reflect concerns of global import, include (1) eradicating extreme **poverty** (those living on less than one US dollar per day) and hunger, with a target of halving the number of people who fall within this definition; (2) achieving universal primary education for girls and boys; (3) promoting gender equality and empowering women; (4) reducing child mortality, with the specific target of lowering the mortality of under-fives by two-thirds; (5) improving maternal health, as measured by lowering maternal death rates by three-quarters; (6) containing the spread of HIV/AIDS, malaria, and other major diseases; (7) committing to environmental care and sustainability, which requires revised or newly implemented environmentally friendly policies, reversing resource degradation and loss, measurable improvement in the lives of at least one hundred million slum dwellers and halving the proportion of people without access to potable water and basic sanitation; and (8) developing a global partnership for development that anticipates a reliable and equable system of trade and finance, debt relief for the world's most heavily indebted countries, cultivating legitimate and enduring employment opportunities for youth, access to affordable pharmaceuticals, and access to new technologies.

Along with the goals came a list of targeted outcomes and a global deadline to be achieved by 2015.

World leaders announced these goals publicly to affirm collective responsibility for the well-being of the planet and its inhabitants—human and nonhuman—because the effects of **globalization** have created a new level of interconnection and interdependence. They acknowledged the need for a universal commitment to the future of humanity, with particular efforts to be made on behalf of the most vulnerable, this in light of increasingly disparate circumstances among the peoples of the world.

Among the hopes that inspired the MDGs are these: (1) universal freedom from hunger, violence, and oppression; (2) opportunities for all people, as individuals and nations, to participate in the benefits of development; (3) the responsibility to share the costs and consequences of global circumstances equitably and justly; (4) a concerted effort to protect the environment by employing sustainable methods of development; and (5) the multilateral management of global efforts and concerns. Africa's special needs were highlighted, along with pledges of support for the continent as it seeks to become an equal partner in global affairs.

Interim gatherings in 2005 and 2008 have allowed progress to be reported and new commitments and strategies to be developed. The 2010 summit had the additional mandate of assessing the effects of the global economic crisis on MDG achievement. As of mid-2010, significant progress had been reported in some areas, although the results vary from goal to goal, and within specific targets. It is increasingly clear that some goals and targets will not be reached by 2015, unless urgent and intense action is taken.

See also Creation, Care for the (Ecology); Economics and the Use of Money; Globalization; Poverty; Rights, Human.

Resources
United Nations. http://www.un.org/millenniumgoals (United Nations website, with links to related documents and data sources).
World Bank. http://web.worldbank.org (World Bank website, with documents and data related to MDGs).

MARY LOU SHEA, THD

MIND OF CHRIST, THE
See DISCERNMENT.

MINJUNG THEOLOGY
See ASIAN THEOLOGY.

MIRACLES/SIGNS AND WONDERS

The phrase "signs and wonders" appears in Christian **Scripture** more than thirty times. It is first used in connection with the plagues of Exodus (Exod. 7:3) and last in Heb. 2:4, which claims **God** used signs and wonders to authenticate the early **church**'s proclamation of the **gospel** (here "miracles" are added to the phrase). The phrase appears in several key NT texts. Peter, for example, uses it in his sermon on the day of Pentecost (Acts 2:22), as does Paul in Rom. 15:19.

Sometimes, as in Ps. 135:9, Scripture says God "sent" signs and wonders without human mediation. At other times, as in Acts 6:8, signs and wonders are performed through human agency.

Appearing about equally often in the two testaments, "signs and wonders" point to miraculous interventions God enacted. In Deut. 4:34-35 God says his distinguishing "signs and wonders," including "terrifying displays of power," make clear "that the LORD is God; there is no other besides him."

However, Matt. 24:24 and 2 Thess. 2:9 tell us that not all signs and wonders come from God.

"Signs and wonders" herald God's sovereignty, including his power to create and redeem, and the ascendency of the heavenly **kingdom** in its conflict with satanic forces (Mark 5:1-20; Luke 8:22-25). Jesus' miracles announce the arrival of the kingdom of God in his person (Matt. 12:28). On the day of Pentecost, Peter tells his listeners that God used deeds of power, wonders, and signs to "attest" that God has made Jesus of Nazareth "both Lord and Messiah" (Acts 2:22-36). In Romans and in 2 Cor. 12:12, Paul writes that "signs and wonders" validated his own apostolic ministry.

In the 1980s "signs and wonders" became a popular phrase in charismatic circles. John Wimber and others taught that signs and wonders are the principal means for making new disciples. Unverified anecdotes of signs and wonders surfaced as the gospel reached various people groups. Wimber said that if evangelists and missionaries want to evangelize in a truly biblical way, they must perform or do signs and wonders. Critics, on the other hand, said framing signs and wonders in that way reduces God's miraculous deeds to a utility under human control. Supporters were accused of sensationalism, while critics were charged with ethnocentricity; if signs and wonders were not happening in the critics' ministries, then they could not be happening in other cultures. Wimber and his supporters have charged their critics with worshipping at the feet of rationalism.

Clearly, signs and wonders have been important in the life of God's people from the beginning. But they are only one way God manifests his glory and interacts with his people. How they are assessed must be guided by Jesus' warnings against an "adulterous generation" lusting for signs (Matt. 12:39; 16:4), instead of seeking him as the "bread of heaven" (John 6:25-40). Signs and wonders have to do with God's sovereignty in history and his witness to Jesus Christ, not with self-serving exhibitionism and coercing or dazzling persons into believing Jesus is the Christ. The church must be careful to frame miracles, signs, and wonders in a way that leads to trust in Jesus—the revelation of God's glory. Signs and wonders have nothing to do with inflating the self-appointed importance of human wonder-workers.

See also Charismatic Theology; Deliverance/Exorcism; Pentecostal Theology; Principalities and Powers.

HOWARD CULBERTSON, DMIN

MISSION, THEOLOGY OF

Theology of mission is a critical reflection on the assumptions, nature, and practice of mission. Strictly speaking, theology of mission is part of the discipline of *missiology*, the study and practice of Christian mission. In another sense, however, mission theology permeates all theological disciplines. This shows a growing recognition that "all theology is intrinsically missiological since it concerns the God of mission and the mission of God" (Corrie 2007, xv).

Thinking theologically about mission can be traced to the NT. But not until the late nineteenth century was missiology formally established as part of the theological curriculum. Since then, the issue of how to define mission has sparked vigorous debate.

Although mission has been diversely understood, a growing consensus is that the *missio Dei* (mission of God) is central to a theology of mission. Inspired by the theology of Karl Barth, Karl Hartenstein introduced consideration of the *missio Dei* to mission discourse in the mid-twentieth century. A *missio Dei* theology emphasizes that the God of Scripture is a missionary God. Mission flows out of the boundless love of the triune God, whose purpose is to restore all of creation, in particular, people created in God's image. The cosmic sweep of the *missio Dei* implies that mission is holistic, embracing such matters as **evangelism**, **social** and economic **justice**, care for **creation**, and compassion for the needy. God's mission is expressed supremely in sending Jesus Christ into the world in the power of the Spirit to achieve **salvation** in every dimension.

What is the role of the **church** in the *missio Dei*? Church-centered theologies of mission have focused on missions as *an activity of the church*, often in building God's kingdom through planting and growing churches. By contrast, a God-centered approach says *the church participates in* God's mission (John 17:18; 20:21) and bears witness to God's kingdom. The church not only *has* a mission but *is* essentially missionary. The church is at the heart of God's missional purpose for the world.

An adequate theology of mission is shaped by a variety of resources, including Scripture, theological and missiological tradition, the specific context of mission, and the experience of those engaged in God's mission. As the foundational source, Scripture is more than a mine for "missionary texts." The entire biblical narrative witnesses to the mission of God and equips the church for mission. At the same time, any theology of mission must be contextually appropriate. Resources drawn from the **social sciences** and comparative religions help the church understand the local context in which it engages in mission theology.

The shift of Christianity's center of gravity toward the **Global South** means that mission theology is no longer done primarily *by* Westerners *for* Christians in the majority world. Rather, the mission field is everywhere; mission is multidirectional. Missiologists such as Lesslie Newbigin have shown the need to treat postmodern Western culture as a missionary context. Churches in all settings are responsible for developing a contextualized mission theology.

Furthermore, a contemporary theology of mission must reflect on the nature of Christian witness in a religiously plural world. A Wesleyan understanding of **prevenient grace** affirms that God is present and working in all human arenas, actively drawing to Christ persons in all cultures and religions.

Finally, a theology of mission must be wedded to mission *praxis*. It needs to critically reflect on the church's mission practice and must lead to participation in God's mission. The goal of mission theology and practice is the transformation of communities of disciples into the full character of Christ.

See also Church (Ecclesiology); Contextualization; Contextual Theology; Holistic Mission; Interfaith Dialogue; Mission and Theological Education; Religions, Theology of.

Resources

Bosch, David J. *Transforming Mission: Paradigm Shifts in Theology of Mission.* Maryknoll, NY: Orbis Books, 1991.

Corrie, John, ed. *Dictionary of Mission Theology: Evangelical Foundations.* Downers Grove, IL: InterVarsity Press, 2007.

Tennent, Timothy. *Invitation to World Missions: A Trinitarian Missiology for the Twenty-first Century.* Grand Rapids: Kregel Publications, 2010.

DEAN FLEMMING, PHD

MISSION AND SOCIAL JUSTICE

The term "mission and social justice" introduces the relationship between the gospel of Jesus Christ and social transformation that promotes social justice. It also introduces the role of missionaries in social transformation.

Many believe preaching the good news of the gospel includes not only offering personal salvation but also changing the social conditions that breed human deprivation and oppose the kingdom of God. They say mission and social justice are two sides of the same coin. The union of mission and social justice is viewed as an affirmation of the dignity of all persons guaranteed by the gospel.

To support their position, advocates of this relationship rely on prophets such as Amos, Micah, and Isaiah who preached that God will not permit love for him to be separated from love of mercy and justice. "What does the LORD require of you but to do justice, and to love kindness, and to walk humbly with your God?" (Mic. 6:8). Proponents believe Jesus fortified the union of mission and social justice in the "Nazareth Manifesto," his first public sermon as recorded by Luke. Jesus declared God's love for and commitment to those who are exploited, oppressed, and enslaved (Luke 4:18-19; Isa. 61:1-2). God unquestionably expresses his solidarity with the poor (2 Cor. 8:9; Prov. 19:17; Matt. 25:31-46; James 2:1-7). Social injustice is just as much a rejection of God as it is of persons. And loving mercy and doing justice is done to God as much as it is to humans. Jesus made this clear in the gospel of Matthew. When expressing love in action for those who are oppressed, the church in mission meets Jesus himself. "Just as you did it to one of the least of these who are members of my family, you did it to me" (Matt. 25:40; see also 5:42; 25:31-46; Luke 4:18).

The gospel of Jesus Christ requires that mission and social justice be joined. This means evaluating and working to change the root causes of injustice that drive persons into poverty and various forms of oppression. It requires identification of social systems such as caste, color, and creed that by their nature reduce many persons to poverty and its many attending ills. Abuse of political and economic power that engenders injustice must also be exposed. John Wesley did this in "Thoughts Upon Slavery" (1774, *Works*, 11:59-79). His analysis is a "plain, unaggravated matter of fact" (70) description of the causes and nature of chattel slavery. Wesley attacked "the root of this complicated villany" and denied that slavery can be made "consistent with any degree of natural justice" (70).

The **early church** evidenced its recognition of the relationship between mission and social justice as a sign of new community being formed by Jesus (Acts 2:44-45). It begins with being transformed by Christ (2 Cor. 5:15) and empowered by him.

From its beginning, the Wesleyan tradition connected mission and social justice. John and Charles Wesley and the early Methodists promoted prison reform, the abolition of slavery, education of the poor, medical care, and loans for cottage industries. They opposed laws and industries that privileged the powerful at the expense of the poor.

See also Christian Ethics/Moral Theology; Contextualization; Holistic Mission; Justice; Kingdom of God; Latino/Latina (Hispanic) Theology; Liberation Theology; Poverty; Rights, Human; Salvation (Soteriology); Shalom; Social Justice; Wesleyan Feminism.

Resource
Basappa, Joseph. "Towards a Theology of Universality: John Wesley's Theological Response to Class Distinctions with a Special Reference to Slavery and Its Relevance to Caste Distinctions." PhD thesis, University of Manchester (Nazarene Theological College), 1999.

JOSEPH SURAY, PHD

MISSION AND THEOLOGICAL EDUCATION

Before the beginning of the nineteenth century, little attention was given to the formal study of mission and mission theology. The early nineteenth-century Protestant and Catholic "awakening to world mission" forms the historical background for the beginning of mission studies. The formal study of mission received the name "missiology."

However, until recently, formal theological education usually treated mission as a separate area of study in the curriculum. Mission was not seen as essential to the church's constitution, and so was not broadly integrated into the theological curriculum. Mission was usually treated as a practical theological discipline distinct from biblical studies, church history, and systematic theology.

Recently, the traditional paradigm has shifted as foundational questions about the bases and priorities of theological education have surfaced. Biblical, historical, and systematic theologians are coming to agree that mission lies at the heart of the church's constitution and hence its whole theological enterprise. Therefore, mission must be placed at the heart of theological education.

Consequently, among churches that see themselves as mission formed, mission is no longer studied as one theological topic among others. A mission-minded orientation for theological education has come to the fore. Mission-formed churches believe that a theology of mission must be integrated into all theological disciplines, including biblical, historical, and systematic theology. At the same time, distinct mission studies make contributions to the whole theological curriculum, as well as to the church's wider theological tasks.

A mission-minded orientation for theological education is a signal development. A formally considered mission orientation and purpose must inform the church's proclamation of the gospel, its commitment to reconciliation, global peace and justice, and economic and social sustainability.

"Mission and theological education" refers also to recent innovative forms of and goals for theological education for mission. An example of *new forms* is a major development called theological education by extension. Piloted in 1963 by the Presbyterian Seminary of Guatemala, it spread rapidly to all parts of the world. Theological education by extension is usually based in residential centers for theological education. It attempts an indigenization of theological education. Most of the students are pastors, many of whom have no prior formal theological education. An example of *new goals* can be observed in China. Churches are emphasizing the role of theological education in training Christian leaders to work alongside government and other social agencies to promote social well-being.

Never before has theological education received such conceptual, pedagogical, and monetary support.

See also Contextualization; Contextual Theology; Holistic Mission; Indigenization; Indigenous Theologies; Mission, Theology of; Mission and Social Justice.

Resources

Roozen, David A., Alice Frazer Evans, and Robert A. Evans, eds. *The Globalization of Theological Education*. Maryknoll, NY: Orbis Books, 1993.

Stackhouse, Max L. *Apologia: Contextualization, Globalization, and Mission in Theological Education.* Grand Rapids: Eerdmans, 1988.

WILLIAM T. YOUNG, PHD

MISSIONARY MOVEMENTS

A missionary movement is an effort by members of one religion to extend it to, and make converts among, other people groups. There are numerous missionary religions. A Christian missionary movement proclaims the **gospel** of **Jesus Christ** to other people groups. Missionary movements are generally most dramatic when they extend across cultural and language barriers.

Missiologist Paul Pierson observes that Christian missionary movements "always seem to arise on the periphery of the churchly structures" and often involve theological breakthroughs marked by discovering or rediscovering unrealized or forgotten dimensions of the Christian faith (Pierson 2009). William Carey, often referred to as the father of modern missions, came to the realization that the "heathen" were really lost without Christ and that Christians in Europe were to take the gospel to them. This was not a new idea but one forgotten by the church in England in the late nineteenth century.

Acts 8:1 records the first missionary movement. It originated in Jerusalem and was prompted by the persecution of the church. Importantly, the apostles did not conduct the first missionary activity. Instead, "all except the apostles were scattered throughout the countryside of Judea and Samaria." Those who were not primary leaders moved out of the city, taking the good news of the kingdom of God with them. Acts 11:19 reports the gospel was heard in "Phoenicia, Cyprus, and Antioch," with the result that "a great number became believers" (v. 21). This was not propelled by an organized church structure sending missionaries. Instead, Christians proclaimed the gospel as they moved into new regions.

Among **Roman Catholics**, the Jesuits, Dominicans, and Franciscans were all missionary movements, even before being given papal permission to exist. Each started on the periphery of Roman Catholicism and originated following renewed spiritual discipline and religious discovery. This was also true of the **Protestant** missionary movements spawned by William Carey and J. Hudson Taylor. They originated on the periphery of organized church structures amid renewal of the church. The so-called haystack prayer meeting (1806) at Williams College, Williamstown, Massachusetts, was instrumental in forming the first North American mission board. Not only was a missionary board established, but its roots also gave birth to the Student Volunteer Movement of 1886. Students challenging other students led to 2,106 students volunteering for mission work and the formal organization of the movement in 1888. Leaders of each of these missionary movements recognized a need to move beyond existing church structures and fulfill God's call to mission service.

From their beginning, churches of the Wesleyan-holiness tradition, with their emphasis on the power and work of the Holy Spirit, sponsored missionary enterprises. The **Church of God** (Anderson, Indiana), for example, began in the early 1880s. However, mission activity did not begin because the Church of God reformation movement's primary leadership decided it would be a good thing but because they believed God called people to speak up and reach out to the world around them. Missionaries went almost immediately to Mexico, England, Germany, India, and China. There were so many that by the early twentieth century the Church of God recognized the need to organize its missionary travel and cross-cultural outreach. Accordingly, in 1910 it established the Missionary Board of the Church of God.

In addition to mission movements from the West, such as Pioneers (1982), Campus Crusade for Christ (1957), and Youth with a Mission (1960), **indigenous Christian** movements have also spawned missionaries who move across cultural barriers: the Friends Missionary Prayer Band of India, the Evangelical Missionary Society of Nigeria, and the growing tent-maker missionaries to the Middle East from Ethiopia and the Philippines. There have also been a large number of Korean missionaries birthed out of the great revivals in Seoul, as well as many missionaries emerging from the house churches of China as part of the Back to Jerusalem Movement.

Christian mission movements continue to rise today in the most unexpected places. **Messianic Jews** and Messianic Muslims are sending missionaries. Rarely do these begin as organized structures; instead, they organize *after* the movement has begun. Most often they occur as individuals and small groups respond to Christian renewal and to God's call to proclaim the gospel to "all tribes and peoples and languages" (Rev. 7:9).

See also Evangelism; Globalization; Global South; Mission, Theology of; Postcolonialism; Proselytism; Religions, Theology of; Tentmakers; World Missionary Conference, Edinburgh 1910.

Resources

Pierson, Paul. *The Dynamics of Christian Mission: History Through a Missiological Perspective.* Pasadena, CA: William Carey International University Press, 2009.
Winter, Ralph D., and Steven C. Hawthorne, eds. *Perspectives on the World Christian Movement: A Reader.* 4th ed. Pasadena, CA: William Carey Library, 2009.

MARYANN HAWKINS, PHD

MODERNITY

Modernity is a period in the history of philosophy and a description of industrial societies in the past two hundred plus years. As a philosophical period, modernity begins with René Descartes (1596–1650) or Francis Bacon

(1561–1626). Modern philosophers, especially Enlightenment philosophers, thought of themselves as moderns in contrast to medieval philosophers and theologians. As describing industrial society, modernity designates how ideas characteristic of modern philosophy eventually became integrated into the social fabric.

Modernity encompasses several intellectual commitments. Preeminently, it champions the power of reason. This confidence is evidenced in the accomplishments of **natural science** and the use of **technology**. Success of scientific explanations and the results of technology have, for many, confirmed reason's capacity to discover truth and solve problems. Modernity is thus often linked to rationalism.

Correspondingly, modern thinkers sometimes contrast reason's power with religious faith. For them, faith is belief supported merely by authority, while reason is knowledge based on evidence and logic. When seen this way, confidence in reason asserts the principle of autonomy, that is, freedom from illegitimate and oppressive authority.

Modernity's emphasis on freedom expresses itself in political theory. Its classic expression is the theory of social contract: political power arises from the people. Social contract contrasts with premodern views in which God bestows political power on monarchs. By contrast, for modernity individuals who agree to create various sorts of communities compose political society. Modernity also gave us the secular state where church and state are strictly separated. This contrasts with the premodern ideal of national and established churches.

Modernity has been thoroughly critiqued. In the nineteenth century the romantic movement and philosophers such as Friedrich Nietzsche (1844–1900) objected to how modernity exalted reason. Nietzsche proposed that feeling and instinct are more fundamental than reason. Martin Heidegger (1889–1976) criticized modernity more broadly. He argued that modernity's emphasis on reason, science, and technology resulted in alienating moderns from the natural world. This, he maintained, was the inevitable outcome of philosophical impulses stretching back to Plato and Aristotle. More recently, the movement known as deconstruction has exposed the totalitarian implications of modernity's exaltation of reason; modernity tended to value identity (sameness) over difference (diversity) in the realm of ideas and society.

Theologians have also critiqued modernity. In the eighteenth century many theologians, including John Wesley, objected to how some modern philosophers contrasted reason and faith. In the nineteenth century the **Roman Catholic Church** reacted to modernity's elevation of reason over authority by declaring papal infallibility (1870) and condemning in the *Syllabus of Errors* (1864) many beliefs typical of modern thought. In the twentieth century, theological **fundamentalism** reacted to modernity by rejecting its confidence in reason and in leading theories of natural science. Recent movements such as **postliberal** theology and **radical orthodoxy** have also sharply critiqued modern philosophy and theology.

Extensive critiques of modernity have led some to conclude that we have moved beyond modernity to **postmodernity**. More likely, postmodernism—at least in its philosophical versions—is more a development of modernism than its repudiation.

See also Enlightenment; Evolution/Evolutionary Biology; Logical Positivism; Religious Pluralism; Secular/Secularism/Secularization; Technology.

SAMUEL M. POWELL, PHD

MONASTICISM

Monasticism is a religious movement of people who withdraw from standard patterns of public life and certain pleasures and commit themselves to more concentrated spiritual growth in pursuit of the highest attainable goal in a particular religion. The twofold movement of separation and concentration is evidenced in the most common monastic activities: asceticism and prayer or meditation. Monasticism has an individualistic or eremitic (from Greek, *erēmia*, "desert," from *erēmos*, "uninhabited") expression. Such monks are anchorites (from Greek, *anachōreō*, "to separate oneself"). A second form is cenobitic (from Greek, *koinobios*, "living in a community").

Buddhism is well known for its monastic tradition and has received much attention in the media because of Zen Buddhism or persons such as the Dalai Lama. Monastic movements are also present in Jainism, Taoism, and Islam but are almost absent in Judaism.

Within Christianity, the monastic movement emerged in the late third century, when ascetics moved into the Egyptian desert to devote themselves to prayer and spiritual warfare. Anthony (d. 356) was the most influential monk, due to Athanasius's biography of him. Pachomius (d. 346), originally more anchoritic, stimulated the cenobitic form of monasticism. He introduced a standard rule, set hours of prayer, and established the authority of an abbot over the monks. Pachomius also established separate monasteries for males and females. Monasteries became places where the ideals of Christian community were practiced.

In the **Orthodox Church**, Basil of Caesarea (d. 379) was the strongest influence for cenobitic monasticism, but anchoritic influences never died out. The famous monastic island Mount Athos in Greece, established in 961, has always represented both kinds of monasticism. Social and cultural activities have never characterized Eastern monasticism; it has always been highly focused on contemplation. Unlike the Western church, Eastern monasticism is not differentiated by orders. Eastern monks were respected as spiritual fathers—very often more so than the official church leaders. This respect is reflected in the importance of starets (elders in Russian Orthodox monasteries) in Russian culture.

Western monasticism emerged in the fourth century with Jerome (d. 420) as one of its influential figures. As the Western Roman Empire collapsed, the monasteries became the centers of learning, preserving many cultural treasures. Monasticism became more closely connected with the official church and contributed to a transfer of certain monastic ideals such as celibacy to the official clergy. Western monasticism has also been more involved in the missionary and social activities of the church than in the East.

The rule of Benedict of Nursia (d. ca. 547) provided the organizational structure for Western monasticism. His rule is moderate and fosters community as well as a balance between prayer and work (*ora et labora*). The history of monasticism contains a variety of different orders and congregations such as the Dominicans, the Franciscans, and the Jesuits. Orders have exercised major influence in different areas of the church such as theology (**Thomas Aquinas** [1225-74]), mission (Francis Xavier [1506-52]), and social work (Mother Teresa [1910-97]).

The **Reformation** assessed monasticism as works righteousness and closed the monasteries. However, the monastic ideals of discipleship and holiness came to be expected of all church members. Since the twentieth century, a reevaluation of monasticism can be detected among **Protestants**.

See also Asceticism; Contemplative Spirituality; Desert Fathers and Mothers; Obedience; Prayer; Self-Denial; Spiritual Direction/Spiritual Director; Spiritual Disciplines; Virtues; Works of Mercy; Works of Piety.

Resources
Dunn, Marilyn. *Emergence of Monasticism: From the Desert Fathers to the Early Middle Ages.* Malden, MA: Blackwell Publishers, 2003.
Wilson-Hartgrove, Jonathan. *New Monasticism: What It Has to Say to Today's Church.* Grand Rapids: Brazos Press, 2008.

ANTONIE HOLLEMAN, DRS

MONISM, DUALISM, PLURALISM

These philosophical terms refer to theories about the nature of reality (ontology or **metaphysics**) and have implications for **epistemology** and **ethics**.

1. *Monism* is the belief that all reality is composed of one substance viewed either as material or immaterial (mind or spirit). Some of the earliest forms of philosophy (pre-Socratic) were monistic. Thales identified the one substance as water, which takes different forms such as liquid, solid, or gas. Heraclitus identified the one reality as fire. Democritus said reality was composed of atoms in motion; the collision of atoms moving about in space explained all things.

Monism can also be interpreted in more complex ways such as the dialectical materialism of Karl Marx, where economic factors constitute what is real. Ideas are epiphenomena of the economic substructure, having no independent existence of their own.

The classic expression of monism is the philosophy of Baruch Spinoza, who identified everything with God—the one reality.

2. *Dualism* holds that reality is composed of two substances. The classic form of dualism occurs in the mind-body dualism of French philosopher René Descartes. Based on his method of doubt, he concluded that he could not successfully doubt the existence of himself as a thinking substance. Since we know a substance by its attributes, and we clearly and distinctly know two quite different attributes (thought and extension), there must be two different substances. Thus Descartes divided reality into "extended substance" and "thinking substance." The former is the subject of science and is characterized by **determinism**, or cause and effect. The latter, thinking substance, is the locus of freedom. The major problem Descartes faced was how to explain the relation between mind and body.

3. *Pluralism* implies that reality is composed of multiple substances. An early materialistic form of pluralism is found in the thinking of the philosopher Empedocles. He argued that everything is composed of some combination of earth, air, fire, and water. Each element had been proposed by his predecessors as the primary stuff. John Wesley followed Empedocles in this theory about the physical universe, while at the same time believing in the real but nonmaterial existence of the soul, thus holding a kind of dualism. G. W. Leibniz, a pluralist, reacted to Spinoza's monism as blurring the distinction between God, man, and nature; he affirmed the existence of multiple substances called monads.

Pluralism is also used in a nonmetaphysical sense to assert that all varieties of belief are equally valid. In religion this means that no one religion can claim an exclusive right to the truth; all religions have equal significance.

See also Epistemology; Greek Philosophy; Panentheism; Pantheism; Religions, Theology of; Religious Pluralism.

H. RAY DUNNING, PHD

MORAL THEOLOGY
See CHRISTIAN ETHICS.

MORAVIANS

The Moravians (or Unitas Fratrum) are an **evangelical** church that began in Bohemia and Moravia (in the present Czech Republic), with roots in the work and teachings of Jan Hus (d. 1415) and **Pietism**. In 1722, refugees from Moravia and Bohemia began to arrive on the lands of Count Nikolaus Ludwig von Zinzendorf in Saxony (Germany). There they built the settlement of Herrnhut. From that base the Moravians launched their **missionary** and **ecumenical** work. Mid-eighteenth-century settlements in the North American colonies included Pennsylvania, New Jersey, Maryland, and North Carolina.

John Wesley first encountered Moravian missionaries as he traveled to Georgia. Wesley was impressed with their **faith**, primitive simplicity, and claims to apostolic succession. Wesley studied German to better converse with them and, in Georgia, lived with them and actively participated in their worship, fellowship, and religious conversions. A Moravian missionary named Augustus Spangenberg served as a **spiritual director** to Wesley. They particularly discussed the nature of saving faith. Wesley came to see faith as a perceptible experience and an instantaneous work of God, wrought by grace alone.

On his return to England, Wesley maintained contact with the Moravians and met the missionary Peter Böhler. Following upon the spiritual direction of Spangenberg and Böhler, Wesley famously experienced the "heartwarming" of personal assurance of salvation at a society meeting on Aldersgate Street (May 1738). Not long after, Wesley traveled to Herrnhut. On his return to England Wesley became involved in a Moravian-**Anglican** society that met in London's Fetter Lane. Despite the Moravians' clear influence on him, Wesley always seems to have had reservations. In 1740 Wesley split from the Fetter Lane Society over differences regarding the **means of grace** and the need for growth in grace.

Moravian influence on Wesley helped shape his understanding of saving faith, assurance, and the order of **salvation**. The Moravians also provided models Wesley used to structure his Methodist **societies**. There is a tendency to overlook the Moravian influences on Wesley because he separated from them and suppressed their influence in his historical accounts. Determining the extent of Moravian influence is made more difficult when other and similar influences are considered (**Anglican, Counter-Reformation**, Pietist, **Puritan**). The Moravians' clearest influence on Wesley was as a catalyst for his personal spiritual development, pressing him to read further about assurance and faith and conditioning his thought as he encountered Puritan practical divinity and the Anglican homilies.

See also Classes, Bands, Conference, Connectionalism, Society; Means of Grace; Pietism; Wesley, John, Theology of; Witness of the Spirit.

Resources

Hutton, J. E. *A History of the Moravian Church*. Charleston, SC: BiblioBazaar, 2006.

Lewis, A. J. *Zinzendorf, the Ecumenical Pioneer: A Study in the Moravian Contribution to Christian Mission and Unity*. Philadelphia: Westminster Press, 1962.

KARL GANSKE, PHD

MUJERISTA THEOLOGY

Mujerista theology is a form of **liberation theology** that has as its goal liberating Latinas in the United States. The term "mujerista" comes from the Spanish word *mujer* and means "woman." Mujerista theology was developed by a group of Hispanic theologians and pastoral workers during the 1980s. Its main proponent was the Cuban-born theologian Ada María Isasi-Díaz (1943–2012). As a liberative praxis (enacted or practiced), mujerista theology analyzes how oppressive forces in society such as ethnic prejudice, racism, exploitation, and systemic violence prevent Latinas from becoming full persons in charge of their own destiny.

The most distinctive feature of mujerista theology is its use of Latina women's **experience** of oppression as its main source. Unlike traditional theologies that expound biblical teachings and church doctrines, mujerista theology seeks to give meaning to the sufferings of Latinas. Although mujerista theology uses the **Bible** in theological reflection, it is not a determining source, because a woman's need to survive takes precedence over biblical texts. The Bible is used only as it aids in understanding oppression and promoting liberation. However, mujerista theology is firmly rooted in the biblical understanding of the ongoing revelation of God in history, which Latinas believe to be the experience of God's intimate presence in their daily lives.

Liberation in mujerista theology entails (1) developing Latina women's moral agency (their consciences) leading to freedom; (2) establishing the "kin-dom of God" (Diaz's substitute for "kingdom of God"), which is the community united in the bonds of friendship, care, love, and pursuit of justice and liberation; and (3) promoting **justice** as a Christian obligation. Justice demands that Christians struggle to bring about a society that promotes the common good and that enables everyone, especially the poor, to participate in social, economic, and political processes that promote human fullness.

See also Bible; Experience, Phenomenon of; Kingdom of God; Justice; Liberation Theology; Women's Role in the Church.

Resources

Isasi-Díaz, Ada María. *En La Lucha/In the Struggle: A Hispanic Women's Liberation Theology*. Minneapolis: Fortress Press, 1993.
———. *Mujerista Theology*. Maryknoll, NY: Orbis Books, 1996.

ELISA BERNAL CORLEY, PHD

MUSIC/HYMNS/HYMNOLOGY

Music is central to Judeo-Christian worship and has been from its beginning. God created, instituted, and blessed music as a means for persons to express their relationship with God both individually and as assembled worshippers.

The OT is especially abundant in its affirmation of the use of vocal and instrumental music for liturgical service. David appointed orders of Levites not of the privileged priestly family to preside over and perform the music of worship in the tabernacle. When the **temple** was constructed, they continued this auxiliary "service of song" (1 Chron. 6:31-32). As their sole responsibility, they formed large choral groups and orchestras of wind, string, and percussion instruments to help offer the community's worship of Yahweh. They lived at the temple because "they were on duty day and night" (9:33). The book of Psalms contains samples of the repertoire used in Israel's worship, including psalms of ascent, prayers, festival liturgies, and **laments**. Though synagogues did not use music, the readings and prayers were no doubt intoned.

The NT, by contrast, offers limited references to music. No mention is made of the use of instruments in worship. Only scant references to song are made, such as when Paul exhorts worshippers to "sing psalms and hymns and spiritual songs" (Eph. 5:19-20; Col. 3:16). Although scholars differ over the meaning of these terms, there is consensus that Paul likely had in mind a variety of song types. This would be consistent with the diverse makeup of the rapidly expanding Gentile congregations, not to mention maintaining continuity with Hebraic faith. Since the Psalms did not make explicit reference to Christ, adding Greek hymnic forms proved especially helpful in creating texts for signifying **Jesus Christ** as **God** and Lord. Some early Christ hymns are visible in Rom. 3:24-26, Phil. 2:6-11, and Col. 1:15-20.

The heart and soul of worship music is congregational song; the gathered community forms the primary choir. The trajectory of congregational song has traveled far during two millennia of worship. "Hymnody" is a category used to describe the church's songs most broadly. But "hymn" also refers to a particular type of congregational song form. From the beginning, Christian hymnists have set poetic texts to music. Various periods yielded their noteworthy types: There is the post-Constantinian flowering of hymnody, including (1) the works of Ambrose of Milan (d. 397), the so-called father of Western hymnody; (2) the development of chant, which, during the Middle Ages, became reserved exclusively for professional cleric musicians; and (3) the polyphony (two or more independent melodic voices) of the High Renaissance.

The Reformers, especially **Martin Luther**, reclaimed hymnody for the congregation as an expression of the priesthood of all believers. Luther authored numerous hymns and tunes. **John Calvin**, taking a more conservative view, permitted singing texts taken only directly from Scripture. Melodious singing characterized the early **Methodists**. They were instructed in how and what to sing. **Charles Wesley**'s vast contribution to Christendom's wealth of hymns can hardly be overstated. His volume of work (estimated at six to nine thousand hymn texts, depending on classification) demonstrates remarkable use of meter, poetic devices, and themes representing both sound doctrinal depth and personal devotion.

The twentieth century to the present has seen an outstanding expansion of congregational songs of all types, especially an explosion of new hymns, hymnals, and hymnological research. The Second Vatican Council (1962-65) resulted in renewed interest in many types of congregational songs among **Roman Catholics**. Songs from all around the world are being sung by many congregations. Organizations that foster serious study of congregational song, such as the Hymn Society in the United States and Canada, are thriving.

See also Liturgical Theology; Liturgy and Worship.

Resources

Charles Wesley Society. www.wesleysociety.org.
Foley, Edward. *From Age to Age*. Chicago: Liturgy Training Publications, 1991.
Hymn Society in the United States and Canada. www.thehymnsociety.org.

CONSTANCE M. CHERRY, DMIN

MYSTERY RELIGIONS

The mystery religions were a variety of religions in the Greco-Roman world that required secret initiation rites. They included the Eleusinian Mysteries at Eleusis (near Athens), devoted to Demeter and Kore/Persephone; the cult of Cybele and Attis, originating in Phrygia; Isis and Osiris from Egypt; the Mysteries of Dionysus; and the Mysteries of Mithras. Though thriving in the first three centuries AD, most were of much greater antiquity (e.g., Cybele had predecessors reaching back to the Mother Goddess of Anatolia in the Neolithic period).

Mystery religions existed alongside and were often related to Classical Greek religion. The gods of the Greek pantheon were primarily fixtures of civic life, invoked for the common benefit of the state and its citizenry. But the mysteries catered to the more cosmopolitan spirit of the Hellenistic age, from which emerged an individual's quest for personal salvation.

"Mystery" was a technical term for a secret rite by which individuals were initiated into a special relationship with a deity, thus securing for themselves salvation from evils both in this life and the afterlife. *Mystērion* ("mystery," "secret") derives from the Greek verb *myein* ("to close"), used in the passive voice to mean "to be initiated." "To close" could have referred to closing the lips (i.e., secrecy) or to closing, then opening, the eyes (i.e., enlightenment).

Ancient authors spoke of three parts to the rite of initiation: "things said" (*legomena*), "things enacted" (*dromena*), and "things shown" (*deiknymena*) — the climax of the ritual. The pattern came from the Eleusinian Mysteries but probably varied in other mystery cults. We know virtually nothing about the particulars of these rites, since initiates—true to form—kept them secret. Hippolytus (ca. 170–ca. 236), however, reported that the secret displayed to those being initiated into the Eleusinian Mysteries was a single head of grain being reaped in silence (*Haer.* 5.3.55).

Most mysteries were founded on a myth that explained the natural cycle of agriculture. Examples include (1) Kore's annual appearance for eight months (growing season) and return to the underworld for four months (summer drought); (2) a mother goddess (Demeter, Cybele, Isis) who represented fertility; and (3) a figure who journeyed to and from Hades (Kore/Persephone, Dionysus). This figure was lord of the underworld (Osiris) or was in some manner restored to life (Attis, Osiris).

Persons initiated into the mysteries believed they somehow participated in divine power over the cycle of life and therefore believed themselves blessed both here and in the underworld. The Mysteries of Mithras stood apart because of their astrological focus: seven levels of initiation to prepare the soul for safe passage to its origin by ascending through the heavenly spheres.

The mystery religions were once viewed as sources for elements of Christian faith and worship, such as the mystery of **salvation**, the **resurrection**, and the **sacraments** of baptism and the Eucharist. However, the proposed parallels with Christianity were found to be exaggerated or distorted. The arguments for Christian dependence on the mysteries have been judged methodologically suspect because of unfounded generalizations about a uniform "mystery theology" and the use of late, scanty evidence (see Ferguson 2003, 297-300).

Resources

Ferguson, Everett. *Backgrounds of Early Christianity.* 3rd ed. Grand Rapids: Eerdmans, 2003.
Meyer, Marvin W., ed. *The Ancient Mysteries: A Sourcebook of Sacred Texts.* Philadelphia: University of Pennsylvania Press, 1999.

KEVIN L. ANDERSON, PHD

MYSTICISM/MYSTICAL THEOLOGY

Mysticism is difficult to define, largely because of its diversification and the commonly loose use of the term. Broadly, mysticism is anything that places one in contact with reality beyond the physical senses. More formally, it is an attempt to become directly connected with the divine, the procedure for doing so, the claim to having achieved it, and the experience itself. Mysticism is present in most religions, including Judaism (Kabbalah and Hasidism), Christianity (the medieval Roman Catholic mystics), Hinduism (Yoga mysticism), Islam (Sufism), and Buddhism (Zen Buddhism).

In Christianity, mysticism has a long and mixed history. There is a difference between Christians who have had a "mystical experience" (e.g., Polycarp [ca. 69–ca. 155] and Justin Martyr [ca. 103-ca. 165]) and those who characteristically follow the "mystical way." The apostle Paul spoke often of being united with Christ and even spoke of mystical experiences, "visions and revelations of the Lord" (2 Cor. 12:1). But he was not a mystic in the more standard sense of the term. His mysticism involved being "in" Christ, the Redeemer, by grace through faith alone, not by any disciplines of his own and not by unmediated contact with God. His "Christ mysticism" knew nothing of union with Christ apart from union with the body of Christ.

There are some identifiable characteristics of most mysticism: (1) It is almost impossible for mystics to describe their experience, it being *ineffable* in nature—incapable of expression. (2) For a deep understanding of mysticism one must experience mysticism. (3) The mystical experience passes, for it cannot be long sustained. (4) After each experience the mystic should return to a level of devotion higher than before. (5) There is progression in holiness gained by increased knowledge of God and the way to God. (6) Mystics experience passivity, a feeling of being suspended by a supreme power and having one's own will united with the divine will. (7) The mystical character is flexible or malleable as opposed to being legalistic. Some would add another characteristic, depending in part upon the mystic's religion: absorption, or losing all individuality or separateness and becoming one with the divine (e.g., in Hinduism the way of knowledge found in the Upanishads and the doctrine of absorption into the One of Plotinus [ca. 204/5-270]).

Some characteristic stages of mysticism can be identified: (1) the purgative stage of self-denial; (2) the stage of illumination where one concentrates completely on God, and God sends light for guidance; (3) the stage in which God withdraws the light, forcing the mystic to rely on God in total or naked faith; (4) the stage in which the mystic reaches the goal of becoming completely united with God, may be identified as "absorption." This goal is not easily or often achieved.

For years, up to his evangelical conversion in 1738, John Wesley unsuccessfully pursued the way of the mystics. Only on learning that reconciliation with God comes by grace through faith *alone*, not through mystical exertion, isolation, and self-denial, did Wesley receive God's peace. He continued to see value in the mystics and included some of them for study by the Methodists, but always corrected by evangelical faith.

See also Desert Fathers and Mothers; Wesley, John, Theology of.

Resources

James, William. *The Varieties of Religious Experience: A Study in Human Nature*. 1902. Reprint, Seattle: CreateSpace, 2010.

Tuttle, Robert G. *Mysticism in the Wesleyan Tradition*. Grand Rapids: Francis Asbury Press, 1989.

Underhill, Evelyn. *Mysticism*. 12th ed. Stillwell, KS: Digireads.com, 2005.

KLAUS ARNOLD, MDIV

MYTH/MYTHOS

A myth is a story involving gods or fantastical beings that expresses mysteries relating to life and the universe. By contrast, in common usage "myth" means something that is false, a reflection of our rejection of such stories. In our modern worldview we are prone to think of such stories simply as bad science. Indeed, we can find instances of ancient thinkers who belittled those in their world who took such stories literally. Such assessments miss myth's more formal meaning and importance.

It is more accurate and helpful to think of ancient myths as poetic *expressions* about the world rather than as *explanations* we expect modern science to produce. Consequently, we should think of stories about Hades kidnapping Persephone more as poetic expressions of the changing seasons rather than as actual reasons for why seasons change. Stoic philosophers who lived in the centuries just before Christ thought of the gods as symbols of virtues and vices. They found profound meaning in stories they did not believe to be historically true.

Christians debate whether they find material in the Bible that might appropriately be called myth in the formal, not popular, sense. For example, is Gen. 1 a poetic expression of God as Creator and the world as orderly, or is it meant as a quasi-scientific explanation of the creation process? The Bible does draw on mythical imagery on occasion, such as when the Psalms picture God crushing the heads of Leviathan (74:13-14) and Rahab (89:10). Psalm 82 describes God's coming judgment of the nations by picturing him in "divine council," pronouncing his verdict on the gods of the other nations. Recent discoveries make it clear that Deut. 32:8-9 pictures God distributing charge over the nations to various gods, while keeping charge of Israel for himself.

The NT speaks negatively of "myths" that seem to be Jewish in nature (e.g., Titus 1:14; 1 Tim. 1:4). Perhaps these were angelic stories like those found in some intertestamental books. Second Peter 1:16 boldly asserts that stories about Jesus, his transfiguration in particular, were not like other "cleverly devised" stories about gods Peter's audience might have heard. Remembering that the most basic meaning of the Greek word *mythos* is "story," it is more the *kinds* of stories these verses reject than mystery-expressing stories as such.

Twentieth-century theologian Rudolf Bultmann suggested that we should think of all the biblical material as mythical, that we must "demythologize" it before it can make sense to moderns. He famously claimed that it is impossible for modern persons to believe in things like miracles and spirits. Rather, he believed these "myths" point to humanity's quest for authentic existence. Bultmann interpreted biblical stories in **existentialist** terms.

The vast majority of Christians disagree with Bultmann, even if they legitimately interpret some biblical material in nonliteral ways. Much of NT scholarship has moved far beyond the limitations on our comprehending the NT as claimed by Bultmann.

See also Cosmology/Cosmogony; Creationism; Science and the Bible; Second Temple Judaism.

Resources

Bultmann, Rudolf. *Kerygma and Myth: A Theological Debate.* Edited by H. W. Bartsch and translated by R. H. Fuller. London: SPCK, 1972.

Finegan, Jack. *Myth and Mystery: An Introduction to the Pagan Religions of the Biblical World.* Grand Rapids: Baker, 1989.

Oswalt, John. *The Bible Among the Myths: Unique Revelation or Just Ancient Literature?* Grand Rapids: Zondervan, 2009.

KENNETH SCHENCK, PHD

Nn

NARRATIVE THEOLOGY

A narrative is a story. Narrative theology teaches that the heart of Christianity is the story of God found in the Bible, not a set of abstract doctrines, propositions, or speculative metaphysics. Not all books of the Bible are explicitly narrative (e.g., Proverbs or Psalms). And no single book tells the whole story. Narrative theology creatively weaves the Bible's major themes into one grand narrative that faithfully tells its story about God, humanity, creation, and their mutual relationship.

While narrative theologies differ from each other in some ways, normally they include the following features:

1. God is the Creator. Humans are part of that creation and have been given a precious gift—finite freedom. The human story has tragic dimensions. Repeatedly humans have misused their freedom and have turned away from fellowship with their Creator. However, God does not simply stand by as the creation turns away. God is the faithful One, always reaching out to fallen humanity, calling humans to repent and return. God reconciles them to himself and makes it possible for humans to live obediently in God's kingdom.

2. By calling out Abraham and Sarah, God creates a people with a special vocation. This people, the Jews, must show the rest of humanity what it means to live faithfully in God's presence so that eventually all nations can once again live in harmony with God. Christians believe that God, in his quest for reconciliation, became incarnate in one of these Jews—Jesus, the Messiah of Israel. Through Jesus' life, death, and resurrection, he made possible God's desired reconciliation. God honored humanity's freedom in this process by making the gift of faith (trust) the single condition for access to salvation. Salvation is freely offered, not imposed, to all, faith being the avenue of response.

3. Through the work of the Holy Spirit, God is especially (though not exclusively) active in the community of believers known as the church, seen as the renewed Israel of God.

4. The people who live in fellowship with the one God of the biblical story can look to the future with a life-transforming hope, even beyond the grave.

When this narrative is taken seriously, obedient readers become part of the biblical story. They live as sinners redeemed by God's grace. For most of Christian history, Christians placed themselves *into* the biblical story; the story shaped their world. But that changed in the modern era. The tendency has been to let the secular, nonbiblical or even nontheistic perception of reality determine the biblical story's meaning and importance. This results in discarding all features of the gospel story that challenge a secular perception of the world. For instance, God as the one who defines what it means to be human, together with the magnitude of sin, is discounted or omitted from human self-understanding. This eviscerates the biblical story.

The contemporary narrative theologian, then, has the challenge of faithfully presenting the story of Scripture in a manner that promotes humble worship of God, embraces Christ the Redeemer, and joyfully serves others. At the same time, he or she must avoid mechanical subservience to the literal words of the Bible. This error can lead to fundamentalism that chokes the life out of the story. Balance can be achieved by guidance from the Holy Spirit.

See also Bible; Biblical Theology; Hermeneutics.

Resources
Frei, Hans W. *The Eclipse of Biblical Narrative: A Study in Eighteenth and Nineteenth Century Hermeneutics.* New Haven, CT: Yale University Press, 1974.
Hauerwas, Stanley, and L. Gregory Jones, eds. *Why Narrative? Readings in Narrative Theology.* Grand Rapids: Eerdmans, 1989.

GREGORY S. CLAPPER, PHD

NATURAL LAW
See ETHICS.

NATURAL SCIENCE

Natural science is the branch of science that studies the natural or physical world and its phenomena. It stretches back into antiquity. For most of its history, the study of nature was based on objective observations and philosophical interpretations. Natural science was known as natural philosophy. During the fifteenth to seventeenth centuries, through the works of such persons as Francis Bacon, Galileo, and Robert Boyle a more methodical and inductive approach to the study of nature was developed. As the study of nature moved beyond philosophical interpretation and began to apply inductive and deductive reasoning to observations of nature, it gave birth to what has become the scientific method. Its adoption and fruitful employment ignited the scientific revolution of the seventeenth and eighteenth centuries. Application of the scientific method to our observations of nature led to the branch of science we today call the natural sciences (astronomy, physics, chemistry, earth science, and biology).

Christians have long linked what they learn through the natural sciences with what they believe about God the Creator. Knowledge of **God** gained by observing nature forms **natural theology.** An interest in natural theology traces back through a long line of church fathers, including Thomas Aquinas, Augustine, and even Paul (Rom. 1:19-20). Many Christians today are able to reconcile the freedom and results of natural science with their faith in God as Creator, Redeemer, and Sustainer. Many Christians who are professional scientists do this.

But many in the sciences believe natural science, when *practiced correctly*, rules out religion. Many Christians believe that only if the natural sciences comply with the Bible can they be *practiced correctly.* The two pit science and religion against each other. The contrast is between **atheistic** scientists/philosophers and religious **fundamentalists.** Autonomous science and religion are believed to be mutually exclusive approaches to truth. This either/or approach has been traced back to the joining of Duns Scotus's (ca. 1266–1308) concept of univocity (one voice) and William of Ockham's (ca. 1285–ca. 1349) razor (when two competing theories are equally explanatory, choose the simplest one). This can lead to the **reductionist** claim that once something is supposedly explained clearly and completely as a natural occurrence, no additional explanations are needed.

Partly due to the enormous success of the sciences, as well as the philosophical influence of naturalism (the material is all there is) and scientism (science is our only path to truth), many have concluded that anything worth knowing must be gained by way of scientific methodology. This highly restricted way of knowing denies that religion has any explanatory significance. Those who draw this conclusion fail to recognize the limits of science and fail to see the philosophical underpinnings that permit a reductionist approach to science. They ignore that naturalism and scientism extend science's explanatory reach beyond its legitimate bounds.

The error is also seen in those who teach that the Bible, as the revealed Word of God, speaks with factual authority on all subjects it addresses—including the natural world. The Bible authoritatively provides a single explanation for all things. Any "natural" explanation of natural phenomena that seems to disagree with the Bible must be rejected. Here we see the overextension earlier imposed on the natural sciences (scientism) now being imposed on the Bible. It is forced to make claims about the world it was never intended to make.

Wesleyan theology rejects both of these extremes. Because of how it understands biblical authority, together with the latitude it assigns to reason and experience of the world, the legitimate explanatory role of science and the Bible are protected. The natural sciences in all their astonishing explanatory power are thought to show the glory of God the Creator. They disclose to faith God's providential activity in the world.

See also Evolution/Evolutionary Biology; Natural Theology; Philosophy of Science; Science and the Bible; Social Sciences; Wesley, John, Theology of.

Resources

Collins, Francis. *The Language of God: A Scientist Presents Evidence for Belief.* Waterville, ME: Wheeler Publishing, 2007.

McGrath, Alister E. *Science and Religion: A New Introduction.* 2nd ed. Malden, MA: Wiley-Blackwell, 2010.

Noll, Mark. "Evangelicals, Creation, and Scripture: An Overview." BioLogos Foundation. Essay presented at the November 2009 In Search of a Theology of Celebration workshop. http://biologos.org/uploads/projects/Noll_scholarly_essay.pdf.

Polkinghorne, John. *Exploring Reality: The Intertwining of Science and Religion.* New Haven, CT: Yale University Press, 2005.

KERRY FULCHER, PHD

NATURAL THEOLOGY

Natural theology is a way to study **God** by drawing only on observations of the natural world (Rom. 1:19-20) and by using reason to reach conclusions such observations support. The sources for natural theology contrast with those of special **revelation** (e.g., a **prophetic** message or the **incarnation**) in which God reveals himself to certain people at particular places and times (John 1:14-18).

The traditional arguments for God's existence (e.g., cosmological, ontological, teleological, and moral) are forms of natural theology. Advocates of the arguments affirm that God's existence can be proved without appeal to special revelation and that the arguments yield a fair measure of accurate knowledge about God. With equal force, counterarguments say the "proofs" fail to achieve their stated goal.

Christians historically have held contrasting estimates of the relationship between natural theology and special revelation—Christ—in which natural theology culminates (Heb. 1:1-4). Søren Kierkegaard (1813-55), for example, insisted that truths revealed by Christ are at odds with what human experience and reason permit us to know. Karl Barth suggested that the conclusions of natural theology will inevitably distort the picture of God found in the Christian Scriptures. **Thomas Aquinas**, however, probably represents the majority Christian view in affirming that special revelation provides truths that go beyond human experience and reason, yet which do not contradict them.

Historically, the most common role for natural theology has been to establish God's existence. Again, Christians do not agree about the extent to which natural theology can succeed. Some have sought to demonstrate God's existence through logical proofs. Others have more modestly attempted to show the probability of God's existence. Still others have been content to show that there are defensible reasons for believing God exists and thus that theists can be rational when holding this belief.

The prominence of natural theology reached its height in the eighteenth and nineteenth centuries, especially in Great Britain. Following discoveries such as the microscope that enabled scientists to observe the complexity within the human body, William Paley and others sought through a study of human and animal biology to demonstrate a benevolent design that demonstrated God's existence.

Given that natural theology can never lead to experiential conviction about the **atoning** work of **Jesus** Christ, an important question arises over whether, and in what quality, general revelation makes "knowledge" of God possible. **John Wesley** spoke of those who do not have access to special revelation but who are nevertheless able through **prevenient grace** to respond to the "light" of general revelation. According to Wesley, when a person exhibits **righteousness** in response to general revelation, even though that person is not yet "properly a son [or daughter]," he (or she) is nevertheless "a servant of God." That person is now in a "state of acceptance" before God and lives to some extent in a positive relationship with him (*Works*, 7:199).

Natural theology continues to be a live and attractive option for many Christian philosophers and theologians. It continues to serve an **apologetic** role. For example, Anglican theologian Alister McGrath has developed a "Trinitarian natural theology."

See also Atheism/Agnosticism; Epistemology; Natural Science; Philosophy of Religion; Reductionism; Secular/Secularism/Secularization.

Resources

McGrath, Alister E. *A Fine-Tuned Universe: The Quest for God in Science and Theology*. Louisville, KY: Westminster John Knox Press, 2009.

———. *The Open Secret: A New Vision for Natural Theology*. Malden, MA: Blackwell Publishing, 2008.

Paley, William. *Natural Theology: or, Evidences of the Existence and Attributes of the Deity*. Reprint of the 1809 London edition, The Complete Works of Charles Darwin Online. Last modified January 1, 2010. http://darwin-online.org.uk/content/frameset?itemID=A142&viewtype=text&pageseq=1 (accessed June 20, 2012).

Wesley, John. "On Faith." In *Works*, 7:326-35.

KEVIN KINGHORN, PHD

NEO-PAGANISM

In Christianity the term "paganism" has usually referred to religions outside the Abrahamic tradition (Jews, Christians, and Muslims) and more particularly to polytheistic religions indigenous to Europe. "Pagan" derives from *paganus* (Latin), meaning "civilian," "rustic," "country dweller," or "outsider." The original meaning is difficult to determine.

"Neo-paganism" is more precise than "paganism"; it refers to movements beginning in the nineteenth century that attempted to recover what are believed to be ancient pagan beliefs and practices. Some of the more prominent neo-pagan religions are Ásatrú, Druidism, goddess worship, and Wicca and witchcraft (a positive term). Although some neo-pagans do not identify themselves as witches, most witches are neo-pagans.

Neo-paganism characteristically emphasizes the (1) veneration of nature in relation to places and seasons and the earth itself, (2) interconnectedness of life, (3) presence of the spiritual realm in all of reality, (4) goddess as the feminine face of divinity, and (5) efficacy of magic. The sacred is pluralistic and diverse; goddesses and gods constitute a community. Their harmonious interaction constitutes the secret of the universe. The interconnection of life and nature manifests the divine from which divination and magic arise. Powers that transcended the world can be made to affect it. Magic is defined as consciously employing the mind to create positive change. Many neo-pagans form their ethic by the Wiccan Rede (Middle English, "advice"): "If it harms none, do what you will."

For neo-pagans, practice and ritual provide the basis for religious identity and community. Rituals unite the human and celestial worlds. They are means for celebrating the cyclical movement of life and death, and the changes of seasons. This happens at new and full moons and at eight seasonal festivals. Rituals are specific to each community and individual. Ritual spaces are usually oriented to the four cardinal directions. In the spaces are statues of deities and also symbols for water, air, fire, and earth.

A ritual is usually conducted in a circle and facilitated by ritual leaders who explain the ritual's purpose, invite the presence of deities or spirits, and monitor the community's energy. The leader concludes the ritual in ways that return participants to normal consciousness.

Neo-pagans seek information from the divine realm by reading its signs. By casting stones and through other means divine signs can be ascertained.

New Age spirituality and neo-pagans are often incorrectly equated. There are fundamental differences. While **New Age** beliefs often picture the natural world as *hiding* spiritual truth, neo-pagans insist the natural world *openly manifests* the sacred. They criticize New Age forms of spirituality, charging that New Age is but an indiscriminant hodgepodge of beliefs borrowed from diverse Eastern and native religions. New Agers, the accusation runs, fail to see the primacy of protecting the living earth. Forms of spirituality that try to escape nature or rise above it violate a central part of Wiccan and neo-pagan belief. Wiccan-pagans interact with "nature." The New Age "gnostic" inclination is to elevate spirit above nature. Neo-pagans see themselves as part of the whole of nature.

See also New Age Spirituality; New Religions.

Resources

Jones, Prudence. "Introduction to Paganism." The Pagan Federation. http://www.pagan fed.org/paganism.shtml (accessed June 20, 2012).

Pike, Sarah M. *New Age and Neopagan Religions in America*. New York: Columbia University Press, 2004.

JOHN CULP, PHD

NEO-PENTECOSTAL THEOLOGY

See CHARISMATIC THEOLOGY.

NEOPLATONISM

"Neoplatonism" is a modern term used for a school of religious and metaphysical philosophy that began with Plotinus (and his teacher Ammonius Saccas) in the third century AD. It lasted until the closing of the Athenian school by Justinian in AD 529. Neoplatonic influences can be identified, however, in Judaism and Islam and in early Christian, medieval, early modern, and twentieth-century movements and individuals. As the term suggests, Neoplatonism is based on the teachings of Plato. Early Neoplatonism constitutes a preservation of his thought instead of its reformulation.

One of the primary documents of Neoplatonism is Plotinus's *Enneads*, collected and published after Plotinus's death (AD 270) by his student Porphyry. The *Enneads*, composed somewhere between 254 and 267, is a series of fifty-four essays divided into six groups of nine essays. Each division is called an *ennead* (Greek, *ennea*, "nine"). The first ennead presents Plotinus's moral philosophy, the second his physics, the third his cosmology, the fourth his psychology, the fifth his philosophy of mind, and the sixth his view of reality. The *Enneads* shares themes common to the Platonic tradition, such as belief in the immateriality of reality; the conviction that the visible and sensible world points to a higher level of being; a preference for intuitive over empirical forms of knowing; the immortality of the soul; belief that the universe is essentially good; and a tendency to identify the beautiful, the good, and the true as one and the same.

Plotinus did not intend to initiate a new phase in philosophy. He intended to teach only what Plato had taught.

Neoplatonists teach that the primeval source of Being is the One and the Infinite, distinct from the many and the finite. The One is the source of all life, is absolute causality, and is the only real existence. The One is the Good. Since it is beyond all Being, it cannot be known through reasoning but through dialectic, a kind of rational, mystical vision in which truth is grasped completely, all at once. The One, as source, as cause, emanates *Nous* (understood as Divine Mind, Intellectual Principle), and from *Nous* emanates Soul, which contains in itself all particular souls, including human. Soul then creates nature (the phenomenal world) according to the archetypical Platonic forms. The whole creation, then, is a succession of creative acts with each lower "principle" imitating the preceding higher one.

The human soul is immortal. Plotinus recognizes two ways for the soul to return to the One—the longer way and the shorter way. The longer way requires the soul's reincarnation through successively higher forms until eventually it passes out of the cycle of birth and death. This requires, however, that the soul live virtuously, giving up sensual gratification of the flesh. The shorter way is the moment of intuition in which the soul experiences union with the One. This can be prepared for by contemplation on nature or beauty—the road to the divine.

See also Greek Philosophy; Mysticism/Mystical Theology.

Resources

Gregory, John. *The Neoplatonists: A Reader.* 2nd ed. New York: Routledge, 1999.
Harris, R. Baine, ed. *The Significance of Neoplatonism.* Norfolk, VA: Old Dominion University, 1976.

PHILIP N. LAFOUNTAIN, THD

NEUROSCIENCE AND RELIGION

Neuroscience concerns the study of the nervous system (mostly the brain) with respect to behavior, stretching from the function of individual neural cells to the social behavior of humans. There is an increasing availability of new and powerful brain-scanning techniques that allow researchers to create images revealing the timing and distribution of activity in the brains of living and thinking humans (e.g., functional magnetic resonance imaging [fMRI]). As a result, neuroscience has been able to study brain activity associated with the most sophisticated and uniquely human forms of mental activity. Thus there has been rapid development in knowledge of the brain activity associated with such human mental processes as comprehension of language, recognition of faces and facial emotion, recalling specific events from the past, empathy and trust in social relationships, and moral decision making.

Neuroscientists have studied brain activity associated with religious behaviors and religious experiences. Researchers have probed the role of brain function with respect to the role of genetics in tendencies to be more or less religious, the evolution of the brain as a contributor to the development of religion, and the mystical religious experiences associated with brain-altering drugs (e.g., peyote) or temporal lobe epileptic seizures. They have investigated the influence of neurochemical systems, patterns of brain activity associated with meditation in Buddhist monks or Catholic nuns, brain activity associated with **glossolalia** or meditation on the Psalms, and so on. The conclusion seems to be that our spiritual and religious experiences and behaviors all have correlates in brain activity. This does not imply that religious experiences and behaviors are not related to something real and spiritual but merely that they are functions of the hypercomplex human neural system.

The ability to make scientific observations of brain activity associated with religious experiences, moral decision making, important dimensions of human interpersonal relationships, and, in fact, all of the highest forms of human cognition has called into question theological and philosophical commitments to either body-soul or body-mind **dualism**. Apparently all realms of human agency and experience have correlates in brain activity. They cannot be significantly disturbed or eliminated by brain damage. The question, "Did I do this or did my brain cause it?" becomes extremely difficult to answer, if not nonsensical. Thus neuroscience is providing increasingly strong reasons to abandon dualism in favor of some form of **monism** or physicalism. According to this view, we are not bodies inhabited by souls—we are bodies. But again, this does not imply that our religious experiences and behaviors are not *in relation to something real and spiritual*.

Such physicalism or monism has its problems, most particularly **reductionism** and **determinism**. However, these issues can be resolved in ways that are both theologically robust and commensurate with modern neuroscience.

See also Altruism/Natural Morality; Anthropology, Theological; Determinism and Free Will; Evolution/Evolutionary Biology; Experience, Phenomenon of; Free Will; Monism, Dualism, Pluralism; Natural Science; Person; Social Sciences.

Resources

Green, Joel B. *Body, Soul, and Human Life: The Nature of Humanity in the Bible.* Grand Rapids: Baker Academic, 2008.
Jeeves, Malcolm, and Warren S. Brown. *Neuroscience, Psychology, and Religion: Illusions, Delusions, and Realities About Human Nature.* Templeton Science and Religion Series. West Conshohocken, PA: Templeton Foundation Press, 2009.
Murphy, Nancey. *Bodies and Souls, or Spirited Bodies?* Current Issues in Theology. Cambridge, UK: Cambridge University Press, 2006.

WARREN S. BROWN, PHD

NEW AGE SPIRITUALITY

The term "New Age" refers to a variety of groups holding eclectic beliefs and practices. Some groups first used the term in the 1930s, but it achieved much greater recognition in the late 1960s and early 1970s. This was demonstrated by "Aquarius," the song from the musical *Hair*, and the book *The Aquarian Conspiracy* by Marilyn Ferguson.

New Age generally refers to a movement growing out of nineteenth-century United States and British religiosity that emphasized subjective, personal spirituality. In the 1960s, New Age accepted and emphasized ecological awareness, feminism, and non-Western religions. In the twenty-first century, New Age thought has been especially associated with the rejection of religion understood as conformity to formal doctrines. Many New Agers claim New Age spirituality has filled a void created by established religion. Instead of the superficiality of established religion, New Age spirituality emphasizes deep personal involvement in the spiritual aspects of reality. New Agers mine all religions, including Christianity, in search for any spiritual resource that will enrich spiritual insight and understanding.

Beliefs commonly associated with New Age movements include (1) the entire cosmos is a great, interconnected web of meaning; (2) consciousness or energy rather than matter forms the basis of the cosmos; (3) humans contain a spark of that energy or consciousness, and it can be used to change reality and create a new world; (4) each person is on a journey of spiritual development, not ending at death, but continuing over many lives (**reincarnation**); and (5) ancient cultures possess valuable insights into the workings of the cosmos and the self.

In the search for a new age, transformation of the self and society is pursued by a variety of practices, including channeling, visualization, astrology, meditation, and alternative healing methods. New Agers frequently travel to "power spots" such as Mount Shasta, California, to change their consciousness.

In some ways, New Age beliefs and practices are similar to evangelical Christian beliefs and practices, some nineteenth-century religious/metaphysical thinkers, and **neo-pagans**. But while similar to evangelical Christianity's concern for personal spirituality, New Age movements differ greatly from evangelical Christians in specific beliefs and mystical practices.

New Age has modified nineteenth-century rejections of materialism found in romanticism and spiritualism by reformulating them as commitments to feminism, ecology, and an appreciation for non-Western religions. While similar to neo-paganism in the emphasis on spiritual realities, New Age movements tend to participate in specialist-client relationships rather than in ritual practices. They anticipate the future actualization of a higher existence. Neo-pagans, by contrast, seek to revive old pagan religions.

See also New Religious Movements; Pantheism; Religious Pluralism; Syncretism, Religious.

Resources

Pike, Sarah. *New Age and Neopagan Religions in America*. New York: Columbia University Press, 2004.

Sutcliffe, Steven J. "Rethinking 'New Age' as a Popular Religious Habitus: A Review Essay on the Spiritual Revolution." *Method and Theory in the Study of Religion* 18, no. 3 (2006): 294-314.

JOHN CULP, PHD

NEW APOSTOLIC REFORMATION/NEW APOSTOLIC MOVEMENTS

Also known as New Apostolic Reformation Missions, New Apostolic Reformation (NAR) designates a loosely connected global community of local churches seeking to reclaim the purpose and methods of first-generation Christians. Special emphasis is given to reinstating the office of apostle and its attendant ministries. Its primary focus is on outreach and church planting through identifying and nurturing apostolic leaders worldwide. Among the hallmarks of these movements is a reliance on **signs and wonders** that allegedly certify authentic teaching and preaching, strategic-level **spiritual warfare**, and worship that is deeper and more sincere than that experienced in Christian communities operating outside apostolic networks.

C. Peter Wagner, a leading proponent of this concept, follows the lead of his mentor, John Wimber of Vineyard Ministries. He argues that apostolic congregations are the visible result of a special outpouring of God's power. They are new, originating as recently as the 1990s, though with antecedents throughout most of the twentieth century.

Wagner claims there is something fundamentally original and different about these networks and their constituent congregations. Supposedly they represent a spirit and works that have not been experienced or enacted since the first century after Christ. Included in these new ways of being the church is the central conviction that Christianity is primarily local and that true Christianity flourishes most easily outside denominational structures and constraints.

Accordingly, apostolic networks are formed through personal connections made among apostolic leaders at the congregational level. Individual parishes restructure their government, financing, evangelistic efforts, missions emphases, and prayer lives around the apostles appointed to lead them. The central concerns of outreach and church planting are most often accomplished through frequent, short-term mission trips arranged among apostles who have formed personal relationships. The trips, led by the apostles and comprised of lay members, are usually one to two weeks in duration and include a variety of activities that are very similar to those undertaken by their denominational counterparts. The positive outcome of these ventures is that local parishioners express greater interest in missions and that participants claim transformed lives, not unlike their denominational cousins.

Critics charge that the movement's accusation that the institutional church has abandoned the faith of the early believers is nothing new. They are also concerned that those identified as apostles, by others who already believe themselves to be apostles, are given near-total control over their parishes and parish funding. Critics contend that God has continued to speak to and through the church across the centuries and that denominations can authentically proclaim the Christian gospel.

As the movement's most ardent advocate, Wagner has written numerous books on the subject, which include aspects of his earlier works on spiritual warfare and church growth. However, these more recent books, written in the 1990s and 2000s, appear to have shifted their audience from the earlier academic readers to today's popular audience. Some might classify these movements as more properly falling under the general categories of **contextualized theologies** and short-term mission movements.

See also Contextual Theology; Early Church; Miracles/Signs and Wonders; Spiritual Warfare.

MARY LOU SHEA, THD

NEW BIRTH (REGENERATION)

New birth is an essential part of the doctrine of **salvation**, embracing the moral transformation of humans and the ultimate renewal of the cosmos.

The Greek term *palingenesia* ("regeneration" or "rebirth") occurs only twice in Scripture. Titus 3:5 refers to the "new birth" (NET) associated with the washing of **baptism** and renewal by the **Holy Spirit**. Matthew 19:28 refers to "the age when all things are renewed" (NET).

Regeneration is represented in other NT expressions relating to God's work of renewal in individual believers: "born again" (KJV) or "born from above" (NRSV) in John 3:3, 7 (Greek, *gennaō* [passive] *anōthen*); "born of the Spirit" (3:5, 8); "born of God" (John 1:13; 1 John 3:9; 4:7; 5:1, 4, 18; cf. James 1:18); and "born anew" (*anagennaō*; 1 Pet. 1:3, 23). Paul's letters speak of believers being "created [*ktizō*] in Christ Jesus" (Eph. 2:10), thus possessing a "new self" (*kainos anthrōpos*; 4:24). They are part of a "new creation" (*kainē ktisis*; 2 Cor. 5:17; Gal. 6:15) and a "new humanity" (*kainos anthrōpos*; Eph. 2:15). Thus personal renewal (individual and corporate) is linked to the eventual restoration of all creation (see Rom. 8:19-23). This is also hinted at in Jesus' insistence that "no one can see the **kingdom of God** without being born from above" (John 3:3).

Cosmic renewal is noted in references to "new heavens [or heaven] and a new earth" where righteousness dwells (2 Pet. 3:13; Rev. 21:1). "See," declares the One seated on the throne, "I am making all things new" (Rev. 21:5).

The new birth is integral to the drama of salvation presented in Scripture. The need for regeneration began in Eden when Adam and Eve disobeyed

God and experienced spiritual death (Gen. 3). Humanity became dead in sin (Rom. 5:12-14; Eph. 2:1) and "alienated from the life of God" (Eph. 4:18). God began creating a new, holy people through Abraham's descendants. The OT prophets expressed the need for moral renewal through divine transformation of peoples' hearts (Jer. 24:7; 31:31-34; 32:38-40; Ezek. 11:19; 36:26) and cleansing by the Holy Spirit (Ezek. 36:25, 27; a need also felt by the psalmist, Ps. 51:10-12). They also foresaw a future age of righteousness when God would obliterate the evil effects of the fall (Isa. 2:1-4; 11:1-9; 35:1-10) and "create new heavens and a new earth" (65:17-20).

Scripture does not present a systematic doctrine of the new birth, but raw materials for theological formulation. For John Wesley, **justification** and the new birth are the two fundamental doctrines of salvation. The new birth is God's act of bringing the inner person back to life, transforming and renewing it after the image of God "in true righteousness and holiness" (see Col. 3:10; Eph. 4:24). It involves quickening the "spiritual senses" that were previously insensitive to spiritual realities. Regeneration creates a new set of affections and dispositions focused on love for God and other persons, rather than on the things of the world. It is having "the mind of Christ" and participating in God's nature (**theosis**). It is the starting point for a process of renewal (2 Cor. 4:16; Col. 3:10) and growth toward maturity in Christ (Eph. 4:13; **Christian perfection**).

The new birth is brought about through **means of grace** such as **preaching** the Word (James 1:18; 1 Pet. 1:23) and **baptism** (Titus 3:5; 1 Pet. 3:21). It is entirely the creative "work of omnipotence." New birth is God's gift received by faith. Precisely how the Holy Spirit transforms the inner, moral life remains as mysterious as the shifting of the wind (John 3:8). Regeneration is essential to attaining **holiness**, happiness, and **heaven**.

See also Faith; Grace.

Resources
Runyon, Theodore. *The New Creation: John Wesley's Theology Today.* Nashville: Abingdon Press, 1998.
Wesley, John. "The New Birth." In *Works*, 2:65-77.

KEVIN L. ANDERSON, PHD

NEW CHURCH MOVEMENTS

Global **Christianity** is characterized not only by traditional denominations but also by many churches and institutions intentionally not aligned with denominations. They are referred to as new church movements or simply NCMs. Often they even reject being identified with historic theological traditions such as **Reformed, Pentecostal, Orthodox**, or **Wesleyan**. As a matter of conviction, many of these movements or churches frown on dividing **Christianity** by denominations and theological differences.

364 * NEW RELIGIONS

Examples of new church movements include the Vineyard movement, the Calvary Chapel network of congregations, and the exploding house **church** movement in China and elsewhere. Add to that base communities in areas where **Roman Catholicism** is strong, African Independent Churches (also called African Instituted Churches or African Indigenous Churches), and the Universal Church of the Kingdom of God, which has sprung up in Latin America. There are megachurches such as Willow Creek Community Church, Lifechurch.tv, and, perhaps to some extent, congregations formed by emergent church strategies and philosophies. A common characteristic is that NCMs usually attract large numbers of youthful followers.

New church movements often offer as proof that they are nondenominational by pointing to the absence of a hierarchy and central headquarters. In reality, however, many NCMs have become collections of congregations that function much like traditional denominations. Other new church movement groups have sought to distance themselves from established denominations by highlighting **beliefs** that differ considerably from the doctrinal statements of denominations. Even so, it is often difficult to detect how most NCM belief systems differ from the historic Christian **creeds**. In reality, the most distinct characteristic of the NCMs is their stated rejection of denominational identity.

There are historical parallels to the NCMs. The twelfth-century Waldensians in France and the mid-fourteenth-century Lollards in England (followers of John Wycliffe) did not initially see themselves as separate denominations (although that is what the Waldensians eventually became). Another parallel would be the free churches that sprang up in Western Europe when the earliest **Reformation** churches became state churches. The new church movements are also evocative of the nineteenth-century American restoration movement that gave birth to groups such as the Christian Church/ Churches of Christ, the Church of God (Anderson), and the late nineteenth-century American **holiness movement**.

At times, some NCMs have been judged heretical. The label **cult** has even been assigned to some. One kinder and perhaps more realistic assessment is that they evidence movements of the **Holy Spirit** that traditional denominational structures could not contain.

See also Church (Ecclesiology); Contextual Theology; Creeds (Nicene, Chalcedonian, Apostles', Athanasian); Indigenization; Indigenous Christian Groups; Indigenous Theologies; Parachurch Institutions; Sect.

HOWARD CULBERTSON, DMIN

NEW RELIGIONS

Some religions have very ancient roots. **Judaism** and Hinduism, for example, go back thousands of years. Others are not so old. Indeed, the past century and a half has witnessed the rise of many new religious movements. Since the 1960s, as many as six thousand new religious movements have emerged. Some have spun off from **Christianity** and other major world religions. Others are syncretistic combinations of **Islam** or **Christianity** or other **belief** systems. Umbanda, for instance, is an Afro-Brazilian religion that blends African religions with Catholicism. The now splintered Moorish Science Temple combines elements of Islam and esoteric Christian and Rosicrucian sources. Others seem completely novel in origin.

After World War II Japanese sociologists coined the phrase "new religious movements," but other phrases are also used, including "alternative religious movements," "emergent religions," and "marginal religious movements."

Because these groups usually view themselves as rooted in ancient traditions, their adherents often resist the label "new religions." For example, Jehovah's Witnesses view themselves as more faithful to the Bible than is orthodox Christianity, which, they say, perverted the Bible. Traditional Christianity, Jehovah's Witnesses claim, added things to Christianity not held by the **early church.** Other well-known new religious movements are the Baha'i Faith, Christian Science, the cargo cults of the South Pacific, Falun Gong, Heaven's Gate, Kimbanguism, Mormonism, Nation of **Islam**, Rastafarianism, Santeria, Scientology, Soka Gakkai, Umbanda, and the Unification Church.

In the past, such groups were usually called **cults.** That term, however, began carrying such negative baggage that it largely fell out of favor. "New religious movement" or NRM is now preferred. Cult is usually reserved for religious groups that are clearly manipulative or exploitative. But the line between the two can be very thin. Scientology, for example, is manipulative.

A study group formed by the **Lausanne** Committee for World Evangelization (LCWE, grew out of the International Congress on World Evangelization, 1974) examined the challenges associated with evangelizing NRM adherents. Its published report noted five elements in the human condition that foster new religious movements: (1) humanity's apparent universal religious urge, (2) the deep desire for community, (3) a need for strong authority figures, (4) a search for transcendent reality, and (5) a desire that religion affect life comprehensively.

The **belief** structures of NRMs vary greatly. Usually they are countercultural. An NRM is usually a minority religion; it presents itself as an alternative to mainstream religions. New religious movements tend to be eclectic and syncretistic, freely combining beliefs and practices drawn from a variety of sources. The founders of NRMs are often charismatic and authoritarian. Often they convince their followers they have extraordinary powers or insights. Notable examples are Joseph Smith of the Mormons, Rev. Moon of the Unification Church, and L. Ron Hubbard of Scientology. New religious movements are usually tightly controlled by an elite core. They make extensive demands on their followers, involving time, loyalty, finances, and lifestyle. Some even consciously try to become substitutes for family and to replace other social bonds.

Sometimes the NRM label is given to renewal movements within traditional religions. By failing to distinguish between a renewal movement and a syncretistic new religion, some have labeled as NRMs all Christian denominations that have arisen in North America in the past one hundred years. However, placing Southern Baptists, the **Church of the Nazarene**, and the Assemblies of God in the same category with Mormonism, Scientology, and the Jehovah's Witnesses confuses the subject and weakens the meaning of the designation NRM.

Resources

Barrett, David B., George T. Kurian, and Todd M. Johnson, eds. *World Christian Encyclopedia: A Comparative Survey of Churches and Religions in the Modern World.* 2 vols. New York: Oxford University Press, 2001.

Clarke, Peter. *New Religions in Global Perspective: A Study of Religious Change in the Modern World.* New York: Routledge, 2006.

Lewis, James R., ed. *The Oxford Handbook of New Religious Movements.* New York: Oxford University Press, 2004.

Partridge, Christopher, ed. *New Religions: A Guide: New Religious Movements, Sects, and Alternative Spiritualities.* New York: Oxford University Press, 2004.

HOWARD CULBERTSON, DMIN

NEW RELIGIOUS MOVEMENTS

New religious movements (NRMs) are religious, spiritual, and philosophical alternatives to traditional religions. Their numbers exploded in the nineteenth and twentieth centuries. Although their origins are relatively recent, their teachings are not. Normally they modify or combine older religious beliefs into unique forms. Some NRMs claim to blaze new spiritual paths while others insist they are restoring ancient faiths. But the dominant religions from which NRMs borrow—Christianity, Hinduism, **Islam**, and Buddhism—view them as deviant. Consequently, NRMs are popularly identified as **cults**.

Attracting a small segment of a local—usually young, well-educated, middle-class people in the West or the exceedingly poor and vulnerable in the South and East—NRMs are a minority option in the increasingly diverse twenty-first-century religious landscape.

New religious movements are difficult to describe. They are characterized more by how they respond to globalization and modernity than by a common set of religious beliefs and practices. Soka Gakkai International (SGI), for example, is a transnational organization. An offshoot of Buddhism, SGI has expanded from its founding in Japan in 1930 into 190 nations and now boasts eighteen million adherents. Other NRMs survive by closely identifying with particular cultural or national identities, not by becoming global religions. The peyote cults in the United States, Umbanda in Brazil, or voodoo in Haiti are illustrative. However, most NRMs fall somewhere between these two extremes.

Globalization and the spread of **modernity** during the last two centuries created the conditions for NRMs to surface. Through increased and intensified interactions between cultures, globalization highlighted the extraordinary differences between societies. At the same time, globalization linked all people and places, forging a new global reality that has undermined differences. In the presence of plurality, people have sought commonality. They have asked, "What makes us all human? What does it even mean to be human?" On the other hand, under threat of absorption into a new global commonality, many have tried to fortify their particularity. They have asked, "What makes me unique? What rituals and beliefs are uniquely mine?" Both sets of questions have theological importance and have fueled NRMs. Globalization allows people to borrow religious ideas from diverse sources and then reconstruct them in unique ways that emphasize particular identity.

The phenomenon of modernity has significantly shaped NRMs, all of which have created their forms of religious belief and practice in response to the forces of modernity. Some have embraced modernity's dramatic changes, with its emphasis on science, **technology**, progress, freedom, and individualism. New religious movements such as Scientology and est use those features in novel ways to serve conventional aspirations such as higher paying jobs, improved personal performance, and enhanced interpersonal relationships. Other NRMs such as the Unification Church, Hare Krishna, and the Family seek to reject and escape modernity. Resisting the individualistic and consumer impulses of modernity, they require their members to live communally and forgo individual property ownership. Most groups, however, both borrow from and boycott aspects of modernity.

The proliferation of NRMs as over against modernity's secularizing tendencies has challenged dominant assumptions about the success of secularization. It was long held by Karl Marx, Friedrich Nietzsche, Sigmund Freud, and many others that the arrival of modernity signaled the inevitable demise of religion. The rise of NRMs indicates otherwise. They continue to multiply, with hundreds being created each year. They claim more than sixty million adherents worldwide. They stand both as heartening evidence of the unquenchable thirst for the divine and as a challenge to the **church** to express the gospel adequately and faithfully in an era of global change.

See also Contextualization; Indigenization; Religious Pluralism; Sect; Secular/Secularism/Secularization; Syncretism, Religious; Traditional Religions; Westernization of the Gospel.

Resources

Chryssides, George D. *Exploring New Religions.* New York: Continuum, 1999.
Clarke, Peter. *New Religions in Global Perspective: A Study of Religious Change in the Modern World.* New York: Routledge, 2006.
Hartford Institute for Religion Research. "New Religious Movements." http://hirr.hartsem.edu/denom/new_religious_movements.html.

DARYL IRELAND, MDIV, WITH FRANCISCA IRELAND-VERWOERD, MDIV

NEW TESTAMENT NAMES FOR CHRIST

See CHRISTOLOGY, NEW TESTAMENT.

NORTH AMERICAN NATIVE THEOLOGIES

"Doing theology" has largely been an oxymoron among Native North Americans. "Thinking" about the Creator has been the domain of Euro-North Americans; "spirituality" the domain of Native North Americans. Hence, until recently, in-depth theological training and reflection have not been greatly in evidence. Concepts such as the "Old Testament of Native America" and the reemergence of the *missio Dei*, whereby the good news ceases to be colonial and becomes indigenous, have encouraged contemporary Native North American theological reflection that is intentional and discerning. Three streams of thought reveal the major foci of Native North American theology at the end of the twentieth and beginning of the twenty-first century.

1. As the twentieth century closed, Native North American theology had embraced as its own the historic Euro-North American perceptions of God, Christ, and the Scriptures. But it did this as conditioned by a Native worldview and value structure. Prior to this, for Native North American Christians theology was a Euro-North American enterprise whose content was largely handed to Native congregants. Variations were limited to theological, **liturgical**, and ecclesial differences among denominations. Only minor **aesthetic** adjustments were made. What's more, only minimal Native theological content and or context were in evidence.

During the middle decades of the twentieth century, as the National Indian Brotherhood (NIB) of Canada and its United States' counterpart, the American Indian Movement (AIM), were expanding, theologically literate Native voices emerged. Formally trained, these men and women sought to understand the impact of **colonialism** and neocolonialism on the struggle for Native identity—in the church and the wider society. Their voices were *deconstructionist* (i.e., dismantling and reformulating the inherited colonial theological constructions). Their reconstructive work included use of **indigenized, liberationist, womanist**, and neoliberal theological frameworks. Rooted almost entirely in mainstream **Protestant** Christianity, this trend continued into the early twenty-first century.

2. In the late twentieth and early twenty-first centuries a deeply **contextualized** set of theologies emerged in the Native **evangelical** community. Using traditional philosophical and worldview frameworks, Native theologians such as Keetoowah Randy Woodley explored the connection between **shalom** and the many variations of "the harmony way" operative in traditional Native cultures. Others, such as Cree theologian Raymond Aldred, investigated Native storytelling technique. Aldred sought to articulate a more appropriate starting place for a Native understanding of the gospel. Lakota missiologist Richard Twiss examined the relationship between **contextual theology** and praxis, while métis religionist Wendy Peterson began work on a more "Native-friendly" **apologetic**. Rounding out the field of those dealing with practical issues, Cherokee theorist and activist Andrea Smith outlined an **indigenous theology** of power and gender in church and community.

3. Other contemporary Native theologians began raising questions about philosophical, biblical, and theological starting points. Advocating a shift away from a dualistic philosophical framework, and treatments of Gen. 3 characteristic of the West, they argue for a Gen. 1 and 2 point of departure because it establishes a more holistic starting point for Christian theology. Not only does this provide a more full-orbed description of past and present Native reality by including it in the overarching narrative of creation, but it also makes available a fuller, more descriptive, nonlinear, and inclusive **eschatology.**

See also Evangelical Theology; Indigenous Theologies; Postcolonialism; Westernization of the Gospel.

Resources

Kidwell, Clara Sue, Homer Noley, and George E. Tinker. *A Native American Theology.* Maryknoll, NY: Orbis Books, 2001.
Wallace, Mark I. *Finding God in the Singing River: Christianity, Spirit, Nature.* Minneapolis: Fortress Press, 2005.

TERRY LEBLANC, PHD

Oo

OBEDIENCE

Obedience and disobedience are key concepts in the Christian faith. From Genesis to Revelation, obedience is described as a hallmark of the faithful. The Hebrew word *shema'* means "to hear," "to listen," "to obey" (Deut. 6:4). The word *marah* means "to be rebellious" or "to be disobedient" (1 Kings 13:21).

In Genesis, God is portrayed as the Creator who deserves allegiance and worship. The key way Adam and Eve were to show their allegiance was by obeying God's command that they not eat the forbidden fruit. They disobeyed. Disobeying God is a fundamental expression of sin.

But God in his great love planned redemption for humanity through a series of covenants. In these covenants God promised to be with his people, Israel, to protect and bless them. The human side of the covenants was that God's people must obey the terms of the covenants by worshipping God alone. Repeatedly, Israel was admonished to hear and obey the word of the Lord (Deut. 6:3; 30:2; Isa. 50:10). Unfortunately, Israel more often than not failed the test of obedience. Much of the OT reveals recurring cycles of disobedience, punishment, repentance and obedience, and then restoration. The cycle repeated until God sent Israel into exile because of its disobedience.

Obedience shows trust in God. Many of the great heroes of faith were noted for their obedience, including Noah, Abraham, Moses, David, Ruth, and Mary. The supreme example of obedience is Jesus Christ, who "humbled himself and became obedient to the point of death—even death on a cross" (Phil. 2:8*b*). In fact, it is because of Christ's obedience to the Father that salvation for all is possible (Rom. 5:19; Heb. 5:8). Because of Christ's perfect obedience, God the Father, through Christ's resurrection, has highly exalted him.

In the Gospels Jesus is described as a Master. Obedience by his disciples is described as following him and being his disciple. Part of Jesus' Great Commission to his disciples is that they are to teach others to obey everything he has commanded. In the Epistles, Jesus is described as Lord and coming King to whom everyone owes the same obedience as that owed to the Father.

In the Scriptures, disobedience to God leads to death; obedience leads to the life God has always intended for humanity (Deut. 30; Rom. 6:15-23). Wholehearted (loving) obedience, as contrasted with heartless and legalistic obedience, is the essence of a sanctified life (Rom. 6:17-19).

See also Covenant; Creation/New Creation; Law and Gospel; Legalism; Love; Repentance; Sin.

RODNEY L. REED, PHD

OBERLIN PERFECTIONISM

See HOLINESS MOVEMENTS: AMERICAN, BRITISH, AND CONTINENTAL.

OLD TESTAMENT METAPHORS APPLIED TO JESUS IN THE NEW TESTAMENT

See CHRISTOLOGY, NEW TESTAMENT; INTERTEXTUALITY.

OPEN THEOLOGY/THEISM

In the 1990s a group of evangelical theologians and philosophers developed a theology that became known as open theology or open theism. Open theology modifies two aspects of the traditional Wesleyan-Arminian doctrine of God.

First, open theism affirms that God is everlasting rather than atemporal (doesn't experience time). God experiences a *before* and an *after* as God relates to humans and other creatures.

Second, open theism affirms *dynamic omniscience*. God knows all that has happened in the past and all that is happening in the present. God knows that future events determined by him will occur. God knows all that might happen. But God does not know with certainty what creatures possessing free will will do.

The term "open" involves two key ideas: (1) God is open to what creatures do freely, and (2) the future is open because in many instances there is more than one possible option (think of a create-your-own storybook). According to open theology, God engages in genuine give-and-receive relations with creatures. For example, God responds to our prayers. God responds to contingencies and, if necessary, adjusts his plans in response to decisions free creatures make. God typically exercises flexible strategies to accomplish divine goals.

Though God's nature does not change, God does have changing emotions and plans of action. Also, because God grants free will to some creatures, it is possible for them to bring about evil that opposes God's will. Creatures with free will can thwart some divine plans.

Open theists support their position biblically and theologically. The Bible portrays God as responding to petitions (2 Kings 20), grieving over sin (Gen. 6:6), and testing people to find out what they will do (Gen. 22). God changes his mind (Exod. 32:14) and predicts specific events that do not happen (Ezek. 26:1-16; 29:17-20). If the Bible's portrayal of God is accurate, then God must (1) be temporal in some sense (experiences a before and an after) and (2) possess dynamic omniscience.

Theologically, open theists argue that divine atemporality logically entails that God does not change at all, for divine atemporality means that God cannot change in any respect. Saying that God doesn't change (doesn't experience time) contradicts the belief that God has changing emotions or plans. Also, they argue that exhaustive divine foreknowledge entails that there be only one deterministic future. Additionally, open theists have raised a new problem: divine foreknowledge is pointless. Once God knows that a specific event will occur, then it is impossible for God to make an event *not* occur. Making a foreknown event not happen would mean that God "foreknew" incorrectly. For example, once God observes that the Nazis will bring about the Holocaust, God cannot subsequently do anything to prevent it. If God has foreknowledge, then intercessory prayer and divine guidance are pointless.

Dynamic omniscience was anticipated by numerous Methodist thinkers, including Andrew Ramsay, a contemporary of John Wesley; Methodist theologian and biblical scholar Adam Clarke (ca. 1760–1832); and American Lorenzo D. McCabe (1817-97).

See also Free Will; God, Doctrine of; Process Theology; Time and Eternity.

Resources
Sanders, John. *The God Who Risks: A Theology of Divine Providence.* 2nd ed. Downers Grove, IL: IVP Academic, 2007.
Pinnock, Clark H. *Most Moved Mover: A Theology of God's Openness.* Grand Rapids: Baker, 2001.

JOHN SANDERS, THD

ORDINARY AND EXTRAORDINARY MINISTRIES OF THE CHURCH

In his *Explanatory Notes upon the New Testament* (*NT Notes,* 2:170-71; comments on Eph. 4:8, 11-12) John Wesley distinguished between the *ordinary* and *extraordinary* gifts of the Spirit, exercised as ministries in the church

(John Calvin had earlier made and discussed a similar distinction in his *Institutes of the Christian Religion* [1536-59], bk. 4, 3.4-5). The "extraordinary officers" are the (1) apostles, who were Christ's "chief ministers and special witnesses"; (2) prophets, "who testify of things to come"; and (3) evangelists, who testify of "things past by preaching the gospel before or after any of the apostles." The "ordinary" ministers or officers are (1) pastors, who "watch over their several flocks," and (2) teachers, who "assist [pastors] as occasion might require."

By relying upon this warrant from Christ in the Scriptures, as early as 1739 Wesley authorized lay evangelists to preach the gospel as extraordinary ministers. As extraordinary ministers, the lay evangelists were free to itinerate widely. Their ministry was among those whom the established church had largely neglected. They were not episcopally ordained and so did not serve in a priestly/pastoral role; they could not administer the sacraments. Pastors (priests) were ordinary ministers who had as their primary responsibility the care of a congregation and celebration of the sacraments; they could itinerate only minimally, if at all.

This warrant was more than a mere formality. It provided a defense against persistent accusations that Methodist lay evangelists were imposters in Christ's church. Wesley and the Methodist evangelists were often persecuted by clergy and magistrates. They were attacked in sermons, books, and tracts and even mobbed by the populace. These extraordinary ministers were accused of being blind and uneducated fanatics, of propagating heretical doctrines, and of fomenting religious disturbances.

See also Wesley, John, Theology of.

Resources
Calvin, John. *Institutes of the Christian Religion.* 1536-59. Translated by Henry Beveridge. Edinburgh: T and T Clark, 1863. Reprint, Peabody, MA: Hendrickson Publishers, 2008.
Wesley, John. "The Ministerial Office." In *Works,* 7:273-81.

ROBERT K. LANG'AT, PHD

ORDINATION

Ordination is an ecclesiastical process whereby certain persons (ordinands) are set apart and authorized to perform specific religious rituals or practices constitutive of a religion. Ordination occurs in at least the following: Judaism, Christianity, Buddhism, and the Latter-day Saints.

Among Christians, ordination—normally involving "laying on of hands" —authorizes a person to engage in particular ministerial (clergy) functions, including publically proclaiming the gospel, administering the **sacraments**, and performing legally authorized rituals such as marriage. The prerequisites and procedures for ordination vary by Christian denomination.

The **Roman Catholic Church** recognizes three "levels" of ordination: bishop, priest, and deacon. It involves two unique features: ordination is one of the seven sacraments, and the actual "laying on of hands" is performed by a bishop who stands in so-called apostolic succession. This assumes a historical and hierarchical continuity with the twelve apostles, who were "ordained" by Christ. Eastern **Orthodoxy** and **Anglicanism** (Church of England) share these assumptions with the major exceptions of not requiring celibacy or harmony with the bishop of Rome; in Anglicanism ordination is not a sacrament.

Most **Protestant** churches assume the ordinand has "received" a call to ministry and has gone through a specified educational process to qualify for ministerial service. Depending on a denomination's **ecclesiology**, the authority to ordain may reside principally in either a congregation or an episcopal structure. Some Protestant groups recognize more than one order of ministry and may ordain persons as deacon, elder, or bishop. Local congregations not part of a denomination (nondenominational) also grant ordination status. Ultimately, Wesley defied his own Anglican tradition that only bishops could ordain; he began to ordain his lay-preacher "helpers" (*Works*, 13:251-52).

Traditionally restricted to men, ordination as it applies to women resulted in a major controversy. The restriction of ordination to men is largely based on Paul's words in 1 Cor. 14:34. **John Wesley**'s view on this matter, in the eighteenth century, was a notable exception. Apparently for practical reasons, Wesley recognized the validity of unordained men and women preachers in his **societies**, believing that God would use extraordinary means to accomplish extraordinary ends in extraordinary times.

After a mixed history, in 1956 the General Conference of the Methodist Church approved full clergy rights for women. Today, approximately twelve thousand United Methodist clergywomen serve the church at every level, from bishops to local pastors.

The holiness movement of the nineteenth and early twentieth centuries recognized the role of women in clergy leadership and freely ordained them. After being influenced by **fundamentalism, holiness denominations** exhibited a more negative attitude toward female ordination. More recently in the holiness churches there has been a resurgence of female ordination.

See also Pentecostalism; Wesley, John, Theology of; Wesleyan Feminism.

Resources
Wesley, John. "An Address to the Clergy." In *Works*, 10:480-500.
———. "The Ministerial Office." In *Works*, 7:273-81.

H. RAY DUNNING, PHD

ORDO SALUTIS

Ordo salutis is a Latin term meaning "order of salvation" and refers to the conceptual steps within the Christian doctrine of **salvation**. It was first used in the mid-1720s by Lutheran theologians. Some recent theologians have called the concept into question as running the risk of "psychologizing" salvation or failing to do justice to its dynamic nature. Another objection is the recent emphasis many NT scholars place on the narrative character of Pauline thought; narrative lends itself to events arranged by story, not by logic. Others, such as N. T. Wright, say Paul's *ordo salutis* is found in Rom. 8:29-30. These steps are foreknowledge, predestination (meaning marking out ahead of time the goal of salvation), calling, justification, and glorification. In the history of Christian thought, various theological perspectives have produced diverse interpretations of the *ordo salutis*.

Although **Roman Catholic** theology did not use the term, Catholic soteriology reflected a definable order of events leading to final salvation. The beginning point is faith (understood as assent to church teaching) followed by baptism and confirmation that begins a lifelong process of **sanctification** (becoming holy). This may culminate in **justification** if completed in this life. Otherwise, the process must be completed in purgatory for final justification.

The Protestant Reformers essentially reversed the Catholic order of **justification** and **sanctification**. They taught that God justifies the unrighteous on the basis of grace through faith alone, after which follows a lifelong process of sanctification, always incomplete in this life. Believing in the absolute sovereignty of grace and desiring to eliminate any possibility of self-salvation, the first step in the *ordo salutis* for **Luther** and **Calvin** was predestination understood as God's decision in advance regarding who would be saved (the elect) and who lost. This was objective in nature, being God's unilateral decision with no human involvement. Calling was universal, but *effectual* calling extended only to the elect. The first subjective step in salvation in the Calvinistic scheme is regeneration, since humanity is conceived as being totally depraved and deprived of any knowledge of God or capacity to respond to him. Repentance follows regeneration, since only a regenerated person can be aware of his or her sinfulness and thus repent. Repentance is a repeated occurrence throughout the Christian life.

The Wesleyan-Arminian view, based on a different understanding of God's essential nature as love, understands **predestination** as a class concept. Those predestined to be saved are those who respond in faith to Jesus Christ. Thus awakening and calling (the function of **prevenient grace**) are extended to all. Prevenient grace enables the awakened to call on God through repentance and faith. Like Protestantism in general, Wesleyans see justification preceding sanctification. It is an act of pardon that settles eternal destiny, conditioned on faith and obedience. Wesleyan uniqueness is its confidence in grace to effect a moment of cleansing from sin in this life, commonly called **entire sanctification**.

Wesleyan and Calvinistic theologies believe the final step in salvation is glorification, which takes place in eternity when the full consequences of the fall are removed and believers are fully restored to God's image.

See also Christian Perfection (Entire Sanctification); Christology; Christology, New Testament; Gospel; Grace; Justification; Means of Grace; Reconciliation; Righteousness; Salvation (Soteriology); Spiritual Formation/Growth.

Resources

Collins, Kenneth J. *The Scripture Way of Salvation: The Heart of John Wesley's Theology.* Nashville: Abingdon Press, 1997.

Weber, Theodore R. *Politics in the Order of Salvation: Transforming Wesleyan Political Ethics.* Nashville: Kingswood Books, 2001.

H. RAY DUNNING, PHD

ORIGINAL SIN

See SIN.

ORTHODOX CHURCH

For most Christians in the Wesleyan tradition, relating to the Orthodox Church requires thinking outside our usual liturgical, experiential, and (to some extent) theological parameters. The Wesleyan tradition is largely a product of Western Christianity (growing in and from the Latin-speaking half of the Roman Empire). However, John Wesley was influenced by various **church fathers** from the Eastern or Greek-speaking half of the empire. The Eastern Church is usually known as the Orthodox Church, or as Orthodoxy. Many of its adherents now live in the West.

The designation "Orthodox Church" refers to a number of self-governing churches that consciously and deeply consider themselves part of the Orthodox tradition. Because of how consistently these churches identify as Orthodox, we can speak of them as composing *the* Orthodox Church as though it were a single entity. But we can also speak in the plural—the Orthodox churches. The patriarchs or metropolitans (heads of ecclesiastical provinces) who lead these churches include the metropolitans of Constantinople, Alexandria, Antioch, Jerusalem, Russia, and Greece.

The historical and doctrinal identity of the Orthodox Church is inextricably tied to the seven **ecumenical councils**. There are other churches similar to the Orthodox Church that did not accept the pronouncements of all seven councils. The **Church of the East** accepted only the first two ecumenical councils and became affiliated with Nestorian Christians. The Oriental Orthodox (Syrian, **Coptic Orthodox**, and **Armenian Apostolic Church**), often referred to as Monophysite, did not accept the **Christological** definitions of the fourth council. A third group accepts the authority of the pope even though the churches follow Eastern traditions. They are known as Greek or Eastern Catholics.

Several historical and theological events help identify and define Orthodoxy. The emperor Constantine (ca. 274–337) became a Christian in 312. He built the city of Constantinople as his capital city, which became the center of Eastern Christianity. Even though the patriarch of Constantinople doesn't have authority over the other Eastern churches, he is looked on as the ecumenical patriarch of all Orthodoxy.

In 988, Prince Vladimir of Kiev converted to Orthodox Christianity. From that time the Slavic churches began to form. The Slavic churches, including the Russian Orthodox Church, now make up the majority of Orthodox Christians. After the fall of Constantinople to the Ottoman Empire (1453), Moscow became the principal Orthodox city.

Differences between the Latin West and the Greek East existed from the start. Differences in language accounted for some of the tension. The growing breach between the Eastern and Western churches included Orthodox irritation over claims of papal authority. In 1054, the conflict culminated in the division between Rome and Constantinople known as the Great Schism.

The word **orthodoxy** has the double meaning of right belief and correct worship. Eastern Orthodoxy claims both, but correct worship is central. Salvation is received through the liturgy where Christ is present and where the church participates in divine realities. The liturgy is the principal location of **theosis** or deification (sanctification), which is the perfection or right aim of Christian development. Mystery, contemplation, and symbol are prominent components of Orthodox faith and worship. Orthodox Christians perceive the real presence of God in the Eucharist. Given the Orthodox emphasis on liturgy, and because of the noticeable influence of monasticism, the church year is highly significant in shaping Orthodox life. Orthodox bishops are selected from celibate clergy, but most parish priests are married.

Tradition is the basis of Orthodox theology and is composed of Scripture, liturgy, and the theological definitions of the **ecumenical councils.** It also includes interpretations of the **church fathers, icons,** and practices by which the **Holy Spirit** has guided the **church** through the ages. The primary value of the councils is their definitions of the **Trinity** and the **incarnation.** The Nicene Creed summarizes the definitions and right understanding of Christian theology, but the Creed was not meant to offer a logical explanation of the Trinity and the incarnation.

Mystical theology and **liturgical theology** are the most common theological approaches. The divine mystery is adored and contemplated. The inability of human reason to grasp the mystery is evident and expected. Consequently, unlike what Christians in the West are accustomed to, language about God is typically negative; it speaks of what God is not, instead of trying to explain who God is.

Orthodox theology and spirituality are distinctly Trinitarian. Orthodox refer to Mary as *Theotokos* (God-bearer). This affirms both the divinity of Jesus Christ and the necessity of Mary's cooperation with God.

Inspired by Methodist theologian Albert Outler (1908-89), there occurred a major trend in Wesleyan studies to trace the origins of much of John Wesley's thought to the theology of the Eastern fathers. In particular, Orthodox influence can be seen in Wesley's more therapeutic and less legal understanding of soteriology (salvation) and in a teleological (design-, purpose-, or goal-related) exposition of **sanctification** and **Christian perfection**. This interpretation is currently being tempered by a reexamination of these Wesleyan doctrinal features in light of various Western precedents. But the basic appreciation of the Greek influence on Wesley will remain. Explanations of tradition that draw upon Orthodoxy are visible in the thinking of some Wesleyan theologians involved in the **evangelical retrieval of tradition**.

See also Christian Perfection (Entire Sanctification); Church (Ecclesiology); Ecumenical Councils; Icons, Images, Iconoclasm; Mary/Mariology; Pseudo-Macarius; Trinity.

Resources

Binns, John. *An Introduction to the Christian Orthodox Churches.* Cambridge, UK: Cambridge University Press, 2002.
Kimbrough, S. T., Jr., ed. *Orthodox and Wesleyan Spirituality.* Crestwood, NY: St Vladimir's Seminary Press, 2002.
Lossky, Vladimir. *The Mystical Theology of the Eastern Church.* Crestwood, NY: St Vladimir's Seminary Press, 1998.
Ware, Timothy. *The Orthodox Church.* New ed. New York: Penguin, 1993.

KARL GANSKE, PHD

ORTHODOXY/ORTHOPRAXIS/ORTHOPATHY

Orthodoxy stems from the Greek words *orthos* (right; correct) and *doxa* (belief; opinion). Christian orthodoxy means right belief grounded in the apostolic faith and the biblical revelation. Right conviction about the truth (orthodoxy) contrasts with erroneous belief, or heresy (*hairesis*). Paul wrote about the folly of those who "exchanged the truth about God for a lie and worshiped and served the creature rather than the Creator" (Rom. 1:25). He warned the Galatians against "turning to a different gospel—not that there is another gospel" (Gal. 1:6-7). The apostle Peter warned of the eternal danger of trading truth for error: "False prophets also arose among the people, just as there will be false teachers . . . , who will secretly bring in destructive opinions . . . bringing swift destruction on themselves" (2 Pet. 2:1).

The term "orthodoxy" first appeared in the second century to refer to theological opinions that are true to the revelation of Scripture. Today,

Christians use the term "orthodoxy" to denote beliefs that constitute the indispensable doctrinal standards of the church.

Orthopraxis is a term derived from the Greek word *orthopraxis* (correct action or right practice). Orthopraxy denotes right doing, as an essential complement to right believing. The book of James links right believing with right acting: "I by my works will show you my faith" (2:18). Jesus said, "Not everyone who says to me, 'Lord, Lord,' will enter the kingdom of heaven, but only the one who does the will of my Father in heaven" (Matt. 7:21). John taught, "Now by this we may be sure that we know him, if we obey his commandments. . . . By this we may be sure that we are in him: whoever says, 'I abide in him,' ought to walk just as he walked" (1 John 2:3, 5-6).

In Scripture, God's commands are always accompanied by his promises to bless. God told Moses to tell the people of Israel, "Now therefore, if you obey my voice and keep my covenant, you shall be my treasured possession" (Exod. 19:5). James wrote, "Those who look into the perfect law . . . and persevere, being not hearers who forget but doers who act—they will be blessed in their doing" (1:25).

Orthopathy is derived from two Greek words that denote a person's attitude or "inmost self." If true religion includes right *belief* and right *practice*, it also includes right *affections*. **John Wesley** often spoke of a right "temper," by which he meant a right attitude. Thomas Chalmers preached about "the expulsive power of a new affection" ([1819-23?]). Jonathan Edwards equated right religious affections with holy dispositions such as reverence and love.

Humankind has the capacity for good or bad inclinations of the heart. Cain was heartless toward Abel; Ruth had a good heart toward Naomi. Paul spoke of the heart as the sphere of divine activity, and he wrote, "God, through Jesus Christ, will judge the secret thoughts of all" (Rom. 2:16). The book of Proverbs counsels, "Keep your heart with all vigilance, for from it flow the springs of life" (4:23). "You will seek the LORD your God, and you will find him if you search after him with all your heart and soul" (Deut. 4:29). Such is the meaning of "orthopathy."

In sum, *orthodoxy* is the right belief of God's revealed truth; *orthopraxy* is the proper implementation of truth in our behavior; *orthopathy* is the expression of holy and loving inclinations. These three concepts refer to head, hand, and heart. Right believing, acting, and dispositions are possible only by the work of God's grace within us.

See also Altruism/Natural Morality; Christian Ethics/Moral Theology; Covenant Service; Ecumenical Councils; Means of Grace; Tempers and Affections; Wesley, John, Theology of; Women's Role in the Church.

Resource
Chalmers, Thomas. "The Expulsive Power of a New Affection." [1819-23?]. https://docs
.google.com/document/d/1DtV3twNfBd_hn027EYxMeFXN5j9_V3mxKV5l8Srk
4bg/edit?pli=1.

KENNETH C. KINGHORN, PHD

ORTHOPATHY

See ORTHODOXY/ORTHOPRAXIS/ORTHOPATHY.

ORTHOPATHY/ORTHOKARDIA

The terms "orthopathy" (right affections or right experience) and "ortho-kardia" (right heart) refer to a central theological and spiritual dimension of the Christian life that is not encompassed by the more familiar terms "orthodoxy" (right belief) and "orthopraxy" (right practice). As used by many Wesleyan and Pentecostal theologians, as well as by some Reformed theologians in the tradition of Jonathan Edwards, "orthopathy" or "orthokardia" designates the third element in the mutual interaction of beliefs, actions, and experiences that shapes Christian lives and communities.

Gregory S. Clapper (*John Wesley on Religious Affections* [1989]) coined the term "orthokardia" to designate Wesley's concern for a heart governed and motivated by holy tempers or affections. It has been subsequently used by Joel Green (*Reading Scripture as Wesleyans* [2010]). Steven J. Land (*Pentecostal Spirituality* [1993]), Henry H. Knight III (*The Presence of God in the Christian Life* [1992]), and Richard Steele (*"Heart Religion" in the Methodist Tradition and Related Movements* [2001]) use "orthopathy" in much the same way—to describe a moral integration of the heart through its being formed and shaped by Christian tempers or affections. Theodore Runyon (*The New Creation* [1998]) uses "orthopathy" epistemologically to designate a transformative experience with God through faith that renews the heart and incorporates persons into God's mission to renew the whole of creation in holiness.

This insistence on a "right heart" and "right affections" is consistent with the Wesleyan rejection of a "dead orthodoxy" and "dead formalism," in which beliefs and actions are disconnected from a transforming relationship with God. In the Wesleyan vision, the heart and its tempers are formed and shaped by experiencing the God orthodoxy describes, and by receiving the new life God promises. Thus renewed in love, holiness of heart provides the character and motivation for the holiness of life orthopraxy requires.

See also Epistemology; Orthodoxy/Orthopraxis/Orthopathy; Tempers and Affections.

HENRY H. KNIGHT III, PHD

ORTHOPRAXIS

See ORTHODOXY/ORTHOPRAXIS/ORTHOPATHY.

P p

PALMER, PHOEBE

Phoebe Worrall Palmer (1807-74) was an American Methodist author, theologian, and **revivalist**. She was born in New York City to devout **Methodist** parents and was raised in the Methodist Episcopal Church (MEC). She joined the MEC as a young girl and was an active member for the rest of her life. In 1827 she married Dr. Walter C. Palmer. The Palmers had six children, three of whom survived to adulthood. Following a deep religious experience in 1837 she assumed a leadership role in a developing movement concerned with keeping **John Wesley**'s doctrine of **Christian perfection** at the heart of Methodist teaching and practice. At the time Methodism in the United States was rapidly expanding both numerically and geographically and undergoing significant changes in social and economic status. By the mid-1840s Palmer had become the primary spokesperson for this **holiness movement**, or holiness revival, which eventually spread beyond Methodism to influence other **Protestant** denominations in North America, the British Isles, and elsewhere. By the end of the nineteenth century this movement had produced a sizeable group of independent **holiness denominations and churches** that claimed to preserve and propagate the teaching and spirit of original Wesleyanism.

Beginning with *The Way of Holiness* (1843), Palmer published nearly twenty books, several of which passed through multiple editions during her lifetime. She also edited an influential, widely read religious journal, *The Guide to Holiness*, for ten years (1864-74). In addition she presided over a popular weekly religious gathering, the Tuesday Meeting for the Promotion of Holiness, in her home for more than thirty years. This meeting inspired hundreds of similar gatherings, and these holiness meetings became a formative feature of the growing holiness movement throughout the nineteenth century. Between 1840 and 1874 Palmer traveled thousands of miles speaking and teaching in churches, camp meetings, religious colleges and seminaries, and public auditoriums. She crossed the United States and Canada several times and traveled to Great Britain and to the European continent. At the height of her popularity she was one of the most widely recognized revivalists in the world.

Central to Palmer's ministry was a creative interpretation of the Wesleyan doctrine of Christian perfection. This "shorter way" to full sanctification provided seekers with a clear path to the "second blessing." Distrustful of religious emotions, Palmer urged seekers simply to follow a series of logical steps: (1) acknowledge God's requirement of, and provision for, perfect holiness; (2) consecrate oneself entirely to God; (3) believe that God is always faithful to fulfill the promise to sanctify what is consecrated; and (4) testify clearly and publicly to what God has done. The third step embodied Palmer's "altar principle" or "altar theology," which became one of her better-known teachings. Its foundation is her interpretation of Matt. 23:19, which she understood to be a promise to Christians seeking to be filled with perfect love. Palmer reasoned that since the passage speaks of the altar of sacrifice that "sanctifieth" the gift placed on it (KJV), the text promises the seeker after holiness that the Christian's altar—Christ (Heb. 13:10)—will unerringly make holy the gift of a fully consecrated life. This inspired the phrase "the altar sanctifies the gift" as a kind of motto within the holiness movement. It served as a source of assurance for those who believed they had fully consecrated their lives to Christ.

Palmer's redescription of faith as trusting that one has received promises in Scripture, thus making a witness of the Spirit unnecessary, was the most controversial aspect of her theology among Methodists. In addition, her claim that entire sanctification is immediate upon consecration and faith moved away from Wesley's emphasis on the freedom of God to determine its timing.

In the 1850s Palmer implicitly addressed the criticism that she had understated the dynamism of divine action. She did this by equating entire sanctification with the **baptism of the Holy Spirit**. Drawing on the Pentecostal language of **John Fletcher** and others, she now understood the baptism of the Spirit as both sanctifying and empowering, enabling women as well as men publically to proclaim the gospel and testify to its blessings.

Palmer's altar theology and language of Spirit baptism would have an enormous impact on the holiness movement, as well as its later Pentecostal offspring.

Phoebe Palmer also invested substantial time, energy, and money in a variety of significant and highly visible charitable and humanitarian works that served the poor and needy. For many years she engaged in a ministry of prison visitation. She supported several orphanages and promoted the care of orphans, one of the most vulnerable groups in mid-nineteenth-century American society. She was also a principal founder of the Five Points Mission. Founded in 1850 and located in one of New York's poorest neighbor-hoods, the mission provided a day school for children, low-cost housing for a number of poor families, and clothing and food distribution. It was also as-sociated with the Five Points House of Industry, a manufacturing enterprise that sometimes employed over five hundred people.

Throughout her public career Palmer was an advocate for the right of women to minister in the churches. In 1859 she published *Promise of the Father*, which marshaled evidence from Scripture and Christian history to support the right of women to minister and which uncompromisingly con-demned the denominations of her day that restricted the full participation of women in the life of the church.

See also Holiness; Holiness Movements: American, British, and Continental; Methodism, American; Methodism, British; Revivalism; Sanctification; Wesley, John, Theology of; Wesleyan Feminism.

Resources

Heath, Elaine. *Naked Faith: The Mystical Theology of Phoebe Palmer*. Eugene, OR: Pickwick Publications, 2009.

Leclerc, Diane. *Singleness of Heart: Gender, Sin, and Holiness in Historical Perspective*. Metuchen, NJ: Scarecrow Press, 2001.

Raser, Harold E. *Phoebe Palmer, Her Life and Thought*. Lewiston, NY: Edwin Mellen Press, 1987.

White, Charles E. *The Beauty of Holiness: Phoebe Palmer as Theologian, Revivalist, Feminist, and Humanitarian*. Grand Rapids: Francis Asbury Press, 1986. Reprint, Eugene, OR: Wipf and Stock, 2008.

HAROLD E. RASER, PHD

PANENTHEISM

The term "panentheism" combines the English equivalents of the Greek terms *pan* (all), *en* (in), and *theos* (God). It understands God and the world as essentially interrelated. Advocates stress God's active presence in the world while maintaining a vital distinction between God and creation. This view contrasts with traditional theism, which tends to stress God's independence (or otherness) from the world. It also contrasts with **pantheism**, which stress-es the identity of God and the world. Although hints of panentheism occur in earlier philosophical and theological writings, important developments have occurred in the past two centuries, especially since Charles Harteshorne's use of the term in *Philosophers Speak of God* in 1953.

There are numerous forms of panentheism.

German theologian Jürgen Moltmann advocates a form of panentheism that involves God in the world and the world in God. The relationship be-tween God and the world is similar to that between members of the Trin-ity, which inherently involves relationship and community. Creation results from God's essential nature and activity as love. Because God is infinite, nothing is outside God. For the creation to exist, God must withdraw (not to be understood as the world existing independently). God's self-emptying (*kenosis*) occurs in both creation and the **incarnation**. The interpenetration between God and creation preserves their unity and difference.

Arthur Peacocke sees the world as a unity composed of complex systems, a hierarchy of levels. He rejects dualism, for the being of God *includes* and penetrates the whole universe. God continuously creates *through* the processes of the natural order, not as an additional, external influence *on* the world. God always works from inside the universe (ruling out creation *ex nihilo*). But God is not to be identified with natural processes; they result from God's creative action. God is infinitely more than the universe. Peacocke combines a strong emphasis on God's immanence with God's ultimate transcendence over the universe by using a model of personal agency.

Philip Clayton, drawing on **process theology**, affirms the interdependence of God and the world. He rejects the notion of God as a distinct substance. God's inclusion of finite being as actual, rather than as a mere idea or potentiality, is contingent on God's decision rather than being necessary to God's essence. The involvement of the world in an internal relationship with God does not completely constitute God's being. Instead, God is both primordial, or eternal, and responsive to the world. The world constitutes God's relational aspect but not God's totality.

One problem panentheism presents for traditional theism is that it holds to an essential and necessary balance between transcendence and immanence. This entails that the world actually affects God. If the world affects or somehow limits God, then, traditional theists argue, God is limited in God's ability to provide salvation for the world.

While Wesleyan theology values careful thought and philosophy, it evaluates philosophical thought according to its consistency with Scripture, Christian tradition, reason, and Christian experience. Accordingly, Wesleyan theology makes a prominent place for God's immanence (Col. 1:12-17; Phil. 2:5-8), for real finite freedom, and for the world's making a (covenantal) difference to God in his relationship to it and in the way he implements his purposes. But also in accordance with Scripture, Wesleyan theology in no sense makes the being of God dependent on the world. In no respect is God's identity, his holiness, his absolute singularity (Isa. 41:18-31), ever confused with or dependent on the world.

See also Creation/New Creation; God, Doctrine of; Monism, Dualism, Pluralism; Pantheism; Process Theology.

Resources

Clayton, Philip, and Arthur Peacocke, eds. *In Whom We Live and Move and Have Our Being: Panentheistic Reflections on God's Presence in a Scientific World*. Grand Rapids: Eerdmans, 2004.

Cooper, John W. *Panentheism: The Other God of the Philosophers—From Plato to the Present.* Grand Rapids: Baker Academic, 2006.

Culp, John. "Panentheism." In *Stanford Encyclopedia of Philosophy.* Stanford University, 1997-. Article revised May 19, 2009. http://plato.stanford.edu/entries/panentheism/.

JOHN CULP, PHD

PANTHEISM

Pantheism is a combination of two Greek words: *pan*, meaning "all," and *theos*, the term for "god." Literally, the word means a "belief that God is all." There are two opposite ways of interpreting the relation between God and the world. One emphasizes God's transcendence and takes the form of **deism**; the other emphasizes God's immanence. Pantheism is its extreme form. A major task in theology involves balancing God's transcendence and immanence.

Pantheism takes philosophical and theological forms. The classical philosophical expression of pantheism appears in the philosophy of Baruch Spinoza (1632-77). He used the formula *Deus sive Natura* to summarize his position. He meant that God and Nature are interchangeable. Using the philosophical discourse of that period, Spinoza argued there is only one substance. By contrast, French philosopher René Descartes argued there are two substances—mind and matter.

For Spinoza the one substance has two attributes—thought and extension. Practically "as the *world* consists of the modes of God's attributes, everything in the world acts in accordance with necessity, that is, everything is determined" (Stumpf 1971, 251). As Spinoza put it, "Individual things are nothing but modifications of the attributes of God [Nature], or modes by which the attributes . . . are expressed in a fixed and definite manner" ([1677] 1883, pt. 1, prop. 25).

A modern adaptation of God's radical immanence, and therefore a form of pantheism, is the theology of Paul Tillich. Tillich insists that "pantheism does not mean, never has meant, and never should mean that everything that is, is God." On the contrary, "Pantheism is the doctrine that God is the substance or essence of all things, not the meaningless assertion that God is the totality of things" (1967, 1:233-34). This explains Tillich's assertion that God is "being itself," or the "ground of being." This is Tillich's alternative to traditional theism, which posits the existence of God as separate and distinct from the material creation. Speaking of God as "existing," Tillich insists, implies that he is a dependent being rather than the power of all beings.

Eastern religions such as Taoism and Hinduism are pantheistic in nature. Their goal is the absorption of individuality in the whole. A modern folk form of pantheism is the **New Age** movement that became popular in the 1960s.

See also God, Doctrine of; Neo-paganism; Panentheism.

Resources

Spinoza, Benedict de. *The Ethics.* 1677. Reprint of the 1883 translation by R. H. M. Elwes, Project Gutenberg, 2003. http://www.gutenberg.org/files/3800/3800-h/3800-h.htm.
Stumpf, Samuel E. *Philosophy: History and Problems.* New York: McGraw-Hill, 1971.
Tillich, Paul. *Systematic Theology.* 3 vols. in 1. Chicago: University of Chicago Press, 1967.

H. RAY DUNNING, PHD

PAPACY
See ROMAN CATHOLICISM.

PARACHURCH INSTITUTIONS

During the twentieth century many agencies known as parachurch organizations/ministries or voluntary societies arose outside traditional denominational structures to recruit and send missionaries. They are called parachurch because they "come alongside" traditional denominations. Organizationally they are independent of denominations. Today they engage in many forms of ministry, including Bible translation, aviation, compassion, medicine, and microbusiness. Their focus is often on particular populations or geographic areas.

Modern parachurch ministries are rooted in church history. For centuries the Christian mission has been carried out by agencies somewhat removed from direct ecclesiastical control. The monastic orders of the Roman Catholic Church and Orthodoxy illustrate this. The Benedictines, Dominicans, and Franciscans all conducted missionary activity. The Society of Jesus (the Jesuits), established in the mid-sixteenth century, combined scholarship and practice to create effective ways of preaching the gospel, establishing indigenous churches, educating the converted, and developing indigenous churches throughout Asia and the Americas.

Among Protestants, early missionary societies not under direct denominational control began to flourish in the late eighteenth century. This began with the Baptist Missionary Society (1792) that sent William Carey and Joshua Marshman to India. Other missionary societies arose, including the London Missionary Society (1795) and the Church Missionary Society (1799). In the mid-1800s J. Hudson Taylor focused on the interior of China. He recruited and sent missionaries as widely as possible, resulting in the China Inland Mission (now known as the Overseas Missionary Fellowship [OMF]).

During the first two decades of the nineteenth century, at least half a dozen missionary societies arose and introduced a model for missions that spawned many institutions and agencies. During the late nineteenth and early twentieth centuries, tens of thousands of students offered themselves for missionary service, many of whom were deployed through the parachurch Student Volunteer Movement. By sending missionaries to world areas, parachurch organizations contributed to what has been termed the great Christian century.

Today the role of parachurch ministries includes some activities normally conducted by denominations. But the ministry of denominations would be weaker were it not for parachurch agencies.

There is, however, a tension between the mission efforts of denominations and parachurch agencies regarding personnel and finances. Two-thirds of the annual monies contributed to missions by Protestants in North America are earmarked for short-term missions within and outside denominational structures. Increasing individualism, skepticism about the efficiency of denominational structures, and the ease with which Christians can identify ministries that match their specific interests add to the tension.

Often, parachurch agencies are more flexible than traditional denominational structures. Fiscal and asset accountability can appear to contributors to be more closely monitored. However, with their smaller staffs and more restricted emphases, parachurch ministries may lack adequate resources for theological education and for caring for and supporting their missionaries. The polity, doctrinal distinctives, and accountability offered by denominations can go lacking in parachurch agencies.

Unlike modern parachurch agencies, the Catholic orders remained within the church and under its care and authority. The current challenge is for denominations and parachurch agencies to demonstrate a harmony in their Christian witness, stewardship of resources, and creative approaches to mission. The challenge is to evidence one holy catholic and apostolic church.

Resources

Willmer, Wesley K., J. David Schmidt, and Martyn Smith. *The Prospering Parachurch: Enlarging the Boundaries of God's Kingdom*. San Francisco: Jossey-Bass Publishers, 1998.

Winter, Ralph D. "Protestant Mission Societies: The American Experience." *Missiology: An International Review* 7, no. 2 (April 1979): 139-78.

WILLIAM L. SELVIDGE, DMISS

PARACLETE

See HOLY SPIRIT (PNEUMATOLOGY).

PARLIAMENT OF THE WORLD'S RELIGIONS

The Parliament of the World's Religions first met in Chicago in conjunction with the World's Columbian Exposition. It opened on September 11, 1893, under the direction of the Rev. J. H. Barrows, later famous as a Christian lecturer in India. Over four thousand people attended the opening session. The event was the birthplace of formal interfaith dialogue.

Since 1993 the parliament has convened every five years in major international cities: Chicago 1993, Cape Town 1999, Barcelona 2004, and Melbourne 2009. The 2009 parliament aimed to renew in people of faith reason to believe world peace is possible. The Council for a Parliament of the World's Religions, based in Chicago, sponsors the parliament.

The world's largest religious gathering, the parliament gathers leaders and communicants from many religious and spiritual communities. They explore peace, diversity, and sustainability in a context of interreligious understanding and cooperation.

During the 1893 Chicago parliament, representatives of ten world religions, including Christianity, addressed the gathering. Among those on the platform at the opening session was Cardinal Gibbons, Roman Catholic bishop of Baltimore. Other major figures were Isaac Mayer, representing Judaism; Mary Baker Eddy, representing Christian Science; Annie Besant, representing Theosophy; and social reformer Frances Willard.

The 1893 parliament keenly impressed the Western world. It was the first time representatives of Eastern religions were welcomed in the West. Equality with their Christian counterparts was extended. The Chinese Confucian delegate Pung Kwang Yu, dressed in the tradition of the Qing Dynasty, was seated in the first row.

The most striking figure was the young Bengali Narendranath Datta, who had taken the name Swami Vivekananda. He eloquently advanced the claim that Hinduism is the mother of all religions. He said the West has much to learn from the ancient wisdom of the East. Swami Vivekananda seems to have coined the phrase the "materialistic West *vs.* the spiritual East."

Today many factors converge to make us more familiar with diverse religions than ever before. This is accompanied by increased religious conflict in many places. The Parliament of the World's Religions reminds us of the importance of dialogue between peoples of different faiths, protection of religious freedom, respect for the God-given dignity of all persons, and our responsibility as stewards of God's creation. This involves study of, interaction with, and care for all persons. Because of how the Wesleyan tradition understands God's grace, it can embrace these values even while proclaiming Christ's lordship and the gospel's universality.

See also Prevenient Grace; Religions, Theology of; Religious Pluralism.

WILLIAM T. YOUNG, PHD

PAROUSIA
See KINGDOM OF GOD; SECOND COMING OF CHRIST/PAROUSIA.

PATRISTICS
See CHURCH FATHERS.

PEACEMAKING

Peacemaking is the process of resolving conflict between parties and establishing safety, tranquility, and individual and communal wholeness. It means acting with the goal of achieving good order for all persons.

Given the long history of conflicts between cultures, races, and religions, the need for peacemakers and peacemaking is unrelenting. Ancient literature records humankind's longing for peace. Aristophanes (ca. 460–ca. 386 BC) tells of how women were implored to use their graces to induce men to cease from warfare. Plato (ca. 428–348/7 BC) longed for simplicity of desire because unbridled human desire leads to greed and often to war. Aristotle (384/3-322 BC) noted that peace should be the result of a just war.

Although a prominent image of God in the OT seems to be that of a God of war, the prophetic tradition highlights God as the God of peace (Hebrew, **shalom**). Shalom comes from a root that denotes completeness and wholeness. It is closely associated with perfection (*shelemut*). Truth and justice are shalom's companion values. Isaiah redefines God as a peacemaker God who judges nations and induces them to "beat their swords into plowshares, and their spears into pruning hooks." Nations are urged not to use the sword and not to "learn [the art of] war" (Isa. 2:4).

In the NT, God is principally a "peacemaker" (Greek *eirēnē*, "peace," "harmony," from which comes "irenic"). Through Christ "God was pleased to reconcile to himself all things, whether on earth or in heaven, by making peace through the blood of his cross" (Col. 1:20). God is the source of all true peace (Rom. 15:33). The Holy Spirit offers the gift of peace (Gal. 5:22). The pursuit of peace is a Christian calling, especially for husbands and wives (1 Cor. 7:15). Those who act as peacemakers will be called the "children of God" (Matt. 5:9). Grace and peace become the Christian greeting and parting blessing (Rom. 1:7).

The pacifist tradition in Christianity—refusing to participate in violence or armed warfare—is an important, but not the only, form of peacemaking. Believing they were following **Jesus**' instructions, early Christians refused to participate in bloodletting of any kind. Prior to AD 170 they did not enter the military. Even after that, Christians who served in the Roman army often occupied positions that minimized the risk of taking a human life. Much later, pacifists such as Peter Waldo (ca. 1140–ca. 1218) and John Hus (ca. 1369–ca. 1415) were often persecuted for their refusal to participate in armed conflict. There emerged Christian denominations known as "the peace churches." They include the Mennonites, who arose under the leadership of Menno Simons (1496–1561), the Society of Friends (later Quakers) founded by George Fox (1624-91), and the Church of the Brethren led by Alexander Mack (ca. 1679–1735).

John Wesley (1703-91), in his "Sermon on the Mount," encouraged Methodists to be peacemakers (*Works*, 5:278-94). He defined peacemakers as lovers of God who struggle to prevent warfare's "fire of hell" or to preserve peace where it is found and to encourage peace where it is not (284).

More recently, Martin Luther King Jr. (1929-68) used nonviolence to achieve human rights and dignity for oppressed people. Anglican archbishop Desmond Tutu (b. 1931) received the Nobel Peace Prize (1984) for his struggle against apartheid in South Africa.

See also African-American Methodism; Anabaptists; Christian Ethics/Moral Theology; Ethics; Fruit of the Spirit; Just War/War; Liberation Theology; Love; Reconciliation; Social Ethics; Social Justice.

Resources

Barak, Gregg. *Violence and Nonviolence: Pathways to Understanding.* Thousand Oaks, CA: Sage Publications, 2003.

Little, David, ed. *Peacemakers in Action: Profiles of Religion in Conflict Resolution.* Cambridge, UK: Cambridge University Press, 2007.

L. BRYAN WILLIAMS, PHD

PELAGIANISM

Pelagianism refers to ideas several theologians introduced in the early 400s. The theologians included Pelagius (ca. 354–after 418), Caelestius (fifth century), and Julian of Eclanum (ca. 386–ca. 454).

In 412 Pelagius and Caelestius engaged in bitter controversy with other theologians, notably **Augustine** and Jerome. The controversy involved original **sin**, human freedom, and **grace**. A main teaching of the Pelagians was that no one inherits from Adam the guilt and corruption of sin. They therefore concluded that baptizing infants is unnecessary to free them from the guilt of Adam's sin. Humans can live without sin, since Adam's sin has not corrupted human nature. The Pelagians acknowledged that Adam's sin has an effect; however, they said Adam's sin affects us by creating a powerful example of unfaithfulness. They interpreted Rom. 5:12 as affirming that everyone sins in imitation of Adam.

According to Augustine, by contrast, this passage teaches that everyone sinned in Adam. Adam's sin completely corrupted human nature; everyone born after Adam was conceived with a corrupted nature.

The difference produced a disagreement about freedom. For Augustine, corruption of our nature resulted in a loss of freedom before God. We cannot know, love, and obey God without a radical infusion of grace. Grace, for Augustine, heals our fallen nature and creates knowledge, **love**, and **obedience**. But Pelagius argued that human nature was not devastated by Adam's sin. Humans still have an ability to know, love, and obey God. Pelagians acknowledged that obeying God is difficult. The human will seems to be turned away from God. But Pelagians saw the problem, not as the will's inability to obey, but as the accumulated effects of sins committed. If we are unable to obey **God**, it is because our past sins have generated a disposition to sin. It is not (as Augustine taught) because our human nature was corrupted by Adam's sin.

There was also a dispute about grace. Augustine said the Pelagians underestimated our need of God's grace. For Augustine, because we can do nothing, God's grace must do everything. Those who do not obey God, he concluded, fail to obey because God has not extended grace to them. The Pelagians took a different view. Pelagius thought of God's grace as the way God illuminates us through teaching, **revelation**, and spiritual gifts. Grace encourages us to obey God. Pelagius rejected the belief that grace is a power that creates obedience within us.

The Pelagian controversy erupted in 412 when a council, meeting in Carthage, condemned Caelestius. By 415 Pelagius was being criticized. However, the bishop of Jerusalem, and later a synod meeting at Diospolis, examined Pelagius and found his theology acceptable. But the bishops of Carthage pursued the matter. Finally they succeeded in getting the bishop of Rome (Celestine) and the Council of Ephesus (431) to condemn the Pelagians. It is notable that the Pelagians' enemies were located mainly in the West (especially North Africa). Their supporters were found mainly in the East.

See also Arminian Theology; Faith; Free Will; Justification; New Birth (Regeneration); Salvation (Soteriology); Wesley, John, Theology of.

Resources
Olson, Roger E. *Arminian Theology: Myths and Realities.* Downers Grove, IL: IVP Academic, 2006.
Rees, B. R. *Pelagius: Life and Letters.* Rochester, NY: Boydell Press, 1998.

SAMUEL M. POWELL, PHD

PENANCE

The origin of penance lies in the disciplinary measures of the early church for dealing with sins committed after baptism. It is one of the seven **sacraments** of the **Roman Catholic Church**, believed to have been instituted by Christ. The Latin Vulgate (late fourth century) translated the Greek word *metanoia* (frequent in the NT and usually translated in English as "repentance") as *poenitentia* ("penance" in English). In the sacrament of penance, priests announce God's remission (absolution) of sins for Christians who in true sorrow confess their sins. Penance requires suitable satisfaction through an act of contrition (certain prayers or actions) and amendment of life through a resolution not to continue in sin. In the sacrament of penance the grace of forgiveness is imparted.

Major changes in the Council of Trent's (1551) understanding of penance occurred after **Vatican Council II**. The sacrament is now called the sacrament of penance and reconciliation.

Those who approach the sacrament of Penance obtain pardon from God's mercy for the offense committed against him, and are, at the same time, reconciled with the Church which they have wounded by their sins and which by charity, by example, and by prayer labors for their conversion. (*Catechism of the Catholic Church* 1993, para. 1422)

Protestants generally view the Roman Catholic understanding of penance as not having biblical support and as at times linked with clergy abuses and doctrinal errors. The Protestant Reformers understood the Greek term *metanoia* to refer to personal and community **repentance**, relying directly on God's grace available to Christians as opposed to grace being mediated through the church and its priests. Penance plays no role in a Protestant understanding of the **atonement**.

However, a proper appreciation of God's love and mercy offered through Christ should foster in all Christians an attitude of penitence, that is, godly sorrow and contrition for sins. Recognizing we are unworthy of God's forgiveness should prompt this. Wesleyans can affirm the importance of repentance and penitence, understood as godly sorrow, as they seek to live holy lives in the power of Christ.

See also Spiritual Disciplines; Spiritual Formation/Growth.

Resources

Catechism of the Catholic Church. 1993. Christusrex.org. http://www.christusrex.org/www1/CDHN/ccc.html.

White, James F. *The Sacraments in Protestant Practice and Faith.* Nashville: Abingdon Press, 1999.

DAVID MCEWAN, PHD

PENTECOSTALISM

The term "Pentecostal" originates in **Scripture** with the feast of Pentecost, and the **baptism with the Holy Spirit** on the day of Pentecost (Acts 2). Worshippers of Christ were baptized with the **Holy Spirit** as **Jesus** had promised. Pentecostalism claims identity with both events.

History. The spiritual history of modern Pentecostalism began with an insatiable hunger for renewal in holiness and the restoration of the manifestations of the Holy Spirit as recorded in the book of Acts.

The most prominent site of renewal occurred in 1906 at the Azusa Street Apostolic Faith Mission (Los Angeles) under the pastoral leadership of William J. Seymour. Worshippers spoke with tongues as on the day of Pentecost. They identified this as the biblical sign of the baptism with the Holy Spirit. God gave other phenomena of NT witness and revelation: healing, other signs, wonders, miracles, and gifts of the Holy Spirit. The news and influence of this restoration spread rapidly—locally, nationally, and internationally.

Experiential distinctives. The source of doctrine for Pentecostal theology is Scripture. Experiences in Christ are the fulfillment of divine promises fulfilled in the power of the Holy Spirit. The Pentecostals emphasized three experiences in **grace**: regeneration (salvation), sanctification, and being filled with the Holy Spirit—the initial evidence being speaking in tongues (**glossolalia**).

The Pentecostals pressed five claims: (1) conversion is a radical change of nature that provides **love** as the new motive for life and cessation of sinning; (2) **holiness** of life through **sanctification** prepares believers for Spirit baptism; (3) baptism with the Holy Spirit is distinct from and subsequent to conversion and sanctification; (4) the first oral evidence of Spirit baptism is speaking in tongues as the Spirit gives utterance; and (5) the Father continues to bear witness to his Son through "signs and wonders, with various miracles, and gifts of the Holy Spirit" given to believers (Heb. 2:4, NKJV). Manifestations of the Holy Spirit were not restricted to the apostolic age.

The Pentecostal message is Christocentric: **Jesus Christ** is Savior, Sanctifier, Holy Spirit Baptizer, Healer, and King soon to return. These doctrinal affirmations became the doctrinal distinctive of Pentecostalism. They are harmonious with Christian orthodoxy. More specifically, these believers identified themselves as being in the **Protestant** tradition on the cardinal doctrines of *sola Scriptura*, justification by grace through faith alone, and the priesthood of all believers. By practice and proclamation, Pentecostals added a fourth—the prophethood of all believers.

Probably the most disruptive claims of Pentecostal preaching are (1) the sequential separation of Spirit baptism from conversion and (2) the initial evidence of the Spirit's baptism as speaking in other tongues.

Theology and process. Pentecostal theology is Christological and pneumatological. As to its Christology, it is Nicene (Athanasian), not Arian. As to its pneumatology, the Holy Spirit is a divine person eternally existing in the Holy **Trinity**. The Holy Spirit as a distinct divine person is essential to Pentecostal theology.

Experience, as governed by Scripture, is essential for Pentecostal theology. It is a theology of worship and witness in the power of the Holy Spirit. Worship and witness are fulfilled in a union of the believer with the Holy Spirit, a union that gives Christians rapport with the Spirit's will, action, and speech. In this environment, speaking in tongues, prophesying, interpretation, and fulfilling other manifestations of the Holy Spirit occur under his sovereignty and at his initiation. This establishes catholicity, a unity of worship in the church in all places and times—temporal and eschatological.

There are significant differences between non-Pentecostal Wesleyan-holiness denominations such as the Church of the Nazarene, the Free Methodists, and the Wesleyan Church, on the one hand, and the Pentecostal Wesleyan-holiness tradition on the other. The non-Pentecostal Wesleyan-holiness denominations do not make a sequential distinction between the experience of entire sanctification and baptism with the Holy Spirit, and they do not affirm speaking in tongues as the initial oral evidence of Spirit baptism. Wesleyan-holiness Pentecostals do make a sequential and definitional distinction between entire sanctification and Spirit baptism. Wesleyan-holiness Pentecostals teach that entire sanctification is prior to and preparation for baptism with the Holy Spirit. They also affirm that speaking in tongues is the initial oral evidence of Spirit baptism.

Even with these distinctions, non-Pentecostal Wesleyans and Pentecostal Wesleyans are united in their commitment to holiness of life as essential to the Spirit-filled life.

See also Charismatic Theology; Christology; Gifts of the Spirit; Pentecostal Theology; Repentance; Trinity; Wesley, John, Theology of.

Resources
Alexander, Estrelda. *Black Fire: One Hundred Years of African American Pentecostalism.* Downers Grove, IL: IVP Academic, 2011.
Alexander, Paul. *Signs and Wonders: Why Pentecostalism Is the World's Fastest Growing Faith.* San Francisco: Jossey-Bass, 2009.
Anderson, Allan. *An Introduction to Pentecostalism.* Cambridge, UK: Cambridge University Press, 2004.
Stephens, Randall J. *The Fire Spreads: Holiness and Pentecostalism in the American South.* Cambridge, MA: Harvard University Press, 2008.
Synan, Vinson. *The Holiness-Pentecostal Tradition: Charismatic Movements in the Twentieth Century.* Grand Rapids: Eerdmans, 1997.

R. HOLLIS GAUSE, PHD

PENTECOSTAL THEOLOGY

Pentecostal theology has roots in the theologies of **John Wesley** and **John Fletcher**. Wesley understood **grace** as unmerited favor *and* transforming power, and **Christian perfection (entire sanctification)** as a work of grace subsequent to regeneration. Fletcher linked Christian perfection with Pentecost and the **baptism of the Holy Spirit**.

Using Pentecostal language for Christian perfection was common among early Methodists on both sides of the Atlantic. By 1850, holiness theologians such as **Phoebe Palmer**, Charles Finney, and Asa Mahan began identifying it with the baptism of the Holy Spirit. "Pentecostal" and "Spirit baptism" soon became synonymous with Christian perfection in most of the **holiness movement**. While most holiness theologians understood holiness *and* empowerment for service as both given through Spirit baptism, radical or "fire-baptized" advocates identified the Spirit's baptism as a distinct gift of power subsequent to entire sanctification. Pentecostalism was born from radical holiness theology. It eventually divided into three camps.

1. Charles Parham (1873–1929), former Methodist minister and **healing** evangelist, was convinced he lacked this third blessing. He believed a global

revival marked by an outpouring of the Spirit duplicating Pentecost would precede Christ's **second coming**. Spirit baptism would enable believers to speak in foreign languages and carry the gospel to all nations. In 1900 Parham and his Bible college students experienced Spirit baptism evidenced by speaking in tongues (**glossolalia**).

Holiness evangelist William J. Seymour (1870–1922), whose roots included **African-American Methodism** and Warner's **Church of God** movement, was convinced by Parham's teaching. In 1906 he carried this message to Los Angeles, resulting in the Azusa Street revival. While sharing Parham's missional urgency, Seymour understood Spirit baptism not only as an enduement with power but also as an overwhelming love breaking down barriers and bringing races and nations together into one Christian family.

For Parham and Seymour, restoration of the "apostolic faith" or "full gospel" consisted of five theological elements: **justification**, entire sanctification, divine **healing**, premillennialism, and Spirit baptism. Most Pentecostals believed glossolalia was the initial evidence of Spirit baptism. However, it was now understood as normally a heavenly language rather than a foreign language.

2. William H. Durham (1873–1912) divided the Pentecostal movement by questioning the three-blessing theology and denying entire sanctification as a second work of **grace**. He argued the "finished work of Calvary" saves and sanctifies; one then progressively appropriates sanctification. Hence there are only two blessings, conversion and Spirit baptism, corresponding to Calvary and Pentecost.

3. Durham's followers subsequently divided over "oneness theology." It held that, as in the book of Acts, baptism should be in Jesus' name. Rejecting Trinitarian theology, it argued Jesus *is* the Father, Son, and Spirit and often equated conversion with Spirit baptism.

In spite of the divisions, Donald Dayton argues that Pentecostal theology shares a common logic: (1) a Pentecostal hermeneutic in which Luke-Acts is the narrative lens for interpreting Scripture, providing a pattern for salvation history and a norm for personal experience; (2) restoration of apostolic faith and power; and (3) an eschatology that understands Pentecostalism as a "latter rain" replicating Pentecost (1987, 23-28).

The 1990s witnessed a revolution in Pentecostal theology, beginning with Steven J. Land's *Pentecostal Spirituality* (1993). Rooted in Wesleyanism and early Pentecostalism, Land argues that spirituality is foundational to Pentecostal theology. It consists of holy affections that integrate beliefs and practices governed by a passion for God's kingdom. In dialogue with contemporary theologians, Land revised Pentecostal theology through a Trinitarian and perichoretic (mutuality as within the **Trinity**) understanding of Pentecostal affections and the three blessings.

Samuel Solivan's *The Spirit, Pathos and Liberation* (1998), a Hispanic Pentecostal theology, is centered on **orthopathos**, a liberating appropriation of suffering, given by the **Holy Spirit**. It incarnates **orthodoxy** and relocates **orthopraxis** by linking them to the suffering poor.

Simon Chan's *Pentecostal Theology and the Christian Spiritual Tradition* (2000) understands Spirit baptism not only as empowerment but also as a new relationship with the Trinity. Glossolalia is a distinctive form of ascetical prayer, and the church is an eschatological community.

Amos Yong's *The Spirit Poured Out on All Flesh* (2005) proposes a world Christian theology grounded in a Lukan hermeneutic, with a focus on experiencing afresh the Spirit's power. This theology has Jesus Christ as its *thematic* motif, and pneumatology as its *orienting* motif.

Frank D. Macchia's *Baptized in the Spirit* (2006) argues the **kingdom of God** is inaugurated at Pentecost. Spirit baptism is an eschatological outpouring of love that integrates the Pauline emphasis on being in Christ and Luke's emphasis on power for witnessing.

See also Charismatic Theology; Gifts of the Spirit; New Birth (Regeneration); Pentecostalism.

Resources

Dayton, Donald W. *Theological Roots of Pentecostalism*. Grand Rapids: Francis Asbury Press, 1987.

Hollenweger, Walter J. *Pentecostalism: Origin and Developments Worldwide*. Peabody, MA: Hendrickson Publishers, 1997.

Jacobson, Douglas G. *Thinking in the Spirit: Theologies of the Early Pentecostal Movement*. Bloomington, IN: Indiana University Press, 2003.

HENRY H. KNIGHT III, PHD

PEOPLE OF GOD

See CHURCH (ECCLESIOLOGY); ISRAEL.

PERSECUTION AND MARTYRDOM

Persecution is the intentional mistreatment of an individual or group by any other individual or group based on differences in origin, race, religion, or worldview. The two most common types of persecution are religious and ethnic. Persecution can take many forms, such as a majority group oppressing or mistreating a minority group.

Jesus told his followers they would be persecuted (Luke 21:12). Persecution is a recurring theme in the ministry of the apostle Paul (2 Cor. 4:8-9). While the Christian church has persecuted others in the course of history (e.g., Muslims during the Crusades, the 1526 Zurich mandate imposing the death penalty on Anabaptists), today the Christian church suffers most under persecution. Particularly, persecution of Christians creeps into some world regions dominated by some non-Christian religions. Jesus told his followers they were to forgive and pray for those who persecute them (Matt. 5:44).

Since the church's beginning, persecution and suffering—evident in the NT—have accompanied preaching the gospel and growth of the church. It is estimated that in the twentieth century more Christians lost their lives through religious persecution than in all previous centuries combined. Incarnational ministry entails that messengers of the cross will share in Christ's sufferings and in the sufferings of fellow Christians (Mark 8:34; 2 Cor. 1:5; Phil. 3:10; 1 Pet. 4:13). Severe persecution infuses a note of authenticity into the Christian message; observers marvel at the willingness of Christians to suffer and die for their faith (Acts 7:54-60).

The month of November is designated for Christians worldwide to participate in the International Day of Prayer for the Persecuted Church, sponsored by the World Evangelical Fellowship. Each year, many believers pray for Christians who are suffering persecution in China, Egypt, Iraq, India, and Iran. They suffer just because they confess Jesus Christ as Lord.

Extreme persecution leads to *martyrdom*. The terms "witness" and "martyr" derive from the Greek word *martyros*. From the time of Stephen, the first Christian martyr (Acts 7:54-60), the term has been used for Christians who bore witness to Christ by shedding their blood. The word "martyr" was used more commonly in the second century, a time of intense Roman persecution of Christians. The term marked Christ's followers who suffered *martyrdom* rather than deny their Lord. When persecution of Christians occurs, one who bears witness to Jesus may become a martyr for Christ.

In some countries Christians are subject to martyrdom because of their faith. Estimates place the number of Christians martyred each year at 150,000. The Voice of the Martyrs website and its monthly magazine provide up-to-date information on the daily persecution, suffering, and, in some cases, martyrdom of Christians, mainly in countries governed by militant regimes.

Martyrdom is certainly not unique to Christianity. Resolute devotees of other religions have sacrificed their lives for their faith and continue to do so.

See also Early Church; Religious Conflict; Religious Freedom; Underground Church in China.

Resources

Buttrick, George A., ed. *Interpreter's Dictionary of the Bible.* New York: Abingdon Press, 1962.

Moreau, A. Scott, ed. *Evangelical Dictionary of World Missions.* Grand Rapids: Baker, 2000.

The Voice of the Martyrs. http://www.persecution.com/public/homepage.aspx?clickfrom=bWFpbl9tZW51.

Whitfield, Joshua. *Pilgrim Holiness: Martyrdom as Descriptive Witness.* Eugene, OR: Cascade Books, 2009.

TERENCE B. READ, PHD

PERSON

The word "person" means today a "human individual." But the word did not exist in the ancient languages of the Bible. It was coined in Latin (*persona*) to refer to the masks worn by actors *through* (*per*) which they *sounded* (*sonare*) their words. "Person" then came to mean a "role" or "character" in a drama. Tertullian adopted *persona* in his doctrine of the **Trinity** to refer to the three "persons"—the Father, Son, and Holy Spirit. To Greek theologians that implied that the one God only played three temporary roles. But they finally accepted the term along with their Greek word *hypostasis*, meaning the "underlying reality" of something. So God really and eternally is three distinct persons in relation to each other.

"Person" was extended from the theological use to refer to humans. Boethius defined a person as the "individual substance of rational nature." That Aristotelian definition categorized personhood in a very impersonal way and promoted the idea that a "person" is the same as an "individual."

Individualism flourished in modern Europe from the Renaissance, until by the nineteenth century, the new political and social philosophy of liberalism strongly advocated the liberty of the individual, individual rights, and democracy. The philosophy of **personalism**, in contrast, emphasized relationships between persons. Personalism influenced American Methodist theology through Boston University. In his book, *Ich und Du* (1923, *I and Thou*), Jewish thinker Martin Buber differentiated between I-thou relationships (which are fully personal) and impersonal I-it relationships.

The recent revival of Trinitarian theology has, however, emphasized that our understanding of the person should be drawn from Christian theology rather than secular philosophy. Whereas the concept of an "individual" emphasizes separate self-sufficiency, a "person" is one who, like the Father, Son, and Holy Spirit, has his or her very being in relationships. A human being becomes a "person" by being shaped by relationships within the family. John Zizioulas has argued that all human relationships are so damaged that true personhood comes only through being born again into the church, the family of God.

"Person" should not be equated with "personality," now a technical term in psychology. People are categorized into "personality types" in accordance with "personality traits." But categorizing depersonalizes. For Christian theology each person is unique (like the Father, Son, and Holy Spirit) and ultimately a mystery that cannot be fully explained (see Emil Brunner, *The Mediator* [1934], chap. 9, and Paul Tournier, *The Meaning of Persons* [1957]). Behind our "personage" (Tournier) or *persona*—the face we present to the world—is the hidden mystery of the person known only to God.

We also cannot categorize the persons of the Trinity as being the same kind of thing as human persons. We apply the word "person" metaphorically or analogically to God, and yet ultimately God is the Source of true personhood. We are only truly personal when by the Spirit we are in God's Image, the Son, and so can say, "Abba! Father!" (Rom. 8:15).

See also Anthropology, Theological; Church (Ecclesiology); Church Fathers; Family, Christian; Humanism; Human Sexuality; Love; Marriage; Personalism/Personalist Theology; Rights, Human; Social Sciences; Spiritual Formation/Growth.

Resources

Schwöbel, Christoph, and Colin E. Gunton, eds. *Persons, Divine and Human.* Edinburgh: T and T Clark, 1991.

Zizioulas, John. *Being as Communion: Studies in Personhood and the Church.* Crestwood, NY: St Vladimir's Seminary Press, 1985.

THOMAS A. NOBLE, PHD

PERSONALISM/PERSONALIST THEOLOGY

Personalism is a philosophy that stresses the central importance, value, and uniqueness of "person" (or "personhood" or "personality") as the key for interpreting reality in all its dimensions, whether ontology, values, or God. It affirms human freedom and opposes any ideology or current of thought that would infringe on, negate, or replace the centrality of "person." Personalism opposes all mechanistic, materialistic, deterministic, and naturalistic interpretations of reality and persons.

As a coherent philosophy, personalism has been most prominent among Anglo-Saxons, especially in the United States. More broadly, personalism designates a wider range of thought united by shared convictions and spiritual emphases.

Personalist theology integrates insights from personalism into Christian doctrine and practice. But there is no unified personalist theology.

Although personalist ideas may be found throughout intellectual history, no founding figure stands in its background. Borden Parker Bowne (1847–1910), George H. Howison (1834–1916), and Mary Whiton Calkins (1863–1930) in America and Emmanuel Mounier (1905-50) in France were prominent proponents. American idealist philosopher Josiah Royce (1855–1916) was closely related to personalism, as was William Ernest Hocking of Harvard (1873–1966). They and other personalists guarded the unique value of each person and the importance of human subjectivity or self-consciousness. They protested against any philosophy, political order, or approach to psychology that jeopardized the centrality and dignity of "person." Personalists saw threats to the person as coming from Hegelian idealism, Marxism, and Enlightenment rationalism.

Personalist philosophy and theology flourished at Boston University, a Methodist university, where Bowne taught. Personalism influenced many in the Wesleyan and Methodist traditions, including Edgar Sheffield Brightman (1884–1953) and Albert C. Knudson (1873–1953).

Personalist theology emphasizes the freedom and responsibility of persons for who they are and what they do. But personalism is not individualism; relationships with others lie at the center of what it means to be human. Love must be freely expressed to others.

Personalist ideas influenced other Christian scholars such as the pragmatist William James and process philosopher/theologian Charles Hartshorne. Martin Luther King Jr., a Boston University graduate, claimed that personalist theology helped shape his emphasis on the human dignity of all persons. Pope John Paul II spoke of personalism's influence on him.

The popularity of personalism has receded. But its emphasis on "person" as pivotal for interpreting reality and on thinking of God as "person" remains important for Christian theology. Personalist theology anticipated the current emphases in relational theologies on personal and interpersonal relations between people and God, between persons, and between persons and the world. Relationality is thought to lie at the core of what it means to be human. Forms of relational theology include **open-theistic** and **process theologies**.

See also Determinism and Free Will; Reductionism.

DON THORSEN, PHD

PERSONALIST THEOLOGY
See PERSONALISM/PERSONALIST THEOLOGY.

PHARISEES/SADDUCEES

Among the numerous religious parties in first-century Judaism, the two most prominent in the NT were Pharisees and Sadducees.

The name "Pharisees" comes from the Hebrew word *parushim*, plural of *parush*, meaning "separate" and "interpret." Pharisees arose around or after the time of the Maccabean Revolt (168-135 BC). Staunch opponents of Hellenism, they were lay teachers, not priests, and were commonly called rabbis (**Torah** could be interpreted and applied by competent laypeople, not only by priests). Pharisees followed the teachings derived from scribal interpretations and were intense defenders of Torah and tradition.

Our main source for understanding the Pharisees is Flavius Josephus (ca. AD 37–ca. 100), a Jewish historian who was himself a Pharisee but who left during the buildup to the Jewish War (AD 66-70). He presents the Pharisees as a party seeking to impose its interpretation of Torah on the Jewish populace. He also describes them as a philosophical school, complete with opinions about determinism and so on. His portrayal was neither completely wrong nor did it correspond to how things actually were (Wright 1992, 52).

The Pharisees were one of several "holiness movements" in the late Second Temple period. Others included the Essenes at Qumran, John and his disciples, and Jesus and his disciples. Consequently, the purity codes played an important role for them. They insisted on rigorous interpretation and strict observation. The laws of temple purity were extended to everyday life in hopes that God would again dwell among his people. In contrast to the Qumran Essenes, the Pharisees separated *within* their society rather than *withdrawing* from it. They "built a fence around the Torah" by enforcing strict Sabbath laws, festivals, oaths, and tithes. The same applied to divorce laws, kosher food, and restrictions on those with whom one could share table fellowship. But they were also concerned about matters much wider than private ritual purity. Politically influential, their interests often involved political and revolutionary action (Wright 1992, 186).

Josephus says the Pharisees began to worship in synagogues, a practice that grew into a powerful religious and political institution. Unlike the Sadducees who were attached to the temple, the Pharisees survived its destruction in AD 70, their form of Judaism subsequently becoming normative.

Pharisees conflicted with the Sadducees (Righteous Ones) over how to interpret the law. Unlike the Sadducees, the Pharisees were open to doctrinal beliefs such as the resurrection of the dead, final judgment, angels, demons, and reward and punishment in the afterlife. The Pharisees expected a great renewal in which the present condition would be radically changed. The Sadducees were content with the status quo (Wright 1992, 328).

The Sadducees were a political-religious sect associated with the temple hierarchy. Their main occupation was temple ritual. Elitists, they maintained the priestly class but became allies of Hellenism and the Romans, thus provoking opposition from the Pharisees. The Sadducees rejected the oral law of the Pharisees and insisted on the literal interpretation of Torah. After the Romans destroyed the temple in AD 70, the Sadducees' religious and political base disappeared.

Together the two parties formed the seventy-one-member Great Sanhedrin, a kind of Jewish supreme court that interpreted civil and religious laws. The Gospels show Jesus in conflict with Pharisees and Sadducees but chiefly with the Pharisees. Nevertheless, he was more in agreement with the Pharisees than the Sadducees on doctrines such as the resurrection of the dead, final judgment, angels, demons, and reward and punishment in the afterlife.

See also Righteousness; Second Temple Judaism; Temple.

Resources

Mullen, J. Patrick. *Dining with Pharisees*. Collegeville, MN: Liturgical Press, 2004.
Sanders, E. P. *Paul and Palestinian Judaism*. London: SCM, 1977.
Wright, N. T. *The New Testament and the People of God*. London: SPCK, 1992.

ISRAEL KAMUDZANDU, PHD

PHILOSOPHICAL THEOLOGY

Philosophical theology is the use of philosophical systems or concepts either to analyze or to articulate a particular theological vision, conviction, or tradition (e.g., **Judaism, Islam,** or Christianity). When philosophical theology is conducted by those who adhere confessionally to a particular religion, the tasks of analysis and articulation typically serve the goals of deepening a religion's understanding of the faith it affirms and of offering an **apologetic** defense to those outside the faith community.

The Christian tradition has a long history of articulating its faith by connecting it with existing philosophical systems. **Augustine** used Neoplatonic philosophy in articulating the Christian understanding of God, **Thomas Aquinas** adapted Aristotelian philosophy, Paul Tillich employed **existentialist** philosophy, John B. Cobb draws from **process philosophy,** and John Milbank has selectively used **postmodern** philosophy. The very task of articulating a religion perhaps requires us to connect it to *some* existing system—given that any community's grasp of a religion must begin with concepts with which it is already familiar. However, there is the ever-present danger for philosophical theologians that adapting a particular philosophical system will lead to an overly narrow interpretation of Christian Scripture and doctrine.

Seeing the dangers that come with philosophical theology, some Christians since the days of Tertullian (ca. 160–ca. 225) have rejected the whole project on the grounds that it compromises pure Christian faith. Søren Kierkegaard and Karl Barth, for instance, saw no legitimate role for philosophical theology.

In addition to articulating the affirmations of a religion, philosophical theology also plays the role of analyzing those affirmations. Analysis takes two forms. First, the tools of philosophers are used to bring clarity and precision to theological discussions. By exploring in detail the concepts used in those discussions—such as personhood, free will, responsibility, and benevolence—philosophical theologians allow us to move beyond a vague and potentially ambiguous use of conceptual terms.

Second, in addition to clarifying individual affirmations within a religious tradition, the tools of philosophy can be used to examine the coherence *among* the various affirmations within that tradition. Philosophical theology in this context does not so much offer conclusions about what *ought* to be believed as it does present coherent possibilities. Still, coherence does represent, philosophical theologians insist, one of three important criteria we should apply when considering a systematic theological view of the world. The two other criteria fall under the respective purviews of dogmatic theology (where we check our affirmations for consonance with **creeds,** canonized **Scripture,** and other Christian norms) and **contextual theology** (where we explore whether our affirmations meet the needs and callings of practicing Christians). The **Wesleyan quadrilateral** would seem to recognize the value of philosophical theology. **John Wesley** taught that a biblically faithful Christianity must be coherent; coherence must inform how we read and interpret the Bible.

Questions of coherence, along with an analysis of an individual concept on which a religious affirmation may rely, can be explored by philosophers both within and outside a religion's "confessional circle." When practicing Christians engage in philosophical theology, they contribute to the tradition's pursuit of "**faith** seeking understanding" (theme of Anselm of Canterbury's *Proslogion* [1077-78]), deepening how Christians understand their faith. The Christian tradition also has a long history of analyzing and articulating the faith for purposes of **apologetics**. The practice of defending and commending the faith to others dates back at least to second- and third-century apologists such as Justin Martyr, Clement of Alexandria, and Origen.

See also Contextual Theology; Doctrine/Dogma; Indigenous Theologies; Natural Theology; Philosophy of Religion; Religions, Theology of; Technology, Ethic of.

Resources
Brümmer, Vincent. *Speaking of a Personal God.* Cambridge, UK: Cambridge University Press, 1992.
Wesley, John. "An Address to the Clergy." In *Works*, 10:480-500.

KEVIN KINGHORN, PHD

PHILOSOPHY OF RELIGION

Philosophy of religion is the philosophical examination of concepts used and claims made by religious traditions. It has a preference for reason and not a particular religion. Intellectual space for philosophy of religion is created by belief that the physical world may not be all that exists. There may be something or someone beyond our natural or phenomenal world that accounts for it. Eastern **religions** such as Hinduism and some forms of Buddhism perceive the supernatural as an impersonal power that transcends the observable world. Western religions such as **Judaism**, Christianity, and **Islam** teach that God, who transcends the world, accounts for it.

Philosophers of religion focus on two general topics: coherence and plausibility. Questions of coherence involve the *meaning* of claims within a religion and whether the claims are logically consistent. For example, philosophers examine whether a **miracle** should be understood as a "violation of a natural law" and whether it is reasonable to suggest that a natural *law* could, by definition, remain a law if it were violated.

Once the coherence of a religious claim is established, philosophers of religion then consider the second issue: *plausibility*. What are the arguments for and against the general claim that **God** exists (or a more specific Christian description of God and God's activity in the world)? For example, if the meaning and coherence of "miracle" can be established, philosophers can then consider the kinds of evidence that would support the claim that a purported miracle has occurred. Philosophy, not religious belief or experience, provides the basis for proceeding.

In addition to the general issues of coherence and plausibility, some philosophers of religion also tackle pragmatic questions about how to live. If, for instance, the evidence for and against Christian theism seems roughly balanced, what course of action would a person be wise to follow?

Philosophy of religion draws heavily from all three parts of philosophy: **metaphysics** (questions of what is real in and beyond our world), **epistemology** (how can/should we come to know about these things), and axiology (what has intellectual and moral value, and why). Philosophers of religion explore such metaphysical questions as whether God exists, whether humans have **souls**, whether they have **free will**, and whether their personal identities consist in more than just their physical and psychological characteristics. In epistemology, philosophers of religion explore the nature of religious experience, the role reason can/should play in forming religious **belief**, and whether moral deficiencies might "blind" one from seeing the truth about God. Axiological questions include how to view God's relationship to what is considered good, whether "morally right" simply means "commanded by God," and whether human rights are grounded in the activity and will of God.

Historically, philosophers of the first fifteen hundred years of the Christian **tradition** tended to focus on metaphysical questions. Over the next several centuries, philosophers tended to be less optimistic about settling metaphysical questions. They turned instead to epistemic questions about the limits and proper methods of searching for truths about God and our world. Some philosophers in the twentieth century became arguably even less optimistic about our search for God, focusing their analysis instead on our use of *language* when talking about God. Nevertheless, in recent decades a growing number of philosophers of religion (such as Richard Swinburne and Alvin Plantinga) have approached the subject with a strong concern for **orthodox** Christianity, ensuring that philosophy of religion will remain connected with the historical philosophical inquiries that have characterized the Christian tradition.

See also Epistemology; Greek Philosophy; Logical Positivism; Metaphysics; Monism, Dualism, Pluralism; Natural Theology; Religions, Theology of; Religious Pluralism.

Resources

Mawson, T. J. *Belief in God*. Oxford, UK: Clarendon Press, 2005.
Peterson, Michael, William Hasker, Bruce Reichenbach, and David Basinger. *Reason and Religious Belief: An Introduction to the Philosophy of Religion*. 4th ed. New York: Oxford University Press, 2009.
Swinburne, Richard. *The Coherence of Theism*. Oxford, UK: Clarendon Press, 1993.

KEVIN KINGHORN, PHD

PHILOSOPHY OF SCIENCE

The philosophy of science is the inquiry into the assumptions and methods of the sciences and into scientific modes of reasoning.

The philosophy of science goes back at least as far as Aristotle (384/3-322 BC), who wrote several works on logic and various treatises on scientific topics. The most important modern contributors to the philosophy of science were Francis Bacon (1561–1626), René Descartes (1596–1650), and David Hume (1711-76). Bacon's *Novum Organon* (*New Instrument* [1620]) directly challenged Aristotle's emphasis on logical method in favor of an empirical and inductive approach to scientific knowledge. He identified two main obstacles to science: (1) forming generalizations (inductions) without a sufficient empirical basis and (2) common prejudices (such as assuming more order in nature than is truly present). For Bacon, the only way to overcome these obstacles is to form scientific generalizations solely from the direct experience of nature.

Descartes rejected the Aristotelian belief that the material universe exhibits purpose (in Aristotle's terms, final causation). For Descartes, the only cause operative in the material universe is efficient causation—the impact of one body on another as they move in space. The emphasis on efficient causation meant that things studied by science could be treated as simple entities with basic characteristics such as spatial location, mass, and speed. As a result, these entities became amenable to mathematical description.

Hume's importance lies in his critique of induction. Hume observed that the principle of induction (the expectation that future effects will resemble past effects) cannot be rationally justified. Attempts to prove this principle must make use of the relation of cause to effect; however, determining this relation assumes the validity of induction. Accordingly, proving the validity of the principle of induction begs the question by presupposing the validity of the principle.

One stream of twentieth-century philosophy of science emphasized the rational character of science. Karl Popper (1902-94) is representative. In his *The Logic of Scientific Discovery* (1959) he attempted to distinguish genuine science from pseudoscience by identifying science's logical features. He also responded to Hume's critique of induction by arguing that science uses deductive (not inductive) logic. Scientists set forth conjectures (hypotheses) and then seek to falsify them by creating experiments designed to see whether the conjectures are false. If the experiment falsifies the conjecture, the conjecture is rejected; otherwise, it is accepted. This is a deductive approach because a single instance of falsification can, in principle, conclusively disprove the theory. Subsequently, Imre Lakatos (1922-74) extended the rationalist approach by noting that scientists accept the validity of theories not simply because they pass the falsification test but also because they help scientists find relevant data and generate theoretical insights.

The other main stream of twentieth-century philosophy of science was represented by Thomas Kuhn's (1922-96) book *The Structure of Scientific Revolutions*. He argued that the normal practice of science takes place within paradigms, which consist of fundamental conceptions and methods. Newtonian physics is an example of a paradigm. Normal scientific investigation inevitably creates anomalies—data that do not fit the paradigm. The result is a condition in which normal science cannot take place because the old paradigm is not adequate to the data. Sooner or later, the scientific community devises a new paradigm that accounts for the data, and normal science resumes within the new paradigm. Kuhn's view of science was a departure from the predominant rationalist view (represented by Popper) because he confined the logical aspect of scientific investigation to normal science within the paradigm. He argued that the transition from one paradigm to another was not governed by strictly logical principles. He further argued that it is a mistake to think of the movement from one paradigm to another as a movement of progress. The history of science, in other words, is not a progressive march toward the truth. Instead, the truth of scientific theories is relative to the paradigms in which they are used.

See also Epistemology; Logical Positivism; Natural Science; Postmodernity; Science and the Bible.

Resource
Cover, J. A., and Martin Curd, eds. *Philosophy of Science: The Central Issues.* New York: W. W. Norton and Company, 1998.

SAMUEL M. POWELL, PHD

PIETISM

Pietism was a seventeenth-century recovery of the religious vitality of the sixteenth-century **Protestant Reformation**. It was a revival of a living Christian **faith** and discipline, of individual devotion to Christ and practical **discipleship**. Pietism's major early proponent was Philipp Jakob Spener (1635–1705), who was well versed in biblical exegesis and often referred to as the father of Pietism.

After **Martin Luther**, Lutheranism lost the vital relationship between Christians and God that characterized Luther's understanding of Christian faith. Faith became intellectual assent to doctrine. Lutheran theology became rigid, assuming the form of a fixed dogma requiring intellectual conformity. The layperson's responsibility was to accept **Protestant** dogma. Pure doctrine and the **sacraments** were believed sufficient for Christian life.

Spener's spiritual and intellectual development was influenced by numerous factors, including Lutheranism, **Reformed** doctrine, some **mysticism**, and **Puritanism**. While pastoring in Frankfurt, Spener gathered small groups for Bible study, prayer, and discussion of the Sunday sermon. The name *collegia pietatis* (and hence Pietism) was given to the groups. Spener stated his plan for developing vital Christians in *Pia Desideria* (1675) or *Earnest Desire for a Reform of the True Evangelical Church*.

Pia Desideria was the first extensive written statement of Pietism. Spener stressed home Bible studies, the active role of laity in church government, and careful instruction in and practice of Christian life. He restructured theological education for pastors and emphasized preaching as leading to new birth in Christ. The *Pia Desideria* also emphasized the fruits of Christian faith.

Interpreters of Pietism disagree over how broadly to apply the term. Some reserve it for the Pietists of the seventeenth and eighteenth centuries. Others apply the name Pietism to all movements, including the one begun through the work of John Wesley and those traditions influenced by him that follow the theological characteristics of Pietism.

Much of the foundation for Pietism was laid by Johann Arndt (1555–1621) in *True Christianity* (four books published from 1605 to 1610). Pietistic leaders in addition to Spener included August Hermann Francke (1663–1727), who influenced Nikolaus Count von Zinzendorf (1700-1760). Zinzendorf later became leader of the **Moravians**. Johann Albrecht Bengel (1687–1752) authored *Exegetical Annotations on the New Testament* (1742). John Wesley was influenced by Bengel and used *Exegetical Annotations* in his *Expository Notes upon the New Testament* (1755). These leaders were Lutherans, but Pietism also had important links to French, Swiss, and Dutch renewal movements.

Never a unified movement, Pietism was separated by geography, liturgy, organization, and doctrine. However, some features were common: (1) a personal relationship with God based on new birth in Christ; (2) renewal in Christ's image; (3) **sanctification**, with the goal of attaining a measure of Christian perfection; (4) Bible study, prayer, and spiritual formation in small groups; (5) **evangelism** and sending missionaries; (6) the authority of Scripture; and (7) expecting the second coming of Christ and rejecting worldliness among Christians.

Moravian Pietists, especially Peter Böhler, played a major role in John Wesley's conversion to evangelical faith. On board a ship bound for America in 1736, Wesley was deeply impressed by the peace they demonstrated amid a storm, a peace he did not have. It was in a Moravian chapel on Aldersgate Street in 1738 that Wesley "felt [his] heart strangely warmed" (*Works*, 1:103).

See also Reformed Tradition; Tempers and Affections; Theosis (Deification); Wesley, John, Theology of; Works of Piety.

Resources

Brown, Dale W. *Understanding Pietism*. Rev. ed. Nappanee, IN: Evangel Publishing House, 1996.

Erb, Peter C., ed. *The Pietists: Selected Writings*. Classics of Western Spirituality. New York: Paulist Press, 1983.

Kisker, Scott Thomas. *Foundation for Revival: Anthony Horneck, the Religious Societies, and the Construction of an Anglican Pietism*. Lanham, MD: Scarecrow Press, 2008.

Lindberg, Carter, ed. *The Pietist Theologians*. Malden, MA: Blackwell Publishing, 2005.

KLAUS ARNOLD, MDIV

PILGRIM HOLINESS CHURCH

The Pilgrim Holiness Church originated from a union of various individuals, congregations, and associations attracted to the message of the Holiness Camp Meeting Association after the American Civil War. The preaching of a "second blessing" that cleansed believers of sinful inclinations and empowered them to live Spirit-filled lives prompted many Protestants to leave their accustomed denominations. They created new alliances that emphasized this experience and its accompanying holy life.

In 1897 two leaders of this **holiness movement** met in Cincinnati. Martin Wells Knapp (1853–1901), a Methodist minister, and Seth Cook Rees (1854–1932), a Quaker convert to holiness doctrine, established the International Holiness Union and Prayer League to promote deeper spirituality among Christians. Organizational structure was minimal, and membership was open to all who desired to experience **entire sanctification**. This experiential aspect was combined with a strong emphasis on **evangelism** and ministry to the urban poor and disadvantaged.

A flurry of mergers and name changes over the next two decades culminated in the formation of the Pilgrim Holiness Church in 1922. Its first general superintendent was Seth Cook Rees, who had parted company with Knapp and subsequently established several holiness congregations in California. Bringing this group of churches to the merger, Rees returned to the denomination he had originally cofounded. The Pilgrim Holiness Church was globally minded from its inception and sponsored numerous worldwide missions. A lack of central organization and the practice of independent fund-raising for its many enterprises (foreign missions, urban ministries, and several Bible colleges) posed a constant threat to the denomination's stability during its formative years. Despite these challenges, the Pilgrim Holiness

Church experienced significant growth, increasing membership by 56 percent between 1930 and 1946.

Gradual centralization of its organizational structure at midcentury prompted merger discussions with the **Wesleyan Methodist Church**. The two denominations united in 1968 to form the **Wesleyan Church.**

See also Holiness Movements: American, British, and Continental; Wesley, John, Theology of; Wesleyan Methodism.

CLARENCE (BUD) BENCE, PHD

PNEUMATOLOGY
See HOLY SPIRIT (PNEUMATOLOGY).

POLYGAMY

Polygamy is the practice of being married to more than one spouse at a time. This is known as parallel polygamy. Serial monogamy, on the other hand, involves marriage, divorce, marriage, divorce, and so on. This is sometimes described as serial polygamy. While parallel and serial monogamy are accommodated in African and Western cultures respectively, both practices undermine the monogamous marriage covenant God ordained. Jesus reaffirmed this:

Have you not read that the one who made them at the beginning "made them male and female," and said, "For this reason a man shall leave his father and mother and be joined to his wife, and the two shall become one flesh"? So they are no longer two, but one flesh. Therefore what God has joined together, let no one separate. (Matt. 19:4-6)

Polygamous practices, parallel and serial, occurred in Bible times. But Jesus said,

It was because you were so hard-hearted that Moses allowed you to divorce your wives, but from the beginning it was not so. And I say to you, whoever divorces his wife, except for unchastity, and marries another commits adultery. (Matt. 19:8-9; cf. Mark 10:5-12).

Although polygamous marriages existed in the OT, and are still practiced in various cultures, it is noteworthy that in most instances the OT depicts stories of dysfunctional relationship(s) and/or unhappy marriages. In general, where polygamy is practiced, social and family conflicts abound and are often accompanied by a high rate of infidelity. Usually, in parallel polygamy wives and children are regarded as the husband's/father's possessions. Women are reduced to objects that can be obtained and tossed aside at will.

While divorce is not God's will for husbands and wives, some may resort to it because physical and/or legal circumstances force the action. In some cultures polygamy is practiced out of ignorance of God's will. In some instances, daughters are forced into polygamous marriages when parents give them as wives without their consent.

Many African Instituted Churches (AICs) or African Indigenous Churches, founded by Africans instead of missionaries, permit polygamy. They see that polygamy was permitted in the OT and adopt that practice as their guide. Very few mission churches permit the practice.

Often the church is faced with the challenge of knowing how best to extend God's grace to persons caught in polygamous marriages, while also educating them about the "good and acceptable and perfect" will of God (Rom. 12:2). In many instances, dissolving a polygamous marriage would generate increased hardship. For example, in parts of Africa most wives and children are wholly dependent on the father for their livelihood. They would likely be left destitute if they were to terminate their polygamous relationship. Several Western evangelical churches urged polygamist men, on becoming Christians, to separate from (divorce) all their wives except one. The policy created hardship for many women and children.

Other evangelical churches do not require that polygamist marriages be terminated. Instead, they teach new converts the biblical model and show that God's grace reaches into polygamist marriages initiated in ignorance of God's will. Evangelical churches also teach that it is sinful for persons who know God's will for marriage to initiate polygamist marriages.

See also Feminist Theology; Indigenous Theologies; Marriage.

FILIMÀO M. CHAMBO, DLITT ET PHIL

POLYTHEISM

Polytheism is the recognition and worship of multiple gods and goddesses. It is the opposite of monotheism, the recognition and worship of one God whose being excludes all other claimants to deity. There are five monotheistic religions: **Judaism**, **Islam**, **Christianity**, the Sikhs, and the Baha'i Faith.

Usually polytheistic gods are members of a pantheon, a group of gods worshipped by a people group. Most *polytheistic* religions are hierarchically arranged, with a primary or "high" god, and many descending gods and goddesses. In ancient Roman mythology, for example, Jupiter was the king of the gods, while Venus, Mars, Mercury, and Apollo were less powerful.

Polytheism should be distinguished from **pantheism**, the belief that God and the world are substantially indistinguishable. The material world constitutes God's multiple attributes. Without the world, God *is not*. God is present *as God* in all things. By contrast, polytheism distinguishes between the world and the gods, even though their associated mythologies depend on the world. Polytheists often see the gods as personifications of natural forces.

Many **African Traditional Religions** (ATRs) are polytheistic. They believe in a "high" creator god and lesser deities. Additionally, ATRs often include ancestors in their worship, usually seen as intercessors between humans and the gods. The unseen, spiritual realm constitutes a hierarchy. The creator (high or supreme) god is highest. Then come the major gods, minor gods, and ancestors at the bottom.

Other current polytheistic religions are voodoo, some forms of **neo-paganism**, some Native American **folk religions, New Age** worship of angels, and the devas of Mahayana **Buddhism**, namely, gods who live in various heavenly realms.

Hinduism is often referred to as polytheistic. However, most devout Hindus would say it is monotheistic, because they worship one god in many manifestations. More correctly, Hinduism is **monistic**. There is finally only a single, impersonal reality; all distinctions, even the gods, are illusory.

The mystery of the **Trinity**—that is, the Christian concept of **God** as one essence, substance, or being in three persons (Father, Son, Holy Spirit)—can be confusing to polytheists and non-Christian monotheists alike. Some Muslims and Jews have misunderstood Trinitarian doctrine and labeled Christianity polytheistic. Likewise, it may seem to a polytheist that Christians interact with multiple gods (e.g., by praying for **salvation** from the Father, through Christ, in the power of the Holy Spirit).

See also African Indigenous Church Theologies; God, Doctrine of; Idolatry; New Age Spirituality; Religious Pluralism.

MARYANN HAWKINS, PHD

POPULAR CULTURE

No commonly agreed on definition of "popular culture" exists. The two terms themselves are contested. One definition of "culture" (Latin, *colere*, "to cultivate") is that it comprises the "shared values and practices of a group of people." "Popular" connotes the "mainstream," the "most accessible and accepted aspects of a culture." Hence, a broad and useful definition of "popular culture" is "the artifacts and practices that constitute and lend meaning to everyday life in a given context."

Popular culture is easily confused with low or folk culture. It is also sometimes generically identified as what remains after the boundaries of high culture are set. Accordingly, popular culture is often used derisively to name the trivial or lowbrow. The postmodern context rejects these common distinctions.

In the early twenty-first century, hip-hop artists sample strains of classical music, trends in high fashion prize folk and bohemian styles, and ad campaigns for mobile phones draw on high-concept environmental art. Still, because of the influence of the mass media in an increasingly global setting, popular culture is inextricably linked to the production, accessibility, and consumption of commercial or mass culture.

Artifacts of popular culture include television, film, literature (fiction, nonfiction, magazines, blogs, etc.), music, and technology. Film and television viewing, attendance at sporting events, reading online and off-line, communicating via information technologies (mobile devices, social networks, etc.), exercise, shopping, eating, and even participating in political processes are features of popular culture.

On close examination, these artifacts and practices belie an inherent religiosity that calls out for interpretation and redemptive engagement. Yet the posture of religious groups toward popular culture is often dismissive. Ironically, the religious faith and practice of people groups often create much of what we call popular culture. The Christian faith, for example, emerged from a religion reviled by many, became a persecuted religion, and then laid the foundations for the culture of half the globe. Yet in spite of its own origins, and in spite of the fact that popular culture in the West often reflects themes commensurate with Christianity, many Christian churches hold popular culture at arm's length in order to avoid "corruption by the world."

Jesus frequently incorporated elements of "popular" Palestinian culture. The people with whom he often associated—disdained by his critics—represented "popular" culture. He took seriously the mundane lives of the populace and used the already familiar to articulate the gospel of the kingdom.

Jesus' followers are called to be astute interpreters of popular culture. The apostle Paul exemplified this in his address to the Athenians in Acts 17. He interpreted their "unknown god" as the Creator in whom "we live and move and have our being" (vv. 23, 28). The Oxford-educated Wesleys were well known for their appropriation of popular culture and the popular reception of their music. A Wesleyan commitment to experience as a source of theology encourages active engagement with popular culture. It is part of the created order through which the Creator is revealed.

See also Capitalism; Dance; Film/Cinema; Media; Music/Hymns/ Hymnology; Technology.

Resource
Romanowski, William D. *Eyes Wide Open: Looking for God in Popular Culture.* Grand Rapids: Brazos Press, 2007.

BRANNON HANCOCK, PHD

POPULAR RELIGIOSITY

Popular religiosity, popular religion, popular piety, or the people's religion describes the unofficial or popular religion that emerges from the interchange between "official" religious doctrine, culture, and socioeconomics and a people's history. Confined to no continent or religion, popular religiosity denotes how ordinary folk go about being religious. It reveals how a culture actually receives and modifies the official religion as taught by the missionaries or educated elites. In Latin America, for example, popular religiosity describes the result of mixing the Christian gospel with a struggle to make sense of life. The resulting combination strives to achieve a measure of justice and to defend the dignity of human life. Popular religiosity is observable in indigenous cultures. It tends toward a decentralization of clerical influence.

Specialists or elites speak for official religiosity. Popular religiosity finds expression among the common people. Official religiosity is transmitted through carefully formulated catechesis and other forms of theological instruction. The common people transmit popular religiosity through their culture, unofficial rituals, language, and symbols.

Popular religiosity is linked to a symbolic language with elements drawn from official doctrine, myth, and the spirit of a nation. Other elements of popular religiosity's symbolic language can include folkloric legends and superstitions. Symbolic language can be nonverbal, as spoken in dances, corporate expressions, and even silence. Its context is the celebrations and challenges of everyday life.

Popular religiosity incorporates both a rural and an urban ethos. It is not the sole possession of any social class but is particularly prominent among poor and marginalized people. It recognizes and cherishes leaders—"the unstudied ones"—perhaps not recognized by the official religious hierarchy. The spirituality of popular religiosity is both similar and dissimilar to an official religion's spirituality. The spirituality of popular religiosity reflects not only official doctrine but also most deeply a people's history; it brings that history to the surface.

Rituals in the form of pilgrimages, processions, vows, and the recitation of prayers for specific purposes (novenas) are important means for expressing popular religiosity. Other avenues include observing designated days and seasons to honor certain people, especially saints. It can give birth to cults that promise cures and liberation from evils.

The Second Vatican Council accented the role of popular religiosity among Roman Catholics. But popular religiosity also exists among Protestants. In Latin America, for example, many Pentecostals and charismatics pray to receive *Espírito Santo* "power" that will enable them to be victorious over the many struggles of everyday life.

In popular religiosity, God and all heavenly agents identify with people's sufferings. Miracles, the search for the cause of evil, and divinely given strength to face it are essential ingredients.

Some scholars say there is a complementarity between official and popular religiosity, that official religion can be influenced or shaped by popular religiosity. Liberation theologians have insisted that **orthodoxy** must be influenced by, or even grow from, **orthopraxis** and not simply be handed down by traditional European theologians for acceptance.

See also Contextual Theology; Deliverance/Exorcism; Divination; Folk
Religion; Indigenization; Indigenous Theologies; Orthodoxy/Orthopraxis/
Orthopathy.

Resource

Zaccaria, Francesco. *Participation and Beliefs in Popular Religiosity.* Empirical Studies in
Theology. Leiden, NL: E. J. Brill, 2010.

BLANCHES DE PAULA, PHD

POSTCOLONIALISM

Postcolonialism refers specifically to a collection of theories in the fields of
literature, sociology, political science, philosophy, and theology and generally
to a broader set of reactions to colonialism. Initially the term was employed
to explore how writers representing newly independent peoples appropriate
the languages colonial powers imposed on them for expressing themselves.
More broadly, it addresses the residual influence of European colonization on
cultures. Thus it is concerned with exposing and neutralizing colonialist attitudes and assumptions about racism, imperialism, and cultural superiority.

While the term "postcolonialism" may appear to indicate that a new reality has replaced colonialism, this is not the case. Rather, the present state of
affairs in many former colonial countries is characterized in multiple, subtle,
and sweeping ways by the colonial past.

This field of study began with the publication of the seminal book *Orientalism* by Edward Wadie Said, a Palestinian-American. He proposed that
Europeans had developed and disseminated inaccurate characterizations
of Western and Eastern cultures. The inaccuracies had permitted Western
powers to impose Western colonial policies. Other leading theorists of postcolonialism include Gayatri Chakravorty Spivak (India), Frantz Omar Fanon
(Martinique), and Homi K. Bhabha (India). They have expanded the conversation and explored related concepts such as subaltern, essentialism, hybrid-
ity, epistemic violence, paternalism, and dependency.

Among prominent theologians and religious scholars entering the discussion of postcolonialism are Andrew Walls, Lamin Sanneh, R. S. Sugirtharajah, Fernando Segovia, Musa W. Dube, Kwok Pui-lan, Mayra Rivera Rivera, and Miroslav Volf.

Given that Christianity reached around the world during the modern
colonial era, the relationship between Christianity and colonialism became
complex—at times mutually complementary and at others marked by conflict. A worldview shared by the colonial powers and Western Christianity,
and language common to both, contributed to the confusion over the differences between colonialism and the Christian faith. Such terms as "advance,"
"conquest," "Promised Land," "civilization," and "progress" marked Western
colonialism. Christians borrowed the language; the result was that the lan-

guage made the two seem synonymous. Western Christianity, shaped by Western culture, became embedded in the cultures and sense of identity of colonized peoples and shaped much of the postcolonial discourse. Recognizing this impact, conversations among postcolonial theologians concentrate on how Western Christianity and culture have shaped their understanding of church history, biblical translation and studies, theology, ecclesiology, leadership styles, and cultural customs and lifestyles.

Early precursors in the postcolonial conversation include Henry Venn (1796–1873) and Rufus Anderson (1796–1880). They advocated developing self-governing, self-supporting, and self-propagating local churches. By the mid-twentieth century, discussions about missiology critiqued the colonial assumptions that lay behind planting **indigenous churches**. The term **contextualization** was adopted to describe a different orientation for evangelism and planting the Christian faith among new people groups. The new orientation is marked by a more inductive and engaging understanding of a host country's worldviews, values, lifestyles, customs, and practices.

Theologies of liberation are more recent expressions of postcolonial dialogue. They emerged within Roman Catholicism in the 1960s and quickly spread throughout other Christian traditions in Latin America, Africa, Asia, and elsewhere. Liberation theologians begin with a hermeneutics of suspicion; that is, they expose colonialist assumptions and engage in deconstructing and reconstructing multiple disciplines from a postcolonial perspective. Liberation raises questions about other marginalized peoples, including women, children, victims of sex trafficking, refugees, immigrants, and other minorities.

See also Christianity and Global Cultures; Contextualization; Contextual Theology; Globalization; Global South; Religious Pluralism.

Resources
Keller, Catherine, Michael Nausner, and Mayra Rivera. *Postcolonial Theologies*. St. Louis: Chalice Press, 2004.
Young, Robert J. C. *Postcolonialism: An Historical Introduction*. Oxford, UK: Blackwell Publishers, 2001.

NORMAN WILSON, PHD

POSTCONSERVATIVE EVANGELICAL THEOLOGY
"Postconservative" is a term first used by Clark Pinnock (1990) and later popularized and defined by Roger Olson. It designates evangelicals who reject theological methods rooted in **modernity** and critically engage **postmodernity**. They typically understand **revelation** to be transformational and **Scripture** to have a narrative or dramatic shape and emphasize the relational and communal nature of **God** and the Christian life. Thus "postconservative" is in many ways a parallel term to "postliberal."

The roots of the postconservative approach lie in **Pietism** rather than Protestant scholasticism. More recent evangelical influences include the later work of Bernard Ramm, Donald G. Bloesch, T. F. Torrance, and especially Lesslie Newbigin.

While critically engaging postmodern thought, postconservatism rejects the relativism associated with its deconstructionist and neopragmatist strands. Instead, it draws much more on the insights of postmodern thinkers such as Alasdair McIntyre and Michael Polanyi, for whom it is our knowledge that is relative, not truth itself. Postconservatives have a critical realist **epistemology** that leads to neither relativism nor absolute certainty but to reasoned confidence.

Postconservatives are critical of the rational **apologetics** and propositionalism that dominated much of **evangelical theology** in the twentieth century. They argue that the purpose of revelation is more transformation than information, and the truth of Scripture is not limited to propositions. It is most centrally and adequately expressed in language such as narrative and metaphor that the Holy Spirit uses to engage the faithful imagination and transform hearts and lives. Thus Scripture is not a book of facts to be arranged by reason into a logical system but a means through which God enables us to encounter Jesus Christ, understand the world rightly, and have our lives, communities, and actions shaped by the gospel. Theology aids in our living out the divine drama or narrative of the gospel.

They insist that neither reason nor experience offer universal foundations on which to ground the truth of Scripture or theology. They believe the rational apologetics typical of much of evangelical theology, along with the experiential apologetics of **liberal theology**, capitulates to the Enlightenment quest for certainty. Instead, theology is grounded in the particularity of the gospel itself. Its truth is seen in how it makes sense of the world and is embodied in lives and communities. Unlike some forms of **postliberal theology**, postconservatives believe the historicity of the events of salvation history is critical to the gospel's truth. But unlike some evangelicals, they do not see the Scripture's truth as dependent on a detailed or precise correlation with history.

Postconservatives distinguish between God's revelation and our theological reflection on it. Because God's redemptive acts are in history, we do not have access to an *ahistorical* revelation (without reference to or regard for history). The gospel is both contextualized in, as well as transforms, culture. This means that, though always rooted in Scripture, there is necessarily growth in theological understanding; the meaning of the gospel unfolds over time and is lived out in many contexts.

Postconservatives reject the autonomous individualism of modernity, embracing instead a community shaped by Scripture that in turn shapes those who participate in it. Relationality is a key concept for understanding **theological anthropology, salvation, church,** and God.

Although not all accept the label, postconservative theologians include Clark H. Pinnock, *Tracking the Maze* (1990); Stanley J. Grenz, *Revisioning Evangelical Theology* (1993) and *Renewing the Center* (2006); Nancey Murphy, *Beyond Liberalism and Fundamentalism* (1996); Henry H. Knight III, *A Future for Truth* (1997); and Kevin J. Vanhoozer, *The Drama of Doctrine* (2005). Others include Roger E. Olson, Rodney Clapp, John R. Franke, John Sanders, F. LeRon Shults and Miroslav Volf.

See also Evangelical Theology; Narrative Theology.

Resources
Dorrien, Gary. *The Remaking of Evangelical Theology.* Louisville, KY: Westminster John Knox Press, 1998.
Olson, Roger E. *Reformed and Always Reforming: The Postconservative Approach to Evangelical Theology.* Grand Rapids: Baker Academic, 2007.

HENRY H. KNIGHT III, PHD

POSTLIBERAL THEOLOGY

Postliberal theology designates a type of theology whose leading proponents were active late in the twentieth century. The term "postliberal" points to its proponents' dissatisfaction with classical liberal theology. It responds to **liberal theological** claims. Representatives include Hans Frei, George Lindbeck, David Kelsey, and Stanley Hauerwas. William Placher and Kathryn Tanner are also sometimes considered postliberal theologians.

Postliberal theology arose in tandem with **postmodern** philosophy. Both recognized that the ideal of universal and absolute truth is illusory. For postliberal theologians, this meant rejecting the assumption that Christian theology can be evaluated by and interpreted in terms of philosophical or scientific discourse. They believe that classical liberal theology portrayed Christian beliefs and practices as but instances of universal religious truths and phenomena. The **God** revealed in **Scripture,** for instance, was thought to be identical with the God discovered by philosophical investigation. By correlating Christian claims with philosophical or scientific claims, postliberals argue, liberal theologians abandoned the autonomy and truth of Christian theology. They submitted theology to an authority outside the Christian faith.

It is questionable whether this indictment applies to all liberal theologians. Nonetheless, the postliberals' concern shows why they embrace Karl Barth's theology. Like them, Barth insisted that the truth and norm of the Christian faith is found only within **revelation;** attempts to understand Christian theology outside of revelation distort theology. Postliberals also appreciate Barth's view that God's revelation is always particular and not general. This agrees with their postmodern skepticism about the possibility of general truths and universal forms of experience. There is, they argue, no such thing as *religion in general* or *universal religious experience.* On the contrary, Christian theology rests on the historical particularity of revelation and on the particular character of the church. Emphasizing particularity and rejecting universal, absolute truth shows the postfoundationalist character of postliberal theology. This means that along with postmodern thinkers generally, postliberals reject the possibility of an absolute, unshakable foundation of human knowledge.

The postfoundationalist stance explains why **narrative** is a central postliberal category. Narrative, postliberals say, is the Bible's preferred genre and the mode of discourse most appropriate for God's revelation; narrative is better adapted to the particularity of revelation than is philosophy. The Bible's narrative, however, despite its realistic character, is not principally a depiction of historical events. Instead, the truth of narrative lies in its power to draw readers into the world the narrative presents and to reshape them according to the narrative's story and characters. Postliberal theologians, therefore, affirm Jesus' resurrection as an essential element of the **gospel** narrative. However, they have little interest in discussing the **historicity** of the **resurrection**. Similarly, they hold that the truth of Christian **doctrines** has nothing to do with how accurately they describe objective states of affairs. Their truth lies instead in their capacity to sustain the beliefs, practices, and character of the church. Doctrines, in other words, are principles that maintain the integrity of the Christian life, not descriptions of objective facts.

See also Modernity.

Resources

DeHart, Paul J. *Trial of the Witnesses: The Rise and Decline of Postliberal Theology.* Malden, MA: Blackwell Publishing, 2006.

Lindbeck, George. *The Nature of Doctrine: Religion and Theology in a Postliberal Age.* Louisville, KY: Westminster John Knox Press, 1984.

Placher, William. *The Triune God: An Essay in Postliberal Theology.* Louisville, KY: Westminster John Knox Press, 2007.

SAMUEL M. POWELL, PHD

POSTMODERNITY

Though a fixed definition of the term "postmodernity" remains elusive, one can identify ideas shared by most thinkers identified as postmodernists. Overall, postmodernism represents a critique of Enlightenment ideals such as strong foundationalism, pure objectivity, and universal norms. In philosophy critiques of these ideals have been made manifest in multiple ways: some stress the importance of linguistic and social contexts (Ludwig Wittgenstein, Thomas Kuhn, and Richard Rorty), some emphasize the role of interpretation in meaning formation (Martin Heidegger, Hans-Georg Gadamer, and Paul

Ricoeur), and some attend to the way that power structures affect human discourse and practice (Michel Foucault, Jacques Derrida, and Gilles Deleuze).

Much of modernity sought a singular foundation or beginning point for all knowledge, and this foundation was to be established with indubitable certainty. Postmodernism challenges foundationalism and suggests that there is no single point of departure for knowing. Rather, to know something is already to be in a particular situation and context. To ask, "What is the first knowledge on which all other knowledge is based?" is like asking, "Which places in Brazil are starting places?" The starting point depends on where one is.

Another modern ideal was absolute certainty for one's beliefs, which was to be achieved by excluding all bias and subjectivity from the process of inquiry and discarding the clothes of particular religious or cultural traditions. Hence, a universal rationality would be available to all people, and timeless truths, truths independent of historical era or geographic location, would be found. These timeless truths would possess indubitable certainty, since no "rational" person could deny them. For postmodern thinkers, however, we do not possess an absolute place to stand because that would require a God's-eye view, rather than a human perspective. Postmodernism claims there is no purely objective perspective by which to adjudicate between conflicting points of view because all persons are embedded in particular historical, linguistic, and cultural contexts. Knowledge is influenced by motives, expectations, and even aesthetic judgments, and these cannot be discarded as "biases," since our very conceptualizing is dependent on them. Accordingly, there is no basis for affirming universal human rationality.

The emphasis on the contextual nature of knowing is very important in postmodernism. A completely neutral perspective would amount to a "view from nowhere." Meaning, truth, and ethics are contextual because these are always produced by communities with traditions. It is particular communities, not isolated thinkers, that determine normativity and meaning. What one takes as a meaningful utterance or normative claim is dependent on particular languages and communities of discourse that shape our perceptions and the very way we ask our questions. We never get "past" or "beyond" a text or experience to a pure, unadulterated meaning because we are always interpreting. There is no historyless, subjectless interpreter. This does not necessarily mean, however, that all interpretations are equally valid. It does mean that the criteria for a "good" interpretation are established by various communities—there are no independent, autonomous, purely objective criteria that all people accept as correct. This is, in part, why postmodernism celebrates difference and otherness, while much of the Enlightenment valued homogenization and uniformity.

The upshot of postmodernism is a call for epistemic humility. Even if it is claimed that God has the absolute truth and that God has given a revelation to humanity, postmodern thinkers would still claim that we do not possess God's understanding of it for two reasons. First, any communication from God is going to occur within particular human languages and the cultural thought forms embedded in them (inescapable perspectivalism). Second, we cannot avoid the necessity of interpreting divine revelation. So hermeneutics is inescapable. Christian postmodernists point out that epistemic humility should be something all Christians affirm because of the doctrines of human finitude and the noetic effects of sin.

See also Enlightenment; Epistemology; Modernity.

Resources
Akkerman, Jay R., Thomas J. Oord, and Brent D. Peterson. *Postmodern and Wesleyan? Exploring the Boundaries and Possibilities*. Kansas City: Beacon Hill Press of Kansas City, 2009.
Lyotard, Jean-François. *The Postmodern Condition: A Report on Knowledge*. Theory and History of Literature, vol. 10. Minneapolis: University of Minnesota Press, 1984.
Sim, Stuart, ed. *The Routledge Companion to Postmodernism*. 2nd ed. New York: Routledge, 2005.

JOHN SANDERS, THD

POVERTY

Human poverty is the condition of having insufficient physical resources to maintain even a minimal standard of human flourishing and dignity. Its specific manifestations differ from culture to culture. It is estimated that half the world's population lives in poverty. The majority of these, or 1.2 billion, live in absolute poverty, surviving on a dollar or less a day. Most of these live in sub-Saharan Africa.

The Hebrew term for poverty, *yarash*, can mean "to disinherit," "to dispossess," "to come to ruin," and "to impoverish." The poor include orphans, strangers, widows, and small farmers exploited by the powerful (Amos 8:4-6).

The **Wisdom** literature of the OT witnesses that laziness and foolishness can cause poverty. But in the **Prophetic** tradition, injustice and exploitation are identified as key causes (2:6; 4:1). God seeks justice for the oppressed and neglected. God's concern for the poor is shown by his giving laws that protect them. Israel was to set free its fellow Israelites who because of economic distress had to sell themselves into slavery (Exod. 21:2). Exploitation of the poor was not permitted (22:22-27). The laws for gleaning required Israelites to leave some of their harvest for foreigners and the poor (Lev. 19:9-10).

In the NT, **Jesus** identifies with those who are at the mercy of the world and advises some of his followers to sell their possessions and give to the poor. According to the gospel of Luke, the poor hear the good news gladly (8:40). Throughout the gospel the poor are defined by numerous criteria: economic standing in society, family heritage, religious purity or impurity, health, and vocation. The poor are persons who eke out a living on the margins of society. In Palestine, there were two kinds of poor people: working poor and begging poor. The working poor consisted of merchants, artisans, farmers, and fishermen who had a measure of self-sufficiency, honor, and respect. The begging poor were destitute of all means of support, strangers to honor and respect. Many of them had at one time been among the working poor. Heavy taxation, illness, or other misfortune had landed them among the begging poor. These were the persons to whom the term "poverty" was most applicable.

Following Jesus' example and command, the **early church** cared for its poor and needy (Acts 2:44-45). When the Jerusalem church was afflicted by poverty, Paul collected an offering among the Gentile churches to care for the Jerusalem believers (1 Cor. 16:1).

The story of the rise of Methodism is laden with its ministry to and identity with the impoverished. Believing that he was simply obeying his Lord, John Wesley extensively used his somewhat privileged social status to find ways to alleviate crushing poverty. He challenged structural evils, including the alcohol industry and the devastating impact on the poor of the enclosure laws, which denied landless farmers use of traditionally accessible land. Repeatedly a renewal of that original Methodist commitment has happened. The rise of the **Salvation Army** was an early instance.

See also Altruism/Natural Morality; Christian Ethics/Moral Theology; Justice; Rights, Human; Social Justice; Wealth; Wesley, John, Theology of; Works of Mercy.

Resources
Greer, Peter, Phil Smith, and Jeremy Cowart. *The Poor Will Be Glad: Joining the Revolution to Lift the World Out of Poverty.* Grand Rapids: Zondervan, 2009.
Payne, Ruby K. *A Framework for Understanding Poverty.* 4th ed. Highlands, TX: Aha! Process, 2005.
Sider, Ronald J. *Rich Christians in an Age of Hunger: Moving from Affluence to Generosity.* 5th ed. Nashville: Thomas Nelson, 2005.

GIFT MTUKWA, MA

POWER (DUNAMIS)
See CROSS; GOSPEL; PREACHING.

PRACTICAL MONOTHEISM
See GOD, DOCTRINE OF.

PRACTICAL THEOLOGY
The discipline of Christian theology has generated various adjectives to characterize its nature and diverse foci. **Biblical** and **systematic** are two prominent ones. Another of relatively recent origin is "practical." The distinction between academic theology and practical (applied) theology was first made

by the faculties of European universities and then imported to the universities and divinity schools of North America.

As a special discipline of study, practical theology seeks to correlate Christian faith (doctrine) with a wide range of contemporary Christian praxis (practice). There is a creative tension between systematic theology and practical theology. Drawing a sharp line between Christian belief and action, theory and practice, would risk separating what inherently belong together. **Orthodoxy** (right faith) **and orthopraxis** (right practice) are inseparable.

Practical theology stresses the correlational, **hermeneutical**, and transformative character of doing Christian theology. It holds in reciprocal relationship the vision and values of Christian tradition, and the current life of the church and state of the world.

"Practical" can be characterized negatively as mere mechanics without theological sophistication. Conversely, theology as an "academic" discipline has been criticized as a hopelessly abstract, ivory-tower exercise. Neither description is correct. Contemporary practical theologians reflect on the transformative nature and intent of Christian theology. Their practical theological work involves far more than mastering skills and applying methods. Practical theology seeks the critical interface between the Word of God in Scripture and the work of God in the church and the world. Practical theology takes as partners the social sciences and cultural factors in its attempt to help shape Christian life and ministry in harmony with Christian convictions.

A central goal of practical theology is to identify action-guiding visions that inspire and instruct Christian discipleship in the church and in public life.

Many North American seminaries offer a doctor of practical theology or doctor of ministry degree that stresses thoughtful, professional practice. This is in contrast to the standard doctor of philosophy or doctor of theology degree that stresses foreign languages, extensive research, and a detailed dissertation on a highly specialized topic.

The word "applied" or "practical" refers to a range of related subject fields, including church growth, counseling, evangelism, homiletics, missions, pastoral psychology, and spiritual formation. Advocacy theologies focus on ethnic, racial, gender, or other particular groups. The Association of Practical Theology, the International Academy of Practical Theology, and the *International Journal of Practical Theology* foster the aims of practical theology.

John Wesley spoke eloquently of "social holiness," with primary reference to the church. But his preaching and example also made clear that Christian beliefs lose integrity unless they are invested in addressing the harsh realities of a fallen world. Like Paul's teachings in the NT, Wesley's theological work was extensive but hardly limited to a systematic or academic theology in the usual sense. For him theology was contextual and mission oriented, often having direct reference to practical circumstances in given congregations.

The phrase "practical divinity" probably originated with John Wesley. His approach to theology was that of a pastor/theologian, making theology a practical discipline, much as it was in its preuniversity Christian setting.

See also Biblical Theology; Christian Ethics/Moral Theology; Contextual Theology; Mission and Social Justice; Public Theology; Social Ethics; Works of Mercy.

Resources

Langford, Thomas A. *Theology in the Wesleyan Tradition.* Vol. 1, *Practical Divinity.* Rev. ed. Nashville: Abingdon Press, 1998.

Maddox, Randy L. "Reading Wesley as a Theologian." *Wesleyan Theological Journal* 30, no. 1 (Spring 1995): 7-54.

BARRY CALLEN, EDD

PRAYER

Prayer (Latin, *preces,* "prayer," "supplication") spans a broad range of religious practices. It overarches eras and cultures. Prayer involves active *communication* (conversation) and passive *communion* (contemplation) with God. It is practiced in private and in public, spontaneously or ritualized. Praising and giving thanks to God, confessing our sins and asking forgiveness, soliciting "our daily bread" (Matt. 6:11) and interceding for the needs of others—all characterize private and communal prayer. Modes of prayer recorded in the Bible include silence, verbal interaction, singing, dancing, and **glossolalia.**

The OT records many individual and communal prayers (Exod. 15:1-18; 1 Sam. 2:1-10; Psalms and Lamentations). The NT portrays **Jesus** as a teacher of prayer (Matt. 7:7-11; Luke 11:1), as providing a model prayer (Matt. 6:9-13; Luke 11:2-4), and as praying often (Matt. 26:39-42; Mark 1:35; 6:46; John 17:1-26). Jesus joined prayer and faith to far-reaching promises (Matt. 7:7-11), conditioned on first seeking God's will (Matt. 6:10; Luke 22:42). Paul admonishes believers to "pray without ceasing" (1 Thess. 5:17). He says prayer requires the Spirit's guidance: "We do not know how to pray as we ought, but . . . [the Holy] Spirit intercedes with sighs too deep for words" and "helps us in our weakness" (Rom. 8:26). The Bible records instances of prayer not being answered as voiced (2 Sam. 12:13-23; 1 Kings 19:4-9; 2 Cor. 12:8-10).

In 1 Tim 2:1-2, four types of prayer are mentioned: supplication (petitionary), worship (doxology), intercession (invocation), and thanksgiving (benediction). Prayer extends, according to these verses, far beyond personal concerns to include "everyone . . . and all who are in high positions." In fact, Christians should understand all of life as prayer. Paul exhorted the Roman Christians "to present . . . [their very] bodies as a living sacrifice, holy and acceptable to God, which is . . . [their] spiritual worship" (Rom. 12:1).

For the eighteenth-century Wesleyan revival, after the Bible, the Anglican Book of Common Prayer was the most influential source for prayers. The extensive poetic works and hymns of Charles Wesley offer a wealth of prayers. The Wesleyan heritage was "born in song" and shaped by "a faith that sings" (Chilcote 2002, 148). Among the **means of grace**, John Wesley considered prayer the most important. He identified prayer as the principal activity in **works of piety** (personal holiness). Correspondingly, **works of mercy** (doing good) that involve social holiness can be seen as expressions of prayer. In the *Plain Account of Christian Perfection* Wesley wrote,

Whether we think of, or speak to, God, whether we act or suffer for him, all is prayer, when we have no other object than his love, and the desire of pleasing him.

All that a Christian does, even in eating and sleeping, is prayer, when it is done in simplicity, according to the order of God. (*Works*, 11:438)

A holistic and confident practice of *informed* prayer petitions God for personal needs, prays for his kingdom's consummation, and intercedes for the salvation of all persons and for justice and peace in the world.

See also Contemplative Spirituality; Faith; Renovaré; Spiritual Disciplines; Spiritual Formation/Growth; Theosis (Deification).

Resources

Chilcote, Paul W. *Changed from Glory into Glory: Wesleyan Prayer for Transformation.* Nashville: Upper Room Books, 2005.

———, ed. *The Wesleyan Tradition: A Paradigm for Renewal.* Nashville: Abingdon Press, 2002.

Foster, Richard. *Prayer: Finding the Heart's True Home.* San Francisco: HarperSanFrancisco, 1992.

Knight, Henry H., III. *Eight Life-Enriching Practices of United Methodists.* Nashville: Abingdon Press, 2001.

ACHIM HÄRTNER, MA

PREACHING

In Christianity, preaching is generally understood as orally delivering a theologically informed address founded on a biblical text or topic, applicable to the present, and hoping to result in persuasion and action. When used as a noun, the term "preaching" refers to the act of such oral delivery. Other religions practice preaching as their doctrines prescribe.

In early Christianity, preaching assumed two forms: *homily* and *sermon*. (1) A homily was a speech that commented on a biblical text verse by verse. It was shaped by rabbinical Judaism and Greco-Roman rhetoric. (2) A sermon was an expository discourse, mostly of a thematic character. It addressed three human dimensions: reason (*logos*), emotion (*pathos*), and character (*ēthos*).

Preaching is a complex activity. Ideally it integrates biblical interpretation, theological reflection, spiritual formation, pastoral counseling, cultural and social analysis, and oratory. Preaching involves interplay between knowledge and skills that employ personal conviction for bearing witness to biblical truth. Preaching depends on guidance by the **Holy Spirit.** The Swiss Reformer Heinrich Bullinger (1504-75) explained that "preaching . . . the Word of God *is* the Word of God" (1561-64, chap. 1). Similarly, Karl Barth (1886–1968) taught that through preaching, the gospel "happens." **Martin Luther** believed preaching involves a mutual responsibility before God, one shared by preacher and congregation. Preaching should evidence a coincidence between the preacher's word and life.

While a cognitive, essay-type paradigm traditionally characterized preaching in Euro-American churches, contemporary discussion of a "new homiletic" seeks a holistic approach. Striving for more than assent to reason, it incorporates intuitive, narrative, imaginative, and performative measures. It aims for a liberating and restorative encounter with the Divine Word. The new homiletic seeks to impact a hearer's entire life.

John Wesley preached approximately forty thousand sermons during his lifetime. A priest in the **Church of England,** he initially preached in liturgical settings. After taking up George Whitefield's (1714-70) method of field preaching in 1739, nonliturgical contexts dominated. Instead of waiting for his listeners to come to a church, Wesley took the gospel message directly to where people lived and worked. His preaching was rooted in the fundamental spiritual discovery he and his brother **Charles** made in 1738: the true nature of God is unconditional **love** and **grace.** Wesley's sermons aimed for individual and social salvation, restoration and **holiness.** The unifying vision for all his sermons is "faith working through love" (Gal. 5:6).

Although Wesley's oral sermons infrequently followed a manuscript, his written sermons evidence structure, logic, and clear intent. His preaching was both theological and practical, meant as "plain truth for plain people" (*Works,* 1:2; in preface to *Sermons on Several Occasions*). Wesley used his preaching for multiple purposes, including evangelizing, teaching, spiritual uplifting, and exhortation. He also employed his sermons for apologetic and even polemic purposes. While some of his sermons have identifiable contexts, others were written and collected deliberately for instruction.

As a consequence of development in Wesleyan missional theology, and the practical needs of the emerging revival, acceptance of lay and female preachers occurred. Preaching by laypersons gained in significance, beginning with John Cennick (1739) and Thomas Maxfield (1740). Sarah Crosby was a female pioneer who complied with an "exceptional call" to preach (1761). Sarah Mallet was the first woman to receive formal approval by Wesley as a lay preacher (1787). From these roots arose today's general conviction within Methodism that God's sovereign call to preach the gospel is *indivisible*—whether responded to by clergy or laypersons, male or female, black or white, young or old.

Preaching in the Wesleyan heritage today rests on an unwavering confidence in the gospel of **Jesus Christ** for individual and social transformation. Urgency, practicality, and applicability to life characterize Wesleyan preaching.

See also Evangelism; Liberation Theology; Liturgical Theology; Liturgy and Worship; Music/Hymns/Hymnology; Revivalism; Testimony/Witness; Women's Role in the Church.

Resources

Bullinger, Heinrich. Second Helvetic Confession. 1561-64. Christian Classics Ethereal Library. http://www.ccel.org/creeds/helvetic.htm.

Craddock, Fred B. *Preaching.* 25th anniv. ed. Nashville: Abingdon Press, 2010.

Härtner, Achim, and Holger Eschmann. *Learning to Preach Today: A Guide for Communicators and Listeners.* Calver, UK: Cliff College Publishing, 2004.

Willimon, William H., and Richard Lischer, eds. *Concise Encyclopedia of Preaching.* Louisville, KY: Westminster John Knox Press, 1995.

ACHIM HÄRTNER, MA

PREDESTINATION AND ELECTION

Predestination is the doctrine that God as sovereign has decreed who will inherit eternal life. *Election* is the same doctrine but viewed from the human perspective. To be among the "elect" is to receive eternal life.

That God preselects individuals for special tasks is evident in Scripture. John the Baptist (Luke 1:13-17), Mary (1:26-35), and Paul (Acts 26:16-18) are among those chosen by God for specific missions. However, the apostle Paul in Eph. 1:11-12 speaks of humans "destined" to "live for the praise of his glory." Likewise, in Rom. 9:22 he writes of "objects of wrath that are made for destruction." These passages move beyond the question of vocation to salvation. Interpreters historically have wrestled with such verses, especially in relation to divine love and justice.

The consensus of theologians in the first three centuries AD was that salvation is contingent on human response to God's universal offer in Christ. **Augustine** of Hippo (b. 354) was the first to teach that salvation is dependent on whether one has been predestined by God to receive eternal life. **Thomas Aquinas** (b. ca. 1225) likewise taught that God orders all things to an end, so those predestined to eternal life are like the "arrows" whom God the "archer" flights to its target. **John Calvin** (b. 1509) in his *Institutes of the Christian Religion* leaned heavily upon Augustine, positing that God has predestined some to salvation but others to destruction.

Among Calvinistic traditions, two major positions on God's decrees have emerged. *Supralapsarianism* teaches that God's first decree was for the election-salvation of individuals. This was followed by a decree to create and ended with God decreeing the fall (Adam and Eve's sin). The opposing view-point, *infralapsarianism*, places creation as God's first decree, followed by the fall, then God's decree regarding who will be elected-saved.

Jacob Arminius (b. 1560) studied under Theodore Beza, Calvin's successor in Geneva. As a professor in Leyden, Arminius set out to defend the Calvinist system against attack, but after careful study of Rom. 9, he modified his view of predestination. Following Arminius's death, his followers published the *Five Points of the Remonstrants*, positing that God's eternal salvation decree was based on divine foreknowledge of those who would believe in Christ and persevere in faith. The Synod of Dort (1618) rejected the Arminian position, affirming "double predestination," that God has chosen both who will be "elect" and who will be "reprobates" (i.e., condemned).

Article XVII ("Of Predestination and Election") of the Thirty-Nine Articles of the Church of England appears to favor the Calvinistic interpretation. John Wesley (b. 1703) was among a minority who adopted an Arminian viewpoint. His 1739 sermon "Free Grace" was the opening salvo in a protracted debate between Wesley and his fellow Methodist, George Whitefield. In the 1752 tract *Predestination Calmly Considered* Wesley excoriates the "horrible decree." While he agreed with Calvin that original sin had eliminated any possibility of merit in the person, including the ability to respond to divine overtures, he was unwilling to solve the problem via a solution impugning God's love and justice. Instead, he affirmed that a "measure of free will" has been "supernaturally restored to every man" (*Works*, 10:229-30). Nonresistance to this divine enablement, or **prevenient grace**, will lead the sinner to conversion.

See also Arminius, Jacob; Calvin, John; Free Will; Grace; Justification; *Ordo Salutis*; Prevenient Grace; Reconciliation; Reformation; Wesley, John, Theology of.

Resources

McGonigle, Herbert Boyd. *Sufficient Saving Grace: John Wesley's Evangelical Arminianism*. Studies in Evangelical History and Thought. Carlisle, UK: Paternoster, 2001.

Schreiner, Thomas R., and Bruce A. Ware. *Still Sovereign: Contemporary Perspectives on Election, Foreknowledge, and Grace*. Grand Rapids: Baker, 2000.

Thuesen, Peter. *Predestination: The American Career of a Contentious Doctrine*. Oxford, UK: Oxford University Press, 2009.

J. GREGORY CROFFORD, PHD

PREFERENTIAL OPTION FOR THE POOR

See LIBERATION THEOLOGY; MISSION AND SOCIAL JUSTICE.

PREVENIENT GRACE

From the Latin *praevenire* (to come before), "prevenient" grace is a metaphor referring to God's reaching love. While God demonstrates favor at many stages of the Christian journey, prevenient grace especially concerns the period before conversion (Rom. 5:8).

The term "prevenient grace" does not appear in the Bible but may be inferred from various passages (John 1:9; 6:44; 12:32). Luke recounts events where prevenient grace was the context, including Saul's conversion in Acts 9 and Cornelius's vision in Acts 10. Romans 2:12-16 speaks of "conscience" in ways that resemble prevenient grace.

Augustine (b. 354) was the first to speak of prevenient grace, and later **Thomas Aquinas** (b. ca. 1225) picked up the theme. The doctrine received further impetus in the English Protestant theology of the seventeenth and early eighteenth centuries, such as the *Apology* of Robert Barclay and selected sermons of William Tilly. **John Wesley** (1703-91) framed prevenient (or "preventing") grace in reference to the **Trinity**, as the drawings of the Father, the enlightening of the Son, and the convictions of the **Holy Spirit** (*Works*, 6:44). Unlike **Calvinistic** predestination, where justifying grace was reserved for the elect, Wesley rooted preventing grace in Christ's **atonement** for all. This grace is necessary because of original sin, which Wesley believed—apart from grace—would have left us incapable of choosing Christ. For those who do not resist this "grace that goes before," like the additional talents given to the faithful servants, God gives more grace, culminating in salvation (Matt. 25:14-30).

Prevenient grace, unmerited and universally available, enabled Wesley to steer a middle course between determinism and works righteousness. This *via media* received fullest expression in Wesley's 1785 sermon "On Working Out Our Own Salvation." He concluded, "So that no man sins because he has not grace, but because he does not use the grace which he hath" (*Works*, 6:512). Grace as a metaphor for universally available divine enablement also appeared in many of **Charles Wesley**'s hymns—a reinforcement of his brother's position during theological controversy.

Recent Wesleyan theologians have shown interest in the doctrine of prevenient grace. Representative is Thomas Langford, who described prevenient grace as "God's active and continuous presence" (1998, 20). Allen Coppedge spoke of the "general grace given to all people that restores in them the ability to accept God's offer of redemption" (2003, 111). Al Truesdale and Keri Mitchell leaned heavily on prevenient grace to formulate a Wesleyan response to **religious pluralism** (2006). Prevenient grace continues to be a useful concept as Wesleyans engage in theological dialogue.

See also Holy Spirit (Pneumatology); Pelagianism; Predestination and Election; Repentance; Salvation (Soteriology); Sin.

Resources

Collins, Kenneth. *The Theology of John Wesley: Holy Love and the Shape of Grace.* Nashville: Abingdon Press, 2007.

Coppedge, Allen. *Shaping the Wesleyan Message*. Nappanee, IN: Evangel Publishing House, 2003.

Crofford, J. Gregory. *Streams of Mercy: Prevenient Grace in the Theology of John and Charles Wesley*. Lexington, KY: Emeth Press, 2010.

Langford, Thomas A. *Theology in the Wesleyan Tradition*. Vol. 1, *Practical Divinity*. Rev. ed. Nashville: Abingdon Press, 1998.

Truesdale, Al. *With Cords of Love: A Wesleyan Response to Religious Pluralism*. With Keri Mitchell. Kansas City: Beacon Hill Press of Kansas City, 2006.

J. GREGORY CROFFORD, PHD

PRIEST AND KING

See CHRISTOLOGY, NEW TESTAMENT.

PRIEST/PRIESTHOOD

See ANGLICANISM; JUDAISM; ROMAN CATHOLICISM; TEMPLE.

PRINCIPALITIES AND POWERS

"Principalities" and "powers" are two terms the apostle Paul uses to refer to forces that wage war against Christ and the church. Other Pauline terms that mean the same thing are "rulers," "cosmic powers of this present darkness," "thrones," "dominions," "world rulers," and "elements of the world." "Powers" is best understood in light of the first-century worldview that pictured various spiritual powers as influencing daily life. Humans could manipulate the powers by using magic, astrology, and religious practices because the spiritual and the physical world were viewed as two sides of the same reality. Spiritual powers acted through their earthly counterparts, and vice versa. Thus, behind all institutions of earthly power there existed parallel spiritual powers. Similarly, for Paul the term "powers" refers to both angelic beings and earthly agents of power. This double dimension should be kept in mind even when Paul occasionally refers to the powers as governing civil authorities ordered by God and thus not to be resisted (Titus 3:1; Rom. 13:1-7).

Spelled out in detail, Paul's theology of principalities and powers includes five dimensions: (1) Principalities and powers subsist in Christ and achieve their fulfillment only in him. "All things . . . visible and invisible, whether they be thrones, or dominions, or principalities, or powers . . . were created by him, and for him" (Col. 1:15-16, KJV). (2) There is currently a breach between Christ and the powers (Rom. 8:38-39; 1 Cor. 2:8; Col. 1:15-20). Created to serve Christ, principalities and powers do not currently fulfill their purpose. On the contrary, they are in a state of rebellion. They foster oppression, slavery, and fear. They are demonic, not because they are essentially evil, but because they have chosen to exist apart from God and contrary to his purposes. (3) The cross was the decisive event in defeating the rebellious powers. There, Christ disarmed and made a public spectacle of them (Col. 2:15; "spoiled" them, KJV). Because of Christ's victory, he is now exalted "far above all rule and authority and power and dominion" (Eph. 1:21). (4) In spite of their defeat, the powers temporarily continue to wage war against Christ and his church (6:12). Nevertheless, their future has been sealed, even though for a while their demonic action continues to afflict humans, especially "among those who are disobedient" (2:2). (5) At the end of the age all principalities and powers will be decisively subjected to Christ as Lord. They will no longer distort and dehumanize; Christ's victory will be thoroughly consummated (1 Cor. 15:24-28; Eph. 1:10).

The ontological character of principalities and powers is a matter of wide disagreement. Some scholars say Paul thought the powers and principalities were demonic beings that control humans. Other scholars consider them to be human institutions and structures that have no personal quality such as demons were thought to possess. In his three-volume work on the subject, NT scholar Walter Wink suggests the powers are both the inner essence of political, economic, and cultural institutions and their outward manifestations. Whatever their ontological status, powers and principalities try to dominate and distort human life. Confronted by their continued hostility, the church must declare to them "the manifold wisdom of God" (Eph. 3:10, KJV). The church must put on the "whole armor of God" in order to stand firm in this battle (6:10-17).

John Wesley discussed the principalities and powers in his Sermon "Of Evil Angels" (*Works*, 6:370-80). He interpreted the "whole armor of God" as "universal holiness" through which we overthrow demonic forces.

See also Angels; Deliverance/Exorcism; Demons/Unclean Spirits; Devil/ Satan; Spiritual Warfare.

Resources

Arnold, Clinton E. *Powers of Darkness: Principalities and Powers in Paul's Letters*. Downers Grove, IL: InterVarsity Press, 1992.

Berkhof, Hendrik. *Christ and the Powers*. Translated by John H. Yoder. 2nd ed. Scottdale, PA: Herald Press, 1977.

Noble, T. A. "The Spirit World: A Theological Approach." In *The Unseen World: Christian Reflections on Angels, Demons and the Heavenly Realm*, edited by Anthony N. S. Lane. Grand Rapids: Baker, 1996.

Wink, Walter. *Engaging the Powers: Discernment and Resistance in a World of Domination*. Minneapolis: Fortress Press, 1992.

———. *Naming the Powers: The Language of Power in the New Testament*. Philadelphia: Fortress Press, 1984.

DAVIDE CANTARELLA, MA

KENNETH L. WATERS SR., PHD

PROBLEM OF EVIL AND SUFFERING
See THEODICY/EVIL.

PROCESS THEOLOGY

Process theology considers all existing individuals and things essentially to be experiences/events. Process theology emphasizes the ultimate significance of time's forward flow and the change of existing things. Although all existing things change, metaphysical principles, mathematical and definitional abstractions, and God's essence do not.

The ideas of process theology have been around since the pre-Socratic philosopher Heraclitus. Many regard philosopher Alfred North Whitehead (1861–1947) as the most important process thinker. Charles Hartshorne (1897–2000) developed Whitehead's metaphysical thought. Hartshorne proposed a philosophical theology largely consonant with process metaphysics.

Process theology is an important branch of relational theology. It proposes that every individual and thing comes to exist through relations with others. Previous events influence each event as it comes to be. Each freely developed event then influences what will come to exist thereafter. Both God and creatures are relational beings.

While process theology says that God is everlasting, it argues that God's experience changes—it is in process. Like other relational theologians, process thinkers believe that God is the best- and most-moved mover rather than Aristotle's unmoved mover. They mean that God influences all others, and all others influence God's experience. However, God's nature remains unchanged.

Most process theologians argue that God cannot withdraw or override creaturely freedom. God does not have unlimited power. This belief solves the problem of evil. Because God cannot entirely control free creatures, God is not culpable for failing to prevent evil.

Christian process theologians affirm basic Christian convictions about Jesus' life, death, and resurrection. However, they use process metaphysics to describe these convictions instead of the metaphysics early Christian theologians presupposed. This sometimes places process theology's views of Christ in tension with theologies supported by other philosophies.

Process theology is congenial to contemporary science and the general theory of evolution. However, it rejects the idea that the laws of nature, genes, or chance entirely determine creatures. Process thinkers believe that God creates through evolution as an ever-present, ever-influential but non-controlling Creator. Process theologians typically embrace theistic evolution.

Process theologians believe that God intimately relates to all things. God is immanent and transcendent. Process thinkers call God's relation to creation **panentheism** (or "theocosmocentrism"), because God is present to and "in" all creation and yet more than creation.

Process theologians affirm that God is Creator. God lovingly makes it possible for creatures to be partly self-creative. Most process thinkers believe that God created this universe billions of years ago from the chaos of a previous universe that God had created. Affirming the opening lines of Genesis, process theologians typically deny that God created the universe from absolutely nothing (*creatio ex nihilo*).

Process theology escapes the "God of the gaps" charge, which is the view that we can only explain gaps in science by appealing to God's special action. Process theology denies that God occasionally interrupts or overpowers the causal processes of the universe. Instead, process theology argues that God always creates and sustains creatures through persuasive love rather than coercion.

See also Determinism and Free Will; Evolution/Evolutionary Biology; Experience, Phenomenon of; Free Will; God, Doctrine of; Natural Science; Natural Theology; Philosophical Theology; Philosophy of Religion; Philosophy of Science; Postmodernity; Theodicy/Evil; Time and Eternity.

Resources
Cobb, John B., Jr., and David Ray Griffin. *Process Theology: An Introductory Exposition.* Philadelphia: Westminster Press, 1976.

Suchocki, Marjorie. *God, Christ, Church: A Practical Guide to Process Theology.* Rev. ed. New York: Crossroad, 1989.

Truesdale, Al, ed. *God Reconsidered: The Promise and Peril of Process Philosophy.* Kansas City: Beacon Hill Press of Kansas City, 2010.

THOMAS J. OORD, PHD

PROMISE
See ISRAEL; VIRTUES.

PROPHECY/PROPHET

Prophecy in the Bible is a speech given under God's inspiration by someone called and commissioned by God to communicate an urgent message from God to an audience. A prophet is a spokesperson for God (Hebrew, *nabi'*; Greek, *prophētēs*). The subject of prophecy may be hope and salvation, or condemnation and judgment.

God called prophets during critical times of Israel's history. The origin of the prophetic movement can be traced to God's call of Moses, Israel's prophet par excellence. The movement also saw the rise in Israel's early history of great OT figures such as Samuel, Elijah, and Elisha, whose words and deeds are recorded. Prophecy in Israel transitioned to a literary stage with the ministry of Amos in the mid-eighth century BC. It continued into the postexilic period and ended with the ministry of Malachi in the fifth century BC. Prophecy and prophets in the OT convey direct revelation from God, which is the basis for their canonical status in the Hebrew Bible.

Prophetic literature in the OT contains various literary forms (genres). The most common genre is the messenger-style speech in which the prophet presents the message with an introductory formula, "Thus says the LORD." Prophets also used other genres such as legal disputes, woe sayings, vision accounts, funeral songs, parables, and proverbial sayings to communicate God's message.

Prophecy, since it contains an urgent word from God, may be directed to an immediate situation that calls for appropriate response from the recipients. Prophecy in the OT often deals with different aspects of Israel's covenantal relationship with God and others in the community. In addition to raising contemporary concerns, OT prophets also speak of events that may happen in the immediate or distant future. These predictions are usually given as warnings from God regarding actions he may carry out depending on how the audience responds to his message calling for reform and proper relationship with him. When prophecies are words of judgment, they are usually followed up by a word of hope and salvation.

The NT has no parallel to OT prophecy and prophets. Of all the NT writings, only the author of Revelation identifies the book as containing prophecy (1:3; 22:7, 10, 18-19). The gospel writers often portray the life and ministry of Jesus of Nazareth as the fulfillment of OT prophecies. Hebrews 1:1-2 claims that God now speaks to his people through his Son, though long ago he spoke through the prophets. All four Gospels preserve Jesus' own implicit claim to be a prophet (Matt. 13:57; Mark 6:4; Luke 4:24; John 4:44). In the Pauline writings, prophecy receives the status as one of the highest spiritual gifts; the office of prophet is the second order of ministry, next to that of apostle (see 1 Cor. 12–14; Eph. 4:11).

Though prophecy as a direct revelation from God is a phenomenon in the OT, it is possible to say that God continues to call and inspire his people to speak on his behalf (see Num. 11:29; Joel 2:28-29; Acts 2:16-21). Prophecy in that sense is a message from God, given through the Holy Spirit's empowerment, "for building up the body of Christ" (Eph. 4:12). In contemporary settings, preaching fulfills this function.

In the book of Revelation the church is identified as a prophetic community. The language of *prophecy* is used not only of specific leaders but also of the community as a whole. Christians bear "witness" (*martyria*); through them the Holy Spirit continues Jesus' prophetic witness in the world (19:10).

See also Gifts of the Spirit; Glossolalia.

Resources

Brueggemann, Walter. *The Prophetic Imagination*. 2nd ed. Minneapolis: Fortress Press, 2001.

Heschel, Abraham. *The Prophets*. 1962. 2 vols. in 1. Reprint, Peabody, MA: Hendrickson Publishers, 2007.

ALEX VARUGHESE, PHD

PROSELYTISM

The term "proselytism" refers to the attempt to convert a person to another religion. In the NT, the word referred to a Gentile who was considering conversion to Judaism. It also referred to the attempts of other religions to convert people to their beliefs. Today, "proselytism" is seen negatively because the word is often used to describe attempts to force people to convert to a religion other than their own.

Some scholars equate conversion with proselytism. Mohandas Gandhi inveighed against missionaries for attempting to convert Hindus to the Christian faith. He told them in so many words, "If you have come to India to make us better Hindus, fine. But don't try to convert us to Christianity." In the 1960s, two states in India passed anticonversion laws, later overturned by the Supreme Court of India. Others in the **Global South** regard conversion as an act of cultural imperialism. Missionaries in many world areas have been accused of "buying" converts by providing food, clothes, money, educational facilities, medical services, and agricultural programs. Some governments have forbidden young people under the age of eighteen to accept Christian baptism.

In the OT, the proselyte was a stranger accepted into the Israelite community. Such non-Israelites are frequently mentioned in listings of the poor, widows, and orphans (Lev. 23:22; Deut. 24:19). There were different categories of proselytes, but only the circumcised proselyte could enter the temple. This apparently demonstrated a full acceptance of Judaism. Others embraced some parts of Judaism but did not become full converts. They were often referred to as *God-fearers* or *worshippers of God* (see Acts 2:5; 13:16; 16:14). God-fearers accepted the theological and ethical teachings of Judaism, attended the synagogue, and observed many of the Jewish ceremonies, but they did not undergo circumcision.

Proselytism flourished in the Hellenistic and Roman periods when many Gentiles abandoned the moral laxity and superstition of their age. Jesus made mention of the Pharisees' zeal in making converts (Matt. 23:15). Proselytism ended in Judaism in the second century when Roman law forbade the Jews the right to proselytize.

Christian missionaries make a distinction between proselytism and conversion. They are commanded by Christ to "make disciples" (28:19) but are never commanded to engage in proselytism. Using force, offering inducements, or promising material benefits in hopes of making a convert must never occur. Missionaries present the claims of Christ and pray that the hearer, moved by the Holy Spirit, will *voluntarily* accept Jesus as Lord and Savior. Beyond that point, following the example of Jesus, the missionary will not go.

See also Evangelism.

Resources

Neill, Stephen, Gerald H. Anderson, and John Goodwin, eds. *Concise Dictionary of the Christian World Mission*. Nashville: Abingdon Press, 1971.

Winter, Ralph D., and Steven C. Hawthorne, eds. *Perspectives on the World Christian Movement*. Pasadena, CA: William Carey Library, 1981.

JOHN WESLEY Z. KUREWA, PHD

PROTESTANTISM

The term "Protestantism" arose in the early years of the **Reformation** of the **church** in sixteenth-century Europe. In 1529 a group of reform-minded princes within the Holy Roman Empire issued a formal "protest" (Latin, *protestari*) at the Second Diet (a meeting of the Holy Roman emperor and the princes of the empire) of Speyer opposing the overturning of an earlier agreement to allow individual German states the right to determine their own form of religion. The term *protestari* signifies not only an objection or opposition to something but also a positive avowal of, or witness to, something. Thus, the "protesting" princes were not only objecting to the injustice they believed was being committed against them but also witnessing to, or confessing, a particular understanding of Christian faith. While originally referring only to churches in the German territories governed by the "protesting" princes, the term "Protestantism" eventually came to refer to all groups that separated from the **Roman Catholic Church** at the time of the sixteenth-century Reformation and since. This includes churches of the **Lutheran**, **Reformed**, **Anabaptist**, **Anglican**, and **Methodist** traditions, as well as numerous smaller groups.

There are several characteristic doctrines or affirmations shared to a great extent by all the traditions and churches associated with Protestantism:

First, Holy **Scripture** is the ultimate source of authority for teaching and practice within the church. Sometimes stated as the doctrine of "Scripture alone" (*sola Scriptura*), Protestants say there is no authority above or equal to Scripture. However, Protestantism has generally valued the accumulated **tradition** of the church as a necessary aid for rightly interpreting and applying Scripture. Thus "Scripture alone" means that Scripture alone has *final* and *ultimate* authority for the church. Nevertheless, some strands of Protestantism tend to understand *sola Scriptura* to mean that Scripture stands alone *in opposition to* all other authority—tradition, reason, or Christian **experience.** In these forms of Protestantism there is often a strong spirit of independence and individualism that may express itself in positive and vitalizing, as well as negative and divisive, ways.

A second distinguishing doctrine is **justification** by **grace** through **faith** alone. This was the fundamental theme of **Martin Luther** (1483–1546) and became a foundation of Protestantism. Protesting against the tendency of the medieval church to frame **salvation** as something achieved by individuals primarily by acquiring "merit" through certain acts of piety, Protestants affirmed that a person is **reconciled** to God solely on the basis of God's free and unmerited grace ("grace alone" [Latin, *sola gratia*]). This is in fact the central declaration of the **gospel**, the good news that comes to the world in Christ: "For by grace you have been saved through faith, and this is not your own doing; it is the gift of God—not the result of works, so that no one may boast" (Eph. 2:8-9).

While Protestantism has always formally held to justification by grace through faith, its history contains branches that have veered in different directions. Some have leaned toward antinomianism in their understanding of the doctrine; others have tended to emphasize the importance of good works almost to the extent of negating salvation by grace alone.

A third distinguishing doctrine is the priesthood of all believers. This Protestant principle has two major implications for the church. First, every believer has the right and privilege of direct access to God. There is no human mediator required to stand between an ordinary Christian and almighty God. Christ is humanity's only necessary Mediator. Second, every believer has the right and responsibility to exercise priestly capacities in service to other believers. Every believer has the right to hear the confession of another; to minister God's Word of judgment and grace to another; to be, as Martin Luther put it, "a sort of Christ, to my neighbor, as Christ has given Himself to me" ([1520] 1998, para. 127). This does not mean that within Protestantism there is no difference between ordinary believers and those set apart for public ministry—preaching the Word, administering the sacraments, and the like. However, any difference is a purely *functional* one; there is no *essential*, spiritual difference between people and their pastor.

See also Anabaptists; Anglicanism; Bible; Church (Ecclesiology); Doctrine/ Dogma; Experience, Phenomenon of; Faith; Gospel; Grace; Justification; Luther, Martin; Quadrilateral, Wesleyan; Radical Reformation; Reconciliation; Reformation; Reformed Tradition; Roman Catholicism; Salvation (Soteriology); Scripture, Theology of.

Resources

Brown, Robert. *The Spirit of Protestantism*. New York: Oxford University Press, 1965.
Luther, Martin. *On the Freedom of a Christian*. 1520. Internet Modern History Source Book. October 1998. Fordham University. http://www.fordham.edu/halsall/mod /luther-freedomchristian.asp.
McGrath, Alister E. *Christianity's Dangerous Idea: The Protestant Revolution—A History from the Sixteenth Century to the Twenty-First*. New York: HarperOne, 2007.
Melton, J. Gordon. *Encyclopedia of Protestantism*. New York: Facts on File, 2005.

HAROLD E. RASER, PHD

PRUDENTIAL MEANS OF GRACE

See CLASSES, BANDS, CONFERENCE, CONNECTIONALISM, SOCIETY; COVENANT SERVICE; LOVE FEAST; MEANS OF GRACE; SPIRITUAL DISCIPLINES; WORKS OF MERCY.

PSEUDO-MACARIUS

The **Holy Spirit** plays a very important role in John Wesley's *ordo salutis*. An important influence on Wesley's *ordo salutis* was someone he believed to be Macarius the Egyptian, born "about the year of our Lord 301" (*Library*, vol. 1, "Of Macarius," para. 1). "[I have] read Macarius and sang," Wesley wrote on his 1736 journey to Georgia (*Journal*, 1:254; journal entry for July 30, 1736). God had "seasoned this holy vessel of mercy with the heavenly odour of Divine grace" (*Library*, vol. 1, "Of Macarius," para. 2).

Today Macarius is referred to as Pseudo-Macarius. Internal evidence establishes a Syrian rather than an Egyptian milieu. His extensive writings, consisting of four principal collections, have a complex history. The date and location of the author are uncertain. He can conveniently be called Macarius-Symeon. But Marcarius of Egypt is untenable.

Studies of the relationship between Wesley and Macarius have concentrated on the similarity between Macarius's soteriology and Wesley's doctrine of prevenient grace, and comparisons and contrasts between their doctrines of Christian maturity or perfection. Macarius taught that **Christian perfection** happens progressively in Jesus' disciples as they gradually, by stages, yield to the **Holy Spirit** and gaze on the Father. After receiving the Holy Spirit, the Spirit must be "perfected in us" (purified from all defilement and stain of sin) in order to persevere (see *Library*, vol. 1, "Of Macarius," Hom. 19). Perfection comes by **prayer** through twelve progressive steps. Christian perfection—a "sober intoxication"—impacts individual Christians, **the church**, and the community beyond.

Although Wesley interpreted the experience of **entire sanctification** as instantaneous, process precedes and follows. Wesley shared Macarius's emphasis on continual growth in grace no matter how high the state of perfection.

Wesley used Macarius's *Spiritual Homilies* (1721 edition) and other writings to fuse the ascetic and **pneumatological** elements of his teaching on holiness. He adapted twenty-two sections of Macarius's *Homilies* for inclusion in the first volume of his *Christian Library*. Wesley was indebted to Macarius in *A Plain Account of Christian Perfection* (1777). He explicitly acknowledged his dependence in his sermon "The Scripture Way of Salvation" (*Works*, 6:43-54).

See also Desert Fathers and Mothers; Discipleship; Holiness; Monasticism; Self-Denial; Spiritual Disciplines.

Resources

Campbell, Ted A. *John Wesley and Christian Antiquity: Religious Vision and Cultural Change*. Nashville: Kingswood Books, 1991.

Kimbrough, S. T., Jr., ed. *Orthodox and Wesleyan Spirituality*. Crestwood, NY: St Vladimir's Seminary Press, 2002.

Maddox, Randy L. "John Wesley and Eastern Orthodoxy: Influences, Convergences, and Differences." *Asbury Theological Journal* 45, no. 2 (1990): 29-53.

Plested, Marcus. *The Macarian Legacy: The Place of Macarius-Symeon in the Eastern Christian Tradition.* Oxford, UK: Oxford University Press, 2004.

TIM MACQUIBAN, PHD

PSYCHOLOGY

See NEUROSCIENCE AND RELIGION; SOCIAL SCIENCES; SOUL.

PSYCHOLOGY OF RELIGION

See SOCIAL SCIENCES; SOUL.

PUBLIC THEOLOGY

"Public theology" is a term Martin Marty (b. 1928) coined to describe the sort of theology Reinhold Niebuhr (1892–1971) exemplified. Niebuhr addressed theological reflection not only to the **church** but also and intentionally to public communities (e.g., a nation) outside the church. As a public theologian, Niebuhr interpreted public institutions in the light of Christian convictions. Niebuhr's aim was to effect the transformation of secular communities according to God's will. Similarly, Martin Luther King Jr. interpreted America's racial conflicts in the light of the Bible's call for justice and liberation. He harnessed biblical interpretation to an agenda for social change. Likewise, representatives of the American religious right engage in public theology; they offer a theological interpretation of America and use it for crafting political and social agendas. Public theology is therefore closely associated with **Christian ethics**.

Theology is normally addressed to concrete situations and is thus **contextualized**. Proponents of public theology argue that theology's context is broader than the church; it includes public communities (often called the public square). Narrowly confessional theologies and **postliberal** theologies, by contrast, see the church as theology's only context. Public theologians typically ask how God is working in their nation's experience. But postliberal theologians generally see the nation only as a danger for the church. They call on the church sharply to distinguish itself from the nation.

David Tracy (b. 1939) has further articulated public theology. He notes that theologians address three publics: the church, the intellectual community (the "academy"), and society at large. Clearly, Christian theology is partly a dialogue with audiences beyond the church. Consequently, theologians adhere to public criteria of rationality. They may also draw on sources of truth not overtly Christian. Paul Tillich's (1886–1965) theology illustrates this. He drew on the Christian tradition and insights from psychology, philosophy, and art. Postliberal theologians oppose the approach to theology Tracy and Tillich embrace, believing instead that Christian theology should employ only Christian norms of rationality. Its single source of truth is **revelation**. Much discussion about public theology concentrates on methodology, such as theology's sources and norms. However, sometimes public theology is simply a matter of the church presenting its message for public consideration, as in the United States Council of Catholic Bishops' official statements on **justice** and **war**. In such instances the Christian community declares its convictions to the public at large, intending to shape public opinion and bring public policy into conformity with God's will.

See also Apologetics; Church and State; Liberation Theology; Modernity; Postmodernity; Radical Orthodox Theology; Secular/Secularism/Secularization; Social Ethics; Social Justice; State Religion.

Resources

Hainsworth, Deirdre King, and Scott R. Paeth, eds. *Public Theology for a Global Society: Essays in Honor of Max Stackhouse.* Grand Rapids: Eerdmans, 2010.
Moltmann, Jürgen. *God for a Secular Society: The Public Relevance of Theology.* Translated by Margaret Kohl. Minneapolis: Fortress Press, 1999.

SAMUEL M. POWELL, PHD

PURITANISM

Puritanism was a **Protestant** reform movement that emerged in Elizabethan England. Those who became known as Puritans were dissatisfied with the distinguishing characteristics of the Church of England (the Elizabethan Settlement [1559]). They believed the Book of Common Prayer did not adequately represent a religion purified of **Roman Catholicism**. Elizabeth I (r. 1558–1603) was not sympathetic to their reform program. At the Hampton Court Conference (1604) it became clear that James I (r. 1603-25) was also not willing to reform the church according to their plan.

Many Puritans criticized the episcopal structure of the Church of England, and some separated from the national church, forming congregations according to presbyterian or congregational polity. Disillusioned over the lack of progress in reforming the Church of England, many Puritans migrated to New England. Under Charles I (r. 1625-49) many elements in the national church that the Puritans opposed actually became stronger. Anglicanism was too diverse; even in the wake of the English Civil War and the abolition of the monarchy, Puritans were unable to capitalize on opportunities the Commonwealth period (1649-60) offered.

Following the restoration of the monarchy, the Act of Uniformity (1662) required the use of a new Book of Common Prayer. Refusal by many clergy with Puritan sympathies to comply resulted in their being ejected from their pulpits. In one sense, Puritanism as a reform movement within the national church ended here. In another sense, the ideals that defined the movement lived on outside the national church (in Nonconformity).

Puritanism was never tightly uniform. But certain common commitments defined it. It was energized by pastoral academics, preachers, and writers of practical divinity. Usually they were **Reformed** in theology and presbyterian in polity. Early in the movement, when expectations for reform ran high, attention was given to ecclesiastical lobbying. From its early days, and increasingly as political and ecclesiastical expectations dissipated, preaching, practical divinity, and an experimental (experiential) piety that stressed self-examination and concern for matters of conscience were central. Its early theologians included William Perkins and William Ames. Defining personalities in the later years included John Owen and Richard Baxter.

John Wesley identified most strongly with the English holy-living tradition. Representatives of this tradition often disputed with representatives of Puritanism. Even so, Wesley had a catholic spirit that allowed him to appreciate aspects of Puritanism and to utilize Puritan literature.

John and Charles Wesley received an impressive Puritan heritage. Both grandfathers were among the Nonconforming clergy ejected in 1662. By contrast, Samuel and Susanna Wesley unambiguously rejected dissent in favor of the Church of England. John Wesley's own reading of Puritan literature seems to have grown exponentially as he prepared to publish *A Christian Library* (1749-55). When commenting on Puritanism, Wesley sympathized with Puritans persecuted for their conscience' sake. He commended their learning and zeal for the Bible. Wesley disapproved of their argumentative bent. He preferred those who were "forced" out of the established church in 1662 to those who separated voluntarily.

Most of the Puritan literature Wesley reproduced falls under the category of practical divinity (devotional literature). There is no conclusive evidence that the Puritans played a decisive role in forming any major doctrine for Wesley. But they and Wesley were drawn to the religion of the heart with its perceptible experience of assurance. They shared concerns about **justification** by **grace** through faith and about the destruction of sin in believers. Wesley heavily edited Puritan material because of substantial differences between Puritan theology and his own.

See also Anglicanism; Arminian Theology; Covenant Service; Protestantism; Reformed Tradition; Roman Catholicism; Wesley, John, Theology of.

Resources

Bremer, Francis J. *Puritanism: A Very Short Introduction.* New York: Oxford University Press, 2009.

Coffey, John, and Paul C. H. Lim, eds. *The Cambridge Companion to Puritanism.* New York: Cambridge University Press, 2008.

KARL GANSKE, PHD

Qq

QUADRILATERAL, WESLEYAN

The term "Wesleyan quadrilateral" refers to the method of theological reflection that affirms the primacy of the religious authority of Scripture and the genuine, albeit secondary, religious authority of tradition, reason, and experience. **John Wesley** accepted the **Protestant** principle of *sola Scriptura* (Scripture alone), but he thought Scripture was complemented by additional types of knowledge. **Church** tradition supplemented Scripture, for example, by providing standards of doctrine and expanding on doctrines not comprehensively addressed in Scripture. Critical thinking aided theological reflection as did consideration of experience.

Experience includes personal experience as well as the collective experiences of the church, people, culture, and advances in science that affect human life. Wesley did not consider himself an innovator in his understanding of religious authority. Instead, he merely intended to clarify how Christians, past and present, determine their beliefs, values, and practices. Indeed, Wesley thought he affirmed the best of theological reflection, extending back to the ancient church. However, Wesley's appeals to experience, in particular, represent a noteworthy contribution to a Christian understanding of religious authority.

Wesley did not explicitly talk about the quadrilateral. Albert Outler (1908-89) coined the term in the 1960s to summarize Wesley's view of religious authority. Outler drew on historic church language that considered the quadrilateral symbolic of a solid foursquare foundation for a building or castle. Unfortunately, the language confused some people because the geometrical metaphor seemed to assign equal authority to Scripture, tradition, reason, and experience. Some even thought the term minimized Scripture, or elevated the other authorities over Scripture. However, based on Wesley's thinking, any explanation of the quadrilateral fails if it does not affirm the primacy of Scripture. An adequate explanation presents the four authorities as dynamic and interdependent, with Scripture remaining superior to the others.

Some critique the quadrilateral as a modern myth that says more about contemporary Christians than about John Wesley. They say that it distracts people from the unilateral authority of Scripture over tradition, reason, and experience or that it distracts from additional important criteria for doctrine and practice. Be that as it may, the quadrilateral has become a useful tool widely used by Christians when engaging in comprehensive reflection about Christian doctrine, values, and practices. Indeed the quadrilateral is today used by Christians far beyond the Wesleyan and Methodist traditions. It helps them articulate multiple dimensions of the Christian faith. It is as useful for personal and church-related decision making as it is for formal theology. In a world increasingly concerned about the contextual dimensions of knowledge, the quadrilateral helps Christians evaluate complex theory and practice.

See also Contextual Theology; Experience, Phenomenon of; Globalization; Indigenization; Orthodoxy/Orthopraxis/Orthopathy.

Resources

Campbell, Ted A., Scott J. Jones, Randy Maddox, Rebekah Miles, and W. Stephen Gunter. *Wesley and the Quadrilateral: Renewing the Conversation.* Nashville: Abingdon Press, 1997.

Crutcher, Timothy J. *The Crucible of Life: The Role of Experience in John Wesley's Theological Method.* Lexington, KY: Emeth Press, 2010.

Thorsen, Don. *The Wesleyan Quadrilateral: Scripture, Tradition, Reason, and Experience as a Model of Evangelical Theology.* Lexington, KY: Emeth Press, 2005.

DON THORSEN, PHD

QUMRAN
See DEAD SEA SCROLLS.

Rr

RADICAL ORTHODOX THEOLOGY

Radical orthodoxy (RO) is a **postmodern** and **postliberal** philosophical-theological movement that responds to modern **liberalism** and **secularism** by repositioning all branches of study and learning within a theological framework. It is "radical" in its attempt to recover the roots of theology through a classical understanding of all knowledge as divine. It is **orthodox** in its conviction that such an understanding is consonant with and sustained by **creedal** Christianity as taught by the **church fathers**.

The genesis of RO lies with John Milbank's *Theology and Social Theory* (1990). Milbank shows how modern liberal social theory depends on secularized versions of theological concepts and argues that secularization operates according to an "ontology of violence," an account of the world determined by contests of power between subjects of consideration (e.g., society) and the disciplines (e.g., sociology) that study them. Denying that there are any unbiased secular standpoints as modernity claims, Milbank reconstitutes sociology from the perspective of Christian theology and its own "ontology of peace." His doing so relates all subjects and disciplines to an original divine harmony.

Central to RO is its critique of the theology of Duns Scotus (ca. 1266–1308) and his rejection of the analogy of being. Scotus assumes a singular or unambiguous ontology that defines the natural, internal being of things apart from their relation to the supernatural, transcendent being of God, thus making possible modernity's affirmation of the "secular" as a realm independent of the sacred. By contrast, RO affirms Plato's doctrine that all being participates in the transcendent Good, as revised by the Christian **Neoplatonism** of **Augustine** and **Thomas Aquinas**. Heavily influenced by the **Roman Catholic** *nouvelle théologie* (French, "new theology"), RO recovers a version of the "analogy of being" that insists that the natural being of all things participates in and is mediated by the supernatural being of God. This recovery has led RO to reassert the **sacramentality** of creation and to emphasize the central role that **liturgy**, culture, and politics play in our relation to the world and God. Catherine Pickstock's *After Writing* (1998) focuses on how the liturgy of the **Eucharist** doxologically (worshipfully) reconfigures the material world as revealing the divine. Graham Ward's *Cities of God* (2000) engages the global city as a way of asserting the inseparability of religious practice and cultural transformation. More recently, RO has turned to **theopolitical theology**. Forging a political vision on the basis of RO's ontology of participation, Phillip Blond and Milbank have argued for a version of "new Christendom" politics that emphasizes the connection between **church and state** and the necessity of re-Christianizing the political order.

As an **ecumenical** movement, RO's relation to the theology of John Wesley and to global Wesleyanism is still uncertain. While D. Stephen Long has argued that Wesley's theology shares many affinities with the Augustinian Thomism of RO, there are many "modernist" elements within the intellectual heritage of Wesleyanism that RO would critique. There are also key aspects of emerging global Wesleyanism, particularly in relation to the "two-thirds world," that challenge the supremacist tendencies of RO's "Western" vision of liturgy, culture, and politics.

See also Augustine; Modernity; Neoplatonism; Philosophical Theology; Postliberal Theology; Secular/Secularism/Secularization; Thomas Aquinas.

Resources

Milbank, John, Catherine Pickstock, and Graham Ward, eds. *Radical Orthodoxy: A New Theology.* London: Routledge, 1999.
Smith, James K. A. *Introducing Radical Orthodoxy: Mapping a Post-Secular Theology.* Grand Rapids: Baker Academic, 2004.

NATHAN R. KERR, PHD

RADICAL REFORMATION

Radical Reformation refers to sixteenth-century reforming movements not aligned with the Magisterial Reformation. Contrasting historical contexts and theologies make it difficult to classify the Radical Reformers. However, three main strands are identifiable: **Anabaptists**, Spiritualists, and Rationalists.

Anabaptists

1. The Swiss Brethren initially were disciples of Huldrych Zwingli, but broke with him for numerous reasons, the most important being his refusal to renounce infant baptism. The Brethren adopted adult or believer's baptism. Adults who had been baptized as infants must be rebaptized. The rebaptisms began in Zurich in January 1525. Believer's baptism became the act of entry into the church, composed only of saved and baptized believers.

Brethren leaders included Felix Manz, Conrad Grebel, and George Blaurock. They charged Zwingli with being too conservative as a reformer and with permitting civil authority to determine the pace of reform. The Brethren adopted pacifism and rejected Christian participation in civil government. Their views were expressed in the Schleitheim Confession (1527), drafted by Michael Sattler. Modern descendants of the Brethren associate themselves with the Mennonites.

2. Revolutionary Anabaptism, stemming from the Zwickau Prophets and Thomas Müntzer, represents one part of South German Anabaptism. Müntzer differed from other Anabaptists because of his participation in the Peasants' War (1525). He developed a doctrine of inner baptism of the Spirit that would eventually influence the Spiritualists. Müntzer's apocalyptic theology inspired Melchior Hofmann, who believed the in-breaking of the **kingdom of God** would soon occur in the New Jerusalem (Strasbourg). Hofmann died in prison. But some of his followers unsuccessfully attempted by force to establish the New Jerusalem in the town of Münster.

3. South German Anabaptists such as Hans Denk and Hans Hut shared elements of the Spiritualist views of Müntzer while rejecting his violence. Balthasar Hubmaier and Pilgram Marpeck had much in common with the Swiss Brethren.

Following the Münster episode, Menno Simons, a Dutch Anabaptist who rejected the Münster violence, reorganized some of Hofmann's followers in northwest Germany and the Netherlands. The Mennonites closely resembled the Swiss Brethren.

The Hutterites, named for their chief founder Jacob Hutter, established communal settlements in Moravia. They practiced the community of goods as described in Acts 2. Due to centuries of sporadic **persecution**, in the nineteenth century most Hutterite communities immigrated to North America.

Spiritualists

Sebastian Frank and Kaspar Schwenckfeld represent the Spiritualist strand of the Radical Reformation. They rejected external forms and outward observances, stressing instead an "inward feeding on Christ."

Rationalists

The Rationalist strand of Radical Reformers emphasized reason in conjunction with Scripture. This led to anti-Trinitarian views. Michael Servetus (burnt as a heretic in Geneva) and Faustus Socinus adopted the radical view that the **Trinity** is inconsistent with Scripture and reason. They rejected infant baptism. Socinus spread Unitarian views in Transylvania and Poland. The Racovian Catechism (1605) was the first declaration of Socinian beliefs.

The Radical Reformers rejected the Christendom model that enforced a single form of Christianity in a realm (later formalized in the Peace of Westphalia as "the religion of the prince determines the religion of the realm"). The number of sixteenth-century Anabaptist martyrdoms was immense, numbering into the thousands.

See also Anabaptists; Church and State; Peacemaking; Reformation; State Religion.

Resources

Liechty, Daniel, ed. *Early Anabaptist Spirituality: Selected Writings*. New York: Paulist Press, 1994.

Williams, George Huntston. *The Radical Reformation*. 3rd ed. Kirksville, MO: Sixteenth Century Journal Publishers, 1992.

GEORDAN HAMMOND, PHD

RATIONALISM

See EPISTEMOLOGY.

RECONCILIATION

At the epicenter of biblical faith stands the gracious and irrepressible action of a holy **God** toward an unholy people to replace the hostility and brokenness of their prior relationship with peace (shalom) and love. The theological word for this exchange is "reconciliation." Although the biblical term "reconciliation" (Greek, *katallassō/katallagē*) is found in the NT only in the Pauline letters, its use there echoes the Septuagint (LXX) where it refers to a fractured relationship being restored to health (2 Macc. 1:5; 7:33; 8:29; cf. Jer. 31:39-40). A much broader resonance is located in the ancient church's Greco-Roman setting where reconciliation includes peacemaking and stories of a mediator who acts to bring reconciliation between two warring parties.

In Pauline thought, the idea of a merciful mediator who exchanges peace for hostility and thereby restores friendship to a broken relationship achieves clear focus. Perhaps the most important biblical text for capturing the dynamic of reconciliation is 2 Cor. 5:16-21, where the divine act and the human effect of reconciliation define the message (v. 19) and ministry (v. 18) of God's people. The source is Christ's death and resurrection, which makes it possible for all people to live for Christ rather than for themselves (vv. 14-15). Christ is the Mediator who alone acts faithfully on God's behalf to inaugurate a new dispensation of divine love (cf. Rom. 5:8-10). This now makes it possible for anyone who is in Christ to understand and practice life as "new creation" (2 Cor. 5:16-17). This is life that complies with the Creator's good intentions for human existence as manifested in Christ's life.

The Pauline vision for Christian existence is thoroughly theocentric (God-centered). God reconciles the entire world through Christ, and he does so for his own glory (vv. 18-19). This divine initiative of peacemaking is not only unilateral, *from* and *for* God, but its full measure is achieved by

Christ while living *in* and *for* a hostile world full of sin (v. 19) and sinners (v. 21). God's reconciling act through Christ not only forgives humanity's trespasses but also promises to transform sinners into instruments of God's righteousness (v. 21; cf. Rom. 6:15-23; 8:3-4). This glorious exchange through the sinless Mediator, Jesus Christ, who stands in the place of sinful humanity to bring about God's reconciliation with the world, creates the possibility of another exchange, namely, the sacrifice of a blameless Christ for us. His death makes it possible for those who now believe in and live in the risen Christ to become as he is, namely, to become instances of new creation.

This pattern of reconciliation shapes how Wesleyans understand Christian holiness. Christians live at peace with a loving God because God alone has acted through Christ. God has done this according to his own purpose and in a holy manner; he is the holy God who nevertheless in Christ became fully engaged in the world. Because this world is inhabited by an unholy people doing unholy things, the purpose of God's engagement is to purify the world, to make peace with it. Through Christ, for those who are "in him," God has exchanged a world of sin for new creation. A principal characteristic of this new creation is holiness—the capacity, through the Holy Spirit, to overcome enmity in its various personal and social forms. Christian holiness sends a living signal to the world that God's reconciling grace is real, for it is being put on display by those who belong to Christ.

See also Atonement; Grace; Justification; Salvation (Soteriology); Theosis (Deification).

ROBERT W. WALL, PHD

REDUCTIONISM

Reductionism is the practice of explaining one kind of phenomenon by a more fundamental, simpler kind of reality. The whole is considered to be nothing but those more fundamental features. The phenomenon under investigation is not considered fully real but is either eliminated as illusory or identified with a more fundamental reality. The phenomenon is described as the product of its underlying features or explained as an epiphenomenon that has no ultimate, independent causal power (Jones 2000).

There are at least three important types of reductionism: ontological, structural, and epistemological. *Ontological reductionism* focuses on the number of substances that constitute reality. Complete reductionism in this category would be a monism that reduces reality to only one type of substance (e.g., materialism, idealism, or pantheism). *Structural reductionism* is based on the view that, in addition to the substance of reality, there are different levels of organization in reality that may also be reduced (e.g., physical, biological, and psychological). *Epistemological reductionism* focuses on the reduction of the kinds and methods of knowledge that cognitively access the substance and structures of reality (Jones 2000).

Religious reduction is a type of *epistemological reductionism*. Important historical instances of religious reductionism were expressed by Karl Marx and Sigmund Freud. Marx *reduced* religion to a social epiphenomena, or illusion that is caused by disordered social conditions. It reveals an alienation of persons from themselves, others, and the product of their labor. Religion offers a false consolation in the midst of material suffering, as well as an exploitive sanctification of political and economic systems (McLellan 1987). Freud's religious reductionism explains the illusion of religion as a form of projection, an immature response to the awareness of human helplessness and the consequent continuation of a childlike desire for protection by a father figure (Freud [1927] 1989).

An important contemporary challenge to Christianity and Wesleyan theology is the reductionism found in secular evolutionary naturalism and scientific materialism. It reduces all knowledge, reality, the universe, the human world, and even God to various forms of natural, material processes (Wilson 2002). This kind of reductionism is at once ontological, epistemological, and structural. Ontologically, everything is reduced to one substance—matter. Epistemologically, the study of reality (in biology, psychology, sociology, religion) is reduced to only those methods and results that give natural explanations. Structurally, the higher level properties of life, mind, society, religious experience, and so on, though conceived as emergent and evolved properties from lower levels of complexity (physics), are still reduced to causal explanations from neuroscience, physics, or historical and moral relativity.

Antireductionist accounts of God and religious experience argue that emergent properties of reality are irreducible and unpredictable to simpler causal explanations. They are not entirely the product of lower-level structures (Jones 2000). Christian antireductionists argue that God is not reducible to the substance of the universe but is the Creator of the universe. They also tend to be antireductionists about high-level structures and properties observed in the creation.

See also Epistemology; Logical Positivism; Metaphysics; Secular/ Secularism/Secularization.

Resources

Freud, Sigmund. *The Future of an Illusion.* 1927. Edited by James Strachey. Reprint, New York: W. W. Norton and Company, 1989.

Jones, Richard H. *Reductionism: Analysis and the Fullness of Reality.* Cranbury, NJ: Associated University Presses, 2000.

McLellan, David. *Marxism and Religion: A Description and Assessment of the Marxist Critique of Christianity.* New York: Harper and Row, 1987.

Wilson, David Sloan. *Darwin's Cathedral: Evolution, Religion, and the Nature of Society.* Chicago: University of Chicago Press, 2002.

LINCOLN STEVENS, PHD

REFORMATION

In its first fifteen centuries, Christianity experienced few schisms. The ecumenical creeds affirmed crucial doctrines about Christ and the Trinity. Affirming the creeds and supporting practices such as clerical celibacy, the medieval church also supported the Roman pontiff. A measure of theological diversity existed, including the meaning of the sacramental bread and wine.

Bishops, rituals, traditions regarding Mary and the saints, and the role of relics in salvation often obstructed faith. Few could read and even fewer had access to a Bible in the vernacular.

In the sixteenth century, dependence on works of penance and devotion for salvation angered Augustinian monk Martin Luther (1483–1546), a professor of theology at the University of Wittenberg. Luther rejected sacred relics as means of grace. Buying and selling indulgences, by which for a price a person could guarantee personal salvation and buy early release of family members from purgatory, incensed Luther. He indicted many church practices, including papal primacy and clergy celibacy, as contrary to Scripture.

Luther thought the Bible must judge every tradition. He intended only to initiate theological discussion when on October 31, 1517, he posted ninety-five theses on the Wittenberg church door. He had concluded that salvation comes by faith alone (*sola fide*), not through works of righteousness.

Luther urged Christians to find personal faith and not to depend on grace mediated through a priest. He taught about the priesthood of all believers and their access to God.

Luther's outcry was timely. Intellectually, scholars such as Erasmus were reexamining the ancient texts of Scripture. Economically, Europe was moving away from feudalism. Politically, German princes were troubled by excessive revenue going to build the Vatican in Rome. Culturally, Northern Europe was separating from Latin Southern Europe.

Luther was not alone. In England, John Wycliffe was arguing for the Bible's translation in the vernacular. Beginning in 1519, Huldrych Zwingli—a priest in Zurich, Switzerland—preached with authority from the Bible and found within it no justification for purgatory, invoking saints, celibacy for clergy, monasticism, relics, and indulgences.

Although Luther retained rituals and Catholic forms (e.g., confession) unless they explicitly contradicted Scripture, Zwingli and his followers jettisoned all church practices not explicitly sanctioned in Scripture. Luther taught "consubstantiation," or coexistence, of bread and wine with the real body and blood of Christ in Communion. But Zwingli taught that the Lord's

Supper is a memorial to Christ's death. Through it Christians, by faith, draw closer to God. Zwingli and Luther retained infant baptism; neither conceived of the separation between church and state.

In the new Protestant territories, some Radical Reformers expected Lutheranism to topple rulers and the oppressive feudal system. When it did not, they reacted violently. Luther instructed rulers to suppress the rebels. Other opponents to the Magisterial Protestantism Luther represented were the Anabaptists. Believing that Luther had not gone far enough, Anabaptists urged Christians to separate from all evil, including the state. Many committed to pacifism. They rejected infant baptism, finding no scriptural justification for it. Instead, they taught baptism of believers only. Roman Catholics, Lutherans, and, later, Calvinists persecuted Anabaptists.

Within a generation, Europe was fragmented. Many German principalities and all Scandinavian countries broke from Rome. England did also, though initially for different reasons.

King Henry VIII severed ties with Rome, declaring himself head of the Church of England. The pontiff had refused to annul Henry's marriage to Catherine, who had borne no son to succeed Henry. In 1534 Parliament passed the Supremacy Act, making the monarch head of the Church of England. Henry confiscated church lands and repressed monastic orders. Only later and gradually, as clergy studied under continental Reformed professors, did the Church of England conform to Reformed theology. The Book of Common Prayer, first compiled by Archbishop Thomas Cranmer in 1549, blended ancient Catholic ritual, liturgies, and creeds with elements of medieval English and Reformed theology. Anglicanism emerged as a *via media*, a "middle way." Still, the Church of England was insufficiently broad for many. Dissenters arose, especially among those influenced by John Calvin (1509-64).

Of a younger generation than Luther, Calvin became a dominant theological voice. In Geneva he shaped a most influential form of Protestantism. While Luther left voluminous works, mostly tracts and sermons written to address particular issues, Calvin, by comparison, wrote more systematically. The table of contents of the *Institutes of the Christian Religion* (first published in 1536 in Latin) seems to promise a carefully ordered systematic theology. A more correct understanding is that he intended to expound the Scriptures, hoping they would take root in the heart. The long-held notion that the doctrine of predestination was central to Calvin's doctrine of God and salvation has now largely dissipated.

Some English clergy, notably John Knox, who introduced the Reformation to Scotland, studied in Geneva under Calvin or his successors such as Theodore Beza. The Calvinists governed their churches through presbyteries made up of elders rather than bishops. They established Reformed or Presbyterian churches in France, Scotland, Switzerland, England, and, later, America.

In the seventeenth century, Pietism arose as a protest against the sterility of Lutheranism and Calvinism. It seemed to Pietists such as Philipp Jakob Spener that Protestant faith had been reduced to assenting to creeds. Faith's personal appropriation and intimate relationship with God was missing. Similarly, Puritans in England desired either to purify the Church of England of remaining Catholic practices or to leave it.

Beginning with the Council of Trent in the 1550s, Roman Catholics launched responses to Protestantism. Luther's doctrine of justification (*sola fide*) harbored dangers of antinomianism—that is, treating the law as opposing the gospel. In its Counter-Reformation, Catholics sent missionaries worldwide.

Churches in the Wesleyan-holiness tradition are thoroughly Protestant, holding to the plain teachings of Scripture as the basis for faith and doctrine and emphasizing the ministry of all believers. But they agree with some aspects of the Catholic response to Protestantism, such as maintaining a lively role for the law as both convicting persons of sin and helping them remain righteous.

See also Anglicanism; Calvin, John; Counter-Reformation (Catholic Reformation); Creeds (Nicene, Chalcedonian, Apostles', Athanasian); Justification; Laity; Law and Gospel; Luther, Martin; Pietism; Protestantism; Puritanism; Radical Reformation; Reformed Tradition; Roman Catholicism; Sacraments; Wesley, John, Theology of.

Resources
Evans, G. R. *The Roots of the Reformation: Tradition, Emergence and Rupture.* Downers Grove, IL: IVP Academic, 2012.
MacCulloch, Diarmaid. *The Reformation: A History.* New York: Penguin, 2003.
Ozment, Steven. *The Age of Reform 1250–1550: An Intellectual and Religious History of Late Medieval and Reformation Europe.* New Haven, CT: Yale University Press, 1980.

FLOYD T. CUNNINGHAM, PHD

REFORMED EPISTEMOLOGY
See EPISTEMOLOGY.

REFORMED TRADITION

Although the designation "Reformed" can refer to all the churches of the sixteenth-century Protestant **Reformation**, it particularly refers to those that emerged from the theology of Huldrych Zwingli (1484–1531), Martin Bucer (1491–1551), Heinrich Bullinger (1504-75), **John Calvin** (1509-64), Calvin's successor Theodore Beza (1519–1605), and the Scottish Presbyterian John Knox (ca. 1514-72). The major confessions are the Canons of Dordt (1618); the Belgic Confession (1618); the Thirty-Nine Articles of Faith of the Anglican Church (1571); the Westminster Confession of Faith (1646), from which came the Shorter Catechism and the Larger Catechism (1647); the Savoy Declaration of Faith and Order (modifying the Westminster Confession to suit congregational polity, 1658); and the Baptist Confession of Faith (1689).

Martin Luther (1483–1546) distinguished his own theology from all of those who promote a Eucharistic doctrine that differed from his. This included Zwinglian, Swiss, and later Calvinist theologies. Twentieth-century Swiss Reformed theologian Karl Barth sharply distinguished between Lutheran and Reformed theology. Barth argued that whereas Lutheranism has the Formula of Concord (1577) by which it expresses officially and publicly its theological foundation in relation to the Augsburg Confession (1540), the Reformed church has no such "closed" confessional position. The motto of Reformed theology is and has been *semper reformanda*, which means that Reformed theology is "reformed and always reforming" or just "always reforming." According to Reformed theologian Michael Horton, the phrase originated in 1674 with Jodocus van Lodenstein, an important Dutch Reformed Pietist (2009).

In contrast to Lutheranism, the Reformed tradition has held that its confessional statements are provisional, mutable, and improvable; though functionally, at least, they have become permanent. Unlike the Scriptures, they are neither to be taken as final theological authority nor assigned the dignity and importance of the early ecumenical councils, thus protecting scriptural primacy.

Central to Reformed theology is the sovereignty and glory of God. God is sovereign in creation and redemption. Because of disobedience, humans have fallen out of right relationship with God, are completely deprived of his redeeming presence, and are radically dependent on his initiative for redemption. God, who is eminently merciful and loving, freely offers salvation to those whom he chooses to redeem. In Jesus Christ, the Father has made atonement for sin, a mighty deed of love that glorifies God. In Christ, humans recover what was lost in Adam's sin.

On the basis of what is believed to be authoritative biblical warrant (Rom. 8:29-30; Eph. 1:4, 9-11; 2:8-10; John 6:37, 44, 65; 15:16; etc.), the Reformed teach that *election* to salvation for some persons—occurring in eternity before the creation—expresses God's sovereign grace. God elected sinners, not directly, but in Christ and on account of Christ. The elect will be justified—reconciled to God—solely because Christ's righteousness is *imputed* to them. This righteousness belongs only to Christ and is completely alien to the elect sinner.

The word "alien" means that the Christian's righteousness is all Christ's and is never to be attributed to human merit. It does not mean that the transforming work of the Holy Spirit ("regeneration," Calvin [1536-59] 1863, bk. 3, 3.10), applying Christ's benefits to Christians, is absent. Calvin made clear that while faith is purely a gift of the Spirit, it is also the work of the Spirit to make Christ present, living, and reigning within Christians in **sanctifica-**

tion. Although the law of sin "must be . . . in [the] members" of Christians as long as they live, it must not "reign"; its "dominion" is "destroyed" by Christ's reign (3.13, 19). And although Christians must practice "ordinary repentance" for sin "during the whole course of [their] lives" (3.18), Calvin says of the work of the Holy Spirit:

O how great the proficiency of him who, taught that he is not his own, has withdrawn the dominion and government of himself from his own reason that he may give them to God! For as the surest source of destruction to men is to obey themselves, so the only haven of safety is to have no other will, no other wisdom, than to follow the Lord wherever he leads. . . . transformation . . . is the first entrance to life. . . . Christian . . . [wisdom entails] complete submission to the Holy Spirit. (7.1)

Calvin understands justification by grace through faith alone *and* a holy life to be "inseparable": "for repentance being properly understood it will better appear how a man is justified freely by faith alone, and yet that holiness of life, *real* holiness, as it is called, is inseparable from the free imputation of righteousness" (3.1). Sanctification is the "third use of the law" (bk. 2, 7.12), the other two being to convict sinners of their unrighteousness and hopelessness apart from God's justifying grace and to restrain those who would otherwise do evil in society (7.6-10).

Reacting against the theology of **Jacob Arminius**, the international Reformed Synod, hosted at Dordrecht, the Netherlands, in 1618-19, developed five points of doctrine that emphasized **predestination**. Eventually, maybe as late as the early twentieth century, the five points were summarized in the now famous acronym TULIP, a kind of theological shorthand for a comprehensive statement of Calvinist or Reformed theology.

T otal depravity. This does not mean that all people are as depraved as they might be but that they are in all parts of their person ruined by sin and utterly helpless apart from God's grace.

U nconditional election. Given humankind's complete helplessness, unable and unwilling to seek God, the only way people can be saved is if God elects to redeem them.

L imited (particular) atonement. Jesus Christ died on the cross to atone only for the sins of those persons the Father has chosen to redeem.

I rresistible grace. True to their fallen nature, sinners will unfailingly resist God's grace. But when God works in those he has chosen to redeem, his regenerating grace will be effectual; it will overcome sin and accomplish salvation.

P erseverance of the saints, or more correctly, the perseverance of God with the saints. The sovereign God will preserve and keep those elected to salvation from falling away from their faith. Perseverance is the ultimate mark of election.

These five points became the mark of Calvinist orthodoxy. The Calvinism of today is conflicted over how appeals to TULIP should be made. For some, TULIP is a sacrosanct, historic theological formula. Other theologians are willing to restate the summarized doctrines and to creatively revise the Reformed tradition's emphasis on the sovereignty of God.

Reformed Christians are characterized by what they believe to be God's cultural mandate. Christians must be actively present in society, seeking its preservation and transformation. Reformed Christians are not always in agreement on the measure of transformation to be expected. But because of what they believe about God's preserving grace, they agree that Christians must not withdraw from the world; they must transformatively engage its institutions. This is no substitute for evangelism. Social preservation and transformation will be truly effective only as persons are redeemed by the gospel of Jesus Christ.

See also Faith; Justification.

Resources

Calvin, John. *Institutes of the Christian Religion.* 1536-59. Translated by Henry Beveridge. Edinburgh: T and T Clark, 1863. Reprint, Christian Classics Ethereal Library. http://www.ccel.org/ccel/calvin/institutes.toc.html (accessed September 20, 2012).
De Jong, Peter Y., ed. *Crisis in the Reformed Churches: Essays in Commemoration of the Great Synod of Dort, 1618-1619.* Grand Rapids: Reformed Fellowship, 1968.
Horton, Michael. "Semper Reformanda." *Tabletalk Magazine.* October 1, 2009. Ligonier Ministries. http://www.ligonier.org/learn/articles/semper-reformanda/.
Leith, John H. *An Introduction to the Reformed Tradition: A Way of Being the Christian Community.* Rev. ed. Atlanta: John Knox Press, 1981.
Rohls, Jan. *Reformed Confessions: Theology from Zurich to Barmen.* Columbia Series in Reformed Theology. Louisville, KY: Westminster John Knox Press, 1998.
Stewart, Kenneth J. *Ten Myths About Calvinism.* Downers Grove, IL: IVP Academic, 2011.

YOUNG-HO CHUN, PHD

REGENERATION
See NEW BIRTH (REGENERATION).

REINCARNATION

The literal meaning of the term "reincarnation" is "entering the flesh again" (Latin, *re-* [again] *in-* [into, in] *carn-* [flesh]). As a belief structure, reincarnation is the teaching that at death one's soul is reborn into another form of existence. The new form may be higher or lower than the previous one, depending on how one has lived in previous existences. Rebirth will follow rebirth until the soul is purged of all that causes reincarnation. In India, reincarnation is known as *samsara.* The cycles of rebirth are known as the "wheel."

Belief in reincarnation seems to answer the question of the origin and destiny of humankind. Numerous religions and philosophies throughout history have taught reincarnation. It is a popular belief among many Westerners, including Christians, as demonstrated by hundreds of books on the subject. The doctrine is closely associated with Hinduism, Buddhism, and Jainism. In Hinduism, the belief dates back to 800–600 BC.

Reincarnation is closely associated with the law of *karma* (action), the law of inescapable consequences for one's actions. The form of life in which rebirth occurs depends on one's actions in previous lives. A person may be reborn as a human, god, animal, or other being, depending on the karma he or she has accumulated. Reincarnation will cease (Sanskrit, *moksha*), and joy (Sanskrit, *ananda*) be achieved only when the soul is finally cleansed of negative karma. At that point all distinctions between the soul (Sanskrit, *atman*)—distinctions that are actually illusory—and ultimate reality (Sanskrit, *Brahman*) will cease. The soul will be unified with or indistinguishably absorbed into Brahman. Until then, cycles of reincarnation will continue.

Buddhism is thought to offer more hope for release from the cycles of reincarnation than Hinduism. Numerous paths to enlightenment (Sanskrit, *bodhi*, "awakening") and release are offered. Unlike Hinduism, for Buddhism the precise individual who dies is not reincarnated. There is no self or ego as is known in Christianity. The self is but an impermanent union of five *skandhas* or states of being (body, perception, feelings, predispositions, and reasoning) that disperse at death. The one who is reborn is neither different from nor the same as the preceding person. Karma-laden character passes over, as though a seal has left its impress on warm wax.

According to Jainism, the consequences of one's deeds are literally deposited in and on the soul. At least eight kinds of karma can "stick" to the soul. The accumulations carry over into the next life and directly affect the course of reincarnation.

See also Monism, Dualism, Pluralism.

Resources

Abhedānanda, Swami. *Five Lectures on Reincarnation*. 1907. Reprint, Bel Air, CA: General Books, 2010.

Atkinson, William Walker. *Reincarnation and the Law of Karma: A Study of the Old-New World-Doctrine of Rebirth and Spiritual Cause and Effect*. 1908. Reprint, Whitefish, MT: Kessinger Publishing, 1997.

JOSEPH SURAY, PHD

RELIGIONS, THEOLOGY OF

A theology of religions accounts for **religious pluralism** by constructing theological categories for **interfaith dialogue**. A Christian theology of religions does this from the perspective of Christian faith and **doctrine**.

The traditional schema of exclusivism, pluralism, and inclusivism is often used to classify theologies of religion according to how they account for two biblical-theological emphases: (1) **salvation** comes through the atoning work of Christ alone; and (2) God desires to bring all persons to **repentance** and salvation.

1. Exclusivism maintains that salvation is found in Christ alone and that only those who hear the **gospel** proclaimed in this life and who explicitly confess **faith** in Christ will be saved. Salvation is found only within institutional Christianity. The exclusivist position is associated historically with the **Lutheran** and **Calvinist** strands of the **Reformation.** Currently it is most often represented by conservative **evangelical** and **fundamentalist** theologies.

2. Pluralism maintains that because "God" or "ultimate reality" is a transcendent mystery, all religions are equally valid responses to that mystery. Christ and Christianity are among many **revelations** that lead to salvation. The pluralist John Hick (1922–2012) insisted the exclusivist position is incompatible with a God who desires to save all persons. Hick identifies a common core in all religions whereby salvation occurs as one turns from "self-centeredness to Reality-centeredness" (2000).

3. Inclusivism maintains that salvation comes from Christ alone but that saving **grace** may be implicitly at work in other religions. Inclusivism is fully articulated by post-Vatican II **Roman Catholicism,** those influenced by the **Arminian** and **Radical Reformation** traditions, and contemporary evangelicals influenced by the Christianity of the **Global South.** Karl Rahner (1904-84) coined the terms "anonymous Christian" and "anonymous Christianity" to refer to how persons of other faiths may have saving grace mediated to them apart from an explicit encounter with Christ.

More recently, some theologians have moved beyond the traditional schema. J. A. DiNoia (b. 1943) argues that the schema cannot take the diversity of religions seriously. He suggests an alternative "Christian theology in dialogue," emphasizing interfaith disagreements to articulate each religion's "particularistic claim to universality" (1992).

Gavin D'Costa (b. 1958), Raimundo Panikkar (1918–2010), and Amos Yong have argued for a more **Trinitarian** and **pneumatological** theology of religions that accounts for the inseparability of the Son and the Spirit in the economy of salvation. They stress the **Holy Spirit**'s work in the diversity of religions and affirm the need to relate the Spirit's work to Christ, without minimizing other religions.

A robust Trinitarianism that grounds the work of the Holy Spirit in **Christology** and emphasizes the doctrine of **prevenient grace** holds the most promise for a Wesleyan theology of religions. The gospel of Jesus Christ reaches no one in whom the Spirit is not already at work. Furthermore, because God's prevenient grace is rooted in Christ's atonement, the Spirit's activity prior to an explicit knowledge of Christ is already, in some measure, the work of salvation. Thus, **Wesley** can express confidence in the possibility of the salvation of persons who have not explicitly acknowledged Christ.

Whatever its character, this "salvation" is *from* Christ and wrought by the Spirit *of* Christ. Because the Spirit witnesses to a person's acceptance by God in Christ, it follows that a life genuinely opened to God will to some extent be shaped by the grace of Jesus Christ and will express faith through love.

A Wesleyan theology of religions is neither exclusivist nor pluralist. Neither is it the inclusivism of "anonymous Christianity" where response to (prevenient) grace by a devotee of another religion must conform to Christian institutional forms. A Wesleyan approach to other religions expects that witness to Christ, though anticipatory of full evangelical faith, will occur there and that such witness will be identifiable beyond the bounds of "Christian" religious institutions. A Wesleyan theology of religions imposes no theoretical or institutional framework on Christianity's engagement with other religions. Instead, it trusts that where the Spirit of Christ is at work, engagement will reveal the ever-new reality of Christlike faith working through love.

See also Atonement; Destiny of the Unevangelized; Interfaith Dialogue; Parliament of the World's Religions; Religious Pluralism; Universalism; Witness of the Spirit.

Resources

DiNoia, J. A. *The Diversity of Religions: A Christian Perspective.* Washington, DC: Catholic University of America Press, 1992.

Gorski, Eugene F. *Theology of Religions: A Sourcebook for Interreligious Study.* New York: Paulist Press, 2008.

Hick, John. "Religious Pluralism and Salvation." In *The Philosophical Challenge of Religious Pluralism,* edited by Philip L. Quinn and Kevin Meeker, 54-66. New York: Oxford University Press, 2000.

Kärkkäinen, Veli-Matti. *An Introduction to the Theology of Religions: Biblical, Historical and Contemporary Perspectives.* Downers Grove, IL: InterVarsity Press, 2003.

Meadows, Philip. "Candidates for Heaven: Wesleyan Resources for a Theology of Religions." *Wesleyan Theological Journal* 35, no. 1 (Spring 2000): 99-129.

NATHAN R. KERR, PHD

RELIGIOUS CONFLICT

Religious conflict (RC) is conflict between adherents of two or more religions or between members of the same religion. Sources of RC include doctrine, religious practice, ownership of land, and worldview. Add disputes about leadership succession, origins, political power, and animosity. A threat to one's beliefs may be seen as a threat to one's being; conflict becomes personalized. Religious conflict nearly always involves misperceptions.

Religious conflict often contradicts a religion's basic teachings, most of which promote peace, justice, and acceptance of others. Most religions hold that war and violence are justifiable only under carefully prescribed conditions. **Augustine** (354–430) was the first Christian theologian to articulate a **just war** theory. **Thomas Aquinas** (ca. 1225-74) built on Augustine's foundation. The **Roman Catholic Church** used Aquinas's writings to control European countries. The Muslim concept of *jihad*, the Arabic word for "struggle," as in "struggling" against temptation, is misinterpreted by some Muslims as a rationale for violence against perceived enemies of Islam.

All religions have their basic beliefs their followers must embrace. In any religion, doing so can lead to inflexibility and intolerance of other religious beliefs, even though the religion's founder may clearly oppose intolerance. Religious zealots, claiming *the* unambiguous will of God for all persons and being unwilling to permit any opposition, use violence to achieve God's "will."

The European Crusades (AD 1096–1272) pitted Christians against Muslims (and other Christians) for control of Jerusalem and the Holy Land. Crusaders were recognized as warriors or knights of Christ. They believed victory came through divine intervention and took great religious pride in their mission. In 1095 Pope Urban II had raised the level of war from just war to holy war. To this day, Jerusalem remains religiously contested between Muslims and Jews. As for Christians, control of the Church of the Holy Sepulchre is divided among six branches of Christianity.

The Thirty Years' War (1618-48), which temporarily settled the religious identities of European nations, was a horribly destructive conflict between **Protestants** and **Catholics**. During the **Reformation**, some Protestants killed **Anabaptists**. Asian history records RC among Hindus, Muslims, Sikhs, and Christians. India and Pakistan, two nuclear powers, have been involved in RC since the creation of their respective nations.

The global media highlights religious conflict but seldom balances it with the way many religious groups play a constructive role in promoting social justice, human rights, compassion, and education for all persons.

See also Religions, Theology of; Religious Freedom; Religious Pluralism; State Religion.

Resources

Grim, Brian J., and Roger Finke. *The Price of Freedom Denied: Religious Persecution and Conflict in the 21st Century.* Cambridge Studies in Social Theory, Religion, and Politics. New York: Cambridge University Press, 2011.

Juergensmeyer, Mark. *Terror in the Mind of God: The Global Rise of Religious Violence.* 3rd ed. Comparative Studies in Religion and Society, vol. 13. Berkeley, CA: University of California Press, 2003.

JOHN WESLEY Z. KUREWA, PHD

RELIGIOUS FREEDOM

Freedom of religion theoretically refers to the privilege of individuals or groups to practice their religious beliefs without interference by an outside influence. The history of this privilege is so diverse and complex that it defies simple summary. In general, this freedom may be formal (constitutionally guaranteed) or informal (absence of peer pressure). Historically, freedom of religion has not been universally granted.

Several later NT documents reflect a situation where Christians were persecuted for their faith, either by the Roman authority or Jews who were themselves given a special dispensation of religious freedom (cf. Hebrews, James, 1 Peter). During the sixteenth century—the period of the Protestant Reformation—political units in Europe were officially supportive of either **Roman Catholicism** or **Protestantism.** The Catholic tendency to resist dissidents by force made the emergence of the **Reformation** difficult. Without state support **Martin Luther** may have been imprisoned or killed. Unfortunately, in most cases Protestants did not grant freedom of religion to non-Protestants in areas over which they had control. Not until the eighteenth-century Enlightenment did the concept of freedom of religion gain significant ground in Europe and America. Many Enlightenment leaders insisted that a fair, just, and productive society depends on religious tolerance.

In contemporary discussion, freedom of religion is addressed within the larger context of human rights. Against the background of history in which the disregard or contempt for human rights resulted in the commission of barbarous acts, the United Nations in 1948 issued "The Universal Declaration of Human Rights." It affirmed the following:

> Everyone has the right to freedom of thought, conscience and religion; this right includes freedom to change his religion or belief, and freedom, either alone or in community with others and in public or private, to manifest his religion or belief in teaching, practice, worship and observances. (Article 18)

On the fiftieth anniversary of this declaration, the Oslo Conference on Freedom of Religion and Belief reaffirmed the original declaration. The basis for this position is belief in the fundamental dignity and worth of the human person that transcends the laws of sovereign states.

When freedom of religion is constitutionally guaranteed, it is interpreted as involving the separation of church and state. This implies that no particular religion has a privileged status. In practice, it does not grant unlimited freedom, since certain religious practices are restricted on the principle that whatever is incompatible with community well-being is prohibited.

John Wesley's attitude toward freedom of religion was ambivalent. He spoke negatively about the effect on the church of the Constantinian establishment (Emperor Constantine's AD 313 recognition of Christianity's legality and his ensuing patronage of the church), but he was always part of the established Church of England (**Anglican**). At times he defended the authority of the crown over the church but ignored the church's canons when it suited him. He admonished the Methodists in America to disentangle themselves from the state. His views were obviously conditioned by circumstances.

See also Church and State; Interfaith Dialogue; Modernity; Religions, Theology of; Religious Conflict; Religious Pluralism; Rights, Human; Secular/Secularism/Secularization; State Religion.

Resources

English, John C. "John Wesley, the Establishment of Religion and the Separation of Church and State." *Journal of Church and State* 46, no. 1 (Winter 2004): 83-98.

Office of the United Nations High Commissioner for Human Rights. General assembly resolution 36/55. "Declaration on the Elimination of All Forms of Intolerance and of Discrimination Based on Religion or Belief." November 25, 1981. http://www2.ohchr.org/english/law/religion.htm.

United Nations. "The Universal Declaration of Human Rights." December 10, 1948. http://www.un.org/en/documents/udhr/index.shtml.

H. RAY DUNNING, PHD

RELIGIOUS PLURALISM

The phrase "religious pluralism" can refer to a simple description of the world in the twenty-first century, namely, that ours is a world of many religions, with an often bewildering multiplicity of subcategories of sects, cults, and denominations. Increases in world communication, travel, and immigration have made our diverse religious world unavoidable. More typically, though, "pluralism" refers to a particular ideology that holds that all (or at least many) religions have saving truth in them.

Even some Christians have been known to embrace this ideology, often in the name of not judging others, with appeals made to Scripture to justify their "tolerance," which sometimes shades off into indifference. The main problem with this understanding is that Jesus' admonition not to judge was aimed at *hypocritical* judging (Matt. 7:1-5). It is certainly not hypocritical to make the judgment that love is better than hate—if you are loving.

What do Christians formed by the Wesleyan tradition bring to the discussion of religious pluralism? First, for John Wesley, any discussion of a religion's truth must include not only its intellectual or belief structure but even more importantly an evaluation of the kind of life it produces in its adherents. His evaluation of religion involves **orthodoxy, orthopraxis,** and **orthokardia** (or **orthopathy**).

Orthodoxy. Wesley assigned normative status to the Church of England's Articles of Religion. He held that certain beliefs are indispensible for Christianity. He agrees with broad apostolic Christian tradition, namely, that for all Christians their understandings of God, humanity, and salvation must be informed by Scripture (especially as interpreted by the tradition) and the church's liturgy and creeds.

Orthopraxis. Wesley was keenly aware that people could embrace orthodox belief but still not live as Christians. Hence, he stressed *right practice* (orthopraxis). Wesley taught that genuine Christians will seek God's grace where God promised it would be encountered—in **works of piety** or **means** of grace, such as searching the Scriptures, taking Communion, prayer, and Christian conferencing. Equally important, love for God and neighbor must be evidenced through **works of mercy**, such as feeding the hungry, visiting the sick and imprisoned, and caring for widows and orphans. Works of piety and works of mercy capture true Christian orthopraxis (practice).

Orthokardia. More important than even orthodoxy and orthopraxis for Wesley is the need for the Christian to have orthokardia—the right heart. Wesley insisted that a person's center—described by the metaphor "heart"— must be renewed and transformed by the Holy Spirit for the person to be a "real Christian." Ultimately, the key "heart" criterion for religious maturity is the presence or absence of agape love.

Wesleyan Christians, then, bring to the encounter with other religions an unshakable conviction that the renewal of the entire person—his or her beliefs, actions, and, most importantly, heart—is the final goal of the religious way of life. Any competing way of life, then, will humbly, but unashamedly, finally be judged by the Wesleyan Christian with the criterion of incarnated agape love. Prevenient grace can operate through any channel that God chooses, including the world's various religions. Wesleyan Christians believe, though, that wherever it is found, this grace finds its full expression in the renewed heart of the believer justified and sanctified by the work of Christ.

See also Creeds (Nicene, Chalcedonian, Apostles', Athanasian); Liturgy and Worship; Orthodoxy/Orthopraxis/Orthopathy; Prevenient Grace; Religions, Theology of; Works of Mercy; Works of Piety.

Resources
Clapper, Gregory S. *The Renewal of the Heart Is the Mission of the Church: Wesley's Heart Religion in the Twenty-First Century.* Eugene, OR: Cascade Books, 2010.
Meadows, Philip. "Candidates for Heaven: Wesleyan Resources for a Theology of Religions." *Wesleyan Theological Journal* 35, no. 1 (Spring 2000): 99-129.
Pluralism Project at Harvard University. http://www.pluralism.org/.
Truesdale, Al. *With Cords of Love: A Wesleyan Response to Religious Pluralism.* With Keri Mitchell. Kansas City: Beacon Hill Press of Kansas City, 2005.

GREGORY S. CLAPPER, PHD

RENOVARÉ

Renovaré (Latin, "to renew") is an ecumenical ministry working for the renewal of the church of Jesus Christ in all her multifaceted expressions. It was begun by Richard Foster and others in November 1988. After writing *Celebration of Discipline* in 1978, Foster became increasingly convinced that a ministry was needed to undergird the concepts that had caught the attention of a multitude of people who had read the book. Renovaré is that ministry. Since 1988, it has matured into a ministry that has a theological base (the "with God life"), a balanced vision (the six formative traditions: **contempla-**

tive, **holiness, charismatic, social justice, evangelical**, and incarnational), and a practical strategy (formation through the practice of **spiritual disciplines**: celebration, chastity, confession, fasting, fellowship, guidance, meditation, prayer, sacrifice, secrecy, service, silence, simplicity/frugality, solitude, study, submission, and worship). Taken together, the vision and the practices are aimed to develop Christlikeness and a life of **discipleship** (understood as apprenticeship and apostleship).

Along the way, such persons as James Bryan Smith, Dallas Willard, Emilie Griffin, and Eugene Peterson have developed and deepened the Renovaré ministry. It remains based in small groups. Today, Renovaré offers persons an attractive website (www.renovare.org) that offers an array of resources (including *The Life with God Study Bible* and related supportive materials) to assist the body of Christ in an ongoing ministry of personal and corporate spiritual formation.

Renovaré is also developing a multicultural influence through its presence in England, Ireland, Brazil, and Korea.

See also Discipleship; Sanctification; Spiritual Disciplines; Spiritual Formation/Growth.

Resources
Foster, Richard. *Celebration of Discipline: The Path to Spiritual Growth.* 1978. Rev. ed., San Francisco: HarperSanFrancisco, 1988.
———. *Life with God: Reading the Bible for Spiritual Transformation.* 1988. Reprint, New York: HarperOne, 2010.

STEVEN HARPER, PHD

REPENTANCE

Repentance means turning away from evil and toward **God**. It includes the recognition of one's sin. In the OT the verb *shub*, "to turn," is typically used to express repentance. The prophets call on Israel to forsake idolatry, oppression of the poor, and other evils and to return to covenant relationship with God. This is the only way to avoid divine wrath (Isa. 30:15; Jer. 18:11; Ezek. 18:27-32; Hos. 12:6; 14:1-2). The offer of repentance is a gift, predicated on God's mercy and willingness to forgive (Exod. 34:6-7; Isa. 55:7; Jer. 3:12; Joel 2:13). God wants to restore, "For I have no pleasure in the death of anyone" (Ezek. 18:32). The prophets' judgment oracles often presume that punishment is conditional: if repentance comes, punishment will be averted (Jon. 4:2, 10-11).

Both John the Baptist (Matt. 3:1-12; Mark 1:4-8; Luke 3:3-17) and Jesus (Matt. 4:17; Mark 1:15) called on people to repent to prepare for entrance into God's **kingdom**. Jesus' mission is to call sinners to repentance (Luke 5:32), and his disciples assist in this (Mark 6:12). After Jesus' resurrection, he tells his disciples that "repentance and forgiveness of sins" are to be proclaimed to the nations (Luke 24:47).

The Greek words for "repent" suggest a change of mind, but the NT use of these terms goes beyond mere remorse or even mental reorientation. The repentance Jesus requires is a radical conversion—turning the whole self to the kingdom in response to the eschatological call of the **gospel**. This is the sense found often in Acts and elsewhere in the NT (Acts 2:38; 3:19; 11:18; 26:20; Rom. 2:4; 2 Tim. 2:25; 2 Pet. 3:9; Rev. 9:20-21). This is always stated within the context of God's gracious offer of forgiveness. The NT also uses "turning" to describe repentance and conversion (Acts 3:19, 26; 14:15; 15:19; 26:17-18, 20; 2 Cor. 3:16; 1 Thess. 1:9).

The word "repentance" may also be used for the contrition and return to right living that Christians exercise if they **sin** following conversion (2 Cor. 7:9-10; 12:21; Rev. 2:5). Paul prefers, though, to deal with turning away from what displeases God by discussing how to live out the new life in Christ (1 Cor. 6:9-20; Gal. 5:13-21; Col. 3:1–4:6).

Hebrews contains the most difficult saying about repentance: it is impossible to restore to repentance a person who has become a believer and then "fallen away" (Heb. 6:4-6; 12:16-17). The author is thinking here specifically of apostasy (6:6), warning of how serious the consequences are if a person renounces the only One who can mediate our redemption with God. Still, no one should ever on the grounds of this verse forsake hope that repentance, even for those who reject Christ, is possible. The One who forgave Peter and who declared that his mission is "to seek out and to save the lost" (Luke 19:10) still holds out mercy until his return.

See also Arminian Theology; Grace; Law and Gospel; Love; Reconciliation; Righteousness; Salvation (Soteriology).

Resources

Goppelt, Leonhard. *Theology of the New Testament*. 2 vols. Translated by John Alsup. Grand Rapids: Eerdmans, 1981-82.
Gowan, Donald, and Francis T. Gench. "Repentance." In vol. 4, *The New Interpreter's Dictionary of the Bible*, edited by Katharine Doob Sakenfeld, 762-64. Nashville: Abingdon Press, 2009.

TERENCE PAIGE, PHD

RESTORATION OF ALL THINGS
See KINGDOM OF GOD; SECOND COMING OF CHRIST/PAROUSIA.

RESURRECTION

Early Christians taught that at the end of the world the dead will receive their bodies back from God, reunited to their souls and transformed. The bodies of the righteous in Christ will be glorified like that of the risen Jesus, fit for eternal life, and sinners will rise to damnation. This has been widely believed among Christians in all denominations.

The OT conceives of covenant hopes as being fulfilled in this present life and is mostly silent about life after death. Nevertheless, it declares that God is the One who delivers from the pit of death, heals, and restores humanity. He vindicates those who trust in him, and he never abandons his beloved or forgets his covenant. This trajectory generated an impulse that may have existed unspoken before it emerged in later texts that mention the resurrection (Isa. 26:19; 25:7-8; Dan. 12:2-3). By the mid-second century BC some Jewish groups believed that the righteous will be raised as a reward (2 Macc. 7:10-11, 14, 23, 29) and that the wicked will be consigned to "torment" to satisfy divine justice (2 Esd. 7:32-38).

Jesus shared belief in a general resurrection (Mark 12:18-27; Luke 14:14; John 5:21-29). But he also believed that he would be raised in anticipation of that future general resurrection. He predicted that he would be rejected and killed in Jerusalem and that God would then raise him up (Mark 8:31; 9:9, 31; 10:34; 14:28; John 2:19-22). After Jesus' death and resurrection, on numerous occasions he appeared bodily to his disciples. Jesus' resurrection is absolutely foundational for the gospel (Luke 24:44-49; Acts 2:32; 17:18; 1 Cor. 15:1-11; 2 Tim. 2:8; 1 Pet. 1:21).

Jesus' resurrection vindicates him as Messiah, Lord, and God's Son (Acts 2:36; 3:13-15; Rom. 1:4). It also completes God's saving work through Christ, which atones for our sins and sets in motion the new creation that encompasses raising God's saints and restoring the whole created order (Rom 4:25; 8:18-23).

The resurrection of Christ and the anticipated resurrection of Christians are inextricably intertwined. Jesus' resurrection is the "firstfruits" of those who have been buried with him in baptism. Because of their corporate identity, believers must rise also, though not yet (1 Cor. 15:20-23; Rom. 6:3-5; 1 Pet. 3:21). Some speak as if this resurrection has already occurred ("realized eschatology" [Col. 3:1; Eph. 2:6]). But this is a metaphorical way of saying the reality of our participation in Christ's resurrection reaches into our present existence.

The resurrection of believers represents God's final triumph over the effects of sin and death. This is necessary for a complete restoration, because in biblical thought persons are a union of soul and body, embodied life. The soul is not destined for an immaterial eternity, as with the Greek notion of immortality. Some creeds, having a concern with the continuity of the person, speak of the same body that was buried being raised again. Jesus' resurrection body was recognizable but was not a normal body (Luke 24:36-40; John 20:19-20, 25-27). Paul says the saints will receive a "spiritual body" like that of Christ, glorified and changed to be suitable for eternal life with God

(1 Cor. 15:44). And his analogy of seed planting suggests both continuity and discontinuity (vv. 39-54).

Parts of the NT seem to speak of the resurrection as God's gift only to those made worthy in Christ (Luke 20:35; Acts 4:2; Phil. 3:11). This is the resurrection "to life everlasting" (1 Tim. 1:16, KJV), the ultimate redemption. The dark side of this event is spoken of mainly as final judgment and condemnation (Matt. 25:41-46; John 5:29; Rev. 20:5, 12-15). Believers are spared from judgment, which by implication is the purpose of resurrection for the wicked (1 Thess. 1:10; 5:9; John 3:36; Rom. 2:5-10; Rev. 11:18).

See also Destiny of the Unevangelized; Eschatology; Hell; Immortality/Life After Death; Jesus of Nazareth; Second Coming of Christ/Parousia.

Resources

Brown, Colin. "Resurrection." In vol. 3, *The New International Dictionary of New Testament Theology*, edited by Colin Brown, 259-309. Grand Rapids: Zondervan, 1975-78.

Dunn, J. D. G. *The Theology of Paul the Apostle*. Grand Rapids: Eerdmans, 1998.

Wright, N. T. *The Resurrection of the Son of God*. Christian Origins and the Question of God, vol. 3. Minneapolis: Fortress Press, 2003.

TERENCE PAIGE, PHD

REVELATION

Revelation refers to the fact that **God** can be known only by being disclosed. Because God is not an object of sense experience and ordinary modes of knowledge, God remains hidden until being unveiled. Theology examines God's self-disclosure.

It is common to distinguish between *revealed* (or kataphatic) and *negative* (or apophatic) theology. Revealed theology is knowledge of God insofar as God has been disclosed to us. Revelation provides words with which to speak about God. Negative theology reminds us that all language about God, even language rooted in revelation, is inadequate. Theology is about what God *is not*, even as it treats what God *is*. Negative theology reminds us that no matter how revelation reaches us, we receive it through the medium of human words; our language about God is always analogical, metaphorical, and symbolic.

It is also common to distinguish between general and special revelation. Revelation is general when it is universally available to humans, such as when Paul spoke of God's law being written on Gentile hearts (Rom. 2:15) or when Thomas Aquinas (ca. 1225-74) and other medieval theologians argued we can know God through the order of the universe. General revelation occurs in ways that make God known regardless of one's knowledge of the **Bible** or **Jesus Christ**. It is thus often associated with **natural theology.**

Special revelation consists of particular historical events and realities that disclose God. Jesus Christ is the principal and definitive example of special revelation; other examples include God speaking to Moses on Mount Sinai and Israel's return from the Babylonian exile. Revelation is considered special when available only to those with access to the revelatory events or to testimony about those events.

Revelation is often associated with mystery. Because God is infinite, we cannot discover the most important truths about God on our own. God must reveal them to us through a medium such as the Bible. Because these truths surpass our natural ability to understand, faith is sometimes understood as submission to the authority of the Bible and the church. This view has traditionally characterized the **Roman Catholic** tradition. More recent Catholic theology has considerably broadened its understanding of faith and revelation.

Karl Barth (1886–1968) offered an alternative to this traditional understanding of revelation and faith. He argued that revelation is primarily the person of Jesus Christ. What is given to us in revelation is God's own self, not information about God. In the **incarnation** and in the Son's obedience to the Father, God is presented to us and is with us. Accordingly, Barth did not regard the Bible as primary revelation. Instead, the Bible is the church's inspired and faithful witness to revelation (Christ) by which God speaks to us.

While for Barth, Jesus Christ is the *objective reality* of revelation—the content of revelation, the Holy Spirit is the *subjective reality* of revelation. Barth meant that revelation is not simply the historical person of Jesus but the event in which the incarnate God is given to us today by the **Holy Spirit.** The Holy Spirit actualizes revelation (makes Christ present) in the hearts of those who through the Spirit hear the Bible and preaching as the word of God, as God's address to them in their particular situations.

Wolfhart Pannenberg (b. 1928) said Barth had defined revelation too narrowly. Drawing on the Bible's **apocalyptic literature**, Pannenberg insisted that revelation consists in the totality of history. Since God is active in history, each historical event reveals God. But the full revelation of God awaits the **eschatological** end of history, which in a sense has already occurred in Jesus' resurrection. The church thus bears witness to revelation by testifying to the resurrection.

The importance of revelation lies in the fact that without it we cannot know God. Our knowledge of God is therefore a result of God's presence in creation and saving grace.

See also Biblical Theology; God, Doctrine of; Hiddenness of God; Prophecy/Prophet; Sacraments; Scripture, Theology of; Systematic Theology (Dogmatics); Torah; Wisdom.

Resources

Barth, Karl. *Church Dogmatics.* Vol. 1, Pt. 1, *The Doctrine of the Word of God.* Translated by G. W. Bromiley. Edited by G. W. Bromiley and T. F. Torrance. 2nd ed. Edinburgh: T and T Clark, 1975.

McGrath, Alister. *A Fine-Tuned Universe: The Quest for God in Science and Theology.* Louisville, KY: Westminster John Knox Press, 2009.

SAMUEL M. POWELL, PHD

REVELATION, BOOK OF
See APOCALYPTIC/APOCALYPTICISM.

REVIVALISM

Revivalism arose in the early nineteenth century and spread among American and British Protestants. It postulated that experiencing salvation need not be agonized over, need not be doubted, and that through abounding grace salvation could occur here and now for anyone. Revivalists sought to redeem society through the same abounding grace. Revivalism undermined Calvinist ideas of election and predestination. It well suited Wesleyanism, which emphasized the gospel's universal scope.

Revivalism employed "new measures" not used by the leading eighteenth-century evangelists—Jonathan Edwards, John Wesley, and George Whitefield—though Church of England preachers had sometimes asked listeners to come forward to the kneeling rail, where Communion was served, to pray in response to a sermon. Scottish Presbyterians, meanwhile, restricted from Communion any whose actions contradicted God's moral standards. Preachers led listeners through a process of self-examination in preparation for Communion and then examined persons individually, giving tokens to those thought worthy of receiving Communion. The Communion table was fenced against those deemed spiritually ineligible.

Persons hungry to partake of Communion followed the examination process during a camp meeting at Cane Ridge, Kentucky, in 1800. Revival ensued. As camp meetings spread, the connection with Communion was lost. But sinners were still called forward to repent and partake of saving grace.

On the Delmarva Peninsula (East Coast, United States), between 1800 and 1803 great revivals swept thousands into Methodist churches. Methodist itinerants invited sinners to come forward to the "altar." The practice quickly became common. Methodists lengthened their already spiritually charged "quarterly meetings" into camp meetings, which multiplied across the United States.

Camp meetings, protracted meetings, and calls for immediate response to the gospel typified revivalism. Revivalists preached persuasively, passionately, and, seemingly, extemporaneously. By showing that willfully breaking God's laws alienated people from God, revivalists induced conviction. The good news of salvation followed. Within one evangelistic service, revivalists thought, hardened sinners could acknowledge their sin, repent, believe, and be reborn. Emotional and corporate outpourings of the Spirit followed.

Belief that revival could come through such methods upset many Calvinists for whom any human efforts beyond petitionary prayer removed divine initiative. Charles G. Finney (1792–1875) argued otherwise, saying Christians must use all available means to lead persons to repentance. His *Lectures on Revivals of Religion* popularized revivalism.

Phoebe Palmer (1807-74), a Methodist laywoman, evangelized widely. Although **John Wesley** had not urged believers quickly to come into or testify to sanctifying grace, Palmer taught a "shorter way" that suited the impatient and pragmatic mood of the times. Palmer urged believers to place their "all" on the altar, in faith believing, as the Bible promised. The "altar" would sanctify the gift.

Finney, Palmer, and Dwight L. Moody (1837-99), among others, found interdenominational revivals an effective method among city dwellers on both sides of the Atlantic. Moody, a layperson like Palmer, urged people toward a higher Christian life. Revivalism in Great Britain found its critics but also successes in such conferences as **Keswick**.

In the twentieth century, revivalism provided common ground among evangelicals. Missionaries used revival methods wherever they were sent. Congregations absorbed its methods. Not only did full-time evangelists conduct yearly or twice-yearly revivals in churches, but also pastors frequently extended "altar calls." In camp meetings and local churches revivalist music prompted persons to "come forward." Hymns such as "Almost Persuaded" and "I Surrender All" softened hearts.

Using "Just as I Am" as his altar call, American evangelist Billy Graham (b. 1918) followed the methods of Finney and Moody. Like them, Graham drew Protestants together in North America and Great Britain and preached worldwide.

Whether occurring through camp meetings or special services, revivalism was a social enterprise demanding personal response. So essential were its methods to evangelicals that by the twentieth century some could hardly imagine persons repenting and coming to Christ in any other way.

See also Evangelism; Grace; Keswick Movement; Music/Hymns/ Hymnology; Reformed Tradition; Social Justice.

Resources
Blumhofer, Edith L., and Randall Balmer, eds. *Modern Christian Revivals*. Urbana, IL: University of Illinois Press, 1993.

Smith, Timothy L. *Revivalism and Social Reform: American Protestantism on the Eve of the Civil War*. Nashville: Abingdon Press, 1957. Reprint, Eugene, OR: Wipf and Stock, 2004.

FLOYD T. CUNNINGHAM, PHD

RIGHTEOUSNESS

The triune Creator whose being and deeds are "righteous" is the Bible's center. The root of the Hebrew word translated "righteousness" is *tsedeq* (tze-dek, "to make straight" and "do right"); it's a term that describes God's character. God's people know God as one who always "makes straight" and "does right." Scripture traces an astonishing array of God's righteous acts (Isa. 59:17; Jer. 9:24), such as preserving creation (Isa. 45:8), disclosing truth and righteousness (Pss. 19:9; 119:142), and justly visiting punishment on the wicked (Deut. 9:4-6). At life's end, Moses summarizes God's work as "just and upright" (32:4-6).

Scripture typically joins God's righteousness to concrete and merciful acts of covenant keeping. God's *right way* of acting results in *straightening out* (redeeming) relationships. Sometimes all creation is targeted for redemption (Rom. 8:18-25; Rev. 21:1-5). Mostly, God acts in faithfulness, loyal love, mercy, and forgiveness to keep covenant with partners (Titus 2:11-14; 3:3-8). God doesn't give up on **Israel**; in righteousness God works to restore right relationship (Jer. 9:24; Hos. 2:19).

Just practices must characterize all human relationships consistent with how Israel experienced liberation from Egyptian slavery (Deut. 25:15). Justice goes beyond legal compliances; it involves practices motivated by reciprocal mercy. Its aim is loving communion between persons, including restoring right relationships.

Usually in the Septuagint (LXX, Greek OT) and the Greek NT, *tsedeq* is translated *dikaioō* (di-kai-o-ō, "to put to right" or "rectify"). *Dikaioō* includes a profound sense of justice, but grounded in grace—justice in unfair amounts!

The way of righteousness exhibited by Israel's God is embodied and proclaimed in Jesus' messianic mission (Matt. 3:15; 21:32). Especially in Matthew, righteousness entails patterns of right living consistent with God's righteous reign (5:20; 6:33). Jesus exhibits this in his teaching, relationships, death, and resurrection (3:15). Moreover, Jesus' manifestation of righteousness is normative for his disciples (5:6; 7:21-26), even at considerable cost (5:10).

The Catholic (General) Epistles elaborate the way of righteousness the gospel entails. In James, for example (whose deep logic resembles Matthew's), faith is validated by works, as modeled after Abraham, whose obedience resulted in his willingness to sacrifice Isaac (James 2:21-24). Friends of God are "rectified" (*dikaioō*) by their works, not by their faith alone (2:24, author's translation). James says the right use of edifying speech will produce "a harvest of righteousness" (3:17-18).

First John offers a synthesis of the biblical concept of righteousness. God, who is "light" and tolerates no "darkness" (1:5), is righteous. God faithfully forgives sinners who confess and establishes loving communion with them (1:9; 3:7). God does this through the merit of Christ's expiatory (atoning) death as the "righteous one" (2:1-2, 29, author's translation). Because believers have been reborn as God's children (3:9), God's righteousness must now characterize their lives—distinguished by the sin they avoid and the love they demonstrate (2:29; 3:7-8, 10-12).

The most expansive portrayal of righteousness is found in Paul's letters. In Romans, "righteousness" occurs thirty-four times, and its verbal form fifteen times. The "righteousness of God" (1:17; 3:21-26; 9:30–10:4) is disclosed in the apostolic preaching of God's gospel (1:16) and is experienced in believers (v. 17).

Paul uses the metaphor of a law court to speak of God's righteousness. God's righteousness targets sinners who are guilty and can claim no merit for acquittal. But God offers the Crucified One as evidence of sublime faithfulness, granting righteousness (acquittal) to all who place their confidence in him.

Paul says those who are acquitted of sin's guilt and released from its power are baptized into Christ by his Spirit. The Spirit empowers them to live as instruments of righteousness (6:11-13; 8:9-17). God's rectifying grace fully integrates justification, new birth, and sanctification into one new creation (Gal. 5:16-26; 1 Pet. 1:13-16).

See also Atonement; Faith; Gospel; Grace; Justification; Kingdom of God; Legalism; Reconciliation; Repentance; Salvation (Soteriology); Sanctification; Trinity.

Resources
McGrath, Alister. *Iustitia Dei: A History of the Christian Doctrine of Justification*. 3rd ed. Cambridge, UK: Cambridge University Press, 2005.
Wright, N. T. *Justification: God's Plan and Paul's Vision*. Downers Grove, IL: IVP Academic, 2009.

ROBERT W. WALL, PHD

RIGHTEOUS SUFFERER
See CHRISTOLOGY, NEW TESTAMENT.

RIGHTS, HUMAN

Human rights are qualities of human existence that persons can expect to have protected by others, governments, and society at large and that persons in turn must protect for others. Though affirmed by the community, human rights protect individuals against excesses by the community.

Human rights may be viewed as *absolute*, that is, rights belonging to all persons just because they are human, or as *relative*, that is, rights belonging to members of a particular group.

Natural, civil, political, and personal are classifications of human rights. *Natural rights* are rights "naturally" belonging to all persons, including the right to life, liberty, and privacy. *Civil rights* are rights associated with one's citizenship in a country. They include the right to property, equal protection under the law, and freedom of contract. Civil rights impose a duty on each citizen, one's country, and its government to fulfill the rights. *Political rights* empower citizens to function effectively in their country. They include the right of petition and the right to hold public office. *Personal rights* are ones that a person morally wills on the community but that might or might not be accepted. They include the "right" to health care or the "right" to succeed. They become enforceable only if a community or country agrees they carry moral force.

The history of human rights emerges out of the need to impose duties on citizens. However, many early civilizations such as Greece had no corresponding term for the modern idea of individual and inviolable rights or duties. The Stoics taught that each person without regard for social rank is capable of reason and hence of living virtuously and wisely. By assigning such importance to all persons the Stoics made their contribution to the development of human rights.

The OT contributed significantly to the development of human rights. Its uniform emphasis on living an upright life in the eyes of the Lord, expected of king and peasant farmer alike, minimized the moral, if not the social, distance between persons. The Mosaic law and the message of the prophets assert that God values and protects persons who would otherwise be crushed by power: widows, orphans, strangers, and the poor. If God assigns such value to the otherwise dispossessed, no human can justifiably ignore it.

Early Christianity, with its emphasis on salvation and the inviolable value this placed on persons, offered a rationale for the emergence of human rights that continued and extended the OT narrative. The moral qualities expected of all Christians, without reference to class or gender, fortified the value of persons without exception.

Those foundations, when built on by the **Protestant Reformation** and the **Enlightenment**, expanded to become the superstructure of **democratic** societies. John Milton (1608-74) could hold that all persons are naturally born free.

John Wesley (1703-91) contributed greatly to the practical growth of individual human rights by championing the cause of the poor against all forms of injustice and by vigorously opposing the institution of human slavery.

Modern expressions of human rights are now codified in documents such as the Bill of Rights of the United States, the Charter of Rights and Freedoms of Canada, and the Universal Declaration of Human Rights by the United Nations General Assembly.

See also Christian Ethics/Moral Theology; Ethics; Justice; Kingdom of God; Love; Peacemaking; Public Theology; Reconciliation; Social Ethics; Social Justice; Works of Mercy.

Resources

Haas, Peter J. *Human Rights and the World's Major Religions.* Westport, CT: Praeger, 2005.
Meeks, M. Douglas. *Our Calling to Fulfill: Wesleyan Views of the Church in Mission.* Nashville: Kingswood Books, 2009.
Runyon, Theodore, ed. *Sanctification and Liberation: Liberation Theologies in Light of the Wesleyan Tradition.* Nashville: Abingdon Press, 1981.

L. BRYAN WILLIAMS, PHD

ROMAN CATHOLICISM

The Roman Catholic Church is Christianity's largest branch. The designation "Roman" refers to the belief that the bishop of Rome (usually designated with the honorific title "pope" [Latin, *papa*]) is the supreme pastor over the "catholic" (Latin, *catholicus*, "universal") church. Roman Catholics believe that Jesus Christ invested his authority solely in Peter and his successors, who act as Christ's "vice-regents." This line of universal authority is claimed to have existed in unbroken continuity until 1054, when Pope Leo IX and Michael I Cerularius (patriarch of Constantinople) excommunicated each other, initiating the schism between Western and Eastern churches.

The importance of the Roman bishop's authority reached its zenith under Pope Boniface VIII (pope from 1294 to 1303), who decreed that submission to the office was "absolutely necessary to salvation" (*Unam Sanctum*, 1302). Traditional Roman Catholic teaching and claims to authority were reinforced at the Council of Trent (1545-63) against the Protestant Reformers and at the First Vatican Council (1869-70) against various errors of modernism. The Second Vatican Council (1962-65), however, lessened the force of many exclusivist Roman Catholic claims; the church expressed a greater openness toward the Orthodox, Protestants, and even other religions.

Roman Catholic dogma is summarized in the ecumenical creeds of the church and detailed in the *Catechism of the Catholic Church.* While believing in the inspiration of Scripture, Roman Catholics hold to a higher view of church tradition than Protestants. Catholic doctrine is safeguarded through the Congregation for the Doctrine of the Faith. When the pope speaks *ex cathedra* (Latin, "from the chair"), that is, as the official teacher of the church on matters of faith and morals, such pronouncements are regarded as infallible.

Roman Catholicism emphasizes the church's role in mediating salvation, dispensed through seven sacraments: baptism, confirmation, Eucharist (in which the bread and wine are "transubstantiated," or changed in substance, into the body and blood of Christ), penance (reconciliation), anointing of the sick, marriage, and holy orders (ordination of bishops, priests, and deacons). Grace is received in the soul through the sacraments, first through baptism, which removes the guilt of original sin. Although Jesus Christ merits initial justification, people must cooperate with grace and bring to fruition the theological virtues of faith, hope, and love, which the Holy Spirit infused in their souls. Works of Christian charity subsequently merit other continuing graces of sanctification.

The Roman Catholic perspective on justification thus differs from traditional Protestant doctrine. Roman Catholics view sanctification as part of justification, while Protestants generally do not (justification is sometimes said to be a "declarative" act whereby God pronounces the sinner righteous). Historically, Roman Catholics have suspected Protestants of minimizing the importance of holy living, while Protestants have suspected that, by including sanctification within justification, Roman Catholics fall back on justification by works. In the 1999 *Joint Declaration on the Doctrine of Justification* (signed by officials from both the Roman Catholic Church and the Lutheran World Federation), the Roman Catholic position affirms the renewal of life by grace but emphasizes that the human "contributes nothing to justification about which one could boast before God" (4.3.27).

Salvation is, in principle, available to everyone, including those without opportunity to hear the gospel. Such people exist in a state of "invincible ignorance" but may still share in salvation if they respond to divine grace in the voice of conscience and attempt to love others. No one, however, may be assured absolutely of their salvation, except by way of special divine disclosure. At the end of one's life, remaining impurities in the soul are cleansed in purgatory, which the *Catechism* defines as a "purification, so as to achieve the holiness necessary to enter the joy of heaven" (*Catechism of the Catholic Church* 1993, para. 1030).

Roman Catholics venerate (not worship) the Virgin Mary insofar as she exemplifies the sanctifying virtues of faith, hope, and love and provides help for the pious. The dogma of the immaculate conception of Mary (the belief that she was born free from original sin) was formalized in 1854. Roman Catholics seek the aid of other saints as well.

The church is organized into dioceses—territories served by bishops. A diocese is composed of smaller areas called parishes, which are served by local churches under the direction of priests and assisted by deacons. Bishops are generally named by the pope. A body of officials known as the College of Cardinals elects the pope. In addition to holy orders, several religious orders (e.g., Franciscans, Jesuits) exist within the church. Members vow to live under a common rule and embrace poverty, chastity, and obedience.

About half of all Christians in the world are Roman Catholics, numbering more than one billion. Approximately half live in Latin America and the Caribbean. In 2010, the Roman Catholic Church had roughly sixty-eight million members in the United States.

See also Counter-Reformation (Catholic Reformation); Justification; Orthodox Church; Reformation; Sacraments; Thomas Aquinas; Vatican Council II.

Resources

Bokenkotter, Thomas. *A Concise History of the Catholic Church.* Rev. and enl., New York: Doubleday, 2004.

Catechism of the Catholic Church. 1993. Christusrex.org. http://www.christusrex.org/www1/CDHN/ccc.html.

Lutheran World Federation and the Catholic Church. *Joint Declaration on the Doctrine of Justification.* October 31, 1999. Vatican: The Holy See. http://www.vatican.va/roman_curia/pontifical_councils/chrstuni/documents/rc_pc_chrstuni_doc_31101999_cath-luth-joint-declaration_en.html.

Vidmar, John. *The Catholic Church Through the Ages: A History.* New York: Paulist Press, 2005.

JONATHAN P. CASE, PHD

Ss

SACRAMENTS

The sacraments were very important to the Wesley brothers. The members of the Holy Club at Oxford went to Communion every Sunday, and John attended or served Communion an average of two or three times a week during his whole career. He wrote a sermon titled "The Duty of Constant Communion" (*Works*, 7:147-57) for his students at Lincoln College, Oxford, because "frequent communion" was not frequent enough (149). And late in his career he took the step, much against the wishes of his brother Charles, to ordain preachers for America because, with the departure of most of the **Anglican** clergy after the Revolutionary War, the eighteen thousand **Methodists** in the former colony had no one to administer Communion or baptize their children "throughout that vast tract of land, a thousand miles long and some hundreds broad" (13:256).

To make the case for *baptism*, especially infant baptism, he republished an essay by his father, Samuel Wesley, on the importance of baptism (10:188-201). The essay explains that baptism cleanses the infant from original sin and incorporates him or her into the church of the new covenant made possible by Jesus Christ. And "baptism doth now save us if we live answerable thereto" (192). But we do not live answerable thereto, and therefore "ye must be born again" (John 3:7, KJV, quoted in *Works*, 6:65, as basis for sermon "The New Birth"). This emphasis on the necessity of conversion has led some of Wesley's followers to assume baptism is not important. Instead, for Wesley baptism does not grant a permanent status, a ticket to heaven, but provides the grace that starts us on a continuing journey. It is *the* sacrament of prevenient grace. But God's faithfulness and the work of the Holy Spirit call from us a response of faith and growth in the Christian life. Wesley says this growth is necessary for **sanctification** that can transform every corner of our existence.

The sacrament that nourishes us in this growth is the *Lord's Supper.* The Wesleyan revival was also a revival of lay participation in the sacrament. Not only did Wesley preach in the fields when churches could no longer hold the crowds, but also wherever he could get the cooperation of local Anglican clergy, he held field Communions, sometimes lasting three or four hours, to serve all the people. Charles Wesley's Communion hymns were sung as people waited, with a song leader lining out the verses and the people responding. The Wesleys had a strong sense of Christ's presence in the sacrament. The English Reformation had banished the Roman doctrine of transubstantiation, but the Wesleys put in its place a strong doctrine of Christ's presence through the Holy Spirit. The Calvinist doctrine of "virtualism," adopted by the Anglicans, had said that in the Supper our minds are lifted up to heaven where Christ is at the right hand of the Father. But the Wesleys turned the direction around. The Spirit brings Christ down to us. As Charles wrote,

> *We need not now go up to heaven,*
>   *To bring the long-sought Saviour down;*
>   *Thou art to all already given,*
>   *Thou dost even now Thy banquet crown:*
> *To every faithful soul appear,*
>   *And show Thy real presence here!* (Rattenbury 1948, 232)

This interpretation also makes the Supper a Trinitarian event. The Spirit and the Son together make palpable through the bread and the wine the event of the Father's love toward us. The Supper is not a mere remembrance of Christ, a subjective memory of his suffering and death, but an objective participation in his resurrection life. And so the Communion is a means of transforming hearts and lives. No wonder John Wesley called it "a converting ordinance" (*Works*, 1:279-80; journal entries for June 27-28, 1740).

Wesley also introduced among Methodists a paraliturgical practice he first encountered among the Moravians, the **love feast**, which recalled the agape meal of early Christians. It did not require ordained clergy for its celebration. It was thus well suited to Methodism as a lay movement. The love feast was not a substitute for Communion but was an informal gathering around tables with bread and water, accompanied by prayers and testimonies about God's mercy and love.

In *The Sunday Service* (1784), which Wesley sent to Methodists in America, he advised the newly ordained preachers "to administer the supper of the Lord on every Lord's day." Evidently he intended "constant communion" (*Works*, 7:149) to be the rule in the new world.

See also Grace; Means of Grace; Wesley, Charles, Theology of; Wesley, John, Theology of.

Resources

Khoo, Lorna. *Wesleyan Eucharistic Spirituality.* Adelaide, SA, AU: ATF Press, 2005.

Knight, Henry H. *The Presence of God in the Christian Life.* Metuchen, NJ: Scarecrow Press, 1992.

Rattenbury, J. Earnest. *The Eucharistic Hymns of John and Charles Wesley.* London: Epworth Press, 1948.

Staples, Rob L. *Outward Sign and Inward Grace: The Place of Sacraments in Wesleyan Spirituality.* Kansas City: Beacon Hill Press of Kansas City, 1991.

Wesley, John. "Duty of Constant Communion." In *Works,* 7:147-57.

———. "The Means of Grace." In *Works,* 5:185-201.

THEODORE RUNYON, DR. THEOL.

SACRED SPACE AND TIME

See CHRISTIAN YEAR; SPIRITUAL DIRECTION/SPIRITUAL DIRECTOR; TEMPLE.

SADDUCEES

See PHARISEES/SADDUCEES.

SALVATION (SOTERIOLOGY)

The branch of theology dealing with salvation is soteriology, based on the Greek word for salvation (*sotēria*). Soteriology encompasses the entire breadth of God's saving work in and for us, from the first effects of **grace** to the **resurrection** of the body and eternal life.

One aspect of salvation is conversion—turning away from **sin** and to **God**. Many Christians experience evangelical conversion as a momentary event; however, a larger work of conversion occurs throughout one's entire lifetime. It begins with God's **prevenient grace**, even before we are distinctly aware of God. Through this grace God strives to bring everyone to **faith** and **obedience**. Prevenient grace creates **conscience** (awareness of God's moral law), illumination (the beginning of our awareness of God), and awakening (the first awareness of our sin). Wesleyans regard these initial moments of spiritual life as part of God's saving work, even though they precede evangelical conversion.

Conversion continues as the **Holy Spirit** leads us to repentance, involving sorrow and change of life, and leading to a lifelong exercise in humility and self-examination.

Repentance, which God's grace enables us to practice, is, accordingly, an essential condition of salvation, for without repentance—a complete change of life's direction—we cannot respond positively to God's grace.

Alongside repentance, the Spirit creates us anew, initially in **regeneration** (the new birth) and over time in **sanctification**. Regeneration denotes the fact that, whereas in a state of sin we were spiritually dead, in Jesus Christ we are brought back from the dead and now live anew in the presence and power of God. Sanctification signifies our growing separation from sin's power and our increasing renewal in the image of God. Although sanctification is completed in the perfection of love, God's grace continues to lead us into a life of increasing knowledge, faith, and obedience.

Besides conversion, salvation encompasses all that God does for us in Jesus Christ, including the following:

- **Atonement**, which describes salvation in terms drawn from the sacrifice of a goat on the Day of Atonement, a sacrifice that covers the sins of the people. This view emphasizes the shedding of Jesus' blood and his vicarious death.
- **Reconciliation**, which portrays salvation as a movement from alienation to friendship, from wrath to peace.
- **Justification**, which depicts salvation as God's act of putting us in the right by virtue of Christ's blood, Christ's obedience, and our faith, which is itself God's gift. From this perspective, salvation consists in God making us righteous.
- Adoption, which represents salvation as becoming God's children and part of God's household.

Each of these metaphors provides insight into how Christians stand in a new relationship to God. United with Christ through his body, the church, we enjoy forgiveness of sin and peace with God and receive God's gift of righteousness.

Salvation has a *completed* dimension. Salvation is God's work, already accomplished, as when Paul noted "we *have been* justified" and "reconciled" (Rom. 5:9-10, emphasis added) and when Hebrews affirms Christ's death "*has* perfected . . . those who are [holy]" (Heb. 10:14, emphasis added). Because of God's decisive act in Christ, salvation is accomplished. Salvation also has an *eschatological* dimension, as when Paul declared that we will be saved (Rom. 5:9-10) from judgment and wrath at the eschatological day (1 Thess. 1:10). Only in the *eschaton* will salvation be completed in **resurrection**. Our bodies will share in the new creation; the final effects of sin on human nature will be erased. The completed dimension of salvation is grounded in the eschatological dimension of the kingdom of God, for while God does not yet rule over everything (1 Cor. 15:12-28), his kingdom has nonetheless already arrived with power (Mark 1:14-15; 1 Cor. 15:12-28; Col. 1:13-14). Although in one sense salvation is finished, in another its completion awaits history's eschatological completion.

Finally, salvation has a *cosmic* dimension. All creation will eventually share in the glory and salvation of the children of God; in Jesus Christ "all . . . things in heaven and . . . earth" are being reconciled to God (Eph. 1:3-14). Salvation, then, is not merely a human reality. It is God's new creation, which remakes the entire created world.

See also Biblical Theology; Christian Perfection (Entire Sanctification); Christology, New Testament; Covenant; Creation/New Creation; Cross; Eschatology; Eschatology, Biblical; Gospel; Second Coming of Christ/ Parousia.

Resources
Gorman, Michael J. *Inhabiting the Cruciform God: Kenosis, Justification, and Theosis in Paul's Narrative Soteriology.* Grand Rapids: Eerdmans, 2009.

Lodahl, Michael. *God of Nature and of Grace: Reading the World in a Wesleyan Way.* Nashville: Kingswood, 2004.

McGrath, Alister. *Iustitia Dei: A History of the Christian Doctrine of Justification.* 3rd ed. Cambridge, UK: Cambridge University Press, 2005.

Runyon, Theodore. *The New Creation: John Wesley's Theology Today.* Nashville: Abingdon Press, 1998.

SAMUEL M. POWELL, PHD

SALVATION ARMY

The Salvation Army is an international Christian church dedicated to meeting the spiritual and material needs of humanity. Its origins trace back to 1865 when William Booth (1829–1912), assisted by his wife, Catherine (1829-90), began a small mission in the poverty-ridden East End of London. Although carrying out their work independently of any denomination, they were profoundly indebted to **British Methodism** (with which he was affiliated at the beginning of his ministry) and to the transatlantic **revivalism** of the mid-nineteenth century. **Wesleyan Methodism** instilled in William and Catherine a passion for **salvation** and a desire for **holiness** of life, while American evangelists such as James Caughey, Charles Grandison Finney, and Phoebe Palmer schooled the Booths in the methods needed to reach the spiritually lost.

At first, William and Catherine had no intention of starting a new denomination; their goal was simply to direct converts to existing churches. Such a strategy, however, failed, chiefly because their unrefined converts received a cold reception in the respectable churches of the day. Consequently, the mission became a spiritual home for the lower working classes. While initially called the Christian Revival Association, by late summer of 1869, as the work spread beyond the borders of East London, it became known as the Christian Mission. Increasingly its growth was couched in military terms; the Booths and their followers considered themselves at war with **sin** and the **devil**. Aggressive tactics were necessary to reach the spiritually destitute, who were headed for the fires of **hell**. This theological conviction, aided by the militarism of the age, ultimately led to a name change in 1878, when William Booth began referring to the Christian Mission as the Salvation Army.

Considerable growth followed as the Salvation Army established new stations—now referred to as corps—throughout the United Kingdom. Success, however, brought persecution from various corners. Criticism from the middle and upper classes focused on the Salvation Army's use of sensational tactics: allowing women to preach, setting sacred words to secular tunes, and parading through the streets with noisy musical instruments. Disapproval from the lower classes came from the organization's condemnation of alcohol, a central feature of working-class lifestyles. From both sources, early Salvationists endured a great deal of persecution. Despite this, or partly because of it, expansion continued, especially to other parts of the world.

During its formative period (1880s) the organization widened its ministry by adding social programs to evangelism. This development reflected William Booth's growing conviction that **salvation** meant not only rescuing people from future damnation but lifting them out of present miseries as well. Among the first to be assisted were sexually exploited young women, slum dwellers, prisoners, and homeless men. Additional aspects of social work emerged after the publication of William Booth's ambitious scheme for alleviating poverty, *In Darkest England and the Way Out* (1890). A dual ministry—spiritual and social—continues to define the Salvation Army, which is governed by a quasi-military system of command. Its leaders are officers (ordained ministers), who receive two years of training at its theological colleges. Salvationists are active in more than 120 countries.

See also Holiness Movements: American, British, and Continental; Methodism, British; Revivalism; Social Ethics; Social Justice; Wesleyan Methodism.

Resources
Howes, Trevor, ed. *The Salvation Army Year Book, 2010.* London: Salvation Books, 2009.
Murdoch, Norman H. *Origins of the Salvation Army.* Knoxville, TN: University of Tennessee Press, 1994.

ANDREW M. EASON, PHD

SANCTIFICATION

Sanctification is God's act of making humans holy.

In its corporate sense, sanctification refers to the **holiness** of God's people. Through **election, Israel** and the **church** are constituted a holy people. They are distinguished and separated from the world. To belong to the church is thus to share in its corporate holiness as the body of Christ and temple of the **Holy Spirit**.

In its individual dimension, sanctification is attained by consecration (or devotion) to God. People (e.g., Nazirites) and things (e.g., the **temple**) can be consecrated to God. They belong to God and are to be used only in God's service. In the NT, a Christian's entire self, including his or her body, must be consecrated to God as expressing worship (Rom. 12:1-2; 1 Thess. 4:1-8).

People and things consecrated to God must avoid impurity; only what is pure has access to God. Impurity originally consisted of avoiding contact with blood, corpses, and other defiling things. Increasingly, however, biblical writers regarded impurity as idolatry and fornication. Purity thus came to have a moral dimension.

Being part of God's holy people requires **righteousness** and holy conduct—above all, love for God and neighbor. Some deeds are specifically demanded of God's people. Correspondingly, some deeds are inconsistent with God's holiness. Sanctification not only separates persons *to* God—to righteousness—but also separates them *from* sin.

Sin has a twofold character. Outward sin consists of actions that knowingly violate God's law. Inward sin (concupiscence, corruption, or depravity) consists of evil thoughts and desires, such as envy, anger, and greed. Every disciple is able, with God's grace, to avoid outward sin; inward sin, however, requires a deeper act of divine grace. Sanctification is this deeper act.

There are distinct moments in the life of holiness. Initial sanctification (which coincides with regeneration, the new birth) is the first moment on the journey of transformation into Christ's image. Sanctification continues as a disciple is progressively transformed—freed from sin and filled with love for God and neighbor. This is the process described in some traditions as **theosis**. **Entire sanctification** is the moment when love is perfected and a person attains complete freedom from intentional sin. In entire sanctification the heart becomes pure—completely devoted to God—and an individual's thoughts and actions are motivated solely by love. God's grace is required for every moment in the life of holiness. A person becomes holy (initially, progressively, and entirely) as he or she cooperates with God's transforming grace through the practice of self-denial and other spiritual disciplines.

While entire sanctification recreates a person according to the *moral* image of God (righteousness, holiness, and love), it does not erase all the effects of sin. Impaired judgment and understanding remain, and these infirmities inevitably affect conduct. So while an individual's love may be pure, his or her deeds may be flawed. Consequently, the life of sanctification continues to be a life of humility and repentance.

While sanctification is effected by God's grace, humans are enabled to cooperate by grace through acts of **self-denial** (mortification) and **means of grace**, including **works of mercy** and **works of piety**. Self-denial is necessary because temptation never ceases. Works of mercy promote sanctification by helping a person grow in Christian virtue. Sharing in the means of grace furthers sanctification by incorporating that person more and more into Christ and enabling him or her to receive the life Christ gives.

See also Christian Perfection (Entire Sanctification); Discipleship; Fruit of the Spirit; Holiness; Involuntary Transgressions; *Ordo Salutis;* Salvation (Soteriology); Spiritual Formation/Growth; Wesley, John, Theology of.

Resources

Dunning, H. Ray. *A Layman's Guide to Sanctification.* Kansas City: Beacon Hill Press of Kansas City, 1991.

Greathouse, William. *Wholeness in Christ: Toward a Biblical Theology of Holiness.* Kansas City: Beacon Hill Press of Kansas City, 1998.

Leclerc, Diane. *Discovering Christian Holiness: The Heart of Wesleyan-Holiness Theology.* Kansas City: Beacon Hill Press of Kansas City, 2010.

Mannoia, Kevin W., and Don Thorsen, eds. *The Holiness Manifesto.* Grand Rapids: Eerdmans, 2008.

Wesley, John. *A Plain Account of Christian Perfection.* In *Works,* 11:366-446.

SAMUEL M. POWELL, PHD

SANCTIFIED CHURCH

The "sanctified church" is a comprehensive term for African-American holiness, Pentecostal, and apostolic churches and denominations in distinction from the black Baptists and Methodists from which they emerged beginning in the late nineteenth century. Those of the sanctified church sought to reform the black church through a recovery of the oral, ecstatic, and embodied spirituality that originated in the religion of the slaves and by an emphasis on entire sanctification and Spirit baptism.

The term "sanctified church" began appearing in scholarly writings in the 1980s through the work of anthropologist Zora Neale Hurston and sociologist Cheryl Townsend Gilkes. But the most recent and comprehensive study is by Cheryl J. Sanders, who provides theological and ethical interpretations of the beliefs and practices of the sanctified church. She describes the sanctified church as a "reform movement that seeks to bring its standards of worship, personal morality, and social concern into conformity with a biblical hermeneutic of holiness and spiritual empowerment" (1996, 5).

The sanctified church includes entire denominations as well as African-American congregations in interracial bodies. Although all three strands of the sanctified church emphasize Spirit baptism, the holiness tradition identifies it with entire sanctification while the Pentecostal distinguishes the two. Unlike the holiness tradition, both Pentecostal and apostolic traditions understand speaking in tongues to be the initial evidence of Spirit baptism. And unlike holiness and Pentecostal bodies, the apostolic tradition rejects the doctrine of the Trinity and baptizes only in the name of Jesus.

All three traditions have a strong emphasis on holiness of heart and life and entire sanctification. Their experience of Spirit baptism encourages egalitarian practices, the rejection of racism, and increased openness to participation and leadership by women and the poor.

See also Baptism with the Holy Spirit; Christian Perfection (Entire Sanctification); Holiness Denominations Worldwide; Holiness Movements: American, British, and Continental; Pentecostalism; Pentecostal Theology; Sanctification; Women's Role in the Church.

Resource

Sanders, Cheryl J. *Saints in Exile: The Holiness-Pentecostal Experience in African American Religion and Culture.* New York: Oxford University Press, 1996.

HENRY H. KNIGHT III, PHD

SATAN

See DEVIL/SATAN.

SCIENCE AND THE BIBLE

Science and the **Bible** have had a long, sometimes complementary, sometimes unnecessarily conflictive, relationship.

Christian theology exercised a determined influence on culture during the Constantinian era of the fourth century. Basil of Caesarea's (ca. 330-79) *Hexameron* was a series of sermons on the six days of creation endorsing the Ptolemaic worldview (geocentric). Nothing controversial emerged from the relationship between the Bible and the Ptolemaic universe. In the West, Ambrose, bishop of Milan (ca. 339-97), restated Basil's view.

When Nicolaus Copernicus (1473–1543) restructured the Ptolemaic system, science took a new direction, although at this point Copernicus's mathematical calculations were not very controversial. But Galileo Galilei (1564–1642) provoked controversy by challenging the interpretation of the Bible that assumed the Ptolemaic cosmology.

Although the **Roman Catholic Church** treated the Ptolemaic cosmology as sacrosanct, **Protestant** theologians were more open to scientific discoveries. Scientists of Puritan background dominated the Royal Society, the famous learned society for scientists established in London by Charles II. Prominent among them was Sir Isaac Newton (1642–1727), who affirmed the calculations of Galileo. Most eighteenth-century theologians, including John Wesley, accepted the Newtonian model as the preferred understanding of the universe, although this gave support to **Deism**. **John Wesley** added his revelational theology, and the Bible and science again lived in peace.

Early in the twentieth century, Newton's mechanical universe gave way to the work of Albert Einstein. The universe was now understood in relational terms. None of this challenged biblical interpretation, except for the mid-nineteenth-century eruption of Charles Darwin's *On the Origin of Species* (1859). Darwin initially received appreciation from theologians such as Frederick Temple of the United Kingdom in 1885 and B. B. Warfield of the United States in 1910. But the American modernist-fundamentalist controversy destroyed the initial harmony. Atheists and humanists followed T. H. Huxley in using Darwin's theory to argue that science and faith have always been in conflict and that evolution disproved divine creation. **Fundamentalists** swallowed this propaganda; they reacted by treating the Christian doctrine of creation as scientific theory, thus producing "creationism."

By the middle of the twentieth century and into the twenty-first century, new hermeneutical models for Scripture and theology offered renewed biblical understanding and authority. Within the narrative, poetic, and literary structure of biblical interpretation now used by reputable biblical scholars, humanity is defined theologically in relationship to God, that is, the image and likeness of God. By this understanding, God assigned humanity the important role of creation's steward, not its exploiter.

Natural science and the Bible are now viewed by many as dialogue partners. The Bible and science together authenticate the importance of preserving creation according to God's intention. From the book of Genesis onward the biblical model supports an integration of the scientific enterprise and humanity recognizing and respecting God's creative activity.

Contrary to charges made by many, leading scientists who are Christians, such as Francisco J. Ayala and Francis Collins, and theologian-scientists, such as John Polkinghorne and Alister McGrath, are demonstrating the compatibility between the Bible and reputable science.

See also Biblical Theology; Biblicism/Bibliolatry; Church Fathers; Cosmology/Cosmogony; Creation, Care for the (Ecology); Creationism; Evolution/Evolutionary Biology; Modernity; Natural Science; Philosophy of Science; Secular/Secularism/Secularization; Social Sciences.

Resources

Berry, R. J., and T. A. Noble, eds. *Darwin, Creation and the Fall: Theological Challenges.* Nottingham, UK: InterVarsity Press, 2009.
Giberson, Karl, and Francis S. Collins. *The Language of Science and Faith.* Downers Grove, IL: InterVarsity Press, 2011.
Polkinghorne, John C. *Science and Creation: The Search for Understanding.* Philadelphia: Templeton Foundation Press, 2006.
Walton, John H. *The Lost World of Genesis One.* Downers Grove, IL: IVP Academic, 2009.

DAVID RAINEY, PHD

SCRIPTURE, THEOLOGY OF

Calling a set of writings "scripture" means they function with authority for a particular religious community. To speak of the theology of scripture, then, is to ask how this authority should be understood and practiced.

In the Christian faith, there are diverse ways to understand the Bible's authority. Some look to the **Bible** for answers to contemporary questions involving not only traditional religious topics but also physical anthropology, geology, medicine, nutrition, and politics. Other Christians assess the Bible primarily as a record of ancient and interesting religious practices having no authority beyond that. **John Wesley**, differing from both of these assessments, understood Scripture in a way informed by his church's interpretive tradition.

Wesley was a loyal son of the **Church of England**, which had a long-standing theology of Scripture. In the Thirty-Nine Articles of Religion (1563) the Church of England described clearly what the Bible offers the church—guidance in salvation and the moral life. In 1784 Wesley edited the Thirty-Nine Articles of Religion down to the twenty-five he sent to the American Methodists. He retained the two articles of religion that dealt with the Bible.

Anglican article 6 (article 5 in Wesley's edition) asserts that the Bible contains "all things necessary to salvation" and that nothing in addition to what the Bible asserts about salvation can be required of believers. Article 7 (article 6 in Wesley's edition) further says the OT remains important for the Christian community. It provides eternal promises and moral guidance. The Bible, then, is an authoritative guide for Christians on salvation and morality.

This doesn't settle all questions about interpretation (**hermeneutics**). But for Wesley and his followers, the articles placed discussion of biblical authority in a defined context—salvation and the quality of life (morality) that evidences salvation. Scripture must be taken seriously (authoritatively) *because* salvation is of ultimate importance.

How does a Wesleyan understanding of the Bible as Scripture play out in practice?

Two contemporary biblical scholars in the Wesleyan tradition have answered the question. Joel Green, in "Contribute or Capitulate? Wesleyans, Pentecostals, and Reading the Bible in a Post-colonial Mode" (2004), says, "The authority of scripture is best discerned in the lives (and not only the assertions) of those communities oriented around scripture" (81-82). Similarly, Richard Hays says that Paul claims "the true meaning of Scripture is made manifest in the transformed lives of the community of faith" (1989, xiii).

Green and Hays faithfully represent Wesley's emphasis on concrete and observable lived obedience. In short, when Jesus' disciples live as though their sins have been forgiven, when they exhibit a radical witness of humble love where their joy arises from serving one another and God, then the divinely inspired nature of Scripture is evidenced.

Wesley himself applied the best scholarly knowledge of his day to the Scriptures to aid his exegesis. Unlike some scholars today, though, Wesley would not try to get "behind" the text to some supposedly more primitive truth but would emphasize the plain reading of the basic story of God and humanity. Wesley recognized that, more often than not, people become convinced of Scripture's authority when they encounter persons who have been

transformed by biblical truth, not through arguments about biblical authority. Wesleyans believe an incarnational witness to the Bible's authority is far
more convincing than arguments about the inerrancy or infallibility of the
text itself.

See also Bible; Biblical Theology; Biblicism/Bibliolatry; Christian Ethics/
Moral Theology; Love; Narrative Theology; Scripture, Wesleyan Approach
to; Wesley, John, Theology of.

Resources

Campbell, Ted A. "Texts of the Apostles' Creed, the Twenty-five Articles of Religion,
and the General Rules." In *Methodist Doctrine: The Essentials*. Nashville: Abingdon
Press, 1999.

Green, Joel B. "Contribute or Capitulate? Wesleyans, Pentecostals, and Reading the Bible
in a Post-Colonial Mode." *Wesleyan Theological Journal* 39, no. 1 (Spring 2004): 74-
90.

———. *Reading Scripture as Wesleyans*. Nashville: Abingdon Press, 2010.

Hays, Richard. *Echoes of Scripture in the Letters of Paul*. New Haven, CT: Yale University
Press, 1989.

GREGORY S. CLAPPER, PHD

SCRIPTURE, WESLEYAN APPROACH TO

The **Bible** is the only authoritative text for Wesleyans. While reason, tradition, and experience are foundational for theology, Wesleyans accept the
Reformation principle of Scripture alone. Scripture is the touchstone for all
matters of faith and practice. Its authority for the people of God is unique
and supreme. It instructs, challenges, guides, and corrects.

For Wesleyans, Scripture's purpose is to reveal God's solution to rebellious humanity's marred relationship with God and each other. Scripture has
a **soteriological** and hence **Christological** orientation.

The Bible's authority in the **ecclesia** is dynamic and active through the
Spirit. It is not understood in a scholastic or **fundamentalist** fashion, the lat-
ter of which attaches authority to the Bible's very words. Its authority for
Wesleyans also differs significantly from the authority the Qur'an has for
Muslims and the Tanak (the name of the Jewish Bible) for Jews.

Almost all who read the Bible do so in translation rather than in the
original Hebrew, Greek, and Aramaic. Translations inevitably differ, making
a literalistic reading difficult to sustain. Thus divine activity in Scripture is
deeper and broader than debates about verbal inspiration imply. The Holy
Spirit has been active throughout the process of Scripture formation. The
Spirit inspired the writers and is active in the Bible's preservation, collection,
transmission, and translation.

Wesleyans are a "people of the book" because they believe that God revealed himself supremely in **Christ** and that Scripture points to him. Scripture is the inspired Word of God because through it the redeeming activity

of the triune God is manifest. Wesleyans are particularly attentive to the story of God's seeking and loving engagement with creation as its Creator and Redeemer. The story spans the catastrophic account of human disobedience all the way to the Messiah's coming. It includes the re-creation of God's holy people in Christ through the Spirit, and God entrusting the mission of reconciliation and new creation to them. The consequence of all this is that Scripture should be read through the lens of Jesus and illuminated by the **Spirit** in harmony with the **hermeneutical** strategy of the NT writers.

Wesleyans consider the Bible as a whole to be authoritative. They focus primarily on the overall direction in Scripture. Hence they shun proof-texting and prefer instead to interpret difficult passages in the light of the big picture of God's revelation in the whole of Scripture. They are not troubled by Scripture's diversity, seeing the particularity of God's engagement with Israel as intended for Israel's rescue and election and for our instruction.

Wesleyans reject using Scripture as a textbook for biology, anthropology, cosmology, physics, or geography. They don't use it as a collection of prophecies to which God can be held accountable. Rather, Scripture is a *performative* word; it continues to challenge those who are reconciled to God, urging them to live to reflect the character of the Holy Trinity and their identity as the holy people of God. Christians are to be a **kingdom** of priests and a holy nation. Scripture is thus a means of grace for God's people. It is part of how God through the Spirit is forming holy people; he retells their ancestral story and forms them as his agents for achieving his purposes in his creation.

See also Biblical Theology; Christology, New Testament; Jesus of Nazareth; Kingdom of God; Revelation; Sacraments; Scripture, Theology of; Wesley, John, Theology of.

Resources
Lodahl, Michael. *The Story of God.* 2nd ed. Kansas City: Beacon Hill Press of Kansas City, 2008.
Wright, N. T. *The Last Word.* New York: HarperCollins, 2005.

KENT E. BROWER, PHD

SECOND COMING OF CHRIST/PAROUSIA

In the Synoptic Gospels **Jesus** predicts his return to earth with divine glory, in the role of cosmic judge (Matt. 25:31-46; Mark 8:38). He takes over the OT notion of the "day of the Lord," when God would come to judge the world, punish the wicked, and deliver and bless those who were faithful to him. Jesus also sees his return as fulfilling the Son of Man figure in Daniel (Dan. 7:9-14; Mark 13:26; 14:62).

Jesus is presented as the Giver of resurrection life. At his return he will command God's angels to gather the elect into God's kingdom. He will welcome into the **kingdom** those who trusted him, and he will reject the unworthy (Mark 8:38; 10:29-30; 13:26-27; cf. John 5:28).

Jesus taught that his return (or *parousia*) would be preceded by social and cosmic woes, including false messiahs and persecution of his followers. This echoes Jewish **apocalyptic** expectations about the woes to precede messiah's coming. He repeatedly warns that the day is unknowable, so disciples ought to live always ready to meet their Lord. Several parables speak of the need to be faithful and watchful, "for the Son of Man is coming at an unexpected hour" (Luke 12:36-40; Matt. 24:45-51; 25:1-13, 14-30).

The **Gospels** do not speculate on the shape of life after Jesus' return. The glory of being with the Lord, and in the kingdom, is hope enough.

In John's gospel Jesus' promised return points in places to its having occurred in the church's post-Easter experience of the Spirit, who mediates the presence of Father and Son (John 14:18-23, 26; 16:7-11, 16-24). On the other hand, John also preserves teaching about a future return of Jesus at history's end to judge humanity and resurrect believers (John 5:25-29; 6:44; 21:20-23; 1 John 2:28; 3:2).

In the Pauline letters, the parousia is the fulfillment of the OT day of the Lord. It will be preceded by a great apostasy led by the "man of lawlessness" (2 Thess. 2:1-8, NIV). Jesus will return in glory to save and transform living believers and to raise the dead in Christ (1 Thess. 4:15–5:3). He will lead an angelic army in a fiery theophany of judgment to punish the wicked, excluding them from the divine presence (2 Thess. 1:6-10; cf. Rev. 19:11-21). However, Jesus delivers believers from this "wrath" (1 Thess. 1:10; 5:9). His return will mean the final triumph of God over sin and death on behalf of his people (1 Cor. 15:24-26). This return is the blessed hope of Christians, who look forward to resurrection life in fellowship with their Lord and Christians who have died (1 Thess. 4:17; 5:10). They pray for Christ's return (1 Cor. 16:22). And the material world will be transformed also at Christ's return, partaking in its own way in the glory of the age to come (Rom. 8:19-25; probably as the dwelling of the saints).

In the remainder of the NT, the hope of Jesus' return is a source of encouragement, especially to believers who suffer (James 5:7-8; 1 Pet. 1:7, 13; 4:13; 5:4; 1 John 3:2; Rev. 3:11). Second Peter defends Jesus' return against doubt arising because of the parousia's delay (1:16-19; 3:4, 9-10). In Revelation, as in Paul, Jesus' return marks God's triumph over the forces allied with Satan, ending their rebellion, violence, and deception of humanity (19:11-21). They are destroyed, this age will be ended, and a new era will be inaugurated where Christ and God will reign with the risen saints on a renewed earth (21:22-23). And so the church prays for Jesus' return (22:20).

See also Christology, New Testament; Destiny of the Unevangelized; Eschatology, Biblical; Hell; Immortality/Life After Death; Resurrection.

Resources

Goppelt, Leonhard. *Theology of the New Testament*. 2 vols. Translated by John Alsup. Grand Rapids: Eerdmans, 1981-82.
Marshall, I. Howard. *New Testament Theology: Many Witnesses, One Gospel*. Downers Grove, IL: InterVarsity Press, 2004.

TERENCE PAIGE, PHD

SECOND TEMPLE JUDAISM

The term "second temple" refers to the **temple** built by permission from Cyrus the Persian following his conquest of Babylon (2 Chron. 36:22-23; Ezra 1:1-4). This occurred under the leadership of Zerubbabel, the governor of Judah, ca. 520 BC. According to the book of Ezra (5:1; 6:14), prophets Haggai and Zechariah were instrumental in the project's effort. Herod the Great significantly expanded the temple precincts and embellished the sanctuary. The second temple and buildings were destroyed at the end of the war with Rome, AD 70.

Second Temple Judaism (2TJ) refers roughly to this period but extends to the beginning of the rabbinic period associated with Jamnia (ca. AD 90s) and even further to the end of the Second Jewish-Roman War (132-35). The term lies behind similar terms: Second Temple period and Second Temple literature. The phrases replace the older "intertestamental period," a Christian designation of the period between the last books of the OT and the beginning of the NT. The designation "2TJ" has the advantage of referring to a more clearly defined historical period. Its beginning is marked by Israel's postmonarchical period; its end is marked by the loss of temple and self-government following disastrous revolts against Rome.

One can still read about the "silent years" between Malachi and Matthew when there was no revelation. But in fact this was a period of immense development and change, with a flurry of literary production. During this period the texts we call the Old Testament developed into collections of authoritative Scripture and achieved the form we recognize today. The nature, form, and interpretation of these Scriptures were the focus of a multitude of other important texts of the period, including those of the NT. The OT period texts that came to be authoritative became part of our canonical **Bible** with the establishment of the codex, or book form, in the fourth century AD.

Discovery of the **Dead Sea Scrolls** in the mid-twentieth century added exponentially to firsthand information about 2TJ, shedding further light on books that compose the Apocrypha and the Pseudepigrapha. The **Dead Sea Scrolls** show the diversity of thought and religious practice as Judaism grappled with its loss of sovereignty under the Persians and Greeks and its eventual domination by Rome. The brief period of independence under the Hasmonaeans (Maccabees) in the second and early first centuries BC promoted competing ideas about what Israel should be.

A major issue was the legitimacy of the Hasmonaean kings for those expecting the return of the Davidic dynasty, the Messiah. From this ferment arose groups known in the NT as the **Pharisees** and **Sadducees**, as well as Zealots and a host of lesser-known parties.

Overall, two factors mark 2TJ: (1) the centrality of the temple for leadership and identity and (2) focus on written Scripture—the Book. Thought and practice of worship focused on the temple's sanctity. All groups tried to live appropriate to its **holiness**. The teachers of each party explained the meaning of holiness, the Pharisaic scribes being most influential. After the temple was destroyed, Judaism had to decide how to continue to survive. The Scriptures, properly interpreted by rabbis, became the focal point of faith and practice. For early Jewish Christians, the focal point of interpretation was **Jesus** the Messiah.

See also Scripture, Theology of; Torah.

Resources

Jaffee, Martin S. *Early Judaism: Religious Worlds of the First Judaic Millennium.* Upper Saddle River, NJ: Prentice Hall, 1997.
VanderKam, James C. *An Introduction to Early Judaism.* Grand Rapids: Eerdmans, 2001.

DWIGHT D. SWANSON, PHD

SECT

A sect is a church branch or offshoot of Christianity. Sects may represent new developments in Christianity or branches off existing denominations. The English word "sect" derives from Latin, which may mean either "to follow" (*secta*) or possibly "to cut" (*secare*). The former word suggests a conventional religious tradition believers follow. The latter suggests disconnection from a tradition and may convey a negative connotation.

In Scripture, references to sects do not convey negative connotations. The Greek word for sect (*hairesis*) is usually translated as party or faction. The **Pharisees** (Acts 15:5; 26:5) and the **Sadducees** (Acts 5:17) were described as being sects or as containing sects. Early Christians were referred to as a Jewish sect (Acts 24:5, 14; 28:21-22) and were at first treated that way by the Romans. However, *hairesis* is also the root word for "heresy."

In the **early church**, sectarianism was rebuked. Paul chastised the Corinthian Christians for their divisiveness, claiming alternately that they belonged to Paul, Apollos, Cephas, and Christ (1 Cor. 1:10-12; 3:3-4). Elsewhere Paul condemned "enmities, strife, . . . quarrels, dissensions, [and] factions" (Gal. 5:20). Factionalism could become apostasy or heresy, representing beliefs, values, or practices contrary to the teaching of Jesus. Heresies were condemned (Gal. 1:8-9; 2 Pet. 2:3, 17-22), and Christians were warned against them (1 Tim. 4:7; Titus 1:10-14; 2 Pet. 3:17).

Sociologist Max Weber (1864–1920) and theologian/sociologist Ernst Troeltsch (1865–1923) devised church-sect typologies that distinguish between historic expressions of religion (church) and alternative manifestations (sect). Traditional religion is thought to uphold longstanding beliefs, values, and practices. Sects supposedly promote unconventional beliefs, values, and practices, or they claim to restore original ones that have been neglected or forgotten. Often sects are identified as practicing exclusive membership, attempting to restore primitive Christianity, opposing or withdrawing from contemporary culture, and looking forward to the imminent end of the world. Sometimes sects stimulate Christianity in constructive, albeit limited, ways.

Rather than a typology, the terms "church" and "sect" may represent a continuum between ideal and radically different manifestations of a religion. For example, the continuum may range from an ideal understanding of the church to a heresy that distorts historic Christianity. In between, the continuum may include existing churches, denominations, sects, and cults. Although the term "sect" often conveys a negative connotation, it is not nowadays associated with heresy.

See also New Apostolic Reformation/New Apostolic Movements; New Church Movements; Third Wave Theology; Traditional Religions.

Resource

Stark, Rodney, and William Sims Bainbridge. "Of Churches, Sects, and Cults: Preliminary Concepts for a Theory of Religious Movements." *Journal for the Scientific Study of Religion* 18, no. 2 (1979): 117-33.

DON THORSEN, PHD

SECULAR/SECULARISM/SECULARIZATION

The term "secular" derives from the Latin *saecularis*, which denotes "relating to an age" or "relating to the world." The "secular" is "other than the sacred." Describing something as secular presupposes a distinction between what is recognized as religious or sacred and the remainder of human life and culture. The distinction assigns no priority to sacred or secular. The secular cannot account for the sacred, and the sacred isn't needed to explain the secular.

The modern era witnessed the process of *secularization*. More and more of what had once belonged to the sacred acquired a secular explanation—the causes of disease, for example. Emergence of the physical and social sciences, the eighteenth-century Enlightenment, modern economic theory, modern political philosophy, the industrial revolution—all played roles. Eventually, approaches to human life and culture developed that made minimal reference to religion. Public policy and discourse came to be seen as inappropriate venues for religious influence and discussion. Reason and pragmatism, not divine guidance, became the guide for arranging and governing society. The role of the sacred increasingly shifted from the public realm to the private.

The religious wars of post-Reformation Europe contributed to secularization. The Crusades had witnessed violent conflict between Christians and Muslims and between Christians in the West and East. But the European Thirty Years' War (1618-48) witnessed a devastating conflict among Catholics, Lutherans, and Calvinists. It was a contest for religious control of central Europe. The brutal competition in God's name profoundly affected many Europeans, especially intellectuals. No longer was it defensible to make major decisions based on ecclesiastical authority or appeal to revealed truth. Instead, a new ground for human life and society was sought by looking to reason and empirical experimentation.

This conviction inspired Scottish philosopher David Hume's *Dialogues on Natural Religion* (1779, which rejects religion as a basis for morality) and Immanuel Kant's *Religion Within the Limits of Reason Alone* (1793). Kant had spoken of "enlightenment" as humanity taking responsibility for its own actions without resorting to divinely imparted knowledge. Kant counseled, "Have courage to use your *own* understanding!" (Kant [1784] 1991, 54).

Secularism is an extreme form of secularization. It names the process by which in a few centuries the West moved from being a society where it was almost impossible not to believe in God to one where belief is optional or often discredited as intellectually and morally deficient. Secularism is the extreme conclusion of the eighteenth-century Enlightenment's demand for freedom from oppressive authorities and freedom for autonomous, critical, rational thought. The term was coined in the 1840s by George Jacob Holyoake, a British atheist and reformist. But its roots lie in the Italian Renaissance and, before that, in Greek and Roman philosophy.

According to secularism, the sacred, understood as transcending the secular, is an illusion. The physical world, human culture, and even religions are best explained in consistently secular terms. Being fully explanatory, secularism has no need to appeal to God, gods, or the transcendent for knowing anything worthwhile. Instead, the natural and social sciences are generally invoked for unlocking the origins of human life, religions and their scriptures, and the universe and for acquiring knowledge about how human societies should be structured. Humans are naturally derived and fully self-determining agents. Secularism is sometimes referred to as *scientism*.

See also Greek Philosophy; Modernity; Postmodernity; Religious Freedom; Religious Pluralism.

Resources

Cox, Harvey. *The Secular City: Secularization and Urbanization in Theological Perspective.* New York: Macmillan Company, 1965.

Kant, Immanuel. "An Answer to the Question: 'What Is Enlightenment.'" 1784. In *Kant: Political Writings*, 54-60. Edited by H. S. Reiss. 2nd ed. Cambridge, UK: Cambridge University Press, 1991.

Taylor, Charles. *A Secular Age*. Cambridge, MA: Belknap Press of Harvard University, 2007.

GREGORY ROBERTSON, THD

SELF-DENIAL

Self-denial is the response we give to Jesus' invitation to follow him (Matt. 16:24). In Christian history the concept has often been misinterpreted and misapplied. Christian **discipleship** has nothing to do with suppressing or eliminating the self. Being designated a *person* is part of what it means to be made in God's image and so is not to be denied. But after humankind's original fall away from God, the God-created self became what some writers (e.g., Thomas Merton) term a "false self," one that is self-centered, self-referential, and self-reliant.

For John Wesley, Christian discipleship was inseparable from self-denial. In his sermon "Self-Denial" Wesley stresses that unlike some aspects of Christian practice that may not be required of all persons, self-denial is

absolutely, indispensably necessary, either to our becoming or continuing his disciples. It is absolutely necessary, in the very nature of the thing, to our coming after Him and following Him; insomuch that, as far as we do not practice it, we are not his disciples. If we do not continually deny ourselves, we do not learn of Him, but of other masters. (*Works*, 6:104)

Self-denial is the act and ongoing process of denying that the self is God and instead affirming that God alone is God. The grand term used to describe such self-denial is "abandonment" (used in the writings of Jean Pierre de Caussade and Oswald Chambers). It means placing oneself in God's hands so that our will coincides with God's will. Created anew by Christ through the Spirit, the self becomes indexed to Jesus' life as manifest in the NT, such as depicted in the Beatitudes.

Self-denial has an affinity with the mystical goal of "union" (**theosis**) with **God**. When Jesus' disciples, by grace, submit themselves in God's will, they are enabled to "take up [the] cross" (Matt. 16:24—our God-given mission and purpose) and follow Jesus. In this way, one of E. Stanley Jones's oft-repeated goals is achieved: "The self in your own hands is a problem and a pain; the self in God's hands is a power and a potential" (1959). For that reason Christians pray, "Thy will be done in earth, as it is in heaven" (6:10, KJV). The prayer requires self-denial.

See also Asceticism; Fruit of the Spirit; Sanctification; Spiritual Formation/ Growth; Works of Piety.

Resources

Jones, E. Stanley. *Conversion*. Nashville: Abingdon Press, 1959.

————. *Victory Through Surrender: Self-Realization Through Self-Surrender*. 1959. Reprint, Nashville: Abingdon Press, 1980.

Merton, Thomas. *The Ascent to Truth*. 1951. Reprint, Tunbridge Wells, UK: Burns and Oates, 1991.

STEVEN HARPER, PHD

SEXUALIZATION OF A CULTURE

The sexualization of a culture refers broadly to the degree to which it becomes generally acceptable to do the following:

- Determine a person's value by his or her sexual appeal and/or behavior
- Elevate physical attractiveness to a central cultural priority and equate physical attraction with being "sexy"
- Sexually objectify other people, particularly women and girls

Sexual objectification occurs when persons are turned into tools for sexual pleasure or exploitation, as opposed to their being treated with love and respect. *Sexualization* involves the implicit or explicit acceptance of sexual objectification as socially and economically normal or tolerable.

Sexualization begins in the imagination but has profound effects on the body. In a sexualized culture, men and women are taught to see each other as objects of sexual desire disproportionate to other ways of perceiving. People are socialized to be attractive, not as whole persons, but as physical bodies. From many quarters, people are pressured to conform to very narrow standards of physical attraction.

Normally, women disproportionately bear the weight of sexual objectification. While men and women are equally corrupted by a sexualized culture, the female body is most often used and abused. Global media and marketing empires disproportionally use women's bodies and body parts to sell products and to stoke appetites. Sexualized media messages even target children, especially young girls, who are socialized to be more "sexy" at an earlier age.

The sexualization of a culture contributes to related social pathologies. It drives thriving global sex trafficking and sex tourism industries. Females, particularly poor women and girls, are the major victims. Among middle and upper classes, obsession with physical attraction has produced new forms of addictions and social illnesses such as anorexia and bulimia.

Marketing of sexual desire is a multibillion-dollar global industry driven by media empires mostly headquartered in the United States. Partially or fully nude images of women's and men's bodies are used to sell everything from hygiene products to cars and running shoes. Advertising proclaims that its products can satisfy desires for acceptance, love, friendship, and sexual gratification. Sexualized marketing works to provoke dissatisfaction with oneself. "Needed" changes in ones sexual attractiveness can supposedly be achieved by purchasing and using a company's products. Advertising has a vested interest in increasing a culture's sexualization—profits increase, even as a culture's moral tone erodes.

Christians are called to sexual holiness. This is certainly true among Wesleyans, for whom Christian **holiness** includes moral purity. In keeping with the NT, Wesleyans have historically taught that holy (virtuous) persons are required to compose a holy (virtuous) people. Christians should be countercultural witnesses to the holy living that the Holy Spirit makes possible. Opposition to the sexualization of a culture should, for Wesleyans—as for all Christians, occur in one's language, thoughts, and lifestyle. Such a counter-cultural ethic demands careful exegesis of the cultural exploitation of sexual desire, open and honest discipleship that takes account of the personal and structural nature of sexualization, and countercultural behaviors lived out in redemptive ways.

See also Fruit of the Spirit; Human Sexuality; Popular Culture; Rights, Human; Virtues.

Resources
Olfman, Sharna, ed. *The Sexualization of Childhood.* Westport, CT: Praeger Publishers, 2009.
Sarracino, Carmine, and Kevin M. Scott. *The Porning of America: The Rise of Porn Culture, What It Means, and Where We Go from Here.* Boston: Beacon Press, 2008.

JAMIE GATES, PHD

SHALOM

The Hebrew term *shalom* is translated "peace" many times in the OT. It is based on the verb *shalam*, which means "to make safe, secure, whole, and complete," as well as "to fulfill or repay." The noun *shalom* denotes a state of contentment and well-nourished security. Along with marking the absence of strife, friction, or imbalance between nations and individuals, shalom includes the positive values of completeness, wellness, wholeness, friendship, restoration, and all that is good, healthy, tranquil, and prosperous.

Often in the Hebrew Scriptures, shalom is used to bless one who is departing. "Go in peace," said Jethro to indicate he blessed Moses' return to Egypt (Exod. 4:18). In connection with covenants and blessings, shalom affirms being on good terms with neighbors or hosts (e.g., Isaac and Abimelech [Gen. 26:26-31]). Shalom also refers to a good death with relationships intact. God promised Abraham that he would go to his fathers "in peace" (15:15). Solomon's name (*Shelomoh*, "his peace") symbolizes the peace with neighboring nations Solomon effected (1 Kings 5:12).

Shalom is related to truth, justice, and salvation: "Let me hear what God the LORD will speak, for he will speak peace [*shalom*] to his people. . . . Righteousness and peace [*shalom*] will kiss each other" (Ps. 85:8-10; cf. Isa. 9:6-7).

Often shalom appears in connection with a covenant the Lord has made, is making, or will make with people (Ezek. 34:25; 37:26).

Later Hebrew speakers have adopted shalom as a greeting. In Israel, "What is your peace?" means "How is it with you?" During mourning rituals the phrase "Upon her (him) is shalom" is spoken, using the name of the deceased. The Greek word *eirēnē* (ā-rā'-nā) is used in the NT as the equivalent of *shalom* (Mark 5:34; Luke 7:50; John 20:26).

See also Ethics; Justice; Liberation Theology; Peacemaking; Reconciliation; Social Justice; Works of Mercy.

KAREN STRAND WINSLOW, PHD

SHEOL/DEATH/GEHENNA

In each of its sixty-six OT contexts, the Hebrew *sheol* is a dark, pitlike underworld below the land of the living. All the dead go there. Each citation augments the meaning of *sheol*, identified with *'abbadon* ("destruction" [Prov. 15:11; Job 26:6]), *maveth* ("death" [2 Sam. 22:5-6; Pss. 6:5; 18:4-5; Hos. 13:14]), and the pit (Isa. 38:18). All the dead go there. Sending to sheol is parallel to causing death in 1 Sam. 2:6 and the suffering of the slain in battle and forsaken dead in Ps. 88:5. Sheol is associated with the earth/ground from which humans came (Gen. 2:7) and will return (3:19), for in Num. 16:30-33, the earth opens and sheol swallows the rebels alive (cf. Isa. 5:14). Biblical characters express dread of descending to sheol but accept it as inevitable (Gen. 37:35). Job's extreme suffering prompted longing for sheol (Job 3:11-19), which demonstrates the depth of his agony while still alive. Psalm 88:3-12 expresses the suffering of one who compares his misery to inhabitants of Sheol, the unmourned dead and the *repa'im* who cannot praise the Lord (cf. Isa. 14:9). Hezekiah claimed that should he die, the gates of sheol would bar him from returning to the land of the living (38:9-10).

Nonetheless, the psalmist imagines that even sheol cannot exclude God's ubiquitous reach (Ps. 139:8; cf. Amos 9:2). Psalm 16:10 reflects the psalmist's hope in God's protection from sheol and death itself: "For you do not give me up to Sheol, or let your faithful one see the Pit." In Hos. 13:14, God promises, "From Sheol itself I will save them, Redeem them from very Death" (NJPS).

The book of *Enoch* (ca. 160 BC) describes sheol as divided into four chambers where the dead, divided according to their behavior in this life, await their rewards at the resurrection: (1) faithful saints rest in the bosom of Abraham, (2) the moderately good wait for judgment day, (3) the wicked are punished, and (4) the wicked who do not warrant resurrection are tormented by fire—*gehenna*. This is the background for Jesus' story about the rich man and Lazarus (Luke 16:19-31).

The term *gehenna*, the place of punishment for sinners, comes from the name of the Valley of Hinnom (Topheth) or Gehenna, a place of child sacrifice to the god Molech outside Jerusalem (Jer. 7:31; 19:4-5; 32:35; 2 Kings 16:3; 21:6), later used for continually burning refuse. Gehenna became the metaphor for fiery penal judgment for the wicked. Although the fires of *gehenna* destroy the wicked (Matt. 5:22; 13:42, 50; 18:9), they are eternal (Matt. 25:41, 46; Mark 9:43, 46).

The Greek translation of *sheol* is *hadēs*. Peter, on the day of Pentecost, declared to the people of Jerusalem, "Foreseeing this, David spoke of the resurrection of the Messiah, saying, 'He was not abandoned to Hades, nor did his flesh experience corruption'" (Acts 2:31). To proclaim God's raising of Jesus, Paul quotes Ps. 16:10, "You will not let your Holy One experience corruption" (Acts 13:35). Between Jesus' death and resurrection, he descended into the prison (presumably of sheol) to preach to imprisoned, disobedient spirits (1 Pet. 3:19). Just as some OT passages overturn the inevitability and finality of death and sheol, so Jesus declared "the gates of Hades [Sheol] will not prevail against [the church]" (Matt. 16:18).

See also Destiny of the Unevangelized; Devil/Satan; Eschatology; Hell.

KAREN STRAND WINSLOW, PHD

SIN

Sin is both rebellion against God and failure to live out the law of love. The study of sin (hamartiology) is foundational to Christian theology, a prerequisite to understanding God's purpose in **salvation**.

The OT uses different words for sin. Most common are forms of *khet'*, indicating a "deviation" or "missing the mark" (Lev. 19:17; Judg. 20:16; Ps. 51:4). Connected to the idea of sin are individuals described as "wicked" (*rasha'* [Job 36:6; Ps. 1:6]) or others practicing "rebellion" (*meri* [Deut. 31:27; 1 Sam. 15:23]).

The NT equivalent of *khet'* is *hamartia* (Rom. 3:23; Harris 1980, 1:638), which in addition to "missing the mark" indicates a governing principle or power (Rom. 6:6; Heb. 3:13). It also designates wrongdoing in a generic sense (John 8:21; 15:22) or sin as an act (Matt. 12:31; Acts 7:60). Other terms for sin are "transgression" (*parabasis* [Rom. 4:15, KJV]), "unrighteousness" (*adikia* [1 John 5:17, KJV]), "lawlessness" (*anomia* [1 John 3:4]), and "ungodliness" (*asebeia* [Rom. 1:18]).

The Bible speaks symbolically about sin's origin. Genesis 3 portrays the unbelief and pride of Adam and Eve as the source of their disobedience. **Augustine** coined the term "original sin" to refer to humanity's initial sin and the depravity inherited from our first parents. In his *Confessions* (1.7.11), he cites as evidence of original sin his hungry cry as a newborn. Augustine identified original sin with *concupiscence* (sinful desires [see Rom. 7:7-8]), its chief manifestation being sexual desire. In this view (traducianism), depravity is communicated to the next generation through procreation. Because of the negative connotations this carries for sexuality, some have espoused the alternative federal head model. As representative of the human race, Adam made a poor choice with enduring consequences for his descendants. Paul saw Adam as pointing ahead to Christ, a foretaste of the One by whose death many would be made righteous (5:12-21).

Most Christian traditions—including **Reformed** and **Wesleyan**—uphold original sin as a truth that captures an important biblical motif. **John Calvin's** 1538 First Catechism speaks of the "corruption of human nature" (Hesselink 1997). Likewise, **John Wesley** considered original sin and its resultant depravity a "disease" that required a divine "cure" (*Works*, 6:54-65). More recent Wesleyan theologians have preferred relational metaphors. Mildred Wynkoop defines "sin" as "love locked into a false center" (1972, 158). Only renewal in grace—first, through divine pardon of sin, then moral transformation—can remedy the selfishness (Luther, *incurvatus in se* [curved in on oneself]) and alienation from God endemic to the human condition. Humans inevitably ratify sin's preexistent power by committing acts of sin.

John Wesley defined sin primarily as a "voluntary transgression of a known law" (1 John 3:4; *Works*, 11:396). While sin is often active (sins of commission), it also manifests itself through neglect (sins of omission) (see Ps. 19:12; James 4:17).

Sin can have a systemic character, evident in groups, structures, and institutions. Hebrew prophets underscored the failures of Israel's leaders, condemning evil cultural practices, such as perverting the court system by taking bribes (Amos 5:12; Isa. 33:15). Jesus' dealing with the woman caught in adultery (John 8:1-11) is a model for Christian engagement in society; the Lord first confronted the systemic sin (i.e., selective application of the Mosaic law by the powerful), then called the woman to individual **repentance**.

See also Atonement; Gospel; Involuntary Transgressions; Justification; Law and Gospel; New Birth (Regeneration); Principalities and Powers; Reconciliation; Repentance; Salvation (Soteriology); Spiritual Warfare.

Resources

Harris, R. Laird, ed. *Theological Wordbook of the Old Testament*. 2 vols. Chicago: Moody Press, 1980.

Hesselink, I. John. *Calvin's First Catechism: A Commentary*. Columbia Series in Reformed Theology. Louisville, KY: Westminster John Knox Press, 1997.

Klaiber, Walter, and Manfred Marquardt. *Living Grace: An Outline of United Methodist Theology*. Translated by J. Steven O'Malley and Ulrike R. M. Guthrie. Nashville: Abingdon Press, 2001.

Powell, Samuel M. *Discovering Our Christian Faith: An Introduction to Theology*. Kansas City: Beacon Hill Press of Kansas City, 2008.

Wynkoop, Mildred Bangs. *A Theology of Love: The Dynamic of Wesleyanism.* Kansas City: Beacon Hill Press of Kansas City, 1972.

J. GREGORY CROFFORD, PHD

SOCIAL ETHICS

Christian social ethics is systematic reflection on and application of the moral dimensions of the Christian faith as they bear on social life. The category of social ethics is distinguished from personal ethics, which deals more narrowly with personal moral action. The two are inseparable; being human is social by definition. Individuals are important for the Christian faith but are members of larger wholes. So an adequate Christian ethic is also a social ethic. But there is no universal agreement among Christians on the applicable range of social ethics.

Historically, social ethics has been the work of Christian thinkers principally concerned with urban life and its complexities, especially industrialized life. For example, Christian social ethicists deployed the Christian faith to oppose the harmful effects of a free-market economic system when it proved unresponsive to the plight of the poor and powerless.

Christians continue to debate whether and how the moral implications of the gospel should impact secular social structures. Should the impact be individual, or programmatic and structural? Historically, "conservative" Christians have tended to insist on personal transformation that, when practiced, eventually leads to broader social transformation. More "**liberal**" Christians are known for recognizing corporate or structural evil that must be addressed head-on. They stress the moral outcomes of communities of persons sharing life together. Harmful or corrupt social structures must be "saved" from their ability to make even good persons do bad things. The **social gospel movement** of the late nineteenth century expressed this conviction; the gospel includes social transformation in accordance with the **kingdom of God**.

There is strong precedent in the Bible for the latter approach to social ethics. The theme of **covenant** speaks to a mutuality of relationships. In giving the Ten Commandments, God initiated covenant with his people. "I . . . will be your God, and you shall be my people" (Lev. 26:12; see Exod. 20:1-17; Deut. 5:4-20). Privilege and responsibility are included in the Sinai covenant. The two tablets of the law include love for God and neighbor. God desired that persons at society's margins—widows, orphans, aliens—have sufficient food to eat. So landowners were not to glean to the edges of their fields (see Lev. 19:9-10). The oracles of the seventh- and eighth-century prophets highlight God's fundamental commitment to the dispossessed.

The social dimensions of covenant are no less intense in the NT, as evidenced in the two greatest commandments (Matt. 22:35-40; Mark 12:28-

34; Luke 10:25-28). Matthew's account of the Sermon on the Mount (chaps. 5–7) and Luke's account of Jesus' first sermon (chap. 4) in which he claimed that God's promises to the poor, the brokenhearted, the captives, the blind, and the oppressed were being fulfilled testify to the inseparable relationship between the gospel and social ethics.

John Wesley and the early Methodists persistently joined the two in their preaching and action. Wesley lived on a small percentage of his earnings in order to feed, house, and educate the poor. He practiced the advice he gave others: "'Gain all you can.' . . . 'Save all you can.' . . . '[G]ive all you can'" (Works, 6:130-33). For Wesley, social ethics was but a faithful expression of belief in the gospel of Jesus Christ as addressed to the complexities of human life.

See also Capitalism; Ethics; Feminist Theology; Hospitability/Hospitality; Justice; Liberation Theology; Love; Mission and Social Justice; Postcolonialism; Poverty; Rights, Human; Wealth.

Resources
Hauerwas, Stanley. A Community of Character: Toward a Constructive Christian Social Ethic. Notre Dame, IN: University of Notre Dame Press, 1981.
Marquardt, Manfred. John Wesley's Social Ethics: Praxis and Principles. Nashville: Abingdon Press, 1992.
Stackhouse, Max L. Christian Social Ethics in a Global Era. Nashville: Abingdon Press, 1995.

JAMES W. LEWIS, PHD

SOCIAL GOSPEL

The social gospel emerged during the period of industrialization and urbanization in late nineteenth- and early twentieth-century America. Its compelling conviction was that the gospel of Jesus Christ involves transforming not only individuals but social systems as well. In fact, personal transformation is incomplete apart from social transformation.

Walter Rauschenbusch (1861–1918) was a chief architect. He was a Baptist minister in a congregation on the edge of Hell's Kitchen, New York City. Rauschenbusch believed churches were obliged to ameliorate the negative impact of industrialization and urbanization on workers and the poor. Laborers from rural America and immigrants populated mills and factories primarily in the Northeast and Midwest. Workers filled the surrounding cities. Rauschenbusch's Christianity and the Social Crisis (1907), despite its advocacy of democratic socialism, synthesized the thinking of those wanting Christian theology to address complicated social issues associated with poverty, public health, housing, and working conditions. Other major figures were Washington Gladden (1836–1918), pastor of the First Congregational Church, Columbus, Ohio, and Congregational minister Charles Sheldon (1857–1946), whose novel In His Steps (1896) inspired Walter Rauschenbusch.

Various segments in American society, principally mainline Protestants, interpreted and implemented the social gospel's objectives in both progressive and conservative programs. Pastors in urban parishes, sometimes in cooperation with practitioners associated with the late nineteenth-century reformist social settlement movement, inaugurated diverse outreach ministries to help workers and their families and the poor. African-American ministers in New York City, Philadelphia, Chicago, and Atlanta spearheaded nationally known programs. Matthew Anderson's Berean Presbyterian Church, founded in Philadelphia in 1880, operated an industrial school and a building and loan association. His wife, Caroline Anderson, a physician, started a medical clinic. In Chicago, Reverdy C. Ransom's Institutional Church and Social Settlement, established 1904, included an employment bureau, kindergarten, nursery, and a men's and women's forum on public affairs. The African Methodist Episcopal Church (AME) provided funds for Ransom to purchase the Railroad Chapel to house the Chicago ministries.

Mill and factory owners often had ulterior reasons to support the social gospel. Through welfare capitalism they used the social gospel to control those whom Rauschenbusch and others wanted to empower. To discourage workers from joining independent labor unions, employers built recreational facilities, provided nurses for worker families, and, in some cases, offered profit-sharing programs. Owners also helped construct church buildings. In the Pittsburgh area, for example, steel industry officials helped finance the purchase or construction of black churches. Sometimes, they employed black clergy to recruit workers. They hired black social workers and placed them in congregations to supervise the social and religious activities of working-class parishioners. Henry Ford, founder of Detroit's Ford Motor Company, authorized pastors to recommend employees and vouch for their character. He mainly used three black Episcopal, Baptist, and AME churches.

See also Social Ethics; Social Justice.

Resource

Rauschenbusch, Walter. A Theology for the Social Gospel. 1917. Reprint, with an introduction by Donald W. Shriver Jr., Louisville, KY: Westminster John Knox Press, 1997.

DENNIS C. DICKERSON, PHD

SOCIALISM

Socialism is a modern political and economic system that aims at creating an economically and socially just society under planned governmental guidance. It advocates a centrally planned economy where the people, in the form of government, own a nation's natural resources, major public services, means of production, and their allocation and distribution. Collective decision making and equitable power relations, as opposed to political, class, or industrial hierarchies and bureaucracies, are to characterize social, political, and economic organization.

There are many types of socialism, including democratic socialism, Marxist socialism, Christian socialism, utopian socialism, and libertarian socialism.

The roots of socialism are many. Modern socialist theory traces to early nineteenth-century Europe. Its motivation derives in part from the eighteenth-century industrial revolution in England, with its attending social problems, and the stated goals of the French Revolution (1789-99): equality, fraternity, and liberty. In 1848 Friedrich Engels (1820-95) and Karl Marx (1818-83) published in England *The Communist Manifesto* (German, *Manifest der Kommunistischen Partei*). Rejecting capitalism as incurably unjust, it became a guide for political socialism. It hugely influenced twentieth-century political, economic, and military history.

With the "fall of the iron curtain" in the late twentieth century and the breakup of the Soviet Union, the political and economic influence of "pure socialism" largely disappeared—with the exception of North Korea and Cuba. China, officially Communist, has experimented with its own mixture of Communism and capitalism.

Modern socialism has Judeo-Christian roots. Many of its observers say modern **secular** socialism is but a post-Christian emancipation from its Judeo-Christian roots, a secularized version of the **kingdom of God** on earth.

In nineteenth- and early twentieth-century Europe and the United States and in mid-twentieth-century Central and South America many Christians embraced socialism in some form. They believed that as a form of social organization socialism best addresses the biblical convictions about social justice as preached by **Jesus**, the apostles, and the OT **prophets**. Christian leaders who have advocated some form of socialism include the so-called liberal theologians Frederick D. Maurice and Walter Rauschenbusch and conservatives such as nineteenth-century German theologian Johann H. Wichern and German pastor Christoph F. Blumhardt. Prominent twentieth-century figures such as Paul Tillich, Karl Barth, and Dietrich Bonhoeffer were socialists. Current Christian advocates of some form of socialism include certain Latin American **liberation theologians**: Gustavo Gutiérrez, Leonardo Boff, and Juan Luis Segundo. The Argentine United Methodist liberation theologian José Miguez Bonino is an advocate of socialism.

A form of socialism was, for a while at least, practiced in the early Christian church in Palestine (Acts 4:32-37).

See also Capitalism; Democracy; Social Gospel; Social Justice; Wealth.

Resources
Newman, Michael. *Socialism: A Very Short Introduction*. Oxford, UK: Oxford University Press, 2005.

Runyon, Theodore, ed. *Sanctification and Liberation: Liberation Theologies in the Light of the Wesleyan Tradition.* Nashville: Abingdon Press, 1981.
Tillich, Paul. *The Socialist Decision.* 1933. Translated by Franklin Sherman. New York: Harper and Row, 1977. Reprint, Lanham, MD: University Press of America, 1983.

KLAUS ARNOLD, MDIV

SOCIAL JUSTICE

"Social justice" is the label typically given the task of fairly providing goods and resources to creatures. From the Christian perspective, social justice emphasizes the biblical themes of the **righteousness** of God and the care for those in need. Social justice emphasizes God's call to humans to promote the well-being of the helpless, poor, disadvantaged, and marginalized.

Poverty and need come in many forms. Those seeking social justice engage in a variety of ways to bring about greater equality among creatures. This may involve working to distribute economic resources more equally and providing social, political, intellectual, or environmental equality. Christians acting for social justice often oppose racism, sexism, nationalism, classism, tribalism, slavery, financial disparity, and human trafficking.

Some people contrast social justice with **love**. They view love as tolerance, permissiveness, or passivity and so do not actively pursue strategies for social justice. They tend to see social justice as a matter of placing boundaries on the harm or excess caused by wealth and privilege.

Others understand social justice as an aspect of love rather than its contrast. For them, love requires acting for the common good, which means pursuing strategies that promote the well-being of those whose well-being is currently undermined. Love requires acting in fair and equitable ways, not simply trying to be tolerant or permissive.

Efforts to achieve social justice have been part of the **church** since its earliest days. In recent centuries, the **Roman Catholic** tradition has called Christians to act for social justice in the light of various social and political problems. Sometimes, Christians appeal to basic human rights or to basic human dignity and value as the motivation for social justice. Other times, Christians appeal to the belief that humans are made in God's image (*imago Dei*). Still other times, Jesus' command to love neighbors and enemies becomes the basis for pursuing social justice.

Roman Catholic priest Luigi Taparelli d'Azeglio apparently first used the term "social justice" in 1840. At the beginning of the twentieth century, a program called the **social gospel** worked for social justice in the Protestant Christian context. The best-known figure of that movement, Walter Rauschenbusch, addressed social problems such as poverty, inequality, crime, racial issues, child labor, inadequate schooling, and war. Other twentieth-century Christians particularly identified with social justice include the Reverend Doctor Martin Luther King Jr., Mother Teresa, and Archbishop Desmond Tutu.

The later twentieth-century movement known as liberation theology is closely identified with Christian social justice. It emphasizes addressing the needs of the poor as foundational for doing theology and acting as Christians. Some Christians call for a "preferential option for the poor," which means that attacking the causes of poverty should receive primary attention. Work for social justice often links with efforts to secure overall well-being or the common good.

Social justice is a common theme in the Bible. Biblical authors often addressed the imperative of acting to secure social justice. An off-quoted OT passage in support of social justice is Amos 5:24: "Let justice roll down like waters, and righteousness like an ever-flowing stream." Christians often identify Jesus' command to love one's neighbor as oneself (see Matt. 22:39) and his story about the good Samaritan (Luke 10:29-37) as key texts supporting commitment to social justice. Social justice is linked directly to NT claims about Jesus establishing the kingdom of God.

Christians in the Wesleyan tradition assign special importance to social justice because they affirm with **John Wesley** that redemption of the whole person begins in this life. Wesley believed that Christian holiness contains an essentially social dimension. In some Christian circles, social justice is synonymous with compassionate ministry.

See also Altruism/Natural Morality; Christian Ethics/Moral Theology; Justice; Liberation Theology; Love; Peacemaking; Poverty; Rights, Human; Social Ethics; Wealth; Works of Mercy.

Resources
Brendlinger, Irv A. *Social Justice Through the Eyes of Wesley: John Wesley's Theological Challenge to Slavery*. Kitchener, ON: Sola Scriptura Ministries International, 2006.
Jennings, Theodore, Jr. *Good News to the Poor: John Wesley's Evangelical Economics*. Nashville: Abingdon Press, 1990.
Weaver-Zercher, David L., and William H. Willimon. *Vital Christianity: Spirituality, Justice, and Christian Practice*. New York: T and T Clark, 2005.
Weber, Theodore R. *Politics in the Order of Salvation: Transforming Wesleyan Political Ethics*. Nashville: Kingswood Books, 2001.

THOMAS J. OORD, PHD

SOCIAL SCIENCES

The social sciences systematically study relationships within society and apply their conclusions in fields such as social work and clinical psychology. Like the **natural sciences**, the social sciences employ strict empirical research methods over **metaphysical** or theological speculation. But unlike the natural sciences, their goal is to understand sociocultural dimensions and dynamics of human behavior within and between human communities.

Emergence of the social sciences is roughly coterminous with the American Republic, both of which emerged during the eighteenth-century Enlightenment. The possibility of scientifically applying to social organization the regularities of the newly discovered laws of nature through the right use of reason was embraced as a reliable guide for organizing human communities and perceiving social trends. The application of natural law would enable scientists to predict and manage such phenomena as political and industrial revolutions. All this emerged from and fostered confidence in human progress.

Beginnings of the social sciences reach back to ancient philosophers such as Plato, Aristotle, and Confucius. They advanced all-inclusive schemes for relating social organization to human well-being. Their social visions included political, domestic, economic, and pedagogical structures, complete with where individuals of diverse rank fit within those structures. During the Middle Ages, Islamic scholars made significant social science contributions, as illustrated by Ib'n Khaldun (AD 1332–1406). His epic "combat cycle" theory explained the patterns underlying the cyclical rise and fall of civilizations.

The term "social sciences" was first employed by French philosopher Auguste Comte (1798–1857), who is considered the father of sociology. Comte argued that social scientists, led by sociologists, should join the captains of industry and rule society. More specifically, Comte thought social scientists should replace clergy and politicians as society's leaders. A new, all-encompassing "scientific religion" must be created.

At the beginning of the twentieth century, two significant changes occurred. *First,* social sciences became quantitative. Societal patterns were reduced to mathematical formulas—making them seem more "scientific." Quantitative approaches were fused with qualitative (nonmathematical) ones. *Second,* the social sciences spawned numerous hybrid disciplines. They include **sociobiology**, neuropsychology, and bioeconomics.

More recently, Karl Popper (1902-93) and Talcott Parsons (1902-79) spurred a movement to form all-inclusive "grand theories" intended to subsume smaller or midrange ones. Grand theories offered usable frameworks for utilizing information held in data banks—making it "research friendly."

In sum, the social sciences encompass related fields that share a common premise: **persons** are not solitary, nor do they exist in a vacuum. Daily life intertwines with and mutually impacts the lives of others.

The major classifications of the social sciences are as follows:

Anthropology (Greek, *anthrōpos,* "human") is the holistic science of humanity—past, present, and future. Anthropology integrates social sciences, humanities, and human biology. It has been described as the most scientific of the humanities and the most humanistic of the sciences. Breadth of scope, subject matter, and methodology typify the field. Its subfields include archaeology, biological anthropology, linguistics, and social and cultural anthropology.

Economics analyzes and describes the production, distribution, and consumption of **wealth**. Its classic definition is the "science which studies human behaviour as a relationship between ends and scarce means which have alternative uses" (Robbins [1932] 1945, 16). Its two broad branches are microeconomics, which concentrates on the individual dimensions of economics, and macroeconomics, which concentrates on general or global economics factors. Economics assumes that (1) resources are scarce, being insufficient to satisfy all wants, and that (2) "economic value" is willingness to pay by way of market transactions.

Political science describes and analyzes political systems and behavior. Herbert Baxter Adams coined the term. It encompasses political theory and philosophy, civics and comparative politics, governance, participatory direct democracy, international relations (law, policy), public administration, judicial behavior, and public policy. Political science research relies primarily on records (e.g., historical documents and official records) and secondary sources (e.g., scholarly journal articles, survey research, and case studies).

Psychology is the scientific study of how the human mind functions and how it affects human behavior. The term derives from the Greek word *psychē*, meaning "soul" or "mind." Psychology applies its methods to diverse spheres of human activity, including daily interchange and the treatment of mental illness. The specialties of psychology are many. They include social, developmental, experimental, educational, cognitive, and industrial-organizational psychology. The groundbreaking field of neuroscience is also part of psychology.

Sociology is the scientific study of human interaction. The field investigates the social rules and processes that bind and separate persons as members of associations, groups, communities, and institutions. The stem *soci* is derived from the Latin *socius*, meaning "companion" or "society." Sociology is an amalgam of (1) Durkheimian (Émile Durkheim [1858–1917]) positivism and structural functionalism, (2) Marxist (Karl Marx [1818-83]) historical materialism and conflict theory, and (3) Weberian (Max Weber [1864–1920]) antipositivism (German, *verstehen*). Its subfields include sociology of religion, education, family, sports, gender, politics, criminality, and demographics.

See also Anthropology, Theological; Capitalism; Democracy; Determinism and Free Will; Economics and the Use of Money; Feminist Theology; Globalization; Human Sexuality; Marriage; Natural Science; Science and the Bible; Sect; Secular/Secularism/Secularization; Sexualization of a Culture; Social Gospel; Social Justice; Sociobiology; Technology.

Resources

Armistead, M. Kathryn, Brad D. Strawn, and Ronald W. Wright, eds. *Wesleyan Theology and Social Science: The Dance of Practical Divinity and Discovery.* Newcastle, UK: Cambridge Scholars, 2010.

Robbins, Lionel. *An Essay on the Nature and Significance of Economic Science.* 1932. 2nd ed. London: Macmillan and Co., 1945.

JON P. JOHNSTON, PHD

SOCINIANISM

See TRINITY.

SOCIOBIOLOGY

Most animals, from ants to humans, are deeply embedded in complex social relationships—depending on them for survival (e.g., mating patterns). Sociobiology focuses on the Darwinian advantages of specifically evolved social interactive behaviors, assumed to be biologically based and genetically encoded.

As its name implies, sociobiology derives not only from biology and sociology but also from **anthropology**, zoology, and population genetics. Applied to human societies, it overlaps with behavioral ecology and evolutionary psychology.

Pioneer biopsychologist J. P. Scott coined the term in 1946. He used it in a different sense from its later use. The term was not widely used until Harvard entomologist Edward O. Wilson introduced it in his epic volume *Sociobiology: The New Synthesis* (1975). Wilson examined the evolution of social behavior across the animal kingdom.

Wilson's final chapter states that common social patterns in human behavior (like subhuman behavior) are adaptations; they exist because they confer fitness advantages. They make privileged possessors of the advantages more fit to thrive in social environments. Accordingly, sociobiologists describe themselves as *adaptationists*.

In addition, sociobiologists are *selectionists*. Their hypotheses about the adaptive functions of social phenomena assume that "advantaged" genes are selectively extracted from ancestral pools and passed down to progeny— guaranteeing their success in social transactions.

Applied to subhumans, these sociobiological assumptions are uncontroversial. But for humans, many sociobiologists contend (e.g., Richard Lewontin) that genes are *not* sole determinants. Though environment plays a significant role, there is a complex interplay between nature and nurture.

By the late 1980s the term "sociobiology" was largely replaced by "behavioral ecology," which encompasses the adaptationist, selectionist approach and refers not only to social phenomena but to asocial (counterproductive) phenomena as well. Decline in the use of "sociobiology" indicates no decline in the paradigm's popularity.

The "problem of altruism" is a central issue for sociobiologists. If Darwinian selection favors only attributes contributing to their bearers' social fitness, how did restraint in aggressive conflict, or active cooperation, evolve? It seems that selection should penalize altruism. But humans in particular perform acts that are clearly altruistic, that is, take great personal risks to save a stranger's life.

Most sociobiologists answer the question in terms of trade-offs. What is sacrificed in power is gained in increased relatedness, especially with kin. Another explanation targets the obvious advantages of reciprocation, such as the monkey who grooms another monkey anticipates being groomed.

Assessed from a Christian perspective, calculated "trade-off altruism" completely misses the meaning of biblical altruism, or love for one's neighbor. The second of the great commandments is to "love your neighbor as yourself" (Lev. 19:18; Matt. 22:36-40). This has nothing to do with trade-off altruism and everything to do with replicating God's love (agape) in community. It requires seeing one's neighbor as created in God's image and as the object of his love. The source of its achievement resides, not in a biological or social disposition, but in the transforming power of the Holy Spirit. Its goal is comprehensive re-creation in Christ's image.

See also Christian Perfection (Entire Sanctification); Love; Person; Sanctification; Science and the Bible; Social Sciences.

Resource
Wilson, Edward O. *Sociobiology: The New Synthesis.* 25th anniv. ed. Cambridge, MA: Belknap Press of Harvard University Press, 2000.

JON P. JOHNSTON, PHD

SOCIOLOGY
See SOCIAL SCIENCES.

SOCIOLOGY OF RELIGION
See SOCIAL SCIENCES; SOUL.

SON OF GOD
See CHRISTOLOGY, NEW TESTAMENT; JESUS OF NAZARETH.

SOUL
The Bible reflects a range of understandings about the soul, some of which stand in conflict with now-popular concepts that mirror aspects of Platonic thought. The Greek philosopher Plato (fourth century BC) contended that the *psychē* (Greek), or "soul," was the eternal, essential element in the hu-

man person, so although bodies perish on death, souls do not, since they then separate from the dead body. In the light of the influence of Platonic thought on early Christian theology, the presence of similar dualistic ideas such as the **immortality** of the soul is not surprising. Although the scattered biblical references to the soul and other aspects of human psychology (e.g., heart, spirit, and mind) provide mostly generalized notions about the soul and give no extended treatment of the subject, even the limited references make clear that biblical thought differs greatly from dualistic understandings of the soul.

In the OT, the soul constitutes what is essential to the human **person**. The Hebrew term *nepesh* (which the LXX translates as *psychē*) frequently refers to the person not as possessing a soul per se but as being a "living soul" (Gen. 2:7, KJV). The soul denotes who the human person truly is, so *nepesh* is often translated "person" or as a personal pronoun (e.g., Gen. 27:25; Lev. 2:1; Jer. 3:11). Although the OT typically considers the soul to be the essential core of the individual in thought, emotions, and will, it views the soul, not as something distinguishable from human life, but as what was necessary for such life or "being" (e.g., Lev. 11:10; Deut. 12:23; Pss. 16:10; 49:15). However, since Hebrew thought understood the human person in holistic terms, the existence of the soul was inseparable from the human body, with no assumed opposition between soul and body. Thus to love God with all one's soul (Deut. 6:5; cf. Mark 12:29-30) is to **love** God completely with all one's total being or life. Conversely, the loss of one's soul amounted to death itself.

The general range of understandings about the soul in the NT is similar to the OT. Nearly two-thirds of all occurrences of the term are found in the Gospels and Acts. Jesus' teachings on human life typically used the term "soul" (*psychē*) as a synonym for human life itself, including references to his own mission and death. Thus Jesus came to "give his life [*psychē*] a ransom for many" (Matt. 20:28; Mark 10:45), and "the good shepherd lays down his life [*psychē*] for the sheep" (John 10:11). Similarly, Jesus' teachings speak about how a person might save and lose his or her life (Matt. 16:25; Mark 8:35; Luke 9:24) or about hating one's soul as a condition for discipleship (Luke 14:26). This hints at a meaning of *psychē* that extends beyond one's physical life to a life provided by God's faithfulness and **grace**. Although reference to those who "cannot kill the soul" but can "kill the body" (Matt. 10:28) has been interpreted as pointing to a soul-body dualism common to Greco-Roman thought, the saying actually parallels Hellenistic Jewish texts that affirm that God, not human opposition, has final authority over the total person. Surprisingly, Paul only infrequently refers to the soul. When he does, he uses *psychē* to describe one's life (e.g., Rom. 11:3; Phil. 2:30; 1 Thess. 2:8) or an individual (Rom. 2:9; 13:1), but never does he use the term to describe life that naturally survives death. For Paul, eternal life is a divine gift, not an independent, eternal entity. Paul seems to use "soul" as paralleling the term *pneuma* (e.g., Phil. 1:27, "spirit"), but nothing suggests the soul is detached from the body, even after death. Thus, although there is no "soul" that possesses inherent existence apart from the human body, associated with the "soul" is the religious life that God gives and that death cannot extinguish. It is due to God's faithfulness that this life triumphs over death (1 Cor. 15:54-55).

See also Anthropology, Theological; Grace; Greek Philosophy; Hell; Immortality/Life After Death; Love; Person; Sheol/Death/Gehenna.

Resources
Green, Joel B. *Body, Soul, and Human Life: The Nature of Humanity in the Bible.* Grand Rapids: Baker Academic, 2008.
Murphy, Nancey. *Bodies and Souls, or Spirited Bodies?* Cambridge, UK: Cambridge University Press, 2006.

RICHARD P. THOMPSON, PHD

SPECIAL REVELATION
See REVELATION; SCRIPTURE, THEOLOGY OF.

SPIRITUAL DIRECTION/SPIRITUAL DIRECTOR
Spiritual direction is the process of helping another person or other persons become increasingly conformed to the image of Jesus Christ. It is a process of listening for the voice of God in all parts of our lives so that we may live as Jesus' **disciples**. The goal of spiritual direction is for a person or group to live the abundant life Jesus offers and to expand that life in endless stages and dimensions.

Spiritual direction is not the same thing as counseling (which aims at therapy) or limited to mentoring (which aims at instructing) or coaching (which aims at advising), even though it shares features of all these. The aim of spiritual direction is the holistic formation of Christian life, not simply problem solving. It seeks discernment, trusting that once God's will is known, God will give grace sufficient to carry it out.

A spiritual director is someone qualified to help a person or group answer the question, "Where, how, why, and in what way is God speaking to me or us?" In truth, the **Holy Spirit** is the Spiritual Director. Human spiritual directors hope to assist the **Holy Spirit** by helping persons discern and follow the Spirit's will. Sometimes spiritual direction will require referral, where more technical and/or professional help can be provided. This might include counseling, psychotherapy, or medication.

An important part of spiritual direction is that the director refrains from making his or her life definitive for another. A wise spiritual director will testify to what he or she has "seen and heard" as a Christian but will not imply that another must simply replicate that. Rather, a wise spiritual director recognizes the particularity of each person. Although Christian discipleship occurs only as part of the body of Christ, each Christian has a ministry and identity in the body. We might call one's identity and ministry a soulprint, just as he or she has a fingerprint. Spiritual directors guide Christians to become the members of Christ's body God intends them to be. While there are universal principles of Christian discipleship, spiritual directors apply them in ways that respect each person's gifts, needs, and characteristics.

Spiritual direction can occur between two persons or with a group as "direction-in-common" (a phrase used by Adrian van Kaam and Susan Muto). It can occur as a formal or "professional" arrangement between a person/group and a certified director. Spiritual Directors International has established a code of ethics for such directors and provides a forum for dialogue among formal spiritual directors.

More often, spiritual direction occurs informally, through conversations among Christian friends. In such settings, spiritual direction is given without the term ever being used and even without realizing that spiritual direction is happening.

Whether formal or informal, the goal of spiritual direction is growth in the grace and knowledge of our Lord and Savior Jesus Christ.

See also Discernment; Discipleship; Sanctification; Spiritual Disciplines; Spiritual Formation/Growth; Spiritual Warfare.

Resources

Guenther, Margaret. *Holy Listening: The Art of Spiritual Direction.* Cambridge, MA: Cowley Publications, 1992.

Jones, W. Paul. *The Art of Spiritual Direction: Giving and Receiving Spiritual Guidance.* Nashville: Upper Room Books, 2002.

STEVEN HARPER, PHD

SPIRITUAL DIRECTOR

See MEANS OF GRACE; SPIRITUAL DIRECTION/SPIRITUAL DIRECTOR; SPIRITUAL FORMATION/GROWTH.

SPIRITUAL DISCIPLINES

Christian life is lived by **grace**, but **means of grace** (avenues) are necessary for God's grace to become active and definitive. Historically, Christianity has rejected any notion of "automatic grace" and has instead spoken of *enacted grace* or a living faith. God's grace isn't so much "stuff" to be accessed at will. Rather, it refers to the active and purposive presence of God that reaches us in concrete ways. Operative in the lives of Christians, grace is made available and effective through historic practices called spiritual disciplines. They are *means* through which Christians not only receive God's grace but also accept the responsibilities it entails.

In the Roman Catholic tradition spiritual disciplines have been viewed according to two categories: **works of piety** and **works of mercy**. While Wesley uses these same categories and names, he also groups these spiritual disciplines similarly but by different names. They are the *instituted means* (prayer, searching the Scriptures, the Lord's Supper, fasting, and Christian conference) and the *prudential means* (doing no harm, doing all the good you can, and attending the ordinances of God).

Practice of these means of grace cultivates social and personal **holiness.** Lists of spiritual disciplines usually contain more items than the historic means of grace, but they describe essentially the same thing.

Spiritual disciplines can be spoken of as *spiritual exercises.* Just as one might go to a gym and use a variety of exercise machines, so we exercise our lives as Christians through diverse disciplines that help establish the rhythm of Christian discipleship—engagement and abstinence. Specific practices yield particular benefits. Taken together, they enable us to produce the **fruit of the Spirit**: "love, joy, peace, patience, kindness, generosity, faithfulness, gentleness, and self-control" (Gal. 5:22-23).

The disciplines are not merits. They are not proofs of goodness or badges of honor. We do not become more worthy Christians by practicing them. If seen in this erroneous way, spiritual disciplines result in the sin of self-righteousness and works righteousness. Most spiritual disciplines will occur out of public view, just as Jesus commanded (Matt. 6:1, 5).

Spiritual disciplines are practiced individually and collectively. When practiced privately, they eventuate in a "heart to Heart" relationship with God. When practiced in community, they provide mutual accountability in the body of Christ and an impetus for mission.

Far from being burdensome, the spiritual disciplines are doorways to liberty. They prepare Christians for joyous service, for doing what needs to be done when it needs to be done.

See also Classes, Bands, Conference, Connectionalism, Society; Discipleship; Means of Grace; Sanctification; Spiritual Disciplines; Spiritual Formation/Growth; Theosis (Deification).

Resources

Foster, Richard. *Celebration of Discipline: The Path to Spiritual Growth.* 1978. Rev. ed., San Francisco: HarperSanFrancisco, 1988.

Harper, Steve. *Devotional Life in the Wesleyan Tradition.* Nashville: Upper Room Books, 1983.

Willard, Dallas. *The Spirit of the Disciplines: Understanding How God Changes Lives.* San Francisco: HarperSanFrancisco, 1990.

STEVEN HARPER, PHD

SPIRITUAL FORMATION/GROWTH

Spiritual formation in the Wesleyan tradition is the lifelong process of being conformed to the image of Christ for the sake of others (Mulholland 1993, 12). God initiates this process and calls persons to responses made possible by **grace** and the power of God's Spirit. Formation involves coming to know God more richly by exploring the **Scriptures**, through support and nurture in the **church**, and **spiritual** practices or **disciplines.**

God's grace and power are at the heart of spiritual formation. However, God does not intend to do this work alone. God gives the individual and the faith community a role to play in the process of formation and spiritual growth.

Early in the Methodist revival **John Wesley** made an important discovery: more than **preaching** was needed for spiritual formation among the Methodists. He determined to fill the need by "joining together those that are awakened, and training them up in the ways of God" (*Works*, 3:144; journal entry for August 25, 1763). Wesley established the Methodist **societies, class** meetings, and **bands** to bring people together for **worship**, instruction, accountability, and support. In this intentional environment, persons were spiritually formed and transformed.

In the societies, early Methodists sang their faith and worshipped. As they listened to preaching, they came to understand "the ways of God." In the class meetings they processed their life experience—their successes and failures. They prayed for each other and were instructed, exhorted, and given words of encouragement. The more intimate communities of the bands focused on deep issues of the heart, the desire to be more fully given to and embraced by holy **love,** or, in the case of the penitent bands, to deal with deeply rooted **sins** and addictions. Accountability was a central formative contributor in the bands and the classes.

In a Wesleyan understanding of spiritual formation, practicing the **means of grace** is also essential. Receiving the Lord's Supper, daily Bible reading, regular times of meditation, fasting, and serious conversations with other Christians are practices that open one's heart and life to the Holy Spirit and God's grace. The means of grace for spiritual formation are as important today as they were for the early Methodists. And what the Methodist societies, classes, and bands provided is still needed.

Congregations that are true to the Wesleyan tradition will take seriously the spiritual formation of children, teens, and adults throughout life. They will intentionally articulate and live out the beauty of a Christlike, holy life, which the indwelling Spirit makes possible for all Christians.

A Wesleyan theology of spiritual formation calls the church to develop contemporary means and structures for drawing persons into community where they can explore the Scriptures, mature in their relationship with

God, and find encouragement and support to live their faith in service to God and others.

See also Discernment; Sanctification; Spiritual Direction/Spiritual Director; Theosis (Deification); Vocation and Calling; Wesley, John, Theology of; Works of Mercy; Works of Piety.

Resources

Henderson, D. Michael. *A Model for Making Disciples: John Wesley's Class Meeting.* Nappanee, IN: Evangelical Publishing House, 1997.
Knight, Henry H., III. *The Presence of God in the Christian Life.* Metuchen, NJ: Scarecrow Press, 1992.
Mulholland, M. Robert, Jr. *Invitation to a Journey: A Road Map for Spiritual Formation.* Downers Grove, IL: InterVarsity Press, 1993.
Watson, David Lowes. *The Earliest Methodist Class Meetings: Its Origins and Significance.* Eugene, OR: Wipf and Stock Publishers, 2002.

CATHERINE STONEHOUSE, PHD

SPIRITUAL GROWTH

See SPIRITUAL FORMATION/GROWTH.

SPIRITUALITY

See SPIRITUAL DIRECTION/SPIRITUAL DIRECTOR; SPIRITUAL FORMATION/GROWTH.

SPIRITUAL WARFARE

Spiritual warfare refers to the belief that God and his people are now engaged in battle against forces that fight against God's will for the church and the world. The NT provides support for this belief. Some texts refer to a spirit world beyond the observable natural order populated by spiritual powers (however defined and whatever their form) that have the ability (however gained) actively to oppose God's will (Eph. 6:12). These forces are evil spiritual entities—**demons**, evil spirits, or **angels**—led by Satan (the devil), God's archenemy.

Most texts that deal with spiritual warfare are found in Paul's epistles. They emphasize the unassailable conviction that because of Christ's crucifixion, resurrection, and imminent return, victory is assured. In Colossians, Paul writes that on the cross, Jesus "disarmed the rulers and authorities and made a public example of them, triumphing over them in it" (2:15). The apostle Paul teaches the Corinthian Christians that Christ "must reign until he has put all his enemies under his feet. The last enemy to be destroyed is death" (1 Cor. 15:25-26).

A principal NT reference that supports the metaphor of spiritual warfare and provides the theological conviction that lies behind it is Eph. 6:10-18. Here Paul uses metaphors of weapons and armor based on a well-armed Roman soldier. So armed by the Holy Spirit, Christians fight "against the schemes of the devil" (6:11, ESV). In this context the Greek word (*methodeia*) means "deceit," "trickery," "conspiracy," and "machination." The "schemes of the **devil**" can take many forms, including demonic possession, suffering and hardship, cultivating discord, greed, and even martyrdom.

Prayers, fasting, and exorcism are some of the "armor" Christians are exhorted to use in spiritual warfare.

The influence of the Enlightenment and modern science on Western Christianity has diminished its consideration of spiritual warfare. But this is not true for many "missionized people" in the **Global South** where **Pentecostal** and **Charismatic** Christians, among others, continue to emphasize a theology and practice of spiritual warfare. Accordingly, during services of **worship** it is common to designate times for liberation. Leaders call on the blood of Christ for victory over threatening spiritual forces in whatever guise they assume—corporate or individual.

This Christian understanding of spiritual warfare must not be associated with cheap exhibitionism, commercial opportunism, and sensationalism. Moreover, spiritual warfare should not be confused with spiritism, that is, communicating with spirits—specifically spirits of the deceased—through mediums (people supposedly able to communicate with the spirit world). Spiritism is unrelated to the understanding of spiritual warfare found in the NT. Christian spiritual warfare can be understood as a form of service to Christ, as participation in his efforts to redeem creation.

Some contemporary Christian groups have developed combat techniques for spiritual warfare. These include war prayers, marches for "territory conquests," spiritual mapping (e.g., determining the influence of evil powers over cities and their inhabitants), and recognizing hereditary curses (sufferings and difficulties in life that come because of evil deeds committed by ancestors). Promoters of these practices are present in several Christian groups. Their critics charge that such practices are the product of syncretism and animism.

John Wesley was no stranger to spiritual warfare. In his sermon "Of Evil Angels" (Eph. 6:12; *Works*, 6:370-80), Wesley exposes evil angels as "'wicked spirits' . . . who mortally hate and continually oppose holiness, and labour to infuse unbelief, pride, evil desire, malice, anger, hatred, envy, or revenge—'in heavenly places'" (371).

See also Deliverance/Exorcism; Folk Religion; Miracles/Signs and Wonders; Principalities and Powers; Spiritual Direction/Spiritual Director; Westernization of the Gospel.

Resources

McAlpine, Thomas H. *Facing the Powers: What Are the Options?* 1991. Reprint, Eugene, OR: Wipf and Stock, 2003.

Wink, Walter. *Engaging the Powers: Discernment and Resistance in a World of Domination.* Minneapolis: Fortress Press, 1992.

———. *Naming the Powers: The Language of Power in the New Testament.* Philadelphia: Fortress Press, 1984.

MAGALI DO NASCIMENTO CUNHA, PHD

SPIRIT WORLD

See SPIRITUAL WARFARE.

STATE RELIGION

Any religion endorsed by a government as its official religion may be considered a state religion. Very often, state religions are synonymous with government involvement in religious affairs. Different models exist, depending on how the relationship between state and religion is viewed. Within Christianity, the term "church state" is often used, even though it is not equivalent to state religion.

In AD 310, Armenia was the first country to declare Christianity its state religion, and the Roman Empire made the same declaration in 380. The Christian rulers saw it as their responsibility to care for the church's well-being, following the OT model of King David. In the eastern part of the empire, this developed into *caesaropapism*; the church was subordinate to the state. This remained the dominant model in most Orthodox countries until the twentieth-century Communist regimes replaced the Christian rulers.

In the West, the position of the pope and the church was much stronger, resulting in the domination of spiritual over temporal power. This is reflected in the rivalry between pope and emperor during the Middle Ages over who grants authority to whom (investiture controversy). The rise of nation-states in Europe during the fourteenth and fifteenth centuries reduced control of the church over the state.

During the **Reformation** the role of the state became more prominent. The Lutheran Reformation enjoyed the protection of German princes and saw the state as a guardian of the faith. In **Anglicanism** the king was head of the church. **Calvinism** was able to maintain a greater degree of independence of church from the state, while the **Anabaptist** movement favored a complete separation of church and state.

During the period of monarchial absolutism (seventeenth and eighteenth centuries), rulers such as the kings of France subordinated the Roman Catholic Church to the state and saw themselves as divinely appointed representatives of God on earth.

As a result of the European wars of religion (late sixteenth and first part of the seventeenth century) and the **Enlightenment**, state and church became more separated. The Constitution of the United States (1787) and the French Revolution (1789) favored freedom of religion and influenced church-state developments in the nineteenth century, resulting in the formal disestablishment of any specific Christian confession from being the official state religion. In some countries this did not happen until after World War II.

Even though an official separation of church and state exists in many countries, a certain level of cooperation is still practiced, reflecting specific historical and contextual circumstances.

See also Church and State; Public Theology; Radical Reformation; Religious Freedom; Rights, Human; Secular/Secularism/Secularization; Underground Church in China; Westernization of the Gospel.

ANTONIE HOLLEMAN, DRS

STEWARDSHIP

The Hebrew Bible does not normally use a distinct term for steward or stewardship. Rather, a more indirect description is commonly used, that is, a person who is "over a house" (Gen. 43:19; Isa. 22:15). The primary term for steward in the NT is *oikonomos* (composed of two root words: *oikos* [house] and *nemō* [manage]). The word for the position of steward is *oikonomia*.

A steward manages property, and a good steward manages it well. The English term "economics" derives from *oikonomia* and is closely related. In churches today a divorce between stewardship and economics often occurs. Economics and wealth creation are often left to the world of business while "stewardship" is often relegated to the church, where the term denotes tithing or giving to missions.

A healthy biblical understanding of stewardship encompasses the entire range of resource management—including wealth creation. One cannot give or care for what one does not have.

Though very important, stewardship is not limited to material dimensions. The apostle Paul understood his office as a stewardship of God's grace (Eph. 3:2; Col. 1:25). Christians are to be "good stewards of the manifold grace of God" (1 Pet. 4:10).

Stewardship is central for our identity as God's creatures. The first command God gave humankind was to "be fruitful and multiply, and fill the earth and subdue it; and have dominion over the fish of the sea and over the birds of the air and over every living thing that moves upon the earth" (Gen. 1:28). Stewardship involves all of life, even procreation. In the ancient world the family unit was the means of production. Thus having many children created a greater "economy."

The Bible makes no distinction between "sacred" and "secular" work. A person's call from God can express itself in a variety of ways. Work is part of one's calling and, if conducted effectively and in the right spirit, is an exercise of stewardship. Some tasks may appear nobler than others, but even "menial" jobs can fulfill the Christian calling. Even when people serve human masters, they are to do it "as to the Lord" (Col. 3:23, KJV). So the call to exercise dominion includes nurture and care of one's life, one's family, and the whole creation.

Wealth created through work is not to be despised or seen as evil. One can misuse wealth, but wealth is not inherently evil. It must be managed carefully, enjoyed properly, and shared with others.

No necessary incompatibility exists between a proper theological understanding of stewardship and participating in a modern capitalistic society. Recent writers have argued that capitalistic systems are more virtuous because they reward the entrepreneur and those who seek to serve others (see Schneider 2002).

Jesus harshly warns those who expect the kingdom of God to come immediately and so do not manage their resources well (Luke 19:11-27). Likewise, Paul instructs that "anyone unwilling to work should not eat" (2 Thess. 3:10).

See also Capitalism; Creation, Care for the (Ecology); Economics and the Use of Money; Idolatry; Secular/Secularism/Secularization; Virtues; Wealth.

Resources

McNamara, Patrick H. *More than Money: Portraits of Transformative Stewardship.* Money, Faith, and Lifestyle Series. Herndon, VA: Alban Institute, 1999.

Schneider, John R. *The Good of Affluence: Seeking God in a Culture of Wealth.* Grand Rapids: Eerdmans, 2002.

KEITH H. REEVES, PHD

STUDENT VOLUNTEER MOVEMENT

The Student Volunteer Movement (SVM) began unofficially in 1886 in connection with a student conference held in July of that year at Northfield, Massachusetts. Approximately 250 students attended. Two years later, the movement officially organized and adopted the name the Student Volunteer Movement for Foreign Missions. Following a brief period of consolidation, this grassroots movement grew rapidly, reportedly swelling in membership to over six thousand volunteers in the 1890s. During its nine decades of life, tens of thousands of students at hundreds of colleges and universities were involved, many of whom were mobilized for mission service from North America and Europe and deployed to Asia, Africa, the Pacific region, the

Middle East, the Caribbean, and Latin America. In addition, the SVM was instrumental in developing missiology as an academic field of study.

Several key leaders were instrumental in the movement's early growth and development. Foremost among them were Luther Wishard, who led the college ministry of the YMCA, and Robert Wilder, whose parents had been missionaries to India. Wishard and Wilder were deeply involved in organizing and leading the Northfield conference. D. L. Moody was one of the major speakers. In 1887 John Forman joined Wilder in touring more than 150 institutions to enlist student volunteers. John R. Mott, a student at Cornell who later presided at the 1910 World Missionary Conference in Edinburgh, was also part of the leadership team. Other early leaders included Robert E. Speer, who followed Wilder as secretary, and Samuel Zwemer, a renowned missionary, scholar, and writer on topics ranging from ministry to Muslims.

During the early and middle decades of the twentieth century, various issues confronted the movement, ultimately resulting in its decline. Foremost was the growing rift in American Protestantism between theologically conservative and theologically liberal Christians. At stake was whether missionary efforts would be judged acceptable and necessary for Christians. As the movement increasingly aligned itself with the **ecumenical** movement, the move toward theological liberalism and cultural relativism left the SVM without a compelling purpose.

Meanwhile, beginning around the middle of the twentieth century, a growing number of faith mission organizations emerged to fill in the gap for thousands of conservative missionaries, including the InterVarsity Christian Fellowship. By the late 1960s the SVM, now known as the National Student Christian Federation's Commission on World Missions, watched its budget and staff dwindle until dissolution of the organization became the only viable option.

See also Mission, Theology of; Missionary Movements.

NORMAN WILSON, PHD

SUFFERING SERVANT
See CHRISTOLOGY, NEW TESTAMENT.

SYNCRETISM, RELIGIOUS
Syncretism means selectively blending elements of one religion with those of another or others. The result is a somewhat integrated mythos and a significant departure from the targeted religion's defining beliefs and nature. Syncretism happens in all religions. It can be seen in such movements as the Baha'i Faith, which integrates elements of **Judaism**, Christianity, **Islam**, Buddhism, and Zoroastrianism; the Druze faith, which integrates elements of Islam with Gnosticism and Platonism; and Sikhism, which blends elements

of Islam and Hinduism. It is also visible in forms of Eastern mysticism, Yoga, occultism, **neo-paganism**, and **New Age spirituality**. Some **liberal theologians** have attempted to identify Christianity itself as a fusion of Hellenistic Judaism, the pagan religions of the Roman Empire, and the simple teaching of Jesus of Nazareth.

Syncretism differs from "bricolage," which names a more haphazard mixing of religions.

In Christian settings syncretism can be confused with **contextualization**. The latter's goal is to remain faithful to orthodox Christian faith while also achieving an authentic local expression of the faith. But even here the danger of syncretism exists. The **early church** faced this danger as it encountered Greco-Roman religions and philosophies. Over time the church developed its biblical canon, **creeds**, and worship to combat syncretistic tendencies, though the struggle against syncretism presents itself in every age.

Today, many Christians reject the historic belief that Jesus Christ is God's definitive revelation and the only way of salvation. Instead, they say there are many effective pathways to God. Tolerance and openness to other religions are the religious values they prize most. Many of them believe themselves free to combine the "truths" of other religions with Christianity. Even supposedly orthodox Christians, insufficiently instructed by Christian doctrine, often mix cultural values alien to Christianity with their Christian faith. The syncretizing element can be a functional worship of a particular form of government, race, political party, or type of economic theory.

The danger of syncretism arises each time the church seeks to make the gospel indigenous. Cultural changes affecting an established church can also pose the danger of syncretism. Churches in many parts of the world have integrated elements of **traditional religions** into their belief structure. Examples are God's Army in Myanmar; Caodaism in Vietnam; the Rastafari movement, voodoo, Candomblé, and Santeria in the Caribbean; and Chrislam in Nigeria. Syncretism often results from a tendency to undercut the full deity and humanity of the incarnate Son of God, or God's revelation to which the Scriptures bear witness.

See also Contextualization; Indigenization; Interfaith Dialogue; New Religious Movements; Popular Religiosity; Religions, Theology of; Religious Pluralism.

Resource

Leopold, Anita Maria, and Jeppe Sinding Jensen, eds. *Syncretism in Religion: A Reader.* New York: Routledge, 2004.

DAVID MCEWAN, PHD

SYSTEMATIC THEOLOGY (DOGMATICS)

In early Christian Greek tradition *theologia* referred to the doctrine (*logos*) of God (*theos*). But two of the greatest patristic intellects, Origen and **Augustine**, synthesized Christian doctrine with Platonist philosophy, and by medieval times the newly founded universities in Christian Europe applied the term to the organized presentation of all Christian doctrine or teaching. Thomas Aquinas's *Summa Theologica* synthesized Christian doctrine and the newly rediscovered Aristotelian philosophy. Following the **Reformation**, when the Reformers rejected Aristotle's influence, Lutheran and **Reformed** theologians preferred the term "dogmatics." This implied the positive presentation of Christian convictions, derived from Holy Scripture and organized according to the Nicene **Creed**, which was the *dogma* (decree) of the **ecumenical councils** of the patristic church. But post-Reformation "orthodox" Lutherans and Calvinists adopted Aristotelian logic once again to defend their dogmatic systems.

Beginning with J. P. Gabler at the end of the eighteenth century, biblical scholars tried to develop a **biblical theology** by using only biblical categories without imposing upon biblical interpretation later church theology and categories. Subsequently Friedrich Schleiermacher defined four major disciplines in the theological curriculum: biblical studies, church history, pastoral or practical theology, and systematic theology. Influenced by Schleiermacher's apologetic interest in addressing people of the **Enlightenment** and by the resulting **liberal theology**, systematic theology became strongly influenced by philosophy (by now a distinct secular discipline) in order to commend "religion" to its nineteenth- and twentieth-century "cultured despisers."

Paul Tillich strongly represented this method in the twentieth century. He worked to "correlate" the doctrinal answers of the Christian faith to the great life questions posed by secular philosophy and culture. Karl Barth, however, led a reaction to liberal theology. He worked to free Christian theology from being shaped by an alien philosophy or metaphysic. Recognizing the uniqueness of God as "Wholly Other," his massive *Church Dogmatics* aimed to restore the Reformation method of shaping Christian theology according to God's self-revelation, his holy Word, revealed through Holy Scripture. T. F. Torrance argued this was a truly "scientific" methodology. Although not narrowly Barthian, contemporary theologians such as Jürgen Moltmann, Wolfhart Pannenberg, and Robert Jenson, together with the so-called Yale school of Hans Frei and George Lindbeck and the ethicist Stanley Hauerwas, stand in this broad trajectory.

John Wesley, representing the **Anglican** tradition, did not develop a comprehensive doctrinal system. After Wesley's death, Richard Watson wrote the first Wesleyan systematic theology, which, in the fashion of his day, was strongly **apologetic**. Later Wesleyan systematic theologies include those of William Burt Pope, John Miley, Olin Curtis, and H. Orton Wiley. The Wesleyan tradition has produced no outstanding theologians with widespread influence across the Christian church.

Today some in the Wesleyan tradition are still interested in a systematic theology allied with or shaped by philosophical or metaphysical questions or systems. Their concern is predominantly with intellectual questions and theological method. Others, aware that Wesley's concerns were to shape his doctrine according to Holy Scripture in order to preach "faith, repentance, and holiness" (see *Works*, 8:472), are more interested in the new cooperation between biblical theology and systematic theology. For them, the **church** and not the academy is the primary context for Christian theology. As with Wesley, they believe theology must primarily serve the church's mission to proclaim the **gospel.**

See also Arminian Theology; Biblical Theology; Calvin, John; Church Fathers; Creeds (Nicene, Chalcedonian, Apostles', Athanasian); Fletcher, John, Theology of; Greek Philosophy; Historical Theology; Luther, Martin; Postliberal Theology; Wesley, Charles, Theology of; Wesley, John, Theology of.

Resources

Grenz, Stanley J. *Who Needs Theology? An Invitation to the Study of God*. Downers Grove, IL: InterVarsity Press, 1996.
Langford, Thomas A. *Practical Divinity: Theology in the Wesleyan Tradition*. Nashville: Abingdon Press, 1983.

THOMAS A. NOBLE, PHD

SYSTEMIC SIN
See SIN.

Tt

TECHNOLOGY

Technology is the human construction and use of material artifacts in any form for practical purposes (Greek, *technologia*: *technē* [skill, craft] and *logia* [study of something]).

Before the twentieth century, "technology" referred to the "study of technical arts." By the early twentieth century, it meant the "practical application of scientific knowledge." More recently, scholars in philosophy and the **social sciences** have identified three distinct meanings.

First, technology is a *means to fulfill a human purpose*. This definition treats the term as applicable to a specific field such as biotechnology. As a *means*, technology plays a practical or instrumental role in achieving some end or purpose. When refining oil, for example, the purpose of technology is clear. In other instances, such as the computer or genomics, the purpose of technology may be vague, multiple, and changing.

Second, technology is also a *collection of techniques, practices, and components*. For example, information technology is a toolbox of individual technologies and practices that combine various skills, processes, and raw materials. Because technology often aims at creating useful artifacts, it is goal oriented and often relies on results and techniques from **science**. This is evident in health technologies, which encompass heart pacemakers, ultrasound, magnetic resonance imaging (MRI), life-prolonging pharmaceuticals, and so on.

Third, technology can refer to the *entire collection of products, devices, and engineering practices available to a culture*. We use this definition when talking about technology's social impact, whether positive or negative.

Given technology's many successes, few would wish to return to a life without it. Many Christian theologians believe technology expresses divinely given human creativity. But technology must be governed by norms, such as wisdom, that transcend technology. All technologies can generate moral questions about their proper use. Equating technological progress with human progress is idolatrous; it turns technology into a god, an error often committed.

Technology is frequently viewed as beneficial and indispensable. For example, current uses of the Internet increase political participation by providing new ways to act in concert with others; it provides new levels of practical accountability for the public speech and actions of political leaders. "Networked citizens" are connected in communities that transcend traditional organizational, political, and geographical boundaries. The Internet provides new means of cooperation and collaboration for social activism in fields as diverse as politics, news media, religion, microfinance, and international development.

Technology has influenced and shaped human life in ways that were unexpected and sometimes unwanted. Communication technology changes how humans think and behave in social contexts. In the 1960s, philosopher Marshall McLuhan warned that "we shape our tools, and thereafter our tools shape us" (1964, xi). A medium, such as television, affects the society not only by its content but also by the characteristics of the medium itself—"the medium is the message," in McLuhan's words (7-21). The rise of cyberculture and the Internet illustrates the point. The rise of communicative power through technology means that face-to-face contact and physical touch are no longer considered prerequisites for belonging to a group or forming human relationships. If the "medium is the message," then we should expect that technologies in the twenty-first century will challenge and possibly alter our notions of friendship, community, and education.

Technology can introduce ambiguity and anxiety into human life. Video culture, for example, can blur the line between reality and virtual reality. Passive electronic entertainment appears to diminish a person's attention span and dull his or her ability to analyze complex problems. The phrase "technology in the workplace" increasingly means that a person can be engaged in his or her work anytime and anywhere.

See also Bioethics; Media; Technology, Ethic of.

Resources

Arthur, W. Brian. *The Nature of Technology: What It Is and How It Evolves.* New York: Free Press, 2009.

Borgmann, Albert. *Technology and the Character of Contemporary Life: A Philosophical Inquiry.* Chicago: University of Chicago Press, 1984.

Genesis 1:26-28, 31.

McLuhan, Marshall. *Understanding Media: The Extensions of Man.* New York: New American Library, 1964.

TERRY FACH, MA, MPHIL

TECHNOLOGY, ETHIC OF

The ethic of technology identifies the morally pertinent features of technology as a whole (especially how it shapes culture and social values). It examines the ethical problems and issues raised by particular technologies such as computing, medical and biological sciences, and information technology.

The moral assessment of technology, which began in earnest in the twentieth century, is increasingly complex. There are two major approaches to such assessment.

According to the first, technology is a morally *neutral* tool (neither morally right nor morally wrong in itself) that has yielded many practical benefits. As an *instrument*, technology is *morally* good or bad depending on its application and consequences.

The difficult ethical questions posed by technology are wide ranging. Cyber ethics examines ethical questions generated by the Internet or cyberspace, especially the privacy, control, and sharing of information. Computer technology gave birth to ethical questions about artificial intelligence and the ability of robots to reason. Biotechnology forces us to examine who should have access to personal genetic information and how to use it. How are we to decide who should and should not benefit from costly medical breakthroughs?

The second assessment considers *all* technology *value laden* because it is the product of human, goal-oriented activity. Even before its application, technology *already* expresses certain human interests and values that carry ethical importance. This assessment urges a more cautious attitude toward technology; it considers how technology shapes our ideas about the "good life" and how it redefines our most fundamental human categories. For example, emerging communication technologies that change the nature of social interaction have redefined concepts such as community and conversation. Many argue that face-to-face conversations, eye contact, and physical touch naturally maximize basic moral virtues essential for forming strong and enduring relationships. Communication technology can minimize these values. Given these questions, an ethic of technology examines whether the new technological forms of communication will support moral development of such virtues as patience, honesty, trust, and empathy as did more traditional forms of communication and social interaction.

Some critics observe a tendency to worship technology and equate technological progress with human progress. This results in decisions about technology stripped of their moral implications. Decisions become merely practical and expedient (Ellul 1990). Similarly, others warn against "the deification of technology, viz., where culture seeks its authorization in technology, finds its satisfactions in technology, and takes its orders from technology" (Postman 1992).

Some ethicists see an ameliorative link between technology and an increase in democracy, social activism, and political accountability. They see a positive relationship between useful information, education, and humanitarian relief.

An ethic of technology will be guided by *a moral point of view*, that is, a set of beliefs about human nature and ultimate goodness. For example, a *Christian* ethic of technology will affirm that all human meaning is grounded in God. Humans are created in God's image. In a special sense, humans are *cocreators* with God and are given dynamic partnership with him. Creativity is a gift to be used for God's glory and for the neighbor's and nature's well-being. This requires that humans be self-critical of their technical achievements. If not, driven by pride or profits, God will be left out of the picture and technology will obstruct God's intentions for his creation. Moreover, Jesus calls his disciples to promote *shalom*. This entails a social vision that promotes the well-being of all people, especially the poor.

See also Bioethics; Creation, Care for the (Ecology); Ethics; Justice; Social Justice; Technology.

Resources

Borgmann, Albert. *Power Failure: Christianity in the Culture of Technology*. Grand Rapids: Brazos Press, 2003.
Ellul, Jacques. *The Technological Bluff*. Translated by Geoffrey W. Bromiley. Grand Rapids: Eerdmans, 1990.
Postman, Neil. *Technopoly: The Surrender of Culture to Technology*. New York: Alfred A. Knopf, 1992.

TERRY FACH, MA, MPHIL

TEMPERS AND AFFECTIONS

"Tempers" and "affections" are terms that, along with "understanding" and "liberty," constitute the natural image of God in John Wesley's **theological anthropology**. They are motivating dispositions of the heart, inclinations of the will. As such they are emotions, not in the sense of passing feelings, but as enduring desires and motivations.

This understanding distinguishes Wesley's anthropology from later nineteenth-century Methodist theology, which assumed a conflict between reason and emotion for controlling the will. Wesley's anthropology presupposes no such conflict and understands the will, not as a neutral capacity for choice, but as inclined and motivated by the tempers and affections that constitute it.

Because tempers and affections constitute the heart and motivate the will, they are crucial to **salvation**. Wesley states their importance: "True religion, in the very essence of it, is nothing short of holy tempers" (*Works*, 7:56). He echoes Jonathan Edwards, who in *Treatise on Religious Affections* wrote, "True religion, in great part, consists in holy affections." Wesley uses the term "temper" much as Edwards uses "affections." There is disagreement over how Wesley himself related the terms. Kenneth Collins and Randy Maddox argue that Wesley used "affection" to describe the onset of an emotion and "tempers" for its habitual presence in the heart. Gregory Clapper says Wesley used the terms synonymously.

The sinful heart consists of unholy tempers, while holy tempers are the **fruit of the Spirit**, centered on **love** for God and neighbor. Although **prevenient grace** partially restores human understanding by providing a moral **conscience**, regeneration (the **new birth**) renews the heart by instilling holy tempers. **Sanctification** consists of holy tempers brought to fullness in **Christian perfection**; they constitute the restored moral image of God.

Holy tempers necessarily exist only within a relationship with God through Christ. Tempers continue to be shaped by this relationship over time, generally through the **means of grace**, including **works of mercy** and **works of piety**.

Tempers also incline persons to see and understand the world in particular ways. Thus an unholy temper such as love of money would lead to one way of relating to God and others, while love for God and neighbor inclines one to recognize and meet the needs of others. **Holiness** of heart thus leads to holiness of life.

Contemporary theologians Robert C. Roberts (*Spiritual Emotions* [2007]) and Don E. Saliers (*The Soul in Paraphrase* [1980]) have developed concepts similar to Wesley's understanding of tempers.

See also Spiritual Disciplines; Spiritual Formation/Growth; Virtues; Wesley, John, Theology of.

Resources

Clapper, Gregory S. *John Wesley on Religious Affections.* Metuchen, NJ: Scarecrow Press, 1989.

———. *The Renewal of the Heart Is the Mission of the Church: Wesley's Heart Religion in the Twenty-First Century.* Eugene, OR: Cascade Books, 2010.

Steele, Richard B. *"Gracious Affections" and "True Virtue" According to Jonathan Edwards and John Wesley.* Metuchen, NJ: Scarecrow Press, 1994.

HENRY H. KNIGHT III, PHD

TEMPLE

The Jerusalem temple played a central role in the religious and cultic life of ancient **Israel**. The OT uses a variety of terms to describe this important structure. The Hebrew word *hekal* connotes a large building or palace that functioned as the dwelling place of God (2 Kings 23:4; 24:13; 2 Chron. 26:16; 27:2; 29:16; Jer. 7:4; 24:1; 50:28; 51:11). Other basic terms such as *bet Yahweh* (house of Yahweh) or *bet 'Elohim* (house of God) refer to the temple as the place of God's residence (1 Kings 7:12, 40, 45, 51; 1 Chron. 9:11, 13, 26; Neh. 6:10; Zech. 8:9). The term *makon leshibteka* referred to the temple as the place where God "sits" (1 Kings 8:13), and the word *ma'on* signified the location of God's holy "habitation" (Jer. 25:30). The term *miqdash*, often translated "sanctuary" or "shrine," came to describe the temple itself (Ps. 74:7) and the surrounding courtyards (Ezek. 44:1).

The history of the temple is extensive, and its existence stretched over hundreds of years. King Solomon constructed the first temple in the tenth century BC (1 Kings 5–8). It was destroyed by Babylonians in 586 BC (2 Kings 25:9; 2 Chron. 36:19; Jer. 52:13) and later rebuilt under the leadership of Zerubbabel in 515 BC (Ezra 1:1-11; 3:1-13; 4:24–6:22; Hag. 1–2; Zech. 1:1–8:13). King Herod (37-4 BC) thoroughly refurbished the second temple complex, but the Romans, under Titus, eventually burned down this structure in AD 70.

Unlike the tabernacle, which served as a temporary, portable shrine during Israel's formative period (Exod. 25–31; 36-40; Num. 7–9), the temple represented a permanent structure based in the holy city of Jerusalem. It was built in a rectangular pattern, 100 cubits long and 50 cubits wide (165 feet by 84.5 feet). The inner space of the temple was divided into three main sections. The *'ulam* represented the forecourt or "vestibule" (1 Kings 7:19) and served as the entrance into the main hall. The *hekal* or main room formed the largest section of the interior space. It housed ten lampstands, a table containing the daily bread of presence, and an altar for burning incense. Much of the daily temple activity occurred in the *hekal*. Two staircases at the end of the *hekal* led into the third room called the *debir* or "inner sanctuary." Often referred to as the holy of holies, this room contained the ark of the covenant, including the two tablets of stone and two cherubim carved from olive wood and covered with gold. The outstretched wings of the cherubim served as the throne on which God's presence resided (Ps. 99:1). The ark of the covenant, on which the cherubim rested, functioned as God's footstool. The *debir* was also known as the "throne room" of God.

The architectural layout of the temple also conveyed an important theological message about God's character and his relationship to the Israelite people. The organization of the temple was arranged according to a hierarchical pattern so that as one moved closer to the holy of holies, one came nearer to the perfect and holy presence of God. This design symbolized and emphasized God's transcendence and separateness from the secular realm of mortals. Only the priests could occupy the sacred areas of the temple and mediate prayers and offerings on behalf of the community. Even among the priests, only the high priest was allowed to enter the holy of holies (Lev. 16). The temple's design thus preserved the notion that Israel worshipped not only a holy God but also a God who graciously permitted access to his presence through proper channels.

See also Second Temple Judaism.

Resource

Myers, Carol. "Temple, Jerusalem." In vol. 6, *The Anchor Bible Dictionary*, edited by David N. Freedman, 350-69. New York: Doubleday, 1992.

KEVIN MELLISH, PHD

TENTMAKERS

The term "tentmakers" refers to those who serve as ministers or missionaries while supporting themselves financially primarily through other means. The concept comes from the example of the apostle Paul, who made tents to support himself in Corinth (Acts 18:3). Key tentmaker activities include employment for self-support while living in a cross-cultural setting for the purpose of proclaiming the gospel and making disciples.

Tentmakers have appeared throughout salvation history, beginning with Abraham, Isaac, and Jacob. They supported themselves with herds of livestock while witnessing to the living God. Whenever God's followers have set out as pilgrims in new lands, they have typically supported themselves as tentmakers.

Beginning in the fifteenth century, explorers discovered and claimed new lands in Asia, Africa, the Pacific, and the Americas. Christian missionaries followed close behind. Of necessity, most of them supported themselves as tentmakers. Roman Catholic missionaries in Latin America supported themselves primarily through agriculture. A renewed emphasis on lay ministry in Protestantism resulted in a growing number of tentmaker missionaries.

Earliest among these were Moravian missionaries to the Caribbean in the mid-eighteenth century. They supported themselves as artisans. Then in 1792, William Carey moved from London to India with his wife, Dorothy, intending to make witnessing for Christ his primary vocation while earning his living as a shoemaker.

With the proliferation of mission agencies during the nineteenth and twentieth centuries, an increasing number of clergy and lay missionaries received external support from their homelands and were able to dedicate more time to ministry. This resulted in a significant expansion of Christianity in much of Africa, Latin America, the Caribbean, the Pacific, and parts of Asia.

But other areas of the world such as Northern Africa, parts of Asia, and countries having a major Muslim presence have not been receptive to missionary efforts supported by external funding sources. Tentmakers help fill this void.

A growing number of tentmakers now live abroad as missionaries while being employed in fields such as medical service, social work, community development, communications, agricultural consultation, economical initiatives, technical specialties, education (e.g., teaching English), and business (known as business as missions).

Many are from new missionary-sending countries and regions, including Korea, China, the Philippines, Africa, the Pacific, Eastern Europe, the Caribbean, and Latin America. A growing number of tentmakers are helping to reach new areas of the world, often through diverse ministry models that include international teams, nongovernmental organizations, and partnerships with local churches and traditional mission agencies.

See also Evangelism; Mission, Theology of; Missionary Movements.

Resources

Lai, Patrick. *Tentmaking: Business as Missions.* Colorado Springs: Authentic, 2005.
Yohannan, K. P. *Come, Let's Reach the World: Partnership in Church Planting Among the Most Unreached.* Carrollton, TX: Gospel for Asia Books, 2004.

NORMAN WILSON, PHD

TERRORISM

Terrorism is the premeditated use or threat of violence by clandestine individuals, groups, or states against a group of innocent noncombatants. By means of violence, terrorism seeks to manipulate another group by creating a significant environment of fear for political or religious purposes. The noncombatant victims are the immediate targets of terrorism. But the main target is always another group, which terrorists seek to intimidate, coerce, or propagandize. The main target may either be opponents of the terrorists' political, ideological, or religious agenda, or persons who could potentially identify with that agenda and be mobilized to support it by participating in terrorism.

Acts of terrorism can be committed by agents of a government (state terrorism), resourced by the indirect support of a government (state-sponsored terrorism), or activated entirely by a subnational political or religious organization, as in the case of Al-Qaeda's attacks. The methods of violence are as multiple as the circumstances and technologies permit. In the modern era, vehicular bombings, suicide bombings, crashing hijacked airplanes, and hostage taking have all been used. The future may include cyberterrorism, bioterrorism, and nuclear terrorism.

Many believe terrorism is a relatively simple phenomenon, caused by the influence of mosque schools, poverty, fundamentalist religion, or political oppression. But there is growing agreement that multiple terrorisms and complex causes exist, not just singular ones. Accordingly, loyalty to charismatic leaders and preexisting political grievances are likely more causal in producing suicide bombers than is religious teaching in mosque schools. Objective poverty is not much of a factor in producing terrorists, but relative economic deprivation is, especially when the latter is connected with restrictions on political rights. Even willful choice by an organization contributes to terrorism. Finally, terrorists such as Osama bin Laden are probably not driven to terrorism by religious fundamentalism but are motivated more by political and economic grievances. Their religious extremism is more the announced justification of terrorism than its true initiating cause.

A Wesleyan ethical response to terrorism derives from the recognition that human sinfulness intertwines with the multitude of personal and social factors that promote terrorism. The Wesleyan optimism of grace accents the possibility and hope for the moral restoration and transformation of persons in the image of God, where holy love for the neighbor and one's enemy actually occurs by the sanctifying grace of God.

Resources

Bjørgo, Tore, ed. *Root Causes of Terrorism: Myths, Reality and Ways Forward.* New York: Routledge, 2005.

Richardson, Louise, ed. *The Roots of Terrorism.* New York: Routledge, 2006.

Schmid, Alex P., and Albert J. Jongman. *Political Terrorism: A New Guide to Actors, Authors, Concepts, Data Bases, Theories, and Literature.* 2nd ed. New Brunswick, NJ: Transaction Books, 2005.

LINCOLN STEVENS, PHD

TESTIMONY/WITNESS

A testimony or witness is confirmation that something claimed to be real or true is in fact so. The Hebrew word *'ed* means "witness," "testimony," and "evidence." The Greek word *martyria* (martyr) means a "witness," "testimony," or "record." Witness/testimony is central to the Bible and Christian faith, both of which witness to the one true **God**. Israel and the church were called into existence as God's witnesses (Isa. 43:10, 12; Acts 1:8; 5:32).

The primary witness to God is God's witness to himself. In mighty deeds and words, in promise and fulfillment, God bears witness to himself. "I, I am the LORD, and besides me there is no savior. I declared and saved and proclaimed. . . . I am God, and also henceforth I am He" (Isa. 43:11-13). God's steadfast faithfulness was definitively displayed in Jesus, in whom God fulfilled all his promises (2 Cor. 1:19-22). In the gospel of John, the Son bears faithful witness to the Father, the Father to the Son, and the Holy Spirit to the Son as having borne faithful witness to the Father (John 16:1–17:26).

God's people bear witness to him as well (Ps. 36:5; Isa. 25:1). Jesus' disciples are to be his witnesses, even to the ends of the earth (Matt. 28:18-20). They are to tell of the salvation God has accomplished in Christ through the Holy Spirit and are to "make disciples of all nations" (v. 19). The Epistles bear witness that in Christ, God has offered forgiveness, reconciliation, and sanctification to the Gentiles (Rom. 15:9-16; Gal. 3:14). In the book of Revelation, the risen Christ, who is the "faithful witness" (*martys*, 1:5; cf. 1 Tim. 6:13), assures suffering Christian witnesses that God will vindicate his people and consummate his kingdom.

The NT speaks often of the **Holy Spirit**, who will himself bear witness to Christ in the **church** and in the world (1 Cor. 12:13; 2 Cor. 3:3; Eph. 4:4). He will bear individual witness (Rom. 8:9-17; 1 John 5:11) by transforming sinners into children of God, by transferring them from the kingdom of darkness into the **kingdom of God** (Col. 1:13-14).

The Wesleyan tradition, marked by a vital and "experimental religion," has made much of the internal and external **witness of the Holy Spirit**. In **John Wesley**'s sermon "The Witness of the Spirit: Discourse II" (*Works*, 5:123-34) we learn that internal confirmation of redemption is "given by the Spirit of God to and with our spirit" (124). The internal witness is accompanied by the transformation of one's life in Christ's image. During **love feasts** and in **class** meetings, early Methodists testified to the presence and power of God in everyday life. Their testimonies reached others with the news of **new creation** in Christ. In parts of the Wesleyan tradition, testifying to the Spirit's internal and external witness became a regular practice in church services.

See also Evangelical Theology; Evangelism; Sanctification; Theosis (Deification); Works of Mercy; Works of Piety.

ROBERT K. LANG'AT, PHD

THEODICY/EVIL

Critics of monotheism say belief in an all-powerful and all-good God cannot be reconciled with evil. A *wholly good God* would want to prevent evil, and an *all-powerful deity* could do so. But evil exists. Therefore God is either not all-powerful or not all-good.

Theodicy is the attempt to explain how evil's presence is compatible with a wholly good and all-powerful God. The term combines two Greek words: *theos* (God) and *dikē* (dee-kay, "justice," "right").

There are two types of evil: moral and natural. Moral agents execute moral evils such as murder and child abuse. Natural forces produce natural evils such as tornados and earthquakes. Such phenomena are considered "evil" when they cause creaturely suffering.

Monotheistic responses to the problem of evil depend on theological commitments such as one's understanding of God's nature, providence, and human freedom.

1. Wesleyans affirm that God is all powerful and wholly good. God exercises general providence but doesn't tightly control all that happens. Also, God grants humans "indeterministic" freedom, meaning that God cannot rigidly determine human actions if they are to remain truly free. This introduces the "free will defense" theodicy. It is compatible with Wesleyan theology. God grants free will to humans so they might freely respond to divine love. But along with the possibility of free obedience, the possibility

of misusing freedom, rejecting God's love, and committing moral evil necessarily follows. It is logically impossible, this defense holds, for God to grant indeterministic freedom and also dictate how humans will exercise freedom. Although God opposes sin and evil, God cannot prevent them while also granting free will.

2. Another common response is the "soul-making" theodicy advanced by Irenaeus (d. ca. 200) and others. According to this theodicy God created humans in God's *image* so they might grow into God's *likeness*. Humans were not created morally mature. Moral development occurs, not in a paradisical state, but under conditions where temptations and real evils can be overcome. Elements of this position can be found in Wesley's sermons such as "God's Love to Fallen Man" (*Works*, 6:231-40).

Developing moral virtues such as patience and courage logically requires the possibility of impatience and cowardice. Hence, some evil is necessary in God's creation. Obviously not all persons mature in response to their encounter with evil and suffering. Some proponents of this theodicy maintain that God continues to work postmortem until everyone achieves God's likeness.

3. Theological determinism that emphasizes divine power is a popular theodicy. God so meticulously controls events that everything happens precisely as God intends. There are no accidents or chance events, and there is no freedom. Humans do what God determines because they possess "compatibilistic" freedom. They are free to do as they desire. However, God determines their desires. Seen from God's perspective, all history proceeds according to a detailed divine blueprint. We might not understand how murders or cancers, sin and evil, fit into God's plan. Nevertheless, humans should believe that God is wholly good and so all events are part of his good plan.

4. **Process theology** affirms that God is wholly good but denies that God is all powerful. Even natural forces are partially autonomous. God cannot coercively control electrons, let alone human agents. Hence, God cannot unilaterally prevent any moral or natural evil.

5. Although the Bible contains no specific theodicy, the life and resurrection of Jesus demonstrate that God loves us and that suffering cannot separate us from his love (Rom. 5:8; 8:35-39). Jesus' death and resurrection definitively establish God's power and goodness. God is now working to overcome evil (8:28) and calls us to participate in his work. In Jesus, Christians find reason for confidence that God will ultimately triumph over evil and suffering (Rev. 21:4).

See also Determinism and Free Will; Free Will; Heaven; Process Theology; Virtues.

Resources
Hasker, William. *The Triumph of God over Evil: Theodicy for a World of Suffering*. Downers Grove, IL: IVP Academic, 2008.

Larrimore, Mark, ed. *The Problem of Evil: A Reader.* Malden, MA: Blackwell Publishing, 2001.

JOHN SANDERS, THD

THEOLOGICAL EDUCATION

See MISSION AND THEOLOGICAL EDUCATION.

THEOLOGICAL METHOD

See CONTEXTUAL THEOLOGY; PRACTICAL THEOLOGY; SYSTEMATIC THEOLOGY (DOGMATICS).

THEOPOLITICAL THEOLOGY

Theopolitical theology is critical analysis of the theological assumptions implicit in various social arrangements and political structures and of the political assumptions implicit in Christian teaching.

The seminal figure for contemporary political theology is Carl Schmitt (1888–1985). Schmitt shows how the concept of sovereignty was transferred in modern politics from theology (an "omnipotent God") to the **state** (an "omnipotent lawgiver"). Furthermore, because the idea of **salvation** entails a sovereign authority, a natural affinity between the political and the theological arises. According to Schmitt, the unity of the "total state" provides the material conditions by which the **church** preserves its own ideal of salvation as a "perfect society." Schmitt thus risks reducing the role of the church to maintaining the well-being of the state.

Shifting the focus to **eschatology**, Jürgen Moltmann (b. 1926), Johann Baptist Metz (b. 1928), and Dorothee Sölle (1929–2003) contributed to what became known as the "new political theology." Rooted in a theology of **hope** in the future reign of God, the church's primary task is to work prophetically against the political status quo and the **principalities and powers** of oppression by working to fulfill the biblical-eschatological promises of liberation, **justice**, and peace. These emphases, combined with a Marxist critique of bourgeois religion and politics, significantly influenced Latin American **liberation theology**, as well as **black** and **feminist theologies**.

More recent theopolitical theology restates the political in terms of the social structures in Christian teaching itself. Retrieving **Augustine**'s idea that politics is concerned with the fulfillment of God's reign in **history**, Oliver O'Donovan (b. 1945) emphasizes how God's reign entails a distinctively Christian society. Stanley Hauerwas (b. 1940) has identified the church as its own counter-*polis*, whose role in contrast to all **secular** societies (such as the state) is to bear God's salvation in history.

If contemporary theopolitical theology considers the social form of the church in terms of the political shape of the eschatological **kingdom of God**, it requires confronting the biblical recognition that the church is not itself the kingdom. "For here we have no lasting city, but we are looking for the city that is to come" (Heb. 13:14). Contemporary theopolitics reminds us that political action cannot be measured and judged by how successfully it maintains the church as a *polis* but by its fidelity to the hope of the kingdom, the New Jerusalem to come.

See also Augustine; Church and State; Kingdom of God; Liberation Theology; Public Theology; Social Gospel; Social Justice; State Religion.

Resource
Cavanaugh, William T. *Theopolitical Imagination: Christian Practices of Space and Time.* London: T and T Clark, 2002.

NATHAN R. KERR, PHD

THEOSIS (DEIFICATION)

Different terms are used to express the meaning of the 2 Pet. 1:4 phrase "partakers of the divine nature" (KJV). They include "theosis," "deification," "divinization," "becoming god," "ingoding," and "partakers/sharers/communicants of the divine nature." They communicate the *purpose* and *process*, or *way*, of **salvation**. The West usually equates theosis with sanctification. The East thinks of transfiguration. Occasionally theosis has meant perfection, divine-human participation, and glorification.

Theosis as *promise* runs throughout the Bible (Gen. 1:26-27; 3:5; Ps. 82:6; Matt. 5:48; John 10:34-35; 2 Cor. 3:18; 2 Pet. 1:4; 1 John 3:1-2). Rich, subtle, and complex, theosis is central to the story of redemption.

Two theological principles have been used to explain theosis. *First, partaking in God's nature* has the quality of "already" and "not yet." Its ground is God's own *koinōnia* (fellowship) that characterizes triune life. The *second* principle joins theosis to the incarnation—that definitive act of God's condescending love *for us* and *in us*. God dwells in humanity so that humanity may dwell in God. When God in Christ acted to redeem the world, he also showed us how to *partake* of his nature.

The early church often used the **incarnation** to explain theosis. Irenaeus (d. ca. 200), bishop of Lyon, said (paraphrasing), "God became what we are so that we may become what God is" (1979, 526). Similarly, Athanasius (d. 373), bishop of Alexandria, said, "God was made man that we might be made God" (1978, 65, author's paraphrase).

For both fathers, *how* God became human is *how* Christians become divine. Not only does the incarnation reveal God, but it also discloses what being fully human means. Theosis entails mutual indwelling—our dwelling in God and he in us. Summarized, theosis means the following: (1) God became what we are, human, so that we might become what he is, divine.

But (2) by becoming what we are, **God** did not cease to be *who* he is, and by becoming what God is, divine, we do not cease to be *who* we are, human.

John Wesley's sermon "The Scripture Way of Salvation" (*Works*, 6:43-54) reveals an understanding of theosis similar to that held by the **Eastern Orthodox**. Because God—whose *"name and nature is Love"* (see Wesley 1982)—created humanity in his image, humanity is *"capable of God"* (*Works*, 6:243). As God has shared in our nature, so we are capable of partaking of his nature. By joining the *promise* of salvation to the *way* of salvation, Wesley echoed the Orthodox pattern of theosis: "We become by grace what God is by nature" (Lossky 1974, 215).

Wesley made explicit the **Anglican** teaching on the relationship between the **means of grace** and the *hope of glory*. The *use* and *practice* of the means of grace in fellowship with the triune God and in the life of the church is how Christians fulfill their potential for theosis. In loving *by* God's grace, Christians become as loving as God is *by* nature. God's commands are clothed in promises. As Christians *use* the means of grace, they *participate* in the hope of glory and become *partakers* of the divine nature.

See also Christian Perfection (Entire Sanctification); Discipleship; Holiness; Means of Grace; Orthodox Church; Sanctification; Wesley, John, Theology of.

Resources

Athanasius. *Incarnation of the Word*. In vol. 4, *Nicene and Post-Nicene Fathers: Second Series*. Grand Rapids: Eerdmans, 1978.

Christensen, Michael J., and Jeffery A. Wittung, eds. *Partakers of the Divine Nature: The History and Development of Deification in the Christian Traditions*. Grand Rapids: Baker Academic, 2007.

Finlan, Stephen, and Vladimir Kharlamov, eds. *Theōsis: Deification in Christian Theology*. Princeton Theological Monograph Series. Eugene, OR: Wipf and Stock Publishers, 2006.

Irenaeus. *Against Heresies*. In vol. 1, *Ante-Nicene Fathers*. Grand Rapids: Eerdmans, 1979.

Lossky, Vladimir. *The Image and Likeness of God*. Crestwood, NY: St. Vladimir's Seminary Press, 1974.

———. *The Mystical Theology of the Eastern Church*. Crestwood, NY: St Vladimir's Seminary Press, 1976.

Wesley, Charles. "Come, O Thou Traveler Unknown"; or, "Wrestling Jacob." In *Wesley Hymns*, 18. Kansas City: Lillenas Publishing, 1982.

K. STEVE MCCORMICK, PHD

THIRD WAVE THEOLOGY

The third wave theology, or the third wave of the **Holy Spirit**, is also called the signs and wonders movement. The names refer to evangelicals who believe signs and wonders of the Holy Spirit should accompany the proclamation of the gospel, instead of ceasing as aspects of the life and ministry of the church at the end of the apostolic era.

The phrase "signs and wonders" refers to supernatural powers and events that accompany the proclamation of the gospel. These may include healings, casting out demons, and words of knowledge. Signs and wonders have become the common denominator in virtually every published third wave testimonial.

The signs and wonders movement began in the late 1970s and early 1980s under the leadership of John Wimber of the Vineyard Christian Fellowship and others. While prayer for healing was a regular feature of congregational life in many holiness, Pentecostal, and charismatic communities, most prominent healing ministries were identified with their leaders. A distinct feature of Wimber's teaching was the "democratization" of healing. The signs and wonders movement emphasized equipping and empowering laypersons for ministry in the power of the Spirit. Wimber's works include *Power Evangelism* (1985) and *Power Healing* (1987).

C. Peter Wagner, a church growth expert and retired professor from Fuller Theological Seminary, created the term "third wave." He is a leading proponent of third wave theology. According to Wagner, the first wave was the Pentecostal movement, the second the charismatic movement, and now the third wave is joining them. The third wave is distinct from, but similar to, the first and second waves. The major differences are the understanding that the baptism with the Holy Spirit is given in conversion and the denial that speaking in tongues authenticates the baptism.

While Wesleyans traditionally affirm the legitimate role of *miracles/signs and wonders* in all levels of mission and evangelism and share the joy of church growth, they point out that the only true test of whether a person or movement is from God is teaching and practice that conform to Scripture and historic Christian faith.

See also Charismatic Theology; Glossolalia; Healing, Theology of; Laity; Miracles/Signs and Wonders; Pentecostal Theology; Scripture, Theology of.

Resources
Kraft, Charles H. *Christianity with Power: Your Worldview and Your Experience of the Supernatural.* 1989. Reprint, Eugene, OR: Wipf and Stock, 2005.
Nathan, Rich, and Ken Wilson. *Empowered Evangelicals.* Rev. ed. Boise, ID: Ampelon Publishing, 2009.
Wimber, John. *Power Evangelism.* With Kevin Springer. San Francisco: Harper and Row, 1986.

WILLIAM T. YOUNG, PHD

THOMAS À KEMPIS
See DISCERNMENT; HUMILITY; WESLEY, JOHN, THEOLOGY OF.

THOMAS AQUINAS

In his brief life Thomas Aquinas (ca. 1225-74) published voluminous treatises on nearly every important theological and philosophical question. He was a member of the Dominican order, which was known as the "order of preachers," one of the first orders not regularly engaged in manual labor. It focused instead on intellectual labor.

Aquinas's greatest work is the *Summa theologiae*, written to provide beginning preachers with knowledge necessary for being good and effective priests. Its overall purpose is to teach knowledge of God, not only as God is in God's self but also as "the beginning and end of things," especially of rational creatures. Hence *part one* (*prima pars*) treats of God and the things of God. *Part two* (*secunda pars*) deals with the movement of rational creatures to God. *Part three* (*tertia pars*) treats of Christ, who as "man" is our way of moving toward God. The third part presents Christ as the "way" (*via*).

Thomas synthesized Christian tradition and was a transitional figure. He drew broadly on the church fathers to present the best of Christian tradition. He also incorporated Aristotle into Christian theology. Aristotle had been largely lost to the West but preserved in Islamic thought. Incorporating Aristotle was controversial. Some of Aquinas's work was condemned after his death.

Aquinas became a leader in a tradition known as scholasticism. Manuals were created that distilled his work into propositions. Learning and repeating them became important to Catholic theology. Martin Luther reacted against scholasticism, claiming Aristotle had become more important than Scripture.

The Thomistic "manual" tradition became very important in the modern era when Catholic theology reacted against **modernity**'s historicism and turn to the subjective self or ego. It reasserted the role of objective reason and logic. In 1914 the Roman Catholic Sacred Congregation of Studies generated twenty-four antimodernist theses culled from Aquinas. All Catholic priests were required to embrace them. However, other Catholic theologians began to question that interpretation of Aquinas. Was Aquinas's thought primarily committed to logic and objective metaphysics, or was it an attempt to return to the rich heritage of the church fathers and Holy Scripture? They began to read Thomas as a return to the church's rich heritage and gained influence in the Catholic Church. They helped make possible the reforms of Vatican II.

We have no evidence Wesley read much Aquinas. He did, however, admonish his clergy to do so. In his 1756 "Address to the Clergy" he asked them, "Do I understand metaphysics: if not the depths of the Schoolmen, the subtleties of Scotus or Aquinas?" (*Works*, 10:492). Such a statement suggests that unlike Luther, Wesley more positively valued what could be learned from scholasticism and Aquinas.

Recent Wesleyan theologians have begun to accept Wesley's admonition and to show the similarities between Wesley's Anglican inheritance and Thomistic theology, especially when interpreted as having its sources in Scripture and the fathers.

See also Church Fathers; Ecumenical Councils; Greek Philosophy; Sacraments.

Resources

Colón-Emeric, Edgardo A. *Wesley, Aquinas, and Christian Perfection.* Waco, TX: Baylor University Press, 2009.

Davies, Brian. *The Thought of Thomas Aquinas.* Oxford, UK: Oxford University Press, 1992.

Gilson, Etienne. *The Christian Philosophy of St. Thomas Aquinas.* Translated by L. K. Shook. Notre Dame, IN: University of Notre Dame Press, 1994.

D. STEPHEN LONG, PHD

TIME AND ETERNITY

Time is the sequential duration of creation and people, both of which have a temporal beginning and ending. Eternity is nontemporal, since it has no beginning or ending. The Bible speaks of God as the One to whom temporal limitations do not apply. God is "everlasting" (Gen. 21:33) or "from everlasting to everlasting" (Ps. 90:2). People are necessarily bounded by the sequential progression of events between the creation and its consummation. God, on the other hand, transcends created time and its limitations (vv. 2-4), except as he chooses to be constrained, preeminently demonstrated in the **incarnation** (Phil. 2:5-11; Heb. 2:10-18).

Christians believe that at the consummation of the **kingdom of God,** time will cease (Rev. 10:6). Eternal life is given to those who believe on Jesus Christ as the Savior (John 3:16; Acts 2:38). Its content is *principally* a matter of "knowing" God through Jesus Christ (John 17:3), not a matter of eternal duration as is popularly believed. Eternal life is both present and future: "Those who eat my flesh and drink my blood have eternal life, and I will raise them up on the last day" (6:54; see Titus 1:2). Life in Christ is also eternal, since it will never end. Neither "things present, nor things to come" can separate God's people "from the love of God in Christ Jesus our Lord" (Rom. 8:38-39). In the gospel of Mark, unending duration is associated with eternal life (10:30).

Time and eternity have long been debated by Christians. **Augustine** (354–430) was a major contributor. He dealt with time and eternity in book 9 of his *Confessions.* Augustine contrasted the temporality of the world with the eternality of God. Time does not apply to God, for God exists outside of time, transcending all dimensions of time and space. Since God is not limited by time and space, there is little reason to think it impossible for God to know everything at all times and places. God does not experience a past, present, or future; for God, there is only the eternal complete present. God created the world, but not *in* time. Rather, *outside* of time God planned and created. God is the fixed point of creation. Temporal things unfold strictly according to God's eternal plan. Time is knowable to humans as past, present, and future. While the past exists in our memory, only the present truly exists.

Additional explanations of God's relationship to time exist. For example, some teachers say Scripture and logic permit a view of God as eternal and temporal. Having created the world and time, God now takes human freedom (and time) seriously. Though God knows all that *can be known*, if finite freedom is to be taken seriously, then things that have not yet happened are unknowable—for humans and for God. The outcome of future contingent events cannot be known if they are truly contingent. This does not mean that God's eternality and freedom to execute his plans are in doubt. It simply means that past views of divine knowledge exaggerated the range of God's attributes and failed to take the creation as seriously as God does. However, it is difficult to correlate this view of God with biblical prophecy and historic theism.

See also Eschatology, Biblical; Heaven; Immortality/Life After Death; Open Theology/Theism.

DON THORSEN, PHD

TORAH

Fundamentally, the term "torah" means a "teaching" and also "instruction in general," a "collection of teachings." It derives from the root *yarah* (Hebrew), "to teach." Torah encompasses the entire range of Jewish discourse—oral and written, narratives and commandments, interpretation and response. Usually Torah refers to the first of three divisions of the Hebrew Bible—Genesis through Deuteronomy. This narrative begins with the Creator and tells the story of Abraham and his offspring—Israel, their descent into Egypt, their deliverance from slavery in Egypt, and their wilderness travails until they are ready to enter Canaan. The Torah ends with Moses' death. Because of Moses' close association with the Torah, a tradition emerged that he wrote it.

Torah as Genesis–Deuteronomy is also known as *Khumash*, or five scrolls (Pentateuch). Among Jews, the Torah retains pride of place as authoritative, sacred Scripture. Within Deuteronomy, the term "torah" refers more narrowly to Mosaic legislation, but the word can also refer to all three divisions of the Hebrew Bible: Torah (Pentateuch); Nevi'im (Prophets); and Ketuvim (Writings). As a whole they are called TaNaK (an acronym composed of the three divisions) or *Mikra* (Hebrew, "what is read") or "Written Torah."

Mikra and "Written Torah" presume the existence of another Torah: "Torah in the Mouth" or Oral Torah. *Mikra* refers to that which is read aloud (not recited, translated, or paraphrased). It contrasts with Oral Torah, which was and may continue to be transmitted orally. Oral Torah includes Jewish law codes, translations, interpretations, and explanations of Written Torah. It also includes rabbinic discourse and debate, and *responsa* (Latin, "rulings") of rabbis up to the present. Subsequently written, Oral Torah comprises the *Mishnah* (repeated traditions), the *Tosefta* (additions to the Mishnah), the Aramaic *Targums*, the *Talmuds*, and *Halakic* (everyday guidance) and *Aggadic* (expositions, legends, and parables) *Midrashim.*

As with Written Torah, Jews believe that God revealed the Oral Torah to Moses at Sinai. They believe Oral Torah was given exclusively to Jews for properly interpreting **Scripture** and for righteous living. "Orality" is part of its special Jewish character. Oral Torah was passed along in the prophetic tradition from God to Moses, to Joshua, to the elders, and then to the prophets; it was next passed to the men of the Great Assembly, to the pairs (such as Hillel and Shammai), and to the sages—the rabbis. Oral Torah emerged through the example, interpretations, and teachings of the rabbis—up to the present. While the rabbinic Oral Torah is concerned with *halakah* (the way to walk, live, or behave), it also addresses questions not dealt with in Written Torah. Oral Torah expands and "rewrites" biblical narratives.

Nehemiah 8–9 depicts the priest Ezra reading the Torah of Moses (possibly a section of Deuteronomy) to Jews of the Persian period (536–330 BC), who had returned to Judah from Babylon to rebuild the temple. The Torah (Genesis–Deuteronomy) became foundational for **Second Temple Judaism** (postexilic). The Jews used this Torah to understand their history as a **covenant** between **Israel** and the Lord. It anchored their identity, their religious and community practices, and their civil government. Groups that emerged because of competing interpretations of Torah all valued it as sacred **Scripture** (see **Dead Sea Scrolls, Pharisees/Sadducees**). The scrolls of Qumran confirm the authority of the Torah prior to the birth of Christ.

In the NT, *nomos* is the Greek term used for Torah in its many aspects: particular commandments, Mosaic legislation, Genesis–Deuteronomy, various scriptural narratives, and the entire set of Scriptures. The range of meanings for Torah is illustrated by Paul's use of *nomos* in 1 Cor. 14:21. He quoted Isa. 28:11, prefacing it with, "In the law it is written." Clearly, Torah means much more than "law." In Judaism, Torah is revelation—a gift of grace. It mediates between God and Israel similar to the way Christians view Christ as the Word of God and their Mediator.

See also Covenant; Dead Sea Scrolls; Israel; Pharisees/Sadducees; Scripture, Theology of; Second Temple Judaism.

KAREN STRAND WINSLOW, PHD

TRADITION, EVANGELICAL RETRIEVAL OF

Evangelical theology has always had a positive relationship with the pre-**Reformation** Christian tradition. However, it usually focused on the first four **ecumenical councils** and **Augustine**. In recent decades some evangelicals have broadened their interests to include patristic and medieval theology and liturgical practices.

Why has the evangelical tradition usually been disengaged from these parts of Christian tradition? *First,* the Protestant commitment to *sola Scriptura* has, in practice, meant the Bible is the only significant source of theological wisdom. For many evangelicals, the postbiblical tradition contributed little to the understanding of God. *Second,* many evangelicals believed Christian thought and practice declined in the postbiblical era. Supposedly, the centuries between the NT and the Reformation were largely marked by error and idolatry. *Third,* evangelicals' view of Christian life, emphasizing revivalistic conversion, had little in common with traditional practices of baptism, confirmation, and Communion.

However, beginning in the 1960s several leading American evangelical institutions journeyed toward traditional Christianity. *Christianity Today* magazine and Fuller Theological Seminary, for instance, have a broadly ecumenical focus. They typify the way many evangelicals connect with other branches of the church. Evangelical publishing houses such as William B. Eerdmans and Zondervan have moved toward an ecumenical slate of authors.

Other signals of the evangelical retrieval of Christian tradition include (1) movement by some two thousand evangelicals into the Antiochian Archdiocese of North America (late 1980s); (2) Frank Schaeffer's (b. 1952) conversion to the Orthodox Church (1990); (3) Richard John Neuhaus's (1936–2009) conversion to the Roman Catholic Church (1990); and (4) formation of the Orthodox Evangelical Church, which emphasizes the ancient Christian faith.

Baker Books recently launched Evangelical Ressourcement, a series that helps evangelicals connect with the theology and practices of the patristic era. InterVarsity Press's Ancient Christian Commentary on Scripture introduces readers to patristic commentators.

These developments are part of a larger trend in theology, namely, moving behind highly scholastic and systematized forms of theology to the less systematic theology of early Christianity. In Roman Catholic theology this means moving beyond nineteenth-century scholastic-Thomistic theology to patristic and medieval sources. For **Methodists** and the **holiness movement** it means moving behind nineteenth-century systematic theologies to **John Wesley's theology** and its historical antecedents. For evangelicals it means supplementing their emphasis on Puritan writers and the Princeton theology of Charles Hodge and B. B. Warfield with patristic theologians.

Alongside the retrieval stands the reappropriation of early church practices and forms of worship. Robert Webber (1933–2007) led in permitting the liturgical tradition to influence evangelical worship. His concept of "ancient-future worship" expressed belief that evangelical worship should include traditional practices such as recitation, singing the Gloria, and the stations of the cross.

Evangelical worship should also make a prominent place for celebrating the Eucharist. Webber's writings came at a critical time, for churches were becoming aware of a generational shift occurring in concert with an emerging postmodern, post-Christian culture. Webber urged evangelicals to deepen their worship by recovering the rich heritage of Christianity's past. The emerging church movement, with its interest in liturgy, traditional forms of prayer, and physical aids to worship (e.g., candles), has put into practice Webber's general vision for renewed evangelical worship.

See also Canonical Theism; Church Fathers; Desert Fathers and Mothers; Early Church; Ecumenism; Liturgical Theology.

Resources
Campbell, Ted. *John Wesley and Christian Antiquity: Religious Vision and Cultural Change.* Nashville: Kingswood Books, 1991.

Oden, Thomas. *Classic Christianity: A Systematic Theology.* New York: HarperOne, 2009.

Williams, D. H. *Evangelicals and Tradition: The Formative Influence of the Early Church.* Grand Rapids: Baker Academic, 2005.

SAMUEL M. POWELL, PHD

TRADITIONAL RELIGIONS

"Traditional religion" (TR) is a term used to speak of culturally indigenous ideas and practices that maintain balance between the spiritual, physical, and social elements of human life according to a society's worldview. Illnesses, death, natural calamities, and so on, are most often seen as instances in which the three elements come into play. Resolution of questions raised by illnesses, death, and calamities must comport with the three elements of human life. **Prayer** and sacrifice are designed to maintain a good rapport with the beings who occupy the spirit world and who control the three elements. **Divination** is often used to determine whose activities have provoked a calamity. Herbs and other paraphernalia are used to assist in healing physical illness.

Societies who practice TR communicate with the spiritual level of creation and use ritual either to assuage the anger of the "spirits" who have been offended by wrong behavior or to persuade the "spirits" to act in ways that will benefit the society. The practices of TR are usually conducted by trained practitioners who hand down beliefs and practices to chosen disciples in culturally accepted and culturally shaping ways. These practices and their foundational ideas do not necessarily remain static from one generation to another. In many TRs the close relationship between death and life is underscored through the veneration of ancestors who are believed to participate in the spirit world after death and, as such, can observe and control aspects of the daily lives of the living.

Ritual and theology are present in all TRs but are distinct in each culture. Most include one or more supreme gods, with additional levels of spiritual beings and mediators in play. Communication with the gods happens through the mediators. The practices of TRs are communal or corporate as opposed to being individualistic or private. This is true even in the case of personal illness. Rites involve religious phenomena and are closely linked to the culture's faith and beliefs about the created order. They are expressed through word, symbol, and action (Deut. 16:1-3). Traditional religion preserves a culture's religious and social structure.

Understanding the traditional religion of a people group is important for effective evangelism. The sense of the divine and other spiritual beings, as well as a sense of moral failure, can open persons to hearing the Christian gospel. On the other hand, the idea of God offering a sacrifice through his own Son, together with a full freedom from sin, is foreign to TR. Furthermore, TR often understands the "spirit's" behavior to be self-centered rather than concerned with loving others. Thus TR often maintains the cultural status quo through fear and intimidation instead of through communally constructive love.

See also Animism; Mysticism/Mystical Theology; Prayer.

Resources

Fink, Peter E., ed. *The New Dictionary of Sacramental Worship.* Collegeville, MN: Liturgical Press, 1990.

Pickering, W. S. F. *Durkheim's Sociology of Religion: Themes and Theories.* Boston: Routledge and Kegan Paul, 1984.

Pontifical Council for Interreligious Dialogue. "Pastoral Attention to Traditional Religions." Letter of the Pontifical Council for Interreligious Dialogue to the Presidents of Episcopal Conferences in Asia, the Americas and Oceania. November 21, 1993. http://www.vatican.va/roman_curia/pontifical_councils/interelg/documents/rc_pc_interelg_doc_21111993_trad-relig_en.html.

BEAUTY R. MAENZANISE, PHD

TRINITY

The doctrine of the Trinity—that God is three **persons** in one being or substance—is regarded by many theologians as the most comprehensive Christian doctrine. But it is implicit, not explicit, in **Holy Scripture**. It emerged in the great debates of the early Christian centuries as the only doctrine of **God** that gives a coherent presentation of the **revelation** found in the biblical narrative. That story of God's action in his *economy* (*oikonomia*) or "stewardship" of his world in **creation** and redemption was summed up in the belief in "Father, Son, and Holy Spirit" that all Christians confessed at baptism. Irenaeus identified the confession as the "rule of faith" (Latin, *regula fidei*). Tertullian devised the Latin words *trinitas, persona,* and *substantia* that were later adapted into many modern languages.

During the great debates of the fourth century over the deity of **Christ** (led by Athanasius and the three Cappadocian Fathers), the **church** advanced from belief in the *economic* Trinity (that God was revealed as Father, Son, and **Holy Spirit** in the biblical story) to belief in the *immanent* or *ontological* Trinity. God not only is revealed as Trinity in **creation** and redemption but, apart from his action in the world, is eternally and independently Trinitarian in being.

Jesus Christ did not *become* Son of God either at his baptism (Adoptionists) or at his birth from **Mary.** Nor was he called that as a courtesy title denoting his being God's first creature through whom the world was created (**Arians**). Nor did the Father become the Son at the **incarnation** and turn into the Spirit at Pentecost (Sabellians or Modalists). Rather, before any revelation in the *economy*, Father, Son, and Holy Spirit were in mutual, eternal relationship. The *Gloria Patri*, which gave equal glory to all three as the one God, affirmed this. The **Nicene Creed** did so definitively.

Augustine accepted the doctrine on the authority of **Scripture** and the **church.** But in trying to understand how to conceive of a "trinity" he used the model of the individual human soul or mind for the image of God: memory, understanding, and will. This is the origin of the so-called *psychological analogy* for the Trinity. Augustine also spoke of the Lover, the Beloved, and the Love between the persons, which employs a *social analogy* of the Trinity. This led to the doctrine that since the Son returned Love to the Father, the Holy Spirit must proceed from the Father *and the Son* (Latin: *filioque*). The Eastern **Orthodox Church** objected, particularly to the West's addition of this double procession to the Nicene Creed without approval by an **ecumenical council.**

The doctrine of the Trinity was not in dispute at the time of the **Reformation.** Thus it was not creatively developed in Protestant theology until Karl Barth proposed that it was rooted in God's self-revelation as the Revealer, the Revelation, and the "Revealedness" (i.e., the consequent knowledge of God attributable to the Spirit). Although he rejected Augustine's psychological analogy, Barth strongly emphasized the unity of God, refusing to speak of three persons, since this was wrongly understood in modernity as three separate individuals.

In contrast, other theologians such as Jürgen Moltmann have strongly emphasized the distinctions among the three persons and consequently the social analogy. Moltmann saw the doctrine as arising from the **cross,** where the Father and Son genuinely suffered, being separated by evil (hence the cry of dereliction). Yet they were simultaneously united in their love for the world so that from the suffering of the cross the Holy Spirit came. Eastern Orthodox theologian John Zizioulas sees the unity of the three, not in an impersonal substance that unites the three persons, but in the Father as the one from whom the Son is begotten and from whom the Spirit proceeds.

To speak of the one *being* of God is probably preferable, since the word "substance" has a complex history in ancient philosophy. But terms such as "substance" and "person" are used metaphorically or analogically with reference to God. Other perspectives on the doctrine have been developed by theologians such as Wolfhart Pannenberg in Germany and Robert Jenson in America, from an Asian perspective by Jung Young Lee, and from an African perspective by J. H. O. Kombo.

See also Christology; Church Fathers; Doctrine/Dogma; God, Doctrine of; Historical Theology; Incarnation; Jesus of Nazareth; Protestantism.

Resources

Cantalamessa, Raniero. *Contemplating the Trinity: The Path to the Abundant Christian Life.* Translated by Marsha Daigle-Williamson. Frederick, MD: Word Among Us Press, 2007.

Coppedge, Allan. *The God Who Is Triune.* Downers Grove, IL: IVP Academic, 2007.

Leupp, Roderick T. *The Renewal of Trinitarian Theology: Themes, Patterns, and Explorations.* Downers Grove, IL: IVP Academic, 2008.

THOMAS A. NOBLE, PHD

Uu

UBUNTU

The term *ubuntu* (uu-Boon-too) means "humanness." It originates from the Bantu languages in Southern Africa. It embodies a perspective on human existence that emphasizes solidarity, reciprocity, communal relationship and justice, mutual support, caring, hospitality, and a sense of belonging to each other. While the exact terms may differ, the ubuntu philosophy of life is expressed in diverse cultural contexts throughout Africa.

Archbishop Desmond Tutu describes ubuntu as "the essence of being human. It speaks of the fact that my humanity is caught up and is inextricably bound up in yours. I am human because I belong." Ubuntu speaks about wholeness and compassion. A person with ubuntu is welcoming, hospitable, warm and generous, and willing to share. Such people are open and available to others, are willing to be vulnerable, are affirming of others, and have self-assurance that comes from knowing they belong to a greater whole. They know they are diminished when others are humiliated, oppressed, or treated as if they are less than human. Since all people belong to one another, each person must strive to build a hospitable, just, and peaceful society for all. The concept of belonging or being a member of the family, community, and society is far more important than personal ambitions and interests.

The concept of ubuntu parallels a range of biblical themes. The communal life of Israel embodied in the holiness code (Lev. 17–26) emerges from the call to be holy as God is holy. The fruit of repentance in Luke demonstrates love of neighbor in an environment of reciprocity and justice (3:8-14). Acts shows solidarity and compassion in the communal life setting of those endowed by the Spirit (2:42-47). Love, compassion, justice, and generosity toward others are gospel imperatives for Jesus' followers who selflessly embrace a lifestyle that springs from Christ (John 15:4). Jesus prays that followers might live in unity with one another as he and the Father are one (17:21-24). They are even invited to participate in the intimate unity of Father and Son, evidenced by living in fellowship and love with one another (1 John 1:7; 3:11). They are called to "[make] every effort to maintain the unity of the Spirit in the bond of peace. There is one body and one Spirit" (Eph. 4:3-4). In short, Scripture and ubuntu emphasize values of humanity that foster mutual support, integrity, and respect and that discourage individualism and selfishness.

Due to the consequence of sin, full expression of ubuntu can only be realized through Christ the Redeemer.

See also Hospitability/Hospitality; Rights, Human; Virtues.

FILIMÃO M. CHAMBO, DLITT ET PHIL

UNDERGROUND CHURCH IN CHINA

The phrase "underground church in China" refers to unregistered assemblies of Christians in the People's Republic of China. They are independent of the government-recognized National Three-Self Movement Committee (NTSMC) and China Christian Council (CCC) for Protestants, as well as the Chinese Patriotic Catholic Association (CPCA) and the unregistered Catholic congregations.

The underground church is also known as the unregistered church or the unofficial church. The designations are somewhat misleading because individual churches are structurally independent of one another and do not constitute a unified body or denomination. Absence of ecclesiastical hierarchy is cited as a reason for less government opposition than might otherwise occur.

Protestant underground congregations are called house churches. They cannot own property for constructing church buildings because they are not officially registered with the government. So they meet in private houses, often in secret for fear of arrest or imprisonment. Registration might lead to interference in the church's internal affairs either by government officials or by NTSMC/CCC officials the Communist Party approves.

The Chinese house church movement developed after 1949 as a result of the Communist government's policy of requiring registration by all religious organizations. The policy requires churches to become part of the NTSMC/CCC. During the Cultural Revolution (1966–1976) Christian worship was forced underground. Even the official churches closed. The house church movement resulted and subsequently witnessed enormous growth. It illustrates an old Chinese poem: "Not even a prairie fire can destroy the grass; it grows again, when the spring breezes blow!"

Protestant house churches are indigenous to mainland China and are usually not under foreign control. Some groups welcome help from abroad so long as it does not compromise their independence. Theologically, house churches are **evangelical**. Many are **fundamentalist**, and many are influenced by **charismatic theology**.

Among Catholics, only the unregistered Roman Catholic Church is called an underground church. It usually recognizes papal authority in contrast to the official CPCA, which does not. The existence of Catholic underground churches is a major barrier against establishing diplomatic relations between the Holy See and the government.

Government opposition to the underground church continues. In 2008, twenty-one pastors of house churches in Shandong Province were sent to labor camps. This was the largest sentencing of house church leaders in twenty-five years. In 2009 the eight-hundred member Shouwang Church in Haiding, a suburb of Beijing, was removed from its rented space and forced to worship in a park.

In 2009 the United States condemned China, North Korea, and Iran for continuing to persecute religious minorities and for restricting freedom of worship. But the US government noted that China has taken some positive steps to increase religious freedom.

Notably, in 2008 the Chinese government for the first time invited house church leaders to attend a house church symposium. It was conducted to recognize contributions house churches are making to China's agricultural development.

In the past two decades, house church networks have developed and are headquartered mainly in Henan and Zhejiang Provinces. The networks have sent missionaries throughout China and into neighboring countries.

See also Asian Theology; Chinese Church, Contemporary; Communism; Indigenization; Indigenous Christian Groups; Indigenous Theologies.

Resource
Aikman, David. *Jesus in Beijing.* Washington, DC: Regnery Publishing, 2003.

WILLIAM T. YOUNG, PHD

UNIVERSALISM

Universalism is the belief that all individuals will ultimately be saved. Early Christians such as Clement of Alexandria (ca. 150–ca. 215), Gregory of Nyssa (ca. 335-ca. 394), and Origen (ca. 185–ca. 254) taught that all creatures possessing a free will eventually will participate in God's salvation. Origen famously speculated that even the devil one day would be reconciled to God.

During the sixteenth century, Radical Reformers Hans Denck, John Pfistemeyer, and others expressed universalist views. Pfistemeyer and his followers were the target of Heinrich Bullinger's 1530 attack that specifically referenced their universalism. These individuals expanded the Reformed doctrine of limited **atonement** to include all humans and then extended the idea of universal atonement to universal salvation.

Although found among some **Pietist** and **mystical** groups, universalism in colonial America was primarily a consequence of the rational religion given birth by the Enlightenment. Boston Congregationalists Jonathan Mayhew (1720-66) and Charles Chauncy (1705-87) were early exponents, as expressed in the latter's *The Salvation of All Men* (1784). But the founder of American universalism is generally thought to be John Murray (1741–1815), who had embraced the views of James Relly (1722-78), an early English Methodist. Relly had expanded the Wesleyan doctrine of "free grace to all" to include universal salvation. Because of his position, he and the Wesleys parted company. Another important early universalist teacher was Hosea Ballou (1771–1852), whose *A Treatise on Atonement* (1805) played a crucial role in the development of American universalism.

In 1803 the General Convention of Universalists of the New England States adopted the Winchester Profession of Belief, which expressed largely orthodox views on a range of doctrines. A child of the Enlightenment, however, universalism proved vulnerable to nineteenth-century German rationalism. After publication of the *Humanist Manifesto* in 1933, American Universalists began moving toward humanism, eventually paralleling Unitarianism in theology. Consequently, in 1961 the two groups merged to form the Unitarian Universalist Association.

Questions posed by universalism continue to be vigorously debated by orthodox theologians not identified with the Unitarian Universalist Association.

See also Salvation (Soteriology).

Resources

Buehrens, John A., and Forrest Church. *A Chosen Faith: An Introduction to Unitarian Universalism*. Boston: Beacon Press, 1998.

Parry, Robin A., and Christopher H. Partridge. *Universal Salvation? The Current Debate*. Grand Rapids: Eerdmans, 2004.

MERLE D. STREGE, THD

UNIVERSITY, CHRISTIAN

A Christian university is an intentional community of scholars, students, and administrators dedicated to integrating Christian faith and formal learning at the college, graduate, and postgraduate levels. It is organized and resourced to discover, advance, transmit, apply, and preserve beneficial knowledge. A Christian university intentionally seeks to form students as wise followers of Christ. It expects its graduates, in diverse fields, to serve as leaders in church and society. Christian universities view service as an act of worship.

Christian universities embrace the Christian faith, that Jesus is the Christ, as their defining vision of reality. In accordance with that faith they protect the integrity of the various disciplines that compose the curriculum, even while offering a Christian appraisal of them all. Not just the acquisition of knowledge, but the acquisition of wisdom and Christian **virtues** is the goal.

Christian universities are guided by the conviction that the Christian faith and a rigorous pursuit of knowledge that advances the world's well-being are not only compatible but inseparable. They affirm the **secular** based on Christian conviction but reject **secularism** as educationally obstructive. Christian faith and a fearless pursuit of knowledge, Christian universities affirm, are not at odds. Rather, they are like two sides of the same coin, supportive and complementary.

Like many institutions of higher education, the core functions of the Christian university are instruction, research, and service. Its educational offerings differ in range from university to university, depending on mission and size. Degree programs can be broad in scope (liberal arts oriented), concentrated on professional preparation (e.g., medicine and education), or even more tightly focused. No matter the program, a Christian perspective intentionally guides.

Christian universities guide students as they seek to understand their gifts, skills, and vocational interests, all within the context of their faith. Christian universities seek holistically to teach, form, and send.

Christian universities can be owned and operated by denominations as integral denominational partners, offered by denominations as gifts to the broader church, or operated as independent, private institutions. In any case, their leaders articulate and promote a Christ-centered vision for higher education, embraced by trustees, graduates, students, faculty, administration, and staff.

The goal is for Christian universities to become wisdom communities in the school of Jesus. However, not all wisdom communities are the same. Different theological commitments, student body compositions, stated purposes, and practices shape these communities. For example, the Wesleyan commitment to **prevenient grace** should extend hospitality to new ideas and others. Wesleyans believe the Spirit of God universally works to bring all persons to Jesus Christ. There is no place for fear, coercion, or withdrawal from the world. A Wesleyan approach to *truth* requires humility (we know in part) and a commitment to disciplined discourse (informed by Scripture, tradition, reason, and experience). Finally, the Wesleyan commitment to Christian holiness requires covenantal relationships, for Christians are called to embody in community what they confess as true. Thus a Wesleyan university works to form persons dedicated to faithful learning and committed to the practice of **hospitality**, openness to others, humility, and holy living.

Resources

Beers, Stephen T., ed. *The Soul of a Christian University: A Field Guide for Educators.* Abilene, TX: Abilene Christian University Press, 2008.

Benne, Robert. *Quality with Soul*. Grand Rapids: Eerdmans, 2001.
Newman, John Henry. "The Idea of a University." 1854. Reprinted in *Essays, English and American*. Harvard Classics, vol. 28. New York: P. F. Collier and Son, 1910. Internet Modern History Sourcebook. Fordham University. http://www.fordham.edu/halsall/mod/newman/newman-university.html.

PATRICK ALLEN, PHD

UTILITARIANISM/CONSEQUENTIALISM
See ETHICS.

Vv

VATICAN COUNCIL II

Vatican Council II was the twenty-first **ecumenical** (i.e., theoretically including bishops representing *all* the church) **council** of the **Roman Catholic Church**. It was convened in Rome on October 11, 1962, and closed on December 8, 1965. The council was called by Pope John XXIII (pope from 1958 to 1963). It was widely assumed that John XXIII would have a short and uneventful reign, by which time the bishops of the church might be united behind a candidate who could give strong leadership for several decades. Unexpectedly, only three months after John assumed office, he called for the first ecumenical council in nearly a century (the last had been Vatican Council I, held in 1869-70). Vatican Council II turned out to be in many ways one of the most significant councils in the history of the Roman Catholic Church.

Pope John XXIII, who was generally regarded by church leaders as a conservative figure, recognized that the post-World War II world had changed dramatically since Vatican I and would continue to change more rapidly than in the past. John XXIII was impressed by the political, economic, social, and—especially—**technological** changes of the mid-twentieth century and the challenges such changes always present the church. It was time, he often said, to "throw open the windows of the church in order to let in some fresh air." He called for the church to undergo *aggiornamento*, an Italian term meaning "modernization" or "adaptation," that is, bringing the church up to date. This created high hopes in some Roman Catholics that Vatican II would bring about a deep reform or renewal in the church. The call for an ecumenical council disturbed others in the church who saw no need for serious reform. Rather, they wanted to defend the unchanging, irreformable nature of the historic church.

Although Vatican Council II ultimately produced something less than what either the most reform-minded Roman Catholics hoped for or most traditionalists feared, it did loosen revolutionary forces that have profoundly affected the church since then.

A series of major issues were addressed at the four major sessions of Vatican II. The council's decisions on these issues were eventually published in sixteen documents or reports—four "Constitutions," three "Declarations," and nine "Decrees." While some decisions of the council simply reaffirmed Roman Catholic **doctrines** and practices that had stood since the pivotal Council of Trent (1545-63) or before, others demonstrated a willingness to change in a rapidly changing world. Among the most significant changes, Vatican II (1) urged that a dialogue be initiated between Roman Catholicism and other Christian churches, other world religions, and **modernity**; (2) recognized non-Roman Catholic Christians as "separated brethren" rather than as heretics; (3) acknowledged authentic elements of truth and **holiness** in other churches—even in non-Christian religions; (4) committed the church to working for unity among all Christians and repented for its own contributions to separation; (5) affirmed the principle of **religious freedom** as practiced in most modern democratic nations (previously condemned by the church); (6) emphasized the central role of the **Bible** in belief and practice and encouraged modern approaches to **Scripture** interpretation; (7) affirmed the value of worshipping in the languages of the various cultures of the world; and (8) approved celebrating most parts of the Mass in those languages rather than in traditional Latin; the council generally endorsed a degree of creative **contextualization** of **worship** practices.

See also Bible; Church (Ecclesiology); Contextualization; Doctrine/Dogma; Ecumenical Councils; Holiness; Liturgy and Worship; Modernity; Religious Freedom; Roman Catholicism; Scripture, Theology of; Technology.

Resources

Hahnenberg, Edward P. *A Concise Guide to the Documents of Vatican II.* Cincinnati: Saint Anthony Messenger Press, 2007.

O'Malley, John W. *What Happened at Vatican II?* Cambridge, MA: Belknap Press of Harvard University, 2010.

Vatican: The Holy See. "Documents of the II Vatican Council." http://www.vatican.va/archive/hist_councils/ii_vatican_council/index.htm.

HAROLD E. RASER, PHD

VIA MEDIA

Via media (middle way) is a term used generally to identify a middle position between two alternatives that preserves the value of both. It may be rooted in Aristotle's virtue of the golden mean. This was not simply a choice between competing options but reflected the right and proper balance between excessive extremes. In theological application, via media expresses the preference for an inclusive, comprehensive approach to theological formulation and a bias against polarity.

In theology, via media expresses a systemic approach to doctrine, faith, and ecclesiology that has become associated with the Anglican Church. From its inception, the English Reformation attempted to occupy a middle ground between the polarizing positions of post-Reformation Roman Catholicism and the Protestant Reformation. The method and spirit of the via media was implicit in Thomas Cranmer's Book of Common Prayer. It became formalized in Anglicanism in the 1559 Elizabethan Settlement initiated by Elizabeth I as a way, through compromise, to settle the religious conflict between Catholics and Protestants that had plagued the reigns of Henry VIII, Edward VI, and Mary I. The Elizabethan Settlement was achieved by way of two acts of parliament: The Act of Supremacy (1559) settled the Church of England's independence from Rome. The Act of Uniformity (1559) established liturgical conformity to the use of the Book of Common Prayer.

Richard Hooker (1554–1600), champion of reason, tolerance, and the value of tradition, made the first formal attempts to develop the via media in a theological system. Although the term *via media* was first used in the seventeenth century, it became part of the common Anglican vocabulary in the nineteenth century when John Henry Newman wrote *The Via Media of the Anglican Church*. It has come to express the self-understanding and temperament of Anglicanism.

The Anglican via media appeals to a balance between the potential excesses of biblical authority and institutional tradition. It appeals to the consensus of the primitive church of the first six centuries. It affirms the primary authority of Scripture while affirming the necessary interpretive roles of reason and tradition, particularly ancient tradition. The via media values a comprehensive consideration of theological perspectives and a willingness to benefit from them in the interest of theological synthesis.

In addition to serving as a theological method, the via media can also be understood as expressing a temperament or spirit. Averse to extremes, and preferring balance, the via media identifies an approach to Christian theology and life that values the center over the margins, consensual agreement over polarizing apologetics.

The method and spirit of the via media shaped the theological development of John Wesley. His catholic spirit, emphasis on agreement on essentials over division because of nonessentials, his approach to biblical authority and interpretation, and his high valuation of the church fathers may be traced to his development in the context of the Anglican via media. The Wesleyan form of the via media is captured in this saying that is likely from the writing of Rupertus Meldenius (Healy 1904) but often attributed to Wesley: "In essentials, unity; in nonessentials, liberty; in all things, charity."

See also Anglicanism; Ecumenical Councils; Ecumenism; Reformation; Roman Catholicism; Wesley, John, Theology of.

Resource

Healy, Patrick J. "Did St. Augustine Write: In necessariis unitas, in dubiis libertas, in omnibus caritas?" *The Catholic University Bulletin* 10, no. 3 (July 1904): 416-17.

CARL M. LETH, PHD

VIRTUES

Virtues are distinguishing features of moral excellence. They characterize persons that promote human flourishing. A truly virtuous person will exhibit moral excellence regularly over time, not just occasionally or in bursts. When well-entrenched or habituated, virtues define one's character. A virtue-centered ethic is also known as a character ethic

Plato and Aristotle describe a virtuous (Greek, *aretē*, "virtue") person as having characteristics that lead to human happiness (Greek, *eudaimonia*). To be happy means functioning well, and functioning well means living in harmony with one's nature. Because humans are by nature fundamentally rational and social beings, when they live rationally in community with others, they lead the lives for which they were created. So for a person to flourish, he or she must exhibit virtues—particularly wisdom, courage, temperance, and justice—that promote social well-being.

These four virtues became known as the classical or cardinal virtues. To them were later joined the three theological virtues: "faith, hope, and love" (named by Paul in 1 Cor. 13:13). The theological virtues are gifts of grace. The cardinal and theological virtues compose the seven virtues often used to provide proper goals for moral and spiritual formation, from the early church to the present.

However, when speaking of human flourishing in the Christian context, some have been wary of using virtue language as their primary ethical idiom. This was true for John Wesley, who lived during a time when some thinkers wanted to establish morality as independent of special revelation. Thinkers such as Anthony Ashley Cooper, third Earl of Shaftesbury (1671–1713), and Francis Hutcheson (1694–1746) treated virtues as springing from a naturalistic and autonomous ethical sense and ability, thus allowing humans to achieve moral righteousness independent of God's grace.

For John Wesley, humans could flourish only when in right relationship with God. A trusting faith in the work of Christ to bring about forgiveness of sins marks a right relationship with God, followed by growth of the **fruit of the Spirit** ("love, joy, peace . . ." [Gal. 5:22-23]). Wesley referred to the fruit of the Spirit as "affections" or "tempers." They define flourishing Christians. Because the fruit of the Spirit grow only as the Holy Spirit is active in the believer's life, virtue language, which by itself connotes a natural and universal capacity for virtuous life, seemed inappropriate for describing Christian discipleship.

Virtue language and fruit-of-the-Spirit language will no doubt continue to coexist. But thoughtful Christians must be careful when using it to describe Christian discipleship. A flourishing Christian can properly be described as virtuous so long as it is remembered that, for Christians, virtue flows from God's grace through faith in his Son. It is life in the Spirit (Rom. 8:9-17).

See also Christian Ethics/Moral Theology; Fruit of the Spirit; Humility; Justice; Tempers and Affections.

Resources

Aristotle. *Nicomachean Ethics*. In *The Basic Works of Aristotle*, 935-1126. Edited by Richard McKeon. New York: Random House, 1968.

Hauerwas, Stanley. *Character and the Christian Life: A Study in Theological Ethics*. San Antonio: Trinity University Press, 1975.

Long, D. Stephen. *John Wesley's Moral Theology: The Quest for God and Goodness*. Nashville: Kingswood Books, 2005.

GREGORY S. CLAPPER, PHD

VOCATION AND CALLING

Christian vocation refers to a life lived in obedient response to God's call to relationship and partnership with him. The origin of the word "vocation" is instructive: *vocatio* (Latin, "a calling") and *vocare* (Latin, "to call"). The Greek equivalent, *proskaleō*, can mean "bid to come to oneself."

God called Adam and Eve to be partners with him in caring for the creation (Gen. 1:26-28). After the fall, God sought partners to participate in his plan to redeem the world. The call (Hebrew, *qara'*, "summon," "invite," "commission") came to Abraham, Isaac, and Jacob and to Moses, Joshua, and King David. In the NT, Jesus called persons to the vocation of discipleship (Matt. 4:18-21; 10:1; Mark 6:7).

In Ephesians, the apostle Paul describes and celebrates the Christian vocation that is principally to make known the riches of God's **grace**. God is in the process of "gather[ing] up all things" (1:10) through Christ, and he calls Christians (v. 18), as members of Christ's body, to participate in the grand mission (vv. 15-23; 4:1-16).

The doctrine of vocation played a prominent role in the **Reformation** by explaining the sanctity of everyday life. Through human labor God intimately and providentially governs his creation. Martin Luther used two words to express Christian vocation: "station" (German, *Stand*) and "calling" (German, *Beruf*). God has given even non-Christians stations in life. But Christians see their stations differently. A Christian's first calling is to evangelical faith. The second calling is to understand one's station, not principally as what one does, but as what God is doing through one's station.

God blesses and governs the world through vocation. He manifests his providence through milkmaids and farmers. God heals through doctors, teaches through teachers, and proclaims his word through pastors. Vocation helps explain the intimate and inseparable relationship between faith and works. The Reformation doctrine of calling was paralleled in the Methodist doctrine of stewardship.

Thus all Christians receive a vocational call. Christian vocation is to be exercised not only in specific testimony to the gospel of Jesus Christ but also through the conduct of one's station in the factory, at school, and on the farm. God gives diverse gifts to all members of Christ's body so that they might fulfill their vocation in the church and beyond (Eph. 4:11-12). The vocation or calling of each Christian should contribute to unity in the body of Christ, to knowledge of the Son of God, and to the maturity of all its members (vv. 11-16).

Vocation is dynamic. As a person grows in Christ and experiences the ongoing sanctifying work of the Holy Spirit, his or her vocation is enriched. Changing circumstances and needs may call for different expressions of our gifts. James Fowler calls Christians to ongoing vocational **discernment**. In various seasons of life we need to discern anew how and where God wants our gifts to be employed (1991, 120-23). Vocation is grounded in the eternal purposes of God.

See also Discernment; Discipleship; Spiritual Formation/Growth; Wesley, John, Theology of.

Resource

Fowler, James. *Weaving the New Creation: Stages of Faith and the Public Church.* San Francisco: HarperSanFrancisco, 1991.

CATHERINE STONEHOUSE, PHD

Ww

WEALTH

Wealth is commonly understood as the abundance of valuable resources or material possessions and the control of them. A Christian account of wealth begins with recognizing that the abundance of God's creation is a gift and by celebrating the self-giving love shared between the Father, Son, and Holy Spirit as the model for Christian discipleship. Additionally, Christian notions of wealth include a reminder of the two greatest commandments: to love God with all that we are and have and to love our neighbor as ourselves. Finally, Christians must take seriously the need to admit and repent of the temptation to hoard wealth and use it for sinful purposes.

Land was the fundamental source of wealth among the ancient Hebrews. God's leading of Moses and Joshua to the Promised Land was a gift of great wealth. Solomon was blessed with great **wisdom** and wealth. The royal traditions in the OT reflect on wealth as a sign of God's blessing. But wealth could also signal unfaithfulness to God. The prophets called the people of Israel to renew their covenant with God, charging them with failing to care for the widows, orphans, and strangers in their midst—evidences of unfaithfulness. They had failed to use their possessions in service to the covenant.

Jesus' assessment of wealth is complicated. Nowhere does he teach that wealth by itself is good or evil. Instead, Jesus taught that when seen as a gift to be used for God's glory and love of one's neighbor, wealth achieves its proper purpose. The woman who poured the expensive contents of the alabaster jar on Jesus illustrates this (Matt. 26:7). The early churches gathered in homes of wealthier Christians. Offerings were gathered from those who had plenty to be given to Christians who had little.

But Jesus constantly warned his followers against the dangers of wealth, of the corroding influence wealth can have on a person's ability to believe in Jesus and rely on God for sustenance. Zacchaeus learned the lesson. As Jesus dined with him, Zacchaeus honored what he had learned from Jesus by giving half of his wealth to the poor and by paying back fourfold those he had cheated (Luke 19:1-10). Jesus' story of the rich young ruler shows how the most ardent faith is tested when asked to give up great wealth to follow Jesus (Matt. 19:13-22). In the letter of James, the wealthy that hoard the wages of those who work for them are told that their riches will destroy them (James 5:1-6).

John Wesley had much to say about wealth and its right use. His famous dictum, "Having, First, gained all you can, and, Secondly, saved all you can, Then 'give all you can'" (*Works*, 6:133), focuses on giving, not on earning and saving as ends in themselves. Wesley preached often on the importance of simple living and against the dangers of wealth. He died with very few material possessions.

See also Capitalism; Creation, Care for the (Ecology); Economics and the Use of Money; Justice; Means of Grace; Poverty; Works of Mercy.

Resource

Jennings, Theodore, Jr. *Good News to the Poor: John Wesley's Evangelical Economics*. Nashville: Abingdon Press, 1990.

JAMIE GATES, PHD

WESLEY, CHARLES, THEOLOGY OF

Charles Wesley (1707-88) was a prolific **hymn** writer whose poetry has made a lasting impact on Christian worship. Yet **John Wesley** judged his poetry to be his lesser talent! Such hyperbole highlights Charles's gifts as a theologian, preacher, and Methodist leader. In addition to poetry, he left a substantial body of prose: tracts, letters, sermons, and journals. Most of it awaits publication.

Much is being discovered about Charles's life and character, but his primary theological contribution remains in his hymnody. Methodism was "born in song" (MCGB [1933] 1954, preface). Early **Methodists** discovered the joy of singing psalms, hymns, and spiritual songs in preaching services and **class meetings, love feasts**, and **covenant services**. Hymn singing was essential for **spiritual formation**, contributing to growth in "knowledge and vital piety" (Wesley 1983, 644). *Singing the faith* and *seeking the faith* were inseparable. Methodist doctrine was proclaimed in verse, even as it was pursued in experience.

John and Charles largely agreed theologically, but since John edited and published many of Charles's hymns, recognizing theological differences between them is difficult. They differed on **Christian perfection**. John tended toward a "relative perfection" available now but also emphasized its gradual attainment. Charles tended toward sinless perfection and stressed the instantaneous gift, usually deferred to life's end. In **Christology**, John was nervous about Charles's emphasis on Christ's humanity, while some think John comes too close to docetism.

Diverse formative influences appear in Charles's hymns: **Puritan** devotion and **Pietist** emphases on heart religion, revivalist expectations of inbreaking spiritual power, and primitivist hopes for union and communion with God. The theology of the hymns shows a pursuit of holiness and perfection shaped by the mystical theology of ancient Christianity but transformed by the soteriology of evangelical orthodoxy and revival spirituality. The language of Scripture permeates the hymns.

In an atmosphere of **deism** and unitarianism, Charles celebrated the triune God, from the **incarnation** and nativity of Christ to the Spirit's transforming presence. Amid controversy with **predestinarians** and antinomians, his hymns upheld the universality of divine love and saving **grace**, to be embraced in a life shaped by **works of piety** and **mercy**. Charles's hymns for the Lord's Supper parallel John's emphasis on the duty of constant Communion. The Eucharist was seen as a confirming and converting ordnance, in which one encounters the real presence of Christ through the heartwarming and eye-opening work of the Spirit. Charles and John drew on Daniel Brevint's analysis of the sacrament as a memorial, a sign of present graces, a means of grace, a pledge of future glory, and an invitation to **discipleship** as a living sacrifice.

The definitive *Collection of Hymns* is a kind of *Pilgrim's Progress* for the Methodist movement. John said the contents are "carefully ranged . . . according to the experience of real Christians," from turning to God in repentance to yearning for evangelical conversion and striving for perfection in love (*Works*, 14:340-41). Singing the hymns was to take a journey through the whole way of **salvation** and across all the contours of the spiritual life, in the company of fellow travelers. The hymns present Christian discipleship as a foretaste of heaven, and Christian fellowship as a pilgrim band journeying home.

Charles and John were not **systematic theologians** in the current sense. John is recognized as a theologian of the Christian life as defined by eighteenth-century **Anglican** theology. Thankfully, Charles is now being assessed as something more than a lyrical expositor of John's theology. Evidence from his other works has helped reveal Charles the theologian "behind" his hymns. By repitching the tent of Methodist theology to include his poetry, however, Charles can be affirmed as a spiritual theologian of the highest caliber, offering a compelling vision of God and implanting a longing to pursue it.

See also Atonement; Christian Perfection (Entire Sanctification); Holy Spirit (Pneumatology); *Ordo Salutis;* Sanctification.

Resources

Cruickshank, Joanna. *Pain, Passion and Faith: Revisiting the Place of Charles Wesley in Early Methodism.* Lanham, MD: Scarecrow Press, 2009.

Kimbrough, S. T., Jr., ed. *Charles Wesley: Poet and Theologian*. Nashville: Kingswood Books, 1992.

Lawson, John. *A Thousand Tongues: The Wesley Hymns as a Guide to Scriptural Teaching*. Exeter, UK: Paternoster Press, 1987.

MCGB (Methodist Church [Great Britain]). *The Methodist Hymn Book*. 1933. Reprint, London: MPH, 1954.

Newport, Kenneth G. C., and Ted A. Campbell, eds. *Charles Wesley: Life, Literature and Legacy*. London: Epworth, 2007.

Rattenbury, Earnest J. *The Evangelical Doctrines of Charles Wesley's Hymns*. 3rd ed. London: Epworth, 1954.

Stevick, Daniel B. *The Altar's Fire: Charles Wesley's "Hymns on the Lord's Supper, 1745."* London: Epworth Press, 2004.

Tyson, John R. *Assist Me to Proclaim: The Life and Hymns of Charles Wesley*. Grand Rapids: Eerdmans, 2007.

———. *Charles Wesley on Sanctification*. Grand Rapids: Francis Asbury Press, 1986.

Wesley, Charles. "461: For Children." In *A Collection of Hymns for the Use of the People Called Methodists*. Edited by Franz Hildebrandt and Oliver A. Beckerlegge. In The Bicentennial Edition of the Works of John Wesley, vol. 7. New York: Oxford University Press; Nashville: Abingdon Press, 1983.

Yrigoyen, Charles, Jr. *Praising the God of Grace: The Theology of Charles Wesley's Hymns*. Nashville: Abingdon Press, 2005.

PHILIP R. MEADOWS, PHD

WESLEY, JOHN, THEOLOGY OF

John Wesley (1703-91) was a priest in the Church of England and leader in the eighteenth-century awakening. Three broad streams shaped his theology:

1. **Anglicanism**, with its sacramental piety, appreciation for the primitive church, and openness to evangelical, Arminian, and mystical influences
2. **Puritan** spirituality
3. **Pietism**, with its focus on heart and life, small groups for formation and mission, and evangelistic and social ministries

Between 1725 and 1735 a series of mystical, Anglican, and patristic writers convinced Wesley that true Christianity was wholehearted love for God and neighbor. Experience in the Holy Club at Oxford demonstrated the value of spiritual disciplines for seeking that goal. Finally, the Lutheran Pietism of the **Moravian** Brethren enabled him to receive **faith** and assurance as a gift of **grace** and to understand **justification** as the doorway to **sanctification**. Through critical appropriation and integration of elements from these traditions in the light of Scripture, Wesley developed the theology that became foundational for the Wesleyan tradition.

Wesley's theology is grounded in a distinctive understanding of **God** and grace. The governing attribute of God is **love**, which shapes all other divine attributes and motivates all divine activity, including judgment of **sin**. The nature and depth of God's love is revealed in the life and especially the cross of Jesus Christ, through which the incarnate God dies for our sins. Out of love the triune God provides salvation for sinful humanity, through what God did in Christ and is doing through the **Holy Spirit.**

Grace is not only divine favor but also the Spirit's transforming power. Unmerited, it is received solely on the basis of Christ's **atonement.** While universally given, grace is otherwise not irresistible, instead enabling and inviting persons into a transforming relationship with God.

Wesley's theology focuses on the way of salvation. Salvation is both instantaneous and gradual. It is defined as the entire work of God in human lives, centered on justification and sanctification. Its goal is restoring persons in God's image. Salvation addresses original sin, through which the moral image of God in humans is totally corrupted. Unholy tempers govern the heart and produce the actual sin for which persons are accountable. Universal **prevenient grace** provides initial awareness of the sinful condition by giving persons a conscience. It also restores a measure of liberty, enabling response to God.

When the gospel fully awakens persons to sin's governing power in their lives, and their guilt before God, they have the faith of a servant, marked by **repentance** as increasing self-knowledge, struggle against outward sin, and attempts to obey God's law. Their inability to overcome sin intensifies receptivity to grace. An awakened sinner yearns for justification and regeneration **(new birth).** Given at God's own timing, this instantaneous work of God lays a new foundation in the heart for the subsequent work of sanctification.

Justification is pardon (or forgiveness) that removes sin's guilt and transforms the faith relationship with God from a servant to a child of God. This normally occurs through a witness of the Spirit, providing assurance of God's pardoning love through Christ's death.

Faith involves *trusting* Christ and *knowing* (being acquainted with) God. Faith is a spiritual sense that enables persons to grow in knowledge and love of God through experiencing God's *present,* unseen reality, along with *past* (e.g., the cross) and *future* (e.g., eschatological) realities.

Regeneration breaks the dominating power of sin by instilling **fruit of the Spirit,** or holy **tempers,** in the heart, the most central being love for God and neighbor. These are in *response* to God's love in Christ. As they grow, they enable persons to *follow* or imitate Christ.

Sanctification is the gradual process of growing in love and other holy tempers through grace. It is marked by the repentance of believers, in which, due to justification, there is no sense of guilt before God but an increasing self-knowledge and dependence on grace due to the continued presence of inward sin in the heart. Those growing in sanctification yearn for **Christian perfection (entire sanctification),** a second instantaneous work of grace. Given at God's timing, it fully restores the moral image of God, and love completely governs the believer's heart and life. All inward sin is replaced by holy tempers. Believers are able, through grace, to fulfill the two great commandments of Jesus (Matt. 22:34-40).

Christian perfection is the goal of salvation. It effects the dispositions of the heart but does not deliver persons from mistakes in judgment, ignorance, or other limitations. **Involuntary transgressions** that violate God's will continue, and so does the need for grace, forgiveness, and continued growth.

Persons can fall away from the path of salvation at any point. While temptation may initiate falling away, its cause is loss of faith in Christ, often because a person puts his or her trust elsewhere. In Wesley's day, persons persisted in the way of salvation through accountability to **spiritual disciplines** (or rules) in weekly meetings of **classes** and **bands**. The rules helped persons avoid things that would draw them away from God; they encouraged participation in the **means of grace**, including **works of piety** and **works of mercy**. Because through the Holy Spirit God is present in the means of grace, the means were central to maintaining relationship with God.

For Wesley, personal salvation stands in the larger story of redemption. Ultimately the entire created order will be transformed in holiness and manifest God's love, renewed to a greater degree than its original state. Because the fullness of God's love was revealed in the cross of Christ, those who know God's love can reflect God's image more extensively than was possible prior to the fall, and the creation can be renewed to a greater degree than was true of its natural state. Affirming the created order's value undergirds Wesley's emphasis on ministering to the body, including his concern for health and **healing** through medicine and prayer.

By renewing persons, God is renewing the universal church in **holiness**. This is a recovery of the primitive church in Acts 2 and an anticipation of the eschatological community to come. The renewed church manifests God's love in its conversations, social and economic arrangements, and mutual care. A church renewed in holiness gives the gospel credibility, making possible world evangelization.

See also Fletcher, John, Theology of; Pilgrim Holiness Church; Quadrilateral, Wesleyan; Scripture, Wesleyan Approach to; Wesley, Charles, Theology of; Wesleyan Methodism.

Resources

Collins, Kenneth J. *The Theology of John Wesley*. Nashville: Abingdon Press, 2007.

Maddox, Randy L. *Responsible Grace: John Wesley's Practical Theology*. Nashville: Kingswood Books, 1994.

Maddox, Randy L., and Jason E. Vickers, eds. *The Cambridge Companion to John Wesley*. Cambridge Companions to Religion. Cambridge, UK: Cambridge University Press, 2010.

Runyon, Theodore. *The New Creation: John Wesley's Theology Today*. Nashville: Abingdon Press, 1998.

HENRY H. KNIGHT III, PHD

WESLEYAN CHURCH

The Wesleyan Church is an evangelical **Protestant** denomination that fully embraces the historical apostolic faith. It affirms the **Nicene, Chalcedonian,** and **Apostles' Creeds** and is more specifically identified as part of the Wesleyan theological tradition. Its doctrines are stated in its twenty-one articles of religion. Currently it holds membership in the Christian Holiness Partnership, the National Association of Evangelicals, and the **World Methodist Council.**

The denomination was created in 1968 at a merging conference uniting the Wesleyan Methodist and the **Pilgrim Holiness Churches.** The Wesleyan Methodist Church was founded (1843) as a breakaway movement from the Methodist Episcopal Church, primarily over issues concerning the abolition of slavery and church polity. Temperance, women's rights, and opposition to secret societies were additional hallmarks of its reforming spirit. The Pilgrim Holiness Church (1922) resulted from an amalgamation of several associations spawned by the late nineteenth-century holiness revivals. Prior to the 1968 merger, the Alliance of Reformed Baptists, located primarily in Maine and the Canadian Maritime Provinces, joined the Wesleyan Methodist Church, significantly increasing denominational membership. The constituent denominations emphasized the sanctified life, entered by a crisis experience engendered by baptism with the Holy Spirit subsequent to regeneration. Entire sanctification was evidenced in conduct that shunned social practices considered sinful or worldly.

Evangelism and **globalization** have become major emphases for the Wesleyan Church. An emphasis on personal soul winning during the 1980s shifted the denomination's focus from a sectarian and exclusive mind-set toward a strong emphasis on outreach and church growth. Large national gatherings and leadership training revitalized the denomination's youth programs and fostered a more conciliatory and transformational approach to contemporary culture. A major demographic shift has been an increase in the size of the average congregation and the growing number of megachurches, with regular worship service attendance exceeding one thousand.

In recent decades, the Wesleyan Church has endeavored to recapture its earlier advocacy of the role of women in ministry, including ordination. At the 2008 General Conference, the church elected its first female general superintendent.

The most significant expansion of the Wesleyan Church has been in its global outreach. In four decades the church has grown from ministries in twenty countries to more than eighty worldwide constituent bodies. Two autonomous general conferences (Philippine and Caribbean) now have federated with the North American General Conference to form the International Conference of the Wesleyan Church. Current North American membership is 139,000, with a global constituency of over 400,000.

Organizationally, the Wesleyan Church combines lay and clergy leadership. Lay and clergy delegates from regional districts compose the quadrennial general conference. This body elects a General Board of Administration and three general superintendents. The denomination's International Center is located in Indianapolis. The Wesleyan Church sponsors five North American colleges and universities: Bethany Bible College (Sussex, New Brunswick), Houghton College (New York), Indiana Wesleyan University (Marion), Oklahoma Wesleyan University (Bartlesville), and Southern Wesleyan (Central, South Carolina). In 2010 the denomination established Wesley Seminary, located at Indiana Wesleyan University (Marion, Indiana). It has recently established several international Bible colleges.

See also Holiness Movements: American, British, and Continental; Wesley, John, Theology of.

Resources

Caldwell, Wayne, ed. *Reformers and Revivalists: The History of the Wesleyan Church.* Indianapolis: Wesley Press, 1992.

Haines, Lee M., and Paul William Thomas. *An Outline History of the Wesleyan Church.* 6th ed. Indianapolis: Wesley Press, 2005.

CLARENCE (BUD) BENCE, PHD

WESLEYAN FEMINISM

Wesleyan and Wesleyan-holiness believers affirmed equality between women and men decades before the term "feminism" was coined at the end of the nineteenth century. Feminism claims that women and men are equals in all areas of life (socially, politically, economically, and spiritually). While Wesleyan feminism mostly represents the spiritual arena, adherents also work to achieve equality in all areas. Some embrace the term "feminism," recognizing its affinities with Wesleyan theology. Others, while supporting equality of the sexes, reject the label.

Rather than reflecting the influence of contemporary feminism, Wesleyan history provides a usable past that Wesleyan feminists continue to utilize. The commitment to equality appears strongly in writings defending women's right to preach. Writers highlighted egalitarian themes from the Bible, beginning with Gen. 1, where male and female are created in God's image and are given dominion over creation. They called Jesus "the emancipator of the female sex" and documented women's ministerial involvement in the New Testament church. The **Holy Spirit** is no respecter of persons but equally gifts men and women as evidenced at Pentecost.

Although early Wesleyan-holiness believers fostered feminism, there was no golden age of Wesleyan feminism. But their endorsement of equality emerged when most other churches were rejecting feminism.

Wesleyan theology encourages a positive appraisal of feminism. **Sanctification**, its defining doctrine, plays a major role. The moment of entire sanctification is a liberating experience that imparts a sense of full personhood and autonomy, rather than sanctioning submission that presumes female inferiority.

Holiness, often defined as purity and power, results from sanctification. **Phoebe Palmer** equated holiness and power. The prominent place of the Holy Spirit in holiness doctrine encourages a feminist agenda. The Spirit's empowerment, sometimes identified as holy boldness, enables women to challenge sexism.

The Spirit's authority supersedes attempts to limit women's equality. This is true for African-American women who face racism and sexism. Relying on the Spirit's power, they challenge racial prejudice and overcome barriers that assert their inferiority. The Holy Spirit emboldens women to claim their God-given equality.

Wesleyan feminism differs from other expressions of Christian feminism because sanctification, with its focus on the Holy Spirit, provides a unique theological basis for equality.

See also Feminist Theology; Palmer, Phoebe; Social Justice; Womanist Theology; Women in the Bible; Women's Role in the Church.

Resources

Hardesty, Nancy, Lucille Sider Dayton, and Donald W. Dayton. "Women in the Holiness Movement: Feminism in the Evangelical Tradition." In *Women of Spirit: Female Leadership in the Jewish and Christian Traditions*, edited by Rosemary Radford Ruether and Eleanor McLaughlin, 225-54. New York: Simon and Schuster, 1979.

Stanley, Susie C. *Holy Boldness: Women Preachers' Autobiographies and the Sanctified Self.* Knoxville, TN: University of Tennessee Press, 2002.

SUSIE STANLEY, PHD

WESLEYAN METHODISM

The roots of the Wesleyan Methodist Church sprang from revivalist fervor in upstate New York and New England during the first half of the nineteenth century. The perfectionist vision the Wesleys had promoted for individual believers was expanded into a zeal for social reform in the American context. Inspired by Charles G. Finney's call for a transformed society and William Lloyd Garrison's antislavery publications, Orange Scott (1800-1847), a presiding elder in the Methodist Episcopal Church (MEC), became a vocal activist for the abolitionist cause. Other Methodists, including Luther Lee (1800-1889), joined Scott in opposing the moderating position of the MEC. In 1843, representatives from the MEC and several other denominations met in Utica, New York, to organize the Wesleyan Methodist Connection. Their primary concerns were abolishing slavery and creating a representative form of polity that substituted significant lay participation for bishop and clergy dominance.

The Wesleyan Methodist Connection (later changed to the Wesleyan Methodist Church) was actively engaged in social movements of the day, including temperance, opposition to secret societies, and advocacy for the role of women in society and the church. The first women's rights convention in America (1848) was convened at a Wesleyan Methodist Chapel in Seneca Falls, New York. Luther Lee preached the ordination sermon for Antoinette Brown, the first woman formally ordained to the Christian ministry (1853) in the United States. Emphasis upon personal holiness was not lost amid social activism. A statement specifically addressing sanctification as an experience subsequent to regeneration was included in the 1848 articles of religion, the first instance of this topic to be incorporated into a denomination's statement of faith.

After the American Civil War, the need to continue as a distinct denomination became a major question. Many members, including Luther Lee, returned to their parent denominations. For others, the focus on entire sanctification, reinforced and modified by the holiness revivals of 1858 and 1867, justified the denomination's continued existence. A strong contingent of churches in the Southern states, organized largely through the endeavors of Adam Crooks (1824-74), remained with the Wesleyan Methodists instead of aligning with the now-divided Methodist Episcopal Church, South.

In the closing decades of the nineteenth century, the Wesleyan Methodists firmly aligned themselves with the holiness movement and its member denominations. Overseas expansion became a primary interest of women and children, with mission activities focused on Africa and South America. Such efforts significantly increased church membership. The denomination established four liberal arts colleges in New York (Houghton), South Carolina (Central), Indiana (Marion), and Kansas (Miltonvale). In 1952, theological concerns over the authority of Scripture led to including specific wording on the inerrancy of Scripture in the articles of religion.

After several unsuccessful merger attempts with the Pilgrim Holiness and Free Methodist Churches, the Wesleyan Methodists welcomed the Alliance of the Reformed Baptists, located in the Canadian Maritimes and Maine, into its ranks (1966). In 1968, the Wesleyan Methodist and Pilgrim Holiness Churches merged to create the Wesleyan Church.

See also Holiness Denominations Worldwide; Holiness Movements: American, British, and Continental; Wesleyan Church.

Resources
Haines, Lee M., and Paul William Thomas. *An Outline History of the Wesleyan Church*. 6th ed. Indianapolis: Wesley Press, 2005.

McLeister, Ira F., and Roy S. Nicholson. *Conscience and Commitment: History of the Wesleyan Methodist Church of America*. 4th ed., edited by Lee M. Haines Jr. and Melvin E. Dieter. Marion, IN: Wesley Press, 1976.

CLARENCE (BUD) BENCE, PHD

WESTERNIZATION OF THE GOSPEL

God's **revelation** of himself first occurred to such Semitic persons as Abraham, Moses, Isaiah, and Ezra. But as **Christianity** spread west into Europe, what began as a Middle Eastern religion was increasingly recast in Western thought forms, language, and cultures. Much of today's **evangelical theology** is constructed on foundations developed in Europe after Emperor Constantine embraced Christianity, the result of which being the Christianization of Western culture. Until the modern era, the terms "Christian" and "West" were inseparable. The West is still incomprehensible apart from its Judeo-Christian past.

This history significantly shaped **missionary** efforts originating in the West. It has shaped how the **gospel** is articulated, the **church** is understood, and Christian discipleship is defined. Theology has been predominantly Western. Churches born in **Asia, Africa,** and **Latin America** have frequently articulated the Christian faith by using local syllogisms and rational "proofs" borrowed from the empirical sciences. One important result is that Christianity has become so identified with Western culture that many non-Westerners think of Christianity as a Western religion.

An example of how theology in non-Western settings has been conditioned by Western culture is the ever-present emphasis on individualism. In non-Western settings it is common to hear, "God loves *you* and has a wonderful plan for *your* life." Another telltale sign is the attraction of the "gospel of wealth" and the paucity of discipleship understood as the "way of the cross."

Too often, Western leaders of global outreach have uncritically assumed that Western theology is not only the best way to frame the Christian faith but the only universally valid way. The attitude is at least partially ethnocentric and colonialistic, motivated by the notion that non-Western cultures are inferior. Supposedly, persons in other cultures, on becoming Christian, should readily see the superiority of Western Christianity. Sometimes this view has even led to demonizing non-Western cultures.

Westernization of the gospel can obstruct its proclamation in non-Western settings. This does not mean that Western ways of reading the Bible are wrong but that they might not be the best way to proclaim the gospel in other cultures. The fullness of God's self-disclosure can best be expressed by using the whole of God's creation, the whole diversity of cultures.

Articulating the Christian faith contextually and developing indigenous theologies become all the more imperative as the Christian center of gravity shifts to the **Global South**. Today the majority of Christians live, not in the

West, but in Africa, Asia, and Latin America. By 2025, Africa will be home to almost 600 million Christians and Asia 456 million. Projections are that by 2100 there will be three times more Christians in the Global South than in the North.

See also Contextualization; Contextual Theology; Globalization; Indigenization; Indigenous Theologies.

HOWARD CULBERTSON, DMIN

WISDOM

Although Israel's Wisdom literature shares traits with that of Egypt and Mesopotamia, for Israel, wisdom begins with knowing and obeying the Lord (Prov. 1:7; 9:10). Unlike biblical narratives about Abraham and the Exodus, Wisdom literature is unconcerned about covenantal interactions. Instead, much of biblical wisdom, such as the book of Proverbs, focuses on maxims, how individuals, including kings, are to live righteously and promote justice. Wisdom (Hebrew, *hokmah*) is conveyed through observations on meaning, order, understanding, and fulfillment.

God creates, orders, maintains, and sustains the world and its creatures through Wisdom. More than a concept, Wisdom is a messenger, a mediating presence, a personification who invited people into close relationship with her. Lady Wisdom claims she was the Lord's first creation and delightful companion through whom God created the world (8:22-31). In **Second Temple Judaism** and beyond, wisdom becomes associated with Torah, whose meaning enlarges to include all understanding and instruction in righteousness (vv. 1-21).

Israel's proverbs, many of which are associated with King Solomon, were probably initially preserved in oral form among families and larger groups until scribes recorded them (e.g., those in royal courts [25:1]). Several psalms, segments of the Prophets, the Wisdom of Ben Sirach, and the Wisdom of Solomon (the latter two appear in the OT Apocrypha) also demonstrate that moral guidance for living—wisdom—is God's gift. People who seek and practice God's wisdom—who live by his will—receive God's direction and develop communities that establish God's peace (3:5-6).

Job and Ecclesiastes are also classed as Wisdom literature. They probe life's enigmas and challenge the formulae for success found in the other wisdom books (some scholars call them "wisdom in revolt"). Ecclesiastes records the musings of a sage who generally disagrees with more traditional sages that a divine order can be discovered and the ways of humans aligned with it (but see 7:19). The book of Job affirms that his trials were not caused by sinning or any omission but resulted from a wager between God and the Adversary (Hebrew, *Hasatan*). The wisdom of Job therefore confesses that suffering can happen without reason but that God remains accessible to sufferers (38–39). God accepts their questions, complaints, and cries about conventional wisdom's claim that suffering results from sin (42:7).

The NT abounds in wisdom themes expressed in the short sayings and parables of Jesus. They are linked to the hypothetical reconstructed source Q used by Matthew and Luke. The prologue to John's gospel portrays Jesus as the Wisdom and the Word of God made flesh, an incarnation of Wisdom, not a literary personification as in Prov. 1, 8, 9 and Job 28. Paul's first letter to the Corinthians includes wise sayings, and the epistle of James is a classic example of wisdom writing.

The *Didache*, or *Teaching of the Twelve Apostles*, is an early Christian manual containing six chapters of wisdom sayings. The *Gospel of Thomas* is an alleged collection of Jesus' wisdom sayings.

See also Hermeneutics; Torah.

Resources

Clements, Ronald E. *Wisdom in Theology*. Grand Rapids: Eerdmans, 1992.
Dell, Katharine J. "Wisdom Literature Makes a Comeback: Pursuing the Good Life." *Bible Review* 13, no. 4 (August 1997): 26-31, 46.

KAREN STRAND WINSLOW, PHD

WITNESS OF THE SPIRIT

This theme has a canonical and noncanonical reference. The former refers to the **Holy Spirit**'s witness to the **Bible**'s authenticity. The latter, based primarily on Rom. 8:16, relates to the assurance of salvation.

Before the Protestant **Reformation**, validation of Scripture was based on the church's authority. The Reformers rejected this belief and found another basis in the *testimonium internum Spiritus Sancti*—the internal testimony of the Holy Spirit. **John Wesley** also subscribed to this authentication.

During the nineteenth century, **fundamentalism** sought to establish the authority of Scripture on inerrancy. Wesleyan theologians generally rejected this argument in favor of the classical doctrine of the internal testimony of the Holy Spirit.

The Spirit's witness to the believer's salvation was "the fundamental contribution of **Methodism** to the life and thought of the **Church**" (Workman, Townsend, and Eayrs 1909, 1:19). Wesley said this doctrine "is [the] one grand part of the testimony which God has given them [the Methodists] to bear to all mankind. It is by His peculiar blessing upon them . . . that this great evangelical truth has been recovered, which had been for many years well nigh lost and forgotten" (*Works*, 5:124).

Wesley taught three levels of witness: (1) inference from the **fruit of the Spirit**, (2) the witness of our own spirit, and (3) the direct witness, which precedes the first two—called the indirect witness. The third is the witness proper—the direct witness. All three are the Spirit's work.

Wesley distinguished between the "assurance of **salvation**" and "the assurance of **faith**." The former implied a knowledge that a person would *persevere* in a state of salvation. Wesley was only willing to claim that a person has the Spirit's witness that he or she is *now* in a state of salvation.

Possibility of the Spirit's witness "involve[s] as a necessary corollary an **Arminian** theory of the **Atonement**" (Workman, Townsend, and Eayrs 1909, 1:34). It depends on a universal provision of Christ's work in contrast to a limited atonement, which postpones assurance of salvation until after death. Wesley taught the witness is the privilege of all believers but came to believe that "a consciousness of acceptance [was not] essential to justifying faith" (*Works*, 14:348).

See also Arminius, Jacob; Calvin, John; Grace; Luther, Martin; Protestantism; Quadrilateral, Wesleyan.

Resource
Workman, H. B., W. J. Townsend, and George Eayrs, eds. *A New History of Methodism*. 2 vols. London: Hodder and Stoughton, 1909.

H. RAY DUNNING, PHD

WOMANIST THEOLOGY

Arising in the 1980s among African-American women theologians, womanist theology combines elements of **black liberation theology** and **feminist theology**. It attempts to voice the particular experiences of black women in the United States. The fusion of theologies has allowed black women to embrace the understanding of **God** as Liberator while recognizing the social realities unique to African-American women. The term "womanist" was coined by theologian Alice Walker. Leading womanist theologians include Delores S. Williams and Cheryl Townsend Gilkes. Womanist theologians from Wesleyan traditions include Jacquelyn Grant (African Methodist Episcopal Church) and Cheryl J. Sanders (Church of God, Anderson).

While foundational biblical passages and common life experiences unite womanist theologians, interpretations fall into two broad categories: survival/quality of life and liberation. The first focuses on supporting African-American women whose lives are harsh and who need practical guidance. The second emphasis promotes active changes in circumstance at personal and communal levels.

Womanist theology seeks to validate the lived reality of black women in the United States as valuable to Christ and worthy of earthly respect. However, the goal extends to women of color everywhere. Additionally, womanist theologians recognize that liberating black women from economic, social, political, religious, cultural, and sexual oppression cannot occur if efforts focus on women alone. Womanists argue that the entire community, including men and children, must participate in liberation that results in freedom from oppression and an improved quality of life. This applies equally to persons who suffer discrimination or oppression due to physical disability, class identity, sexual preference, or caste.

Womanists seek to give voice to those who, in the face of great odds, have acted courageously, selflessly, and communally to advance the common good without public recognition and often at great personal cost. One's personal narrative is central. Womanist theology draws on the African understanding of "conjuring," or calling up power and speaking deep truths about what is normally hidden or suppressed. Womanists encourage speaking out, dialogue, and embracing elements of other **contextualized theologies.** They urge African-American women to claim their own histories and declare their own authority and worth. African-American women are urged to **love** themselves and to acknowledge the goodness and beauty of their bodies and spirits, in spite of centuries of degradation and defilement.

Sin is understood primarily as social—devaluing human beings, land, and resources for the oppressor's pleasure and prosperity. Hagar's story (Gen. 16–21) is important for womanist theology; it encourages those who, since the time of slavery, have had motherhood forced upon them or who have had to act as surrogates or live as single parents.

See also Black Theology; Contextual Theology; Feminist Theology; Liberation Theology; Social Justice; Women's Role in the Church.

Resource
Mitchem, Stephanie Y. *Introducing Womanist Theology.* Maryknoll, NY: Orbis Books, 2002.

MARY LOU SHEA, THD

WOMEN IN THE BIBLE
Women are featured in both testaments as members of the people of God. They receive God's promises, deliverance, commands, covenant, and calls to repentance. Like the rest of Israel, they suffer exile and experience restoration, healing, salvation, Christ's commissioning to make disciples, and the reception of the Holy Spirit (Joel 2:28; Acts 1:14–2:4, 17). Biblical narratives depict both *insider* (to Israel) and *outsider* women as preserving God's people through unusual and even aggressive means. For example, Tamar, a Canaanite, pretended to be a prostitute and thus preserved the line of Judah (Gen. 38). Like the two named midwives who refused Pharaoh's order to kill newborn boys, Moses' mother, sister, and Pharaoh's daughter rescued Moses from infanticide (Exod. 1–2). Zipporah, a Midianite, saved Moses' life when she circumcised their son (4:24-26).

In addition to being assertive wives and mothers, women characters are judges (Deborah [Judg. 5]), prophets (Miriam [Exod. 15:20-21; Num. 12; Mic. 6:4], Huldah [2 Kings 22:14-20; 2 Chron. 34:22-28], and Phillip's daughters [Acts 21:8-9]), apostles (Junia [Rom. 16:7]), deacons (Phoebe [v. 1]), and leaders of churches (Prisca [v. 3] and Lydia [Acts 16:14-15]). They meet God (Hagar, Sarah, Rebekah, and all the followers of Jesus) and have entire books written about their faithfulness and courage (Ruth and Esther). Women characters such as Rahab are models for God's people, confessing their faith in Israel's God and strategizing to join God's people.

In the NT, Mary became Jesus' mother because she said, "Let it be with me according to your word" (Luke 1:38), foreshadowing Jesus' prayer in Gethsemane, which concluded with, "Not my will but yours be done" (22:42). Women befriended Jesus after his ministry began and provided for him and his disciples. Mary Magdalene, among other women, followed him to the cross and rose before it was light to care for his entombed body (Matt. 28:5-10; Mark 16:1-11; Luke 24:10-11; John 20:11-18). Thus women became the first apostles (Greek, *apostolos*, "one sent forth with a message") to bear witness to his resurrection. Gentile women responded to Paul's preaching. They started churches in their homes (Lydia [Acts 16:40]). Paul's letters refer to a number of women colleagues (e.g., Rom. 16).

Nevertheless, the Bible also portrays a patriarchal bias present during the periods of its formation in its law codes that address adult men of Israel (coveting [Deut. 5:21], divorce [24:1-4], rape [22:23-29], vow making [Num. 30:2-13], taking captive women as wives [Deut. 21:11-13], and property inheritance [Num. 27:1-11; 36]). Some later NT epistles appear to accommodate Greco-Roman conventions about women (1 Tim. 2:11-15). First Peter 2:21—3:1 claims that quiet, long-suffering wives would commend the gospel to their husbands. The traditional interpretations of such passages countermand the nondiscriminatory outpouring of the Holy Spirit in Acts 2, the baptismal formula of Gal. 3:28, and the fact that women were colaborers for the gospel with Paul and the other apostles. Although these passages can be interpreted very differently by reconsidering how best to translate difficult terms and by probing their historical contexts, we cannot expect the Bible to say the same thing in every place about women or for cultural conditions and perspectives to be absent from the fledgling churches.

See also Evangelical Feminism; Feminist Theology; Latin American Women's Theology; Social Ethics; Wesleyan Feminism; Womanist Theology.

KAREN STRAND WINSLOW, PHD

WOMEN'S ROLE IN THE CHURCH

Women participated in ancient Israelite and early Christian worship more fully than is generally recognized. In the Hebrew Scriptures, women functioned as redeemer figures (Ruth, Esther, and Abigail) and acted as prophets (Miriam, Deborah, and Huldah). Throughout Scripture women appear as prophets at Israel's most critical junctures: Miriam at Israel's birth (Exod.

15:20-21; Num. 12; Mic. 6:4), Elizabeth and Anna at the Messiah's birth (Luke 1:41-45; 2:36-38), and women present at the church's birth—Pentecost (Acts 1:14). Jesus welcomed women as full disciples; women disciples followed him around the countryside (Luke 8:1-3); he welcomed Mary to learn theology rather than busy herself with hospitality (10:38-42); he discussed theology with the woman at the well and accepted her testimony (John 4:1-26); and he redefined women's blessedness as obedience to God, making their reproductive function secondary to discipleship (Luke 11:27-28). Significantly, women were commissioned at the tomb with the message of Christ's resurrection (Matt. 28:5-10; Mark 16:1-11; John 20:11-18), another critical juncture in God's redemptive work. Women participated in evangelism at Pentecost, hence Peter's use of the Joel passage (Acts 2:16-21). They established churches in their homes (16:40).

Paul refers to Phoebe as a "deacon" and uses the masculine form of the Greek word—the term applied to Timothy. Phoebe is a *diakonos* (overseer) of the Cenchreae church (Rom. 16:1). Prisca is Paul's coworker who risked her life for him (vv. 3-4). Paul even identifies his female relative Junia as an apostle (v. 7). Additionally, Paul affirms that in baptism all classes of people are one (Gal. 3:28). In 1 Cor. 11, he discusses how women should appear when praying and prophesying in public worship. Given Paul's positive references about women's leadership and all the stories in Scripture of God empowering them as prophets, two Pauline passages (1 Tim. 2:8-15; 1 Cor. 14:34-35) cannot be legitimately understood as universal commands that women remain silent in church. Narrow focus on these texts has often left the church advocating female exclusion that God obviously does not endorse and Paul did not practice.

In the early church, women tended the sick, mentored younger Christians, preached the Word, taught theology, and performed liturgical functions. They figured prominently as martyrs in the arena and as monastics engaged in prayer and study. In the Middle Ages abbesses wielded considerable civic and spiritual authority, while other women wrote devotional and theological material. During the **Reformation** some women publicly promulgated **Protestant** teachings, though it fell to the Quakers explicitly to promote the equality of men and women in public worship.

During the eighteenth-century Wesleyan revival in England, women participated as preachers. In the nineteenth century, thousands of American church women engaged in reform activities such as temperance and anti-slavery. Working as missionaries, others established schools, hospitals, and churches around the world. In the mid-nineteenth century, American holiness groups such as the **Wesleyan Methodist** Connection began ordaining women for pastoral ministry. By the early twentieth century, the **Church of the Nazarene**, the **Salvation Army**, the **Free Methodist Church**, and other holiness groups had many women serving as missionaries, church planters, and pastors. In the early decades of the twentieth century, some **Pentecostal** groups, including the Assemblies of God and the Church of God, Cleveland, affirmed women's ordination. Between the 1950s and 1970s many of the mainline Protestant churches began ordaining women in North America and Europe. Some mainline churches in Africa and Asia have begun welcoming women into ordained ministry, although often reluctant to consecrate them bishops.

See also Ordination; Wesley, John, Theology of; Wesleyan Feminism; Women in the Bible.

Resources
Grenz, Stanley J., and Denise M. Kjesbo. *Women in the Church: A Biblical Theology of Women in Ministry*. Downers Grove, IL: InterVarsity Press, 1995.

LaCelle-Peterson, Kristina. *Liberating Tradition: Women's Identity and Vocation in Christian Perspective*. Grand Rapids: Baker Academic, 2008.

Serrão, C. Jeanne Orjala, and Susie C. Stanley. *Faith and Gender Equity: Lesson Plans Across the College Curriculum*. Eugene, OR: Wipf and Stock, 2007.

KRISTINA LACELLE-PETERSON, PHD

WORD OF FAITH THEOLOGY (HEALTH AND PROSPERITY)

Word of faith (WF) or positive confession is a religious movement that teaches the Bible promises health and wealth to those who know the laws for using the "faith force." The process can actually create what petitioners request. Laws governing the faith force operate independently of the will of God, who is himself subject to the laws. Word of faith has its roots in twentieth-century charismatic/Pentecostal Christianity.

E. W. Kenyon (1860–1948) is credited with first articulating "word of faith" theology. Kenyon then influenced Kenneth Hagin, often referred to as the father of the movement. Central to Kenyon's teaching was the "blood covenant." The first biblical blood covenant was the circumcision of Abraham's household. As a result, God made promises to Abraham (Gen. 17). The promises are now available to all God's followers if they "fully obey." The promises include protection against violence, sickness, and poverty.

"Word of faith" adherents consider the Bible to be the Word of God. When it is "confessed" *in faith*, that is, in a "spiritual" or "faith filled" way, the confessor will receive what he or she confesses. This may include divine healing of spirit, soul, and body. This is the "positive confession" or "faith confession," the key to receiving from God what one desires. God wants confessors always to prosper. If someone is not prospering, it means he or she has surrendered authority to Satan.

Word of faith has no formal structure. Its leaders often amend historic Christian doctrine and even the Bible to fit their teachings derived from "revelation knowledge" (new spiritual revelation) they supposedly receive. Current prominent proponents of WF include Kenneth Copeland, Kenneth Hagin (d. 2003), Benny Hinn, Joyce Meyer, Joel Osteen, and Charles Nieman.

Critics of WF describe the movement as "name it and claim it" and "blab it and grab it." It negates a theology of suffering and the way of the cross as a model for Christian discipleship. Physical and monetary success, not the "fellowship of [Christ's] sufferings" (Phil. 3:10, KJV), are WF goals.

Churches of the holiness movement teach divine healing but not as WF does. Early on in Wesleyan-holiness churches the "prayer of faith" was primarily understood as divine **healing**. Obeying the instruction in the epistle of James (5:15), elders (clergy or older congregants) would surround a sick person, anoint that person with oil, and pray over him or her until the "prayer of faith" healed the sick. The practice led some to avoid seeking medical assistance. There was even debate about whether Christians should seek medical assistance. Today, Wesleyan-holiness denominations continue to believe in and practice divine healing. But they also unquestionably think God gives gifts of knowledge and skill to physicians and surgeons.

Although by the standards of Scripture and apostolic Christian doctrine WF shows significant deficits, how the sovereign God will receive and moderate petitions, and work through uneven instruments, must be left to him.

See also Holistic Mission; Pentecostalism; Poverty; Self-Denial; Spiritual Disciplines.

MARYANN HAWKINS, PHD

WORD/WORD MADE FLESH
See CHRISTOLOGY, NEW TESTAMENT.

WORK, THEOLOGY OF

Theology of work refers to a Christian view of the role of work within the larger Christian vision of creation and redemption.

The OT teaches that work is part of the created order. God placed Adam in the garden of Eden and instructed him "to till it and keep it" (Gen. 2:15). He placed Eve beside Adam as his "helper" (v. 18). Together they were commanded, "Be fruitful and multiply, and fill the earth and subdue it" (v. 28). God created humans in God's image, part of which means to work and take care of the creation as God does (vv. 27-28; 2:15). Work functioned as a fulfillment for persons rather than as a curse as some mistakenly view it. The fall made work more difficult; God cursed the ground as a result of Adam and Eve's sin (3:17-19). God made provisions for the Sabbath as a time to cease from labor and concentrate on worshipping God (Exod. 20:8-11). No matter how mundane (1 Cor. 10:31), all work is to be performed "as to the Lord" (Col. 3:23, KJV).

The doctrine of vocation was an important part of Martin Luther's larger theological structure. Vocation refers to a Christian life between baptism and the resurrection at Christ's return. All Christians, in whatever their situations in life, are called to serve God's creative work in the new freedom they have in **Christ**. In this world they engage in the ongoing battle between **God** and **Satan**. Vocation means more than dedicated service to one's occupation. It means that one's occupation—no Christian excluded—in the world is a vehicle through which one glorifies God by participating in God's work. Vocation involves the whole universe of one's life. Luther's doctrine holds creation and redemption together. It stands in sharp contrast to medieval Catholic teachers who thought of vocation as a churchly occupation and as the general calling to be a Christian.

John Calvin believed that all persons, rich and poor, must work; it is God's will. By working, persons serve God as instruments through which God reshapes the world according to his kingdom. By working, humans participate in God's ongoing process of creation. Like John Wesley after him, Calvin warned against lusting after wealth, possessions, or a life of ease. Use of one's increase must include supplying the needs of the poor. The profits of our labor must be reinvested in ways that serve God's purpose.

John Wesley extolled industriousness. But he condemned the accumulation of wealth "for its own sake; not only for the sake of what it procures." "None can *have* riches," he said, "without being greatly endangered by them. . . . After you have *gained* . . . *all you can*, and *saved all you can*, wanting for nothing; spend not one pound . . . for any other end than to please and glorify God" (*Works*, 7:355, 361).

See also Capitalism; Creation, Care for the (Ecology); Economics and the Use of Money; Liberation Theology.

Resources
Cosden, Darrell. *A Theology of Work: Work and the New Creation.* Paternoster Theological Monographs. Eugene, OR: Wipf and Stock, 2006.
Volf, Miroslav. *Work in the Spirit: Toward a Theology of Work.* 1991. Reprint, Eugene, OR: Wipf and Stock Publishers, 2001.
Witherington, Ben, III. *Work: A Kingdom Perspective on Labor.* Grand Rapids: Eerdmans, 2011.

DON THORSEN, PHD

WORKS OF MERCY

For John Wesley, in addition to **works of piety** (instituted **means of grace**), there are works of mercy (prudential means of grace). Works of mercy demonstrate faith in and communion with God. They include everything Christians do to show God's mercy to the "souls or bodies of men" (*Works*, 7:60). Works of mercy are vital parts of holy living and involve a wide range of activities carried out on behalf of others. They can be referred to as good works or works of charity "consecrated to God" (5:328). Works of mercy are essential for pursuing Christian holiness. A sense of mutuality fostered by genuine love for God and neighbor should characterize all works of mercy.

Works of mercy include personal and corporate actions. They span a wide range of activities prompted by Christian love for others. Feeding the hungry, clothing the naked, entertaining or assisting strangers, visiting persons sick or in prison, comforting the afflicted, instructing the ignorant, reproving the wicked, and exhorting and encouraging well-doing are all works of mercy (329-30). They must proceed from pure intentions.

Wesley and the Methodists practiced corporate works of mercy. They lived simply, advocated for social justice, developed schools, provided education, made small loans when needed, and offered pharmaceutical/health care to the poor. Such actions concretely expressed love for God and neighbor. They were essential dimensions of discipleship.

Works of piety (instituted means of grace) and works of mercy (prudential means of grace) are marks of scriptural holiness.

See also Christian Ethics/Moral Theology; Means of Grace; Peacemaking; Social Ethics; Social Justice; Tempers and Affections; Virtues.

Resources
Rack, Henry. *Reasonable Enthusiast: John Wesley and the Rise of Methodism.* 2nd ed. London: Epworth Press, 1992.
Wesley, John. "A Plain Account of the People Called Methodists." In *Works*, 8:248-68.

DEIRDRE BROWER LATZ, PHD

WORKS OF PIETY

For John Wesley, works of piety and **works of mercy** are equally important companions in a Christian's life. Both of them enable Christians to grow in grace, and both of them show what the Lord wants "Christians . . . to be" (*Works*, 5:283, 328-29). Wesley insisted on works of piety that develop from the *general* **means of grace**. However, the *instituted* or particular means of grace emphasize distinct ways to practice works of piety.

Works of piety revolved around attitudes and actions of devotion to God, what Wesley referred to as "religious actions [that] are such when performed with a right intention" (328). In Wesley's day, works of piety included attending public worship and gathering in **bands, classes,** and **societies.** They also included prayerfulness in public and family settings and in private. Searching the Scriptures, reading and hearing the Word, and receiving the Lord's Supper were others. Finally, fasting and abstinence, doing all the good possible, provoking others to good works, and keeping Christian conference are included (6:51; 8:322-23).

Works of piety were, for Wesley, to be carefully protected against hypocrisy. Practitioners were to expect no reward, gain, or interest. They were to guard against vain repetitions in the absence of "feeling what they speak" (5:332).

The purpose for works of piety was to prepare Christians to be willing and ready to receive gifts from God. Their aim was that Christians would willingly, continually, and perfectly obey God. They were part of the pattern of faith Wesley adhered to and exhorted Methodists to practice. Works of piety, works of mercy, and holy **tempers**, woven together, fostered being like Christ. They made it possible for love to be infused into a Christian's heart and life.

See also Christian Ethics/Moral Theology; Discipleship; Holiness; Spiritual Formation/Growth; Theosis (Deification); Virtues.

Resources

Heitzenrater, Richard P. *Wesley and the People Called Methodists.* Nashville: Abingdon Press, 1995.
Knight, Henry H., III. *The Presence of God in the Christian Life.* Metuchen, NJ: Scarecrow Press, 1992.
Rack, Henry. *Reasonable Enthusiast: John Wesley and the Rise of Methodism.* 2nd ed. London: Epworth Press, 1992.

DEIRDRE BROWER LATZ, PHD

WORLD COUNCIL OF CHURCHES
See ECUMENISM.

WORLD EVANGELICAL ALLIANCE
See ECUMENISM.

WORLD METHODISM

From their origins as an English religious movement in the eighteenth century, Methodist and other Wesleyan denominations have evolved into a network of churches throughout the world with almost forty million church members and another thirty-five million affiliated constituents.

Responding to critics of his preaching within the bounds of other ministers' parishes, John Wesley famously wrote, "I look upon *all the world as my parish*" (*Works*, 1:201; journal entry for June 11, 1739; emphasis added). But he consistently resisted efforts within his lifetime for Methodist expansion beyond English-speaking contexts in the British Isles and North America. He believed the pattern "in Jerusalem, in Judea and Samaria, and to the ends of the earth" (Acts 1:8) implied contiguous evangelization; Christians of one nation should evangelize the nations contiguous to it. By the 1760s the Methodist conference under Wesley's leadership had sent pairs of preachers to the British North American colonies. Toward the end of Wesley's life, he approved a mission to the West Indies undertaken by Thomas Coke (1786).

In 1793, two years after John Wesley died, the English Baptist missionary William Carey came to Bengal. His widely disseminated reports led to a groundswell of interest among Protestants in missionary efforts. At least partly due to interest in Carey's work, the nineteenth century became the "great century" for Protestant missionary endeavors. British and American Methodist churches participated in early interdenominational mission-sending groups such as the London Missionary Society (1795) and the American Board of Commissioners for Foreign Missions (1812). In addition, British and American Methodist churches founded their own mission-sending agencies, the Wesleyan Methodist Missionary Society (1818) and the Missionary Society of the Methodist Episcopal Church (1819). Other Methodist denominations would develop their own mission-sending agencies. Methodist women founded societies for missionary support.

As a result of these missionary efforts, in the nineteenth century, Methodist churches were planted in India, China, the Pacific Islands, and a variety of African nations. From these places, missions were extended to other parts of Asia, Africa, and Oceania. By the end of the nineteenth century, missions were also established in Central and South America as Latin American nations began to permit evangelization by non-Catholic church groups. In each location, Methodist groups developed networks of hospitals, clinics, schools, and colleges as an infrastructure supporting the missionary enterprise.

The divisions in world Methodism led to significant problems in countries not only where British and American Methodist churches were working but also where in some cases competing American Methodist denominations were engaged. From the 1930s Methodist communities in Korea and Mexico became independent of their founding American denominations, partly out of frustration caused by slow proceedings to reunite American Methodism and partly because of urgent needs for unity within their own countries. Since that time, many more Methodist bodies have become independent of Western denominations, a trend that has increased since the 1970s. The Methodist Church in Singapore, for example, became an independent Methodist denomination. Others united with other denominations to form united or uniting churches, such as the Church of South India, which incorporated British Methodist churches in southern India.

In 1881, in response to a proposal from the Methodist Episcopal Church, the first Ecumenical Methodist Conference was held at Wesley's Chapel in London. A number of subsequent Ecumenical Methodist Conferences were held until 1951, when the name was changed to World Methodist Conference, scheduled to meet every five years. At that time, the World Methodist Council was formed as an ongoing body to represent common interests among global Methodist churches.

Today the World Methodist Council includes more than seventy member churches and relates to a number of affiliated denominations and organizations. It has sponsored collaborative efforts in evangelism on behalf of global Methodist churches, the preservation of historical Wesleyan and Methodist sites, and common peace and justice initiatives, and it has represented Methodist churches in international ecumenical dialogues such as the International Methodist-Roman Catholic Dialogue. The World Methodist Council has sponsored the Oxford Institutes of Methodist Theological Studies, which brings together Wesleyan and Methodist theologians from across the world every five years.

See also Arminius, Jacob; Ecumenism; Methodist Connectionalism; Wesley, John, Theology of.

Resources

Cracknell, Kenneth, and Susan J. White. *An Introduction to World Methodism*. Cambridge, UK: Cambridge University Press, 2005.

Harmon, Nolan B., ed. *Encyclopedia of World Methodism*. 2 vols. Nashville: United Methodist Publishing House, 1974.

World Methodist Council. http://www.worldmethodistcouncil.org/.

TED A. CAMPBELL, PHD

WORLD METHODIST COUNCIL

The World Methodist Council (WMC), founded in 1951, is an association of seventy-six autonomous denominations representing about seventy-five million people belonging to Methodist and other Wesleyan churches in 132 countries. Its mission is to deepen fellowship among Methodists, advance common theological and moral standards, pray for and support the needs of persecuted Christians, encourage ministries of justice and peace, study union proposals that affect member denominations, and sponsor an exchange program of ministers. In 1953, the council established its headquarters at Lake Junaluska, North Carolina, and erected a stone building that contains offices, a library, and one of the premier Methodist museums in the world.

The WMC is affiliated with the Epworth Rectory, United Methodism's Foundation for Evangelism, the World Methodist Historical Society, and United Methodism's General Commission on Archives and History at Drew University. The Methodist and Wesleyan Archives Center at Drew University houses many published and unpublished materials pertaining to worldwide Methodism. The center's collection includes materials from various denominations within the Methodist tradition, and it houses a large art and memorabilia collection of Methodistica. The council also sponsors the Oxford Institute of Methodist Theological Studies. This society meets quadrennially at Lincoln College of the University of Oxford. It fosters disciplined theological study among global Methodist scholars to enrich their ministries.

World Methodist Council policy is set by a group of five hundred delegates from their respective denominations, which meets every five years. The council does not legislate for member denominations or infringe on their autonomy. Rather, it exists to help them offer a unified witness. Churches in the WMC confess Jesus Christ as Lord and Savior, worship the one God in Holy Trinity, and hold to the authority of the Scriptures and the **ecumenical creeds** of the early church.

See also Holiness Movements: American, British, and Continental; World Methodism.

KENNETH C. KINGHORN, PHD

WORLD MISSIONARY CONFERENCE, EDINBURGH 1910

The World Missionary Conference (WMC) held at Edinburgh in 1910 occurred on the eve of World War I, at the threshold of the twentieth century. Among Protestants, it marked the beginning of the organized **ecumenical** movement. The WMC was the fourth international assembly convened to advance the Christian missionary movement. It was preceded by conferences in Liverpool (1860), London (1885), and New York (1900). They paved the way for the momentous gathering at Edinburgh. The WMC continues to grow in importance.

The WMC met June 12-23, 1910. It broke new ground and became the prototype for subsequent international ecumenical conferences. Beginning in 1907, intensive international planning had laid the groundwork. More than twelve hundred international delegates gathered. Roman Catholic and Orthodox churches were not represented. Only eighteen delegates were from the young Asian churches. Most of Protestantism was represented, ranging from High Church Anglicans to the Salvation Army. The WMC marked full entrance into ecumenical affairs by Anglicans.

The chairman of the conference was the American Methodist layman John Raleigh Mott (1865–1955). He and J. H. Oldham (1874–1969) were major planners and leaders. Mott was never a missionary but was destined to be a Christian statesman who for fifty years played a vital role in Protestant missionary activity. He was the central figure around which much thought and action revolved. For those reasons he is called the father of the World Council of Churches. His name was associated with the theme "the evangelization of the world in this generation."

A large part of the WMC's significance stems from the role it played in shaping eminent missionary leaders, some of whom were Charles Brent, Episcopal Missionary Bishop to the Philippines; V. S. Azariah, the first Indian bishop of the Anglican Church in India; C. Y. Cheng, representative from the churches in China and a champion of postdenominational Christianity; William Temple, renowned teacher and preacher and archbishop of York; and John Baillie, Scottish theologian and Church of Scotland minister.

The WMC not only established the pattern for subsequent conferences but also established the principle that a council is the creation of its member boards and societies. They alone have the right to determine policy. The WMC contributed directly and indirectly to the rise of the major non-Roman ecumenical structures, among them the International Missionary Council and its worldwide network of national Christian councils, the World Conference on Faith and Order, and the Universal Christian Council for Life and Work (Latourette 1975, 2:1344).

The WMC focused attention on "the church in the mission field." The church was championed as "the great mission to the non-Christian world" (Grillo and Cameron 2006, 4). It encouraged unity and church union in Asia and Africa and promoted cooperation among churches in the West.

Edinburgh 1910 was an ecumenical keystone and, along with the Second Vatican Council, may someday be judged one of the two most important church councils in the mid-twentieth century. Kenneth S. Latourette, the renowned missionary historian, had good reason for labeling the period in church history that ended in 1914 "The Great Century" (1975, 2:1061).

See also Ecumenism; Lausanne Movement and Covenant; Millennium Development Goals (MDGs); Missionary Movements; Parliament of the World's Religions; Student Volunteer Movement.

Resources
Anderson, Gerald H., Robert T. Coot, Norman A. Horner, and James M. Phillips, eds. *Mission Legacies: Biographical Studies of Leaders of the Modern Missionary Movement.* American Society of Missiology Series 19. Maryknoll, NY: Orbis Books, 1994.

Grillo, John L., and Ruth Tonkiss Cameron. "Finding Aid for World Missionary Conference Records, Edinburgh, 1910." January 2006. Burke Library Archives, Union Theological Seminary, New York. Columbia University Libraries. http://library.columbia.edu/content/dam/libraryweb/libraries/burke/fa/mrl/ldpd_6306815.pdf.

Latourette, Kenneth S. *A History of Christianity.* 2 vols. Rev. ed. New York: Harper and Row, 1975.

Neill, Stephen. *A History of Christian Missions.* 2nd ed. London: Penguin Books, 1986.

Ross, Kenneth R. *Edinburgh 2010: Springboard for Mission.* Pasadena, CA: William Carey International University Press, 2009.

Stanley, Brian. *The World Missionary Conference, Edinburgh 1910.* Grand Rapids: Eerdmans, 2009.

WILLIAM T. YOUNG, PHD

WORSHIP AND THE CHRISTIAN YEAR
See CHRISTIAN YEAR.

WRATH OF GOD
See DESTINY OF THE UNEVANGELIZED; GOD, DOCTRINE OF; HELL.

Zz

ZIONISM

In biblical and historical terms, Zionism was the Jewish longing for messianic redemption and restoration of a homeland that included gathering exiles from all the nations. The earliest expression of this hope is in the book of Isaiah. Since the second half of the nineteenth century, this yearning has taken on political dimensions, as a movement for establishing a Jewish national state in Palestine.

A distinction must be made between Jewish Zionism and Christian Zionism, although the two are deeply intertwined.

The origins of Christian Zionism are in the dispensationalism that derives from the Plymouth Brethren teacher John Nelson Darby (d. 1882). Basic to his teaching is that for the redemption of the world God is working separately with Israel (the Jews and the state), on the one hand, and with Gentiles and the church, on the other. All the promises regarding Israel in the OT are to be fulfilled in the future, including the creation of a Jewish kingdom on earth, the building of a new temple, and the reinstitution of the ancient sacrifices. The redemption of the church will occur in heaven.

Jewish Zionism, both religious and secular, has its own history of interrelations and conflicts. The secular World Zionist Organization, founded in 1897 in response to increasing anti-Semitism in Europe, functioned as a political body to promote migration to 'Erets Yisra'el (Hebrew, "land of Israel") and, as the basis for diplomatic efforts, to obtain the right of Jews to settle in Palestine.

It is not incidental that the two types of Zionism arose simultaneously.

Religious Zionists were initially opposed to the idea of establishing a Jewish state on two grounds: (1) redemption comes from God; humans should not try to hasten the end; and (2) settlement of the land of Israel cannot be achieved by those who do not keep Torah. These sharp differences remain.

Zionist efforts first achieved success with the Balfour Declaration (1917), in which the British government promised support for establishing a Jewish homeland in Palestine, and finally with the establishment of the State of Israel in 1948.

Darby's teaching was exported to North America through C. I. Scofield's study Bible, spread worldwide via televangelists, and propagated by organizations such as Moody Press and Dallas Theological Seminary. Dallas graduate Hal Lindsey—with his perennial best seller, first published in 1970, *The Late Great Planet Earth*—popularized dispensationalism to the point where it has become the normative view of eschatology for most English-speaking evangelicals.

Christian Zionism's focus on prophecy (dispensationalism) is at odds with historic Christian doctrine, according to which salvation for all persons—Jew or Gentile—comes through faith in Jesus Christ alone (Rom. 1–8), and that God is working in Jesus Christ to create one new humanity, neither Jew nor Gentile (Eph. 2). The OT prophecies about restoring Israel to the land were fulfilled in the **Second Temple** and in the life, death, and resurrection of Jesus Christ. This is the **gospel**.

Dispensationalism undercuts the heart of this gospel by teaching a salvation for Jews outside the **atoning** work of **Christ**. It favors a prophetic determinism that bypasses the teaching of Jesus himself.

See also Eschatology; Eschatology, Biblical; Kingdom of God; Second Coming of Christ/Parousia; Second Temple Judaism.

Resources
Laqueur, Walter. *The History of Zionism*. 3rd ed. London: Tauris Parke, 2003.
Spector, Stephen. *Evangelicals and Israel: The Story of American Christian Zionism*. New York: Oxford University Press, 2009.

DWIGHT D. SWANSON, PHD

ZIONISM, CHRISTIAN

The term "Zion" in the OT often refers to the city of Jerusalem, the nation, or to the spiritual home of God's people. In the NT, the focus is on Jesus himself and those who truly worship God (John 4:20-26; Heb. 12:22-29; Rev. 14:1). Christian Zionism focuses on the promise of a **land** given by God to Abraham and his descendants (Gen. 12:1-7; 15:4-7; 17:1-8; 35:12; Lev. 26:44-45; Deut. 7:1-8). Christian Zionists interpret these scriptures as applying to the modern State of **Israel**, founded in 1948. They claim that Gen. 12:3 must be interpreted literally and that it requires Christians to provide wide-ranging support for modern Israel and the Jewish people. In the famous Balfour Declaration of 1917, British foreign minister Arthur Balfour, himself a Christian Zionist, proclaimed that Palestine would become the homeland for the Jewish people.

Christian Zionism teaches that modern Israel, representing the chosen people of God, will play a central role in ushering in the end of history. Establishing the State of Israel is a prerequisite for the Second Coming. The origin of Christian Zionism lies in **dispensationalism**, a movement initiated by John Nelson Darby (d. 1882) in England. It emphasized the literal and future fulfillment of biblical prophecy associated with Christ's return. It placed a restored Israel at the center of God's plans bringing history to an end.

Darby's **eschatology** became a central feature in the teachings of many of the great evangelical preachers of the nineteenth century and was central in the very popular *Scofield Reference Bible* (1909) still used by many evangelical Christians.

Christian Zionist teachers interpret political developments according to the prophetic schedule of events that should, by their view of Scripture, unfold. When Israel captured Jerusalem and the West Bank in the 1967 Arab-Israeli war, many believed this was further confirmation that history had entered its last days. Christian Zionists expect a series of wars and disasters before the return of Christ. He will judge the nations and individuals by how they have treated Israel (Gen. 12:3).

Christian Zionism is found primarily in North America and Britain. It finds significant support among **charismatic** Christians and **Pentecostal** and independent Bible churches. It has had a global impact on conservative Christians through such books as Hal Lindsey's *The Late Great Planet Earth* and the best-selling novels and films of the Left Behind series. Christian Zionism's views about Israel and those who embrace them have fed distrust between many Muslims and the Christian West.

See also Eschatology; Eschatology, Biblical; Fundamentalist Theology; Second Coming of Christ/Parousia; Zionism.

Resource
Sizer, Stephen R. *Christian Zionism: Road-Map to Armageddon?* Downers Grove, IL: InterVarsity Press, 2004.

DAVID MCEWAN, PHD

SCRIPTURE INDEX

Old Testament

New Testament

2:5	Discernment
2:5-7	Empathy
2:5-8	Panentheism
2:5-11	Time and Eternity
2:6-7	Humility; Kenosis
2:6-11	Christology, New Testament; Music/Hymns/Hymnology
2:8	Biblical Theology; Humility; Kenosis
2:8*b*	Obedience
3:6	Legalism
3:9	Faith
3:10	Persecution and Martyrdom; Women's Role in the Church
3:11	Resurrection
3:12-16	Discipleship
3:14	Biblical Metaphors for Salvation
3:20	Ecclesiology, New Testament

Colossians

1:2	Holiness
1:5, 27	Hope, Christian
1:12-17	Panentheism
1:13-14	Salvation (Soteriology); Testimony/Witness
1:15-16	Principalities and Powers
1:15-20	Creationism; Music/Hymns/ Hymnology; Principalities and Powers
1:16-17	Evolution/Evolutionary Biology
1:17	Contemplative Spirituality
1:19	Incarnation
1:20	Biblical Theology; Peacemaking
1:25	Stewardship
1:27	Eschatology
2:13-15	Eschatology
2:15	Demons/Unclean Spirits; Principalities and Powers; Spiritual Warfare
3:1	Resurrection
3:1–4:6	Repentance
3:5	Idolatry
3:10	New Birth (Regeneration)
3:10-11	Creation/New Creation
3:12-16	Church (Ecclesiology)
3:12-22	Family, Christian
3:16	Music/Hymns/Hymnology
3:23	Stewardship; Work, Theology of

1 Thessalonians

1:9	Idolatry; Repentance
1:10	Resurrection; Salvation (Soteriology)
2:8	Soul
2:14–3:10	Jesus of Nazareth
2:18	Devil/Satan
4:1-8	Discipleship; Holiness; Sanctification
4:3	Christian Perfection (Entire Sanctification)
4:3-8	Human Sexuality
4:15–5:3	Second Coming of Christ/ Parousia

4:17	Second Coming of Christ/ Parousia
5:9	Resurrection
5:10	Second Coming of Christ/ Parousia
5:17	Prayer
5:19-22	Discernment
5:24	Christian Perfection (Entire Sanctification)

2 Thessalonians

1:6-10	Second Coming of Christ/ Parousia
2:9	Devil/Satan; Miracles/Signs and Wonders
2:1-8	Second Coming of Christ/ Parousia
3:10	Stewardship

1 Timothy

1–6	Doctrine/Dogma
1:4	Myths/Mythos
1:10	Human Sexuality; Marriage
1:16	Jesus of Nazareth; Resurrection
1:20	Devil/Satan
2:1-2	Prayer
2:4	Destiny of the Unevangelized
2:8-15	Women's Role in the Church
2:11-15	Women in the Bible
4:7	Sect
4:10	Calvin, John
5:14-16	Marriage
5:15	Devil/Satan
6:13	Testimony/Witness

2 Timothy

1–4	Doctrine/Dogma
2:8	Resurrection
2:20-21	Ecclesiology, New Testament
2:25	Repentance

Titus

1–3	Doctrine/Dogma
1:2	Hope, Christian; Time and Eternity
1:10-14	Sect
1:14	Myths/Mythos
1:15	Conscience
2:9	Second Coming of Christ/ Parousia
2:11-14	Righteousness
2:13	Hope, Christian
3:1	Principalities and Powers
3:3-8	Righteousness
3:5	Love; New Birth (Regeneration)
3:7	Hope, Christian

Philemon

1:16	Family, Christian

Hebrews

1–13	Religious Freedom
1:1	Prophecy/Prophet
1:1-4	Natural Theology
1:5	Gospel

"The *Global Wesleyan Dictionary of Theology* lives up to its name in every respect. It is truly *global*, thoroughly *Wesleyan*, and resolutely *theological*. This is a one-stop shop that will repay careful reading and repeated use. I plan on having it close at hand."

—Brent A. Strawn, PhD
Associate Professor of Old Testament
Candler School of Theology
Emory University

"The wide range of global contributors has brought the richness of the true Wesleyan understanding of the world as a parish. . . . This remarkable book will compel many thoughtful readers throughout the world to look afresh at their own understanding of ministry and spirituality."

—Beauty R. Maenzanise, PhD
Dean, Faculty of Theology
Africa University

"This dictionary is timely, global, clear, and inspiring. . . . I recommend this book for teachers and learners alike, whether one is a follower of the Methodist way or a curious interlocutor."

—Amy Laura Hall, PhD
Associate Professor of Christian Ethics
Duke University

"El *Global Wesleyan Dictionary of Theology* llega en un momento que exige abrir fronteras intercontinentales debido a la globalización. Hoy día es necesario ampliar perspectivas bíblico-teólogicas y conocer más allá de la tradición local. Por eso, el *Global Wesleyan Dictionary of Theology*, elaborado por eruditos de tradición wesleyana de todo el mundo, es una herramienta excelente no solo para conocer la riqueza de la tradición sino para vivir de acuerdo a la fe y como wesleyanos en el contexto global del siglo XXI."

—Elsa Tamez, PhD
Emeritus Professor, Universidad Bíblica Latinoamericana
(Latin American Biblical University)

"This dictionary is much more than a reference book. It is a unique and ambitious attempt to map the common language of a pan-Wesleyan family. . . . This book deserves to be consulted, browsed, and studied by those interested in the history of Wesleyan traditions, or seeking to understand their relevance for contemporary Christianity."

—Philip R. Meadows, PhD
Lecturer in Missiology and Wesleyan Studies
Cliff College, England

"These writers come from four corners of the global village, representing the richness of the tradition framed in diverse particularities of cultures, languages, and symbols. The result is richer and deeper than expected."

—Young-Ho Chun, PhD
Professor of Systematic Theology
Saint Paul School of Theology

"Marked by sound scholarship, a distinctively Wesleyan orientation, and a global sweep, the *Global Wesleyan Dictionary of Theology* is an indispensable resource for teachers and leaders in the Methodist, Holiness, and Pentecostal movements and a gift to the church worldwide."

—Steven J. Land, PhD
President and Professor of Pentecostal Theology
Pentecostal Theological Seminary
Cleveland, Tennessee